ROBERT FROST

A BIOGRAPHY

I enjoy sharing
my books as
I do my
friends, asking
only that you treat
them well and see
them safely home

ROBERT FROST

A BIOGRAPHY

BY LAWRANCE
THOMPSON
and
R. H. WINNICK

the authorized life of the poet
condensed into a single volume
edited by Edward Connery Lathem

NEW YORK
HOLT, RINEHART AND
WINSTON

Published in 1982 by Holt, Rinehart and Winston,
383 Madison Avenue, New York, New York 10017.

Published simultaneously in Canada by Holt, Rinehart and
Winston of Canada, Limited.

Library of Congress Cataloging in Publication Data
Thompson, Lawrance Roger, 1906–1973.
Robert Frost, a biography.
Includes bibliographical references and index.
1. Frost, Robert, 1874–1963—Biography. 2. Poets,
American—20th century—Biography. I. Winnick, R. H.,
joint author. II. Lathem, Edward Connery. III. Title.
PS3511.R94Z954 1981 ~811'.52~ [B] 80–28337

ISBN: 0–03–050921–1

Designers: P. J. Conkwright and Nancy Dale Muldoon
Printed in the United States of America

Grateful acknowledgment is made to the following for permission to reprint excerpts from their publications:

Holt, Rinehart and Winston, Publishers, for excerpts from *The Poetry of Robert Frost* edited by Edward Connery Lathem. Copyright 1916, 1923, 1928, 1930, 1934, 1939, © 1967, 1969 by Holt, Rinehart and Winston. Copyright 1940, 1942, 1944, 1945, 1947, 1951, © 1956, 1958, 1960, 1961, 1962 by Robert Frost. Copyright © 1967, 1968, 1970, 1973, 1975 by Lesley Frost Ballantine. Reprinted by permission of Holt, Rinehart and Winston, Publishers. For excerpts from *Selected Letters of Robert Frost*, edited by Lawrance Thompson; copyright © 1964 by Lawrance Thompson and Holt, Rinehart and Winston. For excerpts from *The Letters of Robert Frost to Louis Untermeyer;* copyright © 1963 by Louis Untermeyer and Holt, Rinehart and Winston. For excerpts from *Interviews with Robert Frost*, edited by Edward Connery Lathem; copyright © 1966 by Holt, Rinehart and Winston. For excerpts from *Selected Prose of Robert Frost*, edited by Hyde Cox and Edward Connery Lathem; copyright 1939, © 1967 by Holt, Rinehart and Winston. For excerpts from *Robert Frost and John Bartlett: The Record of a Friendship* by Margaret Bartlett Anderson; copyright © 1963 by Margaret Bartlett Anderson. For an excerpt from *Robert Frost: The Trial by Existence* by Elizabeth Shepley Sergeant; copyright © 1960 by Elizabeth Shepley Sergeant. For excerpts from *Robert Frost: Poetry and Prose*, edited by Edward Connery Lathem and Lawrance Thompson; copyright 1972 by Holt, Rinehart and Winston.

Mrs. Valerie Eliot and Faber & Faber Ltd., for excerpts from a formal toast by T. S. Eliot; copyright © 1976 by Valerie Eliot.

Russell & Volkening as agents for the author, Faber and Faber (London) for excerpts from *The Letters of Ezra Pound*, edited by D. D. Paige, copyright 1950, renewed © 1978.

Little, Brown and Company, for excerpts from *Robert Frost in Russia* by F. D. Reeve; copyright © 1963, 1964 by F. D. Reeve.

The Macmillan Company for excerpts from Robert Frost's Introduction to *King Jasper* by Edwin Arlington Robinson, copyright 1935 by The Macmillan Company, copyright renewed 1963 by The Macmillan Company.

Middlebury College, for an excerpt from "The Doctrine of Excursions," a Preface by Robert Frost to *Bread Loaf Anthology*, published in 1939.

American Academy and Institute of Arts and Letters, New York, New York, for an excerpt from remarks delivered before the Institute in 1939 and printed in the *National Institute of Arts and Letters News Bulletin*, Vol. 5, 1939. All Rights Reserved.

The New York Times Company, for excerpts from various editorials, interview-articles, feature articles, book reviews and news stories appearing in *The New York Times* between 1922 and 1966; copyright © 1922, 1939, 1950, 1954, 1958, 1961, 1962 by The New York Times Company.

New York University Press for an excerpt from Robert Frost's Introduction to *A Swinger of Birches: A Portrait of Robert Frost* by Sidney Cox, copyright © 1957 by New York University.

The State University of New York Press, for excerpts from *Family Letters of Robert and Elinor Frost*, edited by Arnold Grade; copyright © 1972 by The State University of New York.

A special acknowledgment is made to Alfred C. Edwards, sole trustee of the estate of Robert Frost and former chairman and chief executive officer of Holt, Rinehart and Winston, Inc., for permission to quote from works by Robert Frost unpublished or uncollected prior to the appearance of this biography in its original, three-volume form, as issued by Holt, Rinehart and Winston, Inc., in the years 1966–1976.

CONTENTS

❧❦

CONTENTS

THE LATER YEARS

ILLUSTRATIONS

꘏꘏꘏

EDITOR'S PREFACE

⫸⫷

"ROBERT FROST as personality and poet," declared Lawrance Thompson, "enchanted the American people, and won a deservedly special place in their hearts. His charm was heightened by his manner of seeming to be so natural, direct, and confiding in all forms of communication; but he was never as natural as he seemed. Even as the majority of his admirers misunderstood the apparently simple artistry of his poems, so they failed to recognize the dramatic masks he wore." And it was clear that, as Thompson went on to point out, ". . . after the poet's death important adjustments would have to occur in the public response to the man and his work."

Lawrance Thompson's formal concerns centering upon the time when the making of these "important adjustments" would be both in order and possible began in the summer of 1939. (He had in 1937 been appointed Curator of Rare Books at Princeton University and was subsequently, throughout the remainder of his career, a member of the university's Department of English, devoting himself to teaching and, variously, to productive scholarship in the field of American literature.) His efforts to record the events and developments of Frost's life, and in general to scrutinize and analyze "the man and his work," were to continue for well over a quarter of a century.

"The prime mover," Thompson wrote, "was Robert Frost himself. On 29 July 1939, he asked me to become his official biographer, with the stipulation that no part of the proposed biography would be published during his lifetime. Until shortly before his death on 29 January 1963, he worked closely with me, and yet he gave me complete freedom to arrive at my own conclusions. He never asked to see any part of the biography. . . ."

As something of a "curtain-raiser" for his biographical narrative, Lawrance Thompson published during 1964, the year after Frost's death, a substantial collection entitled *Selected Letters of Robert Frost*. Then, in 1966 the initial volume of the "official biography" itself came forth, *Robert Frost: The Early Years*; and this was followed four years later by *Robert Frost: The Years of Triumph*.

R. H. Winnick, who was to become Thompson's associate in the completion of his biographical enterprise, has sketched how it was that their collaboration came into being: "In August 1971, some three months after receiving a Pulitzer Prize for the second in his projected three-volume biography of Robert Frost, Professor Lawrance Thompson suffered a cerebral hemorrhage that interrupted, at an early stage, his work on Volume III. Although he had all but completed the task of assembling the biographical data needed to write this last volume, and had recorded at length in private notebooks what he had heard, seen, and provisionally concluded during and after twenty-five years as the poet's biographer and one of his intimate friends, his illness made it difficult, if not impossible, for him to continue alone."

A graduate student of Thompson's at Princeton, Winnick entered into an arrangement under which, as he has recounted, ". . . I would serve him full-time as research assistant; and, together, we would work on the Frost biography." In April of 1973, however, after months of joint labor and the preparation of only a rough, preliminary draft of the final volume, Lawrance Thompson died; and Roy Winnick was turned to for a continuation of the project, alone. Based on their previous discussions, on the existing draft, and on the extensive research materials in Thompson's files, as well as upon consultation with individuals who had been close to the poet and were especially knowledgeable about various aspects of the Frost story, Winnick completed Volume III; and *Robert Frost: The Later Years* was published in 1976.

The three volumes of the Thompson-Winnick study approach a total of two thousand pages, including their elaborate indexes and some four hundred pages of notes. Even before the writing of the third volume was embarked upon, a decision had been made to have, ultimately, a one-volume version of the overall work, for "general readers"; and the present editor was asked by Lawrance Thompson to assume responsibility for its preparation.

The basic effort, in this undertaking, has been to condense by means of excision, and without rewriting—through the deletion of passages long and short, of sentences and phrases, of individual words—attempting to retain the authors' essential coverage, with regard both to informational content and to interpretation or assessment, while at the same time reducing the extent of their main-text sections by nearly sixty percent. This compression and other factors have, in turn, prompted an editorial restyling of the text, respecting punctuation, capitalization, and the like. Errors discovered within the biography's earlier printings have been corrected, and all quotations have been given a special review (items of correspondence having been compared with their manuscript or typescript originals, where possible). Consistent with the practice followed by Messrs. Thompson and Winnick, mistakes and irregularities in spelling, punctuation, and suchlike within quoted matter have not been altered, except that in certain instances missing elements and, occasionally, an explanatory word or phrase have been entered—set off by square brackets—in order to avoid causes for puzzlement or misapprehension.

Readers of this single-volume edition who desire greater biographical detail, or who wish access to documentation and other data treated by Thompson and Winnick in their notes, are directed to the three volumes of the work as initially issued. An appendix herein provides an approach to the full texts of verse and prose compositions by Robert Frost mentioned in this condensed form of the biography, and the appendix will serve to identify, also, principal sources for reference to Frost's published writings generally.

All of the instances of indebtedness and the circumstances of appreciation heretofore cited by the authors, in their acknowledgments statements within each of the separate volumes, continue to relate, quite fundamentally, to the existence of this biography. Emphasizing such to be the case, the editor wishes to record warmly, in addition, his own sense of obligation, as well as his deep gratitude, for the kindnesses and the assistance accorded him by many institutions and individuals —including, very particularly, by members of the special-collections and reference-services staffs of the Dartmouth College Library. He tenders, moreover, heartiest personal thanks to Edward Hyde Cox, Alfred C. Edwards, Prof. and Mrs. Theodore Morrison, Mrs. Lawrance Thompson, and R. H. Winnick.

E. C. L.

Dartmouth College
Hanover, New Hampshire

THE
EARLY
YEARS

OF BACKGROUND AND BEGINNINGS

(—1874—)

CALLED IN HASTE to the Frost home, on that part of Washington Street, between Polk and Larkin, near the western foot of Nob Hill, the doctor was met at the door by the expectant father, William Prescott Frost, Jr., who flourished a Colt revolver and warned that if anything happened to his wife while the child was being delivered, the doctor would not leave the house alive. Frost had purchased the revolver less than a year earlier, almost as soon as he reached San Francisco in search of newspaper work. Many told him, and for good reasons, that it was the habit of San Francisco reporters and editors to carry such a weapon, concealed, for self-defense. He was daredevil enough to like such instructions.

A good shot, fond of firearms, and a sportsman, Frost had twice tried to become a soldier. Brought up in Lawrence, Massachusetts, where the cotton mills were dependent on raw materials from the Southern states, he had developed strong sympathies for the Confederacy. As a teenager he ran away from home to enlist in the army of Robert E. Lee, and managed to get as far south as Philadelphia before police picked him up and sent him back. After the War Between the States, and near the close of his high-school days, he applied for admission to West Point, and became embittered by his conviction that unfair political influences had thwarted him.

A fighter anyway, and fond of roaming the streets looking for trouble, he had earned a reputation, while still a boy, for being wild and unmanageable. His troubled father, a foreman in one of the Lawrence mills, repeatedly applied harsh forms of discipline—without success.

Failing to become a West Pointer, he entered Harvard College, and Cambridge and Boston gave him new latitude to indulge in more sophisticated forms of play. Bright enough to finish his academic assignments hastily, he became a successful poker player, a heavy drinker, and a frequenter of brothels. Throughout his Harvard years Frost led a double life, as playboy-scholar; and he was graduated, with honors, Class of 1872, bitterly scornful of the puritanical mores he associated with New England.

Having become interested in political history and fascinated by the chicaneries of law and politics, he had difficulty deciding whether to make a career in law or journalism. Only one thing had been certain: he must shake the dirt of New England from his heels as fast as he could. California beckoned, and San Francisco appealed strongly (perhaps because it had already been decried as the wickedest city in the world). But to cross the vast continent required so much money that the young Harvard graduate decided to work for a year as principal of a small private school in Lewistown, Pennsylvania.

Journalism, he had decided, would serve as a stepping-stone to a political career; and, soon after he began his duties as principal of Lewistown Academy, he arranged to take private lessons in stenography —under peculiar circumstances. The circumstances involved Isabelle Moodie, the only other teacher on the staff of the academy.

A native of Scotland and inclined to preserve, still, more than a hint of a burr in her lively conversation, Miss Moodie carried herself with aristocratic bearing. Strong, tall, and graceful in her motions, she expressed an extraordinary intensity of response to anything that attracted her. Her beautiful dark-brown eyes were deep-set, beneath a high forehead; her auburn hair, parted in the middle, was gathered loosely in a large roll at the back of her neck. She had been only twelve when brought to Columbus, Ohio, in 1856, to live with a financially prosperous and socially prominent uncle.

Isabelle Moodie, fathered by a sea captain who went down with his ship in a storm not long after his only daughter was born, and mothered by a hussy who ran away from the arduous duties of motherhood, had been reared by her father's devout Scotch-Presbyterian parents; and from early childhood she had been sharing the religious convictions of her grandparents and developing mystical sensitivities. Her intense concern for spiritual matters made her face light up with a glow that increased her natural beauty—and found expression in her fondness for writing poetry and for singing hymns.

Almost as soon as the new principal of Lewistown Academy began to teach with Miss Moodie, he fell in love with her. But the discrepancy between their attitudes toward religious matters created an unfortunate hindrance to courtship. Fortunately, his colleague placed an advertisement in a local newspaper soon after school began:

"Any one desiring instruction in the art of Phonography will please apply to Miss BELLE MOODIE, teacher at the Lewistown Academy. . . .

"The method taught is that invented by Isaac Pitman, . . . being that adopted by first class reporters both in this country and in England."

The principal immediately applied for private instruction—and very quickly began to introduce a subtle kind of lovemaking, which became so effective that only five months after they met he wrote a formal proposal of marriage.

In the letter he said: ". . . As I became better acquainted with you, I saw in you a nearer approach to my ideal of a true woman, joined with the native cultivation and refinement of a lady, than I had ever chanced upon among any of my lady friends." He dealt gracefully with their differences in attitudes toward religion, by stressing the spiritual effect of his love for her. And insisting his unbelief contained no obstinacy, he implied that their love for each other might convert him to the true faith.

In his letter of proposal he also faced some other hindrances to the success of his courtship. Miss Moodie was six years older than he, and he reminded her that other lovers had successfully ignored such a problem. Then, he touched gently on another possible barrier, implicit in Miss Moodie's frequent hints to him that she had reasons for feeling she "should never marry." (She had once refused to accept an offer of marriage, made to her by a Presbyterian clergyman; she had felt she was not worthy of him. But repeatedly thereafter she had experienced mystical intuitions of divine punishment, apparently visited on her for having rejected the noble man of God for whom she had been intended.) Her new suitor impetuously urged that their only concern should be with the present and future: ". . . do you see in me that which you can love? that which you can rely upon as a support in the rugged ways of life?"

Without too much reluctance, Miss Moodie apparently had seen exactly what her suitor wanted her to see in him. He was extremely capable, gifted, strong-minded, and handsome. He had the carriage of an athlete and the features of a hero. Demonstrating powers of leadership, he gave the impression that he would make his own way successfully, even if at present he had no money except his immediate earnings.

They were married at Lewistown on March 18, 1873, approximately six months after they first met, and long before the school year reached its end the Frosts submitted their resignations and let it be known they were planning a move to California. As soon as their duties at the academy were completed in June, they went to Columbus, Ohio, and spent several weeks visiting with friends and relatives of the bride. Then, Frost made the journey alone to San Francisco, with the understanding he would establish himself in newspaper work and find a home for them both.

On July 9, 1873, he reached the railroad terminus in Oakland and made the picturesque voyage by ferry across San Francisco Bay. In less than a week he wrote his beloved, proudly, that he had submitted editorials to the best San Francisco newspapers, the *Evening Bulletin* and the *Chronicle,* and each of his first six offerings had been accepted. It seemed certain that one of these papers would hire him and he would have no difficulty in earning an excellent living. So, she must come at once.

A few days later, after the *Bulletin* completed arrangements for him to work as an editorial writer and stenographic reporter, he wrote his wife that he had already taken part in a new kind of excitement much to his liking: a street riot, with gunplay. The fun began after the *Bulletin* published a series of articles attacking and exposing certain wildcat silver-mining stocks. When the market quotations tumbled, a roaring, screaming mob gathered before the *Bulletin* office and shot out all the windows. (Police dispersed the crowd, and nobody suffered serious hurt.)

From the start, Frost's adventurous temperament thrived on San Francisco. It is doubtful any place on earth could have been more congenial to his tastes than this city, which had been a mere frontier town only a few decades earlier and mushroomed in spectacular fashion soon after gold had been discovered at Sutter's Mill, near Sacramento. By 1873 the helter-skelter beginnings had given way to an ordered arrange-ment of broad streets—some paved with cobblestones and others with planking—along which board sidewalks ran. Back of the bayside water-front—thick with warehouses, docks, fish markets, ferry slips—the business section had expanded into row on row of three- and four-story offices and stores, many of them cheaply built, others constructed of brick and stone. Farther inland the residential sections began crowding together thousands of homes, while the ornate mansions of millionaires began to vie with each other for prominence on the southerly slope of Nob Hill. Keeping pace, the slum region developed along Leidesdorff Street, which became known as Paupers' Alley.

Fascinated by all he saw and heard, the newly arrived writer for the *Bulletin* quickly learned that law and order, such as it was in San Francisco, no longer rested in the hands of self-appointed vigilance committees. Still, if law enforcement had greatly improved, there re-mained an atmosphere of rawness and corruption.

By the time Isabelle Moodie Frost made the long journey, in November of 1873, her husband was well acquainted with the past and present of San Francisco. He had also found and furnished a small apartment at 737 Pine Street, within easy walking distance of the *Bulletin* office; and from the moment of his bride's arrival in the city, Frost showed a genuinely protective attentiveness. Because his wife was not an experi-enced cook and housekeeper, he gallantly insisted that any form of housework was too menial and exhausting for one in her delicate condition. As a result, they soon moved from Pine Street to a good hotel, the Abbotsford House, on the corner of Broadway and Larkin Street.

After they grew tired of hotel life, they found another apartment, at 14 Eddy Place. But before their child was born, they apparently found an even-better place, on Washington Street, only a few blocks south of the Abbotsford.

The nearer the day came, the greater the show of the husband's devotion. And by the night of March 26, 1874, he became far more upset than his wife by the prospect of the imminent ordeal. Fortunately, the brandished revolver was not needed—and the obstetrical skills of the doctor were not too much impaired by the threat of violence. But it was characteristic of this impetuous, New England–hating Yankee that his Copperhead sympathies led him to name his son after the Confederate hero, Robert Lee. (Mrs. Frost, given little choice in the matter, may at least have consoled herself—as a poetess and as a Scot—that Robert was a name that had for her some cherished associations.)

The mother had, indeed, shown less fear than Robert Frost's father at the time their son was brought into the world. Yet, the event had scarcely occurred before she was almost overwhelmed with fright—and, even, panic.

Her husband had restrained his vices so honorably during the first year of their marriage, that he had earned her adoration. But she noticed that, for causes more easily felt than articulated, he no sooner became the father of a son than he began to slip into habits of drinking, gambling, and dalliance. For a time the purity and innocence of his very religious wife, absorbed as she was with the care of her first child, may have helped to protect her from any awareness of his dalliance. His extraordinary fondness for whiskey ("strong-man's food," as he liked to call it) was another matter. Whiskey seemed to turn this apparently devoted husband into a dangerously brutal man—who, often, went into a rage and smashed furniture if his wife so much as implied her disappointments and protests. (Years later, after she became a widow and after her son was old enough to share confidences, she told him that during the first few months of his life she had more than once snatched him from his cradle and carried him into the street, then into a neighbor's home, for fear his father's drunken violence might otherwise cause the death of child and mother.) To her, it seemed tragic and inexplicable that the man who had wooed her with promises of support in "the rugged ways of life" could have become transformed, as she said, "into a Heathcliff."

During those days when she lived in constant dread, she found her greatest consolation in prayer and in church work. Immediately after her arrival in San Francisco, she had for several months been accompanied by her husband as she visited various churches, before deciding to establish affiliation. Inclined toward the Scotch-Presbyterian liturgy since childhood, she was dissatisfied with the California variations of it.

Her next choice had been stimulated not only by the faith of her uncle in Columbus, but also by the writings of the late Thomas Starr King, the distinguished pastor of the Unitarian church in San Francisco. Briefly, the Frosts attended what had been King's church. But Mrs. Frost was far too mystically inclined to gain any lasting sustenance from the rationalistic fare of Unitarian sermons. She craved an atmosphere more congenial to her gift of "second sight," and happily she found it in the Society of the New Jerusalem. (Emanuel Swedenborg had established the foundations of the society only after his own powers of second sight had enabled him to converse with spirits and angels—through dreams and visions and mysterious conversations.)

In San Francisco the Swedenborgian minister was the picturesque and vigorous John Doughty, whom the Frosts had met as a neighbor during the brief period when they were living near his home, at the foot of Nob Hill. Doughty had in 1852 helped to erect an attractively small house of worship on the north side of O'Farrell Street, between Mason and Taylor. To that church, after she became a member of it, Mrs. Frost took her son for baptism. To this very sympathetic friend she also took her burdens when she began to fear that her marriage would end in ruin.

She was hurt when her husband refused to join the Swedenborgian church. Soon after their child was born, she began to notice how easily her husband found excuses for being unable to attend church with her and how openly scornful he became of spiritual matters. She was also troubled to find that his tastes were better satisfied by the "low jinks" and "high jinks" rituals of the Bohemian Club, newly organized in San Francisco to promote social and intellectual rapport between journalists, other writers, artists, actors, and musicians.

Not all of the friendships made by her husband at the Bohemian Club were displeasing to Mrs. Frost. One of its most serious members was an attractive Philadelphia-born adventurer, a giant of a man, Henry George. George had in the summer of 1871 published a pamphlet entitled *Our Land and Land Policy,* in which he urged that every man had a natural right to apply his labor to the land; that when the land is privately owned and man must pay rent to use it, he is robbed of some of his labor; that taxes should be on land values only, thus taking for the community what the community has produced and relieving industry of the incubus of all other taxes. His pamphlet won him a position as part-owner and editor of a newspaper primarily designed to attack and expose public abuses, the *Daily Evening Post.*

As editor-in-chief of the *Post,* Henry George gradually attracted Mr. Frost away from the *Bulletin* and gave him work as city editor, a position Frost kept for nearly nine years. George had a steadying influence on Frost, even after the *Post* changed hands, forcing George out. The George and Frost families became close friends and frequently visited in each other's homes. (Long before the private printing of *Progress and Poverty,* the Frosts became converts to the "single tax" doctrine, and they never relinquished their firm belief in it.) The growing intimacy of the two families may have enabled Mrs. Frost to share confidences with Mrs. George and to seek advice concerning the problem of living with a man who, while becoming a success as a newspaper editor, repeatedly failed as husband and father. Perhaps she even confided that a new crisis had driven her to an awkward decision.

Carrying her second child and fearing that her husband's violence, under the influence of whiskey, might cause her injury, she was determined to leave him. It must have been difficult to explain her plans and to secure money for travel. But in the spring of 1876 she made the journey across the continent, with her two-year-old son, Robbie, ostensibly to visit friends and to meet for the first time the parents of her husband, in Lawrence, Massachusetts. Probably more by accident than design, she was still in Lawrence visiting the Frosts when, on June 25, 1876, she gave birth to the second child, a girl—for whom she could not immediately find a name.

Nothing is known of how Mrs. Frost was received by her in-laws, how she explained her extraordinary visit, or what she said about her marital difficulties. One hint of awkwardness may be surmised from the fact that she left Lawrence, with her two children, as soon as she could.

There was a haven in New England where Isabelle Moodie Frost knew she would be welcomed. It was a farm in Greenfield, Massachusetts, the family home of a close friend named Sarah Newton, with whom Belle Moodie had taught school for several years in Columbus. Sarah Newton always spent her summer vacations with her parents in Greenfield, and it is probable that Mrs. Frost had made arrangements to reach Greenfield, with her son, well before the time her second child was expected. Under any circumstance, she did receive affectionate and considerate attentions from all of the Newtons, whose urgings kept her in Greenfield throughout the summer of 1876. And because the family atmosphere at the Newton farm was devout and pious, it was well suited to the needs and temperament of their somewhat-forlorn summer visitor.

It must have been to the farm in Greenfield that the husband of Belle Frost addressed contrite and apologetic letters—letters so persuasive they finally convinced her it might be safe to return to him. Even so, she attached certain conditions, for she did not go back, with her children, alone.

After traveling from Greenfield to Ohio by train, she spent the entire autumn of 1876 in Columbus with friends and relatives. (The attention paid her children by two of her Moodie cousins helped her to decide on a name for her daughter: her Cousin Jeanie, who during mid-March had married Alexander Procter, and her Cousin Florence, who in 1879 would marry William G. Harrington. The name chosen for the child was Jeanie Florence.) In Columbus she renewed acquaintance with an intimate of high-school days there, Blanche Rankin. Miss Rankin had been living precariously, even desperately, with a dipsomaniac father, a widower. She welcomed the invitation to accompany the Frost trio to California and to live with the Frosts in San Francisco until she could establish herself there. The arrangement worked well, over a period of several years, and the Frost children grew up calling her Aunt Blanche.

Many new adventures had engaged the attentions of William Prescott Frost, Jr. during his wife's long absence from San Francisco. With the help of Henry George he had aligned himself with the machinery of the Democratic Party in the campaign on behalf of Samuel J. Tilden, Governor of New York and Democratic candidate for President. Mrs. Frost, while still in Ohio, took cognizance of these matters when writing to her husband on November first:

". . . I sincerely hope that such severe labor will not make you sick. It scarcely seems wise for you with so many duties pressing on evry side to do so much. I know how deeply interested you are in the present campaign, but you should not entirely forget that excellent proverb suited to all kinds of warfare. 'Discretion is the better part of valor.' I hope for your sake that the Democrats will win. As for myself I would like a change just to satisfy my curiosity. I wish to see if the Democratic party can get public affairs out of their present mess."

Mrs. Frost was well aware that the "present mess," national and local, had its roots in glaring malfeasances throughout both terms of President Grant's administration. Also contributing were the financial panic and depression that followed the collapse of Jay Cooke's powerful banking firm in New York City on September 18, 1873. Another "mess" had developed in San Francisco on August 27, 1875, when W. C. Ralston's seemingly impregnable Bank of California had closed its doors during a "run" carefully engineered by Ralston's enemies. Ralston had taken the last of his famous swimming exercises in the bay, and to the many citizens of San Francisco who suddenly found themselves bankrupt it made little difference whether Ralston's drowning had been accidental or suicidal. The ensuing collapse of California industries, and consequent destitution among the unemployed in San Francisco, became widespread. Then, the California Workingmen's Party began to frighten San Francisco by holding protest meetings and threatening violence unless political graft ceased and restrictions were placed on the importation of cheaply paid Chinese laborers. This cumulative "mess" caused the Democrats to hope for local and national successes in the fall elections.

The Democrats were disappointed. When the electoral votes were counted, announcement was made that the new President was Rutherford B. Hayes, who had won, over the Democratic candidate, Tilden, by a single vote. Embittered, Henry George soon turned to writing his inquiry into the causes of industrial depressions, while William Prescott Frost, Jr., equally embittered, dedicated more and more of his energies to working for the Democratic Party in San Francisco.

When Mrs. Frost wrote her warning that it scarcely seemed wise for her husband to do so much when so many duties pressed on him from every side, she had not been aware of one folly that had already wasted much of his energy. Among the sporting events of those years, walking races had become extremely popular, and during his Harvard days Frost had indulged sufficiently in this game to pride himself on his abilities. When the celebrated walker Dan O'Leary challenged San Franciscans by making the public boast that he could give any man a half-day start and overtake him in a six-day-and-night walking race—each man to sleep during the race as much or as little as he chose—Frost accepted the challenge. Bets were placed, arrangements were made for the contest to be held at the Mechanics' Pavilion in San Francisco, and the race was carried through.

The city editor of the *Post* finished in first place, but O'Leary refused to pay his bet. He claimed Frost had repeatedly violated the rule that the walker's forward heel must always touch the ground before the other foot was lifted from the ground. The hard feelings that grew out of this were not nearly so important to Frost as the ailments he suffered as a result of his exhausting ordeal. By the time his wife returned to San Francisco he was undergoing medical treatment for consumption (not yet called tuberculosis).

Casual and scornful in his references to his illness, the young man insisted he would throw it off. As soon as he could make his fortune, from Comstock silver-mine investments, he would take the popular cure, by going to Hawaii, with his family. For the present, he was too busy to do more than allay the symptoms with his favorite medicine, whiskey.

SAN FRANCISCO
CHILDHOOD YEARS

(1876–1885)

As A grown man, Robert Frost said his earliest memories of his childhood in San Francisco were of romping, with his mother, up and down the dimly lit corridors of the Abbotsford House, the relatively small, yet somewhat barnlike, hotel on the northwest slope of Nob Hill. It became home again for the family as soon as Mrs. Frost returned, with her children and Aunt Blanche, late in November 1876. The boy's mother, always trying to shield Robbie and Jeanie from hurts, concealed her own apprehensions and did her best to make circumstances seem brighter than they were. Nevertheless, because the intermittent ardor and cruelty of her husband soon created new situations not unlike those that had caused her to leave him, she had so much love to spare that she nearly smothered her children with it.

If she saw the danger of spoiling them by being overly protective, she also felt the need for giving them extra attention and love. Both of them showed early signs of nervous and physical ailments. From the first, as babies, they were nurtured on fear.

Somewhat blindly, perhaps, Robbie's father had boasted in a letter written only seven months after the child's birth, "We are all well, particularly the little boy, who, in fact, has never seen a really sick day in his short life." Similarly, four months after their daughter's birth, the mother had written to the father, from Ohio: "Of the baby I can only write ditto to what I have already written[:] healthy, pretty and good. I am sure she will be good with her papa if he will not tease her." Her hint about teasing was not unrelated to emotional difficulties unintentionally conveyed from father to son. Before Mrs. Frost separated from her husband, she had been troubled by the clumsy ways in which the humorless man, trying to play with the boy, seemed to take pleasure in rough handling that often caused tears.

In the same letter, she had written, "Robbie keeps pretty well at present." Pretty well. In spite of her attempts to put unpleasantness aside at all times, she had already become aware that her son's extraordinary sensitivities were closely related to frequent upsets and ailments. The child had clearly suffered much. There could have been little that was soothing during the long journey back East, the brief visit with his paternal grandparents, the decrease of attention from his mother at the time of his sister's birth, the protracted stay in Greenfield, the visits made in Ohio, and the long return trip to San Francisco. Years later Aunt Blanche told him that throughout the early days of his boyhood he had seemed so constantly the victim of mysterious aches and pains, in his head and stomach, that she and his mother feared he would never survive to manhood.

In all these California years the sustaining atmosphere of even a relatively serene and well-ordered home was unknown to the Frost children. Tidiness was not one of Mrs. Frost's concerns. She never became a good housekeeper or a good cook. Her loyal friends excused her by saying her devout nature was far too spiritual to allow her to be bothered with worldly details. It is probable that the repeated insistence of her husband on moving from apartment life to hotel life was caused, at least in part, by these limitations.

Another problem was the frequently precarious state of the family budget. In trying to alleviate that condition, Mrs. Frost earned some money by reviewing books for her husband's newspaper. Some of her poems also appeared in the *Post,* the longest being a two-hundred-line, blank-verse dramatic monologue in a Browningesque manner, "The Artist's Motive." She even tried her hand at writing stories for children.

As soon as Robbie and Jeanie were old enough to be interested, their mother combined storytelling with devout moralizing, for the purpose of teaching them the fundamentals of religious and theological truth. Bible stories provided a daily fare, and particular emphasis was given to the Genesis stories. Over and over they heard the story of Adam and Eve, the story of Cain and Abel, the story of Noah and the ark into which the paired animals marched. Mrs. Frost made the stories illustrate moral truths that also involved pairs of opposites—evil and good, chaos and order, darkness and light—until Robbie developed a habit of thinking in terms of paired images. (Throughout his life he was inclined to build his thinking, and his poetry, around these pairs.)

Mrs. Frost advanced her storytelling to include narratives of heroes and hero-worship: classical myths, battles and leaders of her native Scotland, battles and leaders of the American Civil War. One story, which took on cumulative meanings for both children through retelling, was of the brave French girl named Joan whose very sensitive ears helped her listen to the voice of God speaking directly to her.

A skillful teacher, their mother was also eager to give them early exposure to classroom discipline, and when Robbie was five years old, arrangements were made to have him attend a kindergarten privately conducted in the home of a Russian lady, Madame Zeitska. The shy, sensitive boy was so frightened by the prospect of leaving his mother that her reassurances scarcely persuaded him he would enjoy playing with other children in the school. The Frosts were then living at 1431 Steiner Street, at some distance from Madame Zeitska's home; and even the enticement of a pleasant ride in a horsedrawn omnibus, halfway across the city of San Francisco, did not appeal to him.

On the first day, when Robbie made the strange journey, he felt, before he had reached the school, unpleasantly lost; and the day was not half over when someone pushed him too high and too long in a backyard swing, with the result that he was sick to his stomach. A further agony occurred when the omnibus driver on the home journey had so much difficulty in finding Robbie's house that the boy wept for fear he would never see his mother again. The next day, when it came time for him to get ready for school, he developed a severe pain in his stomach and was permitted to stay at home. Thereafter, whenever attempts were made to send him back to Madame Zeitska's, the pains returned. Pleading and cajolery were in vain. His first day of kindergarten was his last.

Similar pains returned soon after he was given his first taste of public school, in the autumn of 1880. The Frosts were living once again at the Abbotsford House, and the public school was almost across the street from the hotel. At first Robbie seemed completely charmed by the first-grade teacher, Miss Fisher; but after little more than one week of rough-and-tumble among boisterous companions, he again began to complain of pains in his stomach. Even if his mother suspected the ailment was nothing more than nervous tension, she was sure the child was miserable. So, she permitted him to stay at home until he felt well enough to want to go back. He never did feel well enough, and his mother reluctantly decided to let him carry on his first-grade studies under her guidance.

Unintentionally pampered and spoiled, the boy showed so much distaste for mastering "the three Rs" that he progressed very slowly. If there was one exception, it was in the early phases of his learning to write his letters and words and sentences. After he progressed far enough to be given a fine new copybook with a sample at the head of each page, he worked with such eager industry that he became greatly upset whenever he made a mistake. One serious slip of the pencil would be enough to send him into such a rage of disgust with himself that he would tear the page out of the book, so he could begin again with a perfect sheet. His mother's idealism, thus reflected, had already caused him to give sympathetic ear to those exacting biblical words, "Be ye therefore perfect, even as your Father which is in heaven is perfect." The older he grew, the more he puzzled over that exhortation.

Under his mother's supervision, Robbie finished enough of his first-grade work to be qualified for entrance to the second grade of the nearby public school. His new teacher, Miss Radford, immediately heightened his liking for geography and managed to keep him more or less tolerant of school discipline, until February of 1882. By the time St. Valentine's Day arrived, he had become so bold and enterprising that he crawled on hands and knees across the back of the schoolroom to retrieve a Valentine from an empty desk—and was caught by Miss Radford. Punishment, administered before the entire class, took the form of a few slaps across the palm of his right hand with some pieces of rattan. The pain inflicted was nothing, compared with the shame and indignity of this public disgrace and with his resentment over what seemed to him a gross injustice. The next day he firmly refused to go to school. His mother tried as firmly to overcome his arguments, but his stomach pains returned with such severity that Robbie was once again permitted to carry on his studies at home.

Entering the third grade, in another school, in the fall of 1882 he submitted pleasantly to a new teacher named Miss Dudley, until inevitable tensions and difficulties offended him. That was the end of his public-school education in San Francisco. Such schoolwork as he could be persuaded to do—and it was not much—he completed at home.

While Robbie was learning during these early years to take advantage of his mother's leniency, he found that his father's characteristic impatience, quick temper, and severity of discipline soon dressed the balance. Engrossed in his own work and seeming to find little time or inclination for play with his children, Mr. Frost restricted his function as father, primarily, to tasks of correction and punishment. Sometimes blows fell without warning—and, as it seemed to the children, without just cause. Frequently, when the boy indulged his creative skills by improving accounts of his exploits and by adding imaginative embroideries, he found he ran the risk of being called a liar by his father and of being punished accordingly. Robbie's mother tried to make the boy understand that earthly obedience was inseparable from obedience to heavenly dictates; that all forms of earthly naughtiness were seen by the Heavenly Father, who would one day call each individual to account and would mete out punishment. The Frost children were made to understand quite clearly that the fear of the Lord was the beginning of wisdom. But in Robbie's experiences cumulative fear of a distant, mysteriously punishing Heavenly Father became inseparable from his firsthand knowledge and fear of his earthly father, whose punishments were so inconsistent and severe.

His mother tried to help Robbie accept, with stoicism, whatever punishment came his way—either from his earthly or his heavenly father. Although it was a hard lesson to learn, he was given innumerable opportunities to practice the Christian doctrines of humility, submission, acceptance, and obedience. The older he grew, the surer he became that there was little enough he could do about some matters, except submit. But there were times when submission to his father's punishment made him puzzle anew over the relationship between his just deserts and what he got.

One of the most baffling and grievous incidents occurred on a memorable Halloween, spoiled early for the children by their father's insistence that he would not tolerate the clutter caused by the messy business of scooping out pumpkins, with knives and spoons, prior to cutting eyes and noses and mouths. The best the Frost children could do was to visit friends and enjoy the process vicariously. That evening, hours after he had shared his disappointments with neighboring children, Robbie answered a knock at the door and found his best friend standing there, with a present: a handsome, grinning jack-o'-lantern, complete with candle burning inside. Too much embittered by his father's edict, Robbie forgot his manners. He blurted out the fact that his father would not let him have a jack-o'-lantern and, so saying, slammed the door. His father, accidentally witnessing the dramatic scene, and perhaps more enraged by this exposure of his own selfishness than by Robbie's bad manners, reached for the nearest weapon handy. It happened to be a metal dog chain. With it he lashed the boy's legs until they bled.

During some of the crises that threatened to cause paternal beatings, Robbie was helped by his mother, as on one occasion when he lost a ten-cent piece. His father, working at home on editorial writing, had sent the boy up to Mr. McPartland's grocery store for a package of cigarettes; and all had gone well until Robbie started home, playfully tossing and catching some change. As the dime fell from his hand, it bounced on the board sidewalk and rolled some distance downhill before it disappeared through a crack. Dreading the consequences of that loss, Robbie tried his best, with two sticks, to recover the dime. Failing, he went back to the store and asked Mr. McPartland for another dime. The storekeeper refused, the loiterers laughed, and the boy fled to his mother. Apparently sharing her son's apprehension, she had one last recourse. She took the boy into his bedroom, where they knelt and prayed. Then, she let him go alone to deliver the cigarettes and to explain the accident as best he could. His father, scarcely raising his head, reached for the cigarettes and dismissed him with a distant "Never mind." To Robbie, thus miraculously spared, it seemed clear he and his mother had demonstrated the wonderful power of prayer.

On later occasions, however, he was perplexed to find that prayer did not always work miracles. Again and again he asked his mother about this discrepancy, and she always explained it to him in terms hard for him to understand. The gist of what he learned was that the ways of God were very mysterious and it was wise not to inquire too closely into them.

Mrs. Frost constantly tried to teach her son that he should count only the sunny hours. She was the first to arouse his enjoyment of geography, and she did it by calling his attention to the natural wonders and beauties of those physical features they could actually see from the lookout points of three hills they climbed in their walks: Telegraph Hill, Russian Hill, Nob Hill. And their ventures around San Francisco were not all devoted to the study of geography. Much to the liking of Robbie and his sister was the splendid horsecar ride through the sand dunes and across the peninsula, to the Cliff House, below Land's End; then, the walks over paths along the cliffs to hear the ocean roaring and watch it shattering into foam against the nearby Seal Rocks. To the south of the Cliff House was a long wooden stairway, down which they walked to play on the white sands of the beach and, even, to wade in pools left by outgoing tides.

Other adventures were enjoyed by the children when their mother took them to Woodward's Gardens, which combined the attractions of a botanical display, an amusement park, and a zoo. It occupied the entire block from Mission to Valencia Streets. Mr. Woodward's splendidly kept exhibits of California trees, shrubs, and flowers, which must have appealed to Mrs. Frost, were not nearly so fascinating to her son and daughter as were the menagerie, aquarium, museum, hippodrome, roller-skating rink, and picnic grounds. As Robbie grew older the menagerie pleased him most of all. It was there he once conducted a little experiment, using a newly acquired "burning-glass" to tickle the noses and paws of two monkeys begging for peanuts. The playful experiment went well enough until one monkey reached out through the bars, snatched the glass, retreated to the back of the cage, and buried the mysterious torture instrument in straw, well out of the boy's reach.

Another kind of outing occurred annually for the entire Frost family: the summer conclave of the Caledonia Club of San Francisco, organized for the encouragement, practice, and preservation of the games, customs, and manners of Scotland. As soon as Robbie grew old enough to overcome his shyness, he entered into the Caledonia Club footraces, with other children his own age. His athletic father, eager to encourage the boy, bought him a pair of spikeless running slippers and began to coach him on fine points of sprinting and distance running. After one period of energetic preparation, which consisted of a daily workout on board sidewalks near his home, Robbie attended the next Caledonia Club picnic so thoroughly prepared for his race that he won it and returned home, proudly, with a cash prize. In various activities he was gaining poise, as he gradually overcame his bashful discomfort in the presence of strangers.

The last phase of Robert Frost's boyhood in San Francisco began splendidly, when he was six years old; it ended in darkness, when he was eleven. During these five years he did his best to cope with experiences that alternately exhilarated and depressed him, experiences sometimes as precipitous as those San Francisco streets that climbed steeply up over Nob Hill and plunged as steeply down the other side.

On an important morning in June of 1880, when the fortunes of the Frosts were ascendent, neither the six-year-old Robbie nor his sister, Jeanie, could mistake the evidence that something important was about to happen. They watched with wonder as their mother helped their father complete preparations for a long journey. He had been elected a member of the California delegation being sent to Cincinnati, Ohio, to the national Democratic convention; and they were going with him, on the ferry, at least as far as the cavernous Oakland train sheds, where they would hear a brass-band send-off of the delegation.

Having earned this honor through his energetic work with the Democratic Party, their father had reason to believe he was well started up the ladder of a political career. He confided that before too many years passed he hoped to make an even-more-significant departure from San Francisco—to the capital of the nation, as a Representative or, even, Senator.

Early in the summer of 1880, Robbie's father was given another honorable assignment. William Starke Rosecrans, Union hero of the Chattanooga campaign, had been nominated as candidate for Congress from California. In support of that nomination the journalistic skills of Mr. Frost were requested by the party, to write a campaign booklet on the life and accomplishments of Rosecrans. The general himself provided materials for Mr. Frost; the pamphlet, skillfully written and quickly published, enhanced the political standing of the candidate and of the author.

Robbie was excited when the campaigning for the fall elections burst into a frenzy of parades, brass bands, and rhetoric. Robbie's father honored the boy by sending him on little errands to ward politicians in the neighborhood and, then, by letting him ride on a float in a parade. Near election day he marched with his father in a torchlight procession and enjoyed the hullabaloo—until sparks from the torches fell into his hair. All these adventures brought a new sense of closeness between father and son.

Descent into a new kind of darkness occurred as soon as the election results were announced that fall. Garfield defeated Hancock in the Presidential race, and Robbie suffered because disappointment transformed his father into a silent, brooding stranger. The boy was hurt by the way this dour man came home from work, night after night, with no word of greeting for anyone, and even more hurt by the way he often sat in silence through the evening meal. Morning after morning Robbie watched his father eat breakfast alone, toss off his jigger of whiskey, and depart without a gesture of farewell to son or wife or daughter. It gradually became apparent that part of the man's discouragement was caused by his debilitating illness, made worse by the amount of energy he had poured into the futile campaign.

A new buoyancy was given to all of the Frosts, in the early summer of 1882, when Aunt Blanche proposed a vacation from city life. In the fall of 1880 she had taken a position as teacher, and soon afterward she had married a man named Eastman and moved to Napa Valley, some fifty miles to the north of San Francisco. Urging that the Frosts bring their children to Napa and spend several weeks, Aunt Blanche found rooms for Mrs. Frost and Robbie and Jeanie at a ranch near where she and her husband were working. Mr. Frost seemed content to be left alone in the city.

For the children these weeks were enough to open an entirely new world of experience, which delighted them. There were perpetual wonders to be seen and admired. Robbie and Jeanie were permitted to play at helping to feed the horses, the cattle, the chickens. They were, even, allowed to play at gathering eggs. Under their mother's guidance they also took long walks into the countryside and marveled at the fertile river-valley fields, the vineyard-covered foothills, and the forests on the surrounding mountains.

Only once before had the children been given a summer vacation from the city. When Robbie was five years old his father had taken the family up into Marin County, north of San Francisco, and they stayed for a short time at a hotel in the town of Nicasio, surrounded by mountains and forests. Robbie, too young to remember much about the natural beauty of that region, had been most impressed by the hotelkeeper's daughter, a girl his own age, who had caught him cheating at croquet—and had swiftly punished him by hitting his head with her mallet. No such unpleasantness happened to him at Napa. Instead, his first taste of farming caused him to make a boyish resolve that some day he would own a ranch in Napa Valley.

A far-more-adventurous summer vacation was planned by Robbie's father the next year, when the boy was nine. Several of the journalists who were charter members of the Bohemian Club organized country outings for members and friends who enjoyed roughing it. One of these outings, designed as a convenient retreat from the summer dust of San Francisco, was held by pitching tents on the beach at the edge of the bay, near the village of Sausalito. Each morning the men who were not on vacation took the ferry from Sausalito to San Francisco for their day's work.

Robbie's mother would never have consented to take her children to this Bohemian Club camp if she had known beforehand what she was going to find. Her husband's cronies amused themselves, evenings, with cardplaying, gambling, tippling, and revolver practice—using as targets empty whiskey bottles thrown out into the bay.

For Robbie, these brief days at Sausalito were marred by his father's mania for long-distance swimming. When well, he had been a powerful swimmer, and he was convinced this form of exercise would help cure his consumption. Several times, after he returned from San Francisco in the evening, he walked with his son along the beach and around a shoulder of land toward the Golden Gate, until they reached his favorite spot. Robbie, left alone on the shore as guardian of his father's coat and towel and whiskey bottle, would watch the man begin his long swim through cold water to an offshore bell buoy. As the choppy waves began to hide the swimmer from view, Robbie's fears would mount—and would continue to mount until he could, finally, see his father climbing the metal ladder on the buoy. The man would stand there just long enough to catch his breath and, then, would dive off to start toward shore. Fear would surge over Robbie, in wave after wave of apprehension, until he could see his father again. With mingled relief and pride, the boy would run down to the edge of the water, offer the towel, follow his father's labored steps up to dry sand, and watch the man reach for the bottle of whiskey.

Another kind of fear, evoked by a different ocean-water setting, remained memorable to Robbie. Whenever his father chose to celebrate a minor streak of luck in gambling, in politics, or in the stock market, the impetuous man splurged by taking his family to dinner at one of his favorite restaurants. For the children, the best of these was the Cliff House, with its lofty view out over the Pacific. After one particularly cheerful dinner there, the entire Frost family descended to the beach for a walk along the shore in the dusk. Robbie, soon absorbed in a solitary game of lashing stone targets with a seaweed whip, unintentionally dropped so far behind the others that they passed out of sight beyond outcroppings of rock and ledge. When at last the boy turned to look for them and realized he was alone under the cliff, he was frightened. The roar of the waves seemed hostile. The towering wall of rock leaned out and threatened. Dark clouds reached down with crooked hands. Overwhelmed with terror, he ran and kept running until he overtook his parents. (Years later, in the poem "Once by the Pacific," he tried to capture the mood of that moment; he endowed with prophecy the menacing images of waves, clouds, and cliff.)

A far-more-subdued sense of fear and wonder was experienced by Robbie whenever his mother revealed her own prophetic and mystical belief in her powers of second sight. She taught her children to understand that they were always in close rapport with the spiritual world, even when they were least aware of it, that between earth and the heavenly realm of the angels was the realm of fairyland. She loved to tell them fairy stories, and the more fantastic they were, the more they appealed to Robbie's imagination. He particularly liked to hear about children his own age who established contact with elves.

As Robbie developed his own capacities for second sight and second hearing, he almost scared himself out of his wits. He was still a child in San Francisco when he first began to hear voices. If left alone in a room for some time, he was often simultaneously fascinated and terrified by hearing a voice, which spoke to him. At such moments, if he were playing on the floor, he would retreat to the protection of the largest chair and kneel in it with his forehead pressed against the back, his eyes shut, his hands over his ears. But he could not shut out the sounds of the voice, and the harder he pressed his hands over his ears, the clearer and louder the voice came. Sometimes he could hear whole sentences. At other times the words were so indistinct he understood only such meanings as were conveyed through the tones of the voice. At still other times he clearly heard the voice repeating something he himself had said a few minutes earlier—repeating, yet endowing his own words with tones so different from his that the effect seemed to be one of mockery.

When he told his mother about these perplexing experiences, she seemed to understand them better than he did. Sympathetically, she hinted that he shared, with her, mystical powers; but she warned him not to tell others about these experiences. Anyone else might misunderstand.

His mother helped him to feel that the different voices he heard when he was awake were somehow related to voices he heard in his dreams. She always endowed her own dreams with meanings that related the worlds of the seen and the unseen. One particular story was finally written out by Mrs. Frost and published, in a booklet entitled *The Land of Crystal; or, Christmas Days with the Fairies*. Although the story may have attracted only slight attention when printed, it is valuable as a reflection of how Mrs. Frost used stories as parables for the moral education of her children.

The storytelling of Robbie's mother may have inspired him to try his hand at the only story he wrote out during his San Francisco boyhood. The details had all come to him in one of his dreams: Alone, after running away from home and after having become lost in the mountains, he had followed a scarcely visible trail, which led through a cleft between two mountaintop cliffs. The trail led him down, down, down into a beautiful green valley where he was welcomed and honored as a hero by a tribe of Indians who were the only inhabitants of the secret valley. The Indians themselves had escaped from their enemies by retreating through the narrow pass into this valley, where life was always serene. Occasionally, their braves made sorties back through the secret pass, in order to make surprise attacks against their enemies. But these braves always returned, victoriously, to their happy valley.

This much of the dream-story Robbie wrote out as his first narrative composition. Later, on nights when he was sent to bed while still suffering from the hurts of the day, he consolingly told the story to himself, over and over, adding to it new episodes, which he never wrote out.

Some of his worst hurts, suffered during his years in San Francisco, occurred after the Frost family made the last of many moves, this time to an apartment on the ground floor of 1404 Leavenworth Street, just a short distance from the house where he had been born. From this relatively unfashionable district, on the back side of Nob Hill, the boy frequently walked with his mother and sister up Leavenworth Street to the high shoulder of the hill and on down the southern slope to where the truly fashionable "nobs" and nabobs had built or were building their spectacular mansions.

Between these pretentious abodes and the Frost apartment stood a natural barrier. It was an undeveloped block-square mound of rock, dirt, and clay—the true "knob" or height-of-land for this particular hill, too precipitous for any kind of building other than the forlorn shacks squatters had erected near the very top. Into the sides of this knob had been cut the straight lines of four streets that encroached as much as they could, streets that required retaining walls of varying heights to keep the mound in its place. (Washington Street cut into it on the north, Leavenworth on the west, Clay on the south, and Jones on the east.) The scrub brush on the steep flanks of this wasteland provided excellent hiding places for youngsters in the neighborhood. They formed little gangs, staked claims to different parts, then drove off any intruders who lacked proper membership.

For at least two years after the Frost family moved to Leavenworth

Street, Robbie was neither old enough nor bold enough to mingle with these tough youngsters who made a playground out of the hilltop. But by the time he was ten years old he had acquired enough experience, while playing on the streets in his neighborhood, to become envious of the boys his own age who had been granted membership in the Washington Street gang. He set his heart on being accepted by them—at any price. Finally, he mustered courage enough to ask if he could join the gang. The leader was a tough, overgrown teenager named Seth Balsa, who studied Robbie with suspicion, before asking if he knew how to fight. The very sound of the word made Robbie wince, but he managed to say yes. All right, said Balsa, could he lick that kid over there? He pointed to Percy McPartland, son of the Leavenworth Street grocer. Robbie concealed his fright by answering, boastfully, that he could lick two boys the size of Percy. Balsa, to be obliging, called to another boy, and the challenge was explained; Robbie was given his chance to fight them both at once.

As a spectator of street fights, Robbie had learned that the game of fisticuffs in San Francisco was catch-as-catch-can, with no holds barred. At a safe distance from these fights, he had even come to admire the efficiency of wrapping one arm around the neck of an opponent, holding the head in a convenient position, and punching at the eyes with the free fist. Desperately now, he dove at Percy and tried to employ this familiar strategy. He did succeed in getting his right arm around Percy's neck and in throwing one punch, but he quickly found he needed his left hand for warding off blows aimed at his own face by Percy's partner.

The cheering and jeering watchers wanted to see blood. They were soon satisfied. In no time, all three fighters were on the ground, as they punched, kicked, and scratched. It was no contest. By the time Seth Balsa had seen enough and stepped in to separate the warriors, one of Percy's eyes was well marked; but Robbie's nose was bleeding, both of his cheeks were bloody, and his lower lip was badly split. Nevertheless, the Washington Street gang had been impressed by Robbie's courage, and Balsa welcomed him into full membership, before sending him home to get his face patched up.

Painfully hurt and on the verge of tears, Rob started home—filled with misery and elation. He had not expected that he would have to pay such a price and take such a beating, but before he reached 1404 Leavenworth Street he began telling himself this was the most important day in his life so far. His courage had conquered his cowardice. Suddenly, he had grown up. Some kind of transformation had occurred through this baptism of blood, and he was ready to serve his leader, Seth Balsa, in whatever battles lay ahead. What actually lay ahead, Robbie soon discovered, had less to do with fighting than with the finer points of acquiring and handling portable property.

Many of these daring hill-children coasted recklessly down any negotiable street in little four-wheel wagons. The wear on wheels was severe, and Seth Balsa's wagon needed a new pair. He knew where a pair could be found, in the cellar of a house on Leavenworth Street; but the cellar window was too small for Balsa to enter, and he flatteringly sought Robbie's help. Eager to demonstrate his courage in another way, Robbie went to the house with Balsa by twilight. Together they crawled under the porch, and then, Robbie watched with admiration as Balsa quietly jimmied the narrow window. Robbie eased himself in through the small opening, feet first. With matches provided by Balsa, he found the wheels and passed them out. It was too easy; and, just to show his courage, Robbie looked around for more plunder. Through the window he presented several offerings (including a boxed croquet set) until Balsa finally drew the line—by rejecting Christmas-tree ornaments. A few days later, when Balsa's cart appeared on the street with all four wheels newly painted, no questions were asked. The crime had been perfectly executed, and Robbie was proud of the part he had played in it.

Only once, after that, was Robbie asked to play cat's-paw for Balsa in an act of thievery: the stealing of a small pig from a pen near the San Francisco slaughterhouse. The pig was easily caught and almost as easily disposed of, for a reasonable price, in Chinatown. Robbie's share of the proceeds was less than half; but, again, he gloried in this new demonstration of his prowess.

Another brief sequence of ups and downs occurred when ten-year-old Robbie gained the reluctant permission of his parents to sell newspapers on the streets of San Francisco. There were several paperboys in his gang, and one of them guided him through the initial procedures. He learned which papers sold best, how to get them, where to find likely customers, what tone to use in shouting the most attractive headlines, and how to make the financial accounting. He had looked forward to this new adventure, and as long as the novelty of it lasted, he enjoyed the grown-up feeling of being on his own among the pedestrians in downtown San Francisco. But the hours were long, the competition stiff, the profits disappointing. A few days were enough, and he simply quit.

While still a paperboy, reveling in his ability to make his way back and forth between his hillside home and the business section, Robbie discovered the need for ingenuity in learning to confront unexpected dangers. He was making his way downtown one afternoon, to pick up a supply of papers, when he boldly risked a shortcut through streets he usually avoided because the boys in that neighborhood carried on sporadic warfare with the Washington Street gang—and they knew Robbie as one of their enemies. He had almost completed his passage through this hostile territory, when four boys recognized him and gave chase.

Counting on his ability to outrun his pursuers, he was not immediately frightened. But his pursuers very quickly showed they had longer legs. As they began to gain on him, Robbie realized the need for emergency tactics. Inspired by desperation, he dodged off the board sidewalk, fled up the steps of the nearest house, opened the door, entered, closed the door quietly, and slid the bolt lock into place. Frightened and panting, he heard the pack stop at the foot of the steps; and he cringed as one of them shouted, "That's not where he lives." Footsteps upstairs seemed to approach a window, as though to investigate the racket; but the footsteps did not descend. Minute after minute passed, and the puzzled voices on the other side of the door gradually faded away. When it seemed safe, Robbie unlocked the door, opened it, stepped out, closed it softly, and tiptoed down to the sidewalk. His enemies had disappeared, and he went on downtown without any further trouble. On many occasions thereafter, when he passed the house that had provided him haven, he looked up at it appreciatively and wondered who lived there.

Beginning to think of himself as lucky, he felt as though a great streak of luck occurred in the summer of 1884. Again free from school, through default, he was available to serve as his father's errand boy and messenger during a political campaign. The Democrats throughout the nation had nominated Grover Cleveland for President. The Democrats in San Francisco had nominated William Prescott Frost, Jr. for the important office of city tax collector. And as Robbie became more useful to his father, the boy acquired a new sense of his own importance.

If handbills needed distribution to a streetcorner crowd, prior to one of his father's impromptu soapbox speeches, he proudly managed that. Staying to listen, he did wish his father could be more colorful and appealing in his remarks. The cold presentation of facts, the dry reticence, the complete lack of playfulness or wit or humor disappointed Robbie. He tried to excuse his father, by noticing new signs of illness. There was no question but that the chronic ailment had grown worse, and even his father seemed to acknowledge it, in a strange way. In his campaigning, whenever he passed near the slaughterhouse, he would stop just long enough to buy and drink a cup of warm blood—while Robbie, watching, would fight against nausea.

He was happier when his father took him into saloons, where the boy could display skill in tacking small posters to the ceilings by pressing a tack through the middle of the card and, then, tossing it upward with a silver dollar flat beneath the tack (to serve as a flying hammer). If his father lingered in any saloon for a drink, Robbie was always permitted to make samplings from the free-lunch counter and to study the strange variety of such fare.

His participation in all of these activities gave him an awareness that he had grown up a great deal since the last Presidential election. (He had been six years old then; now he was ten.) As the tempo of this campaign built to the frenzied phase that brought out the parades with floats, by day, and the processions with torchlights, by night, the boy entered into these activities with far more zest, far more energy, far more knowledge than he had formerly displayed. But it was his new knowledge that made him worry more and more about his father's chances for political success. There was, of course, the power of well-oiled party machinery, which brazenly fought corruption with corruption; and more than once Robbie heard his father say the Democrats were justified in stuffing ballot boxes with illegal votes—the Republicans were so notoriously dishonest that to throw the rascals out of power was an end that justified any means.

On the day of reckoning, when all votes were counted, not quite enough of them had been cast to elect William Prescott Frost, Jr. tax collector. Even the triumphant election of Grover Cleveland could not assuage the sick man's bitter personal disappointment.

For days after his defeat, he did not come home. At last he appeared, in a drunken rage, waving at his wife a ballot that had been cast against him by, he said, the minister of the First Church of the New Jerusalem, the Rev. John Doughty. He reminded his wife of her assurance that Doughty had promised to vote for Frost; he now told her she could see with her own eyes (if she believed the offered evidence) that Doughty was exactly the hypocrite and liar her husband had long accused him of being. Unconvinced, Robbie's mother did her best to soothe and placate the broken man. It was far too late for that.

So sure had he been of his approaching political success, that in June of 1884 he had resigned his position as city editor of the *Post*. After the election, the *Post* could find no work for him. Late in 1884 he was hired by another San Francisco newspaper, the *Daily Report,* but he was never well enough to carry out his duties with any consistency there. What hurt Robbie most during these gloomy months, which dragged through fall and winter and spring, was the pathetic sight of his father's apparently complete surrender to his irrevocable defeat. Whether it was illness or whiskey that made the man's eyes seem glazed, the boy could not be sure.

Perhaps his father realized how near the end might be. It was foreshadowed for his children, with frightening vividness, one afternoon in May of 1885, as they were playing on that part of the steep bank that overlooked the corner of Leavenworth and Clay streets. They saw their

father being helped off the cable car; they saw the bloodstained handkerchief he held to his mouth; they saw a friend put an arm about him to
help him walk the short distance to their home. After a doctor had been
called, after whispered conversations and frightening silences, even the
children knew what to expect. They were kept out of the sick man's
room, but during that same evening he called for Robbie. The boy went in
and sat on the bed, too frightened to understand very much of the pale
man's whispered admonitions. Afterward, he could remember only one
stern command: Never, never should Robbie hang around streetcorners
in San Francisco after dark.

The next morning the same hushed atmosphere shrouded the Frost
home. The children were given their breakfasts, sent out of the house to
play, and told they must be very quiet, because their father was terribly
ill. For the next few hours they tried to keep busy and, finally, joined
other children playing at the edge of the familiar claybank. Toward noon
one of the neighbors' boys said to them, bluntly, "There's crepe on your
door."

Their father's last request, before he died, was that his body be taken
back to New England for burial—back to the New England he had so
often said he hated. The funeral was held in the First Church of the New
Jerusalem, the service conducted by the Rev. John Doughty, whom the
dead man had detested. Then, it was necessary to consider the size of the
estate he had left, before any plans could be made.

There had been a $20,000 insurance policy, but it had lapsed because
he failed to make his payments. A bank account contained some money,
but after the widow had settled the funeral expenses and sold the
furniture in the rooms at 1404 Leavenworth Street, she had only eight
dollars in cash. The dead man's parents forwarded enough money to
defray the cost of travel. The widow and her children said good-bye to
friends; they accompanied the coffin across the bay by ferry to Oakland,
saw the coffin placed in the baggage car of their train, and started East
for another funeral service and the interment.

A RETURN TO NEW ENGLAND

(1885–1886)

FOR THE widow, dressed in black and accompanied by her two children as she made the ritualistic pilgrimage from California to Massachusetts, the future threatened to be more frightening than, even, the past had been. Nine years earlier she had cast herself and her children on the mercy, such as it was, of her husband's parents; and they had seemed to reproach her with their silence. Now she dreaded the likelihood they might somehow blame her for the wasted life, the failure, the death of their only son.

She may have tried to console herself with the thought that after she reached her destination with the coffin, and after the ordeal of the interment ceremonies, she need not stay long in New England. But where could she go? She had relatives in Ohio, and she must have considered the possibility of returning to Columbus. For obscure reasons of pride or of estrangement, she did not consider that prospect a good one. More attractive to her was the hope that she might return to San Francisco. But where could she find the money she would need for the return trip? And could she earn an adequate living for her family there?

Many times during the long journey to Massachusetts she must have sought the comfort of hoping God would provide. Here again, as she repeatedly told her son in later years, her griefs and worries were complicated by her feeling that God had *already* provided. She tortured herself with fears that she had indeed been responsible for what had happened; her immediate predicament seemed to reflect divine punishment. And if these fears were based on spiritual truth, she thought, it was her duty to bear the trials with submission.

Her greatest worries must have been for her children and for what would happen to them. Jeanie, from the time she was three years old, had suffered from ailments the doctors in San Francisco had not satisfactorily diagnosed or alleviated. No mother could have lavished more love on her child than she had given Jeanie, and yet, it seemed as though that love had made the girl too dependent. Jeanie suffered from prolonged periods of crying and hysteria, and intermittently refused to play with other children, refused to go to school, refused to leave the house. The older she grew, the more content she seemed with books.

Robbie had been another kind of care and worry in his early years; but the older he grew, the stronger and healthier he seemed to become. His mother was also certain her own religious idealism and perfectionism had taken root in Robbie. Proud of him, and constantly reassuring him that she expected him to make a name for himself someday, she had even taken the risk of telling the boy that, with his father's death, Robbie was now the man of the family, the one on whom she and Jeanie must lean more and more.

Throughout the tedious journey from California, and for years thereafter, Mrs. Frost did her best to make the children remember and revere all of the fine traits in their father. She told them his story in ways that enabled her to represent him as a brave and noble man whose great gifts and great promise had been cut off, tragically, by consumption at the untimely age of thirty-four. She reminded them that they were taking his body back to his own home for burial, because he had asked them to do so.

The two children did not look forward to their New England visit. They could see that the long train ride was, indeed, an adventure in geography, as their mother kept assuring them; but the more they saw of the United States, from the train windows, the more convinced they became that the most beautiful parts of it were those they had grown to love in California. And by the time they were in Boston—the capital of Massachusetts, and said by some to be "the hub of the universe"—Robbie found a way to express his homesickness. He held up a bright silver coin for his young sister to admire, pointed at it proudly, and called it "San Francisco!" Then, he held up a dirty copper penny—a coin rarely seen at that time in San Francisco—pointed at it with disgust, and called it "Boston!"

After the California Frosts reached Lawrence and suffered through the second funeral sermon, and the ritual at the Bellevue Cemetery, they lingered as uncomfortable guests of the bereaved parents. Robbie's responses, from the start, were hostile. His grandfather seemed to be a stiff and prim old gentleman; and his home, at 370 Haverhill Street, seemed in the same character. It was a severe, white-painted, clapboard house, disproportionately narrow and tall. Robbie's grandmother dramatized another kind of figurativeness, at least for the boy. Her stern and unsmiling face was accentuated by a peculiar nervous disorder that made her head twitch as though she were saying no, no, no to everything.

For years this odd pair had lived on the first floor of their home. Although financially comfortable, they had thriftily rented the second-floor rooms. The apartment on the second floor happened to be vacant when the California Frosts arrived. But, of course, it was possible someone might soon want to rent the rooms. So, the three poor relations were given the two small rooms, under the gable roof, on the third floor.

Both Robbie and Jeanie resented the discipline of daily routine and cringed before the watchful eyes of their grandfather. He scolded them when they tried to play on his neatly tended lawn. He scolded them whenever they approached the trim flower beds. He scolded them when they touched anything without his permission. The children also disliked their grandmother's demands that they rise early for breakfast, appear promptly at mealtime, wash their hands before sitting down at the table, and never wipe half-washed faces on her snow-white towels. She nagged at them for tracking mud, on unwiped feet, into her house. She nagged when they left screen doors half-closed.

Robbie soon made the complaint that his grandfather was cruel. As evidence, the boy told of watching the old man hide behind a corner of the house, horsewhip in hand, waiting for a bold youngster who kept slipping into the yard, unasked, to pick a few flowers. Robbie had indignantly watched his grandfather creep up on the intruder and lash the child's bare legs with the horsewhip. According to Robbie, another kind of cruelty occurred a few days later. Given some firecrackers by his Great-Uncle Elihu Colcord, a brother of Robbie's Grandmother Frost, Robbie had understood the instructions that these treasures should be put away until the Fourth of July. But the boy had to set off just one, to see how it worked. His well-satisfied ears had not stopped ringing before he felt, rather than saw, a presence that disturbed him. He turned to find his grandfather staring down from his ice-cold, gray-blue eyes—so much like Robbie's own eyes, and like those of Robbie's dead father. No word came from the old man's twitching lips; but the reproach in those eyes was cruel, said Robbie.

It was part of the routine, in this rigorous atmosphere, to set Sunday aside as truly a day of rest, in which no frivolous activities were permitted, even in the conduct of children. The entire household paraded solemnly to the Universalist church for morning and evening services. The children were required to remain for the morning sermon and were expected to gain some edification from it. From later evidence it is possible that eleven-year-old Robbie was, indeed, old enough to acquire more edification from this exposure to Universalism than he cared to admit. He later built into his heterodox and homemade religious beliefs the very central Universalist notion that although there is the certainty of just retribution and punishment for all sinfulness, God's ultimate purpose is to save every individual from the tortures of hellfire.

The mounting tensions between the children and their grandparents forced the penniless widow to make plans for leaving. She had hoped that

Uncle Elihu Colcord might help her with an application she had already made for a teaching position in Lawrence, that she might at least stay where she was until she found work in the fall. Instead, Colcord made another suggestion. Perhaps she would like to take her children for a visit with Benjamin and Sarah Frost Messer, another uncle and aunt of her late husband's, who had a small farm in the town of Amherst, New Hampshire, some forty miles northwest of Lawrence. The invitation was accepted; it offered escape from the awkward situation in Lawrence.

For the poor relations from California this move provided the first glimpse of the rural north-of-Boston region in southeastern New Hampshire. Ben Messer was a genial, outgoing man whose considerateness made the transition less awkward. His wife, worn by her endless routine of daily chores, still managed to preserve a cheerful and kindly disposition. The warmth of these two appealed strongly to the forlorn California trio, and in spite of the strangeness and loneliness of their new surroundings, Robbie and his sister found life on this New Hampshire hillside very pleasant.

As midsummer wore into early fall, Mrs. Frost tried once again to secure a teaching position, this time in one of the local district schools. There were no vacancies, and she was persuaded by the Messers to stay on at the farm, so she might send her children to the nearest schoolhouse —all eight grades in one room. Robbie had scarcely begun school before he complained he could not get along with his teacher, and Jeanie soon joined him in finding fault. Perhaps it would be better, their mother decided, if they went back to Lawrence, where the schools might be more to their liking and where she might find some kind of steady employment.

Back they went, and this time into the home of Uncle Elihu and Aunt Lucy Frost Colcord. More sophisticated and affluent than the Haverhill Street Frosts, the Colcords seemed to accept their obligations with scarcely more grace. Mrs. Frost did manage to borrow some money from the Colcords, so she could rent two shabbily furnished rooms on the second floor of an apartment house on lower Broadway and move there, with her children. The arrangements made for their schooling required examinations, to determine the grade in which each child should be entered. To Robbie's consternation he learned that while his younger sister qualified for work in the fourth grade, he would have to start in the third. Vainly he protested, and his mother brought him around to a grudging acceptance of his plight. He did spend the rest of the fall term with the third-graders—in spite of his repeated complaints against the indignity of being herded in with eight-year-old "babies."

For these Californians, their first New England winter seemed unbearably cold, but no amount of discomfort could dim for the children the wonder and excitement of witnessing their first real snowstorm. If the winter temperature dropped too low for games outside, Robbie amused his sister by conducting scientific experiments of his own devising. On one occasion he borrowed a well-worn thimble from his mother, filled it with water, put it out on the windowsill, and watched, with Jeanie, the slow formation of ice crystals. The next morning, when he recovered the thimble from the sill and tapped out the bulging mold of ice, he placed it on the lid of a stove and watched with delight as it danced around the lid on its own melting.

The many attempts of Isabelle Moodie Frost to get a teaching position brought her something before the end of the first winter in New England. She learned of a sudden vacancy, and was asked to fill it, in a district school in Salem, New Hampshire, only ten miles northwest of Lawrence, not far beyond the state boundary. She made the move early in 1886.

Back in colonial days the original townships of both Salem and Lawrence had been parts of a single plantation, known as Pentucket. Settlers, developing scattered communities within this plantation, had gradually established Lawrence and Methuen and Haverhill in what became the State of Massachusetts and had, also, established Salem and neighboring Derry in what became the State of New Hampshire. While Lawrence gradually developed into a flourishing mill city, Salem and Derry remained rural, devoted to farming.

The railroad built between Lawrence and the New Hampshire cities of Manchester and Concord had bypassed the Salem village by about two miles, with the result that a new community in the township had grown up, at Salem Depot. It was to this community that Mrs. Frost brought her children, taking rooms just across the tracks from the depot. The little cluster of buildings included a general store, not more than twenty dwellings, two small shoe factories, a grain mill, a livery stable, two churches, and Salem District School Number Six.

Although the Colcords and Frosts in Lawrence seemed to hold the widow's teaching potential in low regard, the Salem school board was deeply impressed. Mrs. Frost was expected to carry children through work suitable to grades five through eight. After they completed grammar-school education, most of the young people returned to useful occupations on outlying farms or started to work in the local shoe factories. Rarely did any child who was graduated from District School Number Six go on to high school. Mrs. Frost hoped to implant new ideals. Before she had been teaching more than a few weeks she was stimulating her brightest students to seek further education. Her proposals were sufficiently novel to arouse the suspicions of parents who were farmers and tradespeople. By contrast, some of Mrs. Frost's best pupils came from the homes of doctors and ministers, who admired and supported her objectives. They invited her into their homes to share and compare ideas on rural teaching.

The Frost children, with their mother's assistance, easily made the transition from the third and fourth grades of the Lawrence system to the fifth grade in District School Number Six. The new teacher informed all her pupils that those who earned the highest marks would be allowed to take seats in the back of the room; those needing more help or more discipline would be seated nearer the front.

Her insistence on averaging deportment with scholarship worked to the disadvantage of her son. Robbie, consistently bored by assignments, made his own amusements. His newly learned skill at whittling was indulged, in the classroom, when his mother was too busy to notice. For protection he opened a large geography book, as a shield, and whittled away to the amusement of his schoolmates.

Not often reprimanded by his mother for anything, Robbie came under the law enough to find he was making steady progress toward the front of the room. This punishment had no corrective effect on his distaste for scholarship. It merely encouraged him to employ another device, which permitted him to escape beyond reach. Several times each morning and afternoon he would hold up the proper finger signal and frantically wave his hand until his mother nodded permission for him to be excused, so he could, presumably, hasten to the outhouse toilet in the back of the schoolyard.

In that same schoolyard, during spring term, Robbie developed a passion for baseball. Never before had he set his heart on a career, but in the spring of 1886 he decided that someday he would become a hero as a major-league pitcher. And by dint of persistence the boy soon established himself as a "regular" on his school team. Robbie's mother tried to use his new passion as an instrument for encouraging him to complete his schoolwork. She failed. He was content to let his sister be the student in the family.

Before spring term ended, it became clear that Robbie's best friend was a boy his own size and age named Charley Peabody. No other boy in the school had such zestful initiative for mischief in the classroom, such sauciness with girls, such fearlessness in performing schoolyard stunts. In Robbie's eyes these were attractive traits, because they contrasted so markedly with his own shyness, caution, and hesitancy.

Before long, Charley began to invite Robbie to the Peabody house. Charley had already demonstrated skill as a hunter, but he was enough of a naturalist to prefer bringing his game back alive. His bedroom was his menagerie and museum. Along one wall stood screened boxes, which housed a hawk, an owl, two snakes, a flying squirrel, and a raccoon. Out in the woods, back of the Peabody home, Charley began to teach Robbie a whole new lore of adventure: how to climb birches and ride them down, how to track and trap animals, how to skin a woodchuck, how to collect a bird's nest from the most precarious vantage point.

During the summer of 1886 the friendship of the two boys was interrupted by Mrs. Frost's decision that her son was old enough to earn a little money. Several other boys his age had found work in the shoe factories at Salem Depot, and Rob—as his mother began to call him —was sent to look for a job. Hired as an apprentice in the larger factory, he was at first taught nothing more difficult than the process of hammering three nails into the leather soles of partly made shoes. Before long he was transferred to a more exacting and dangerous task, as assistant to a man who manipulated an automatic heel-nailing machine. The boy's duty was to place nails, upright, in the holes of a metal rack that was mechanically held out just long enough to permit the swift placement of the nails, then drawn back as the automatic hammer was tripped to drive the nails in place. The new apprentice was warned that one of his recent predecessors had lost a finger by reaching in to straighten a misplaced nail. Frightened by the warning, Rob soon guessed the injured boy's effort to straighten that nail might have been caused in part by the man who worked the machine and cursed whenever a nail slipped. This nerve-racking assignment was made even more tedious because the chances for rest were so few. After only a few days Rob had had enough.

Following his experiences as a shoemaker, Rob found a less-strenuous and more elementary form of leatherwork in the backyard of what had become his new home. After Mrs. Frost and her children had grown tired of boardinghouse life they moved briefly to the home of a family named Emerson and, then, accepted the more satisfactory offer of rooms and the use of a kitchen in the home of Mr. and Mrs. Loren E. Bailey. Loren Bailey was currently farming a bit and operating a little sweatshop leather business on the side, with several men cutting and assembling heels (most of them wanderers and some mere tramps, content to earn only a little money before moving on). There was usually a spare cutting block, and Rob was given the chance to work there whenever he wanted, as soon as Bailey had taught him how to hold the metal pattern, how to trace around the edge of it with the sharp cutting knife, and how to assemble, nail, and trim the pieces of leather.

That summer, occasionally, Rob found pleasant diversion by walking down to Charley Peabody's, for an hour's visit or, even, for a whole day of adventure in the woods. During these visits he came gradually to realize there was another member of the Peabody family who also appealed to him: Charley's sister, Sabra, a bold and carefree tomboy, who at the same time was very pretty. Mischievous and fun-loving, she had a knack for gently teasing Rob in ways he liked.

By the time school opened in the fall, Sabra had become even more important to him than her brother. He was in love, and he overcame his shyness enough to admit the fact to Sabra herself. That he was only twelve years old, and she ten, in no way diminished all the bliss and anguish of his passion. And at twelve Rob had already begun to taste the bittersweet of uncertain courtship. He simply could not understand Sabra's tantalizing way of making him try to guess whether she loved him as intensely as he loved her. Each of them seemed to have special gifts for making the other jealous, to such an extent that their romance was devoted very largely to quarrels, silences, and reconciliations. Rob's passion was so fierce and uncontrollable that it kept driving him into actions calculated to hurt Sabra, partly because he felt he had no way of measuring her interest in him, save through her furious jealousy.

The anguish of love was not Rob's only problem during the fall and winter of 1886. His mother seemed to be suffering from some kind of illness, and other children in the upstairs classroom of District School Number Six noticed marked changes in her appearance. Although she never missed a day of school and never complained, she seemed to grow thin, haggard, gaunt. Her hair had always been carefully drawn into a knot at the back of her neck, but now she paid less and less attention to strands that escaped the knot and hung about her face in a manner that made her appear disheveled. Her dresses, some of them castoffs given her by friends, no longer conveyed the air of proud fastidiousness she had shown when first she came to Salem Depot.

The more sympathetic pupils carried home troubled stories of how Mrs. Frost sometimes sat at her desk so completely absorbed in her own thoughts that she failed to notice the scuffles of mischief-makers in the back of the room. Her more critical students began to complain to their parents that she was a poor teacher who couldn't keep order. They said she spent too much time helping her favorites, particularly Rob and Jeanie. They also complained that Rob was a lazy good-for-nothing who seemed to stay in bed each morning as late as he pleased and, then, came drifting into school without a word of reprimand from his mother.

Town gossips took up the hue and cry, saying Mrs. Frost should not be kept as teacher beyond the present year. These attacks evoked a countercampaign in defense of Mrs. Frost, by parents and children who had grown extremely fond of her. They granted she was impractical and at times careless in matters of appearance and dress. They even granted she was not the best disciplinarian the school had known. Nevertheless, they insisted, she was so good that in her first half-year she had enabled four students to pass entrance examinations at the high school in Lawrence. Nothing like that had ever happened before in District School Number Six. Moreover, she was a beautiful-spirited, Christian woman whose holiness shone through her eyes.

Two families in Salem Depot proved to be most helpful to Mrs. Frost during this difficult time: Dr. E. W. Wade, chairman of the school board of Salem township, and his wife and Mr. and Mrs. Fred W. Chase. To Mrs. Chase, after they had become intimate friends, Mrs. Frost confided much concerning her two children. Jeanie, she said, had always been high-strung, easily given to tears and hysterics, from early childhood. At times, she admitted, Jeanie did not seem to be quite normal. Perhaps the good Lord had given the child more brains than she needed. Too bright for her age, she was inclined to make a world of her own out of her imaginings and her reading.

As for Rob, his mother told Mrs. Chase, the dear boy seemed to grow more shiftless each day. She explained her fears that she herself had unintentionally hindered him from developing good habits of reading and study. Perhaps she had been too fond of reading aloud to her children. Rob was a good listener, but so odd in things he said about what she read. He would not let her finish reading aloud the last chapter of *Tom Brown's School Days* because, he said, he could not bear to think that such a good story should end. Had he finished the book by reading the rest of it to himself? No, he never read anything unless his mother sat with him and encouraged him. She also admitted that the boy was as stubborn and hot-tempered as his father had been. At times he was very difficult to manage. Often Mrs. Frost wistfully said to Mrs. Chase, "I don't know what will ever become of that boy."

Others in Salem Depot told of a different attitude. More than once they watched Mrs. Frost put an arm around the boy's shoulders, draw him close, and say with pride, "I have great hopes for Rob." Scornfully and cynically, gossips passed mean comments about silk purses and sows' ears. Most of the townspeople were agreed that the Frost boy was, indeed, a lazy good-for-nothing and that there was not enough promise in him to justify any hope.

"HE CONQUERS
WHO CONQUERS HIMSELF"

(1887–1889)

EVEN WHILE many Salem townspeople were viewing the Frost boy as a hopelessly lazy good-for-nothing, Rob became aware his interests were undergoing a profound change. The cause was not unrelated to his insistence that his mother read and reread to him certain chapters in the story he could not bear to finish, *Tom Brown's School Days*. Although Mrs. Frost naturally viewed Hughes's famous narrative as a vehicle well designed to inculcate muscular Christian morality, Rob was probably more inclined to enjoy it as an heroic adventure story that had particular appeal because he could so easily identify himself with Tom, a boy proud of his skills as runner, fighter, ballplayer—even though Rob knew, for certain, that cricket must be inferior to baseball. Here also was a story in which fighting was honored far more than Rob's mother was willing to honor it. This was no book for women and girls. Passages in it made his blood tingle with approval. Even the garrulous, masculine tone of the narrator pleased Rob, who felt that his own life was too heavily subjected to feminine influence.

Tom Brown as hero had a further effect. Clearly, Tom was not ashamed of study and did not consider schoolwork sissified. All the discussion concerning Latin and Greek came as a foreshadowing for Rob. He knew that his first year of high school would introduce him to these, and what was good enough for Tom was good enough for Rob. The book became an incalculable inspiration.

Mrs. Frost may have realized that the change in her son's attitude toward reading and study, as it became increasingly noticeable during the summer of 1887, was partly due to her years of storytelling and story-reading. Her passion for the color of Scottish folklore and history, her delight in the cadences of Scottish dialect, and her admiration for the courage of Scottish heroes had influenced the choice of books she read to her children. During the previous winter, 1886–1887, she had read them

Sir Walter Scott's *Tales of a Grandfather,* knowing that these glimpses into the history of Scotland were designed for youthful ears. She supplemented Scott's *Tales* with border ballads, some of them drawn from Percy's *Reliques.* Reaching back even further, she exposed her children to pertinent selections from *The Poems of Ossian.*

It is easy to understand why Mrs. Frost should have taken Scottish pride in the Ossianic epic of *Fingal*; but it would be difficult to overemphasize the strong impact on Rob of his mother's readings from *Ossian*, this work with themes she wanted her son to cherish—such as the theme of regret for the pathos of noble bygone days, the sadness of modern times, the leavening effect of visionary melancholy.

A poetess herself, and a Swedenborgian poetess, Mrs. Frost made her children feel by example, rather than by precept, that romantic nature-poetry was at its best when it suggested correspondences or analogies between the seen and the unseen worlds. "In our Doctrine of Representations and Correspondences," Swedenborg had written, "we shall treat of both these symbolical and typical representations, and of the astonishing things which occur, I will not say in the living body only, but throughout nature, and which correspond so entirely to supreme and spiritual things, that one would swear that the physical world was purely symbolical of the spiritual world. . . ." Each of the romantic poets whom Mrs. Frost loved had been fascinated by his own sense of resemblances between the physical and the metaphysical: Emerson, Wordsworth, Bryant.

Her frequent repetition of Bryant's "To a Waterfowl" sank in so deeply that Rob discovered with astonishment, one day in the summer of 1887, that he could begin at the first line and say the poem all the way through. What surprised Rob most was that he was certain he had never tried to learn "To a Waterfowl." With even-greater surprise he made another discovery, years later: Of these three poets to whom his mother had first exposed him—Emerson, Wordsworth, Bryant—his favorite was hers, Ralph Waldo Emerson.

Among Mrs. Frost's favorites, too, was Edgar Allan Poe, whom she quoted so often that her children knew several of his poems by heart before they entered high school. For her the special appeal of Poe could not have been the jingling quality of the rhymes and meters nor the morbid preoccupation with the death of a beautiful woman. It is more probable Mrs. Frost had the capacity to discover in Poe's romantic lines certain mystical and metaphysical correspondences that helped her to illustrate some of her favorite Swedenborgian truths.

The same religious ideals Mrs. Frost conveyed to her children, through poetry, were supplemented by her way of keeping pace with their growing pleasure in prose tales of romantic and heroic adventure. Back in the San Francisco days, when she had introduced them to her beloved George Macdonald, by reading from *At the Back of the North Wind,* she may have had no plan in mind to take Rob and Jeanie all the way up the ladder of Macdonald's Scotch novels. It was not until they reached Salem that she exposed them to the entire series.

So long as Rob's mother pleased him with the narratives she read aloud, he had sufficient reason for not developing his own reading habits. It was apparently true that, as he often boasted, he did not read through any book, by himself, until his fourteenth year. The stimulus that finally overcame his resistance was provided accidentally during the summer of 1887. One day when he was working in desultory fashion, cutting leather in Loren Bailey's shed, he and Mrs. Bailey were alone. On this particular day Mrs. Bailey began to talk of her relatives in Scotland. In an effort to match her, Rob drew proudly on all he knew about his mother's family. Then, their conversation veered to the history of Scotland, and again Rob was adequately informed. But when Mrs. Bailey said that he should read her favorite historical novel, Jane Porter's *The Scottish Chiefs,* which started with the murder of Wallace's wife and ended with the Battle of Bannockburn, the names themselves were enough to tempt him. He borrowed her dog-eared copy, began to read it by himself, gave up leather-cutting, and devoted his time exclusively to the narrative until he had finished it. Thereafter, his prejudices against reading were ended.

Rob's mother must have been relieved by his change in attitude. Knowing that both her children could complete their grammar-school work during the next school year, she was certain that by spring of 1888, Jeanie could easily pass the high-school entrance examinations. But she was equally certain that Rob, who would be fourteen by that time, might not pass them all. One factor that worked to his mother's earlier disadvantage, in teaching Rob to read and study, had been his passion for baseball. Now it worked in her favor—and his. Lawrence High School had an excellent baseball team, and the nearer Rob drew to high school, the more he dreamed of playing on such a team. Of course he would not be permitted to play if his marks were not good; so, his goal justified his making a little extra effort in the line of study.

Almost slyly, as though ashamed, Rob applied himself quite seriously to his studies in the autumn of 1887. Having begun to study, he complained of being forced to poke along at the rate set by the poorer students. He also complained that his interests were not satisfied when he was asked to prepare a few pages of several different assignments, day after day. Why shouldn't he be permitted to concentrate on one subject at a time, intensively, and go straight through the year's work in that subject? His mother assured him that if he thought he could learn better and faster that way, she would give her permission. Proudly developing his own methods, he chose, first, to read completely through Fry's *Geography* and to pass examinations set by his mother. Next, he chose Eaton's *Arithmetic*. He moved on to Higginson's *Young Folks' History of the United States*. Last of all, he braced himself for wading bravely through all of Swinton's *Grammar* and Franklin's *Higher Reader*.

The *Grammar* bored him, but to his surprise he found himself lingering over the *Higher Reader*. Some of the stories he read again and again. Then, he deliberately settled in to memorize several poems and proverbs and mottoes. Until this time he had repeatedly teased his sister by saying he disliked poems, particularly the kinds of poems she adored. He said that some of the poems in the *Higher Reader* were just as bad, just plain silly. (One of them prompted him to make his first try at writing a rhymed answer, as a mocking parody.) But when he found in the *Higher Reader* the poem on the Greek struggle for freedom, Halleck's "Marco Bozzaris," he liked it so much he quickly memorized it.

With the coming of spring in 1888, Rob found that no books could keep his thoughts from baseball. As soon as April weather dried the playing field, he threw all his energies into session after session of baseball practice with his team. Number Six did so well that year, in competition with other nearby district schools, that the boys ambitiously overextended themselves, by challenging one of the best grammar-school teams in Lawrence. The results were almost catastrophic.

The opposition played havoc with Rob's pitching; and, removed as pitcher, he boasted—loudly enough to be heard by the enemy—that if only he could get on base he'd show the big boys how easy it would be to bring home at least one run. When Rob next came to bat, the catcher called for a parley with the pitcher; they'd give the boaster a base on balls.

There was pride in Robbie's bearing as he trotted to first. As the pitcher started his next throw, Rob scampered for second and was safely there before the catcher's throw arrived. It was easy. Of course, the steal to third might be a little harder, but he felt sure he could make it. He pranced off second, as the pitcher again faced the batter; he came back and tagged base, when the pitcher turned around. Then, he took an even-more-daring lead, and was off with the pitch. But when Rob came sliding into third, headfirst, he saw the gloved ball waiting for him; he knew he was out. Disgusted, he picked himself up, dusted himself off, and walked to the bench—amid the humiliating jeers and catcalls.

Other humiliations overtook Rob that spring. When he and his sister went down to Lawrence to take the first of their high-school entrance examinations, Rob was almost panic-stricken. The subject was arithmetic, and Jeanie said afterward the examination was easy. Rob had trouble with it from the start. In less than a quarter of the time allowed, he raced through all the problems he felt he could handle and, then, turned in his paper. The teacher called him back. Wouldn't he like to take a little more time? Had he checked his answers? No, he said; no. Then, he bolted.

When the examination marks were mailed to Salem Depot, Rob learned that although he had barely passed arithmetic, he had done well enough in all the other tests and would be admitted as a freshman in good standing, with his sister—whose standing was much better.

The greatest humiliation of the Salem days occurred that fall, soon after Rob and Jeanie had begun to commute by train to the Lawrence High School. While their attentions were being absorbed by the newness of this experience, their mother began to have her worst troubles in District School Number Six. New gossip revived smoldering enmities, and her critics now insisted that if she were not replaced they would hire a teacher of their own. Gradually made aware of the trouble, Rob felt it directly when he went into the general store and was met with the proprietor's curt threat, "Get out of here, you little Frost." He did as ordered, indignantly resenting all that was implied. His chagrin was heightened by his deep sense of loyalty to and love for his mother. The situation hurt him so deeply he began dreaming of ways to wreak physical vengeance on these enemies.

The school board called a special meeting for the announced purpose of considering "the Frost case," and Rob attended. He sat alone in the back of the room and watched his mother come in, escorted by Mrs. Wade and Mrs. Chase. Rob felt the complaints made were unbelievably insulting. But after the opposition had been permitted to vent its complaints and faultfindings, loyal friends of Mrs. Frost's stood up to defend her. Then, the school board voted that Mrs. Frost should continue as teacher. A few days later, in retaliation, the plaintiffs carried out their threat and set up a provisional classroom, over the barber shop; and by the end of the term it was apparent, even to her closest friends, that it was wise for Mrs. Frost to resign, as she now desired to do. She wanted to move away from Salem Depot, with her children, as quickly as possible.

On the night before their departure, Rob went with his mother to pay a farewell call at the Chase home. He refused to go in, and his former schoolmate Agatha Chase came out to talk with him as he stood waiting beside the gate. Fighting back tears, he condemned all who had treated his mother so cruelly. Then, with proud scorn he raised the questions that hurt him most: Who did these people think they were? And who did they think the Frosts were? "You wait," he said. "Someday, I'll come back to Salem Depot—and show them."

The first day of his high-school career was a frightening ordeal for Rob. There was nothing unpleasant in the brief and familiar journey by rail from Salem Depot to Lawrence, and there was nothing to disturb him in the outward appearance of the gaunt and ugly three-story brick building.

He had seen the inside of the school during the previous spring, when he had gone there to take entrance examinations; but it had been nearly empty then. Now, lost among strangers and caught in the press of chattering students who milled and jostled on the stairs and through the corridors, he was treated as an outsider, a country bumpkin, a nobody.

The worst insult of this first day was provided by three of his classmates who stopped him in the corridor, just long enough to ask a taunting question: Wasn't he the Salem smarty who had been thrown out at third last spring, after boasting he could even steal home? Their jeers were enough to make Rob decide, then and there, that he couldn't possibly compete for a position on the high-school team. It was a painful decision, and it seemed as though no other misery could have hurt so much as this rude shattering of his cherished baseball dreams.

For the Salem boy it was fortunate that all the preliminary confusion and excruciation were quickly counterbalanced by well-ordered routine and discipline in the classrooms, by the competence of his new teachers, and by his worries over assignments. Of the three programs offered—the college-preparatory or classical program, the general or English program, and the mixed or commercial—Rob and his mother had decided he would choose the first. Aware of his brilliant father's career in this same high school and at Harvard, the boy planned to give special emphasis to the classics and history. It was an ambitious choice, made by relatively few of the students in his class, and that further isolated him. He knew it would also exclude any immediate possibility of a course in English literature and of going on to read the kinds of novels that had begun to fascinate him. He was taking Latin, algebra, a course in the history of Greece, and a course in the history of the Roman Empire.

In studying his assignments, night after night, Rob admitted to himself that his unexpected display of industry was motivated in part by fear. He could not bear the possibility that he might be humiliated in the presence of his fellow students by questions he could not answer. Having disciplined himself to read without his mother's help, he was now driven by motives of fright and self-defense to reread and, even, to memorize names, dates, facts. Surprised to find his assignments interesting, he took further satisfaction in discovering his ability to complete work without his mother's help.

In classroom recitations he was painfully self-conscious, but whenever he became absorbed in discussions where he could use newly acquired information, he participated eagerly. Still easily hurt by any form of criticism or correction, he was occasionally jolted back into silence.

Reading in his textbooks the myths and legends and stories about Greece, he began to glory in the Golden Age, the rule of Pericles, and the subsequent vicissitudes of the noble Athenians during the Peloponnesian

War. He sided passionately with Athens. Not expecting that the Athenians could possibly be defeated by Sparta, he agonized over the outcome. He wished he could change history, if only for a little while, just to see what might have happened if the Athenians had never sent their fatal expedition to Sicily.

He was surprised to find that even his elementary work in Latin gave him satisfaction that eclipsed his dislike for memorizing declensions and conjugations and rules. For the first time, he began to understand his mother's reasons for arranging the parts of English sentences in diagrammatic forms on the blackboard. English words he had for years been using took on new significance for him, as soon as he recognized their Latin roots. Scraps of Latin found in his collateral reading suddenly came to life.

At the very first meeting of the freshman class the proposal had been made and accepted that the motto for the Class of '92 should be *"Vincit qui se vincit"*; and he was proud to sense the meaning before the words were translated. The choice of this motto touched him, partly because it gave him words for something he had been trying to articulate, on his own. If conquest had to begin with self-conquest, he had already started in the right direction, and he was willing to persevere.

He would need a good deal of perseverance, he feared, if he were to conquer his prejudices against mathematics. He had already made up his mind that he would hate algebra. But, here again, his dread of appearing to be stupid in class helped him overcome an initial distaste. Before long, the little problems acquired the charm of puzzles. It was a new game for him, and at one phase of it he became so absorbed that his sheer concentration brought him through a public performance before he had time to grow self-conscious.

The incident occurred on a day when the superintendent of schools visited the algebra class and pleasantly challenged the students to take one step beyond what they had learned. The visitor wrote on the blackboard an algebra problem that required a new process. He assured the students they knew enough about algebra to solve the problem, and to recognize the new process, if they would only try. Troubled and uncertain, the entire class stared in silence until Rob impulsively exclaimed, "I can do it."

The boy was so intent on describing each of the separate steps that, for the moment, he was not bothered by shyness. Even the superintendent's interruptions, for the purpose of leading him on, seemed like stimulating countermoves in a game of wits. When he finished and was praised for his ability to make mental rearrangements of algebraic facts already learned, Rob was proud of his accomplishment. More than that, it dawned on him that he had suddenly discovered something about the process of original thinking. It was always a matter of putting together known quantities in fresh ways.

Somewhat vengefully, he applied the process further, by deciding he could use his newfound abilities as a means of getting back at those classmates who had mocked him as the boastful base-runner who didn't reach third. Desperately needing any self-confidence he could acquire, and welcoming praise as a counterbalance to his persistent sense of being an outsider, Rob soon hid shyness and uncertainty beneath a self-protective shield of pride and scorn. Largely because of diffidence, he made no lasting friends during his first year. But his inner and outer responses were undergoing such rapid change that his new posture was not wholly a shield.

Shortly before Memorial Day 1889 he watched his homeroom teacher, Katharine O'Keeffe, making preparations one morning before school began. She went to the blackboard and wrote, word after word and line after line, until she completed a poem. Having no way of knowing that Miss O'Keeffe was quoting, Rob was convinced he was watching her unfold a poem she herself had composed. And he felt a growing sense of admiration, even amazement, as he noticed how nicely each word seemed to fall into place for the development of her thoughts. Aware that Memorial Day was approaching, he considered his teacher's reminder a fitting tribute to the soldiers who had fought and died in the Civil War. More than that, he saw this dramatic act, of putting words together to make a poem, as a new game—requiring a skillful control, in much the same way a pitcher has to manipulate the ball in throw after throw: "How sleep the brave, who sink to rest, / By all their country's wishes blest! / When Spring, with dewy fingers cold, / Returns to deck their hallow'd mould. . . ."

Rob's misunderstanding kept him from realizing that Miss O'Keeffe was borrowing, but through his error he gained insights important to him and to his future. For the first time, he saw that any good poem could be admired purely as a performance. It was enough to make him want to try the game, for his own amusement. Several years later, when he learned that "How Sleep the Brave" had been written by William Collins, in praise of those who had fought and died on Culloden Moor in 1746, he merely transferred his earlier admiration from Miss O'Keeffe to Collins.

By the end of this first year, the Salem boy took a justifiable pride in what he had already accomplished. His final grades placed him not only above his bookish and pedantic sister, but also at the head of his class, with ninety-five percent in each of his history courses, ninety-six in Latin, and ninety-nine in algebra. His elation inspired enough arrogance to let him confront his Roman-history teacher, with an indignant demand for an explanation of his low mark. He felt certain he had never failed to answer any of her questions correctly, in either oral or written work, and had always been among the first to volunteer answers. Hence the self-assurance with which he demanded: "Why didn't I get a hundred for my final mark? Were any of my answers wrong in my final examination?" She dodged the bold questions by asking, "Do you think you know all of Roman history?"

Unable to find an answer that seemed to have bearing on the problem as he saw it, he stood silent before her, staring. Then, he turned away, without saying a word, and carried her question home to puzzle over. Although he was willing to admit he didn't know all of Roman history, he had known enough to answer all the questions asked, except this last one. He wished he had told her that she seemed to penalize him for his failure to know more than she had demanded. There was the answer! Why hadn't he thought of it while he was standing tongue-tied? At least, he told himself, his afterthought did more than relieve his puzzlement. It also fitted into his newly discovered definition of thinking: a process of putting this and that together, with enough originality, to solve a problem.

Rob spent the summer of 1889 trying to catch up on some of the reading he might have done if he had been able to take the freshman course in English and American literature. For the moment his interests were concentrated on the American Indian. His search for Indian stories brought him to a current best seller, Mary Hartwell Catherwood's newly published *Romance of Dollard,* built around the heroic self-sacrifice of the celebrated Frenchman who had gone down in history as the savior of the colonies of New France when they were threatened by the Iroquois. Francis Parkman, the historian who actually lived for a time with Indians, had written a preface for the story about Dollard. The boy might have gone on to read the classic account of Indians in *The Oregon Trail.* Instead, because they happened to be at hand, the three volumes of Prescott's *History of the Conquest of Mexico* provided the next romance, all centered around the picturesque Aztec Indian sovereign Montezuma and the daring Spanish conquistador Hernando Cortés.

Prescott's chapters on the Aztec Indian civilization exposed Rob for the first time to early phases of American archeology and established a foundation for his lifelong delight in Mayan, Toltec, and Aztec cultures. Then, the account of Cortés's ruthless massacres and butcheries caused Rob to throw all his sympathies with the bewildered natives. It was inevitable that he become most deeply moved when Montezuma's people conducted their vengeful uprising against the Spanish, in reaction to the atrocities of Alvarado. He found his favorite episode in Book V ("Expulsion from Mexico"), particularly Chapter 3 ("Noche Triste"). He reveled in the vivid account of the retreat Cortés arranged after the death of

Montezuma, the stealthy exit from the beleaguered fortress and through the sleeping city of Tenochtitlan.

Rob's extraordinary burst of reading in the summer of 1889 helped to stimulate the beginning of his poetic career, but there were other experiences during the same summer that gave him a start in another direction. Loren Bailey's little farm in Salem was crested with a field that supplied all the hay his horse and cow could eat during any winter. The task of harvesting this crop required the help of only one other man. This year he called on Rob for help—and introduced the boy to farm rituals and mysteries that eventually became doubly useful.

Bailey's old grindstone stood in the shade of a gnarled apple tree; the first of Rob's new lessons started there. The expert taught the novice how to give just the right speed to the stone, with one crank-turning hand, while intermittently pouring, from a tin can held in the other hand, just the right trickle of water to keep the stone moist under the pressure of the scythe blade. Bailey was not the kind of man to be satisfied with anything less than a razor-sharp blade edge. Before the process was complete, Rob learned that the nice handling of stone and blade requires time—enough to give any novice wheel-turner aches in both arms. (Years later, in his poem "The Grindstone," he was able to smile at his memory of this experience, but his immediate response seems to have been a natural boyish impatience with Bailey's fussiness.)

Next, Rob learned that while the delicate process of hanging a scythe blade on the snake-shaped snath is a ritual in itself, the most important scythe-ritual of all is the proper swinging of this ingeniously constructed tool. He was also given lessons in the correct and delicate handling of a pitchfork and taught himself how to drag a huge wooden bull rake, to gather scatterings.

The boy felt that this was the first real man-sized work he had ever done. These days of haying were so strenuous they filled Rob's nights with pitchfork dreams, but he took pride in having stayed with the task to the end. It had given him a new sense of his own strength. He had found muscles he never knew he had, and the pain in them was a reminder that he was entitled to carry himself like a man.

5

MORE STRIDES
IN SELF-DISCIPLINE

(1889–1891)

When Robert Frost again began to commute from Salem Depot to Lawrence High School, in the fall of 1889, he knew the difference a year of growth had made. The shyness and fear, which had bothered him so much at the start of his freshman year, were now concealed (if not controlled) behind a self-protective posture of arrogance. If any of his classmates still wanted to think of him as a rube from Salem, they at least would have to admit that he had proved his academic superiority to all of them, in the most difficult program offered by the school.

Shortly after the beginning of his sophomore year, Rob discovered that he had already built the foundations for a close friendship with a student beyond his own class, a senior named Carl Burell. Carl, almost ten years older than Rob, had belatedly made up his mind to continue his education. He had somehow established himself in Lawrence as a janitor and a jack-of-all-trades. He had become acquainted with Rob's grandfather and also with Rob's great-uncle, Elihu Colcord, both of whom gave him work occasionally. For a time he lived in the Colcord home. Carl and Rob may have met first during Rob's freshman year; but during the fall of 1889, when Carl was nearly twenty-five and Rob fifteen, these two, who were very largely ignored by most of their schoolmates, began to build their friendship—more through loneliness than through shared interests.

Before Carl returned to school he had tried to educate himself by taking books from the public library and by purchasing books that particularly interested him. His tastes were unusual, and from him Rob soon began to extend his own interests along lines not taught in school. Among many books Rob saw for the first time in Carl's room at the Colcords' were illustrated volumes devoted to Carl's two favorite botanizing specialties, ferns and orchids; a little collection devoted to American humor; and a representation of works dealing with evolution and the consequent battle between science and religion.

One book in Carl's library attracted Rob's attention because he knew his mother treasured a copy of it: *Our Place among Infinities*. The author was the British astronomer Richard Anthony Proctor. Starting in the fall of 1889, Rob began reading *Our Place among Infinities*. It was hard going, and the polemical tone puzzled him. The first essay begins: "The subject with which I am about to deal is associated by many with questions of religion. Let me premise, however, that I do not thus view it myself. It seems to me impossible to obtain from science any clear ideas respecting the ways or nature of the Deity, or even respecting the reality of an Almighty personal God." Uncertain how he should take these assertions, Rob was fascinated by the subject under discussion in this first essay, "The Past and Future of Our Earth." Although Proctor's apparent rejections of certain accepted beliefs may have confused the young man on first reading, he must have found at the end of the essay statements that made him realize why his mother kept the book: "Science is in presence of the old, old mystery; the old, old questions are asked of her,—'Canst thou by searching find out God? . . .' And science answers these questions, as they were answered of old,—'As touching the Almighty, we cannot find Him out.'"

Here Rob was back on familiar ground, made plain to him by his mother throughout his childhood: The ways of God are indeed strange and mysterious and past finding out. Thus reassured, Rob could continue to the next essay, entitled "Of Seeming Wastes in Nature," and could find there further reassurances: "In a word, our faith must not be hampered by scientific doubts, our science must not be hampered by religious scruples."

To the boy, at the time, there was reassurance in this way of handling the otherwise unpleasant conflict between science and religion. Throughout most of his life, thereafter, the same resolution continued to satisfy him.

Our Place among Infinities had another immediately important effect on Rob. It was not enough that Proctor's essays led him to become acquainted with the positions and movements of stars and constellations. He insisted that he was going to get a telescope powerful enough to let him see with his own eyes the rings around Saturn. An advertisement he found in *The Youth's Companion* offered exactly what he wanted and made the promise that the telescope would be sent free to anyone who obtained a certain number of new subscriptions to the magazine. Encouraged by his mother, he immediately began a house-to-house canvass of the Lawrence neighborhood where they were then living.

The Frosts had moved back to Lawrence in February of 1890, after

Mrs. Frost had an opportunity to teach at a district school in Methuen, the town lying between Salem and Lawrence. For the convenience of her two high-school children, she had rented a cheap and drafty apartment in a slum section on East Haverhill Street, unpleasantly near the Boston & Maine Railroad freight yard, and yet, within a mile of the high school. Even if the Frosts had not been strangers in this forlorn neighborhood of Lawrence, it would not have been a good area for selling subscriptions to *The Youth's Companion*. After he had given up, completely discouraged, his indulgent mother completed the campaign for him, by making appeals to friends in Salem and Lawrence. Eventually, the telescope arrived, and Rob quickly began to learn more about his own place among infinities.

Carl Burell's very important stimulus to Rob in scientific matters was closely bound up with Carl's contributions, of verse and prose, to the *High School Bulletin*. In his library he carefully preserved the issues containing poems and essays he had published so far. If they made Rob feel jealous, he must have supposed that the achievements represented by Carl's balladlike poems could easily be surpassed. Measured against the ballads Rob's mother had read aloud, over a period of many years, Carl's work needed improvement.

The inspiration for writing a ballad of his own came to Rob one blustery and cloud-darkened evening in March 1890, as he walked from school to the home of his grandparents. Something reminded him of the story he had found in Prescott's *Conquest of Mexico*—of the night made sad and terrible for the Spaniards by the Aztec Indians during the disastrous retreat across the causeway over Lake Tezcuco from the island city of Tenochtitlan. What he remembered of Prescott's account began composing itself into lines and ballad stanzas as he walked. The schoolbooks he carried at the end of a strap were useful as a metronome; he kept swinging them to give him a proper sense of the ballad rhythm he wanted. It seemed to him he could hear the lines spoken, almost by the same voice that had puzzled him years ago in San Francisco.

Quatrain after quatrain kept coming to him, and with the completion of each new one his rapture mounted. Just as soon as he could sit down to write, with much excitement he put on paper one line after another, until he had twenty-five stanzas. Appropriately, he entitled his poem "La Noche Triste," and he introduced the ballad with a prologue—twenty-seven unrhymed, irregular, three-stress lines—which bore the subtitle "Tenochtitlan." He separated the prologue from the ballad proper by using another subtitle, "The Flight." In his conclusion, as though remembering what Halleck had done in "Marco Bozzaris" or how Collins in "How Sleep the Brave" had built the last couplet around the word "freedom," Rob paid tribute to the liberty-loving Aztecs who had fought so desperately for their own freedom that they triumphed, at least temporarily, over their Spanish oppressors.

The intoxication of this new accomplishment was so great Rob sat gloating over his manuscript, convinced that it prophesied his future as a poet. The next day he took to school with him a fair copy of the ballad, carried it to the senior homeroom, where he hoped to find the chief editor of the *Bulletin*, Ernest Jewell, and left the manuscript on Jewell's desk before the editor arrived. Although Rob had some doubt whether a senior would condescend to accept a poem written by a sophomore, he was superstitious enough to hope that his having written it during his birth month would be a lucky omen. Apparently it was. Jewell published "La Noche Triste" on the very first page of the *Bulletin* for April 1890.

The double success of writing and publishing his first long poem spurred Rob to another effort. It resulted in a lyric, "Song of the Wave," a mood piece fashioned from vivid memories of his vigils at the Cliff House and the sight and sound of Pacific Ocean water shattering against ledges in the twilight. Again, Jewell accepted the sophomore's offering, which appeared in the *Bulletin* for May 1890. Rob's poetry-writing mother was almost as greatly elated as he was.

As Rob came to the end of his sophomore year, he knew he had made important strides toward his ideal goal of inner and outer discipline. Faithfully, he had carried out his class preparations in Greek, Latin, European history, geometry; he had made his own explorations in the field of astronomy; he had spent many hours with Carl Burell, discussing the conflict between science and religion; he had written two poems that had been published; he had acquired the friendship of Ernest Jewell; and he had been welcomed into the debating society. His final marks for the year placed him once again at the head of his class, and he could not resist the enjoyment of noticing that some of his classmates who had treated him as the dumb country boy were now deferential.

During the summer of 1890 the financial problems of the Frosts became so serious that all three of them were glad to find work in a hotel at Ocean Park, Maine, some twenty miles south of Portland. But almost as soon as they reached Ocean Park, Mrs. Frost regretted the venture. The chambermaids with whom she and Jeanie worked seemed shockingly coarse, and low in their moral standards. The kitchen help, the waitresses, and the waiters with whom Rob was thrown were not people she would have chosen as associates for her son.

More painful to Rob was his discovery that as errand boy and handyman he was at the beck and call of everyone. Having anticipated daily opportunities for spending some time on the beach and swimming in the ocean, Rob was disgusted to find that by the end of each day he was far too exhausted to need or want exercise. Even worse, when he did go swimming for the first time, he discovered the temperature of the Maine ocean water was even colder than it had been at Sausalito, near the Golden Gate.

The only innovation that intensely aroused Rob's faculties this summer was tennis. The servants were permitted to use the hotel courts in the evenings, and Rob was frequently drafted to make a fourth for doubles —with a borrowed racquet. Although the game was entirely new to him and he was ashamed of his initial clumsiness, by the end of the summer he had developed enough skill, and appreciation of the game, to make him decide tennis was almost as much fun as baseball; and both games remained lifelong passions with him.

Aside from tennis, so many unpleasant incidents marred the days at Ocean Park that all three of the Frosts eagerly returned to Lawrence as soon as they could after the Labor Day weekend. To his surprise, Rob found he was even looking forward to the start of the fall term and classes.

A new intensity of seriousness was reflected in Robert Frost's plan to concentrate fully on classical studies at the beginning of his junior year in high school. He had foreseen the drudgery awaiting him if he took a third year of Latin, a second year of Greek, a course in Latin composition, and a course in Greek composition. But he was deliberately giving himself further exercise in self-discipline.

By this time he was convinced his position at the head of his class was so important to him that he was willing to approach any assignment as an exacting test of his ability to overcome ingrained laziness. Whenever he was in the mood for self-indulgence, he secretly—even furtively—stole time for writing another poem. But even here, he found that after his first rapture of seeing "La Noche Triste" and "Song of the Wave" in print, he was more and more inclined to be slow and cautious in revising and polishing anything he wrote.

He anticipated that his most pleasant hours of extracurricular work during this year would be provided by the activities of the debating society. Having worked closely with Ernest Jewell in the task of suggesting topics for debate the previous spring, he found that the society leaned even more heavily on him now Jewell had been graduated. At the first meeting in the fall of 1890, Rob offered for a subject, "Resolved: That the Chinese Exclusion act is just and is a benefit to our country." Although not one of the formal participants in the eventual debate on this topic, he did take part in the general discussion and (perhaps because he was a native San Franciscan) spoke strongly for the affirmative side.

Later in the fall the following topic was proposed: "Resolved: That Bryant is a greater poet than Whittier." Rob spoke formally as the second affirmative, and the affirmative side won.

On the subject of ". . . a bill for removing the Indians from Indian Territory to more fertile districts and ceding said districts to the tribes forever; and for giving them some compensation for the losses already suffered," as first speaker on the affirmative side in this debate, Rob came well prepared. His factual information was drawn from a book he had read especially for the occasion, Helen Hunt Jackson's bitter and impassioned indictment entitled *A Century of Dishonor: A Sketch of the United States Government's Dealings with Some of the Indian Tribes*. But the evening was spoiled by the boisterous disorder of members who preferred to clown. The uproar grew so offensive the junior vice-president of the society resigned, and Rob was elected to take his place temporarily.

Far more crucial to his future plans was the taking of preliminary examinations for admission to Harvard. (His father's affiliation with Harvard made Rob assume that he would go there, if the money could be found.) Harvard offered to high-school juniors the opportunity to take seven hours of preliminary exams in March and in June—examinations in Greek, Latin, Greek history, Roman history, algebra, geometry, and English literature. Warned that those who had not taken courses in English literature were expected to develop a reading acquaintance with each title in a long list of books, and awed by so many strange titles, Rob decided to tackle only six "prelims" at Cambridge in the spring of 1891 and to ask for a postponement of the English-literature examination until fall. The arrangement was acceptable; an excursion to Harvard was made in March, another in June; and, to his great satisfaction, Rob passed all six.

A new stimulus was given to Rob's writing that spring, when his class met to elect *Bulletin* editors for the following year. Traditionally, the senior class assumed responsibility for the management of the school paper, and the Class of 1892 elected Rob chief editor. In the meeting, as soon as the vote was taken, Rob rose to his feet and warned that he would accept only if he were given more support than previous editors had been given; he urged that the usual number of five assistants or literary editors should be increased to seven. The terms were immediately met.

Rob, as though he felt called upon to live up to expectations, submitted to the retiring editor a new poem, which was published on the first page of the *Bulletin* for May of 1891: "A Dream of Julius Cæsar." Distinctly different from his two earlier offerings, this one was cast in blank verse, nearly seventy lines in length, and for Rob it marked an important achievement with which to end his junior year.

Early in the summer of 1891, perhaps through such a friend as Loren Bailey in Salem, New Hampshire, he obtained work on a farm in the nearby township of Windham. The farmer was an easygoing Scotchman named Dinsmoor, who made extra money by taking in a few summer boarders seeking rural escape from the city. Having prospered so well that he needed hired men on his place each summer, Dinsmoor had built bunkhouse quarters for them.

In many ways the farm offered an idyllic setting for guests or hired men, and when Rob arrived he was delighted with the prospect. The summer might have passed in truly idyllic fashion for the young man from Lawrence had his bunkhouse companions not been too much like the people with whom he had worked at Ocean Park a year earlier. And the roughest and rowdiest was Dinsmoor's own son.

Among the guests at the Dinsmoor farm was a very pretty stenographer from Lawrence, who soon provided romantic diversion for young Dinsmoor. For them both, the most pleasant evening's entertainment came to be a casual and leisurely voyage down the lake in a rowboat. The men in the bunkhouse were quick to notice that Dinsmoor never brought the girl back until long after dark. He answered their jests with boasts—and Rob was not amused. His bunkmates explained that if their ribaldry offended him, they would gladly teach him the facts of life, so he could enjoy their wit. In their crude way, they taught him more than he could tolerate concerning sexual matters.

Rob might have had difficulty in explaining, even to himself, that the insinuations and obscenities of his bunkmates offended him most because they cut sharply against the grain of his idealistic and romantic notions of love and womanhood.

Unintentionally, he discovered something when he assumed the heroic task of defending, against young Dinsmoor's boasts, the morals of the stenographer. All this evil talk, he said, was an attempt to besmirch a pure and innocent girl. Rob could tell that much about her from his own brief conversations with her.

Oh, he could, could he? Then, perhaps he should take the girl down the lake for a moonlight voyage some night when Dinsmoor was otherwise engaged.

The challenge was accepted, the arrangements were made, and on the scheduled evening Dinsmoor and his companions gathered at the dock to give the two a raucous send-off. For the next hour Rob found that the girl's spirited and witty conversation made him feel at ease. He had decided he could not prove his point to his lascivious bunkmates unless he brought the girl back long after dark, and so, he kept rowing slowly down the lake.

He was merely amused when the girl urged him to keep nearer to the eastern shore, so she could tell where they were; but he did as she asked. He was not even troubled when she asked him to row into a small cove. But in the cove he suffered an unexpected shock. The girl suggested it would be nice if they went ashore a little while. Something about the tone of her voice frightened Rob more than what she said—and forced him to realize that young Dinsmoor and the others knew more than he did about this girl. Suddenly feeling miserable and ashamed of himself, he fumbled for excuses as he turned the rowboat back into the lake and started for the farm. If the girl noticed how her companion lapsed into silence after all his easy talk, she gave no sign of it. Nothing seemed to bother her, and she merely kept on talking. When they reached the dock, Rob gallantly helped her out of the boat, tied it up, escorted her to the lamplit house, said a hasty goodnight, and fled.

By the time he reached the bunkhouse he had established a posture from which to answer all taunting questions amicably and triumphantly. He insisted his innocent evening with the girl proved his claim that they had lied about her. But after the lewd comments and laughter had stopped, after the others had gone to sleep, Rob lay in his bunk overwhelmed with a frightening suspicion. Suppose young Dinsmoor had gotten the girl in trouble and knew it. Suppose he had made a scapegoat of Rob by arranging this evening voyage. What was the law in a situation like this? If the girl and Dinsmoor both lied, might Rob be the one who would have to marry her? It didn't seem possible—and yet!

As a result of that night's experience, Rob's feeling grew into loathing for everything and everybody at the Dinsmoor farm. What had appeared idyllic, now became repulsive. He had liked the farmer, old Dinsmoor, until he began to notice that he drank whiskey and occasionally came home under its influence, from vegetable-selling trips to Lawrence.

After only three weeks at the farm, Rob found a good excuse for quitting, and slipped away without asking for his wages. Late that same night he walked, wretchedly, into his home and answered his mother's questions as he had done when he quit the shoeshop in Salem: He couldn't stand the coarseness, the profanity, the filthy talk of the hired help at Dinsmoor's. No more was asked—or told.

Conscience-stricken by his failure to bring home any money after three weeks of work, Rob quickly found employment at a woolen mill, pushing a bobbin-wagon among the rows of machines. But the hours were from seven until six, with a half hour for lunch, six full days a week; and Rob had not worked long in Braithwaite's mill before he found his sympathies were allied with the labor organizations that had been stirring up the city with protest meetings. His personal reasons for wanting a successful culmination of labor pressure made him delighted when all of the Lawrence mills were forced to grant Saturday afternoons off, starting in the middle of this summer.

Except for the long hours, Rob enjoyed the mill. He liked mingling with the men and women. Their friendliness, their harmless practical jokes, their witticisms, their laughter kept the drudgery from being unbearable. He did not make the familiar complaint to his mother that some of the loose talk and profanity shocked him. If he had needed it as an excuse for quitting, he would have used it (and there were many times when he wanted to quit); but, for the sake of the money, he stayed until fall—and, then, was glad to return to school.

Robert Frost was proud of his standing when he returned to Lawrence High School as a senior in the fall of 1891: head of his class, chief editor of the *Bulletin,* prominent member of the debating society, and one of the college-preparatory students who had already passed six preliminary examinations. He liked being treated with more and more respect. He was not unhappy when one of his teachers reproached other students by assuring them that they had as many hours for preparation as Robert Frost did, and when she urged them to imitate his way of putting time to good use. He also enjoyed the fact that sitting next to him in his homeroom a very pretty girl expressed her admiration in shy glances, which were all the more appealing because he so fully understood shyness.

The girl's name was Elinor Miriam White, and she was the daughter of a backslidden Universalist minister in Lawrence. Rob had not met her previously, because she was enrolled in the general or English program. A chronic illness called "slow fever" had hindered her regular attendance at the high school until the middle of Rob's sophomore year. But she had managed to study at home, to take examinations, and to do so much extra work that she had qualified for membership in the Class of '92. She made herself even more attractive to the chief editor of the *Bulletin* when she submitted to him, early in the fall, a few manuscript poems from which she hoped he would select at least one for publication. He did.

When the first issue of the *Bulletin* appeared under the management of the new staff, Rob filled several of his editorials with optimistic observations, exhortations, and announcements. His most important editorial announcement was that a group of alumni was enabling the *Bulletin* to offer a series of prizes for the best literary works in poetry and in prose. Serious in his attempts to encourage competition for these prizes, Rob returned to the subject in a later issue. He complained that the response to his first announcement had been "far from satisfactory" and went on to make a special plea for the writing of more poetry:

". . . In our colleges, students of English are advised to make use of verse composition for increasing their general vocabulary. . . . Perhaps we speak too flippantly of our subject; but we are not here to persuade any one that the poets (so-called) of our school journals are all to harp among the nation's bards; far from it. We know that our school is not now made up exclusively of future poets, yet we venture to say that there is not a scholar, who, with some little practice cannot surmount our literary columns with a capital of no mean proportions, (mechanically speaking). . . ."

Although the plea apparently went unheeded, the pleasantries in it did not conceal the earnestness of the editor's concern for the writing of poetry. He had heightened his demands on his own technical skill, and he could have offered an example to the others by publishing a poem he wrote soon after he made his October visit to Harvard to take his seventh examination, the one in English literature. The poem, "Clear and Colder," was a skippingly anapestic song inspired by his early-morning walk through Boston Common on the morning of his examination.

For Rob, the writing of "Clear and Colder" was a particular exercise in further adapting to his own needs a ballad stanza he had been hearing since first his mother showed him her favorites in Scott's *Border Ballads* or in Percy's *Reliques*. His first published poem, "La Noche Triste," had been built into a four-three ballad stanza, common measure. Now, he had advanced far enough to enjoy experimenting with another familiar pattern, working his own variations on a simple refrain, taking more liberties with meter so he could make the lines skip along with the mood of the piece, and drawing his images directly from his own observations. He had reason to be proud of all he was teaching himself about the mechanics of prosody, and he certainly could have published "Clear and Colder" in the *Bulletin*. Instead, he put it aside, as though he were content to view it merely as an exercise.

Although he enjoyed his work and play as editor-scholar-poet, he was no bookworm. And he welcomed a coincidence that led him back into athletics early in the fall of his senior year. Having lost none of his enthusiasm for baseball and none of his pride in being able to run fast, he had wistfully followed the activities of his schoolmates in their various games. But his pride still felt the wound of those insults that had greeted him on the first morning of his arrival at Lawrence High School, and he had reached his senior year without having tried to earn a place on any team.

One afternoon he happened to visit the football field when the team was practicing, and happened to be within calling distance when the discovery was made that one player was needed to give adequate opposition to the first-string team. Maybe Frost would fill in, someone said. Provoked just enough by the tone of the jest, Rob peeled off his coat and asked for a helmet. The position assigned him was at right end, where the speed of his defensive motions, the shrewdness with which he anticipated the strategies of the offense, and the unexpected savagery of his flying tackles surprised the regulars. By the end of the afternoon he had won himself a place on the first team, and he held up so well that he played in every scheduled game that fall. The team finished the regular season unbeaten.

Anyone playing football in the nineties could count on being bruised all over—if nothing worse—before the end of a game. And all of Rob's keen sensitivities were so easily injured—or, at least, offended—by the ruthlessness of the play, he always felt sick to his stomach whenever the hammering excitement was over. Toward the close of one game, when the strain and punishment were almost more than he could bear, he managed to last until the final whistle. Then, he walked off the field into tall grass, knelt where nobody could see him, and relieved his nervousness with a prolonged fit of vomiting. It was all a part of the price he was willing to pay for the fulfillment of his ideals of power and honor and glory. It was all part of the self-discipline that could and did assert courage and daring as the best way to overcome his own fears, lest they grow to be paralyzing and self-crippling.

From his own experience he had acquired all the evidence he needed concerning temporary psychological states that could render an individual a victim of uncontrollable forces. If he needed any further evidence, he had it near at hand and painfully apparent in the sad predicament of his sister. Back in Salem it had seemed as though her bookishness might give her an adequate realm of retreat from whatever she could not bear in the world of reality. But in the four years since then, it seemed as though Jeanie's desperate retreat into books had failed her. As long as she had asserted superiority over her brother, scholastically, she seemed to derive adequate sustenance from pride alone. When he surpassed her, during their first year in high school, all her defenses began to collapse.

Jeanie suffered through moods of depression, spells of tears, hysteria, ravings. Her many problems were discussed repeatedly and at length by her mother and brother. Neither of them understood the causes of her weakness. Rob understood enough, however, to take warning from his sister's condition. He kept reminding himself that unless he could keep his own potentially self-destructive sensitivities, fears, rages under control, he might become the victim of problems even more serious than those that had already overtaken his sister.

The most severe accumulation of nervous upsets that threatened Rob during his high-school years was caused by his involvement in too many activities during the late fall of 1891. Football practice and regularly scheduled games used up so much of his time and energy he could not do so much work as he wished in preparing classroom assignments, but he drove himself hard. The steadying influence he exerted on the debating society heightened the dependence on him of that partly serious and partly nonsensical group. He was elected to the office of senior vice-president and, then, president.

Even before these new honors were voted to him, Rob had so much difficulty finding time enough for his duties as chief editor of the *Bulletin* that he began delegating some of his tasks to assistant editors. They gave him insufficient support. As a result, the November issue was distributed in December. At nearly the same time, Jeanie's hospitalization with typhoid fever required Rob's absence from school for several days. Again, he asked the staff of the *Bulletin* to help; again, they failed him. Returning to school in January, he discovered that the December issue had not been published and that there was scarcely any copy in hand. Enraged, he took what copy he had, went to the printer's office, asked for a cubbyhole where he could work, and spent one whole day in hiding, while he wrote enough to fill out the issue. In this way, he decided, he could fulfill his obligations before resigning as chief editor, in protest against the failure of his staff to carry out their duties.

The preparation of the December 1891 *Bulletin* was a major literary accomplishment for Robert Frost. At least, it seemed to him to be an enormous tour-de-force, as he tossed off piece after piece, on that day in the printer's office, until he had enough to make up the required eight pages. This desperate method of acquiring copy by creating it firsthand resulted in the perpetration of a thoroughly successful hoax. Most of the students who, finally, received the December issue on January twenty-ninth were never permitted to realize he had written most of it himself. The new editor took cognizance of Rob's resignation, referring to it in the January issue:

"We are sure that the whole school and especially the senior class regrets the resignation of Mr. Frost as editor of the BULLETIN.

"After having lavished the wealth of his intellect on the paper for four months, the gentleman has decided, for purely personal reasons, to relinquish his editorial labors; and with much sound advice and the proper amount of tears has transferred to us the official shears and waste basket. . . ."

OUT OF HIGH SCHOOL— AND COLLEGE

(1892)

DURING THE last semester of his senior year at Lawrence High School, Robert Frost deliberately voyaged into deep waters of hope and doubt, to extend his intellectual and spiritual horizons. Although he prided himself on the courage required to venture independently through strange seas of thought alone, he was troubled by his growing awareness that he could never return comfortably to the harbor provided for him by his mother's serene religious beliefs.

The problems uppermost in his consciousness, and his attitudes toward them, were revealed in a brief essay he contributed to the *Bulletin* for May 1892. After resigning from his duties as editor he had apparently been asked to serve briefly as a substitute for his successor, and in complying he had written three editorials, signed with his name. In the third of these he defended a position not unlike that which Carlyle had honored in *Sartor Resartus*: the need to rethink any conventional belief in order to make it one's own. There were three possible categories of response to the customary or conventional attitudes, Rob explained— categories represented by groups of individuals who might be called followers, enemies, and rethinkers. Rob went on to praise the rethinkers and to attack those enemies who make the mistake of trying to identify rethinkers with unthinking followers and of trying to fashion liberalism into a dogma.

His motive for writing this editorial may have been provided in part by arguments between Rob and his friend Carl Burell. Carl had become disillusioned with religion and impatient with Rob for continuing to maintain even a rethinker's religious position. Mrs. Frost knew that Rob, having reached this rethinking phase of growth, took pride in teasing her by saying such things as that the evolutionists might be correct; if God had made man from a monkey, He had merely made man from *prepared mud,* instead of from dust. She did not enjoy this kind of wit and reproachfully asked her son if he, like Carl, had become an atheist as a result of reading those dreadful scientists. No, he said. Then, how did he explain his new and flippant attitude toward sacred matters? What did he call himself? He wasn't sure, he said, how to describe his position, except to say that he enjoyed being a wanderer among ideas. Perhaps he could be called a freethinker. His mother was shocked. "Oh, don't use that word," she protested. "It has a dreadful history."

She needn't have worried too much. Her son could have told her that his kind of freethinking was merely an expression of his desire to rethink and to form his own opinions about religion, quite apart from tradition, authority, or established belief. So far, all of his freethinking had not destroyed his essential piety. Furthermore, his attitude toward the findings of science (as opposed to the beliefs of religion) remained one of strong and stubborn hostility toward materialism.

Mrs. Frost's immediate worries might have been assuaged if she had noticed a particular sentence in Rob's guest-written editorial. It referred sympathetically to literature in which "the traveller reviews God's thoughts (nature) and praises them." Here was evidence that he had indeed preserved, in spite of his doubts, a basic piety, even when making his extensive travels through Carl Burell's library. Ahead of him lay some deeper and more dangerous expanses of religious doubt. Ahead, also, would be occasions when he might boastfully pretend that he was more heretical in his freethinking than he actually was. Throughout his life Rob's best anchor, in stormy moments of doubt, was the assurance he found in manifestations of metaphysical design.

As it happened, Rob did catch a new glimpse of metaphysical design, while in the very act of doubting, one day in the spring of his senior year. As he walked alone toward high school, troubled by problems in his own home, he puzzled over the old questions concerning whence and why misfortune is. He seriously doubted, now, whether all the griefs, sorrows, pains, and evils that had darkened his loved ones, since the death of his father, could be made to fit positively into any larger design. Suddenly an answer came to him, as a flash of second sight, while he continued to walk. If our souls do come to this earth from heaven, he thought, then each must choose to come. Heroically and courageously, each must want—and must, therefore, choose—to be tested or tried by the ordeal of earthly existence. Reassured (for the moment) by this insight, Rob ventured further. He imagined related elements in such a metaphysical design.

This ordeal could not be a valid test unless the soul, in making its departure from heaven, should agree to surrender the memory of having chosen to be tested. If, on the other hand, the memory of the choice did remain, there could be no real danger of ultimate defeat and failure, no valid trial worthy of man's spiritual and God-given capacities.

These answers to his doubts were new—at least for him—and he began to search for vivid poetic images with which to dramatize them. Because he knew that this undertaking was the most ambitious poetic leap he had so far tried to make, he was not surprised to find he had difficulty with it. But he was troubled when new doubts interfered. Years passed before he was able to finish this poem, which he eventually called "The Trial by Existence."

Rob's independent reading of poetry during the last half of his senior year gave another direction to his wandering among ideas. One stimulus to these adventures came from his gradual realization that Elinor White not only wrote poetry, but knew many good poems new to him. He was jealous because her wide reading made her better informed about the history of English poetry than he was, which gave impulse to his reading. And as soon as he began to admit he was truly in love with her, he discovered he was enthralled by love poetry.

In related ways, other phases of his own growth were marked that spring by his eagerness to find for Elinor White some good poems new to her. It was part of his courtship, and it provided occasion for his first gift to her: two pocket-sized books of poems by Edward Rowland Sill. Rob seemed to be touched most deeply by Sill's death poems. His favorite by far—and which remained a favorite with him throughout his life—was "Truth at Last." This was one of the poems Rob pointed out to Elinor when he gave her the volumes. (He knew her well enough to understand that her maturity—greatly surpassing his own—did not spare her from frequent moods that were dark and melancholy.)

Only weeks after Rob made his discovery of Sill, he heard for the first time of another New England poet who had died a few years earlier and whose verse, published posthumously, had attracted so much attention that the little volume had gone through six editions in six months: *Poems* by Emily Dickinson. To his surprise, Rob found himself more thoroughly captured by his new find than he had been by Sill. Although her terse, homely, gnomic, cryptic, witty qualities appealed strongly to him, he was fascinated to find that this author was also "troubled about many things" concerning death. It seemed to him that while she had developed an extraordinary capacity for running the gamut of moods, in her various imaginative confrontations with death, the poems that cut deepest for him were those that expressed her doubt whether any reasons fashioned by the mind, concerning life in heaven, could compensate for the heart's passionate and instinctive regrets over the transience of earthly bliss. Rob shared his discovery with Elinor and was happy that her admiration for Emily Dickinson was as great as his.

An entirely different adventure in ideas, and in argument, took place for Rob near the end of his senior year. Elinor White was very much in his consciousness on the day when he obeyed a summons from Mr. Goodwin, the high-school principal, and listened with satisfaction to the confidential announcement that valedictory honors in the Class of '92 had been won by Robert Lee Frost. The only competitor, it seemed, was a student who had taken the general course, not the classical. Although it was true, Mr. Goodwin explained, that the competitor's marks were at present very high and that some teachers thought the competitor's marks might excel Rob's by the end of the term, Goodwin was convinced the requirements in the general program were not so difficult as those in the classical. Hence, his decision that the honor should go to Frost. His curiosity piqued, Rob took the liberty of asking who his competitor was. A girl, he was told; a girl named Elinor White.

Immediately, Rob suffered mixed feelings of delight and jealousy. But his prompt reaction was to insist that if anyone thought it probable Miss White's marks would be higher than his in the final record, the award should not be made now—or the award should be given to her immediately. Demurring, Mr. Goodwin again explained his prejudices in favor of a student who had specialized in the classical program. Rob continued the argument so heatedly that Goodwin finally proposed a compromise, which was acceptable: Frost and Miss White would be co-valedictorians, but the valediction to the class would be made by Frost.

To the superstitious young man, thus paired with his beloved, the decision seemed prophetic. His love for Elinor had been growing throughout the year. Their courtship had progressed unevenly, but as soon as they began comparing notes as co-valedictorians, conditions were changed. Before the commencement exercises took place they had pledged themselves to each other and were secretly engaged to be married.

The annual high-school graduation exercises were traditionally held in the auditorium of city hall; and on Friday afternoon, July 1, 1892, the thirty-two members of the graduating class marched down the center aisle and up the steps to the platform, where all the speakers were seated in the front row—much to Rob's embarrassment. (He had carefully arranged that he be at the very end, and he planned to escape into the wings if he grew nervous.) Studying the program and trying to console himself that he would have nothing to do for at least an hour, he counted the speakers ahead of him. Twelve; and he was the unlucky thirteenth. But he noticed with satisfaction that his name appeared again on the program. Elected class poet, he had written a "Class Hymn," which was to be sung at the very end of the ceremonies. The words were printed in the program.

At the start all went well enough. One after another, the speakers rose and declaimed. Instead of listening, Rob spent most of his time going over his own speech, just to be sure he would not stumble when he said it all from memory.

He had chosen to address cherished ideals and discoveries that had been articulated by the experiences of these four years, particularly as the ideals touched on relationships between poetry and afterthought. It was his hope that the listeners would recognize the tribute paid to the poetic career he had already chosen for himself. He had thought to build the entire address around one discovery he began to make at the very moment in his freshman year when he had found no immediate answer for the question, "Do you think you know all of Roman history?" Although he had often suffered the discomfort of being late in finding the right thing to say, he had taken great consolation from his discovery that, in afterthoughts, he could at least figure out what he should have said. His best thoughts were always afterthoughts, in a Wordsworthian sense; his most poetic and most deeply felt insights came when his emotions were recollected in tranquility. Hence, his decision to build his address around this far-reaching discovery and to dramatize it by striking the imaginative posture of being an orator invited to speak at the unveiling of a marble monument newly erected in honor of "After-thought" (the hyphen was important to him, because it accentuated the meaning). His title: "A Monument to After-thought Unveiled."

Confident as he was in what he had to say, he found that as the other speeches dragged on, his nervousness increased. It had always been agony for him to appear on any stage for any reason. Made unbearably nervous, now, by his apprehensions, he felt so suffocated he began to watch for a chance to bolt. He found it at the end of the next-to-last speech before his, and he made a quick exit—knowing that Elinor came next, then he. Down the back stairs he ran, searching for a sink. He found it, soaked his handkerchief in cold water, sopped his face and neck and head, then dried himself off as best he could with the sleeve of his coat. For several minutes he paced back and forth in the lower corridor, near enough the staircase to hear Elinor speaking, firmly and calmly. He knew her address almost as well as he knew his own (they had helped each other rehearse, hour after hour). Her subject was "Conversation as a Force in Life," and it seemed to him that there was unintentional irony in it. Elinor's specialty was meaningful silence.

As Elinor approached her concluding remarks, Rob tiptoed back up the stairs, hiding in the wings until she finished. With the start of the applause, he slipped back into his seat. The clapping stopped; the rattling of the programs diminished. Almost overpowered by fright, he jumped up, hurried to the center of the apron, took a deep breath, and began to rattle off his words—like bullets. He knew he was speaking too fast, but there was nothing he could do about it.

Safely through the main address; now, the valediction to his class-mates. He took one step to the side, half-turned, and continued. Deliberately, he had constructed his valediction so that it would interlock with his "Class Hymn."

Back in his seat—flushed, trembling, out of breath—Rob was con-scious of the familiar and frightening pains of nausea in his stomach. But there was further embarrassment for him a few moments later, when the superintendent of schools unexpectedly called him back to the center of the stage to receive the Hood Prize, a small gold medal, awarded for general excellence and deportment during his four years.

The next day one of the Lawrence newspapers described Elinor White's co-valedictory address as "a most thoughtful and praiseworthy piece of work, full of sound sense and original thought, and showing fine mental power and culture." Then, the same account went on to say that Robert Lee Frost's address "combined in a rare degree poetic thought, a fine range of imagination, and devotion to a high ideal, and evinced intellectual compass much beyond the usual school essay." In another paper the reporter found fault with some of Rob's elocutionary manner-isms. Conceding the valedictory was a "splendid effort, showing research and thought," the critic said that "in the opinion of some its merits might have been shown to better advantage in a more natural delivery."

Rob's own afterthoughts were keen with swift regret over the nervous way he had raced through the address. If the reporter could have had any idea of how frightened the valedictorian had been, from the beginning to the end, some allowance might have been made for the unnatural quality of his presentation.

On the morning after his graduation, Robert Frost sold the gold medal presented to him for "general excellence," at a jewelry shop in Lawrence. The transaction was motivated not by poverty, but rather, by his idealistic, rebel scorn for conventions. As a junior in high school he had written an editorial defending rethinkers who return to conventional beliefs after challenging them; but one year later, in his valedictory address, he had expressed his new conviction that men form the habits that result in "the heroism of genius" only when they turn their backs on everyday conventionalities and make up thoughts and "after-thoughts" of their own, in converse with themselves. The elaborate process of formulating his valediction had helped him to certain decisions, not the least being that the time had come for him to declare his independence of the mob. The excellence he now dreamed of could not be represented adequately by the Hood Prize.

If others might not understand his pride and scorn, if his enemies might mistakenly call it arrogance—if even his mother might feel more and more separated from her son by his actions—he could not help it. Elinor White's love provided all the assurance he needed. Together they had already begun to create a world of their own, a place apart.

It seemed to Rob that his newly achieved distinction enabled him to find work, immediately after graduation, not merely as a common laborer, but more nearly as an administrator. He was given a position as clerical assistant to the gatekeeper at the Everett Mills in Lawrence—a dignified task involving the careful recording of absence and tardiness. The work was so easy it even gave him time to read, intermittently, and it enabled him to continue his arduous courtship during the long summer evenings and weekends.

Elinor White had the capacity to match her beloved's rebelliousness. She had been brought up in a home atmosphere made liberal by her father's independence of spirit. He had not flinched when circumstances convinced him that he did not believe in the dogmas of the Universalist church—or of any other church. Much to his wife's chagrin he had given up his career, had found what seemed to him a more honest way of earning a living, and quite comfortably supported his resentfully disapproving wife and their three daughters by cabinetwork. His influence on his youngest daughter, Elinor, was reflected in the ease with which she adapted herself to the unconventionalities of her fiancé.

Throughout the summer, whenever they could be together, the two lovers made their evenings and weekend days idyllic, by taking leisurely walks into the country or by making excursions up the Merrimack River, above the Lawrence dam. In these voyages by rowboat Rob and Elinor soon found favorite and secret hiding places. But the serious flaw in these days of riverbank courtship was caused by Rob's passionate, importunate lovemaking.

For some time Elinor thwarted and embarrassed him by her shyness and reticence, until the poetry of Shelley came to Rob's aid. Together they read aloud not only the lyrics, but also "Prometheus Unbound," "The Revolt of Islam," "Queen Mab," and—most important of all— "Epipsychidion." It was Rob's pleasure to point out that Shelley placed love at the core of the universe, but with a special emphasis on the need of lovers to rebel against the social conventions. Before the summer was over, he convinced her that Shelley had been right in saying love withers under constraint, that the very essence of love is liberty, that it is neither compatible with conventional attitudes nor with fear, that love is most pure and perfect and unlimited where its votaries live in confidence, equality, and unreserve.

Priding themselves more and more on being freethinkers, they even came to agree with Shelley that the institution of marriage—the licensing of love through civil or church rituals—is a shamefully degrading thing. Secretly, they conducted their own marriage ceremony during the summer of 1892, promised themselves to each other eternally, and with the exchange of plain gold wedding rings sealed their pledges.

This privately conducted marriage was motivated in part by the shared dread of impending separation. Each had completed arrangements for college. Elinor's plans for attending St. Lawrence University at Canton, New York, had been strengthened by the award to her of a scholarship that would cover most of her expenses. Rob's hope that he would attend Harvard was modified by the proselytizing activities of a Dartmouth graduate, newly appointed to teach chemistry and physics at Lawrence High School. Although Rob had not taken any science courses, he had been permitted by this teacher to conduct informal experiments in the school laboratory. The teacher became so impressed with Rob's attainments that he encouraged the boy to consider attending Dartmouth —and had even talked to Rob's grandfather about the probability that most of the expenses at Dartmouth could be defrayed by scholarships. The campaign was assisted by Rob's grandmother, who did not want the boy to go to Harvard, lest his life be ruined by habits she felt her own son had acquired there. Dependent on his grandfather's financial backing, Rob had to accept the decision that he should go to Dartmouth.

During the journey Rob made from Lawrence to Hanover, New Hampshire, in the autumn of 1892, only one important event occurred. The trip involved going by train to Manchester, New Hampshire, and waiting several hours for a train that would take him across the state to White River Junction and, then, up to Norwich, Vermont. His science teacher had stressed the literary attractiveness of Dartmouth, had perhaps mentioned the poet Richard Hovey, who had been graduated in 1885, and certainly the novelist Arthur Sherburne Hardy, a professor of mathematics there. Rob decided he would go to the Manchester public library, to spend his hours of waiting, and see if he could find any of Professor Hardy's novels. It might be well to know something about them before he met the distinguished mathematician-novelist. But because Rob remembered only the last name of the professor, he drew from the Manchester circulation desk two of *Thomas* Hardy's novels. Unaware that any mistake had been made, Rob diligently skimmed both volumes, and looked forward to meeting the author of them.

From Manchester to Norwich and, then, by horsedrawn conveyance across the Connecticut River and up the hill to the elm-tree-shaded Dartmouth campus on the Hanover Plain, Rob could feel his excitement mounting. Assigned quarters in Wentworth Hall, where he had a study and a small bedroom on the third floor, he found that his first task was to buy enough secondhand furniture to make his rooms livable.

He was one of only a few freshmen in Wentworth, and the sophomores wasted no time before starting to haze. During the first evening someone opened his door and threw into the room some kind of weapon that upset and put out his lantern. By the time he got the lantern lighted again, he could hear someone doing something to the outside of his door, which opened into the hall. Before he tried opening the door, he guessed what had happened. It had been fastened with enough screws to hold it firmly closed. Frost took it pleasantly as part of the game, and the general hubbub of noise in the corridor gave him courage to shout for help. At last someone came up the stairs to reprimand the sophomores. He could hear the noise abating as soon as a man's voice called out, "Boys, boys, be easy on them." Before morning the screws had been removed.

As soon as classes started, he was pleased to find that his assignments were relatively easy. He had chosen to take only three courses: one in Greek, with readings in Plato and Homer; one in Latin, with readings in Livy's history of Rome; one in mathematics, which started with advanced algebra and went on to solid geometry.

The routine of study soon became monotonous. Much more to Rob's liking were the rituals of warfare between the freshman and sophomore classes. On the greatest occasion of all for Rob, the freshman strategy, during the "pennant rush," was to get near enough to the pole to tear the flag from it and, then, to carry it triumphantly through the mob to a waiting freshman runner so fleet of foot he could outdistance the enemy. It was Rob's accomplishment to be among the freshmen who succeeded in penetrating the ranks of the massed sophomores, to have his hand on the pennant when it was torn down, and to help carry it to the sprinter who successfully ran off with the prize. His experiences as a high-school football player enabled him to stand up well under the bruising of these battles—but he still suffered the old sense of nausea after each new excitement.

Rob gradually came to find that his closest friend among the freshmen at Dartmouth was Preston Shirley, a spirited youngster whose asthmatic ailments and slightly hunched back could not restrain him from entering into the thick of every brawl. They were invited to join the same fraternity, Theta Delta Chi. Perhaps because of information furnished to the fraternity, Frost was persuaded Theta Delt was really a literary society—or, at least, as good as one—because so many of its members were interested in writing. When he tried to explain that he could not afford to join, one of the seniors paid his small initiation fee. Further honors came to him when he was elected, by the other freshman initiates of Theta Delt, to make the speech for the freshman delegation at the fraternity banquet that followed the initiation ceremonies.

If there was anything about Frost that disturbed and perplexed his fraternity brothers it was his way of indicating that he was not quite so fraternal as they wished him to be. He liked walking, but he liked to walk alone. He had the feeling he could somehow assimilate his experiences better if he used this method of getting off by himself. His fraternity brothers became suspicious enough to challenge him. What did he do, they asked, when he went off into the woods alone? The question seemed insolent enough to deserve his mocking retort, "Gnaw bark."

If he could have found one sympathetic ear among his questioners, he might have wanted to say that during these walks he also gnawed the bare bones of his longing for the presence of Elinor White. He wrote to her regularly, and he almost devoured each letter she sent him. But he was strangely troubled by his fear that she was settling in with almost too much satisfaction at St. Lawrence University. He could be made jealous by any references to friendships newly established, even friendships with her own sex. There was something about this separation that seemed more cruel to him than to her, and this knowledge troubled him. St. Lawrence was coeducational; she might fall in love with someone else.

These fears had no foundation, he kept telling himself; he and Elinor were bound by ties of love and loyalty that transcended any possible interference from anyone else. Still, the constant uncertainty shook his confidence in himself.

Under the circumstances, it would not have been surprising if he had taken consolation in translating his passion into verse that he could send her. He did not. The nearest he came to such was his reading of poems written by others. Quite by accident he found and bought in the local bookstore Palgrave's *Golden Treasury*; and in his room, hour after hour, when he should have been preparing assignments, he seemed impelled to read and read again from Palgrave the outpourings of poets who had previously suffered from love, just as he was suffering now.

There were times when he decided that the most important part of his Dartmouth experience, so far, was his discovery of Palgrave. But he came at least to the edge of English literature in other ways. One of the orientational talks to the freshmen, to acquaint them with possible fields of specialization, was given by Charles Francis Richardson, Winkley Professor of Anglo-Saxon and English. He talked particularly, on this occasion, about the importance of becoming acquainted with literature, and he gave special emphasis to poetry as the highest literary expression. Frost was deeply touched when Richardson invoked Shelley in order to define poetry as being the realm ". . . Where music and moonlight and feeling / Are one." In his present mood, Frost thought, that would do as one definition of poetry. But he had already discovered that poetry could and did get its arms around things more important to him than music or moonlight.

One of his discoveries, during this fall term at Dartmouth, made him newly aware of poetic range and influence. While browsing in the college library he noticed a periodical he had never seen before, *The Independent*. The entire first page of this issue for November 17, 1892, was given over to a new poem by Richard Hovey, "Seaward: An Elegy on the Death of Thomas William Parsons"; and an editorial in the same issue praised Hovey's elegy, by drawing favorable comparisons with Milton's "Lycidas," Shelley's "Adonais," and Arnold's "Thyrsis."

The Dartmouth freshman was almost as much impressed by the editorial as by one American poet's salute to another. At the time, he was not sure he would ever be able to realize his secret ambition to write a poem that could compare with Hovey's. But as he sat there in the Dartmouth library, reading, he stored up impressions that later made him hope that someday he would see a poem of his own published on the front page of this periodical.

Not long after Frost found Hovey's elegy, he went by train to Sutton, Vermont, to visit Carl Burell. Much had happened to Burell since he and Frost had attended Lawrence High School together. He made a trip alone to California soon after his parents died, but he had been so bitterly disappointed by his lonely experiences there that he soon returned to New England, settling on the small farm of his widower grandfather, Jonathan Eastman, in Sutton. It was to the Eastman farm that Frost went for his Thanksgiving vacation.

As soon as cold weather required the Dartmouth students to stock their fuel closets with wood and coal, so they might keep fires burning day and night in their rooms, Rob yielded to lazy habits. It was a nuisance to carry coal up two flights of stairs, and it was an even-greater nuisance to carry buckets of ashes back down to the dumping ground assigned for student use. It was far easier to rake ashes out on the floor beside the stove and let them pile up.

Rob's lackadaisical attitude toward housekeeping in his dormitory room was akin to the young man's general attitude toward all other phases of academic life. The rebel streak began to assert itself with increasing strength. He had hoped Elinor would return to Lawrence at Christmastime, if for no other reason than to see him. But winter weather and expenses had caused her to forgo the trip—and Rob's response was one of exceptional disappointment. He had the feeling that while he was growing bored with the routine of classroom assignments and dormitory life at Dartmouth, Elinor was becoming too deeply enthralled by social and academic affairs at St. Lawrence. Her letters continued to make him jealous. They heightened his growing impatience with being told what to study, when to study, and just how to meet deadlines for written assignments. Depressed, lovesick, homesick, he had not completed his first semester of study at Dartmouth before he began to tell himself he had had enough of higher education. All he needed now was an excuse for quitting. His mother unintentionally provided it.

Mrs. Frost's three years of teaching in Methuen, following all the unpleasantness at Salem Depot, had been made miserable, once again, by her weaknesses as a disciplinarian. Even worse, this year she had been transferred to an eighth-grade room and had found that among her students were some older boys who were repeating eighth-grade work. Rob heard about the difficulties experienced by his mother in trying to handle these "numbskulls," as he called them; and his resentment gradually mounted. What those Methuen boys needed was a firm, masculine hand, and there seemed to be no reason Rob should not take over the school for his mother. Convinced that there was nothing worthwhile for him at Dartmouth, and aching to escape from an imprisonment made worse by snow, he confided to his friend Preston Shirley that he was about to depart.

When Shirley realized nothing could dissuade Frost, he offered one last night of bacchanalian feasting. The two freshmen barricaded themselves into the room and sang and carried on—and ate Turkish fig paste. Late at night they heightened the atmosphere of celebration by opening the window just long enough to bellow insults at sleeping sophomores. The next morning, without any other farewells, Frost strapped up his small trunk and casually made his permanent departure from undergraduate life at Dartmouth. The decisive act was no more significant to him than were the days he had spent at the school. If he had learned anything useful enough to serve him in later years, it was that for him education was likely to be a matter of self-teaching, rather than of classroom learning.

What others might think of his quitting was not nearly so important to him as what he himself thought. If there were any fear at all, it was caused by his uncertainty about Elinor White's reaction. But she was the one who was more responsible than anyone else for his leaving college.

7

FRUSTRATIONS AND PUBLICATION

(1892–1894)

ROBERT FROST had some difficulty in convincing his mother that he had better things to do than waste his time at Dartmouth College. But it was not easy for her to resist his explanation that he had come home for the express purpose of helping her deal with the "numbskulls" who had been pestering her for months. His plan was to call on the chairman of the school board in Methuen, a family friend, the Rev. Charles H. Oliphant, who was a Congregationalist minister. He would explain that his mother's health was being endangered by the nervous exhaustion of trying to deal with brutes, and that he wanted to serve as a substitute teacher.

Oliphant had doubts. Another, less-demanding assignment could be found for Mrs. Frost without difficulty. But how did her son propose to handle the serious problem of discipline? With force, if necessary. All right, but was the young man familiar with the materials he would have to teach eighth-graders? Yes, he had discussed these matters thoroughly with his mother. If Oliphant heard any arrogance in the tone of these answers, he was not too greatly troubled by it. In a few days, he said, he could get the approval of the school board.

Grimly satisfied with the prospects, Frost made further preparations for his task. He purchased a supply of stout rattans, and by the time he learned the school board had approved his appointment, he had aroused himself to an ugly pitch of resentment. On the first morning, he brought the boys and girls to order and bluntly explained his presence. He scolded the older boys for having bullied his mother, and made it clear he was ready to even the score.

Classwork had not even begun when he saw an excuse for descending on a culprit—yanking him out of his seat and shoving him through the door into the entryway, where he laced him soundly with a handful of rattans. While he was executing justice in the hall, pandemonium broke loose in the classroom. There was no choice now. He had to tackle the ringleaders. He did; and one of them resisted punishment, by drawing a knife. Frost caught the boy's wrist, twisted it hard enough to make him drop the knife, and then, flailed away with the rattans.

That evening the new teacher visited Oliphant to make a report. He admitted he had been forced to use more physical persuasion than he had planned, but he urged that Oliphant give him a few more days to test the success or failure of his methods. The request was granted.

The stern physical punishment continued, until gradually the atmosphere of this previously chaotic room became conducive to moderately successful teaching. Nevertheless, Frost soon grew so weary, from strenuous disciplinary measures, that he did not continue teaching beyond the end of the term, which closed late in March. He had planned to stay at least through the spring, and when he failed to appear the big boys spread the word that they had beaten their tormentor so badly they had forced him to resign. His own rationalization for quitting was that he had stayed long enough to accomplish revenge.

A family crisis developed at the home of Elinor White very early in the spring of 1893, while she was still absent at St. Lawrence University. Elinor's sister Ada, suffering from physical and psychological ailments, began to complain about the city noises and pleaded that she be taken into the country. Mrs. White enlisted Rob's aid. He suggested it might be possible to rent an empty homestead, the Oliver Saunders place, in Salem, New Hampshire; and because Mr. White refused to accompany his wife and daughter, Rob volunteered as caretaker and protector. After Ada was brought to the Saunders place, Mrs. White depended on Rob for innumerable tasks. It pleased and flattered him to be so much in demand, and he took his duties seriously.

Into this isolated rural hideaway, unexpectedly, descended Leona, oldest daughter of Mrs. White—and said by some to be by far the most vivacious and beautiful of the three girls. She had recently married a farmer in Epping, New Hampshire, and she arrived at the Saunders place with the announcement that, although pregnant, she had run away from her husband. Leona's problems were discussed at length, and because Frost was acting as male head of the White family, he was consulted about even the most intimate details.

Leona seemed to depend more and more on Rob's sympathetic attentions, and it soon became apparent that Mrs. White had a problem on her hands. Somewhat desperately, she sent a telegram to Elinor, saying (with an understandable disregard for truth) that Ada was terribly ill and Elinor should come home from college immediately. Her request was followed. Rob immediately turned his attentions to Elinor, and before long Leona went back to her husband.

Rob, able to resume his courtship of Elinor, insisted she should not go back to St. Lawrence that spring—or ever. Ideally, they should announce to the world that they were married. And if the demands of society made it seem advisable, they should condescend to perform the simplest public ritual of legalizing their relationship. Elinor asked how, if she should grant his wish, he planned to earn a living to support them; and she made him understand she was not the only one disappointed in his apparent willingness to betray the promises he had made as valedictorian, not the only one surprised that he could give up his studies, for no good reason, and be content with idling.

Hurt and resentful, Rob was willing to admit he had no plans—only the hope that someday he might become famous as a poet. Otherwise, he did not know what he wanted to do with his life. As for earning the necessities of life, there were any number of ways in which he could make money without becoming enslaved to a profession: teach school for a while, work in one of the mills occasionally, do odd jobs.

Elinor protested that if she did not go back to college soon, she might lose credit for much of the work she had already done. It was clear, Rob insisted, that he meant less to her than something or someone at St. Lawrence University, that already she had somehow violated her pledge to him. Again, she protested; but, finally, she sent word to St. Lawrence that she would be unable to return until fall.

It was not a good start for the long summer Rob and Elinor spent with Mrs. White and Ada at the Saunders place. He had won some kind of advantage, and he was happy with it. Nevertheless, Elinor's silences perplexed him more than ever before. When fall came and the Whites made arrangements to leave, Frost announced he would stay on for a few days alone. No use going back to Lawrence if Elinor insisted on returning to college. And it may have pleased him to think he could make her sorry to leave him there all by himself.

He took pleasure in feeling sorry for himself, a pleasure he later caught in a poem that described his loneliness and fear each night when it began to grow dark at the old Saunders place: "Bereft."

Rob felt "bereft" in the sense that he had been robbed by the loss of someone dear. Hence he was lonely, sad, forlorn—luxuriating in self-pity. But after he had indulged these miseries for a few days, he returned to his own home, where his mother and sister had been getting along as best they could without him. Conscience-stricken by the unspoken criticism he could feel in the glances of those who had expected—or, at least, had hoped—he would return to Dartmouth, he searched for work sufficiently unusual and honorable to impress friends and enemies alike.

Ultimately, he humbled himself by accepting work as a light-trimmer in the Arlington woolen mills. He was one of the menials. He had to stand on the very top of a ladder while reaching up, with both hands, to replace burned-out filaments in the arc lamps. His duties were not arduous (they brought him only eight dollars a week); and on clear, sunny days there was little need for artificial light. Whenever his boss found him idle, he gave him a broom, to sweep up, or a cloth for polishing. These labors hurt Rob's pride, and he learned to keep out of sight after his light-trimming tasks were finished. Exploring various hideaway places, he chose as his favorite a sort of hen coop, built to house a large belt wheel, on the roof of the main building. In this isolated place, Frost lounged and read and slept.

For his reading in this lofty wheelhouse Rob carried a pocket-sized book, usually a volume from a set of Shakespeare. Never before had he read any of the plays carefully. Now, he began to study, pencil in hand, making marginal notes on how passages should be spoken if the lines were to convey, dramatically, the essential meanings. Soon, he began to admire the give-and-take of Shakespeare's lean, sharp dialogue, made most effective when the thread of thought and action was not snarled into a maze of metaphor and adjective. For the first time, he realized that in Shakespeare's poetry—and, he supposed, in any good poetry—there was an interplay between the basic rhythm of the metrical line and the natural intonations of the spoken sentence. In his own writing, he decided, he would try to achieve these qualities. Day after day, he continued to study Shakespeare's dialogues, searching for hints and clues that might help him understand and master these technical aspects of poetry.

He continued in the Arlington Mills from late September 1893 until February of 1894. Difficult to handle was the discovery that several of his former students whom he had disciplined too harshly in the grammar school in Methuen were now working in the mills; and, as the weeks slipped by, they began to threaten Frost with insinuations that the day would come when they would get revenge. For protection, Frost fell into the habit of approaching and leaving the mills in company with some of the more trustworthy workers. But in the dusk of one winter evening a group of his tormentors waylaid him as he was walking home from work alone. They knocked him down, rolled him into the slush of the gutter, punching and kicking and hammering him until he was certain their intent was murder.

A passing Good Samaritan waded into the fracas, with shouts for help, while swinging a heavy walking stick. The tormentors ran, and as Frost rose to his knees, trying to mumble his thanks, he saw two figures standing there above him. One of them was a young man who had formerly been his classmate in high school. Only a few words were spoken, and Frost continued home, doubly the victim of humiliation.

What hurt more than the physical pounding was the remembered expression of disdain on the face of his former classmate—perhaps disgust at the thought that a Hood Prize–winner and valedictorian could have degenerated so soon into a good-for-nothing mill-hand street-fighter.

Rob, while nursing his own soul-bruises, suffered oblique effects from his mother's cumulative misfortunes. After she had been shunted through four Methuen schools, she was completely relieved of teaching duties. The loss of her salary forced her to give up the comfortable apartment where she and her children had been living in Methuen; and for Rob's sake they moved to Lawrence, finding an inexpensive tenement near the tracks of the Boston & Maine Railroad, at 96 Tremont Street.

Then, one morning late in the winter of 1894, Rob was approaching the gate of the Arlington Mills when he heard the mill bell shift from its vigorous clang to a funeral toll. The gate would soon be shut; the laggards, for their tardiness, would be made to stand idle throughout the next half hour and would find a few cents less in their next pay envelope. He had often experienced the humiliation—the price he had to pay for his incurable habit of late rising. This morning, as the main gate clanged shut just before he could reach it, he vented his mood of resentment by making a Shelleyan gesture of scornfully rebellious defiance. The time had come to strike, and he was willing to stand apart from the herd as a lone striker.

As he turned his back on the gate, he knew this was more than a strike. He was putting an end to his life as a mill hand. The assertion of independence gave a lift to his spirit and made him feel more like a man than he had felt for months. He would find something else to do, more dignified than being a light-trimmer in a dirty mill.

The path he soon found himself walking was a bitterly familiar one. A replacement was needed for a substitute teacher in tiny District School Number Nine in South Salem, only about a mile below Salem Depot and not far from the Methuen-Salem boundary line. The pay was no better than he had received at the mills, but the hours were shorter. In addition, his work with children in the first six grades was more to the young man's liking, and the deference with which he was treated by pupils and parents alike was balm to his wounded pride.

Secretively, shyly, he stole time during the spring term of 1894 to explore another path. Almost surreptitiously, he had clung to the direction his steps had begun to take during his sophomore year in high school, when he had begun to compose the ballad stanzas of "La Noche Triste." In spite of the discouragement that had beset his many attempts to write verse, he continued to cherish his dream that he might eventually become known as a poet. He was almost ashamed to admit his hopes, his ambition—even to himself. Whenever the mood came over him to take out his sheaf of poems, to make fresh starts or revisions, he concealed his activities from his mother and sister, as though he dreaded to let them know what he was doing.

One such concealment occurred in the Tremont Street apartment on a Sunday evening soon after he had begun teaching school in Salem. He had carefully locked himself in the kitchen to work on a poem inspired by a moment that had occurred late in the fall of his few months at Dartmouth, a moment when he had found a fragile butterfly wing lying among dead leaves. Because the delicate wing seemed to him so perfect an image, representing the brevity of life, he had been trying to build an elegy around it ever since he left college. This evening the words and thoughts intermingled so successfully he felt a sense of power and triumph that carried him through to an almost-satisfactory end.

But as he worked, his sister tried the door to the kitchen and, finding it locked, began to pound on it in anger. What was he doing? And why had he locked the door? He gave her no satisfactory answer; he kept on writing. The mystified and impatient Jeanie walked out the front door and around the house, until she could climb the steps and turn the handle of the back door—also locked. Again she hammered and complained, to the amusement of her brother. He was through now, and all her noise did not hinder him from making a fair copy of "My Butterfly: An Elegy" before he opened the kitchen door to Jeanie, and retired to his own bedroom feeling a sense of elation over his newest and best poetic accomplishment.

What pleased him most about this evening was that he had discovered within himself unexpected ability to fuse elements of observed fact, impassioned rhythmical tone, and heartfelt personal theme. Although he had built his lament primarily around images of the butterfly, briefly alive and now dead, he had given depth to the poem by hinting at literal and figurative analogies between certain things happening simultaneously to himself and the butterfly.

As he read the lines, immediately after he had written them, he cried inside with the joy of his knowledge that at last he had caught poetic qualities that had seemed beyond his reach. Suddenly, all his ambition was justified and reinforced. Now he had something he could submit to a magazine editor. Remembering Hovey's "Elegy" published on the first page of *The Independent,* and feeling that *The Independent* might be particularly sympathetic to poetry, he sent off his manuscript without any covering letter, simply with his name and address at the top of the first page.

Quicker than Frost dared expect, the editor replied, with a check for fifteen dollars, with praise for "My Butterfly," and with a request for some biographical information about the author's "training" and "line of study." The event was so exciting that Frost in his answer, dated March 28, 1894, did not even try to strike a posture of calm. All he had needed by way of encouragement was exactly the kind of response given by the warm praise of an editor so distinguished as the Rev. William Hayes Ward, whose specialty was not so much poetry as theology and Assyrian archaeology.

The learned man's sister, Susan Hayes Ward, usually served as literary editor of *The Independent*. She had been the one who had called attention to "My Butterfly," and after the formalities of acceptance she wrote to the newly discovered poet, expressing her own admiration. She also made some comments on weak places in the poem, urged him to make a few revisions, and sent him a copy on which he might make changes. Her well-intended criticisms depressed the young poet almost as much as her genuine praise heartened him. He answered, enclosing three more poems and managing to combine both sides of his reaction in his opening paragraph:

"It is just such a letter as you wrote me that I have been awaiting for two years. Hitherto all the praise I have recieved has been ill-advised and unintelligent. . . . So that something definite and discriminating is very welcome. My thanks unlimited! Yet this consideration is hardly due me. Take my word for it that poem exaggerates my ability. You must spare my feelings when you come to read these others, for I haven't the courage to be a disappointment to anyone. Do not think this artifice or excess of modesty, though,—for, to betray myself utterly, such an one am I that even in my failures I find all the promise I require to justify the astonishing magnitude of my ambition."

He concluded his letter to Miss Ward by admitting that certain lines in "My Butterfly" did need revision, as she had suggested, but for the present he did not find adequate inspiration for correcting or improving the faults.

His next letter, dated June 10, 1894, revealed a darker and more discouraged mood: ". . . It has been painful for me trying to induce a passion like the one that is the spirit of my poem. I am afraid I cannot revise the thing. I am greatly dissatisfied with it now. Do you not think it would be well to suppress it. . . ." Apparently Miss Ward knew how to cope with these passing moods of despondency. She continued writing to him, she waited patiently for his revisions, and she made arrangements to keep the poem until the appropriate time to publish it in autumn.

Both of the Wards were unusually impressed with "My Butterfly." They showed it with pride to Bliss Carman (who had just collaborated with Richard Hovey in publishing the exuberant *Songs from Vagabondia*), and Carman praised the poem. Another copy was sent to the

Hoosier novelist Maurice Thompson, who responded with a glowing tribute. Ward also sent a note to an acquaintance of his in Lawrence, a Congregationalist minister named William E. Wolcott, asking Wolcott to visit the poet and help him in any way possible.

Calling on Frost to congratulate him on the success of "My Butterfly," Wolcott offered to serve as adviser-critic. Flattered, Frost showed several of his manuscripts to Wolcott, who found nothing that seemed to compare with "My Butterfly." He complained that the other poems lacked the same high lyrical music of true poetry, suffered from a flatness of tone, and sounded "too much like talk."

Some afterthoughts were needed before Frost could make any constructive use of Wolcott's criticism. He remembered that he had liked the dramatic qualities of the poetic dialogues in Shakespeare's plays *because* those dialogues actually sounded so much like "talk" that they characterized the individual speakers, and he was convinced part of Shakespeare's greatness in ordering words was that he made the words themselves convey the sound of talk. His afterthoughts enabled him to make use of Wolcott's criticism, which accidentally threw light on something he had been groping toward. A poem well handled could not possibly sound "too much like talk"; all the best lines and sentences should clearly convey tones of voice that rooted poetry deep in human experience. From now on he would try harder than ever to make his poetry sound "like talk."

But it was one thing to fashion an ideal poetic theory out of Wolcott's faultfinding; it was another thing to confront the discouraging fact that whenever Frost yielded to the mood and wrote poetry, nothing worthwhile came of it. Self-protectively, he kept making the excuse that teaching the boisterous children in District School Number Nine had worn him down until he was on the verge of illness.

Irritabilities marred his anticipation of Elinor White's return from St. Lawrence University for the summer vacation of 1894. Throughout the year he had tortured himself with fears and dreads that her college interests were drawing her further away from their vows of eternal love. But Elinor insisted her college friendships had no bearing on her love for Rob; he had no reason to be jealous. Back and forth through the mail went the shuttle of their discord, Frost pressing more and more on what he considered the disloyalty of Elinor's dalliances. He even wrote and sent to her a poem entitled "Warning," in which he summed up his ultimate fear.

By the time Elinor did come home from St. Lawrence that summer, her lover was ready to number all her college friends among his enemies, and he was crushed by her insistence that she must finish her college studies—that, even then, she felt they should not marry formally until he had found reliable means of providing at least a minimum of financial support for them both.

He tried to explain that love came first, that as for their future and his capacity to earn money, if she really meant what she said about her faith in his poetry, she should be able to see significance in his having sold "My Butterfly" for cash. Gently resisting all his pleas, Elinor returned to St. Lawrence in the fall of 1894, after making only one concession. She would continue to accelerate her program of studies, so that she could be graduated a full year ahead of schedule, in June of 1895; if by then he had established himself relatively well, she would marry him.

Dissatisfied with her plans, and yet unable to change them, Frost made several listless attempts to find work congenial to him. He went so far, on three separate occasions, as to accept positions in Boston, but quit each one after only a few days. More pertinent to his ambition was his briefly obsessive speculation concerning all he had read and heard about poets who found artistic stimulus through drugs and alcohol. As an experiment, he made a trip to Boston, rented a room in a boardinghouse, bought two bottles of wine, drank as much as he could, and began to write poem after poem. Late in the night he went to bed, happy in the thought that his experiment had been a success. The next morning, when he read his new creations in the sober light of day, he could not understand how he had been so thoroughly deceived by the wine. Disgusted, he tore up his manuscripts and went back to Lawrence.

As he continued to drift from one odd job to another, Frost apparently worried his grandfather. The elderly gentleman finally cornered him during one of his rare visits to his grandparents' Haverhill Street home. There was no unkindness in the tone with which his grandfather began to talk. The old man said he had been pleased to learn Rob had sold a poem to *The Independent*. He was well aware, he said, that the attractions of a literary life seemed to be keeping Rob from settling down to a wage-earning career or profession. If the boy needed a little more time to try his wings as a poet, money could be found to support him for one more full year, on one condition: If at the end of the year he had not established himself as a self-supporting man of letters, he would stop wasting time. Rob, instead of making a tactfully grateful answer, rose to his feet, struck the posture of an auctioneer, and began to chant: "I have one, who'll give me twenty; I have one, who'll give me twenty; one, give me twenty-twenty-twenty-twenty. . . ." The arrogance had its desired effect. While Rob was still chanting, his grandfather abruptly left the room.

During his troubled courtship of Elinor, Robert Frost made a romantic gesture in the fall of 1894, with almost-disastrous effect. He thought his beloved could be made to understand that the sale of "My Butterfly" to *The Independent* truly foreshadowed the time when he could earn a living for both of them by publishing book after book of poetry, and he wanted to place in her hands a symbol of this future. Inspired by new hope, he sorted through his manuscripts to find four poems that might accompany "My Butterfly" in a little book made especially for her.

Each of the four poems must have been chosen with a view to what Elinor could read between the lines; each may have had reference to places made sacred by shared experiences. One was entitled "An Unhistoric Spot," another "Summering," and another "The Falls." In the final poem, "Twilight," the lonely lover addresses the personification of twilight—one who, like himself, is sadly looking for someone else. (It echoes the address to the moon uttered by Sidney's lonely lover in the familiar sonnet from *Astrophel and Stella*, which begins, "With how sad steps, O Moon, thou climb'st the skies!")

Having made his selection, he carried fair copies of these four poems, with "My Butterfly," to a job printer in Lawrence. He asked that a very special little book be made of them, in an edition of just two copies. One would be for Elinor, the other for himself. The work was done and the books delivered to him—the title word, "TWILIGHT," stamped in gold on the brown pebbled-leather binding.

Each poem was so subtly a love poem that he hoped Elinor might dare show them to her college friends, who would then know that her lover was by no means the failure they might think him. Before the book was ready to mail, however, Elinor's letters overcame him with new and dreadful fears that his cause might already be lost.

Her letters, as he interpreted them, provided proof that she was welcoming the attentions of a new suitor, a handsome and charming senior—the Beau Brummel of his class—Lorenzo Dow Case. From Mrs. White, Rob learned that this charmer was so serious in his attentions that he had asked for, and Elinor had granted him, permission to spend one evening a week with her. Rob was frantic.

He made secret plans to go to Canton as soon as possible. He would assault the citadel, and he would use *Twilight* as his best weapon. He confided all of his hopes to Mrs. White, who expressed her sympathy in several ways. She gave him money for a round-trip railroad ticket. She even accompanied him to a haberdashery and helped him buy a new suit for the venture. Finally, she went with him to the station and gave him her blessing as he departed.

The journey was overnight, and as Rob sat in the coach throughout the long, dismal hours, he tried to prepare himself for any eventuality. Early in the morning he found his way to the campus and began asking directions to the house to which he had addressed so many letters. It was a private home, rather than a campus dormitory, but campus regulations made it a punishable offense to entertain any young man there except during the proper evening hours. Hence, the surprise of the girl who answered Rob's knock; hence also, the expressions of distress, reproach, and indignation in the eyes of Elinor when she came to the door to face her unexpected visitor. Before she said a word, her eyes managed to wound her lover so deeply that all the fight went out of him. The best he could do was explain he had been impelled to come so that he might talk face-to-face with Elinor about very important matters that concerned them both. Elinor said she simply could not talk with him here. Then, could they meet and talk somewhere else? Yes, when next she came home. Awkwardly, he began to plead. She stopped him.

Before he fully realized how it had happened, he had surrendered his precious weapon, *Twilight*. Elinor took it from him as casually as if it had been the morning paper and, then, closed the door firmly. She had commanded him to take the very next train out of Canton. He did not wait for it to arrive. Instead, he started walking down the railroad tracks, toward home, completely overcome with chagrin and mortification. Needing an object on which he could vent his disappointment, he found it in his pocket. He had planned to show Elinor his own copy of *Twilight*, just to make her understand that between them they had all the existing copies. As he walked along the tracks, he took his out of his pocket, tore the pages into handfuls of confetti, and tossed it along the cinderbed.

At the next station Rob waited for a train, and during the homeward journey he suffered through agonies more intense than he had ever experienced before. For years he had been trying to find himself, trying to choose a direction or goal for his life, trying to develop confidence in his own abilities. Elinor's love had seemed to be the mainstay of all his hopes, the foundation on which he had been building. But so closely entwined were his different kinds of faith that when she had dismissed him so unexpectedly and curtly at her door, the act had undermined faith in self, faith in his future as a poet, faith in others. He had been trying, courageously, to rid himself of his deep-seated sense of insecurity and his lack of confidence, and he had made good progress throughout his high-school years, particularly after he had met Elinor. His falling in love had been a venture shyly made, without any realization that it would help him develop his own capacities, through the strength she could and did give.

All these gains were lost now, and it seemed suicide was the only fitting end for such a catastrophe. He would make Elinor feel sorry throughout her life for what she had done. It may have crossed his mind that he could secretly arrange death by plunging into some such Slough of Despond as the Dismal Swamp in Virginia, and that the desired effect would be heightened if Elinor could never find out where he had gone or how he had died.

Elinor did write soon, but if she made any apologies or any comments on *Twilight* or tried to correct Rob's mistaken notions concerning the possibility that she was now engaged to Lorenzo Case, her words were not persuasive. Instead, they seemed to precipitate Rob's conviction that he might as well throw his life away, with her letter. In a rage of jealousy, injured pride, and discouragement, he packed his bag and left home, without telling even his mother where he was going. If he had not so nearly made a beeline for the Dismal Swamp, it might be possible to imagine he did not know for certain where he was going.

On the morning of November 6, 1894, he took a train from Lawrence to Boston, crossed the city, and took a train to New York City. On the evening of the same day, he boarded a Merchants & Miners Line steamer for Norfolk, Virginia. Early the next morning he disembarked and began asking directions to the Dismal Swamp.

Slowly he worked his way out of Norfolk and through a scattering of suburbs, along the Elizabeth River. It took him all day, and he had had nothing to eat since breakfast. He continued in a southerly direction toward the place where the swamp actually began to look like wilderness. As darkness settled in, he became aware that an almost-full moon was going to give him light. He saw ahead, rising high at the end of farmland fields, a forest wall. The lofty trees grew so rank that their branches spread out over the narrow road from both sides, so he seemed to be approaching a dark tunnel.

Rob would have had good reason to stop at the edge of the swamp-forest. His fear of darkness had been an obsession as far back as the San Francisco days; he still hated to go into an empty house alone after dark. He certainly would have turned back, now, if his immediate course had not been so grim and desperate. Driven forward by pressures more powerful than his fears, he kept on walking, out of the moonlight, into the forest-tunnel. He knew that on either side of the narrow road the underbrush might be providing hiding places for dangerous wild animals, that on the occasional shoulders of dry ground beside the road he might step on a late-prowling rattlesnake. He didn't care.

Before he had groped his way far into the swamp, he came to a place where mud holes gave way to a thin expanse of water, which seemed to block his way. But as his eyes grew accustomed to the moon-softened darkness, he saw a narrow plank walk, supported a foot above the water by posts, stretching into the darkness along the roadside farther than he could see. He inched his way along, step after step, wondering what might happen if he lost his balance. If he fell off so that his head hit the plank walk hard enough to knock him unconscious, he might sink deep enough into water and mud so nobody would ever find his body, so nobody would ever know what had happened to him.

He seemed to want exactly what he feared. He was trying to throw his life away, as a kind of retaliation against Elinor's treatment of him; and all he needed was a push. Mile after mile he continued, deeper into the swamp, waiting for something to happen.

At last, it did happen. Somewhere near midnight, after he had covered a distance of nearly ten miles, he saw ahead of him on the side of the road a light not cast by the moon. Then, he heard voices. For all he knew, he was approaching the hideaway of bandits and murderers. But he kept walking toward the light and the voices, unable to guess what he would find—and, apparently, not caring. He did not know he had, since he had entered the forest, been walking within a stone's throw of the Dismal Swamp Canal and that sooner or later he would reach the northwest lock. As he mounted to higher ground he saw more lights, heard more voices, and slowly came into a lighted opening where a boat was being raised in a lock.

He may have decided, then and there, that he had tried hard enough, for one night, to throw his life away. Whatever he thought, when he could be sure he had a voice, he called to a group of men standing on the afterdeck and asked where they were going. Elizabeth City. Did they need an extra deckhand? No. What would they charge to take him as a passenger? There was a brief consultation before the answer was given. One dollar. Out of his pocket he pulled the money—almost the last he had—and in a few moments he was helped, across a makeshift gangplank, to the deck.

One of the crew told the unexpected passenger that the boat was making this run to pick up a party of duck hunters, that these hunters made an annual festivity of going by boat from Elizabeth City to a place called Nags Head, near Kitty Hawk, on the Outer Banks. These geographical names meant nothing to Rob, who was tired and uncomfortable enough to ask if there were any place aboard the vessel where he could take off his wet shoes and stretch out.

At Elizabeth City, by the time he awoke late in the afternoon and climbed back on deck, he saw the duck hunters piling up the gangplank, with guns held in the crook of their arms and with food hampers or demijohns of liquor in their hands. Nobody paid much attention to Frost. He stood there, still feeling this all belonged in the realm of dreams.

Under way for Nags Head, the hunters gathered on the benches of the afterdeck, opened the demijohns, and seemed to be settling in for festive drinking. Before the boat had cleared the harbor one of the passengers took notice of the stranger, introduced himself as "Ed Dozier, owner of the bes' goddam bar in Elizabeth City," and offered Frost a drink. No, thank you. Then, some fried chicken? He was too hungry to refuse any kind of food, and very soon he was trying to cope with Ed Dozier's questions. He couldn't bear to tell the truth in his answers. It would have sounded silly to say he had come all the way to the Dismal Swamp just to kill himself or just to make his sweetheart worry about him. Instead, he explained that he was looking for work; he had come down from Norfolk on this boat and had accidentally slept too long, so that the boat had got under way before he realized what was happening. Well, if it was work he wanted, Ed Dozier could help him, just as soon as they got back from this little ole duck-hunting expedition. Frost protested. He couldn't let Mr. Dozier bother with him—after all, how did he know Rob wasn't an escaped convict? Ed laughed. "You're all right," he said. "You look so much like a child that nobody'd be afraid of you."

In the twilight, several hours later, the old tub docked at Nags Head, and the passengers stormed ashore near a small hotel locked up for the winter. Ed Dozier had the key; and the men made a noisy game of opening shutters, filling lamps with kerosene, carrying in supplies, and making themselves comfortable. In the lobby they put tables together, spread out a slapdash supper, and urged the stranger to help himself to either food or drink. Frost sampled the demijohns offered to him, without finding liquor mild enough to be palatable. But he ate slabs of chicken and ham.

Nobody seemed interested in sleep. By dawn, most of the men had scattered to choose blinds in the long grass or behind sand dunes; and when the ducks began to fly through the gray dawn, the hunters opened fire with such casual earnestness that birdshot rattled like hail on the tin roof of the hotel porch, where Frost stood watching. He thought bitterly that if Elinor White learned her beloved had met death at the hands of drunken duck hunters at Nags Head in North Carolina—and all for love of her—it would serve her right.

Well before noon the hunters came straggling into the hotel, with only a few wilted proofs of their marksmanship. Still jovial, they packed their gear and paraded down to the boat. On the return voyage most threw themselves on deck to sleep, but Ed Dozier resumed conversation with Frost. Just what kind of work did the boy want? Rob didn't know exactly; he had taught school and done some writing. Well, back home in Elizabeth City, Ed said, there was a newspaper and a female academy. Chances were good that Frost could take his pick. Or he could, at least, stay for a few days in the Dozier home while he looked over the town for some other kind of work.

The next few days the runaway from Massachusetts was given more evidence of Southern hospitality, exemplified affably and generously by the Doziers. Keeping his word, the host took his guest about the town, calling first on editor, then headmaster. Each offered the Northerner a chance to go to work immediately, but it is probable that no kind of work would have tempted him at this time. He had run far enough away to feel twinges of homesickness. He lingered for only three days with the Doziers and, then, made an odd departure. Watching for a chance to escape when nobody was looking, he slipped out of Dozier's back door, without saying good-bye.

Nearly out of money, Frost decided to try his luck at leaving Elizabeth City hobo-fashion, by stealing a ride in a freight car. In a short time he was on his way somewhere (he neither knew nor cared, for the moment, whether North or South) in an empty boxcar, the door of which he had carefully shut to exclude fellow travelers. Bothered for a time by the vibration, the noise, the darkness, he finally made himself as comfortable as he could, in a corner, and slept.

When he woke, he found that his car had been shunted onto a siding near a North Carolina lumber camp. It was already evening when he slid the door open, carefully studied the scene, and jumped to the ground. In a short time he had his bearings well enough to discover a store, where Negroes were standing, sitting, chatting, and playfully wrestling with one another. As he bought crackers in the store (with almost the last few pennies he had), a white boy roughly his own age asked if he was looking for work. Well, yes. The boy was a scaler, a specialist in stripping bark off logs; he offered to teach Frost about the process, to let him get work. He also showed Frost a bunk where he could sleep. That was enough!

The next morning he was back near the railroad tracks, carefully coached about waiting for a freight that would take him North, straight through to Washington, D.C. He kept out of sight until the long train had started, tossed his bag into the first open door he saw, and jumped in after it. Hours later he crawled to the open door and watched for station signs. The first one he saw gave a jolt to his memory and imagination, long ago stimulated by poring over the pages of *Battles and Leaders of the Civil War*: Bull Run. Shades of his namesake, Robert E. Lee.

He spent that evening in a hobo jungle outside Washington, studying the grizzled and shabby veterans who crouched or sat around a little fire made of sticks and branches. For the first time, he heard the lore and tales of hoboes, their ballads and songs. This experience might have been tolerably entertaining for Frost if some of his companions had not asked too many questions, and frightened him so much that he finally said he'd get out if they didn't like his company. Nobody demurred when he stood up; a few shouted taunts as he walked down the tracks in darkness. He had the feeling that some of them were following him, might even kill him for what they thought they could get out of his pockets or bag.

No longer interested in suicide, he was so frightened that, after he had climbed up the embankment to the nearest street, he approached the first policeman he saw and asked for protection. Was there any chance of getting locked up for the night in a jail? There was, under the circumstances, and Frost was instructed on how and where to proceed. (Years later he liked to boast that he had spent his first night in Washington behind bars, in a jail.)

The next morning he went back to the freight yard. His cronies of the previous night were already on their way. But when he tried to climb into a freight car, he was caught by a railroad policeman and warned to get out of the yard. Suffering from a new kind of fright, he would have gone, as ordered, if a more experienced hobo had not calmed him with advice to stay out of sight and wait for the next freight. The policeman was nowhere in sight as he made his next run for the partly opened door of an apparently empty boxcar.

For a few minutes his eyes were so unaccustomed to the darkness that he was startled when he suddenly realized that crouching against the wall, across the car from where he had stretched out, was a sullen Negro. Neither tried to say a word to the other, above the clatter of wheels. But before the train had left the yard, it halted; and voices could be heard, as a group of inspectors moved down the tracks, glancing in the doors. Growling to himself, the Negro stood up and drew a revolver as he walked to the half-closed door. He reached it just before someone outside shoved the door wide open. He was trying to raise the revolver when hands pulled his feet from under him and yanked him to the ground. Frost could not see what was happening, but he could hear the blows, the curses, and the Negro screaming for mercy. Another searcher climbed into the car, roughly dragged the white boy to his feet, pushed him out of the door, and ordered him up the tracks—away from where the Negro lay. Suffering from his old nausea, Frost ran as fast as he could—and did not even remember, until it was too late, that he had left his satchel in the boxcar. For hours he hid in bushes, until he managed to get up courage for another successful run at an opened door.

When he crawled out of the train he found he was in Baltimore. Having gone without food for a day and a half, he was desperate enough to throw himself on the mercy of relatives. He knew that his mother's Cousin Fannie had married a man named Thomas Baldwin and that the Baldwins had recently moved to the Baltimore suburb of Towson.

It took him all afternoon to walk to Towson, where he asked for directions at a small grocery store. The grocer, named Williams, seemed touched by the forlorn appearance of the young man. When it became clear nobody in the store knew of any family named Baldwin in the neighborhood, he offered Frost work delivering groceries. For a few days he did stay with Williams, earning scarcely anything except board and room. By this time he was so tired of his runaway venture that he swallowed his pride and wrote to his mother, asking for money enough to purchase a railroad ticket home. Within a week he was back in Lawrence.

The trip had been a failure, so far as he was able to determine. True, he had succeeded in worrying Elinor White, but if any change had taken place in what he took to be the engagement of Elinor to Lorenzo Dow Case, there was nothing to indicate it in the letters waiting for him. His only consolation was that during his absence—almost on the day he passed through New York en route to the Dismal Swamp—the issue of *The Independent* for November 8, 1894, had carried on its first page his poem "My Butterfly: An Elegy."

As soon as he could recover energy and interest enough to send thanks to Miss Ward, he did so. In a letter dated December 4, 1894, he explained the tardiness of his acknowledgment by saying he had "just returned from experiences so desperately absorbing that I am nothing morbid now"—and so could enjoy the poem as freshly as if he had but lately written it, as though he had not "wasted eight months in ineffectual aspiration" since he wrote it.

His absence "in Virginia, North Carolina, and Maryland, very liberally and without address," had certainly given him the raw materials for poetic inspiration, and he used some of them almost immediately. In his attempt to be, as he had said to Miss Ward, "nothing morbid" over an apparently hopeless situation, no matter how reluctant he might be to accept his apparent loss of Elinor White's love, he could at least sing his grief. He did sing it, in a poem about dead ends, dead leaves, dead hopes. When finished the poem was called "Reluctance."

RECONCILIATION AND MARRIAGE

(1894–1895)

ROBERT FROST knew he was not quite telling the truth when he assured Susan Hayes Ward that he was "nothing morbid now," although he had "just returned from experiences so desperately absorbing." Assertively, he tried to convince himself and others that because he had survived those Dismal Swamp adventures, the task that now confronted him was to pick up whatever was left of his life and put the pieces together as best he could. But he also knew his posture of elation over the appearance of his poem in *The Independent* was merely an attempt to overcome his persistent brooding over disappointment and heartbreak.

For the first time he saw in Carl Burell's favorite word, "disillusionment," a terrible depth of meaning. Even his mother could not comfort him with biblical quotations and paraphrases. Refusing to be consoled, Rob answered her by endowing some words from *Hamlet* with his own bitter meaning: "So have I heard, and do in part believe it."

Believe, believe! From the earliest days of childhood he had been nurtured and strengthened by many related kinds of belief. His deeply ingrained religious belief, taught him by his mother, had made him confident that of his own choice he had entered into a private relationship with God, whereby his efforts would help to fulfill a positive future in this world and the next. His God-belief had strengthened self-belief. Although his enemies might continue to scoff, he had gradually acquired a conviction that his gifts and skills—and his determination—would enable him to realize his immediate hopes. Inseparable, and yet quite distinct, was his own private literary belief, on which he depended instinctively whenever he wrote a poem—inspired, from the very first line, by something intuitively foreseen, the final goal always achieved not so much through contriving, but rather, through believing the poem into existence. Until recently he had derived a fourth kind of strength from his love for Elinor and from what he had believed to be her love for him.

Now, the frightening collapse of this cherished love-belief had caused him to doubt the validity of all his other beliefs.

One disturbing effect of his disillusionment was his feeling that if he were now able to measure the difference between illusion and reality, he was also inclined to suspect that what he presently viewed as reality might soon become, for him, another kind of illusion—and this fear drove him to the verge of a nervous breakdown. Almost hysterically, he felt that his eyes now gave him a double image of everything. Under the circumstances, it was fortunate that he had inherited from his grieving mother the balancing instinct for enjoying the comic aspects of life. But it pained him to realize that his double vision now forced him to see something comical in what he had previously viewed seriously, and something serious in what he had formerly laughed at. Desperately, he tried to fashion a new kind of self-defense (or, at least, a makeshift palliative) by combining grief with humor, to express his awareness of discrepancies between his old and new ways of seeing, hearing, speaking, writing, acting. He later admitted, however, that such a resolution of his problem was not spiritually consoling:

". . . Belief is better than anything else and it is best when rapt[,] above paying its respects to anybody's doubts whatsoever. At bottom the world isnt a joke. We only joke about it to avoid an issue with someone; to let someone know that we know he's there with his questions: to disarm him by seeming to have heard and done justice to his side of the standing argument. Humor is the most engaging cowardice. With it myself I have been able to hold some of my enemy in play far out of gunshot."

He could not always engage humorously the darker side of his own nature, his worst enemy, which often assured him that the ultimate form of escape from self-doubt and self-hate was suicide. When he had gained enough perspective on the causes and aftereffects of the Dismal Swamp crisis, he did represent them humorously in the poem he built around the metaphor of bumping his head against "The Door in the Dark." But he could never forget his initial sense of pain and his consequent feeling that people and things didn't pair anymore with "what they used to pair with before." Immediately after his return from the Dismal Swamp, the best he could do to conceal his pain and grief was to pretend that he was just as he had formerly been.

After he had re-established himself with his friends, and after he had apparently made excuses for his long absence, Rob looked around for work as a newspaper reporter. He had luck when he approached the editor-in-chief of a Lawrence paper, the *Daily American*. But the staff of the *American* taught him more about unscrupulous newspaper policy than about writing; and when, sent to cover a private wedding, he was ordered to threaten the father of the bride by saying that if Frost were not permitted to attend he would write and publish a story about it anyway, it took a little time for him to realize he had been asked to perform a kind of blackmail. But he stayed away from the wedding—and quit his job.

Having worked as a reporter for the *American* little more than two weeks, Frost had not yet exhausted his willingness to do this kind of job. Among the Lawrence papers was a weekly that seemed to have a literary flavor, and Frost took a more congenial position on the staff of the *Sentinel*. Again, he lasted for only a few weeks.

Although he may have told himself repeatedly that it was useless for him to write letters to Elinor White, he had been unable to stop. Nor could he avoid the inconsistency of crowding into letter after letter his plaintive fear that she no longer loved him and his desperate hope that perhaps she still did. He tried to probe her motives for rejecting him for another, and he kept asking Elinor to reconsider her decision—or, at least, to tell him when she would next come home, so they might talk matters out.

She did come home, apparently in mid-March of 1895; and they did meet, in the kitchen of her home. Rob's greatest fear was that Elinor had arranged this meeting in order to give back to him the plain gold ring he had placed on her finger more than two years earlier. His greatest hope was that in their conversation he could somehow persuade her that she still did love him. Awkwardly, he spoiled his plea for reconciliation by upbraiding Elinor for the way in which she had changed. When she tried to defend herself, by blaming him for his refusal to give direction to his life, he lost his temper. She had once believed in him enough to love him and to give herself to him; if she no longer did believe in him, she was the one who had spoiled everything.

In the midst of his outburst, he saw exactly what he feared. Elinor held out her hand and said that if he was going to talk like this he should take back the ring he had given her. She put the ring in his hand. He took the ring, lifted the cover from the coal range, tossed the ring on the fire, declared she had really given him reason enough to kill himself, this time, and stormed out of the house.

Wild with mingled rage and grief, he took the train to Boston the next day. He thought he knew where he might find more sympathetic ears. Ernest Jewell, his friend of high-school days, was a student at Harvard College, and Rob found him in his dormitory room. He poured out the story of his quarrel with Elinor and confided that this was the end of everything, darkly hinting he had decided to throw his life away. Jewell knew Rob too well to take these hints seriously, but he did humor his lovesick visitor. Then, Rob walked to the Harvard Medical School, where he located another friend, Charles Carden. Merely having unburdened himself—first, to Jewell; then, to Carden—Rob felt better.

As he made his way back to the North Station in Boston, he veered far enough to stop in at the Old Corner Book Store. On a shelf devoted to new volumes of poetry he found a pamphlet that bore the name of an English author new to Rob, Francis Thompson. The pamphlet contained a separate printing of "The Hound of Heaven," and as he stood there reading, Frost was in the proper mood for using the poem as a mirror of his own predicament. He could read into this poem of escape and pursuit a great many reflections of his own story. It may even have seemed to echo some of the mood he had tried to express in his own lines entitled "Bereft," which had concluded: "Word I was in my life alone, / Word I had no one left but God." Retrospectively, he always viewed as a special event this occasion when he had accidentally made discovery of "The Hound of Heaven."

Home he went, that evening, and found a Swedenborgian religious service in progress in the living room of the Frost apartment. His mother, noticing his entrance, passed to him a letter Elinor had delivered by hand during his absence. Rob opened the envelope and read words he had scarcely dared hope to find. Elinor said she was sorry that misunderstandings had been caused by anything she might have said or done the night before. She wanted to see him as soon as she could, to explain and ask his forgiveness. Abruptly, Rob left the prayer meeting and was on his way.

The reconciliation was not all he had hoped it would be. Elinor had a habit of making him realize that she was almost two years older than he was. On such an occasion, she had a way of preserving her dignity and reticence. It is not likely she threw herself into his arms. She apparently began the reconciliation by holding out to him the gold ring she had rescued from the fire of the coal range; she had cleaned off the ashes and had put the ring back on her finger. It was a kind of poetry that said better than words that she did love him, still, and that she had never stopped loving him, even during the trial by fire. She admitted he had frightened her with the possibility that this time he might actually carry out his suicidal threat or that he might, at least, disappear again as he had done last fall. But she did not say she was now ready to marry him, publicly, whenever and wherever he wished. She still insisted that their marriage must be postponed until he could find some way to earn a living for them both. Under the circumstances, Rob may have been willing to admit that such a way would need to include something more than the writing of poetry, even to admit that during the past few years, since his graduation from high school, he had self-indulgently made up excuses for quitting Dartmouth, for quitting work—and just plain loafing. But his mother had been talking, recently, about plans that might provide him with a new kind of livelihood.

After Mrs. Frost resigned from her duties as a public-school teacher in Methuen, she had begun to conduct an informal private school in the Tremont Street apartment. Jeanie had helped her from the start, and Mrs. Frost was convinced that if Rob would join them, they could develop a program with eight grades. Many of the best citizens in Lawrence were dissatisfied with the public-school system, and these prejudices worked to the advantage of Mrs. Frost in her plan to extend her school.

In his attempt to persuade Elinor that he could and would immediately settle down to earn a living, he assured her he was already helping his mother develop her plan, that during the spring term, soon to begin, he would earn a salary by tutoring some of his mother's older students in Latin and in mathematics. Elinor must have been pleased with this new display of resolve; and Rob, not long after she returned to St. Lawrence University to finish her four-years-in-three, set to work seriously in his mother's school. By the time Elinor returned with her diploma in June, she found he had succeeded in helping his mother obtain fairly sure promises that there would be at least twenty students that autumn. He also assured her that he would earn a little extra money, near the end of the summer, by tutoring two boys who needed help in English and mathematics.

Because Elinor's summer plans had been made so far in advance that she could not easily change them, Rob adapted his accordingly. Leona White Harvey had again left her husband and was supporting herself as a portrait painter. She had accepted an invitation to spend the summer at Ossipee Mountain Park in New Hampshire, with the understanding that she might be accompanied by her sister Elinor, who was also a talented artist.

Rob could not bear the thought of being separated from Elinor throughout the long summer of 1895. He offered to go with the White sisters on their journey to Ossipee Mountain and to stay for at least part of the summer. He did accompany them by train to Alton Bay, by the steamboat *Mount Washington* around Lake Winnipesaukee to Moultonborough, and by carriage up the mountainside to the hotel in the park. It was his first visit to this part of New Hampshire, and he immediately came under the spell of the region.

Leona and Elinor were given a cottage near the hotel, leaving Rob to shift for himself. He asked about places where he might stay and was told that not more than a mile up the mountain, beyond the park, there was a scattering of houses owned by natives. Rob walked up the road to explore the possibilities.

The first house he found was a forlorn, one-story clapboard cottage with a piece of metal stovepipe sticking through the ridgepole, in place of a chimney, with uncurtained windows and a battered, lockless door. Rob knocked and was admitted by the owner, Henry Horne, a bearded and unwashed giant who lived there alone when he could find nothing better to do. Just now he was getting ready to spend the summer as a hired man on a farm down on the shore of Lake Winnipesaukee. Would he care to rent? Yes, he'd be glad to rent if the city boy didn't mind roughing it. As a matter of fact, he said, he'd like to have someone in the house to serve as "guardeen" of his most valuable possession: several barrels of hard cider in the cellar.

Amused and still feeling adventurous, Rob settled in to enjoy himself. As soon as Elinor and Leona had worked out their daily routine, the three newcomers began exploring mountain trails. Whenever Leona was busy with her painting, the walks were better for the two lovers. But Rob could feel there still remained a distance in Elinor's attitude toward him.

He had not counted on being left so much alone during this summer, and he disliked the emptiness of the shabby Horne house, particularly at night. His fear of darkness had remained so intense that his mother had continued to let him sleep with her, from the time they left San Francisco until they moved to Lawrence from Salem. After that, throughout the remainder of his high-school years and during their many moves from one apartment to another in Lawrence and Methuen, his cot was always set up in his mother's bedroom. Never before had he been forced to be so brave as to sleep in a forest-shrouded house all by himself, night after night.

Throughout that summer he slept with his trousers on, ready for flight if necessary. At first his only consolation had been that he had brought with him from Lawrence an old, single-shot pistol and plenty of ammunition. Later, Leona lent him her St. Bernard, which had been sent up by express to keep the girls company in their cottage. But the huge dog was more trouble than he was worth. Let a thunderstorm come up during the night, and the first bolt would drive the panic-stricken beast into bed with his master. The dog proved to be such a nuisance that Rob returned it to Leona, assuring her he was not afraid to stay alone.

His boast was made too soon. In the dark of one night an uninvited visitor nearly frightened him out of his wits. He had been asleep for hours when he was suddenly awakened by what sounded like a sharp knock or two on the door. Startled, he lay there trembling in his uncertainty. Had he heard a knock, or was it part of a dream? After a few moments he heard three unmistakable knocks. Now he was nearly petrified. Forgetting his loaded pistol, he crawled to the open kitchen window at the back of the room, climbed out over the sill, called a "Come in" through the window as bravely as he could, and trembled anew as he waited to see what would happen. He could hear the creaking of the rusty hinges, and he could feel his hair standing on end. Someone was actually coming in.

That was enough for Rob; he fled. Barefooted, clad only in his trousers and underwear, he circled through the edge of the woods to the dirt road and ran toward the hotel, until he had recovered enough courage to stop.

In his condition he was too embarrassed and ashamed to ask for help at the hotel. After a few moments of indecision he began to walk cautiously back toward the house, half-suspecting he would find someone with a lantern, stealing hard cider from the cellar. But the house was still dark when he located it by starlight. Through the remainder of the night, he walked back and forth along the road, perplexed and frightened. When daylight came he crept to the window for one glance inside. For a moment he was again overwhelmed with fear. A man lay stretched flat on the kitchen floor, as though dead. But it was one of the most harmless of his neighbors, and he was quietly snoring. When Rob went in and woke him up, the man explained he had not meant to bother anyone; he had merely wished to spend the rest of the night in the Horne house, so he could sober up from too much drink with friends down in the village, before going home.

So terrifying to Rob were the experiences of this night that they intermittently haunted his dreams for years. At last, perhaps motivated in part by the hope that he might rid himself of the whole thing, he made a poem out of it and called it "The Lockless Door." In the poem the pivotal image is the act of escape from something feared, an act Frost dramatized repeatedly throughout his life and art. But it is probable that during the summer of 1895 the courage that overcame his fear of the dark and of loneliness was motivated by pride and desperation. He could not bear to let Elinor see any evidence of what he himself belittled as cowardice.

Perhaps his desire to stay near Elinor caused him to modify his arrangements for tutoring. Instead of going back to Lawrence, as planned, he invited the two boys to spend three weeks camping with him in the Henry Horne house. They accepted the invitation, made the best of primitive conditions, and combined study with mountain climbing.

As soon as Rob returned to Lawrence with Elinor and Leona, late in the summer, he began helping his mother make arrangements for expanding her school. It was obvious that more space would be needed than was available in her Tremont Street living room, and there was also the need to find a better location. The green or common marked the center of the city, and Mrs. Frost wanted to establish her school near it. With Rob's help she found two rooms to rent on the third floor of an attractive new stone structure designed primarily for offices, the Central Building, only three blocks southwest of the green. For living quarters the Frosts rented two other rooms in the same building, and to this odd home they moved before the school year started in the fall of 1895.

For reasons that are not clear, Robert Frost did not immediately continue his work as teacher or tutor in his mother's school. He once again took charge of the small Salem District School Number Nine, where he again taught twelve pupils (in varying numbers per subject) reading, spelling, penmanship, arithmetic, grammar, composition—for a monthly wage of twenty-four dollars. Simultaneously, however, he continued to help his mother, by serving as her general manager of finances. And Elinor White joined the staff of Mrs. Frost's Private School that fall.

The atmosphere of this new school was extremely informal. The children were delighted with the arrangements, particularly the strangeness of classrooms in an office building, and they all admired and loved Mrs. Frost. The success of the school caused Rob to increase his importunate claim that Elinor no longer had reason for postponing their public marriage. But she knew her father still disapproved of the match, and she may also have been made hesitant by other elements, not the least being Rob's ingrained habits of laziness, which made him almost as casual about schoolteaching as his mother was indifferent about housework. Whatever her motives, she put off giving any answer to Rob during most of the fall. Then, she consented.

The choice of day for the marriage was Thursday, December 19, 1895. It was apparently determined by the start of the vacation between the fall and winter terms at District School Number Nine. The choice of place for the marriage—one of the two offices converted into schoolrooms in the Central Building—is easily understood. Neither Elinor nor Rob had any church affiliation; but this particular room had been used throughout the fall of 1895 as the meeting place for the Swedenborgians in Lawrence, and the ceremony was performed by the longtime friend of the Frosts, the Rev. John A. Hayes of Salem, Massachusetts. Among the guests at the wedding, Mr. White was conspicuously absent.

The bride, when she had been an undergraduate at St. Lawrence University, had impressed several of her friends there as a girl who was always reaching for the unusual. She had spoken to many of them about Robert Frost as a "boy back home" who wrote poetry; but for some time she had never suggested that she was in love with him, that he had given her a ring, or that she thought she might marry him. When the attractive Lorenzo Dow Case began paying her particular attention, she may have hoped, romantically, that he would become a white and shining knight, that he would sweep her off her feet and carry her away. She may even have written to Robert Frost saying (as he insisted to the end of his life) that she was formally engaged to marry Case. If so, she was at least premature, for Case continued his attentions, week after week, without ever proposing marriage and without ever saying he was in love with her. In the last term of her senior year Elinor did finally say to Case that she thought they should no longer continue to see each other as they had been doing for so long, that she had decided she would marry the boy back home.

If Elinor White had been reaching for the unusual, and if she had wanted some cause to champion—even if the cause required martyrdom on her part—she could have set her heart on the possibility that she was marrying an attractive young man who, in spite of his spoiled-child ways, in spite of his temper tantrums and his attempts to hurt her by threatening to kill himself whenever things might go too much against his wishes, did seem to her to have the true capacities of a poet. She may also have felt she did love him so much that she would be willing to endure his failures as a human being and that she wanted to help him prove her belief in his ability to succeed as a poet.

As for the bridegroom, there were some things he himself did not like too well about this wedding. He would never forget, and he would never quite forgive, the fact that while he had been courting Elinor—and even after he thought he had completely won her, and had privately married her—she had hurt him so deeply and terribly by making him think she loved and wanted to marry someone else. It seemed to him she had indeed driven him to the verge of suicide on two occasions and that the injury he suffered as a result of those wounds was one from which he could never completely recover. It had been partly to save himself, and to save his own proud belief in himself, that he had refused to give up the courtship. And beneath all his gentleness, from the time of their reconciliation to the day of their wedding, he had made her well aware of his quality of ruthlessness, self-centeredness, and—even—of cruelty. She must have wondered whether he wanted to triumph over her doubts and hesitancy, merely to retaliate.

For better or worse, he had persuaded her to marry him. He did love her deeply, and she did have the qualities to inspire love. Yet, each of them knew, as they swore their vows to each other, that there were ominous elements in this union. Elinor White did have a craving for the unusual, and she had chosen a dangerous way of achieving it.

9

EARLY MARRIED YEARS
AND HARVARD

(1896–1899)

THE BRIDE and groom had, for reasons of financial economy, decided to postpone their honeymoon trip until the summer vacation, and not long after their marriage they were back at work as teachers—he in Salem and she in Mrs. Frost's Private School. But within a few weeks the groom had become so despondent over what meant most to him that he wrote pathetically to Susan Hayes Ward, who had long ago assured him she wanted more of his poems for *The Independent*: "Perhaps you had better not waite any longer. I have done my level best, in the time that has elapsed since last you heard from me, to make good my promise as a poet. But I fear I am not a poet, or but a very incomprehensible one. . . ."

Although this particular mood of discouragement did not last long enough to interfere seriously with the carrying out of his responsibilities as teacher, as son, as brother, as husband, the strain on his nerves did have a serious effect. Before the end of the school year, he began to complain of a curious ailment he did not understand. There were times when he could not eat, because he suffered from pains in his stomach or solar plexus—it was hard to tell which. There were other times when he awoke in the night to discover he was sweating heavily, as though from fever, although he had no fever. When he sought medical advice, he was not at all surprised to have the doctor say that he seemed to be suffering from acute nervous tension.

Quite a variety of nervous tensions had been building up in him during the spring of 1896. His mother had become ill, and he had been needed to help carry the teaching load in her school. He had resigned from his duties in Salem, where boredom had been the greatest strain; but as soon as he began teaching older children Latin, algebra, and geometry, for his mother, he found that the work made heavy demands on his nervous energies. The unsatisfactory living arrangements in the makeshift apartment shared by Rob's mother and sister and the newlyweds created an entirely different kind of nervous tension. Closely related was the fact that the financial problems of renting four rooms in the Central Building soon made it clear that unless more students were enrolled, it would be impossible to make ends meet.

Even more deeply troublesome was his feeling that he had somehow won his bride under the false pretense that Mrs. Frost's Private School could provide a living for all four teachers, and that Elinor had already foreseen the general drift of affairs toward another failure. Worse than that was the grimness of Elinor's silence, which implied (at least to Rob) she might already be sorry she had married him. The accumulation of these tensions contributed to a nervous condition that Rob coped with as best he could during the spring term. Then, he nearly collapsed.

It may have been during his recovery that he wrote a slight love poem for Elinor in playful self-defense, "The Birds Do Thus." Susan Hayes Ward bought it for publication in *The Independent*, where it appeared before too long.

For their delayed honeymoon they decided they would like isolation in the country, and they enlisted the assistance of Carl Burell. Their friend of high-school days was working in a box factory in the village of Pembroke, New Hampshire, and he found for them exactly what they wanted, in the neighboring village of Allenstown. And Carl had taken pleasure in planting flowers around the rented cottage prior to the arrival of his friends, had even started a kitchen garden.

Quite unexpectedly, this honeymoon vacation in the country had a lasting effect on the entire life of Robert Frost, because Burell's passion for amateur botanizing proved to be contagious. From the experiences of this summer in Allenstown, New Hampshire, came not merely the Frostian tendency to scatter flowers through his later poetry, but also his new delight in having his eyes opened to details of nature he had not previously noticed.

Carl began to interest Rob in the color and structure and fragrance of flowers. He showed Rob and Elinor blossoms they had not even seen before—particularly, spiked flower clusters from Carl's favorite family: orchids. Rob soon asked for permission to borrow a few books from Carl's library, to advance his limited knowledge of botany. Carl sensibly started him with a primer, Mrs. William Starr Dana's *How to Know the Wild Flowers: A Guide to the Names, Haunts, and Habits of Our Common Wild Flowers*. Very much to Rob's taste was the enriching lore of literary quotations scattered through the volume—snatches of poetry from Emerson, Bryant, Whittier, Longfellow, Wordsworth, Scott, Shakespeare, Spenser—and many well-chosen prose passages from Thoreau's *Journal*. He also found that Mrs. Dana's prose had a distinctly poetic quality of its own.

Frost very quickly became so keen that he began to notice all kinds of mysteries and wonders during walks he took in the neighborhood of his Allenstown cottage—with or without Elinor. She accompanied him less and less in his wanderings as the summer days passed, for the reason that this bride who had started on the delayed honeymoon some seven months after the wedding was nearly seven months pregnant. No longer in the mood for walks, and more inclined to take midday naps, she insisted Rob should not hesitate to leave her alone in the cottage while he went exploring. These separations heightened his sense of guilt, particularly if he returned to find he had been so long absent that Elinor had begun to worry. Usually, her reproaches for his late returning were expressed through her characteristic reticence or complete silence, and one such occasion inspired Rob to write her an apology, while they were still in Allenstown. It was a poem entitled "Flower-Gathering."

The almost-idyllic honeymoon-vacation of the Frosts in Allenstown was marred by a serious accident that nearly cost Carl Burell his life. One day while he was at work in the small factory where planks were sawed and planed and cut into shooks (the units of wood used in assembling a single box), the metal lacing on a leather pulley-belt caught the sleeve of his coat. Carl, pulled into the air, tried to hold fast to the belt, and succeeded until he was thrown over a pulley, near the ceiling, in such a way that his feet struck the roof girders. Falling to the floor heavily and knocked unconscious, he seemed to be dead. When he recovered consciousness, he felt as though he had broken almost every bone in his body. The doctor's verdict was that his feet were so badly smashed it might be necessary to amputate them both, but no decision could be made for some time. He was confined to bed at his boardinghouse, where Rob visited him repeatedly. They both realized that all of Carl's devotion to the quest for his beloved flowers and plants would be curtailed pathetically if he were never able to walk again.

As it happened, Rob himself became a witness to the scene in which Carl was paid a relatively small sum of money by an insurance representative, prior to the time when anyone could know for certain just how badly injured he might be. Amputation was not necessary, and Carl did regain the use of his feet, but he was so badly crippled by the accident that he always limped thereafter. Years later, Rob still felt so much of his own acute agony over the accident that he dramatized the heart of it in a blank-verse narrative that he entitled, with deliberate irony, "The Self-Seeker."

Frost's intensity of response—the almost-religious quality of awe and worship—he then (and always thereafter) associated with bog-trotting for orchids was later given a self-deprecatingly humorous statement in the poem eventually called "An Encounter." The more serious poem

"The Quest of the Purple-Fringed" may even have been written at Allenstown during the summer of 1896.

When this unusual summer in Allenstown was done, the Frosts returned to Lawrence. The first important event of the fall was the part they played in helping move their own belongings and those of Mrs. Frost's Private School to new quarters, next door to the high school, on Haverhill Street. The house was a tall, bay-windowed, two-and-a-half-storied frame residence, oddly shaped to fit the long, narrow lot on which it had been built. It offered more living space for the Frosts than they had enjoyed before; but, when classes began, the staff of teachers was reduced to three, because Elinor was so near her confinement. (For the first time since their marriage, Rob and Elinor had an apartment of their own, on the second floor of the house, and enough other rooms on that floor for rental if they wished.)

Their child was born in the apartment on September 25, 1896, a boy whom they named Elliott. Inheriting his father's light-blue eyes and his Aunt Jeanie's blonde hair, the newcomer very soon won continuous adoration and attention. If Elinor had previously harbored any reservations concerning the wisdom of her marriage, it seemed that all her doubts disappeared with the arrival of her first child. Her entire attitude toward life seemed to undergo a noticeable change, and she became so completely wrapped up in caring for him that the father could not entirely resist moments of jealousy.

Rob took in stride the duties of fatherhood, partly because his attentions were diverted by his many other responsibilities and by the renewal of a friendship that dated back to his mill days. While he worked briefly in the Arlington Mills he had become moderately well acquainted with a fellow worker, a young man named Herbert Parker, whose father was a prominent officer in the Pacific Mills. A rebel, estranged early from his father, young Parker had further complicated his family relationship, recently, by marrying a girl who was considered socially disqualified for membership in the Parker family. Frost's discovery of this awkwardness aroused his sympathies. After consultation with his mother and Elinor, Rob offered to rent his friends the extra rooms at the back of the second floor in the Haverhill Street house. (The rooms had been similarly used before, and there was a separate, outside-staircase entrance to them.) The arrangement worked amicably until the Frosts began to have doubts concerning the respectability of a particular friend whom the Parkers entertained. A crisis developed when Rob went so far as to warn Mrs. Parker that if a certain Mrs. Hindle were permitted to visit the Parkers anymore it would be necessary for them to move. Unpleasant words were exchanged, and Mrs. Parker accused Rob of being a coward for insulting her freely at a time when her husband was absent.

The use of that word "coward" seemed to precipitate the crisis. Rob could and frequently did call himself a coward, deprecatingly, but he couldn't bear to have anyone else do so. Enraged by Mrs. Parker's use of the word, he blurted out that if her husband uttered it, matters would take a serious turn. Well, she said, her husband would use exactly the same word—as soon as he returned from work.

Rob, stirred into a frenzy of anger, could scarcely bear waiting. As soon as he was sure his friend had come home, Rob went storming into the Parker apartment. He found Parker sitting in a chair, and he asked point blank if he would dare call Frost a coward. Yes, he would—particularly if, during his absence, Frost had insulted Mrs. Parker. Very well, then, if Parker would step down to the backyard, they could settle this question of cowardice with their fists. No, said Parker, he didn't think that would settle anything; and he made no move to rise. Frost, losing control of his temper, threw a punch that hit the seated man hard enough to start the makings of a black eye. Parker jumped from his chair to defend himself, and a free-for-all continued until Frost's mother and sister and wife entered the apartment to separate the assailant from his victim.

Parker immediately carried his complaints to the police. A warrant was sworn out for Frost's arrest, and he was required to appear in court on Monday morning, December 28, 1896. The judge turned to Frost. "Did you hit him?" Frost scornfully glanced at Parker's half-closed eye and answered, "Looks like it, doesn't it?" Given the choice of going to jail for thirty days or of paying a fine of ten dollars, Frost chose to pay the fine; and the judge closed the case with an epithet obviously aimed at the assailant: "Riffraff!"

Frost was ashamed and humiliated. He had not reached the courtroom door before he was overtaken by a young man who had been a classmate through high school. In answer to the young man's questions, Frost poured out the whole story of the circumstances that had led up to the one-sided punching match. The sympathetic questioner did not say he was now a reporter, covering court cases for the *American,* the newspaper for which Frost had briefly worked. The afternoon edition of the *American* devoted a full column to the story, and Frost was further embarrassed by another Lawrence paper, the *Weekly Journal,* which made flagrant use of sarcasm in its version of the scandal.

This public disgrace, turning on the words "coward" and "riffraff," had a profoundly unsettling effect on Rob's already-shaken confidence in himself, and he continued to brood miserably over the judge's epithet. There were times when Rob had the suspicion that the judge was correct, even as there were times when he could admit to himself that Mrs. Parker had been correct in calling him a coward. Torturing himself, he began to review circumstances in which his extraordinary sensitivities had made him cringe, and he looked back to his attempts to assert at least enough courage and daring to counteract his fears. Riffraff? If he had descended that low in the eyes of the public, where did the truth lie? Was he the only one, now, who still believed he was better than riffraff?

If there was any single consolation for him at this time, it came from his mother. He felt that she understood him best, that—now, as always—she was encouraging him to assert his talents as poet and leader, that she still idealized him as her hero. She showed her admiration for the way he had come to her assistance in helping her establish a private school, and she was constantly praising him for his abilities as a teacher. But he was troubled by the fear that this new scandal, so prominently treated in the newspapers, would hurt the reputation of the growing school. Besides, he wanted his life to be different from what it was becoming, and he knew he had gone back to teaching, not so much because his mother needed his help, as because he needed hers in proving to Elinor he could earn a living.

Discouraged and humiliated by the Parker affair, he was in a mood for running away once more or, at least, for going away so he could start again somewhere else. But he didn't know where or how to find a new foothold, and Elinor seemed indifferent to all of his talk about possibilities.

Frost liked to remember as a turning point in his life his decision to become a special student at Harvard College. It occurred while he and his wife were living in the house they rented for the summer of 1897 at Salisbury Point in Amesbury, Massachusetts. He had come downstairs from his study, holding in his hand a Latin text of the historian Tacitus, wherein he had found so much to admire that he thought he would really enjoy teaching Latin and Greek at a high-school level, if only he could go back to college long enough to prepare himself for such. Harvard, under President Eliot, had developed a reputation for encouraging individual students to shape special direction for study, by means of the elective program; and it seemed to Rob that if he could gain admission to Harvard he need not spend four years in qualifying for a good position as a high-school teacher.

At the time, he may not have told Elinor that he had another reason for wanting to attend Harvard: his desire to study psychology and philosophy with the celebrated William James, whose latest work, *The Will to Believe,* had attracted much attention after its publication early in 1897. It is probable Rob had become acquainted with some of the essays in that volume prior to their appearance as collected. The second essay, "Is Life Worth Living?," had been published in a professional journal in 1895, had been widely quoted, and had even been issued as a pocket volume in 1896. As the title indicated, this essay came to grips with the question of whether persuasive counterarguments could be given to any fellow mortal who had reached the verge of suicide.

The tone of the essay implied that James had firsthand experience with the problem under consideration. Truth was that this brilliant and distinguished man had very seriously contemplated suicide at the age of twenty-eight; and, writing to assist others, James did manage to convey a quality of optimism and fervor through the printed words of "Is Life Worth Living?"

Assurances and encouragements were particularly needed by Robert Frost at the time William James published *The Will to Believe*; and it may have seemed to Frost that James was speaking directly to him, at precisely the time when Frost was determining to give more scope to his own higher faculties—to go to Harvard. But when he was voicing his decision to Elinor, she made no response, in speech or in gesture, and her apparent indifference sent a chill through Rob. There came the renewal of his fear that she had completely lost hope for his future—or for hers—and that she was merely taking refuge in a stoical resignation to whatever might happen.

He knew there was no time to waste if he were to gain admittance to Harvard in the fall. He would be rusty for any entrance examinations that might be required, but the prospect stimulated his energies and gave him a buoyancy that was reflected in his letter to Dean Le Baron Russell Briggs.

Dean Briggs informed the applicant it would be necessary to take a group of entrance examinations: Greek, Latin, ancient history, English, French, and physical science (astronomy and physics). Rob had never taken any courses in French or in the physical sciences, and yet, he saw ways of appearing not to be an ignoramus in these two final examinations. Out of curiosity, he had studied Elinor's elementary French textbooks while she was teaching in Mrs. Frost's Private School. Now, with his wife's help, he hastily improved his knowledge of French conjugations and declensions. His early interest in astronomy had led him to continue reading in that field, and he hastily read through a high-school textbook on physics. The challenge of the ordeal pleased him. He took it in stride; and he managed to pass all of the examinations, so that he was permitted to enter without condition.

Not so well solved were problems concerning finances. Uncomfortably, he went to his grandfather and borrowed money for his tuition. He did not want to leave his wife and child in Lawrence, nor did he want to try commuting. His mother-in-law's marital difficulties worked to his advantage here. Mrs. White proposed that she take temporary leave of her husband and live with Rob and Elinor in Cambridge, that she would undertake the task of finding an apartment and would help pay the rent.

Until those arrangements could be made, Rob took a single room at 16 Rutland Street, within ten minutes' walk from the Harvard yard. He also found work as principal of the Shepard Evening School in North Cambridge—two hours, three nights a week. These obligations enabled him to make ends meet, but they took more time from his study than he anticipated.

The Harvard system of electives did not give him the immediate latitude he sought. He was particularly annoyed to discover he was required to take a course in elementary German and in English composition. He accepted the German course as unavoidable. But his instructor in English was an effeminate assistant, Alfred Dwight Sheffield (known among the students as "the bearded lady"), who very quickly infuriated Frost. Hoping that he was qualified to take Barrett Wendell's course in advanced composition, he found enough courage to approach Prof. John Hays Gardiner, head of the course, and to ask permission to change. Gardiner seemed offended. He asked Frost what "pretentions" might be prompting such a request. Well, there was nothing new in Hill's *Principles of Rhetoric,* because the supplicant had already devoted several years to literary work. He had been a newspaper reporter and had even published some verses in *The Independent.* Frost was not prepared to have the professor draw back his chin and make the sarcastic observation, "Oh! So, we're a *writer,* are we?"

Hurt and flustered, Frost tried to smile as he said he guessed he wouldn't press the point further. Gardiner agreed; it would be as well if he didn't. And Frost left, vowing silently that he would never forgive or forget this rudeness.

Sheffield had his own form of belittlement, equally aggravating. In class, one day he asked each man to write a short lyric. Searching around in his memory for a poem he had previously composed, Frost found one that seemed appropriate to the autumnal season, "Now Close the Windows." Sheffield, when Frost appeared for his next conference, asked if the poem had actually been composed in class or merely written from memory. Well, it was his own poem, although he had to admit he had not worked it up on the spur of the moment. Then, it was not acceptable. Other poems submitted (including "The Tuft of Flowers") did not please Sheffield, who gave Frost his best marks for prose pieces, written inside or outside the classroom. But always the penciled comments were infuriating. They implied that the first requirement of the student was to learn how to write, that only later on would he have something to say. Sheffield obviously assumed that his task was to drill the students meticulously through their writing of "exercises." Frost's final grade in the course was "B"—and, again, Frost was outraged.

Far more pleasant—and rewarding to his later poetic career—was the course in Latin, divided between composition, under the guidance of Maurice W. Mather, and readings in Livy and Terence and in lyric, elegiac, and iambic poetry, with Charles P. Parker. What meant most to him (as he later revealed in *North of Boston*) was his discovery of Virgil's eclogues, which opened up the entire range of pastoral poetry. In Greek, his acquaintance with Virgil's inspirer, Theocritus, had to be postponed until the second year. But in his freshman year he was particularly happy to study the *Iliad* and the *Odyssey*, favorites in translation since his boyhood. His instructor was Frank Cole Babbitt, almost as young as some of his students and capable of inspiring a special quality of enthusiasm.

Frost's loneliness was relieved late in the fall of 1897, when Mrs. White finally found an apartment to her liking—one side of a house on Ellery Street. As soon as Elinor and her mother and the baby were established in their new home, where a special room was available as a study for the Harvard freshman, he found his entire attitude underwent a decided improvement. (The study was a cupola room, perched on the roof and far enough away from the baby's room to provide complete escape from Elliott's occasional fussiness and caterwauling.) The quality of his work improved so much during the second semester, he was awarded a scholarship of two hundred dollars in recognition of the "marked excellence" he had demonstrated as a freshman.

At the start of the summer vacation Frost again rented the house at Salisbury Point in Amesbury. He was so exhausted by his duties as student, as principal of the Shepard Evening School, as husband, as father, as son-in-law, that he looked forward to weeks of idleness. But the exhaustion may have helped to cause a strange illness.

The trouble seemed to begin as the result of an accident that occurred soon after the Frosts reached Salisbury Point. Their water supply was provided by a well in the front yard, and the well bucket, raised and lowered by rope, was used for keeping the baby's milk cool. It was a process that required careful placing of the milk pail into the bucket and careful lowering of the bucket until it barely rested on the surface of the water. During a too-hasty lowering Frost let the bucket sink so far it tipped over, and the milk spilled into the well. After consultation with neighbors, he feared that typhoid germs might develop and pollute the water. Under the circumstances, he had no choice except to empty the well as much as possible, by bailing. With the help of a neighbor who provided a ladder long enough to reach the bottom of the shallow well, Frost went to work. He stayed too long in the well, filling pails lowered to him by rope and standing in the spring-cold water until the work was done. That night he suffered slightly from chills, but by morning he had recovered so completely he accepted a neighbor's invitation to make a rowboat voyage down the Merrimack River.

For Frost the venture was a new kind of outing. They went down the river with the outgoing tide, reached the clam flats at the mouth of the river at low tide, dug all the clams they wanted before the incoming tide covered the beds, fished for flounder in relatively shallow water, then rowed home with the incoming tide. The freshness of the entire experience made the day so enjoyable that Frost was not prepared for the unpleasant aftereffects.

Belatedly, he realized that his standing barefooted in the ocean water to dig clams had aggravated the condition caused by his standing barefooted at the bottom of the well the day before. This time, the chills that made the night miserable for him were followed by severe pains in his stomach and chest. A doctor was called, medicine was prescribed, and improvement was anticipated. But the pains continued, and when the doctor returned he asked Frost if there had ever been tuberculosis in his family. Yes, his father had died of it. The doctor shook his head ominously and said this confirmed his fears. The symptoms indicated Frost might have become the victim of the same terrible disease. The best advice was to move back from the river, preferably to a mountain climate and dry air. If the pains had continued for many days, Frost might have taken the advice more seriously, but within a few days he seemed to return to normal.

In the fall of 1898, Frost returned to Harvard as a sophomore, leaving his wife and child with the Whites in Lawrence. He looked forward with particular eagerness to taking philosophy with William James and was greatly disappointed to learn that, because of illness, James had been granted a year's leave. Frost signed up for two full-year courses without him: "General Introduction to Philosophy" and a survey course, "History of Philosophy." The introductory course began with the study of logic, under the distinguished chairman of the department, George Herbert Palmer. It continued with a study of psychology, under the guidance of Prof. Hugo Munsterberg, who used as his text the one-volume *Psychology* by William James. As a result, Frost came directly under the influence of James, through his textbook, even during James's absence from the campus.

If James had fashioned his textbook as a mere physiological approach to the study of psychology, Frost's interests would have been stimulated, by his own problems. But because James deliberately extended the subject to include ethical applications, some of his remarks had special relevance—a kind of preaching made palatable because the utterances occurred in a scientific textbook in which the provisional Jamesian pluralism and (still-incipient) pragmatism constantly invoked skeptical attitudes congenial to Frost's own doubts, hopes, and fears concerning himself and his relations to others. The mirror-value of passage after passage in *Psychology* must have made strong appeal to him. And the chapter on "The Self" may have proved especially useful to Frost, because so many passages in it were pertinent to his own gropings.

Frost's most difficult problem at this time remained his awkward relationship with his wife, whose responses troubled and sometimes baffled him. In her silences he still feared hints of her disillusionment and disappointment, caused by his own inadequacy and failure. While he was studying James's *Psychology,* the problem still confronting him was one of trying to achieve self-confidence, and James had much to say on the point:

". . . A man with a broadly extended empirical Ego, with powers that have uniformly brought him success, with place and wealth and friends and fame, is not likely to be visited by the morbid diffidences and doubts about himself which he had when he was a boy. 'Is not this great Babylon, which I have planted?' Whereas he who has made one blunder after another, and still lies in middle life among the failures at the foot of the hill, is liable to grow all sicklied o'er with self-distrust, and to shrink from trials with which his powers can really cope."

The literary references, particularly the echoes from *Hamlet,* were not missed by Frost, who found another mirror of disillusionment in the Prince of Denmark. But always, in James, the ability of this celebrated scientist to combine with skepticism a reassertion of belief in religious matters must have made a particularly strong appeal.

If the skeptical believer, James, had merely preached to Frost the Christian doctrine of self-giving or self-sacrifice, without reference to the need for self-fulfillment, he would not have been so useful to this Harvard sophomore. But James and Frost saw eye to eye on the need for a certain kind of selfishness—which had to be asserted by the artist, in particular, for his fulfillment.

For Frost, needing all the encouragement he could get, William James offered many different kinds of enlightenment, justification, and reassurance. Most stimulating of the elements in this textbook may have been the constant affirmation of gains to be achieved through heroic assertions of will, courage, effort. And the book made a particularly appropriate introduction to the study of philosophy, because James was, indeed, bold enough to combine a study of physiology and psychology with the study of philosophy and, even, of metaphysics. In his "Epilogue," James endowed the word "metaphysics" with a practical meaning. This was the way Frost wanted to hear a scientist talk, and one of his strongest reasons for admiring William James was the ability of this particular scientist to make his own approaches "pluralistic" enough to encompass physics and metaphysics.

In Frost's other course, devoted to the history of philosophy, he was exposed to an entirely different approach. The lecturer was a relatively young man, only eleven years older than Frost, and formerly a pupil of William James's during the days when James, fresh out of medical school, had been teaching a course in physiology. He was George Santayana (who had already asserted his interest in poetry and esthetics by publishing *Sonnets and Other Verses* in 1894 and a prose treatise entitled *The Sense of Beauty* in 1896). There were a patrician grace and eloquence in Santayana's oral presentation of his material, and Frost immediately responded with warmth to the literary qualities. But Santayana had not finished his survey of the Greek philosophers before Frost began to realize that this former pupil of James's represented a viewpoint decidedly at odds with that of his teacher.

It was clear that Santayana considered the expressions of religious belief particularly interesting as forms of poetry or fiction—valuable if taken in a symbolic, rather than in a literal, sense. And Santayana's amused and quietly sarcastic handling of matters of religious belief was not lost on Frost. To the artist-philosopher Santayana, the creative imagination had a sacred significance. So, he liked to approach the history of philosophy as an ambiguous study of human tendencies to create idealistic illusions, and of human eagerness to believe in these illusions as truths.

As the lectures Frost heard him give at Harvard continued, Frost could scarcely believe his ears, particularly when Santayana began to make specific applications. To Frost, utterances such as these amounted to downright blasphemy, and he was thoroughly shocked to hear them. Nothing Santayana could say to justify his position was acceptable to Frost. He might have been attracted to Santayana's representation of philosophy as a literary act, created through the combined impulses of imagination and reason, if Santayana's detached and humorous and ironic viewpoint had not cut so squarely across the serious and inspirational exhortations of James. Faced with the choice, Frost asserted his rightful will to believe in the utterances that had the greatest relevance to his immediate needs. Like James, Frost wanted to be "pluralistic," in the sense that he could combine naturalism and idealism, physics and metaphysics, skepticism and mysticism. It was a feat he managed to maintain throughout the rest of his life, although the consequent fluctuations between these extremes produced some inconsistencies that puzzled him almost as much as they puzzled the intimate members of his family and, eventually, some of his readers.

Throughout the first semester of his sophomore year at Harvard he applied himself to his studies in philosophy and in the classics with so much energy that he was presented with a prize *"pro insigni in studii diligentia*." He was proud of the honor, and yet, he had already begun to feel he might soon leave Harvard, as he had left Dartmouth.

Elinor, before the beginning of the school year, had told him she was again with child and that it might be better if she and Elliott stayed with her parents in Lawrence. As a result, he had taken a room at 61 Oxford Street in Cambridge. But because he had agreed to assist his mother in giving night classes in her private school one night a week, he made regular trips between Cambridge and Lawrence. Harvard had recently instituted the experiment of granting students "unlimited cuts," and Frost fell into the habit of lingering in Lawrence, during each visit, longer than he knew he should.

In the spring semester of 1899, Frost audited the first lecture in a course devoted to John Milton, given by George Lyman Kittredge, newly appointed to the English department. The hour began with a spirited reading of Milton's poem "On Time," and Frost was prepared to enjoy every minute of it. The poem was enriched by Kittredge's way of going back over it, line by line, to point out the significance of images, figures, allusions. But just when Frost's pleasure had reached such a peak that he became curious to see how the other students were responding, he was dismayed to find that every head was bowed—over notebooks in which the students were trying to record every single word. They seemed to feel that the ultimate test of their profit from such a course would be the proof they could give, in the next examination, that they had captured and memorized every one of Kittredge's observations and insights. Disgusted with this attitude toward the study of literature, Frost was content to let the first day with Kittredge be his last.

Quite different was his response to the celebrated lectures of Nathaniel Southgate Shaler on historical geology. The course opened new vistas in time and space for Frost, and he stored up for future use as metaphors the various images of geological building, erosion, rebuilding. Here was science that interlocked, also, with his early passion for astronomy and his later concern for the Darwinian concept of evolution. Best of all, for him, was the grace with which Shaler seemed to give an esthetic quality to lectures, by casually unfolding and shaping his materials into carefully structured units.

Nevertheless, before the spring term was halfway through, Frost became increasingly troubled by many different things that made him feel he should not continue his studies. His mother needed him more and more to help with her school; his wife became increasingly dependent on him as she drew nearer to the time when their second child was expected; and his own energies seemed to be placed under both physical and nervous strain. He was particularly worried by the recurrence of the same ailment that had overtaken him during the previous summer, at Salisbury Point, and he could not help fearing that the doctor might have been correct in guessing the ailment was tuberculosis.

Although he made up his mind to withdraw from Harvard without waiting to finish the year's work, he resisted the impulse to walk out without saying a word to anyone. On March 31, 1899, he stopped at the office of Dean Briggs and was touched to hear the dean say, with genuine sympathy, he was sorry Frost felt he must leave, that he should not go without taking with him some kind of statement that might be useful in obtaining work as a teacher. While Frost waited, the dean wrote a brief letter that said all that was needed, and more.

Armed with this letter, Frost made his departure, inspired with new hopes and beset by old fears. He was convinced he had learned most from the man whose courses he had been unable to attend. He was still uncertain whether he had the power to apply to his own predicament —his own failures, past and present—what he had learned. During the ten years since the death of his father more than his share of hurt had come his way; and it was not his fault, he told himself. Nevertheless, James had shown him one way in which he could and should blame him- self. His own responses to disappointment—his own resentments and rages—were the immediate causes of his going to the edge of self- destruction. In that sense, he had been his own worst enemy.

Perhaps he had acquired from James new ways of confronting his inner and outer enemies—ways that justified sweeping aside the rubble of any idealistic notions, if they did not work for him; ways that required digging down to the bedrock of tested fact and, then, of rebuilding on that foundation. He hoped, henceforth, he could be a realistic idealist. But, at the same time, he feared he was running out of time for any kind of planning and rebuilding. The first real problem was his physical health —and if his trouble was consumption?

In spite of all James had done for him, all he had tried to do for himself, he was frightened now—worse than ever before.

10

ENTERING UPON A
FARMER'S LIFE

(1899–1900)

EARLY IN the spring of 1899, and soon after he had returned to Lawrence from Harvard College, Robert Frost again consulted his family physician. The doctor listened patiently to the review of symptoms Frost had been reporting for several years. The puzzling thing about these symptoms, Frost said, was that they came and went so unpredictably.

This time, when they began he had been living alone in his rented room in Cambridge, and he told himself that the only cause of his malaise was Elinor's absence—he didn't like to live alone. Gradually overwhelmed with a mounting sense of fatigue, he had tried taking naps in the daytime, tried going to bed early. But he never seemed to get a restful sleep. At times he felt that his feet must still be chilled from the well water he had bailed so desperately at Salisbury Point the previous summer. Occasionally, even now, he felt the return of the same old pains in his chest or stomach or solar plexus. He had hoped his condition might improve as soon as he resigned from Harvard. Instead, it had grown worse.

The doctor said there was no sure way of telling whether these troubles were caused by nervous fatigue or by consumption. In either case, no cure could be effected by medicine. The best remedy would be an entire change in Frost's living habits. Sedentary work, either as a teacher or as a student, could only heighten the physical and nervous strain. It would be best if the young man could engage in some activity such as farming, which would keep him out of doors and give him plenty of exercise. By this time Frost was so frightened he was ready to accept the familiar advice.

During one of his walks, botanizing, he had gone to the outskirts of Lawrence and into the Methuen countryside. Quite by accident he had noticed and admired an attractive arrangement of chicken coops in a field behind a house not far from the Merrill School, where his mother had first taught after leaving Salem. If Frost had to be a farmer, he supposed the least unpleasant specialty might be feeding chickens and collecting eggs. Under the present circumstances, there could be no harm in taking another walk, to ask the advice of the Methuen farmer who seemed to be a very capable poultryman.

The farmer was a French-Canadian, a veterinarian by profession, Charlemagne Bricault, a dapper little man, only seven years older than Frost. Bricault explained that his specialty was breeding pedigreed birds (some Barred Plymouth Rocks, mostly White Wyandottes) to increase egg-laying. By keeping records for each generation and by using "trap nests," he could prove he was making gains. His roosters were all from hens that had laid 200 or more eggs a year.

Frost was told that incubator eggs from Bricault's hens usually sold for the high price of ten cents apiece, but if the visitor really wanted to start a good-sized brood of Wyandottes, a better price could be given. Furthermore, Bricault promised to help find markets for Frost's eggs and poultry. Statistics were cited to prove that if Frost seriously went into the business of raising Wyandottes "bred-to-lay," he could be assured of making a very handsome profit on his investment.

With some wry hesitation, Frost gradually convinced himself that, because he wanted to carry out doctor's orders by earning an out-of-doors living, the possibility of becoming a poultryman was not unappealing. Once again he swallowed his pride and called on his grandfather, to ask the loan of enough money to get started. The two men spent some time making estimates and writing out figures for costs—including those for a year's rental of a suitable place in the neighborhood of Bricault's farm. Then, William Prescott Frost made a formal business arrangement with his grandson. The money was lent, at interest, and promissory notes were drawn.

After a brief search for a place with plenty of room for coops and runways, Frost found what he wanted at 67 Prospect Street in Methuen, a mile or so north of Bricault's farm and only about three miles from the center of Lawrence. The house and barn, perched on a gently sloping knoll called Powder House Hill, were backed by fields that could be used for movable chicken pens and shelters. The property commanded a pleasant view of surrounding meadows and woodlands. The owner was a spinster, Mary Mitchell, who agreed to rent part of her two-story, box-shaped colonial house, with the understanding that she would keep some rooms for herself and share the kitchen.

By the time the Frosts moved into their new home there were four in the family. Their nearly-three-year-old son, Elliott, now shared attentions with a baby sister named Lesley, born in Lawrence on April 28, 1899.

Rob immediately went to work to build shelters for the incubators. As soon as all was in readiness Bricault delivered 200 eggs, showed the novice how to regulate the heat of the kerosene lamps, instructed him concerning the important ritual of turning each egg once a day to improve the chances of proper hatching, and promised to stand by in case of emergency. It was a humble start in a new way of life, yet Rob found it much to his liking.

Before the eggs began to hatch he had ample time for spring botanizing, particularly with an eye to orchids in the lowlands. These activities had such a good effect on his health that he was encouraged to think he might soon be cured of his mysterious ailments.

His elation was soon marred by the serious illness of his mother. When she had been deprived of his help in teaching school, while he was at Harvard, Mrs. Frost had not seemed strong enough to carry on well with Jeanie's assistance. The enrollment had fallen so sharply she had been obliged to find new and smaller quarters. At first, they moved the school from the Haverhill Street house to rooms they rented on Jackson Street. But after only one year there, they had moved again, to even-smaller quarters on Summer Street. During the spring of 1899, Mrs. Frost had visibly lost weight and strength, from some kind of illness she refused to discuss. Only after her son insisted did she agree to seek medical advice. Her doctor seemed worried, arranged for her to enter a hospital in Boston for an exploratory operation, and thus confirmed what she already suspected. She was dying of cancer, and the specialists said she could not possibly live more than a year. As soon as she was permitted to leave the hospital she was invited to live with Rob and Elinor in their new home on Powder House Hill. Jeanie closed the apartment in Lawrence and went to live with friends.

Well aware that her illness was fatal, Mrs. Frost accepted it with the same quiet serenity and courage she had shown during all the years since the death of her husband in San Francisco. She seemed particularly interested, however, in her son's new activities as a poultryman and was pleased to watch the progress of the flock, as the chicks grew rapidly to pullets and, early in the fall of 1899, began to lay eggs.

Bricault kept his word, bought all the eggs Frost offered for sale, and made arrangements for taking the live broilers and fryers. (Frost could not bear to become involved in the butchering end of the business.) As winter approached, Frost found that more work was required to make the coops winter-proof, and before long he was shoveling paths through the snow to feed and tend his brood. Yet, he enjoyed all these rituals. By the time spring came he was even bold enough to decide he wanted another batch of eggs for incubation, and so closely did Bricault work with him that there was a sense of partnership in the whole enterprise. Rob's health continued to improve; the prospects for a steady increase of his financial returns were at least calculable; and within little more than a year after he had begun this new way of life, he found good reason for thinking that his decision had been a wise one. However, early in the summer of 1900 the Frost household on Powder House Hill was distressed by a serious illness that overtook Elliott.

Until this time he had seemed to come through all the ailments of babyhood and childhood with surprising ease. As soon as he had learned to walk he became a companion to his father, and he liked to make occasional trips to the chicken coops, to feed and water the Wyandottes. For a full year the child's Grandmother Frost had been helping to care for Elliott, much to the relief of Elinor, who had her hands full with her baby girl. It was from his grandmother that Elliott heard many of the same Bible stories that Jeanie and Rob had heard when they were young.

Rob's mother, regularly visited by a doctor, got the first medical advice concerning the child. Her doctor examined Elliott and left some homeopathic pills, which were given without improvement. The child soon grew so much worse his parents called their own doctor. The stern old man seemed to be annoyed that he had not been called sooner. With harsh reproach he turned from the bed, faced the parents, and said: "This is cholera infantum. It's too late, now, for me to do anything. The child will be dead before morning."

Elliott died that night, and the shock of his death crushed his parents beneath a grief that seemed unbearable. Rob blamed himself and said he had been guilty of neglect that amounted to murder. By failing to call the doctor, he had in effect killed his own son. Frantically, he kept saying this was God's just punishment of him.

Elinor suffered inconsolably and in silence for days. When she could finally bear to talk, she reproved Rob for saying this was God's punishment. How could he, at a time like this, be so unreasoning and so self-centered as to wallow in thoughts of punishment for himself, without seeing the injustice in the notion that the child's life had been taken from the child—and from her—as a way of punishing *him*? How could he think there was any divine justice or any benevolent oversight of human affairs? There was no God, she said; there couldn't be. The world was completely evil, and she hated all life that was left, including her own.

For the time, at least, her husband was inclined to agree with her, and his bitterness provided the notion of metaphysical indifference in the ending of a poem he may have started a winter or two earlier. When it was finally published, in *A Boy's Will*, the poem was entitled merely "Stars." But the gloss on it, in the table of contents—"There is no oversight of human affairs."—amounted to his own bitter restatement of Elinor's dark words.

Still crushed by the anguish of their loss, Rob continued his task of tending his chickens, and Elinor went on caring for their fourteen-month-old daughter, Lesley. It seemed to both of them that they had lost whatever meaning or purpose or direction life might have had, and that it was only with indifference that they could perform their daily obligations. It even seemed unimportant to Rob that all of his old ailments suddenly returned, that his sleep was wracked with nightmares, that he frequently awoke to find his nightgown discolored from heavy sweating, that his old sense of weakness overtook him, that the cold returned to his feet, that the pains returned like knives in his stomach, solar plexus, chest.

As the summer dragged on and the hay-fever season returned, his ailments pointed, at least in part, to a diagnosis of tuberculosis. During the previous summer he had for the first time suffered distress from hay fever; but in the summer of 1900 pollen dust seemed to poison him until he was almost exhausted with choking, coughing, sneezing, crying.

In the midst of these troubles, as Rob's mother became steadily weaker, her doctor tried to encourage her with reports that some miraculous cures for cancer had been effected in a sanatorium not far away. Although it is doubtful Mrs. Frost took these statements seriously, she permitted her son to arrange for her to be entered as a patient at the sanatorium in Penacook, New Hampshire, that summer.

While all these troubles were proliferating, their landlady announced she had tolerated the Frosts long enough in her home. They were far behind in paying rent; she wanted them to get out before fall—and to take with them the hundreds of chickens that were permitted to invade every sanctuary on her property, including her house.

By this time there were nearly 300 White Wyandottes prowling over Miss Mary Mitchell's premises, and the spinster had good reason for losing patience with her tenants. Frost knew he needed more space in which his flock of hens and pullets could range, and he consulted the real-estate agent who had previously given him help. In the meantime, on her own initiative, Elinor's mother had been asking questions about other farms that might be rented or bought. She learned that an unusually attractive property of thirty acres, with a relatively new house and barn, was on the market in the town of Derry, New Hampshire, just to the north of Salem; and she was very anxious that Elinor and Rob should look at it before they came to any decision. Elinor made the next important move, by going alone to visit Rob's grandfather. Whatever she said, she was so persuasive that he offered to buy the Derry farm for his grandson if, after careful inspection, it seemed to be worth the price.

Rob was not impressed with the offer. Instead, his immediate response was resentment. Repeatedly, he made the claim that his grandfather's offer to set him up on the Derry farm was a way of saying: "Go on out and die. Good riddance to you. You've been nothing except a bother to me, for years, and you're not worth anything except as a disappointment."

Part of the immediate trouble was hay fever, which made him feel so miserable he could easily transfer resentment to anyone or anything around him. Closely related was the unhealed wound of his grief over Elliott's death. Inseparable from that grief was his puzzled awareness that his relationship with Elinor had not developed as he had hoped. He was now convinced he loved her much more than she loved him. Underlying all these fears and resentments were his ingrained responses. Impatient with conflicts between what he wanted and what he had, he more than ever resented his need to depend on the generosity of his grandfather.

Even the possibility of the move to a Derry farm caused him contradictory emotions of elation and resentment. His grandfather, too old to make the inspection trip, enlisted the aid of the more sprightly Elihu Colcord. A shrewd politician, experienced in appraising real estate, Uncle Elihu hired a carriage and took Rob and Elinor with him when he made the twelve-mile drive from Lawrence, through Methuen and Salem, to the township of Derry. The farm, locally known as the Magoon place, they found on the Londonderry turnpike, two miles south-southeast of Derry Village. The small house, shed, and barn seemed to snuggle down between the protecting hills and ridges that flanked it on the north and south. The large bay window at the front of the house faced west and overlooked two small pastures.

A good-sized orchard of apple trees and a vegetable garden stood to the north of the house. Behind the barn, to the east, a long hayfield stretched back toward a hardwood grove or woodlot. To the south, between the house and the long ridge that crested in a knoll at the turnpike roadside, alders concealed a small, west-running brook, which drained out of a little cranberry bog. The brook, flowing under the turnpike through a culvert, was fed by a pasture spring. The lowlands in the neighborhood of the cranberry bog suggested places where orchis might be found blooming in season.

Close against the southern side of the barn, patches of cultivated raspberries and blackberries flourished. A former owner had improved the little farm by setting out a few peach, pear, and quince trees. Rob immediately saw the possibility of using the orchard and at least part of the long hayfield behind the barn as places where coops could be built and hens could be permitted to run without too much need for fencing —if one were willing to risk the depredations of hawks and foxes.

Inside the house, Elinor and Rob studied the arrangements with satisfaction. Granite steps led up to the roof-covered front door. The door opened into an entryway from which stairs on the left led to three second-floor bedrooms; a door on the right gave access to the bay-windowed parlor, from which another window looked out on the piazza, to the south. Beyond the parlor a door led to a living-dining room with three other doorways; one opened to the piazza, another door gave access to a corner bedroom, another led to the ell, which housed the kitchen, the pantry, the grain shed, the privy.

Elinor and Rob, thoroughly satisfied, reveled in the possibilities, while the suspicious Uncle Elihu grumbled over details, poked his cane into foundation timbers, critically tried the pump in the dooryard, and sniffed at the water he caught in a tin cup. His final conclusion was that the asking price of $1,700 would be fair enough and he would recommend that Rob's grandfather agree to add $25 for the few tons of hay in the barn loft.

On the return to Lawrence, Uncle Elihu may have explained to Rob that the title to the property would be held in the name of the purchaser, William P. Frost. He may even have hinted that someone like Carl Burell would be needed as a helper for a year or so, until Rob had learned more about how to run a farm. Colcord may have also hinted that Grandfather Frost had suspicions that Rob's previous and brief experiments with so many occupations might foreshadow the temporariness of this latest splurge, in poultry farming.

Soon after the visit to Derry, Rob's grandfather began the legal proceedings for purchase. He also got in touch with Carl Burell and asked if he would be willing to help the younger people get started on the farm. Still working and living in East Pembroke, Carl replied he would be delighted to accept the offer if he could bring with him his eighty-four-year-old grandfather, Jonathan Eastman, in whose home Rob had spent Thanksgiving Day of 1892.

Although Rob grudgingly accepted these arrangements, he was furious with his grandfather and with Carl when the two men worked out satisfactory terms without really consulting him. Carl and "Jont" Eastman were to be given rooms on the second floor of the small house and were to eat their meals with the Frosts. Carl was to have charge of the cow, the horse, the fruit trees, and the vegetable garden. His financial returns would come from whatever he could realize on the sale of fruit and vegetables. It was understood that Rob would, thus, be free to devote most of his time to the care of poultry, from which he would realize his profits.

That the arrangement seemed sensible enough to other members of the family merely heightened Rob's resentment. Carl had now joined in a "conspiracy" with Rob's grandfather! "I take a long time to wreak vengeance, when I've been wronged," Frost later said of this arrangement, "but I never forget, and I never forgive a wrong." Carl was completely unaware that in trying to help his friend, he was letting himself in for what Rob liked to view as fair punishment.

The move to Derry was made around October first (the event was noted in *The Derry News* for October 5, 1900), and the first visitor who stayed overnight at the farm was Jeanie, who seemed to come not out of love or curiosity, but to scold her brother because he had let weeks go by without making the short trip to Penacook, where their mother was slowly dying.

It was easy enough to make excuses, but after Jeanie's prodding, Rob did get up there—just once. His mother, completely bedridden by this time and wasted away to such an extent that her face was unpleasantly cadaverous, showed the same serene resignation Rob had admired for so many years. In her attempts to console her son and daughter-in-law after the death of Elliott, she had become thoroughly familiar with their scorn for religious matters. She was even aware that Rob had expressed his disbelief in any life after death, and she smiled confidently at him as she said that very soon she would know whether he was right or wrong on that point.

None of her friends or relatives was with her when she died. Funeral services were held in Lawrence. Her Swedenborgian pastor paid tribute to her as "one to whom religion was a way of life," and her Swedenborgian friends joined the family in taking her coffin to the hilltop cemetery in Lawrence, where she was buried between the graves of her husband and her grandchild Elliott.

Another early visitor at the Derry farm was Elinor's mother, the indefatigable Mrs. White. She knew her daughter was not a good housekeeper; and yet, she was surprised to discover that, even after the Frosts had been settled on the Derry farm for weeks, no curtains had been hung, no rugs spread, no furniture arranged in the living room. Elinor's plea was that she had been too busy to bother with frills—too busy caring for the baby, too busy getting meals and washing dishes for three hungry men. There were deeper reasons, mutely expressed in Elinor's manner of listless indifference, and her mother must have understood them.

To Rob it seemed at times that his wife and grandfather must have arrived at a secret agreement that this Derry venture would not last long, that not many months would pass before another grave would be dug and filled. His physical exhaustion, brought on by even a minimum of work in collecting eggs, carrying water, scattering grain, was enough to make him prey to a welter of annoyances that aroused new resentments. In his lowest moments he told himself that maybe it was just as well he should die soon and get it over with. He didn't care, if Elinor didn't care; he didn't care, if God didn't care. More than once he told himself, sarcastically, that he knew God *did* care; this was all part of the punishment meted out to him because of the way he had treated his wife, his mother, his sister.

Self-abasement and guilt accumulated in him until they became a despairing kind of self-hatred. Overwhelmed, he found that he didn't even want to struggle any longer against the waves of pain and sickness that washed over him. And why wait for this lingering death, when there were easier ways to the same end? Each time he drove from his farm, with his old horse and wagon, along the backcountry road to Derry Depot for provisions, he passed an isolated pond deep enough for drowning.

During the late fall and early winter he found that the temptation was becoming more and more attractive. Although none of his moods had found outlet in poetry since he left Methuen, this one did. It inspired a dark sonnet into which he poured thoughts of suicidal death by drowning. He called the sonnet "Despair."

The mood of "Despair" vividly reflected his almost-overwhelming certainty that circumstances left him with no favorable outcome. He had hoped to accomplish so much, back on that day of his greatest triumph when he had figuratively unveiled a monument to "after-thought" and poetry. He had even seemed, when *The Independent* printed "My Butterfly: An Elegy," to be well started on the road he had chosen. Now it *all* seemed elegy, in the sense of lament for ideals lost in the degradation of chicken manure and cow manure and horse manure on a backcountry farm. The question that he framed in all but words was "what to make of a diminished thing."

But it was all his own fault, he told himself; he deserved the punishment he was receiving. His illness could be suffered with, to the end, if it were not for his guilt in feeling that somehow he had unintentionally betrayed and disappointed Elinor.

NEW ATTITUDE—
NEW RESPONSES

(1900–1906)

IN RETROSPECT, Robert Frost could never understand how or why he managed to climb out of his despairing preoccupation with suicide during the first phase of his life on the farm in Derry. That long winter, he continued to suffer with mingled feelings of anger, resentment, and hopelessness, almost luxuriating in his miseries.

But a change occurred in his attitude when he began to notice evidence that the winter was being broken by spring. He could not resist the lift he felt when he saw how the March sunlight, still bleak, had power enough to melt windswept patches of ice and to uncover the ground. With exultation he watched for signs that warm rains and winds were gradually defeating a stubborn enemy. He welcomed the first robin. He admired the first green spike of skunk cabbage pushing up through dead and matted leaves in the alders beside the brook.

Carl and he, when they should be tending to farm work, joined forces in digging up clusters of adder's tongue, lady's slipper, yellow violets, jack-in-the-pulpit, so they could carry each one gently, on a shovel, for transplanting beside the brook or along the edge of the alders.

Part of the lasting change that gradually overtook the farmer-poultryman-poet, without his being aware of any effort on his part, was simply his discovery that it was good to be alive, after all, for another springtime. Almost with a sense of surprise, he found he cared for things and people more than he had thought he could ever again care.

Even Frost's reading came to his rescue. He had begun his acquaintance with Thoreau's *Walden*. It gave him all the encouragement he needed for doing and not doing things that, he well knew, his grandfather would never understand. Thoreau helped him understand more clearly the business of the poet, and Frost understood Thoreau's insistence that contemplation of facts was for him the best form of religious worship.

Having been forced by circumstance to see himself driven into a corner and reduced to lowest terms, Frost had known moments when he had denied that there was any oversight of human affairs or any reason for reverence. But all of his deeply ingrained elements of religious belief were stimulated anew by the experiences of the first spring on the Derry farm.

Thoreau's way of talking about facts could not help but remind him of Emerson's "there is no fact in nature which does not carry the whole sense of nature. . . ." Emerson had also said that the farmer makes worshipful responses to facts. Emerson had even spelled out more clearly what Thoreau had only implied concerning the contemplation of fact as involving a form of prayer: "Prayer is the contemplation of the facts of life from the highest point of view. It is the soliloquy of a beholding and jubilant soul. It is the spirit of God pronouncing his works good. . . . As soon as the man is at one with God, he will not beg. He will then see prayer in all action. The prayer of the farmer kneeling in his field to weed it, the prayer of the rower kneeling with the stroke of his oar, are true prayers heard throughout nature. . . ."

When Frost took these familiar ideas into reconsideration during the spring of 1901, he was approaching them from that new direction that had stripped life down to the foundation of very hard fact. Having been given the choice of death or life, he had found he preferred to stay alive. More than that, he found that his irrational acts of caring and cherishing were signs of his willingness to settle for imperfection—including the wistfulness of loving one who might not love him as much as he loved her. Whatever the limitations of circumstance, including his health and his questionable capacities, he was ready to go about his business, as farmer and poet, with a new depth of pleasure in caring and cherishing, expressed in the humble duties even.

In the summer of 1901, while Frost was still trying to explain to himself his new attitude toward life and death, his grandfather unexpectedly died, leaving an odd will. So much attention was paid in the will to Robert and Jeanie Frost that it seemed necessary for Rob to revise his previous estimates of his grandfather's attitude toward his poor relations. The estate was valued at more than $17,000, not including the farm in Derry. Minor bequests were followed by larger ones: $200 "to my sister Lucy A. Colcord" and $500 each to the First Universalist Society of Lawrence and the Lawrence Home for Aged People. The will continued:

"THIRD: It is my will that all my personal effects . . . be given to the following named persons, viz: , , , all silver ware marked 'F', one teaspoon marked 'Willie', two tablespoons marked 'J. Colcord', one napkin ring marked 'Will', and my gold watch and chain, be given to my grandson Robert Lee Frost. And that all other silver ware however marked together with my other gold watch, which formerly belonged to my wife, shall be given to my grand-daughter Jeanie Florence Frost. Also . . . that my said sister . . . shall have the privilege of selecting any other articles . . . , to the value of about twenty-five dollars . . . ; and all the remainder of such articles be divided equally between the said Robert Lee Frost and said Jeanie Florence Frost, as they themselves shall agree. . . .

"FOURTH: As my said grandson Robert Lee Frost is now living on my farm situated in Derry . . . and is now making a home there for himself and family, I give to him the free use and occupancy of said farm for and during the first ten years beginning at the time of my decease. . . . At the end of said ten year term, I devise to him the fee in said farm. . . .

"FIFTH: All the rest and residue of my estate . . . I give, devise and bequeath to my said TRUSTEES . . . to carefully hold and invest the same, and of the income thereof to pay certain annuities as follows, viz:—To the said Jeanie Florence Frost an anuity of four hundred dollars annually for and during the term of her natural life. To the said Robert Lee Frost an anuity of five hundred dollars annually for and during said ten year term, and from and after the expiration of said ten year term an annuity of eight hundred dollars annually for and during the term of his natural life. . . ."

Rob received a further sign of his grandfather's affection and generosity when Wilbur E. Rowell, the lawyer serving as executive trustee of the estate, informed him that his grandfather had destroyed several promissory notes covering loans used in starting the poultry farm on Powder House Hill.

If he felt any gratitude, any change of heart and mind as a consequence of these unexpected revelations, Rob found a peculiar way of expressing it. He complained that his grandfather had cheated him out of what would have been his if such large and "silly" gifts had not been made to the Home for Aged People and the First Universalist Society. Moreover, he quickly tried to arrange for advance payments from the trust fund and was resentful when he was told that, by the terms of the will, no annuities were to be paid in advance, that the first annuity would not fall due until one year after the death of his grandfather.

Rob's difficulty with Carl Burell built to a peak late in the second winter at Derry. Arguments developed repeatedly between them and would have sooner or later forced Carl off the farm, in spite of his good-natured efforts to parry and tolerate Rob's criticism. But matters were brought to a head by the unexpected death of Carl's grandfather on March 8, 1902. Within three weeks Carl took his leave of the Frosts —under pressure, but without bitterness.

Only after Carl had gone did the new owner of the Magoon place realize how much he had been dependent on him. Carl's departure had been so hasty he had not even instructed Rob in the nice points of milking the cow, and Rob was surprised to find he lacked the peculiar dexterity of fingers and wrists. Stripping was another matter. Not aware he could dry up the cow by neglecting this aspect of her care, he soon did just that. When it became clear she would need to be bred again, well ahead of the usual time, he felt embarrassed to lead her up the road to visit with a generous neighbor's bull, and awkward at having to buy milk from the same neighbor during the next few weeks.

There were many other ways in which Frost was made conscious of Carl's absence, not the least of them being his fear of night sounds in the house and barn. He had purchased a revolver in Lawrence before he came to the farm, and he kept it loaded at all times on a shelf in a kitchen cupboard. More than once, long after Elinor and Lesley were asleep, leaving him free to write at the kitchen table, mysterious noises in the shed or barn or cellar sent chills up his back. At such times he sought the consolation of taking down the revolver.

In spite of all the difficulties caused by Carl's forced departure, Rob and Elinor and Lesley did manage to survive unaided. But by the time spring came, financial assistance had to be found. Running more and more into debt, and yet, hating to borrow money from the bank in Derry, Rob solved the problem in another way.

Ernest Jewell, his friend of high-school days, had returned to the Lawrence High School as a teacher of mathematics, and Jewell occasionally came out from Lawrence to visit the Frosts. In the spring of 1902, Frost explained to Jewell his feeling that the so-called "bred-to-lay" business offered sure possibilities of substantial profits, but that he needed cash. Papers were drawn up, and Jewell turned $675 over to Frost. But the poultry business never did flourish as Frost hoped, and Jewell never did receive any interest on his investment—in fact, he never recovered the full amount of the principal.

Largely through making mistakes, Frost acquired new insights from his experiences on the farm. And the better he came to know backcountry New Hampshire people, the more he admired their practical knowledge. Gradually, he paid them the tribute of trying to imitate them—even trying to imitate the careless way they talked.

There was a man named John Hall who was especially appealing, not merely because he had a picturesque vocabulary and a ready wit, but also because he was an expert poultryman. Frost met Hall at a poultry show in Amesbury, Massachusetts, and learning that Hall lived in Atkinson, New Hampshire, a town bordering on Derry, Frost arranged to call on him. Hall was not married, but he lived in relative peace and comfort with a common-law housekeeper-wife and her mother. The barnyard sheltered a surprising congregation of plain and fancy birds; blue-ribbon prizes were tacked up all over the kitchen. It was clear that Hall got extraordinary pleasure out of prize-winning. But he wasn't in the business to make money. His life seemed to be built on the same kind of caring and cherishing Frost had just begun to understand.

All of Frost's newly acquired insights about backcountry responses to human experience gave new impetus to his life. These self-reliant people had something casually stoic about the way they took all their hardships as a matter of course, without complaining and without seeming to find any reason for the expectation that circumstances should change.

Just south of Frost lived a French-Canadian farmer named Napoleon Guay (pronounced—and sometimes spelled—"Gay"). The boundary line between his rented property and Frost's farm was marked by the stone wall that separated his grove of white pine from one of Frost's apple orchards. (Guay was the man who would not "go behind his father's saying": "Good fences make good neighbors." He was also the man who literally stole up behind Frost and caught his axe "expertly on the rise," as a preliminary to condemning machine-made axe helves and to showing Frost the lines of a good helve.)

More than once, in talking to his neighbors, Frost learned facts that had, to his ears, the ring of pure poetry, and heard inflections of voices that captured meanings better than words did. Thoreau had been there before him: "A true account of the actual is the rarest poetry. . . ." Emerson had been there before Thoreau: ". . . there is no fact in nature which does not carry the whole sense of nature. . . . Besides, in a centred mind . . . the . . . chief value of the new fact is to enhance the great and constant fact of Life. . . . The world being thus put under the mind for verb and noun, the poet is he who can articulate it. . . . So the poet's habit of living should be set on a key so low that the common influences should delight him. . . ."

These were ideals for which Robert Frost was beginning to have strong sympathy and understanding. Nevertheless, he seemed to feel that his Derry farm meant less to him now that he was bound to it than it would mean when he could look back at it across a gulf of time and space. Part of the irritation that marred his enjoyment of "a key so low" came from his increasingly impatient ambition to gain recognition for his literary work. He also needed to find other sources of income, so many bills accumulated prior to the payment of the first annuity from his grandfather's estate. He tried to shift from poetry to prose, to make money, and ultimately sold a sketch or short story entitled "Trap Nests" to *The Eastern Poultryman,* which printed the piece in its issue for February 1903. But the sketch earned him only ten dollars, and by that time it was clear the growth of his family would require more solid ways of increasing his income.

Elinor had given birth to a son, Carol, on May 27, 1902, and she was expecting another child in June of 1903. Perhaps it was partly to give Elinor some kind of diversion, before her next confinement, that Rob took his wife and two children to New York during March 1903. They rented a small, furnished apartment in midtown Manhattan, on Sixth Avenue, and Rob's most important activities were unsuccessful calls on editors of various periodicals. After a full month the Frosts returned to the farm, glad to be out of the bustle. On June twenty-seventh Elinor gave birth to their second daughter, Irma.

Showing less interest in farming than in literary matters, Rob seemed hopeful the poultry journals he read faithfully might be amenable to printing a few more pieces true to the life of a farm. In short order, he wrote and sold eleven, which were published. He might even have continued, if one had not misfired in a way that made him the butt of an unintentional joke.

The troublemaking article was straight reportage, "Three Phases of the Poultry Industry." It began by describing Dr. Bricault's White Wyandotte farm; then, gave praise to a Lawrence carpenter who, tired of city life, had bought six acres in the countryside near the village of Salem, New Hampshire; and ended with a description of John Hall's farm. The blunder occurred through Rob's casual way of letting his imagination supplement his knowledge, in this passage about John Hall's theories and practices: "As for vigor, it is easier to get this right than not. What the stock need is a little judicious neglect. Mr. Hall's geese roost in the trees even in winter. Such a toughening process would be too drastic for hens, but these have to take it according to their strength."

More than one poultryman, reading in *Farm-Poultry* the reference to geese roosting in trees, must have chuckled over the obvious error. It may be that several subscribers wrote in to ask questions. A query published in the issue for January 15, 1904, was playfully sarcastic, and the editor added his own comment, saying Mr. Frost would have to explain the "evident error." It was an embarrassing predicament, best handled with humor. But in the process of trying to excuse himself, Frost compounded his difficulty by further revealing his amateur status: ". . . what more natural, in speaking of geese in close connection with hens, than to speak of them as if they *were* hens? 'Roost in the trees,' has here simply suffered what the grammarians would call attraction from the subject with which it should be in agreement to the one uppermost in the mind. That is all. But the idea will have to stand, viz., that Mr. Hall's geese winter out,—and that is the essential thing. . . ."

This time, the editor immediately assumed the obligation of educating his correspondent, without the assistance of letters from subscribers: "Mr. Frost seems not to be aware of the fact that geese generally remain out of doors by choice practically all the time. . . ." And the incident might have ended there had not Frost tried, in self-protection, to enlist the aid of the celebrated John Hall.

Having had little schooling, and even less experience in polemical letter-writing, Hall permitted Frost to write a letter for him, and it was published in the issue for March 1, 1904. This letter brought the incident to a lame close for Frost, who seemed to lose heart in asserting further knowledge of poultry lore. (It is probable that two sketches of his, published in *Farm-Poultry* after the geese-in-trees embarrassment, had been accepted previously.)

During the period from the spring of 1902 to the spring of 1906, Frost brought himself out of the fears and discouragement and heartbreak that had followed hard on his departure from Harvard. From his neighbors and from his reading, he had learned a new attitude. From the reality of his experience as an amateur farm-poultryman, he had found new subject matter and themes for his poetry. From characters like John Hall, he had discovered anew that the talking tones of voice should determine an important part of form in prose or verse. And there was another element in his recovery: his instinctive, outgoing response of love and affection for his children. (His third daughter, Marjorie, was born March 29, 1905.) The children somehow helped lead their parents out of sorrows that had seemed insurmountable.

As a parent, Robert Frost took very seriously and with pleasure the task of helping his children to discover the joys of new experiences. Even before they were old enough to walk, he carried them into one adventurous journey after another, starting in their own dooryard.

In winter, when the snow was wet he asked them for help in building a snowman strong enough to wear a felt hat, bright enough to see with stone eyes, and brave enough to carry a wooden gun. If ice lay under the snow, he shoveled a path all the way to the cranberry bog and uncovered enough ice to let them slippery-slide on it. When the snow had settled and packed under the winter sun, he called their attention to mysterious signs made by birds and animals; he taught them how to read the tracks of chickadees, partridges, rabbits, skunks, foxes, and squirrels. When new snow began to fall, he showed them how to catch big flakes on their mittens and marvel over the different crystal patterns.

Between winter and spring came mudtime, but as soon as spring began to blossom, the father and children went across the road, into the pasture, and along the wall, hunting for the best plants to bring back roots and all. Their treasures were placed in special beds along the base of the porch, facing south, and under the bay window, which faced west: bluets, hepaticas, white violets. Added in their turn, as they flowered, were lady's slipper, bloodroot, and two kinds of trillium. Each spring, newly transplanted discoveries gave the garden beds in the Frost farmyard a fine range of color and fragrance—long before the little cranberry bog was in blossom and, even, before the first delicate spikes of orchises began to show in the alders beside the stream they had named Hyla Brook.

Spring brought other exciting adventures to them in the farmyard. Whenever anyone saw the widespread wings of a chicken hawk lazily coasting high above house and barn, it was the signal for everyone to hurry through the barn to a hiding-place and lookout near the hen houses. If the hawk swooped down, the hens made a great racket and flapped their wings as they ran. If the children could find their father when the hawk was in sight, he would sometimes shoot at it with his revolver. He never hit it, but he always gave it a terrible scare and made it fly away.

Spring was also the time of year for raking up dead leaves in the yard and picking up dead branches, for burning. The great bonfire was always built in the middle of the nearer pasture, across the road from the house. After the children had piled brush and leaves higher and higher, until the heap was taller than their heads, their father put a match to a handful of dry grass, tucked it in at the base of the heap, and pushed the children back. Slowly, the flames began to work their way in, making wet branches crackle and whistle. The flames would start to climb until one tongue of fire came out of the top. Just for a minute it looked like a big candle. Then, it was all on fire, and the roar of the flames was frightening.

The best bonfire of all was one that got away. Flames, pushed along by the wind, began racing toward the stone wall, the road, and even toward the house. The frightened children, herded to windward, were sure that only the heroic efforts of their father saved their house and barn. He used his old work coat to reach into the smoke and beat out the fire. When the last smoldering spots had been doused with pails of water from Hyla Brook, the children could scarcely believe so much of their pasture had been burned black in so short a time.

As the children grew older they enjoyed hearing stories, told them by their father, before they went to bed. His stories were always about things that happened in or near their own dooryard. Several of them were about their collie dog, Schneider, and the adventures he had with woodchucks and rabbits and squirrels and birds. Others were about elves and goblins and fairies who lived very near their farm. And sometimes their father read some of his own poems about the little people he had known when he was a boy. One told about his own powers of second sight, which helped him to communicate with the little people. He had begun to write this poem while he was in high school, and it had some old-fashioned ways of saying things. It was called "In a Vale."

Their father knew almost as much about the moon and planets and stars as he did about fairies, elves, and goblins. On summer evenings, soon after the sun had gone down, he liked to sit on the front steps, with the children, and get them to watch for the stars coming out. The children learned to find the North Star, the Little Dipper, the Big Dipper, Orion.

Among the many games their father taught them, the Frost children liked best his way of playing school. As soon as Carol and Irma and Marjorie were old enough to enjoy it, he showed them how much fun they could have that way. Autumn evenings, as the sun went down earlier and earlier, he would call them in from the yard and let them sit in a line on the sofa in the parlor. He would start by telling them a story. Then, he would count with them. And, then, he would sing a song with them until recess time. After recess, they would all play a spelling game. A little word was written on a big card, and anyone who could spell it right could have the card; if not, they could all look at it. Then, they would sing another song, do exercises to make their muscles strong, march around the room once or twice, and keep right on marching out into the kitchen for their supper of bread and milk.

There were oh-so-many other kinds of excitement, on birthdays, the Fourth of July, Halloween. But the children said Christmas was the best day of all, and they learned from their father that Christmas meant more than toys and candy. Each year, long before the day arrived, he told them the story of the Nativity, read it to them from the New Testament, and sang "Away in a Manger" with them.

At Christmastime, a special grace was said before meals and a special evening prayer replaced the one that concluded: "And if I die before I wake, / I pray the Lord my soul to take." Perhaps the religious beliefs of the Frost children were planted most firmly through their observance of Christmas festivities, but the same beliefs were nurtured carefully throughout the year. As they grew old enough, each of them took turns reading aloud stories that, often, had a religious flavor.

It was part of their father's Christian discipline to make the children understand the meaning of such words as "obedience" and "acceptance." Like his father before him, he seemed to believe in the adage "Spare the rod and spoil the child." There was a Victorian earnestness in his conviction that children should be led to understand that the moral life entails a desperate struggle and that resistance to temptation is the first step in training the will toward the fulfillment of life's great end.

The children could not see any inconsistency, perhaps, between what their father preached and practiced. He behaved badly, at times, under circumstances unfortunate for the children. Lesley was never able to forget a mysterious performance, the meaning of which nobody ever explained to her. She could remember being abruptly and roughly awakened by her father, in the middle of a night, when she was about six years old. She was told to get out of bed and to follow her father down the unlit stairs to the parlor, through the parlor to the dining room, and through the dining room toward the kitchen, where she could see a light burning. As she entered, she saw her mother sitting at the kitchen table, crying, her hands pressed against her face. Bewildered, Lesley turned to look at her father and noticed he held his revolver in his hand. Waving the revolver toward her mother and, then, toward himself, he said wildly to Lesley: "Take your choice. Before morning, one of us will be dead."

She wanted them both, she said, and started to cry. Her mother got up from the table, led her back to bed, and sat beside her until the child had cried herself to sleep. In the morning she remembered all the facts and wondered if they had actually happened. Perhaps she had only dreamed them. But no. There was evidence enough to make her certain this experience had not been a dream.

Their father could not explain to them that even the pleasure he took in the freshness of their responses to life was not enough to protect him completely from his intermittent moods of uncertainty and darkness. He did not enjoy, any more than they did, the periods when he was depressed by his notion that he was a failure.

Somewhere near the beginning of 1906, Frost sorted through his batch of manuscripts and notebooks, to find a poem he had begun to write in the spring of 1892. So far, he had not been able to finish it. But during the nearly fourteen years since its start he had slowly acquired images and insights he hoped could be brought to bear on what he had first tried to say. Now he thought the poem would serve as an expression of newly achieved and hard-earned affirmations.

It had grown out of his hurts and doubts and hindrances. He could vividly remember the moment of the initial inspiration. He had, on that spring day in 1892, doubtfully been wondering whether any satisfactory explanation could be given for the grief, pain, and evil that had destroyed his father's life and had repeatedly beset him, his mother, his sister, since his father's death. A flash of insight provided answers that morning.

In retrospect, he could perhaps see how some elements in those answers had been based on his mother's religious faith. She had taught him that all human souls come to earth from heaven. But the originality of his insight seemed to spring from his imaginative conviction that each soul, in coming, must heroically choose to come; each soul must ultimately dare to be tested or tried by the ordeal of earthly existence. He also imagined afresh that each soul, in making the departure from heaven to earth, must be required to surrender the memory of the choice—that if the memory remained, there could be no real trial, no real danger of ultimate defeat, no valid testing worthy of man's God-given spiritual capacities.

He now told himself that he might sooner have found appropriate images and metaphors through which to give these insights poetic statement, if he had not been overtaken by so many failures and disappointments soon after his graduation from high school. For a time he had tried to rationalize the failures, by repeating his mother's warning that griefs are meted out by a just God as punishment for wrongdoing —also, that human beings are often tortured by evil forces that are all instruments of the divine plan. But as his failures accumulated, he became disillusioned with religion, to the point where he doubted whether there really was any justice, any divine oversight of human affairs, any connection man could figure out between his just deserts and what he gets.

The death of his mother heightened his bitter awareness of all the unmerited miseries in the world and caused him to reconsider the old claims concerning salvation through freely willed actions. Years later, in a mood that reflected the recurrence of disillusionment, he paid poetic tribute to his mother by dramatizing poetically what he sometimes viewed as the unmerited injustices that had ruined her noble life. This tribute, "The Lovely Shall Be Choosers," ironically and sarcastically represented all her freely willed choices as illusions, arranged by higher powers to mete out retribution or punishment for her refusal to accept the proper kind of marital love.

As he returned to his work on the unfinished poem that eventually became "The Trial by Existence," Matthew Arnold's five quatrains entitled "Revolutions" may have provided stimulus to the gradual revision of pictorial elements. A more powerful incentive to thematic concerns came from William James. But, important as James may have been to Frost in encouraging him to formulate a cautiously skeptical, personal, eclectic set of beliefs, the immediate stimulus for the revision of "The Trial by Existence" probably was the maturing of Frost's attitude toward moral courage and bravery, daring and heroism. To its author, "The Trial by Existence" was more than a milestone; it marked a turning point in his attitude toward the kinds of promises he wanted to keep, toward himself and others, and the attitude that would be necessary, for him, if he were to keep them.

Almost as soon as he had finished his revision of the poem, Frost made a fair copy and sent it, with some other poems, to William Hayes Ward, in the first letter he had addressed to an editor of *The Independent* during a period of five years:

"I trust I do not presume too much on former kindness in addressing these verses to you personally. Sending MS to the Independent can never be quite like sending it anywhere else for me.

"I often think of you and your sister in my work. . . . Please remember me to her either formally or by showing her any of my verses—whether you can use them or not."

Ward immediately decided he could use "The Trial by Existence," which he characterized as "uncommonly good." But there was far more importance for Frost in his having been able to finish the poem than in its being publishable.

Such an affirmation was no guarantee, as he well knew, that he might not subsequently waver in his religious belief, that he might not again be reduced by discouragement and pessimism. Even when he tried as hard as he could, it was impossible for him to close all the doors and windows of his inner life against discouragement that came at him from outside. They kept getting in past his guard, especially when he was asleep, and they kept turning his dreams into nightmares.

Just beyond his bedroom window grew a white-birch tree with branches long enough to scrape against the house and, in the wind, even against the panes of glass. In his dreams these harmless branches became horrible things. Years later he commemorated this particular tree in a poem that may serve to represent the darkest of his moods on the Derry farm, "Tree at My Window."

Whenever the storms of his "inner weather" grew too violent, he was almost lost to his recurrent wish that he might run away—steal away, stay away—and never come back. It was a mood against which he had to fight or a mood he could slake at times merely by getting out of the house and off the farm—particularly if he and Elinor had built up too much abrasive tension between them. Often, he would plunge into the woods behind his farm and walk until he was almost exhausted. Then, he could come back, repentant. So, he was of two minds about running away as a release from nervous fury: whether good or bad, brave or cowardly. During one of those ambiguous states of mind he wrote a defensive sonnet entitled "Into My Own."

In later years he could and did place this poem in a context that treated it ironically, as reflecting his youthful, runaway mannerisms that implied, "I was right, and you'll be sorry when I'm gone." Perhaps these ironic possibilities of meaning, in the poem, were brought to his attention obliquely by Elinor's tart comments. Although she puzzled others as much as she puzzled him, there was never any question concerning her ability to make observations that went like bullets to their mark. Sometimes, and in ways that interrupted his self-pity, she was able to draw him back from his habitual acts of escape or withdrawal. He acknowledged as much, in one of his most intimate love poems, implicitly addressed to her, "A Dream Pang."

Much of what was written by Frost in his renewal of poetic activity, during this phase of his life on the Derry farm, were unmistakably love poems, written to Elinor as gestures of courtship. Whatever they might mean to others, through valid symbolic extension, they first meant to him a way of increasing the intimacy that was so important to him. Even after they had been away from the farm for years, the memory of moments of lovemaking at Derry continued to inspire poems, one of the most famous, "The Pasture," having a particular value here. The speaker, on two different occasions, asks the beloved to go with him just long enough to enjoy and cherish two little experiences made especially meaningful if shared by lovers:

> *I'm going out to clean the pasture spring;*
> *I'll only stop to rake the leaves away*
> *(And wait to watch the water clear, I may):*
> *I shan't be gone long.—You come too.*
>
> *I'm going out to fetch the little calf*
> *That's standing by the mother. It's so young*
> *It totters when she licks it with her tongue.*
> *I shan't be gone long.—You come too.*

There is no way of knowing just what effect this kind of poetic lovemaking had on Elinor Frost. It may have helped her to overcome the natural darkness in her nature, which had been increased by crushing disappointments and griefs. She did enjoy the romantic isolation and the homely pleasures of wandering afield, to cherish, just as much as he did. She may also have realized that her puzzling love caused him to make reassuring efforts that found expression in poems of lasting beauty. She knew the need for renewing love and poetry by discovering fresh ways of saying it. She could have told him that, but in his poems to her he made it clear that she didn't have to.

TEACHING AT
PINKERTON ACADEMY

(1906–1911)

SOCIAL AND financial embarrassment drove Robert Frost into some desperate remedies during the spring of 1906. He had avoided contact with his neighbors, whenever possible, from the day he arrived in Derry; and in Derry Village he was on speaking terms with only a few people. He did most of his shopping at Derry Depot, and he came to resent the occasional insolence he felt from the merchants and businessmen.

During the previous summer, 1905, he had gone to the local bank to deposit the fourth $500 paid him from his grandfather's trust fund. The teller had studied the check and said, "Some more of your hard-earned money." The teller may have intended the remark pleasantly, but Frost resented the insinuation.

Some of the storekeepers annoyed him by the way they raised their eyebrows and cocked their heads at his dapper mare, Eunice. (He had been extravagant, he admitted, in purchasing a fancy stepper like Eunice, but he did enjoy a good-looking horse.) Eunice and a pretty little sulky had played a crucial part in his worst embarrassment in the spring of 1906. He was in the butcher shop and had just finished buying a few good cuts of meat. When the package was wrapped and placed in his hand, Frost told the butcher to charge it and started to walk out. The butcher stopped him. Stepping around the edge of his counter, just far enough to look out of the display window at Eunice and the sulky, he turned and addressed other customers who were waiting: "Anyone have a lien on that mare and sulky?" Silence; then, laughter. All right, the butcher said, just this one more time. In a rage, Frost dumped the package on the counter and stormed out of the shop.

All this finally shamed Frost into reconsideration. Perhaps it was time he stopped pretending he was a farm-poultryman. Everyone in the region knew he did very little farming and not much with hens. After the annuities had begun to come in, he had gradually permitted his brood of

Wyandottes to decrease. And he had come to feel that there must be some better way for him to earn a living.

Looking around somewhat desperately, he decided he could at least apply for a position as a teacher in one of the several district schools. So far, he had avoided sending Lesley to school, although she was seven years old. Part of his reason had been that he was sure he could teach her better and faster than anyone else could. But if he should begin teaching school, she could go and come with him, while they continued to live on the farm. He could not afford to sell the farm—in fact, it would not be legally his for at least five more years. Having made up his mind, he knew that he should not approach the chairman of the local school board until he had acquired a copy of his high-school record and a few letters of recommendation.

Early in 1906 a pleasant coincidence awaited him in Lawrence. As he was walking along Essex Street, he was stopped by Pastor Wolcott. Wolcott said he had heard Frost owned a poultry farm in Derry. Yes, but he was growing tired of it and was thinking that maybe he'd go back to teaching school, perhaps even in Derry. Good, said Wolcott, there's a fine old academy in Derry. He had been there as a speaker for graduations, was well acquainted with the Congregational minister in Derry, Charles Loveland Merriam, and would be glad to write him on Frost's behalf; Merriam was a trustee of Pinkerton Academy. Frost shook his head. He would like to teach at Pinkerton, but he had no college degree. Even worse, he admitted, he was known in Derry as only a "hen-man"—and a poor one at that. He'd better start by not assuming anything. Perhaps he could work up to Pinkerton after he had taught for a while in one of the district schools. Wolcott disagreed, and he not only wrote to his friend Merriam, after urging that Frost should call on him, but also gave Frost a general note of recommendation.

After his return to Derry, armed with records and letters, Frost visited the chairman of the school board, a local dentist. Giving his name, the visitor spread out his documents on a desk and explained that he was applying for a position as a grammar-school teacher. To the dentist the name seemed to carry unpleasant associations. He picked up the documents, handed them back unopened, made a casual remark to the effect that anyone could get letters of reference, and very curtly ended the interview, saying there were no vacancies in the Derry schools. Hurt more by the surliness than by the bad news, Frost was not inclined to look further. But after he had licked this wound for several days, he thought he should at least try Wolcott's suggestion.

He found the Congregational pastor one evening, busy with a group of boys in the vestry of the church. Told to wait until the boys had been dismissed, he braced himself for the same kind of treatment he had received from the dentist. But when Merriam was free and the two men began their conversation, all was friendly and encouraging. Wolcott had been correct; there might be something at Pinkerton. Wolcott had also written that Mr. Frost had published some poems. As a way of getting acquainted in Derry, perhaps Frost would be willing to read a few before the Men's League of Merriam's church. The next meeting, coming soon, was the annual spring banquet. Frost cringed. Never, he explained, had he read any of his poems before a public gathering. He doubted if he would ever have the courage to do that. Then, how would it be, Merriam asked, if the pastor read one of them for him, just by way of introduction?

A few days later Frost visited Merriam again, to submit a poem by no means newly written. (It had been inspired by an experience that occurred while he was haying for Joseph W. Dinsmoor, at Cobbett's Pond near Salem, New Hampshire; it had been written early enough for use as a theme paper in English A at Harvard in 1897.) And on the evening of the Men's League banquet, Frost sat beside Merriam and tried to hide behind a too-thin metal post while "The Tuft of Flowers" was being read. Self-conscious, nervous, and embarrassed, he would have preferred not to be there at all. But the poem was well received, and the men and women to whom he was introduced were cordial. Several of them were teachers at Pinkerton. Another was John C. Chase, owner of a local woodworking factory.

Chase, who was secretary of the Pinkerton board of trustees, urged Frost (almost secretly) to apply at once for a position at the academy. He explained that in the English program the woman teaching the sopho-mores had been forced to resign because of illness, and her place was being filled temporarily by a retired local minister. Frost's record had been shown to Chase by Merriam, and there was every reason for Frost to feel confident he could get the part-time position.

At the end of his evening with the Men's League, Frost walked back down the road to his farm, aware that "The Tuft of Flowers" had, indeed, served its purpose. He had not let himself realize how hungry he had grown for exactly the kind of attention the poem had earned from these staunch Congregationalists, and he had felt the honor when asked if a local paper might print the poem in its next issue. Having sold only five poems in twelve years, he was in no mood to care whether he would be paid or not, so long as "The Tuft of Flowers" appeared in print. Furthermore, part of his excitement at the end of this evening came from the possibility that he might soon be drawing a regular salary. During the ten years since his marriage, this was an experience he had never had.

When Frost visited the academy to make application for a teaching position, he was shown into the office of the principal. The Rev. George Washington Bingham, making it clear that he had been expecting his visitor, came to the point without wasting time. If Mr. Frost would start teaching two sections of an hour each, five days a week, during the remainder of the spring, it was probable a full-time position could be given him at the beginning of the fall term. Fine. As for salary, would it be all right to calculate it on two-sevenths of each day's normal seven-hour teaching load, at a full-time basis of, say, 1,000 or $1,100 a year? Yes, that would be all right. Very well: 1,000. (Chagrin—and the vision of money lost merely by failure to say that 1,100 would be fine!) Now, let's see; two-sevenths of $1,000 would come, roughly, to $285. All right? Yes.

With these arrangements, Frost began at Pinkerton Academy late in March of 1906, and he quickly sorted out his friends from his enemies. With scorn, his fellow English teacher, Arthur Warren Reynolds, a Harvard graduate, went out of his way to commiserate that Frost had been unable to spend even as much as two full years at Harvard—and that he was forced to teach without having a college degree.

Reynolds's hostility and apparent jealousy may have been heightened when *The Independent* carried in its issue for October 11, 1906, the poem entitled "The Trial by Existence." Principal Bingham read and admired the poem. The Rev. C. L. Merriam flatteringly discussed the poem with its author. The affable John Chase frankly said he cared less for poetry than for the excellent publicity given Pinkerton by the appearance of such a poem in a nationally distributed periodical.

All of this attention had a stimulating effect on Frost's writing, some of which he shared only with the community in Derry. After he had been reading Longfellow with his students in the classroom, he may have proposed that because February 27, 1907, was being celebrated throughout the nation as the centennial of the poet's birth, a chapel service be devoted to Longfellow. Plans were made, and Frost wrote a commemorative poem for the occasion. The poem was printed as a broadside, distributed to the students at the service, and was sung to a suitable tune of a familiar hymn.

Frost had shared an entirely different kind of poem with the larger community five days prior to the celebration of Longfellow's birthday. Once again invited to attend the annual banquet of the Men's League of the Central Congregational Church at Derry Village and to read a poem, once again he agreed to attend if Pastor Merriam would read for him. The poem was "The Lost Faith," and the subject matter would have made it more appropriate for a Memorial Day service. The theme was the poet's regret that the ideals for which the Union soldiers had fought so heroically during the Civil War had become so nearly forgotten.

"The Lost Faith" implied quite plainly that its author had relinquished at least some of those Copperhead sympathies taught him by his father.

Nevertheless, it also implied that Frost still preserved his early conviction that heroic combat and bloodshed are the highest measures of man's self-sacrifice for his ideals. In addition, Frost was continuing to write with an increase of religious fervor, now that his initial leanings, fostered by his mother, were being fortified by the Congregational ministers with and for whom he was teaching. There was no trace of the hypocritical in this fervor; and it never abated in him for long, even though there were intermittent spells when the pressures caused by his skepticism forced him to make statements that offended the orthodox, statements that were sometimes mistakenly interpreted as "proofs" Frost was an "atheist."

For the moment, while the Congregationalists among the Derry townspeople were becoming more favorably impressed with the new teacher at Pinkerton Academy, some of his students were not so easily persuaded to like him. A few mistook his early nervousness and gravity as proof that Mr. Frost was lacking in any sense of humor. Several complained he put too much stress on composition and on memorizing poetry. Others discounted his abilities as a teacher, passing the word that he was down on his luck, that he was merely a failed "hen-man." One of these went so far as to scrawl that epithet across the blackboard in his classroom one morning, before anyone else appeared.

Frost arrived early enough to have erased it, but he had reasons for leaving it. As he waited for the students to come, he sorted through his batch of corrected compositions. Whose handwriting matched the scrawl on the board? He found it, unmistakably. The students filed in, glanced at the board, and began to whisper. He pretended not to notice. But as soon as the bell rang and the hour of instruction had formally begun, almost unable to keep his wrath under control, he pointed an accusing finger at the culprit and said, "For writing that, get out of my class—and don't ever come back."

Before the end of the day there was no member of the school who had not heard the news. Frost was called into the office of the principal, who was duly sympathetic. But, of course, Bingham explained, it would be impossible to keep the boy from attending Frost's classes indefinitely; he would fail the course, and would have to leave Pinkerton. "Then, he will have to leave Pinkerton," said the hen-man.

More consultations were held. Opinions were sought from members of the board of trustees, and the boy was expelled. After that, the new teacher had no trouble with discipline; and, much to their surprise, the students very soon learned that their seemingly dour English teacher had a very fine sense of humor—at least until something made him cross.

His best students praised the relaxed manner in which he soon began to conduct his classes and his way of getting them started on compositions. Instead of asking them to write about subjects they had been studying, he told them to base their sketches or essays on their own experiences, on facts observed, on ideas all their own.

When he read their papers aloud, he convinced them that the most interesting ones were those based on closely observed facts "common in experience—uncommon in writing." He added another rule: "Don't write unless you have something to say. If you don't have it, go and get it." The best students realized that their teacher wanted them to have ideas of their own and to reach beyond their grasp. They could not always keep up with or follow him in all he said, but they recognized the freshness of his approach to originality, and they liked it.

They also liked his way of combining instruction in reading, elocution, and rhetoric. He insisted that their appreciation could be measured by the qualities of expression when they read aloud in class, rather than by their analytical comments. He set them examples by reading aloud poems and short stories and chapters of assigned novels. He made them understand how many different meanings were implicit in the word "dramatic"; and he taught them subtle forms of pace, volume, emphasis in conveying dramatic shadings when each took his turn at reading aloud. His goal, he said, was to increase the pleasure they derived from reading. Again and again he wrote on the blackboard, and asked them to remember, his favorite instruction for doing assignments: "To be read —to be enjoyed / Not studied—not skimmed."

But Frost did stir up trouble while coaching second-year students for participation in the interclass debates. The prospect of coaching the sophomore class aroused in him a fierce spirit of competition, when he discovered that the "worthy opponents," drawn from the senior class, would be coached by his enemy Arthur Warren Reynolds. Forcing his best sophomores to work overtime, Frost assured them they could triumph over the seniors. He required them to write out the full texts of their arguments and to submit them for his consideration. He revised and strengthened, until the arguments were more nearly his than theirs. The extra work required of him (and the tedious after-school practice sessions) seemed more exhausting than any work he had ever done on the farm; but when the debate was held, the sophomores were the winners.

The hen-man was satisfied. He had vindicated himself as a teacher, and he had avenged himself against the insinuative deprecations of Reynolds, in this first round of a continuous battle. But at the very moment of his triumph Frost was also aware that he was ill, largely as a result of nervous and physical strain. At the end of the two-week spring vacation, he was flat in bed. *The Derry News* for April 5, 1907, carried a brief reference: "The spring and summer term of Pinkerton academy opened on Tuesday with the usual number of students in attendance. All regretted that the teacher of English[,] Mr. Robert Lee Frost, is unable to be at his post. He has been very sick with pneumonia."

Robert Frost's bout with pneumonia during March and April was very nearly fatal. Before he could regain his health, it became apparent that Elinor (who was expecting another child in June) was being physically dragged down; and just as Frost was beginning to get his feet under him again, she became ill. It was his turn to care for her; and by the time she had recovered, he was down again.

Early in June of 1907 arrangements were made for Mrs. Frost to move to Derry Village, to stay with a practical nurse. It was there that Elinor gave birth to her fourth daughter, on June 18, 1907. Named Elinor Bettina, she died soon after she was born. Elinor took the loss with the despairing fatalism that had become habitual with her. Frost blamed himself for the child's death. He said he never should have let Elinor take care of him when he had been sick with pneumonia. His grief was entirely different from the grief he had felt when Elliott died, and yet, his deep sense of guilt was genuine.

Now there were two invalids at the Frost farm, and memories of his pleasant experience in the White Mountains, during the hay-fever season of the summer before, made him suggest a temporary escape. Suppose they took the children up to Bethlehem, New Hampshire, this year and stayed until the ragweed had finished the worst of its dusting, down in the valleys? They might even stay until near the time classes began at Pinkerton. This was the plan he had almost put into effect the previous summer.

He had gone to Bethlehem in August of 1906 without making any reservations. The hotels were already filled with summer visitors, including those hay-fever victims who claimed Bethlehem was the best of all retreats for his kind of ailment. Through luck or guidance, he had stepped into a drugstore to ask where he might find an inexpensive place to stay; and the druggist had immediately introduced him to a customer standing near, an Irishman named Michael Fitzgerald. Fitzgerald owned a small hotel some four miles outside Bethlehem, on the high part of the South Road to Franconia. His rooms were all taken, but Frost could have meals with his guests and rent a room in a nearby farmhouse owned by another Irishman, John Lynch.

So it had worked out, but he had grown so lonesome for his family that the Lynches had taken pity on him. They said that if Frost wanted to have his wife and children join him, a couple of extra rooms could be found for them in the farmhouse, and the Frosts could have use of the living room, as well as the kitchen. He had been ready to carry out the plan, when called home by illness. Why not carry it out now, in August and September of 1907, if the Lynches were still able to rent the rooms? They were; and before leaving Derry, Frost made arrangements with his reliable neighbor, Guay, for taking care of the hens and the cow; and the Lynches welcomed the strangers as though they were long-lost members of the family.

Six weeks high in the White Mountains was a glorious experience for all of the Frosts, and one memorable part of those summer weeks with the Lynches was the gathering of old and young on the porch of the farmhouse each evening for songs and storytelling. Frost entered into all the fun and nonsense with gusto, partly because he took so much pleasure in being the center of attention. But after the children had been sent to bed, he liked to draw out the Lynches, whose Irish accents and viewpoints gave special flavor to accounts of neighborhood events, past and present.

Mrs. Lynch blended scorn with sadness when she told the story of a local girl who trained as a nurse in Boston, married there, fell in love with one of her patients, and ran away from her Boston husband to live in hiding with her lover on a small farm not far down the road from the Lynches. Frost prompted the telling of that story when he asked Mrs. Lynch to explain an event that puzzled him.

He had taken Carol for an evening walk along the South Road. Returning in the twilight, they heard the approach of a horse and carriage, saw the carriage lamp on the dashboard of the approaching vehicle, and stepped off the narrow dirt road to let horse and carriage pass. Frost noticed the way the driver, a woman, had touched up the horse with the whip, to hurry him on. He had seen the carriage turn in at the very next house on that lonely road and heard a man and woman talking beside the carriage in the farmyard as he and Carol walked past. Then, the woman called to them, came forward in the darkness carrying a lantern, and asked what they were doing, prowling around her house at night. Frost explained that they weren't prowling. He was merely taking his son for an evening walk, and they were returning to the Lynch farm, where they were staying. The woman apologized, but Frost gathered from her tone of voice that there must have been reasons behind her suspicions. When he asked who the woman was, Mrs. Lynch told the story, and added that the woman seemed to live in mortal terror of being found—and possibly murdered—by the husband whom she had forsaken. To Frost, these were raw materials for poetry, and he later used them in his dramatic narrative "The Fear."

The Frosts lingered at the Lynch farm far into September—as late as they could. The air seemed to be medicine for Frost, and so charmed had he become by the vistas of rock-strewn fields, woods, valleys, and mountain ranges that he would have been willing to stay in that wilderness indefinitely, if he could have found a way to earn a living—

perhaps by sending his poems out from there to eager publishers. But the publishers weren't eager; and for want of any better way to make ends meet, he took his family back to Derry, to start teaching at Pinkerton again when the fall term of 1907 began.

For Frost, his happiness over memories of Bethlehem was inseparable from his intense cherishing and caring. It gave a new lift to his spirit, and he threw himself into his teaching that fall with energy and capacity greater than during his two previous terms. Bingham, almost ready to retire, had been so impressed with Frost's work in teaching literature, elocution, and rhetoric that he had invited him to reorganize the entire English program. The results were not immediately noticeable, and yet, within the next four years, Frost's methods of teaching attracted the attention of authorities outside the academy. When Bingham made known his wish to have the trustees look for a successor, the secretary of the board, John C. Chase, felt that Frost was the man for the position —and Frost seriously considered the possibility. Part of his eagerness in this regard was caused by his knowledge that Chase and others were also considering Arthur Warren Reynolds as a candidate. When consulted by Chase, Frost was content to make insinuations enough concerning Reynolds to be certain his enemy should not be given the position—and, then, was willing to admit that he himself could not take it, because his lack of a college degree would cause too much criticism and jealousy.

When additional funds were given the academy by the New Hampshire legislature in 1908–1909, because neighboring towns without high schools sent so many students to Pinkerton, it became common practice for inspectors to appear. In the spring of 1909 a stranger quietly walked into one of Frost's classes and took a seat in the back of the room. That same afternoon, the stranger appeared again and sat through another class. He was Henry Clinton Morrison, superintendent of public instruction for the state, and he was so impressed by all the innovations of classroom method used by Frost that he stayed after school for a long conversation. The upshot of Morrison's interest was that he asked Frost to give a talk on his methods of teaching English. A convention of New Hampshire teachers would be held in Exeter later in the spring, and Morrison felt that Frost could assist him—and the teachers—by explaining how he ran his classes at Pinkerton.

With some trepidation Frost accepted the request. On his way to Exeter by train, he made notes of what he wanted to say. He would build his talk around his notion of teaching students to *absorb* and *impress* ideas. This seemed to be the gist of his educational theory. He wanted to tell them books should be used in English classes so that students would be lonely forever afterward without books of their own, that students should be made so interested they could never again leave books alone.

There were various ways of catching their interest, and he would explain some of the ways he had discovered. As for the matter of expression, students should be taught the satisfaction and pride in conveying an idea so well, in either oral or written form, that anyone would remember how the idea had been conveyed and what it was.

By the time he reached Exeter, an hour before his scheduled talk, he found he was so frightened by the ordeal facing him that he doubted whether he would have the courage to stand on the platform and deliver his talk. After going and making sure of the room where he was to speak, he tried to walk off his fright. As a desperate way of getting his mind away from his worries, he put one pebble in each of his shoes, in the hope that the pain would be useful. It didn't work. Somehow he managed to go through with the talk, and it was well received. Morrison heard such good reports of it that he immediately scheduled other talks for Frost.

The gradual process of throwing more time and energy into the practice and theory of teaching led Frost to feel he should move his family off the farm and into more convenient quarters near the academy. By the summer of 1909, when the move was made, he had already given up any pretense of being a farmer. But Elinor, not socially inclined, liked the isolation of the farm and had resented the gradual intrusions and demands made on her husband's time by his duties as a teacher. For the sake of the children, primarily, their mother accepted, not without reluctance, the move of the family to the upper floor of a large house on Thornton Street in Derry Village.

As the hay-fever season approached, Frost delighted his family by proposing that they should all go with him on a camping expedition, far enough north in Vermont to escape—he hoped—any ill effects from ragweed pollen. They would buy tents, mattresses, and cooking equipment. They would find a site high above some lake, and the lake he had in mind was Willoughby. His interests were prompted by much he had learned about the region from Carl Burell; the dramatic arrangement of mountains and lowlands along the shores of Lake Willoughby made the region a paradise for botanists. The children were elated by the prospect, and the early part of the summer was largely devoted to making preparations.

After the equipment had been sent by express to the town of Westmore, at the northern end of the lake, Frost went up alone, hoping to get the tents pitched and in readiness before the rest of his family arrived. He was impressed by what he found. Viewed from the northern end of the lake, Willoughby stretched serenely for two or three miles among fields and woods to the south and, then, closed dramatically between the sheer cliffs of two mountains with biblical names sacred to Aaron and Moses: Hor and Pisgah. Frost knew at once where he would be botanizing.

As soon as the children made friends in the neighborhood and began to entertain themselves, he set out daily to the lower end of the lake. His findings on the cliffs gave him a new enthusiasm: ferns. Never before had he known or really cared that this flowerless plant had so many varieties and sizes and shapes. He found himself growing more and more fascinated.

Of all the casual acquaintances made by Frost that summer, among visiting botanists and year-round residents, only one of them touched him deeply enough to inspire a poem. In his repeated visits to the Conley farmhouse, to buy milk and eggs, he sometimes lingered to talk with the farmer's wife. Haggard and careworn from her daily rounds of cooking for her husband and his hired men, Mrs. Conley feared that she could not keep up the pace demanded of her. Frost was touched by her fears more than by her predicament. She admitted that insanity ran in her family, that her father's brother "wasn't right," and she herself had been "put away" for a short time. Recently, she had begun to fear that the same thing might happen again. Frost's pity found expression years later in the dramatic monologue "A Servant to Servants."

For the Frosts, camping at Willoughby was marred by a too-long stretch of rainy weather. It gave a good excuse for getting in under cover of roof and walls, renting a cottage (as soon as the near-end of summer made one available) on a ledge-covered point of land thrust farthest into the lake on the northwest side. Immediately, swimming became the special order of play. But it did not hinder Frost from developing a new hobby: looking at property to buy—which he continued to indulge throughout the rest of his life. The sense of affluence he had developed through the combined salary from Pinkerton and his annual check from the trust fund made him feel he could afford to have a summer cottage at Willoughby. And when he failed to find just the kind of cottage he wanted, he began to make inquiries about the possibility of buying a small farm that overlooked the lake. Nothing quite satisfied his ideal of what he should have.

The time came to get the children to Derry for the beginning of school, and the trip back may have given Frost time enough to reconsider his eagerness to purchase real estate on the shore of Lake Willoughby. But he had become convinced that summer ventures in the mountains of New Hampshire and Vermont were good for him and his poetry. He was determined that someday he would actually buy a house in the mountains and earn his living by sending down a steady flow of poems for publishers in Boston and New York.

Robert Frost's last two years at Pinkerton, beginning in the autumn of 1909 and ending in the spring of 1911, taught him something new about his own capacities. His private awareness of gradually increasing success in the classroom gave him one kind of confidence he needed. The visits made by Henry C. Morrison and the subsequent praise expressed through Morrison's request that Frost talk at teachers' conventions gave another. Previously there had been times when he had told himself that his inability to get ahead with anything he undertook must be traceable to some lack of animal magnetism in his own nature. He feared that a great many people who met him simply did not like him as a human being, hence their scornful way of noticing or ignoring him.

Perhaps he was never aware that since his boyhood days in Salem, when he had been thrown on the defensive, he had protected himself with a proud kind of arrogance. It was a way of trying to combat scorn with counterscorn; but it gave him an unpleasant manner. Some of his closest friends and relatives had long felt the hurt of this arrogance, which they could not combat. His sister, Jeanie, repeatedly finding fault with him for his treatment of their mother and herself, had too many problems of her own to be much help to him. Ernest Jewell, who had known him since high-school days and who had given him friendship and money during the early years at Derry, had become so deeply offended by Rob's failure to pay his debts that a coldness had developed between them. Carl Burell, who had the clumsy affection of a St. Bernard dog and the capacity of a martyr for generous forgiveness, may never have understood all the inconsistencies of Rob's responses to him.

Elinor had suffered most from Rob's furious, quick-tempered rages, his easily wounded sensitivities, his pride, his vengefulness. She seemed to find her best defense in silence. But she could at least understand, sympathize with, and pity the cumulative frustrations of his ambition to establish himself as a poet. She may even have been amazed that he had survived all the vicissitudes of disappointment and grief that had battered him from so many directions during their thirteen years of marriage. Better than anyone else, she must have seen that he refused to give up his own hopes, his own belief in himself. She may have been the one who felt the greatest sense of relief in observing the gradual increase of self-confidence that came to him through those years of teaching at Pinkerton. It was derived particularly from the satisfaction he took in being admired and looked up to by his best students.

Morrison's praise also took Frost backstage to share in the new plans for Pinkerton. In spite of John Chase's notion that Frost would make a good principal, Morrison had other ideas. The trustees wanted to reorganize the curriculum by introducing new programs in agriculture, domestic science, and stenography; and Morrison probably recommended the candidate who was accepted, Ernest L. Silver.

Two years younger than Frost and a graduate of Pinkerton and of Dartmouth College, Silver had acquired special teaching and administrative experience that seemed to make him excellently qualified to replace Bingham in the fall of 1909.

Frost did not become acquainted with Silver until just before the fall term started, but the two men established an immediate rapport. Among their many common interests were athletics; and it was not long before Frost and Silver made their appearance on the football field, behind the academy, to watch practice and try their own hand at passing the football. Occasionally, they even violated seasonal routine by throwing a baseball.

It was clear to the students that under the new regime the tone and atmosphere of Pinkerton Academy were undergoing pleasant changes. Relations between students and teachers and the new principal became much more informal and practical. And the success with which Frost had established so many innovations for the teaching of English litera-ture and composition gave him the courage to extend his own program. At his request the academy set aside money for prizes to be offered each semester to those who wrote outstanding compositions, to be read aloud before the entire student body. Also, he was permitted to stimulate participation in the debate program. (The consistency with which his class won debates led to repeated charges that he prepared much of the material and offered many of the best arguments. There was some truth in the accusation.)

In the rearrangement of duties at Pinkerton it was natural that the faculty member in charge of the program in English literature, composi-tion, elocution should be asked to take over supervision of the student literary paper, *The Pinkerton Critic,* and of dramatic productions. As former editor of the *Bulletin* at Lawrence High School, where there had been no faculty guidance, Frost informed the editorial staff of the *Critic* that theirs was the task of selecting copy for publication, that they had to assume the obligations and responsibilities of their office. But he did meet regularly with the staff to discuss policy, and he was willing to be consulted whenever problems arose. He went even further than that and permitted the *Critic* to publish two of his own poems. One, originally written as a love poem for Elinor, reflected the perennial mood of regret when autumn came to the Derry farm, and it was entitled "A Late Walk."

Frost's warm friendship with the editorial board of the *Critic,* and his estimate of their capabilities, led him to propose that they should present a series of five plays, representing dramatic art over four centuries, plays he would adapt and compress, so that the task of learning lines would not be too burdensome. The suggestion was accepted, and he set to work.

He had often explained to his pupils the difference between "speaking passages" and "rhetorical passages." His own gradually developing theory of poetry-at-its-best was based on his conviction that "talk" was most dramatic and poetic when the sentences were lean and sharp with the give-and-take of conversation, wherein the thread of thought and action ran quickly in words and did not become lost in a maze of adjectives and metaphors. His task as editor of these plays was to strip them down to essentials. It was a time-consuming labor of love, and yet, he found it an exercise that convinced him his basic theory of poetry was correct.

His undertaking was ambitious, and the requirements he placed on the students were exacting, because some of the students played more than one part. They all worked hard, and the rehearsals were carried out secretly, during hours that seemed to be devoted to meetings of the editorial board of the *Critic*. A few members of the faculty were taken into confidence, together with Principal Silver, for practical reasons. No announcement was made until within a week of the time when *Doctor Faustus* was scheduled for production. Then, Frost prepared a release, which appeared in the local papers:

"Beginning Thursday, May 26, and continuing at intervals of a week, the editorial board of the Pinkerton Critic will give in Academy Hall a series of noted plays illustrating four periods of English dramatic literature, Marlowe's Faustus of the sixteenth century, Milton's Comus of the seventeenth, Sheridan's Rivals of the eighteenth, and Yeats' Land of Heart's Desire and Cathleen ni Hoolihan of the latter nineteenth. The set, five in all (two of which will be given the same evening as being by the same author) will constitute a good short course in literature, intended to cultivate in school a taste for the better written sort of plays. But while all are literary and the object in staging them is largely educational, it must not be inferred that they have not been selected without regard to the entertainment they are likely to afford. All belong to the class of good acting drama as distinguished from the kind that is only meant to be read. All were written for the stage and have won and held a place on the stage. . . ."

Students and townspeople were so impressed by the presentation of these plays, by the *Critic* staff, that they may have recognized Frost's part as representing the zenith of his many contributions to the new level of teaching at Pinkerton. Planning to continue the process the following year, by starting a series of productions with Ben Jonson's *The Silent Woman*, he wrote out a revised version of this play, omitting all except the best scenes and lines. But on the day he brought his manuscript copy to the academy to request it be typed, he learned that one of the other teachers was working against him. She had announced that the play he had chosen was too "heavy" for the students and that she was going to coach a group who would produce a lighter piece of dramatic entertainment, *The Village School*. In an outburst, he then and there tore up his abbreviation of *The Silent Woman,* threw it in the nearest wastepaper basket, and said this ended his attempt to supervise dramatic productions.

Frost had become intimately acquainted with many members of the Class of 1910, and it is probable he attended the graduation exercises for the thirteen girls and four boys. His favorite student, John T. Bartlett, served as marshal, and Frost had already told Bartlett that he could give his teacher vicarious satisfaction if he continued the kind of prose writing he had published in the *Critic,* and went on to make a name for himself in literature. Bartlett planned to enter Middlebury College in the fall of 1910, and Frost was pleased with that decision.

A few months later, Frost had scarcely returned, with his family, from another hay-fever season in Bethlehem, to start teaching again at Pinkerton, when he learned that Bartlett had walked out of Middlebury, in much the same way that he had walked out of Dartmouth, simply because he couldn't take it. He was back home in Raymond, only two townships away from Derry, and Frost immediately expressed his sympathy by walking over to call on him. Additional similarity between their lives was revealed when it became known that part of Bartlett's trouble was an obscure pulmonary illness, which might be tuberculosis. For a time he remained on the family farm in Raymond, occasionally visiting Frost in Derry during the school year 1910–1911.

During the summer of 1911, Ernest Silver accepted an invitation to become principal of the New Hampshire State Normal School in Plymouth, and he wanted Frost to go with him, as one of his teachers. Back of both moves was Henry C. Morrison. There was no opening in the field of English literature, but Morrison insisted that Frost's value to the normal school would not be determined by the titles of his courses. Let him teach anything, so long as he was on the staff.

Frost was extremely reluctant to accept the Plymouth offer on any terms. From the time he had begun to gain confidence through his teaching at Pinkerton, he had been writing more and more poetry. To his surprise, he found that the harder he worked, the greater the stimulus to his writing. His ideal was to continue as a teacher until the time when, by the terms of his grandfather's will, he could legally sell the farm (which he had been renting since the move to Derry Village), then use the proceeds for taking at least one year of leave from teaching and get on with his writing. He also counted on the fact that, starting in July of 1912, the payment from the trust fund set up by his grandfather would be increased. His present salary at Pinkerton was $1,000; the promised salary at Plymouth for part-time teaching was also $1,000. If he did not teach at all, the $800 annuity would be only $200 less than the salary now earned at the expense of much nervous and physical energy. After considerable thought and long discussions with his wife, he informed Silver and Morrison that he would accept the Plymouth offer, with the understanding that he might possibly resign at the end of one year.

The sale of the Derry farm caused some difficulty. When the farm had been mortgaged for $750 on March 24, 1906, the terms of the mortgage required annual repayments, at interest semiannually of six percent, with the unpaid balance due on March 24, 1911. This mortgage had not been approved by the trustee of his grandfather's estate. (The farm did not technically become Frost's property until July 1911.) With his usual carelessness about money matters, Frost had gone ahead, but he had failed to make his payments when due. In August of 1911, when he accepted the Plymouth offer, he still owed an overdue amount on the mortgage. To pay it, he arranged another mortgage for $1,200, out of which he realized (after the payment and other expenses) $627.45.

The farm had been so badly neglected, during the five years that followed the first mortgage, that he was apparently unable to find a buyer who would pay anything like the original price. He finally sold, in November 1911, through a transference of the mortgage to a Boston real-estate agent. Delighted to get rid of the farm, Frost could not fail to appreciate that he had mixed memories of what it had meant to him. In one sense, that farm represented the years of his most complete abasement and humiliation, the years when he had been forced to strip his life down to the verge of nothingness and to rebuild. In another sense, the experiences on the farm had provided him with the raw materials for important rebuilding—spiritual, emotional, psychological, poetical. He could already tell that the farm, when viewed from a greater distance in time and space, would acquire for him a romantic luster unequaled by anything else in his life so far.

13

PLYMOUTH AND THE EVE OF DEPARTURE

(1911–1912)

SPECIAL IMPULSES were given to the life of Robert Frost during the single year he and his family spent in Plymouth, New Hampshire. He devoted part of the year to preparations for the boldly venturesome leap he was about to make. But his most significant actions were dramatized on the stage of his inner consciousness. He had been hired to teach a course in psychology and another course in the history of education. The newness of the task stimulated him to do some intensive reading; and here, once more, his reading proved far more important to him than to his pupils.

The offer that led him to move northward, into the foothills of the White Mountains, brought him into contact with an educational-industrial community no larger than the three villages in Derry, and yet, distinctly different. Plymouth, a county seat, was snugly perched on a hillside overlooking a wide intervale. The green meadows, ironed flat by spring freshets of the Pemigewasset River, were flanked by forest-covered hills. The natives of Plymouth were proud of its history, which dated from a skirmish between colonists and Indians prior to the Revolution. Artists and literary figures had been attracted to the town. Hawthorne had visited it more than once, and he had died there.

At the state normal school (the enrollment was a little more than one hundred—all girls), Frost knew that his position as an educator had been advanced considerably, but the primary advantage he gained was the reinforcement given his new sense of confidence. As he made his rounds at Plymouth during the early autumn days of 1911, he had the gait and the carriage of a man going somewhere. This very touchy man of moods had brought his arrogance and grouchiness under at least temporary control. In offhand conversations, inside and outside the classroom, his remarks were usually cheerful, witty, mischievous, playful. Even his speech was different.

His habit of careful pronunciation, encouraged by his well-educated father and mother, had been well developed before he moved East, and the sensitivity of his ear to differences between Western and Eastern ways of talking had made him resent the Yankee vernacular, long after his move from California. But during the Derry years he became fascinated by witty, picturesque, backcountry ways of implying meaning through sly inflections and modulations of voice, and Frost had gradually modified his way of talking. He deliberately imitated the manner in which his neighbors unconsciously slurred words, dropped endings, and clipped their sentences. By the time he reached Plymouth, glad to be rid of the farm, he was still perfecting the art of talking like a farmer.

When he met his first class at the normal school, Frost found that the janitor had already placed on the desk a stack of textbooks for distribution to the students, Monroe's *History of Education*. As soon as the girls had taken their seats, Frost said he would begin by giving the first assignment. He wanted a few volunteers who would carry these dog-eared textbooks right back down to the basement and leave them in the stockroom. Monroe would not be used in the course this year. Instead, their instructor preferred that the girls become acquainted with a few original works that contained some better approaches to the history of education. They would start by reading Pestalozzi's *How Gertrude Teaches Her Children*. After that, they would read and discuss Rousseau's *Emile*. And before the course was through, they would even read some selected passages on education in Plato's *Republic*. He hoped the girls would like these books well enough to buy copies of them for their own shelves, to reread at leisure after they had begun their careers as teachers.

Carrying his nonconformist methods over to his course in psychology, Frost never lectured. Informally, he discussed with his students the assignments he made in two books by his beloved William James: *Talks to Teachers on Psychology* and the one-volume text he himself had studied at Harvard, *Psychology* (the "Briefer Course"). In these discussions, the assignments served as a springboard for their instructor's observations, drawn from his own classroom experiences, concerning ways to stimulate interest, attention, memory, and valid associations of ideas.

Early in the course he read an amusing story by Mark Twain, called "The Celebrated Jumping Frog of Calaveras County." For the girls this was a delightful approach to the psychology of teaching—though it seemed to have no bearing on the subject. But when their instructor finished reading, he closed the book and drew from the story a moral, half in jest, half seriously: Some teachers always load their students so full of facts, that the students can't jump; other teachers know better, and they tickle the students into having imaginative ideas of their own, just by saying, in effect, "Flies, Dan'l."

On one occasion, when Frost learned that nobody in the history-of-education class had read Mark Twain's *A Connecticut Yankee in King Arthur's Court,* he said that such a weakness should be corrected, and for the next several days he read aloud to them from the book.

The girls considered Frost "quite a character" and even suspected he liked to get time for reading to himself, in class, by handing out blue books in which he asked them to write essays on any subject they found interesting while they were studying their latest assignment. The essays were handed in, but seldom returned.

The new principal of Plymouth Normal School and Frost, back at Pinkerton, had worked and played so congenially that Silver had made an unusual offer to provide special living arrangements for the Frost family at Plymouth. A large cottage served as the residence for the principal, but Silver's wife was an invalid, living temporarily with her parents in Portsmouth. Because he was planning to live alone, Silver offered to share his furnished cottage, rent free, with the Frost family. Silver had his own rooms and took his meals with the Frosts, but he soon learned Mrs. Frost, extremely casual about housework, was completely indifferent to serving meals at regular hours. Whenever she made a special effort there might be an unusual supper—with a huge roast of beef, and not much else except tea and bread.

Silver found Mrs. Frost's informalities as cook and housekeeper particularly embarrassing on the few occasions when he tried to entertain visiting dignitaries. But when he made even the most guarded protest to Frost, the criticism aroused furious resentment. Once, Silver indiscreetly reported to Frost that one of the visitors had said Mrs. Frost seemed lacking in personality. Enraged, Frost lectured Silver on the fact that what anyone else did or didn't find to like about Mrs. Frost was entirely beside the point: "She's *mine!*"

Characteristically, Frost soon convinced himself that Silver was an enemy. He reinforced his bitterness by imagining that Silver had tried to have him discharged during the Pinkerton days, that Silver had been forced by Morrison to bring Frost to Plymouth—even to take the Frosts into his house. He began to watch for ways of getting revenge, while Silver continued his attempts to maintain harmony in their relationship.

In spite of these awkward tensions, the Frosts liked their new surroundings. All the children were now of school age and could go to the Plymouth Normal School, which provided complete instruction for a limited number of children in the town. The campus of the school gave ample romping ground for Lesley, Carol, Irma, and Marjorie—and offered the older children a chance to learn tennis.

For tennis competition more skillful than his children could offer, Frost began playing Sidney Cox, twenty-two-year-old Plymouth High School teacher. During their initial conversation, Frost had teased Cox enough to anger the young man. When they met on the street, soon afterward, Cox avoided speaking to Frost. As though in retaliation for Frost's teasing, Cox went out of his way to ask their mutual friend Silver whether alcohol was the cause of Frost's having made so little progress in life. Silver, amused, reported the question to Frost, who was indignant. Retrospectively, Frost said of his way of dealing with Cox: ". . . his seriousness piqued the mischief in me and I set myself to take him. He came round all right, but it wasn't the last time he had to make allowances for me."

Cox was so flattered by the continuous attentions paid him by Frost that he very soon came under the spell, and grew to be a worshiper. The two men walked the hills, back roads, and intervales around Plymouth; they played tennis; they devoted many evenings to long conversations in the parlor of the principal's cottage. Particularly memorable to Cox were evenings when Frost read aloud such newly discovered favorites as Synge's *Playboy of the Western World* and Shaw's *Arms and the Man.*

During these readings, Cox was unconsciously witnessing an important phase in the self-education of Robert Frost. From the time Frost had begun to read Yeats in Derry and to follow accounts of the Abbey Players, the intensity of his response was determined in large part by his finding an articulation of esthetic theories he himself had been trying to formulate (and practice). This was corroboration of his private convictions—incentive to continue in the direction he had already marked out for himself.

In one of his walks with Sidney Cox he hinted at the subject uppermost in his mind, by saying there are only three grades of tasks. The most servile and the one that demands least from the worker is the assigned task, done under supervision. Freer and more exacting is the task assigned by another, left to be carried out at the discretion of the worker. But the one that takes most character is the self-assigned task, carried out only at the instant urgency of the worker's own desire.

The artist, he had long realized, has to make heavy demands on himself. He has to draw his own strength and courage from his inner resources. As a result, the artist has to be selfish. If he works under supervision, for others, he spends for them the energy he needs for his own work. His creative originality has to assert itself independently, apart from any other compulsions. It can be curbed, sacrificed, subordinated to the wishes and needs of others; but to the extent that it is thus used, it is diverted from its proper goal. Frost had been taught by his mother that self-giving and self-sacrifice are the noblest and most heroic forms of human effort. He had honored that belief throughout his boyhood, and he still wanted to honor it. But his own problem, now, was to justify artistic selfishness without minimizing heroic self-giving.

During one of his last talks at a teachers' convention, he had taken pleasure in shocking the audience by saying that the first concern of the teacher has to be with self, the responsibility to save his or her own soul. The second responsibility of the teacher of literature is to the art of the author of the poem or story or novel under discussion. Finally comes the responsibility to the student. These were the kinds of provocations he liked to flaunt, knowing that some of his listeners would not understand them.

Back in Derry he had written a poem about a problem not unrelated. The inspiration had been provided by the first tramp who stopped at his farmhouse and asked if he could sleep in the barn overnight. It was late in the fall, the night was cold, and the tramp looked as though he might set fire to the barn if the answer was no. With mixed feelings of fear and pity, Frost had let this tramp sleep on a bed of rugs and blankets in the kitchen, beside the stove. He gave the man food that night and breakfast in the morning. After the stranger was gone, Frost puzzled over his own inner turmoil. All men are created equally free to seek their own rights in their own way, but how does one draw the line between the rights of the property owner and the rights of the tramp to make claim on the sympathy (or fear) of the property owner?

For artistic purposes, Frost sharpened the problem by changing the facts, just a little, to make them more dramatic and ironic. The poem became a ballad (with Yeatsian echoes) entitled "Love and a Question." The question of individual rights involving the claims of "the poor of God" continued to bother him. In his own case he saw the question as inseparably related to the selfish preoccupation of the artist who hoards his energies to do his own work well, in contrast to the preoccupations of the altruist who spends his energies to do good. And he gradually came to admit that his artistic prejudices were helping to shape his social views. His primary sympathies for individualism were against any concept of the welfare state.

A few days after Christmas 1911, Frost went by train to New York City. In his suitcase was a newly published translation of a work by the French philosopher Henri Bergson, *Creative Evolution*. By the time he reached Newark, New Jersey, to spend a night with William Hayes Ward and his sister, Frost was eager to share his excitement over this new discovery. He knew that the Wards were devout Congregationalists, and yet, he probably felt he was on safe ground when he assured them that Bergson had found splendid poetic images for endowing with spiritual meanings the scientific theories of the evolutionists. Frost explained Bergson's insistence that the life force cannot be accounted for in material terms, that the vital spirit is a dynamic and creative force that struggles to achieve richness and complexity through matter and beyond matter. Frost particularly liked Bergson's gathering metaphors, and liked Bergson's claim that the instinctive and intuitive consciousness of the creative individual—the poet, the saint, the prophet—is always helping to place man in the right relationship to the Source, always trying to make the properly creative and spiritual responses—through expressions of spiritual change, growth, freedom—to liberate the soul of man from the enslavements of matter.

William Hayes Ward listened silently to the enthusiastic praise given Bergson by his guest. When he had the opportunity, however, Ward said he himself had already taken occasion to read some of *Creative Evolution* and that he had found it to be a thoroughly atheistic tract. Oh, no, Frost protested; Bergson was a deeply religious man. Impossible, said Ward —and he changed the subject.

On the return trip to Plymouth, Frost continued reading *Creative Evolution,* without realizing that he was planting in his memory images and ideas that would later serve as raw materials for his own metaphors. Bergson's dualistic viewpoint helped to corroborate and articulate some half-formed notions congenial to Frost, and he was delighted.

From his high-school days, Frost had never been so heretical as he liked to think; but by the time he reached Plymouth, brimming with more health, confidence, self-reliance, courage than he had ever possessed before, he was again intent on asserting his originality through various skeptical disagreements with orthodox Christian belief. His renewed pride in viewing himself as a nonconformist had made him ripe for the discovery of Bergson's very subjective and individualistic and romantic poetry. It had also made him ripe for the discovery that he might further strengthen his position as heretic and skeptic if he should read (or perhaps reread) a book he had been in no mood to digest sympathetically when it made its first appearance in 1907, *Pragmatism* by William James.

Pragmatism begins in a way that has a direct bearing on Frost's interests at this time. After quoting G. K. Chesterton, James comments: ". . . I know that you . . . have a philosophy, each and all of you, and that the most interesting and important thing about you is the way in which it determines the perspective in your several worlds." And a primary goal of James was at one with Bergson's. Each wanted to uphold metaphysical idealism, not from a Christian viewpoint and not from a scientific viewpoint, but rather, from a subjective and personal viewpoint, which might claim to be founded on a practical and "utilitarian" observation of the facts.

There may have been another reason *Pragmatism* appealed to Frost after he had reached Plymouth. His new confidence, which had increased his pleasure in displaying bold and skeptical views, had also, paradoxically, revitalized his religious beliefs. For years he had been trying to construct a way of belief that would provide assurance that God was in His heaven and all was right with Frost's part of the world. At the same time, like James, he wanted his way of belief to be so heretical and skeptical that he could stand in a place apart, from which he could mock the "abstract" misuses (as he saw them) of the intellect by logical philosophers, by materialist scientists, and by dogmatic Christian system-builders. Earlier, Frost had found that the rebellious idealism of Shelley provided a basis for such a posture. Now, the metaphors and insights of Bergson and James helped him to build a superstructure on that Shelleyan foundation.

Frost wanted to scoff at a narrow-minded and literal God-concept that left no room for the poetry of Bergson's insights. In *Pragmatism,* James came to Frost's aid. The James view of the properly changing and growing human response to what is true was very attractive to Frost. So was James's definition: "The true is the name of whatever proves itself to be good in the way of belief, and good, too, for definite, assignable reasons."

This beautifully flexible definition of "the true" could be made to work just as well for a mystic as for a pragmatist; and, like James, Frost wanted to be both at once. Furthermore, it pleased Frost to find James wittily mocked the old-fashioned claim that God had designed every minute physical detail in nature for a special end. And James, having disposed of what he refers to as the "abstract" or "rationalistic" principle of "design," concludes: " 'Design' . . . becomes, if our faith concretes it into something theistic, a term of *promise.* Returning with it into experience, we gain a more confiding outlook on the future. . . . This vague confidence in the future is the sole pragmatic meaning at present discernible in the terms design and designer. . . ."

Such a neat cleavage between the "abstract" and the "concrete" meaning for the concepts of designer and design, Frost—immediately concerned with gathering metaphors with which to support his own beliefs—seems to have admired. After his return from New York, still smarting under Ward's dogmatic insistence that Bergson was an atheist, Frost sent, in his letter of thanks to Susan Hayes Ward, a sonnet later revised for publication as "Design." William Hayes Ward, reading the first draft of this poem, might have thought he found in it a confirmation of his fear that Robert Frost had come powerfully under the influence of "atheistical" writers and had, thus, become an atheist himself. But he would have been incorrect.

Frost, habitually the prey to dark moods, so desperately needed the consolation of positive religious belief that he was never long without it. Although he could briefly and intermittently entertain the notion that the Designer might be evil, he preferred to manipulate the notion in a detached way, to tease and mock those whose religious beliefs seemed to him to be sentimental. Even in teasing, however, he still very firmly agreed with James and Bergson that all the important purposes of the Designer are benevolent.

These literary gestures that Frost made while at Plymouth represented one kind of breakaway. They were closely related to another, which he had been planning since the day he sold his farm. He was convinced that if ever he was to assert himself artistically with success, he must find the time and place to be completely selfish. Financially, he had gained advantage merely through the passage of years. By the terms of his grandfather's will, the amount of the annuity to be paid him in July of 1912 would be increased to $800. If he were careful, he could live on that amount. But where should he go?

John Bartlett came into the considerations of where. He announced he was leaving for Vancouver Island, British Columbia. Frost confided that such a romantic hideaway sounded so attractive the Frost family might join him there. The Frosts and Bartlett talked at length about Vancouver. But while the family continued their discussions, Frost began to find reasons for feeling that perhaps he should stay at home.

There were many signs in literary circles that a new day had arrived for poetry in the United States, and one of the signs was that Frost began to have more success in selling poems to magazines. He had been discouraged, briefly, by a letter of rejection by Ellery Sedgwick, editor of *The Atlantic Monthly.* (In returning six poems—including "Reluctance" —Sedgwick wrote, in part, "We are sorry that we have no place in *The Atlantic Monthly* for your vigorous verse." Frost wondered whether the word "vigorous" was intended as criticism. Was his verse too vigorous or not vigorous enough for the *Atlantic?*) But while he was still in the process of resenting what Sedgwick had written, he received a letter from Thomas Bird Mosher, offering to buy the poem "Reluctance" for use in *Amphora,* one of Mosher's publications. Frost knew that for more than ten years Mosher had shown a taste for fine printing, as reflected in his many pocket-sized editions; that Mosher also published a monthly anthology, *The Bibelot,* each issue containing short pieces of prose and poetry, usually reprints. His answer to Mosher was filled with overtones of the excitement caused by the turn of events he was experiencing —and planning:

"I was just saying of my poetry that it didnt seem to make head as fast as I could wish with the public, when the letter came in which you said almost the identical thing of your Bibelot. But you could add of your own motion that you were getting, you supposed, all that was coming to you. Not to be outdone by you in philosophy (which is my subject of instruction) I made myself say it after you for a discipline: I suppose I am getting all that is coming to me. (These are harder words for me to pronounce than they ever could be for you—for reasons.) And then see how soon I had my reward. The very next day what should my poetry bring me but a check for twenty-five dollars, which is more than it ever brought before at one time. Some part of this belongs to you in simple poetic justice. Five dollars, say. You wouldn't tempt me to spend forty dollars on the Bibelot or anything else if you knew the ambitious schemes I have at heart, imposing habits of the strictest economy for the next ten years. But I can, and herewith do, send five dollars for books; and without impropriety, I trust, to satisfy my sense of the fitness of things, I copy on the inside of this sheet the poem by which I earned it, glad of the chance to show poem of mine to one whose life is so conspicuously devoted to the cause of poetry."

Mosher had apparently given Frost the right to make a double sale of "Reluctance," by offering it to periodicals for use prior to Mosher's publication of it. In less than a month Frost wrote again, to say he had sold "Reluctance" to *The Youth's Companion* and that he had sold another poem to *The Forum*. A third poem was sold to the *Companion* a little later. But none of these favorable signs deterred the Frosts from continuing their plans for going abroad. Somewhat romantically, Elinor urged that they should go to England and "live under thatch." Frost, still inclined to join forces with John Bartlett, suggested they toss a coin: England or Vancouver. The coin chose England.

Frost broke the news to Silver, who seemed incredulous and gave reasons against such a ridiculous course. Frost was adamant, and his pleasure in rejecting all of Silver's well-intentioned advice amounted to exactly the kind of revenge he had been wanting, to even the score with this man who, he imagined, had been his enemy from the start.

Late in the summer of 1912 he took passage on a steamer bound for Glasgow, the *Parisian*; and the family mounted the gangplank, eager for adventure.

14

IN ENGLAND—
A BOY'S WILL

(1912–1913)

NOT LONG after the Frosts were settled in England, Mrs. Frost wrote to Mrs. Lynch, partly to explain why she and her family had not spent the hay-fever season of 1912 in Bethlehem, New Hampshire. She began:

"I know you have wondered many times what has become of the Frost family, and I am sure you will be very, very much surprised to learn that we are way across the ocean, in England.

"You see, last summer we spent several weeks trying our very best to decide where we wanted to go, and gradually we came to feel that it would be pleasant to travel about the world a little. And finally we decided to come to England and find a little home in one of the suburbs of London, and two weeks from the day of our decision, we were on our way out of Boston Harbor. We stored our furniture, and brought only bedclothes, two floor rugs, books and some pictures. We sailed from Boston to Glasgow, and enjoyed the ocean trip on the whole, though Mr. Frost, Lesley and I were quite seasick for a few days. The younger children escaped with only a few hours discomfort. . . . We landed at Glasgow in the morning, and travelled all day across Scotland and England, arriving at London about seven oclock. From the station, we telephoned for rooms at the Premier Hotel, and after securing them, drove in a cab to the hotel, feeling greatly excited, you may imagine, at being all alone, without a single friend, in the biggest city in the world. We stayed in the hotel a week, while Mr. Frost was busy looking for a house in the towns about. I took the children about the city as much as I was able during the day, and nearly every evening Mr. Frost and I went to the theatre. London was splendid. The absence of elevated railways and trolley cars make it a much more beautiful city than New York. . . ."

An obvious lift had been given to Mrs. Frost's perennially subdued outlook on life by all these events, and her delight in the bold venture was shared by her entire family.

The search for a little cottage in the suburbs caused some difficulty. Although Frost had no idea how to tackle the problem, he had read in the English newspaper *T. P.'s Weekly* a "highways and byways" column that clearly implied the author of it was well informed concerning the rural areas in the vicinity of London. Taking the liberty of calling at the office of *T. P.'s Weekly,* Frost found that the columnist was a genial ex-policeman eager to have someone draw on his knowledge. Appointing himself as guide, he showed Frost a few unsatisfactory houses and, finally, took him twenty-one miles north of London to Beaconsfield. No thatch-covered cottage turned up, but the last house on the right-hand curve of Reynolds Road was for rent, and Frost was pleased with it. Locally known as The Bungalow, it was an attractive little five-room, vine-covered stucco house with "a large grassy space in front, and a pretty garden behind, with pear trees, strawberry beds and lots of flowers" (as Mrs. Frost described it in her letter to Mrs. Lynch).

In the Beaconsfield setting, when all the excitement of new surroundings had lessened, Frost was able to get into the mood for serious writing, and he began the first chapter of a novel. He progressed only far enough to feel that his beginning might better be reshaped into a play or a poem; and, disliking the novel, he found himself writing lyrics, some of them based on his new observations and insights. The lyric pleasure of his response to England was very soon counterbalanced, however, by Frost's growing awareness that he missed what he had left behind in New Hampshire.

Alone one night, he sorted through the sheaf of manuscripts he had brought with him, to see if he had enough to make up a small volume. Never before had he found the courage to begin preparing a manuscript for submission to a publisher, and even now, he was not sure he was doing more than playing a game. He spread the pages out across the floor in the lamplight, occasionally crumpling up a sheet and tossing it into the fireplace.

His first thought was that he could find no unifying thematic element. The many different moods in the lyrics he had written during a period of twenty years were obviously inconsistent and self-contradictory. But he could shape a group into a spiral of moods, and such a pattern might be reinforced if he made his responses to the changing seasons of fall and winter and spring and summer reflect different phases of his own spiritual growth.

From his new position of detachment he could look back with enough perspective to see how his early lyrics represented his having been scared away from life—his having been scared almost completely out of life, through suicidal temptations—and his having gradually found thought-felt justification for returning to assert so many different kinds of love and cherishing. In a sense his affirmative poems were all love poems, and perhaps the best pattern he could express through the arrangement of them might be a motion out of self-love and into his love for others.

His reticence would not permit him to make such an arrangement too self-revealing. Nevertheless, he became more and more attracted by the possibility that the grouped lyrics might express a figurative truth through metaphysical fiction. His book would represent his achievements up to the age of thirty-eight—and a selection from them could suggest the "long, long thoughts" of a youth who had struggled to find his own direction. (Longfellow's phrase came to mind as justification for inconsistencies; the fluctuating moods of a boy's will are as unpredictable and varied as the moods of the wind, which blows wherever it cares to blow.)

Having made a start at the game by spreading out his manuscripts on the floor, he gradually worked at his ordering, until he achieved a threefold structural pattern that did have the personal significance of spiritual and psychological growth. In this arrangement, part one began with a dramatic and symbolic act of complete withdrawal, but it ended with a special kind of return. Part two was built out of lyrics that carried forward the theme of return, by representing various poetic expressions of affirmation. Part three was made up of a few lyrics that viewed wistfully, even passionately, those withdrawals that were inevitable— such as the end of a life or a love or a season.

In all three structural parts, seasonal elements were deliberately invoked to add a special dimension. Part one began with a late-summer poem and moved quickly into fall and on through winter into spring. Part two built a cluster of meditative lyrics around the summer poem "The Tuft of Flowers," which provided the central affirmation of the entire volume: " 'Men work together,' I told him from the heart, / 'Whether they work together or apart.' " The seasonal cycle was continued in part three, so that the poems carried on through summer, again, to fall—ending with "Reluctance."

Finally, he strengthened the continuity of his arrangement, by giving a brief gloss or note under each title as it occurred in the table of contents (with only two exceptions). Frost felt that the unifying effect of these little commentaries did help him to derive special overtones of relevance —and a gathering metaphor—from the title he borrowed out of the familiar refrain in Longfellow's "My Lost Youth": "A boy's will is the wind's will, / And the thoughts of youth are long, long thoughts." He was not entirely satisfied with his attempt at unification through notes, and he later dropped them. His immediate consolation was that the notes and the ingenious pattern in his arrangement did endow the almost-too-personal lyrics with some degree of detachment.

As soon as the manuscript of *A Boy's Will* was completed, he could think of only one way to search for a publisher: seek advice from the one who had helped him find a house. Taking the manuscript with him, he went down to London to lay his problem before the retired policeman. He was told that Elkin Matthews published many books of poems for a price. Politely, Frost tried to explain he was not seeking that kind of publication. Very well, then, the policeman-columnist said, the firm of David Nutt also handled a certain amount of poetry.

Frost found the office of David Nutt and Company at 6 Bloomsbury Street. The best he could do was to make an appointment, and the formality of this procedure seemed cold enough to discourage him. Even on his return he found little reason to expect he had made any significant progress. The interview was conducted by a sad little woman dressed in black, who spoke with a French accent. (Frost was not aware David Nutt had died, that the publishing business had been carried on by Alfred Nutt, now also dead, and that this woman was the widow of Alfred Nutt.) With some misgiving he left the manuscript of *A Boy's Will,* accepting her assurance that she would let him know the decision in a few days. She kept her word, in a letter dated October 26, 1912:

"I have looked through your MS and I am personally interested in the treatment of you[r] theme. I am therefore disposed to bring out your poems if the proposal I can put before you and which would be on the principle of a royalty payment will suit you. I cannot put a dry and cut proposal before you as yet, as I wish to think a little about the most suitable form to give to the book but I hope to be in a position to do so very soon."

Suddenly, with the arrival of this brief note, so many hopes deferred seemed realized—or, at least, realizable. On his next visit to London, Frost called again on Mrs. Nutt, to discuss terms, and was not too greatly troubled to have her say that when the contract was drawn up it would contain a clause that would let the firm of David Nutt have the first right to publish his next four books of verse or prose. A few days later, further encouragement was given him when he received a letter from Thomas Mosher, who said he would like to publish a book of Frost's poems. Unable to avoid boasting, Frost answered on November 19, 1912:

". . . The Dea knows I should like nothing better than to see my first book, 'A Boy's Will', in your Lyric Garland Series. It even crossed my mind to submit it to you. But under the circumstances I couldn't, lest you should think I was going to come on you as the poor old man comes on the town. I brought it to England in the bottom of my trunk, more afraid of it, probably, than the Macnamara of what he carried in his. I came here to write rather than to publish. . . . If I ever published anything, I fully expected it would be through some American publisher. But see how little I knew myself. Wholly on impulse one day I took my MS. of A Boy's Will to London and left it with the publisher whose imprint was the first I had noticed in a volume of minor verse on arriving in England, viz., David Nutt. I suppose I did it to see what would happen. . . ."

Nor could he refrain from making something of it when next he wrote to Silver in Plymouth:

". . . When I ask myself in the words of the song 'Oh why left I my home, Why did I cross the deep', I have to confess it was to write prose and earn an honest living. Poetry is not a living. It is not even a reputation to-day. It is at best a reputation next year or the year after. And yet I always feel as if I was justified in writing poetry when the fit is on me—as it was last January. Very little of what I have done lately goes to swell the first book, just one or two things to round out the idea. You may look for a slender thing with a slender psychological interest to eke out the lyrical. Call it a study in a certain kind of waywardness. My publisher is David Nutt of London and Paris, a friend as it turns out of Bergsons."

Soon after Christmas of 1912, only three months before the publication of A Boy's Will, Frost undertook a subtly waged campaign, and it brought him into contact with several British and American poets whose alliances and rivalries and literary battles were at least hinted at in various London periodicals of the day. The first round of a new battle, into which Frost walked quite innocently, was foretold by Harold Monro, a moody Scotsman, poet, Cambridge graduate, and editor of The Poetry Review, the offical monthly publication of the Poetry Society. Monro made the following announcement in the November 1912 issue: "On January 1, 1913, we shall open, at 35 Devonshire Street, Theobalds Road, in the heart of old London, five minutes' walk from the British Museum, a Bookshop for the sale of poetry, and of all books, pamphlets and periodicals connected directly or indirectly with poetry. . . ."

There was nothing in this announcement that gave any indication of the battles Monro had been waging with the Poetry Society during his brief editorship. He had aroused the ire of its elderly members by publishing representative offerings from newcomers, and soon the authorities exercised their power by discharging Monro. In return, he exercised his power by renting the building at 35 Devonshire Street with his own money, designating it as the headquarters for his own quarterly, Poetry and Drama, and opening a bookshop at the same address.

The skirmishes between Monro and the Poetry Society represented only one facet of growing literary warfare. Monro was associated with a group of poets who, scorning leftover Victorians—even scorning the Edwardians—took their name from the coronation of George V in 1911. The leader of this group was Edward Marsh. By the time Frost reached

England, Marsh had already begun to collect poems for a volume he planned to edit and publish as *Georgian Poetry 1911–1912*.

Another group, gradually separating itself from the Poetry Society and from the incipient Georgians, had begun to rally under the leadership of Thomas Ernest Hulme. His interests were largely devoted to a philosophical concern for theories of art. A translator of and lecturer on Henri Bergson, Hulme had found in F. S. Flint a poet who was well informed concerning the French Symbolists and contemporary French poetry. As early as 1908, Hulme had tried to wean Flint from the catholicity of his tastes, by advancing a theory that was intended to refresh the vitality of the image as the basic element in poetry and to reinvigorate the uses of analogy, stated or implied, as the basic instrument of thought in poetic expression. Sympathetic, and yet, not greatly influenced by Hulme, Flint had published in 1909 his first volume of poems, *In the Net of the Stars*.

Far more strongly moved by Hulme's theories was the Idaho-born Ezra Pound, but the group of Imagistes soon gathered by Pound had very little to do with either the theories of Hulme or the poetic practices of Flint, nor did the group hold Pound's interest for long. Pound had already passed through several phases of his literary career, and his versatility and scholarship made him attractive to various individuals and groups without binding him to any one of them.

Before Frost met Pound in London, Harriet Monroe of Chicago had felt that the resurgence of interest in poetry justified her plan for establishing an American periodical devoted to poetry, and she wrote Pound, asking if he would serve as London representative. The first number of *Poetry: A Magazine of Verse* was published in October 1912, with contributions by Pound.

All of these literary stirrings were in the process of development when Frost arrived in England, and yet, he was very largely unaware of them. On the night of January 8, 1913, when he found his way to the opening of Harold Monro's Poetry Bookshop in Kensington, the place was so crowded with guests that he had to witness the ceremonies from a seat on the staircase leading to a balcony. Those who sat around him were sufficiently talkative and friendly to make him feel not too uncomfortable. A stranger introduced himself as Frank S. Flint, and he continued his talk so pleasantly that during the evening Frost bought a copy of *In the Net of the Stars*. Before they parted, Flint learned that David Nutt would soon publish *A Boy's Will*, and gave Frost some assurance he would find a chance to review it. He strongly urged, however, that Frost should make the acquaintance of Ezra Pound, and promised to approach Pound on Frost's behalf.

There was reason to cultivate the attentions of F. S. Flint, and Frost wrote to him soon after their meeting:

"I trust there was nothing ambiguous in my rather frank enjoyment of an unusual situation the other night. Considering certain gentle gibes you dealt me, I am not quite sure in the retrospect that you didn't think I was laughing at someone or something, as the American newspapers laughed (some of them) at Yeats. You will take my word for it that there was nothing in my sleeve: I showed just what I felt. I was only too childishly happy in being allowed to make one for a moment in a company in which I hadn't to be ashamed of having written verse. Perhaps it will help you understand my state of mind if I tell you that I have lived for the most part in villages where it were better that a millstone were hanged about your neck than that you should own yourself a minor poet."

Apparently conscious of Flint's literary influence, Frost ingratiated himself by devoting, next, more than a page of his letter to flattering technical comments on his favorite lines and rhymes in Flint's volume of poetry. Flint was touched by the tone of this letter; it transformed their acquaintance into a warm friendship, which found reflection in Flint's review of *A Boy's Will* when it was published.

Before that, there was the pleasure for Frost of correcting galley proofs and, then, page proofs of the book. When he had finished, he could not resist a playful show of pride: the set of page proofs given to him as his property (identified as "FIRST REVISE" and date-stamped by the printer "30 JAN. 1913"), he sent to his former student John Bartlett, on faraway Vancouver Island.

More pertinent to his immediate campaign was the need for cultivating the attentions of Ezra Pound. Flint not only carried out his promise by mentioning Frost to his fellow countryman, he also got from Pound and sent to Frost a curiously worded invitation. It was a calling card bearing Pound's address—10 Church Walk, Kensington—beneath which Pound had written and initialed a curt message: "At home—sometimes." Frost's pride was hurt by the arrogance of the wording; but he knew that, under the circumstances, he could not afford to be rankled. Waiting for more than a month—and for just the right time—he eventually sought out 10 Church Walk. To his surprise, the door was opened by a young man —with a tousle of red hair and a neatly trimmed red beard, blue-gray eyes and a nervous manner.

Pound immediately began the conversation by scolding Frost for having taken so long to answer his card. It was clear he had learned from Flint the news that *A Boy's Will* would soon be published, and he hoped Frost had a copy of the book with him. No, he had not yet seen a copy of the book; he supposed it must be bound and ready to be sent to reviewers. Then, said Pound, he and Frost would make the brief trip over to the office of David Nutt and demand a copy. They did, with Pound taking charge; so that when Frost saw the first bound copy of A Boy's Will, with its attractive, pebble-grained and copper-colored cloth binding, the thin volume was being placed in Pound's hands, not Frost's.

Back they went to Church Walk. Pound sat down to read, directing Frost to find a magazine and keep himself busy for a while. Before long, the silence of the room was broken by Pound's chuckling, just before he said, in a pompous tone that amused Frost, "You don't mind our liking this?" "Oh, no," Frost answered; "go right ahead!"

Pound singled out as one of his favorites "In Neglect." There was quite a story behind these lines, Frost said; and in a few moments he was pouring out an overdramatized, not-too-accurate version of how his grandfather had mistreated him by sending him out to die on the Derry farm, of how his grandfather and his Uncle Elihu Colcord had also mistreated him by drafting wills that deprived Frost of monies that should rightfully have come to him as part of his legacy. He also told of all his difficulties in trying to find magazine editors who would accept his poems for publication.

This was enough to arouse Pound's sympathy. Almost brusquely, he said Frost had better run along home, so Pound could get to work immediately on a review of A Boy's Will for Harriet Monroe. A few days later he wrote Miss Monroe:

"Sorry I can't work this review down to any smaller dimensions! However, it can't be helped. Yes it can. I've done the job better than I thought I could. And it's our second scoop, for I only found the man by accident and I think I've about the only copy of the book that has left the shop. . . .

"I think we should print this notice at once as we ought to be first and some . . . here are sure to make fuss enough to get quoted in N.Y. . . ."

After he had sent his review, Pound apparently gave Frost a carbon copy of it. The event should have occasioned joy. Instead, Frost was horrified to discover that some of his own remarks about the inhumanities of American editors and some of his dramatic fictions concerning the inhumanities of his grandfather and uncle had been paraphrased in it.

While Frost groaned over these indelicacies (first his, then Pound's), Elinor Frost wept. It was difficult to know whether his new friend would do more harm than good, but there was no stopping him now. To his own father Pound wrote: ". . . I'll try to get you a copy of Frost. I'm using mine at present to boom him and get his name stuck about. . . ." One particularly valuable use of this copy was that he lent it to Yeats, who may have been flattered by some internal hints that Frost admired him. Pound reported to Frost that Yeats had pronounced A Boy's Will "the best poetry written in America for a long time" and that Yeats wanted to meet him.

Such an honor deserved a place apart from any other response. (Frost had made up his mind during the Derry years that Yeats was his favorite living poet, Meredith having died in 1909.) Taken to Yeats's London apartment by Pound, who wore a velvet jacket for the occasion, Frost was less surprised by the appearance of Yeats, whose photographs he had often seen in American periodicals, than by the dark-curtained, candlelit atmosphere of the room in which they sat and talked. Pound, showing himself very much at home, stretched out on the floor at the feet of Yeats, who seemed to enjoy adoration. Yeats had recently become preoccupied with psychical research, and the conversation meandered through the realms of ghosts and little people.

During the course of the evening, Frost made bold to advance the claim that he could tell from the behavior of words in a poem whether the author had struggled to get it written or whether he had carried the whole thing off with one stroke of the pen. Yeats seemed to be doubtful, and Frost said he could illustrate. He was certain that Yeats must have written with one stroke of the pen his pure lyric that begins: "I went out to the hazel wood, / Because a fire was in my head. . . ." Ah, no, said Yeats; he had written "The Song of Wandering Aengus" in agony during his terrible years.

As Yeats talked on, through the candlelit evening, he seemed to Frost much older than his forty-eight years. He spoke as though his work was all behind him, and he seemed to be completely wrapped up in his own memories and thoughts and actions. The evening came to an end, leaving Frost with the feeling he had failed to establish any rapport with the man whose poetry he had so long admired. He did accept Yeats's invitation to attend the weekly Monday-nights, when Yeats was "at home." He went twice, and felt lost in the crush of strangers. The hoped-for friendship was never established.

Pound continued to boom Frost. He took him to visit the novelist May Sinclair, after Pound had lent her his copy of A Boy's Will and been told that she found an admirable quality in it. A few years earlier she had done much to increase the reputation of Edwin Arlington Robinson by praising him, along with William Vaughn Moody and Ridgely Torrence, in The Atlantic Monthly. Frost expressed his opinion that Robinson was the best of the three, and was pleased to have Miss Sinclair say she remained interested only in Robinson.

A Boy's Will was published on or about April 1, 1913, and Frost was on edge to discover how the reviewers would treat him. The first notices were not entirely favorable. The Athenæum for April fifth contained two sentences: "These poems are intended by the author to possess a certain sequence, and to depict the various stages in the evolution of a young man's outlook upon life. The author is only half successful in this, possibly because many of his verses do not rise above the ordinary, though here and there a happy line or phrase lingers gratefully in the memory." *The Times Literary Supplement* for April tenth, again, used only two sentences: "There is an agreeable individuality about these pieces: the writer is not afraid to voice the simplest of his thoughts and fancies, and these, springing from a capacity for complete absorption in the influences of nature and the open air, are often naïvely engaging. Sometimes too, in a vein of reflection, he makes one stop and think, though the thought may be feebly or obscurely expressed (as in the last stanza of a poem, otherwise striking, called 'The Trial by Existence')."

These were the most important mentions of *A Boy's Will* in British periodicals during the first two months following publication. Frost's hopes melted into discouragement, and some of his bitterness apparently found reflection in a letter from Mrs. Frost to John Bartlett's wife:

"I am very glad you and John like Roberts book. Of course I love it very much, and have been somewhat disappointed that the reviewers have not been more enthousiastic. How can they help seeing how exquisitely beautiful some of the poems are, and what an original music there is in most of them? Rob has been altogether discouraged at times, but I suppose we ought to be satisfied for the present to get the book published and a little notice taken of it. Yeats has said to a friend, who repeated the remark to Robert, that it is the best poetry written in America for a long time. If only he would say so publicly, but he won't, he is too taken up with his own greatness."

For Frost this new disappointment brought back old doubts he had thought he was done with. But gradually—and after Robert Frost had almost given up hope—some encouraging, even flattering reviews of *A Boy's Will* appeared in British and American periodicals.

In September of 1913 three reviews, including one in *The Dial* (Chicago), gave him new heart—and gave earlier reviews more importance. He had been inclined to discount the kindliness and generosity of Flint's review in *Poetry and Drama,* but he apparently needed and liked it now:

"Mr Robert Frost's poetry is so much a part of his life that to tell his life would be to explain his poetry. I wish I were authorized to tell it. . . . Be it said, however, that Mr Frost has escaped from America, and that his first book, *A Boy's Will,* has found an English publisher. So much information, extrinsic to the poems, is necessary. Their intrinsic merits are great, despite faults of diction here and there, occasional inversions, and lapses, where he has not been strong enough to bear his own simplicity of utterance. It is this simplicity which is the great charm of his book; and it is a simplicity that proceeds from a candid heart. . . .

". . . Each poem is the complete expression of one mood, one emotion, one idea. I have tried to find in these poems what is most characteristic of

Mr Frost's poetry, and I think it is this: direct observation of the object and immediate correlation with the emotion—spontaneity, subtlety in the evocation of moods, humour, an ear for silences. But behind all is the heart and life of a man, and the more you ponder his poems the more convinced you become that the heart is pure and the life not lived in vain."

For the time being, he also relished the anonymous review that appeared in *The Academy* (London):

"We wish we could fitly express the difference which marks off 'A Boy's Will' from all the other books here noticed. Perhaps it is best hinted by stating that the poems combine, with a rare sufficiency, the essential qualities of inevitability and surprise. We have read every line with that amazement and delight which are too seldom evoked by books of modern verse. Without need of qualification or a trimming of epithets, it is undoubtedly the work of a true poet. We do not need to be told that the poet is a young man: the dew and the ecstasy—the audacity, too—of pristine vision are here. At the same time, it is extraordinarily free from a young poet's extravagances; there is no insistent obtrusion of self-consciousness, no laboured painting of lilies, nothing of the plunge and strain after super-things. Neither does it belong to any modern 'school,' nor go in harness to any new and twisted theory of art. It is so simple, lucid, and experimental that, reading a poem, one can see clearly with the poet's own swift eyes, and follow the trail of his glancing thought. One feels that this man has *seen* and *felt*: seen with a revelatory, a creative vision; felt personally and intensely; and he simply writes down, without confusion or affectation, the results thereof. Rarely to-day is it our fortune to fall in with a new poet expressing himself in so pure a vein. No one who really cares for poetry should miss this little book. . . . We have not the slightest idea who Mr. Robert Frost may be, but we welcome him unhesitatingly to the ranks of the poets born, and are convinced that if this is a true sample of his parts he should presently give us work far worthier of honour than much which passes for front-rank poetry at the present time."

15

ISSUANCE OF *NORTH OF BOSTON*

(1912–1914)

IN THE fall of 1912, as soon as Robert Frost received word from Mrs. Nutt that the manuscript of *A Boy's Will* had been accepted for publication, he began writing in an unexpected burst of energy. And when Mrs. Nutt asked about his plans for a second volume, which she would publish in accordance with the terms of his contract, he had already advanced far enough to offer a provisional title.

Earlier, when Frost began to select and arrange poems for his first volume, he had held back three written at least as early as 1905 and 1906 on the farm in Derry: "The Death of the Hired Man," "The Housekeeper," and "The Black Cottage." In each the objective characterizations were achieved through a combination of dramatic dialogue and narrative. These poems were closely related to his hopes that someday he might also write psychological studies in the form of novels, short stories, and plays.

As he returned to the writing of blank-verse narratives and character studies, Frost discovered he could not possibly crowd out occasional moods that demanded expression in new lyrics. He was not troubled by such inconsistencies. Long ago he had found that even the shortest lyric could be endowed with some element of the dramatic, and would be the stronger for it. He had also noticed that there was at least an element of dialogue in the kinds of lyrics he liked best to write. It would have been difficult for him to say how far back in his own experience he had become conscious that his inner hopes and fears acquired poetic voices that talked back and forth. He had learned, particularly during the painful years of his courtship, that the opposed voices and postures of his divided consciousness were as vivid to him as any voices of actors on a stage, that out of these inner tensions the lyric voice that triumphed—no matter how briefly—might find expression in a poem he felt and heard before he could ever try to write it down.

Dramatically regarded, the arrangement of the lyrics in *A Boy's Will* amounted to an implied dialogue between opposed sides of his own consciousness. He had arranged to let the separate parts of the pattern become a study in the psychological phases of his own self-destructive negations and his constructive affirmations. If both of the voices did not speak in all of those lyrics, he had often tried to imply, dramatically, a listener who is addressed and silenced by the speaking voice.

This element of dramatic dialogue, involving themes that were for Frost perennial subjects for inner debate, asserted itself in a revealing poem he began to fashion at Beaconsfield. The inspiration had occurred shortly before Christmas of 1912, on a freezing-cold evening when he had gone alone by train to the nearby town of High Wycombe to do what little Christmas shopping he could afford, for Elinor and the children. On the streets of High Wycombe the sad faces of many working men and women reminded him that a strike of colliers, then in progress, was having widespread effects on many laborers. As he shopped, one incident hurt him enough to make him cry inside. He walked toward a store window filled with toys, and for a moment he did not notice that he was looking over the heads and backs of two very small children who stood with their noses pressed against the window glass, saying nothing. Touched by their silence, he asked what they liked best in the window. By way of answer, one of them took his finger out of his mouth to point; and where he wet the windowpane, the moisture froze almost as soon as he took his finger away. That was all.

The little incident carried Frost back, in his thoughts, to the previous winter in Plymouth, when he had questioned whether he and his family had any right to make Christmas merry while so many seemed to have no such opportunity. Now the old questions returned. What part should he be taking in the suffering of others? How much did he owe to others? Should he throw in his lot with them? And if so, how far? He knew the Stoic notion that a man must not allow himself to be moved by the misfortunes of others, but he found that he could not help being moved. How could an artist cultivate a life of selfishness? What was the justification? On the other hand, what kind of relief—individual, social, governmental—would be adequate relief? All these elements came together somehow, for Frost, in lines he began writing at Beaconsfield and called "Good Relief."

But the suffering that concerned him most at this time was his own homesickness. It drove his memories back, wistfully, to the Derry farm. His longings intensified his recollections, with the result that he contin- ued to write some meditative lyrics at a time when, in accordance with his plans, he should have been working on his dramatic narratives and dialogues. One of them began, after revisions: "When I see birches bend to left and right / Across the lines of straighter darker trees, / I like to think some boy's been swinging them. . . ." Another began: "Something there is that doesn't love a wall, / That sends the frozen-ground-swell under it / And spills the upper boulders in the sun. . . ." (Years later Frost said: "I wrote the poem 'Mending Wall' thinking of the old wall that I hadn't mended in several years and which must be in a terrible condition. I wrote that poem in England when I was very homesick for my old wall in New England. Now I'll read another which I wrote while I was a little homesick: 'Birches.' ")

Homesickness brought back, with a special vividness, a great many other firsthand memories of neighbors—and tones of voice—that were imaginatively (sometimes literally) built into dramatic dialogues. And before the summer of 1913 had passed, the second volume was beginning to shape up, although many poems were still in first-draft state and needed further revision.

Near the end of October, Frost proudly announced that the title of the book was "about the only part not ready to go to press." Having considered *Farm Servants* and *New England Eclogues,* he relinquished both because they were too restrictive; not all of his poems fitted the meaning Virgil had assigned to the term "eclogue" when he had adapted it from Theocritus to include his bucolic poems about Arcadian shepherds. For a time Frost thought he might call the book simply *New Englanders* or *New England Hill Folk*. But a more homely title suggested itself to him one night as he walked around and around the dining-room table in The Bungalow at Beaconsfield, after everyone else was in bed. He remembered that a Boston newspaper advertised properties for sale by saying they were located "North of Boston." When he suggested to British friends his determination to call the volume *North of Boston,* they resisted, on the ground that British readers would associate the title with Boston in Lincolnshire. Frost remained adamant, perhaps because homesickness heightened his belief that the title would be received well in New England.

When Frost explained to Mosher that in writing the dramatic narratives for *North of Boston* he had "dropped to an everyday level of diction that even Wordsworth kept above," and yet, that the "language is appropriate to the virtues I celebrate," he was hinting at his new discoveries of old truths. As in his earlier experiments with poetic lines that "sounded like talk," the practice came first and his principles of ordering were derived from his practice.

It was almost with the excited tone of discovery that he continued to describe those principles. Having boasted to John Bartlett, "I alone of English writers have con[s]ciously set myself to make music out of what I may call the sound of sense," and having claimed that the audial imagination of the reader must collaborate with the poet to the extent of hearing shades of intonation captured between the lines and controlled by the entire context of a poem, Frost kept finding more he wanted to say on the subject. "I wouldnt be writing all this [in a letter] if I didn't think it the most important thing I know," he told Bartlett. "I write it partly for my own benefit, to clarify my ideas. . . ." Some of his best clarifications were written at this time:

"A sentence is a sound in itself on which other sounds called words may be strung.

"You may string words together without a sentence-sound to string them on just as you may tie clothes together by the sleeves and stretch them without a clothes line between two trees, but—it is bad for the clothes.

"The number of words you may string on one sentence-sound is not fixed but there is always danger of over loading.

"The sentence-sounds are very definite entities. . . .

"They are apprehended by the ear. They are gathered by the ear from the vernacular and brought into books. Many of them are already familiar to us in books. I think no writer invents them. The most original writer only . . . catches them fresh from talk, where they grow spontaneously.

"A man is all a writer if *all* his words are strung on definite recognizable sentence-sounds. The voice of the imagination, the speaking voice must know certainly how to behave[,] how to posture in every sentence he offers. . . .

". . . The ear is the only true writer and the only true reader. I have known people who could read without hearing the sentence sounds and they were the fastest readers. Eye readers we call them. They can get the meaning by glances. But they are bad readers because they miss the best part of what a good writer puts into his work.

"Remember that the sentence sound often says more than the words. It m[a]y even as in irony convey a meaning opposite to the words. . . .

"To judge a poem or piece of prose you go the same way to work—apply the one test—greatest test. You listen for the sentence sounds. If you find some of those not bookish, caught fresh from the mouths of people, some of them striking, all of them definite and recognizable[,] so recognizable that with a little trouble you can place them and even name them, you know you have found a writer."

As applied by Frost in his *North of Boston* poems, these principles were calculated not to displace the underlying and recurrent metrical patterns of a poem nor to justify *vers libre*, but to achieve an enrichment and complexity through a poetic arrangement of two factors: ". . . there are the very regular preestablished accent and measure of blank verse; and there are the very irregular accent and measure of speaking intonation. I am never more pleased than when I can get these into strained relation. I like to drag and break the intonation across the metre as waves first comb and then break stumbling on the shingle."

In his best moments Frost never claimed these principles were new; but he did insist that modern poetry had a tendency to forget the brilliant adaptations made of these principles by Virgil in his eclogues, by Shakespeare in his dialogues, by Herrick in his best lyrics, by Wordsworth in choosing for poetry the humble and rustic life, wherein the essential passions of the heart speak a plain and emphatic language.

In the poems of *North of Boston*, Frost made extremely bold demands on the "audial imagination" of his readers. It is to his credit that so many of his readers heard so clearly what he was trying to say. The dialogue between negation and affirmation—even between death and life—in *A Boy's Will* was carried over directly to *North of Boston*. The virtues he celebrated in each were those that enable individuals to confront and to survive the worst, by and with and through the strength of affirmative, outgoing love. He hinted at this carry-over, in his one-sentence introduction: "*Mending Wall* takes up the theme where *A Tuft of Flowers* in *A Boy's Will* laid it down."

Having waged a subtle campaign on behalf of *A Boy's Will* before it was published, Frost prepared the way for *North of Boston* even more effectively. He circulated several manuscripts, starting perhaps with a visit he made to Wilfrid Wilson Gibson. Under ordinary circumstances Frost might have been repelled immediately (as he was eventually) by the crude way in which Gibson handled his own techniques and themes. But it is probable the friendliness and warmth of Gibson's personality meant so much to Frost at the time of their meeting that certain normal hindrances to friendship were ignored.

Almost five years younger than Frost, Gibson had seemed thoroughly rooted in Victorian mannerisms while composing his first four books of poetry, but by 1910, when he published *Daily Bread*, he had "caught the stormy summons of the sea" and begun to sing what he called "the life-song of humanity." In *The Poetry Review* for January of 1912 an essayist who hailed Gibson indiscriminately as "a new force in English letters" explained how Gibson had found the raw materials for his ballad-echoing narratives: ". . . he went down into mines and through factories and tenements and the squalor of sunless slums—the disease-ridden, evil-smelling styes of humanity—and there, where little children perish of want . . . ; there, where women, the mothers of the race, . . . are battered and broken by the merciless grinding of the wheels of labour, the relentless and inhuman greed of manufacturer and consumer; there, in the places where strong men starve because they cannot get work, he listened. . . ."

Gibson had already become one of the most popular and highly praised versifiers on either side of the Atlantic—and Frost had set his heart on the idea of achieving recognition not only with the discriminating few, but also with the common man. He confided as much while writing a letter from Beaconsfield in the fall of 1913:

". . . there is a kind of success called 'of esteem' and it butters no parsnips. It means a success with the critical few who are supposed to know. But really to arrive where I can stand on my legs as a poet and nothing else I must get outside that circle to the general reader who buys books in their thousands. I may not be able to do that. I believe in doing it—dont you doubt me there. I want to be a poet for all sorts and kinds. I could never make a merit of being caviare to the crowd the way my quasi-friend Pound does. I want to reach out, and would if it were a thing I could do by taking thought."

Frost was indeed "taking thought" when he reached out to meet W. W. Gibson. He made the first move by calling on the humanitarian poet almost as soon as he learned that Gibson was living alone in one of Harold Monro's rented rooms above the bookshop in London. And Frost took with him a few of his own manuscripts, poems to be published in *North of Boston*. Apparently Gibson thought well enough of these samplings, for he reviewed *North of Boston* in the London *Bookman*. Long before that, however, he introduced Frost to Lascelles Abercrombie, Gibson's closest friend, whose poems and plays had deservedly won more discriminating praise than anything Gibson had written.

Abercrombie was the leader of the Georgians and a character who appealed to his friends as unprepossessing in his picturesqueness: "a small, dark, shy man, with spectacles and straight, slightly greasy-looking hair" and "a queer little green hat which tipped up preposterously in front."

Frost quickly came to admire Abercrombie and to envy him because he lived "under thatch," with his family, in Gloucestershire. Gibson had his own plans to take up an abode "under thatch" nearby, just as soon as he could win and marry the attractive lady who served as secretary at Harold Monro's bookshop. Flatteringly, and yet sincerely, both Gibson and Abercrombie insisted the bucolic Frost should not be living in the suburban town of Beaconsfield, that he should let them find him an inexpensive cottage in the countryside near them. Persuaded by the warmth of their friendliness, Frost promised to join them if he could manage to sublease The Bungalow in Beaconsfield. None of the other acquaintances he had made in London, up to that time, meant enough to him to hold him there.

Frost did not succeed with his sublease plans until the spring of 1914; and, as it happened, there were good reasons for staying near London until spring. During the fall and winter, at least prior to Gibson's marriage, Gibson enabled Frost to meet several other prominent literary figures whom he would have regretted not meeting. Among them was Ralph Hodgson, whose best-known poem Frost had discovered in an extraordinary way several months earlier. While sitting in the Beaconsfield station, waiting for a train, Frost noticed that the discarded newspaper between his feet contained a poem apparently reprinted as a filler. He bent over to read the lines. Pleased with the freshness and musical grace of Hodgson's "Eve," Frost picked up the newspaper, tore out the poem, and kept it. (Hodgson had lived in the United States for a time, and for a man who wrote lyrics he had led an extraordinarily unpoetic life—as a pressman in Fleet Street, professional draftsman, member of a pictorial staff on an evening paper, editor of a magazine, and as a fancier of bull terriers.)

Early in October 1913, at St. George's Restaurant in St. Martin's Lane, Hodgson introduced Frost to the essayist-biographer-critic Edward Thomas, who had reviewed *A Boy's Will* anonymously and favorably in *The New Weekly*. Frost was immediately sympathetic toward this moody and handsome man. Their casual meeting began what later became a very important friendship for both of them.

Continuing to cultivate old and new acquaintances during the fall and winter of 1913–1914, Frost became, through Flint, acquainted with T.E. Hulme, whose home at 67 Frith Street he visited repeatedly, to attend the famous Thursday-night gatherings. Hulme's knowledge of Bergson's writings provided a special bond.

Through Gibson and Flint, Frost became well enough acquainted with Harold Monro to sell him two poems, "The Fear" and "A Hundred Collars," for use in *Poetry and Drama* prior to their publication in *North of Boston*. The sale was based on terms Frost suggested: Just prior to the time for the departure of the Frosts for Gloucestershire, he and his family would be permitted to spend a week in a pair of furnished rooms above the bookshop. Other sales were made for cash. Ezra Pound surprised Frost by purchasing the right to publish "The Housekeeper" in his newly acquired magazine, *The Egoist*. Pound was also instrumental in enabling Frost to sell "The Code" to Harriet Monroe's *Poetry* magazine. These were the only four poems from *North of Boston* that appeared in print prior to its date of publication.

An entirely unexpected privilege was afforded Frost in the fall of 1913, when he accidentally met newly appointed Poet Laureate Robert Bridges. The death of Alfred Austin on June 2, 1913, had set people guessing who the new laureate would be. Thomas Hardy's name was mentioned, and the consequent public shudder was reflected in a *Daily Mail* headline: "DO WE WANT A PESSIMIST?" Frost thought the popular vote would have given the laureateship to Kipling, but the more austere rejection of this possibility was reflected in *Poetry and Drama,* where Monro caustically observed that the general public "is taught its imperialism with sufficient impressiveness, if without Rudyard Kipling, in the columns of newspapers, in the halls, and on the cinematograph." Approving of Bridges's appointment, Monro said, "The benefit to the public by his selection consists in the fact that its attention is thereby drawn to his poems."

Frost was not sufficiently familiar with Bridges's poetry to have an opinion at first, but within a short time he heard—and disliked—certain theories advanced by Bridges. Their accidental meeting occurred in the home of Laurence Binyon, another of the many poets to whom Frost had been introduced by F. S. Flint. Calling on Binyon unexpectedly one morning, Frost was told Bridges was to be there soon. Binyon was taking him to lunch and urged Frost to go with them. He did, sheepishly, and very soon found himself arguing with the poet laureate. Frost's account of the occasion braids their two opposed poetic theories, with no attempt to do justice to the laureate:

"... He's a fine old boy with the highest opinion—of his poetry you thought I was going to say—perhaps of his poetry, but much more particularly of his opinions. He rides two hobbies tandem, his theory that syllables in English have fixed quantity that cannot be disregarded in reading verse, and his theory that with forty or fifty or sixty characters he can capture and hold for all time the sounds of speech. One theory is as bad as the other and I think owing to much the same fallacy. The living part of a poem is the intonation entangled somehow in the syntax idiom and meaning of a sentence. It is only there for those who have heard it previously in conversation. It is not for us in any Greek or Latin poem because our ears have not been filled with the tones of Greek and Roman talk. It is the most volatile and at the same time important part of poetry. It goes and the language becomes a dead language[,] the poetry dead poetry. With it go the accents the stresses the delays that are not the property of vowels and syllables but that are shifted at will with the sense. Vowels have length there is no denying. But the accent of sense supercedes all other accent[,] overrides and sweeps it away. I will find you the word 'come' variously used in various passages as a whole, half, third, fourth, fifth, and sixth note. It is as long as the sense makes it. When men no longer know the intonations on which we string our words they will fall back on what I may call the absolute length of our syllables which is the length we would give them in passages that meant nothing. The psychologist can actually measure this with a what-do-you-call-it. English poetry would then be read as Latin poetry is now read and as of course Latin poetry was never read by Romans. Bridges would like it read so now for the sake of scientific exactness. Because our poetry must sometime be as dead as our language must[,] Bridges would like it treated as if it were dead already. . . ."

Knowing as much as he did about Mark Twain's grouchy ways of tickling the British lion's nose, Frost may have felt a special kinship with Twain while in England. He was bold enough to differ with the poet laureate face to face, but he needed more than boldness in dealing with his publisher, Mrs. Nutt. Early in 1914 he called on her, to say that he would like to make arrangements for the publication in the United States of his first two books. That was her business, she said, not his. So far as publication was concerned, he had no legal rights other than those stated in his contract with her. At this time she informed him that he had no right to publish even one of the *North of Boston* poems in a magazine. Frost needed all the tact he could muster to retire in good order.

A different set of problems marred the winter for Frost and his family. The two older children, Lesley and Carol, complained so bitterly over the teaching methods in their Beaconsfield school that Frost withdrew them. As a consequence, attempts to continue their schedule of teaching at home brought a special burden on their mother. Frequent visits from newly acquired friends taxed her energies even further. Matters were made worse by various kinds of illness, which had plagued her intermittently since their arrival in Beaconsfield.

All of the Frosts became increasingly homesick during the winter months, and as a kind of consolation their father tried to reassure them by saying they would return to the United States as soon as he had written and published one more book after *North of Boston*. Nobody seemed quite satisfied.

The entire family was glad when it was time to begin packing for the move to Gloucestershire. The plan made with Harold Monro was carried out. For a full week they lived in rooms above the Poetry Bookshop in Devonshire Street, and the children, at least, enjoyed sightseeing in London. Then, they took the train to Gloucester.

For Frost, the only regret in the move was that he would be far out in the country when the hoped-for reviews of *North of Boston* might begin to appear.

16

A RURAL-ENGLAND SETTING

(1914)

THE WELTER of daffodils in the fields of the Dymock region in Gloucestershire charmed all six members of the Frost family when they arrived there in April of 1914. This countryside, so different from anything they had seen during their walks outward from Beaconsfield, was a surprise and a wonder. They rode to the hamlet of Dymock on a train that wound northward around broken hills and beside green hollows of grazing land that cradled flocks of sheep and herds of cattle. There was a startlingly vivid quality in glimpses of white petals from pear trees, lazily falling like huge flakes of snow on unbelievably bright grass. From the train window they marveled at flowers they could not name.

At the Dymock station Abercrombie and the Gibsons formed a welcoming committee. It had been decided the Frosts themselves must choose the cottage they wished to rent, and that while the choice was being made they could live comfortably with the Abercrombies not far from Ryton. A pair of cottages joined, the place was called The Gallows, and it had become a meeting place for a cluster of Georgian poets.

After fully enjoying his house-hunting, Frost rented for a year a cottage on a farm two miles to the south of the village of Ledbury in Herefordshire. Known as Little Iddens, the cottage was homely and boxlike, built of black timber and whitened bricks. It stood with its back to a southerly rise of ground in the Leadington region of Dymock. If the children were disappointed to find that Little Iddens was not crowned with thatch, they quickly found compensations. Orchards of pear and cherry and apple covered the hill at the back of the house. From the front, the view was a picture. The foreground of sloping hayfields, pastures, meadows, each with its hedgerow elms, provided an exquisite setting for the forest greenery of May Hill four miles away.

Inside the cottage the Frosts explored the tiny kitchen, with its old-fashioned stove and baking oven, the worn and undulating pavement of bricks on the downstairs floors, the shed to the rear of the kitchen, the stiff iron pump near the shed door, the narrow staircase to the second floor, and the low-posted bedrooms, each with its window of leaded panes in a hinged casement. To the children it seemed like a fairyland house.

The first visitor was Edward Thomas, who had been invited to bring his teenage son and daughter, Mervyn and Bronwen. The Frost children gladly entertained the Thomas children while both fathers were free to roam the countryside. Thomas knew the region well. As a start, he insisted on taking Frost over back lanes to flower-sprinkled groves on the side of May Hill and on up to the top. The best part of the panoramic view, for Thomas, was to the west, where he could point out and name some of the highest peaks in the mountains of Wales. So, the friendship between these two men continued to develop.

Mrs. Frost, writing to her sister Leona after this visit, said of Thomas: "Rob and I think every thing of him. He is quite the most admirable and lovable man we have ever known." She also tried to give her sister a glimpse of Little Iddens, and confided part of her response to this new life.

The ailments that plagued her during the second winter in Beaconsfield were caused largely by the fatigue of caring for a difficult husband, four children, and unexpected guests. She had tried to warn John Bartlett's wife against unnecessary housekeeping and had written from Beaconsfield:

"I hope, my dear, that you do not try to do too much housework. I think it is *very necessary* for you to take good care of yourself for several years to come, and you must learn the art of 'letting things go' just as I had to learn it long, long ago. How could I ever have lived through those years when the children were little tots if I had been at all fussy about my housework? Do not try to cook much—wash dishes only *once* a day and use no rooms except kitchen, bedroom and sitting-room, and hire someone to come in and sweep up once in two weeks. . . ."

At Little Iddens, even the art of "letting things go" could not save Mrs. Frost from strain. As she wrote her sister, she had not been feeling well for three or four weeks: ". . . The housework and teaching and the excitement of meeting so many people constantly, has been almost too much for me. Three weeks ago I felt that I was on the edge of complete nervous prostration, but I pulled out of it and am feeling considerably better now."

The visitors kept coming, not all of them cordially received. One was the supertramp-poet William Henry Davies, whose childlike versifications on the wonders of nature had won the praise of George Bernard Shaw as early as 1905 (and he had been rescued from poverty by Shaw and other admirers who arranged a pension for him). Now, staying with the Gibsons, he called too often on Frost at Little Iddens.

In London, during a dinner given in honor of Davies by Harold Monro,

Frost watched the hero of the evening drink too much wine, excuse himself from the table, wander drunkenly out of the room—and forget to return. Throughout his protracted visit in the Dymock region, Davies conducted himself more soberly; and yet, as Frost wrote: ". . . his conceit is enough to make you misjudge him—simply assinine. We have had a good deal of him at the house for the last week and the things he has said for us to remember him by! He entirely disgusted the Gibsons. . . . His is the kind of egotism another man's egotism can't put up with."

Far more to Frost's liking was a Gloucestershire barrister and botanist, John Haines, by marriage a relative of Abercrombie's, by avocation a shrewdly perceptive lover of poetry and a rabid botanist. Frost was immediately attracted to this unassuming and lively admirer of plants and verse, and Haines continued the work begun by Thomas, educating Frost about British flowers. Together, they wandered through the Leadon Valley and as far away as the ridges of the Cotswolds, discovering blossoms that delighted Frost. One night they even hunted rare ferns by matchlight—and found them.

A careful reader of periodicals, Haines became the harbinger of glad tidings. He brought or sent to Frost, from Gloucester, reviews of *North of Boston,* as they kept appearing throughout the summer of 1914. The first excitement was provided by the consistency of praise for these modern "eclogues" in "this book of people." Characterizing the "stark concentration" in the volume as "vivid and effective," the anonymous reviewer in *The Times Literary Supplement* added, "Poetry burns up out of it as when a faint wind breathes upon smouldering embers."

For Frost, a fresh kind of satisfaction was realized from the pointed evidence that his new-made friends had rallied strongly to his aid. Abercrombie reviewed him in *The Nation,* Gibson in *The Bookman,* Thomas in *The English Review,* Monro in *Poetry and Drama,* Ezra Pound in Harriet Monroe's *Poetry.* (Frost had not felt sure Pound would fall in line.) Many of the reviews reflected the care with which Frost oriented his friends in regard to his theories about "the sound of sense."

To Haines, who had sent him the clipping from *The Nation,* he wrote: "Thank you for the review—Abercrombie's work as your wife thought. I liked it very well. The discussion of my technique wouldn't have been what it was if Abercrombie had had nothing to go on but the book. He took advantage of certain conversations in which I gave him the key to my method and most of his catchwords. 'Method' is the wrong word to call it: I simply use certain principles on which I accept or reject my own work. It was a generous review to consider me in all ways so seriously and as I say I liked it. . . ."

He had liked it; but the note of disparagement in his remarks reflected his characteristic tendency to be jealous of all competitors, even when they were being praised for praising him.

Fortunately, special attention was paid to Frost throughout four good weeks of that summer. It happened as a result of his having urged Edward Thomas to bring Mrs. Thomas and their children and rent a cottage next door to Little Iddens for the month of August. The suggestion pleased Thomas, whose admiration for Frost was based on the conviction that nobody else had ever before understood so deeply his dark spells of anguish.

Thomas and his family had been there only three days when the feared news arrived that Britain had declared war on Germany, and it was immediately clear that the future might hold disastrous effects for both men. "The war is an ill wind to me," Frost wrote to Cox. "It ends for the time being the thought of publishing any more books. Our game is up. . . .

"So we may be coming home if we can find the fare or a job to pay the fare after we get there. . . ."

Thomas was aware that he might be drafted into military service at any time. Even if not immediately drafted, he knew the meager living he had made as a hack writer would be curtailed severely by the war. But it still appeared to be so far away from Little Iddens that the two men refused to spend all of their time worrying about it.

The interest shown by Thomas in Frost's practice and theory of poetry was extremely flattering. "Thomas thinks he will write a book on what my new definition of the sentence means for literary criticism," Frost wrote to Cox. "If I didn't drop into poetry every time I sat down to write I should be tempted to do a book on what it means for education." He repeated to Cox the gist of one point he had already conveyed to Bartlett: ". . . the sentence as a sound in itself apart from the word sounds is no mere figure of speech. I shall show the sentence sound saying all that the sentence conveys with little or no help from the meaning of the words. I shall show the sentence sound opposing the sense of the words as in irony. And so till I establish the distinction between the grammatical sentence and the vital sentence. . . ."

It was the distinction that fascinated him, and he was willing to employ hyperbole in order to make his point. In a postscript to Cox, he said as much: "Words are only valuable in writing as they serve to indicate particular sentence sounds. I must say some things over and over. I must be a little extravagant too." In his poems, in his prose, and in his arguments, Frost enjoyed indulging the luxury and extravagance of hyperbole.

Try as they would, neither Frost nor Thomas could go very long without finding that their talk turned back to the overwhelming crisis of the war. Rupert Brooke had not yet enlisted, but he had made it clear he would become involved somehow. "Well, if Armageddon is *on*," Brooke said, "I suppose one should be there." Frost almost felt the same way: "If I were younger now and not the father of four—well all I say is, American or no American, I might decide that I ought to fight the Germans simply because I know I should be afraid to."

Two months later he wrote: "No one quite knows what the war has done to him yet. We may be dead, the whole crowd of us, and not able to realize the fact. It is as hard to know how the war has affected us individually as it is to tell off hand what the war is all about, or to understand a modern battle."

The sense of brotherhood and comradeship Frost experienced with Thomas while they had been in each other's company through at least part of every day in the month of August 1914 made their parting an especially sad one. Thomas would not say good-bye. He promised that within a month or two he would return for another visit.

Soon after the Thomas family had gone, Frost accepted the invitation of the Abercrombies to share the combined cottages at The Gallows during the winter months—or at least until Frost decided whether he would try to make arrangements for a passage home, through seas made dangerous by mines and submarines. By mid-September the move to The Gallows was completed. For the Frosts, there was the pleasurable sense of returning to an abode they had admired and enjoyed immediately after they came to the Dymock region.

The joined cottages were perched on a bluff above the road. The older of the two was the smaller: half-timbered, with a thatched roof, the straw at the eaves only shoulder-high. They called this older cottage The Study, because Lascelles did his writing in the main downstairs room. The Abercrombies used the upstairs bedrooms for themselves and their two small children. From The Study there was a passage into the larger cottage, solidly built of red sandstone. To the rear of this cottage had been built a large annex, housing the kitchen and pantry and shed, with three upstairs bedrooms that had been given to the Frosts on their arrival in April and to which they returned in mid-September of 1914.

There was a casual, easygoing, gypsylike manner in the way the Abercrombies lived. Weather permitting, they cooked and ate most of their meals out of doors on the large terrace or in the garden. Catherine Abercrombie and Elinor Frost, enjoying each other's company, shared the conviction that housework was best handled by avoiding it. But Catherine was disturbed by the ways of the Frost children. To her they seemed fretful and troublesome, particularly when Lesley and Carol spent so much time talking about their desire to get back to the United

States. Catherine was also troubled by the inability of the Frost children to get along with other children in the neighborhood.

Frost was jealous in his attitude toward his host and toward the daily caller, Gibson. Each had established a considerable reputation as a poet before Frost came on the scene, and he seemed to resent being treated as an outsider. Gibson had a jocose way of annoying Frost by reading him praise he got from America and, then, calling Frost's attention to bad grammar and misspelled words in the letters. Teasingly, Gibson wanted to know whether Frost's difficulty in getting attention at home might be caused by the high level of illiteracy in the United States.

The game of teasing was one Frost enjoyed only when he was on the giving end. So, there was double pleasure for him when Mrs. Nutt forwarded to The Gallows, belatedly, a letter of praise from a stranger. It bore as a heading "Four Winds Farm," Stowe, Vermont, and was signed "Florence T. Holt." It read:

"Your book 'North of Boston' interests me very much. Do you live in Vermont? If so, you may know my brother's book 'Stowe Notes'. If you don't know it, & would care to, as your book makes me think you would, & will let me know your address, I will send the book to you. My Mother knows the people about here better than I do, & she finds many similar to them in your verses: certainly you have New England in them!

"I hope I am not taking too much of a liberty in writing this note, but probably you will not be displeased to know of our interest."

Now he had a weapon to use on Gibson and Abercrombie. If their poems elicited illiterate responses from the United States, let them look to the causes. Here was a letter from a Vermont farmer's wife—and who could ask for anything in better taste?

At the time, Frost did not know that this first letter of praise from a stranger was written by a lady whose husband was a distinguished and successful publisher in New York City, Henry Holt. Nor did he know that she had already begun to work on his behalf. A representative of Henry Holt and Company mentioned her in writing a cautious letter to David Nutt and Company on September 2, 1914:

"Mrs. Henry Holt, who is very enthusiastic over Robert Frost's NORTH OF BOSTON, has very kindly loaned us her copy. The two readers we had look at these poems found them uncommonly interesting and, while we cannot see a paying market here for this particular volume, still we are so interested in this author's work that if you have some later book of his for which you would care to offer us the American rights, we would be most happy to consider it. . . ."

Mrs. Nutt evidently had a hand in the reproachful answer:

". . . We think that if you recognise the value of Mr Frosts work you must also see that his books will make their way steadily. We could not offer you rights of his new book if you do not push the present volume to some extent. . . .

"We consider that under present political circumstances american publishers ought to show some willingness to help english publishers who have had sufficient daring and intelligence to recognise the talent of one of their own countrymen. . . ."

Fortunately, this reprimand was not needed. On exactly the day it was written, a representative of Holt wrote to David Nutt and Company: "Following our letter of September 2nd in regard to . . . 'North of Boston;' we are inclined on further consideration to take a small edition of this book, say 150 copies in sheets, if it has not already been placed in the American market, and if you can supply them at a reasonable price. . . ."

So, the negotiations began. But Mrs. Nutt seemed anxious to keep Frost in the dark about them. At the same time, he was doing all he could to marshal the assistance of his friends. Eventually, he was helped most by Edward Thomas, who enlisted the persuasive support of one of England's most influential critics, Edward Garnett.

Twice during the fall of 1914, Edward Thomas visited Frost at The Gallows, and each time he stayed for several days. Outwardly, it might have seemed that the common interest that bound these men in friendship was their delight in the Gloucestershire countryside. Elinor Frost and Helen Thomas saw deeper into the psychological significance of this relationship, and approved. So did Catherine Abercrombie, apparently, for she wrote of Edward Thomas: "It was quite a shock on first meeting him unless one had been warned. He suffered very much from recurring melancholy, which stamped itself on his face but only made his beauty more apparent. It was only when Robert encouraged him to turn to writing poetry that he became happy in the delight of his new-found powers."

Robert Frost did more than that for Edward Thomas. In trying to understand the deeply important relationship between these two men, particularly for the light it throws on Frost, there is value in noticing analogies between the kinds of suffering they experienced, analogies that enabled Frost to save the life of Edward Thomas very shortly before Thomas gave his life for his country in combat.

Four years younger than Frost, Edward Thomas was born of Welsh parents, and the pronounced streak of puritanical fastidiousness in his nature seemed to be part of his inheritance from his Welsh ancestors. Although he grew up as a normal boy, he showed an early bent toward introspectiveness and brooding. This tendency gradually developed into what Catherine Abercrombie accurately described as "melancholy," and it became a disease against which he fought throughout his life. One of his weapons against it was his early pleasure in the lore of the naturalist.

Quite early he began to write poetry, but his father discouraged him, and he turned his creative literary interests to essay-writing.

He entered Oxford University in the fall of 1897 and felt that his disillusioning experiences there marked the beginning of serious depression. He admired Walter Pater, described himself as "all Shelley and sunsets," and was utterly repelled by Whitman, whom he believed to be "an added fiend to Hell." He gradually forced himself to mingle with other students at Oxford, to drink with them, and to participate in some of their wildest parties; but, beneath the surface, he maintained his austere and ascetic fastidiousness.

During his third year at Oxford, Thomas married his boyhood sweetheart soon after she told him she was pregnant. He left the university and tried to earn a living as a hack writer. His increasing sense of failure heightened his melancholy. Trying to escape from the nameless thing that tormented him, he frequently ran away and stayed away for several days without letting his wife know where he was.

Any little encouragement or sign of progress in his writing would enable him to reveal the most attractive side of his nature. Briefly he would be contented, even reckless in his newly recovered happiness. But before long he would slip back into despondency. He drove himself ruthlessly, but none of his volumes achieved financial success. Intermittently, he suffered from headaches so painful that he took opium as another might take aspirin, and yet, his asceticism restrained him from acquiring the drug habit.

In the fall of 1912, when the Frost family reached England, Thomas was suffering from an acute phase of neurasthenia and was threatening to kill himself. His wife confessed to friends that he once put a revolver in his pocket and disappeared for hours. Many of his letters written at this period contain hints of panic and hysteria. He acted as though he were caught in a trap and were fighting to get out. Among the literary friends who cared deeply for him and did their best to help him were Walter de la Mare, Joseph Conrad, W. H. Hudson, and Edward Garnett.

By the fall of 1913, Thomas seemed to be headed toward unavoidable disaster. He was in this condition when he met Robert Frost, on October 5, 1913. When first their almost identically light-blue eyes met, each may have felt he saw himself mirrored. Obviously, they had more in common than a love of literature.

Frost had not seen Thomas's review of *A Boy's Will*, but in their conversation about the book it quickly became apparent to Frost that this stranger saw more deeply than anyone else the psychological theme of attempted escape, and necessary return, in the arrangement of the lyrics. The admiration shown Frost by Thomas implied an awareness that Frost himself had gone down to the bottom, like a drowning man, and had somehow learned the secret of how to save himself. It was almost with desperation that Thomas reached out to Frost for help.

Frost quickly discovered that the immediate problem for this obviously tortured man was caused by marital difficulties. Thomas made it clear he wanted to preserve his marriage, that he loved his wife and children, but that he blamed himself for the failure of his marriage and there was nothing he thought he could do to overcome that failure.

Frost was always at his best as a human being when he felt himself needed by someone whose psychological difficulties were in some ways analogous to his own experiences. Under these circumstances he had an extraordinary capacity for drawing out exactly the details he wanted to get at. During the early meetings of these two men it was not long before Frost recognized and understood the similarities between their stories. Frost, in his wife's presence, had flourished a revolver and had threatened to kill himself—or her. Frost had repeatedly tried to run away from himself—and from Elinor. He had fought off major fears and depressions and suicidal yearnings. In part he had been helped by his ability to take warning from the psychological deterioration dramatized in the hysterical actions of his sister, Jeanie.

Now, in his desire to help Thomas, he spread out the pieces of his own story and tried to explain them as best he could. He made it clear that he was by no means certain he was out of the woods. If he had saved himself from going under, on different occasions, he couldn't say he would always be able to save himself.

Frost could tell Thomas a great deal about the vicissitudes of marital relations, but he was not willing to talk about them as grounds for divorce. If he had learned the mistaken aspects of walking out, running away, escape, he was not yet convinced that the ambivalence in these terms should be reduced to one pejorative meaning. He was certain that while some of his actions had been weak and childish gestures, others had saved his life—at least his sanity—by providing necessary kinds of retreat for reorganizing his feelings and thoughts.

To Frost, marriage was only one kind of struggle involving alternations of love and hate—and not the most important. As long as he lived, he thought he'd be fighting a continuous battle on various fronts, and he felt he'd have to settle for nothing more or less than temporary victories. The wounds borne, the suffering, the anguish experienced in all these different conflicts could be survived if anyone possessed a sufficiently intense desire to accomplish one particular thing, come hell or high water.

The particular thing to which Frost had clung for more than twenty years—without seeming to make much headway until recently—was his ambition to succeed as a poet, by gaining public recognition. There had been times when some of his faults had worked to his advantage: his quick temper, his resentments, his uncontrollable rages. His most terrible fight had been against his own fears. At almost any time he could frighten himself almost to death. And there had been times when he had been paralyzed by his fear that he would never succeed as a poet. He was a quitter, but he had never permitted his fears to make him quit hoping on that score. Fortunately, even fear could be counterbalanced by rage, by resentment over a seeming or actual wrong, or by anyone who tried to discourage him with disparagement. He was not trying to convince Thomas that such countermeasures were admirable; he was merely saying that in desperate phases of conflict some things happened unavoidably, and their value had to be measured by the consequences.

Thomas stopped talking about divorce, and returned to his wife. He brought his wife and children all the way from his poverty-stricken home in Hampshire to meet Frost's wife and children in Beaconsfield. Later, he went so far as to talk about moving from Hampshire to New Hampshire, to live near Frost and establish himself, before bringing his wife and children across the ocean; but he gave up that plan as being unfair to his wife and children. With Frost's encouragement and praise he went back to his writing, with a new determination. After he finished another book, he took a cycling vacation in Wales with his son, Mervyn, and they stopped with the Frosts at Little Iddens. By that time he had accepted the suggestion, made by Frost, that he should bring his wife and children to Gloucestershire for the entire month of August.

In the course of his protracted campaign to save the life of a man he loved as a brother, Frost gave Thomas the greatest psychological assistance merely by reading aloud from essays in Thomas's *Pursuit of Spring* and saying to Thomas that it was poetry, not prose; that all these years Thomas had been denying himself the right to be the one thing he couldn't help but be; that if this meant so much to him—if he still wanted, more than anything else, to be a poet—then, his already-proven abilities ought to give him the incentive he needed for developing these abilities.

It worked. Thomas began to steal time from the necessity of hack writing, so that he could get on with his recovered desire to make a name for himself as a poet. And he began this phase of his literary career by quite unashamedly imitating Frost, even boasting to Frost that "this one sounds like Frost." The older man protested. He pointed out the ones that sounded most like Thomas—and the idiom that should be cultivated, because it was Thomas's.

During his last visit with Frost at The Gallows, Thomas accidentally enjoyed the spectacle of seeing Frost demonstrate, with completely unconscious and unintentional impulse, what he meant by saying that some of his most cowardly fears were, often, overcome by rage. The incident occurred as the two men were returning from a long, aimless walk around the neighboring parts of Lord Beauchamp's estate. As they came out of the woods, on a narrow lane, they saw and passed by the gamekeeper—who held his shotgun threateningly. Thomas was frightened and Frost was furious. They walked on.

To Thomas there was no satisfactory explanation for the gamekeeper's performance; something should be done. Inflamed by Thomas's words, Frost was caught up in one of his glowing rages. Something would be done right now, he said, and Thomas could come back with him to see it done. They did not find the gamekeeper until they had tracked him to his cottage, where Frost gave him a piece of his mind. If ever he acted like that again Frost would beat the daylight out of him. The gamekeeper blustered, and Frost repeated his threat as he withdrew.

That evening the town constable knocked at the door of The Gallows. He said he had been sent with orders to arrest Frost, but that he had no intention of doing so. He was amused by Frost's threat and described the gamekeeper as a known bully. It would be necessary, however, to make a report to Lord Beauchamp concerning the incident, and he hoped Frost wouldn't mind. A few days later Frost received a note of apology from Lord Beauchamp.

When Thomas left The Gallows he made arrangements for a subsequent visit that never took place. Years later Helen Thomas made her own comment: ". . . Between him [Robert Frost] and David [Edward Thomas] a most wonderful friendship grew up. He believed in David and loved him, understanding, as no other man had ever understood, his strange complex temperament. The influence of this man on David's intellectual life was profound, and to it alone of outside influences is to be attributed that final and fullest expression of himself which David now found in writing poetry. There began . . . a kind of spiritual and intellectual fulfilment which was to culminate two years later in his death. . . ."

HEADING HOMEWARD

(1914–1915)

IN HIS persistent campaign on behalf of his poetry, Robert Frost had begun correspondence with more than one American publisher shortly after Mrs. Nutt informed him that her firm would publish *A Boy's Will*. The physical attractiveness of Mosher's books had prompted him to look with particular favor on Mosher's overtures, at least until Mrs. Nutt sternly informed him that she and she alone had the legal power to make arrangements with an American publisher.

New impetus given to this campaign after the entry of Britain into the war was reflected in letters to friends at home. By mid-August, Frost had mailed to several of them clippings of various laudatory reviews that appeared after *North of Boston* was published. A group of clippings sent to Sidney Cox was accompanied by a crisp and businesslike note: "I should take it kindly if you would pass these along. Anything you can do for me just at this time will be a double service. My only hope is that some interest will be taken in the book in America: here none can be from now on: people are too deeply concerned about the war. . . ."

As soon as Mrs. Nutt permitted Frost to know that he did have an American publisher, a new element was added to his campaign. It involved the windup of his affairs in England, the arrangement for a passage home, the possibility of taking with him the son of Edward Thomas, and the proper leave-taking of those who had helped him so much.

In spite of serious talk of possibilities that London would be bombed at any moment by German zeppelins, Frost made several brief trips to London. He had explained his attitude on such matters to Edward Thomas; he said it again in a letter to Sidney Cox: "What a man will put into effect at any cost of time money life or lives is what is sacred and what counts." What he would put into effect at any cost was his ambition to increase his foothold as a good American poet.

The war had not yet touched him deeply; but he followed with sympathy and interest whatever war poems he could find in periodicals, and he felt the tension between his own selfishness and the self-giving of Englishmen who were enlisting by the thousands:

". . . I have my work to think of too—though I dont get on with it to speak of in these unsettled times. The war has been a terrible detriment to pleasant thinking in spite of all I can do to approve of it philosophical-ly[.] I don't know whether I like it or not. I don't think I have any right to like it when I am not called on to die in it. At the same time it seems almost cowardly not to approve of it on general principles simply because it is not my funeral. It seems little minded. There we will leave it. I hate it for those whose hearts are not in it and I fear they must be many. . . ."

In London, Frost saw soldiers everywhere—even in Harold Monro's bookshop, where he talked at length with a young poet in uniform who introduced himself, Robert Graves. The subject of their talk, according to Graves, was the debate in Frost's mind as to whether he should or should not enlist in the British army. If he did seriously consider that possibility, his final decision was that he should not.

His more immediate concern was the less-and-less-distant reaction of American publishers to his unpublished verse. And some of his brief trips to London were made to sell a few more poems there. To Harold Monro he managed to sell four, which appeared in *Poetry and Drama* for December 1914: "The Sound of Trees," "Putting in the Seed," "The Smile," and "The Cow in Apple Time."

In making farewell calls, Frost carefully avoided Ezra Pound. Explaining the awkwardness of this relationship, Frost wrote to Sidney Cox:

". . . I fear I am going to suffer a good deal at home by the support of Pound. This is a generous person who is doing his best to put me in the wrong light by his reviews of me: You will see the blow he has dealt me in Poetry (Chicago) for December, and yet it is with such good intention I suppose I shall have to thank him for it. I don't know about that—I may when I get round to it. The harm he does lies in this: he made up his mind in the short time I was friends with him (we quarreled in six weeks) to add me to his party of American literary refugees in London. Nothing could be more unfair, nothing better calculated to make me an exile for life. Another such review as the one in Poetry and I sha'n't be admitted at Ellis Island. This is no joke. Since the article was published I have been insulted and snubbed by two American editors I counted on as good friends. I dont repine and I am willing to wait for justice. But I do want someone to know that I am not a refugee and I am not in any way disloyal. . . ."

More and more, his thoughts were on getting home, and by mail he completed arrangements with Edward and Helen Thomas to include fifteen-year-old Mervyn Thomas in his family, with the understanding that the boy was to live in Alstead, New Hampshire, with a Thomas relative. After considerable difficulty, Frost booked passage on a ship scheduled to sail on February thirteenth. In haste, the Frosts moved back to Little Iddens, to collect their belongings and close the cottage. After some confusion, Mervyn and the Frosts arrived at Liverpool, with time enough to spare for the writing of just a few more farewell notes.

On the night of February 13, 1915, the SS *St. Paul* worked her way out of Liverpool harbor and took her position in convoy with the enormous SS *Lusitania,* guarded by British destroyers that combed the waters with searchlights. Mines and submarines were feared. The passengers were told not to undress. Everyone was nervous.

After the tension of the first night there was general relaxation, and Frost was able to return in his thoughts to his own particular fears—and hopes—for what lay ahead in America. The prospect involved entering upon an entirely new phase of his life, and he was troubled not only by how the American publication of his books would be received, but also by questions of whether the royalties from them would provide a living. He assumed he would have to find work, and he had already written to Cox: "I should awfully like a quiet job in a small college where I should be allowed to teach something a little new on the technique of writing and where I should have some honor for what I suppose myself to have done in poetry." Yet, it was obvious that the vested interests of college professors would resist innovation.

In another letter to Cox, calling the university approach "the worst system of teaching that ever endangered a nations literature," Frost spelled out his complaint more specifically:

". . . Everything is research for the sake of erudition. No one is taught to value himself for nice perception and cultivated taste. Knowledge knowledge. Why literature is the next thing to religion in which as you know or believe an ounce of faith is worth all the theology ever written. Sight and insight, give us those. I like the good old English way of muddling along in these things that we cant reduce to a science anyway such as literature love religion and friendship. People make their great strides in understanding literature at most unexpected times. . . . I dont see how you are going to teach the stuff except with some . . . light touch. And you cant afford to treat it all alike, I mean with equal German thoroughness and reverence if thoroughness is reverence. . . ."

If he was able, however, to earn a living without teaching, simply by remaining true to the writing of poetry, as he dreamed he might, there still remained the problem of where he would live, returning to America without any home base and free to choose. During the homesickness in England, he noticed that the images that came to view were remembrances of places and people and things in Derry and Plymouth and Bethlehem, New Hampshire; and he had said, from Beaconsfield, to

Silver, "My dream would be to get the thing started in London and then do the rest of it from a farm in New England where I could live cheap and get Yankier and Yankier." Even earlier, he had said more: "We can't hope to be happy long out of New England. I never knew how much of a Yankee I was till I had been out of New Hampshire a few months. . . ."

In all these dreams about where he would live when he reached home and how he would earn a living, one fear kept bothering him—a paralyzing fear. He had indiscreetly confessed it to one of his new literary acquaintances in London, under awkward circumstances; and he had regretted the confession ever since. The fear was that now, at the age of nearly forty-one, he had exhausted his creative powers as a poet.

In his darker moods he kept telling himself, incorrectly, that the little reputation he had made in England had been based too heavily on poems written in Derry around 1906, or before, and that the really fresh poetic response had somehow died nearly ten years ago. The best he had done since then was to take his early wares to market. If he received any recognition at home after the American edition of *North of Boston* appeared, he would naturally be asked to produce more of the same or something better. He could go back to his Derry notebooks and dig out poems. He had enough for one more book. He might even write a few—only a few—new ones. But what then?

The prospect frightened him. He foresaw that what lay ahead would severely test his belief that he had adequately worked out defenses against almost any overwhelmings. In a sense he was back where he had started, long ago; and he knew he would need all he could muster of skill and courage and valor and daring and heroism. Even then, perhaps the gulfs would wash him down.

All right, let the test come! This was his own private war, and he liked it. Something inside him seemed to want him to fail; but something a little stronger than that seemed to want him to win. He still had the power to consist of the inconsistent, the power to hold in unity the ultimate irreconcilables, the power to be a bursting unity of opposites, and the power to make poetry out of these opposites. He would always be back where he had started, and he was ready to say again that what a man will put into effect at any cost of time or money or life or lives is sacred, and what counts.

THE
YEARS OF
TRIUMPH

ARRIVAL BACK IN AMERICA

(1915)

DURING THE slow voyage across the Atlantic from Liverpool to New York City in February of 1915, Robert Frost was worried less by the danger of German submarines than by his difficulty in choosing where he would make a home for his wife and children. Fortunately, there was one place where the family knew they would always be welcomed: the farm owned by John Lynch on the South Road between Bethlehem and Franconia, New Hampshire. And when Frost suggested it might be possible to rent rooms at the Lynch farm, as soon as they got to America, so they could use it as a temporary base while he searched for a farm they might purchase in that region, the children and their mother were delighted.

Long before the SS *St. Paul* entered New York harbor, plans had been made to get in touch with the Lynches by telephone. If there were no hitch, their father told the children, they might all be in Bethlehem within twenty-four hours after they reached New York. There was a hitch.

No immigration difficulties had been foreseen when the Frosts volunteered to serve as traveling companions for Mervyn Thomas, whose father had wanted to get him out of England during the war. At Ellis Island, however, soon after the *St. Paul* made the routine stop there, on the morning of Washington's Birthday 1915, immigration officers frightened Mervyn and his protectors by quoting the law: No alien under sixteen could be admitted to the United States unless met at the immigration office by at least one parent—or by a suitable sponsor who could offer acceptable evidence of financial means that would keep such an alien from becoming a public charge.

The pronouncement was made with such arrogance that Frost was enraged. Wasn't it clear enough that Frost himself was qualified to be sponsor and guardian? No, because he had already admitted he had neither a remunerative position nor a sufficient income. Brusquely, the immigration officer explained that the case would be referred to a judiciary board that would meet the following day; the boy must be detained in a cell at Ellis Island until that time. The Frosts were so upset they could talk of nothing else while the steamer moved across New York harbor and was warped to her pier.

There was no reception committee. The few friends who knew they were on the *St. Paul* were too far away to make an occasion of their arrival. If America knew Frost had scored a literary triumph in England and that both of his books had been accepted for publication by the firm of Henry Holt and Company in New York City, there seemed to be no sign that anyone cared. (Frost did not even know whether either of his books had yet been published in America.) He did find a sort of greeting in print, however, soon after he shepherded his family through customs and made arrangements for baggage and furniture to be held a few hours until he knew for certain where they were going.

As he walked up Forty-second Street toward Grand Central Station, he stopped at a newsstand, casually lifted the cover of the current issue of *The New Republic,* and found on the first page a table of contents that listed a review of *North of Boston.* He stopped long enough to buy a copy and scan the review, written by Amy Lowell—the Imagist poet whom he had declined to meet in London, when Ezra Pound had given him the chance. Although it was exciting to find that Miss Lowell viewed this "modest little green-covered book" as "certainly the most American volume of poetry which has appeared for some time," some of the comments that followed were annoying:

"The thing which makes Mr. Frost's work remarkable is the fact that he has chosen to write it as verse. We have been flooded for twenty years with New England stories in prose. The finest and most discerning are the little masterpieces of Alice Brown. She too is a poet in her descriptions, she too has caught the desolation and 'dourness' of lonely New England farms, but unlike Mr. Frost she has a rare sense of humor, and that, too, is of New England, although no hint of it appears in 'North of Boston.' And just because of the lack of it, just because its place is taken by an irony, sardonic and grim, Mr. Frost's book reveals a disease which is eating into the vitals of our New England life, at least in its rural communities.

"What is there in the hard, vigorous climate of these states which plants the seeds of degeneration? Is the violence and ugliness of their religious belief the cause of these twisted and tortured lives? Have the sane, full-blooded men all been drafted away to the cities, or the West, leaving behind only feeble remainders of a once fine stock? The question again demands an answer after the reading of Mr. Frost's book."

It was plain that the city-bred sister of the president of Harvard College did not entirely understand the poetry of Robert Frost. How could she be so ignorant concerning those persistent virtues he had poetically honored in the backcountry people of Miss Lowell's native New England? At least, he was pleased that she had liked *North of Boston* well enough to give it nearly three full columns of review.

At Grand Central Station, Frost made two long-distance calls. The first, to John Lynch in Bethlehem, resulted in assurance that the Lynches would be glad to welcome the Frosts as paying guests and would be ready for their arrival the next day. The second was to Russell Scott, in Alstead, New Hampshire, to explain the difficulties that were holding Mervyn Thomas on Ellis Island, and to ask for help. Scott, an Englishman, had assured Edward Thomas the boy could stay with him indefinitely, but there were reasons Scott did not want to be named, formally, as Mervyn's sponsor. Scott did, however, have a brother, Arthur, living in New York and married to an American girl who had influential friends. She could be of help if Frost would ask her assistance.

Mrs. Arthur Scott, when reached by telephone, showed immediate sympathy. If Mr. Frost would come directly to the midtown apartment where she and her husband were living, she would explain the hesitancy of Russell Scott to serve as formal sponsor for Mervyn and would also try to get in touch with someone who could solve the difficulty.

As soon as Frost had bought tickets for the rest of his family and made arrangements for them to depart, en route to New Hampshire, he continued his campaign on Mervyn's behalf. Mrs. Arthur Scott had felt certain a friend of hers, the prominent New York lawyer Charles Burlingham, would be willing to corroborate Frost's statement that he was financially able to serve as sponsor for Mervyn. She was correct. Burlingham, when approached, telephoned the commissioner of immigration, Frederic C. Howe, who said he would advise the Ellis Island authorities that Robert Frost was acceptable as the sponsor. Assurances were given that all would be in order by the time Frost returned to Ellis Island the next day.

Free to spend the intervening time as he liked, Frost immediately decided to make a brief visit to his American publisher, Henry Holt and Company. When he reached the Holt office, he was received far more cordially than he had expected. Alfred Harcourt, head of the trade department, said Frost must hear the whole story of how Holt had become the American publisher of *North of Boston*.

During the previous summer, Florence Taber Holt, the publisher's wife, had somehow acquired a copy of the English edition and had liked it so much she urged her husband to print an edition. Henry Holt's favorite on his list of authors was Dorothy Canfield Fisher, who was asked to give her opinion. It was extremely favorable, but the decision was made to proceed cautiously, by importing from David Nutt and Company only 150 sets of unbound sheets. Although this request had been sent to Nutt early in September 1914, the sheets had not arrived until January 1915. Publication date had been set for February twentieth.

Holt, prior to publication date, acquired enough orders to exhaust the small edition, and Harcourt had immediately sent a cable to Nutt, ordering 200 more sets of sheets. But weeks would pass before that new supply of sheets could arrive. The situation was absurd. Orders were coming in steadily for the newly published *North of Boston,* and no copies were available. If Nutt delayed too long, Holt might be forced to print its own edition.

Harcourt had one other bit of news for Frost. Well in advance of the publication date, Harcourt had sold to *The New Republic* the poem entitled "The Death of the Hired Man," and it had appeared in the issue for February sixth. At this point in his account Harcourt took from his desk *The New Republic*'s check for forty dollars, in payment for the poem, and presented it to Frost.

Harcourt told Frost that, for business reasons, the newly returned poet should remain in New York City for at least a few days. It might be advantageous to let Harcourt take Frost to lunch with the editors of *The New Republic*; and, in addition, Frost should attend the meeting of the Poetry Society of America scheduled for the very next night. Ready to participate in any campaign that might advance his reputation, and held by his obligation to Mervyn Thomas, Frost accepted these proposals.

The next morning, when he returned to Ellis Island, matters did not go easily. The poet was led into a courtroom where Mervyn was waiting his turn to have someone plead his case. The three-man board, listening to one case after another, finally invited Mervyn's sponsor to answer questions. If Frost were to serve as guardian for this underage alien, how did he plan to earn a living? Well, he was a teacher and a poet. Did he have a position now as teacher? No, but he was sure he could get one. Until he did, would he be able to support himself, his family, and this boy on the earnings from his poetry? Perhaps. He had recently published two books in England, and one of these books had just been republished in the United States. How much money had he received for these books so far? Well, none so far; but——.

The three men were amused—and Frost was infuriated by their smiles. Desperately, he went on to say he had explained his case to friends, a lawyer named Charles Burlingham had vouched for him as sponsor, and Mr. Burlingham's word had been accepted by Mr. Howe, the commissioner of immigration. The men announced they had received no word from the commissioner. Then, Mervyn was asked if he had anything to say in his own behalf concerning why he should not be sent back to England. Bewildered and frightened, the boy glanced at

Frost. Now disgusted, he answered Mervyn's mute plea by shouting, "Tell them you wouldn't *stay* in a country where they treat people like this!"

The case was deferred until after lunch, so some test could be made of the assertion that the commissioner of immigration knew about the case. Fortunately, the message from the commissioner was found, and Frost was given papers certifying that he was authorized to serve as Mervyn's sponsor. A few hours later Frost put the boy on a train that would, with changes, take him to Alstead, New Hampshire, to be met there by Russell Scott.

Alfred Harcourt, told about the Ellis Island difficulties, may have had them in mind when he secured Robert Haven Schauffler to serve as companion for Robert Frost at the meeting of the Poetry Society of America. Schauffler's humanitarian poem "Scum o' the Earth," which dealt with various hardships suffered by enterprising immigrants, had attracted much praise when it appeared, a few years earlier. What Harcourt did not know, when he made this arrangement, was of the harsh comments aimed at two of Frost's *North of Boston* poems that had been read aloud at the December meeting; and Frost, if he had known how his name and poetry had been abused by the society two months before, might have refused to attend the February meeting. But the crowd of nearly 200 was large enough for him to hide in, and he insisted to Schauffler that this first visit should not be marred by any formal presentation. (The subject under discussion was free verse, and the visitor was conservative enough to enjoy hearing various members of the society heap condemnations on this so-called new art form.)

Less enjoyable was Harcourt's promotional campaign with the editors of *The New Republic.* At luncheon a day or so after the meeting of the Poetry Society, Frost became acquainted with Francis Hackett, Philip Littell, Walter Lippmann, and Herbert Croly. If each of these editors projected his own socialistic and humanitarian prejudices into his reading of "The Death of the Hired Man," either before or after it appeared in *The New Republic,* and if each had failed, therefore, to guess at the unreconstructed political or social conservatism of its author, one lunch with him may have been enough to reveal his hostility to their liberalism.

During this unexpected lingering in New York City, Frost did call on Mrs. Henry Holt, who had been the first stranger in America to send him a letter of praise for *North of Boston.* When she learned, during Frost's visit with her, that he had just returned from England and he hoped to buy a small farm in northern New England, she insisted he should reach no decision until he had explored possibilities in the Green Mountains, around the village of Stowe. She was so persuasive in describing the attractions of Vermont that he did later extend his search to the Stowe region, before he decided to settle in the White Mountains.

As soon as Frost completed his round of campaigning in New York City, instead of starting for New England he made an impulsively compassionate journey to visit his sister, Jeanie. She was teaching in Wildwood, New Jersey, when last she had written him, and he went there by train without trying to give her any hint of his coming. He knew the nervous instability that had troubled her since childhood had been reflected recently in her failure to keep any teaching position for more than a year, but she had told him in her letter that this, her first, year at Wildwood had started well. When he got there, he was upset by his discovery that she had been discharged and was now teaching in South Fork, Pennsylvania—a coal-mining town not far from Pittsburgh.

He could easily have made excuses to himself for avoiding the long trip to South Fork; his wife and children were waiting for him in New Hampshire, and he had little cash. Nevertheless, to South Fork he went. When he found Jeanie, there, she was already distraught from what she described as the rudeness—even, brutality—in her new school. He listened to her wild account of all she had suffered since he last heard from her. She regretted she had not made better uses of the annuities from her grandfather's estate and that she had not continued her education to a point where she could obtain a first-rate teaching position.

Her brother, trying to comfort and encourage her, insisted it was not too late for her to earn a college degree. She was so bright, he told her, she could do the necessary work in three years. He also assured her that most of her expenses could be paid from the funds continuously provided by the annuity, and he offered to give her additional financial aid as soon as he was established. Deriving fresh hope from her brother's practical suggestions, Jeanie at once began making college plans, which she later carried out. She was so grateful for his visit that he was glad he had made the effort to find her. At the same time, he was equally glad to take leave of her and set out for New England.

The expense of his journey to Wildwood and South Fork caused him to rearrange his route northward. He went first to Lawrence, Massachusetts, important to him as the home of Wilbur E. Rowell, who had already served for fourteen years as executor and trustee of the William Prescott Frost estate. When he reached Lawrence, early in March of 1915, he was given such a cordial reception by Mr. and Mrs. Rowell—and was so quickly granted an advance of $200—tha. he could not refuse their invitation to stay with them for an extra day or two. Nor could he deny himself the pleasure of walking along the familiar streets of Lawrence and of calling briefly on a few of his old friends.

Some of these visits were more embarrassing than he had anticipated. Ernest Jewell, with whom he had been closely associated during and after their high-school days, received him coldly. Neither one of them mentioned the considerable debt Frost had owed Jewell since the Derry period, but it was obvious from Jewell's manner that he had neither forgotten nor forgiven the twelve-year lapse in the promised payments. A far more affable reception was given him by several of his former high-school teachers, into whose classrooms he cautiously intruded. One persuaded him to set a precedent by reading aloud to her literature class—or, rather, by saying from memory—a few of his poems.

Before leaving Lawrence, Frost decided he had reason enough for delaying still longer his departure for New Hampshire, so that he might call on at least one literary figure in Boston: Ellery Sedgwick, editor of *The Atlantic Monthly*. For years Frost had been unsuccessful in attempts to place his poems in the *Atlantic*. Now, partly for spite, he wanted to visit Sedgwick, to see if recent developments might have softened his attitude. Impulsively, Frost started for Boston on Friday, the fifth of March.

The visit to the editor of the *Atlantic* turned out to be far more of an adventure than Frost had expected. Sedgwick, informed that the caller was Mr. Robert Frost, came forward from his inner office with a seemingly hypocritical display of warmth. He stretched out both hands in greeting, as though he were welcoming a long-absent friend.

Sedgwick said he had first heard about *North of Boston* from Amy Lowell, and now he wanted the whole story. Frost began talking, and in a short time he succeeded in charming the editor, to such a degree that Sedgwick made a surprising gesture. He hoped Frost was free to be a guest in the Sedgwick home that evening, at a little dinner party already planned. Frost hesitated only a moment before accepting.

The two other guests at the Sedgwicks' that evening were Mr. and Mrs. William Ernest Hocking. Only one year older than Frost and newly appointed as a professor of philosophy at Harvard, Hocking had gained wide attention three years earlier with his first book, entitled *The Meaning of God in Human Experience*. In it he had pointedly emphasized the religious aspects of his philosophical idealism. Although Frost was often shy about acknowledging his own religious beliefs, he always responded with eagerness to any practical idealist like Hocking.

Hocking's attractive Irish wife surprised Frost by saying she was a daughter of the poet John Boyle O'Reilly. Frost, priding himself on his own Scottish-Celtic heritage and genuinely fond of the Irish, impressed Mrs. Hocking by demonstrating his knowledge of her father's poetry.

The Hockings regretfully left the dinner party early, because they had previously committed themselves to attend a lecture; and Frost did not stay late with the Sedgwicks. Before his departure he apparently asked for more details connected with one story Sedgwick had told at the dinner table. That morning, soon after Frost made his visit to the office of the *Atlantic,* Sedgwick had learned that two of Boston's literary notables, Nathan Haskell Dole and Sylvester Baxter, already admirers of Robert Frost's poetry, were going to read from *North of Boston,* and talk about the poems, that very day at the weekly luncheon of the Boston Authors' Club. Sedgwick, unable to attend the luncheon, could not resist boasting that he was to be the host of Robert Frost that evening. This was circulated as news at the club, the first announcement that the newly discovered poet was in Boston. That afternoon Dole and, then, Baxter telephoned Sedgwick to protest that Frost should not leave Boston until they could meet him.

Frost made a phone call to Dole that evening. He introduced himself and asked if it were too late for Dole to receive a visitor. Dole expressed his delight; Frost should come right along—and spend the night.

The next morning Dole insisted on bringing to his home, to meet Frost, the poetry editor of the *Boston Evening Transcript,* William Stanley Braithwaite. Dole was correct in his prediction that Braithwaite would jump at the chance to obtain an interview, and Frost's conversation with the poetry editor began pleasantly. He had read and liked "The Death of the Hired Man" in *The New Republic.* He had also read Amy Lowell's review. Although he had not previously seen *North of Boston,* he insisted on buying an extra copy Dole possessed. Frost, touched by these indications of sympathy, promised to send Braithwaite a copy of *A Boy's Will,* together with some biographical facts that might be useful in the article Braithwaite did, indeed, want to write.

At noon Dole took Frost to meet Sylvester Baxter, and the three men discussed literary matters during luncheon. Although Frost insisted he must catch an early-afternoon train for Lawrence, so he might start for New Hampshire that night, circumstances again caused him to change his plans. Escorted by his two new friends, he progressed only as far as the North Station when the trio happened to meet Mrs. Hocking. She exclaimed with ardor that she and her husband had been sorry to leave Ellery Sedgwick's dinner party so early the night before; they both had belatedly wished they had thought to invite Mr. Frost to have tea with them in their Cambridge home before he started northward.

Frost met the occasion with impulsiveness, and Professor Hocking later gave his own account of what happened as a result of that accidental meeting: "He came, and we began talking; he stayed the night, he stayed the next day and the next night. When I had to go to class, Agnes Hocking took him on; and when she had to get a meal, I took him on. We had a great time. In three days, we had done a fair two-years' job of ripening friendship. . . ."

Something other than this friendship caused Frost to linger with the Hockings in Cambridge. Saturday afternoon he had telephoned Amy Lowell in Brookline, simply to express his thanks for her review of *North of Boston*. She responded with typical imperiousness. She was having a small dinner party Monday night, she said, and he *must* be her guest on that occasion. He promptly accepted the invitation.

On the afternoon of his departure from the Hockings' home, he had no difficulty in following directions to Miss Lowell's house. Waiting for him in the library, Miss Lowell rose from the sofa to greet her guest. He had been warned that she was a huge woman, whose corpulence was caused by a glandular ailment, but he was quickly put at ease by the liveliness of her manner and the genuine cordiality of her welcome. Frost surveyed the elegance of the spacious room. Never before had he seen such a library; never before had he been entertained in such a mansion. Although he was inclined to scorn any such display of wealth, he was impressed.

The only other guests at dinner that evening were poet John Gould Fletcher and retired-actress Ada Dwyer Russell (the latter a permanent member of Miss Lowell's household). The conversation began with literary gossip, and Frost was thoroughly entertained by the raucous prejudices of his hostess. She had gaily participated in every important literary battle since the beginning of the New Poetry movement, three years earlier. Very few people were able to outtalk Robert Frost on occasions like this, but Amy Lowell did; and before Frost left he had acquired a new understanding of how and where the battle lines were drawn between the liberal and the conservative poets in America. He was convinced that, although he did admire the gusto with which Amy conveyed her prejudices, his old-fashioned ways of making new poetry placed him apart from the immediate lines of battle.

Just how successful he had been in making an impression on the literati of Boston, during his unexpected tarryings, he did not know until he reached Bethlehem. His new friend Sylvester Baxter wrote enthusiastically in *The Boston Herald*:

"Boston's literary sensation of the day has been the home-coming of Robert Frost. Three years ago a young New Hampshire schoolmaster went over to England, lived in retirement for a while, and published a volume of poems which won him many friends in a quiet way. Some time ago another volume of verse went to the same publisher and one morning Robert Frost found himself famous. His work was hailed as striking a new note in modern poetry. He was sought on every hand in the circles where literature values count and was acclaimed one of the elect—ranking with Masefield, Gibson, Abercrombie and others of that high grade in the younger generation of British poets. The book was called 'North of Boston,' and its contents bore out its title, being a series of vivid pictures of New England life and character. . . .

"In due time copies crossed the water and appeared in the bookstore[s] and the libraries. Readers began to discuss the remarkable work and ask, 'Who is Robert Frost?' . . .

"Then came the news that Frost had just landed in New York with his family, on his way back to New Hampshire, to take up farming again—he had been a farmer as well as a school teacher.

"Last Friday they were discussing Frost at the monthly 'shop talk' of the Boston Authors' Club; one of the members[,] reading from his work, said that Frost was doing for New England in verse what Alice Brown, Mary Wilkins and Sarah Orne Jewett had been doing in prose. Another member announced that Mr. Frost was in Boston that day, and was dining that evening with Mr. Ellery Sedgwick and some literary friends. It seems that he had come to Boston from friends in Lawrence, the home of his youth, and had expected to spend only a few hours in the city, for he had with him only the clothes he had on. But his new friends insisted upon his staying over, and meeting various people he ought to know and who wanted to see him. So he did not get away until last evening. . . .

"Mr. Frost is expected to return to Boston in the near future. He is a most agreeable personality—'one of the most lovable men in the world'—declared one of his new literary friends, prominent in New England letters. He is still in his thirties, but remains youthful in face and figure. . . ."

Frost was not embarrassed by such advertising. It was proof enough to him that the initial phase of his campaigning had not been a waste of time. As soon as he reached the Lynch farm in Bethlehem and could look back at all he had done since his arrival in New York, he could even risk boasting, to one of his old friends:

"I didn't get through New York and Boston without more attention than you may think I deserve from my fellow countrymen. The Holts are splendid. If you want to see what happened in Boston, look me up in the Boston Herald for Tuesday March 9 under the heading Talk of the Town. . . ."

MORE CAMPAIGNING
IN BOSTON

(1915)

AFTER HIS adventures in New York and Boston, Robert Frost was in a mood to relish the solitude of winter life on John Lynch's farm in the White Mountains. Never before had he seen the place with icicles on the eaves, with rounded and wind-carved caps of snow on the roofs, with deep paths shoveled about the yard, and with snow piled high along both sides of the driveway. In England, where winter brought so much rain that back roads and paths too much resembled mud time in New England, he had missed the sparkle of landscapes and dooryards buried under snow. Homecoming, for him, had little to do with getting back to New York or Boston. He had been homesick for the rural scenes and people in New Hampshire, for such warmth of greeting as was given him by these affectionate friends the Lynches.

His children, giving him only time enough to get one good night of sleep, insisted that he must accompany them on various explorations —on well-used snowshoes and skis found for them by John Lynch in his attic. Frost was in the mood for letting his children show him how to celebrate their return to the region they loved as much as he did. It was only after he had begun to relax at the Lynch farm that he discovered how tired he was. Yet, he did not deny to himself or to his friends that there was a continuing excitement in his beginning to realize some of the hopes he had nurtured secretly and persistently through more than twenty years of discouragement. To the closest of his old friends, John Bartlett (who had by now returned from Vancouver, with his wife and child, to Derry, New Hampshire), he gave some hints of how he responded to "the wearing subject of the fortunes of my book," *North of Boston*:

"You can't wonder that it is a good deal on my mind with a review appearing every few days and letters coming in from all quarters. I wish I could describe the state I have been thrown into. I suppose you could call it one of pleasurable scorn when it is not one of scornful scorn. The thought that gets me is that at magazine rates there is about a thousand dollars worth of poetry in N.O.B. that I might have had last winter if the people who love me now had loved me then. Never you doubt that I gave them the chance to love me. What, you ask, has come over them to change their opinion of me? And the answer is What?—Doubtless you saw me noble countenance displayed in The Herald. . . . The Transcript will . . . [do] me next. The literary editor of The Chicago Post writes to say that I may look for two columns of loving kindness in The Post in a day or two. It is not just naught—say what you will. One likes best to write poetry and one knew that one did that before one got a . . . reputation. Still one can't pretend not to like to win the game. One can't help thinking a little of Number One. . . ."

He might have confided to Bartlett that after all these years of neglect, in which it was easy to imagine that he had fewer friends than enemies (and, even, some enemies among his friends), his delayed victory aroused a retaliatory sense of vindictiveness he did not try to restrain. But matters that seemed more practical required attention, including the urgent need to find and buy a home.

No attempt had been made to hurry Lesley, Carol, Irma, and Marjorie into classrooms after they reached the Lynch farm in February. Frost insisted they had been out of school so long in England that there could be no harm in letting them stay out for the remainder of the year. If their father had had his way, he might also have insisted that the desultory education given them by their parents was far better suited to their needs than the humdrum boredom of usual classroom teaching.

Mrs. Frost had other views, for she had carried the heavier burden of trying to work with them, as teacher, in spite of their very strong resistance to studying. Now she wanted them out of the house and in a school near enough for walking. At the western foot of the Lynch mountainside, the village of Franconia could provide a grammar school and, in Dow Academy, a complete high-school program. If the Frosts could find a place to live there, their mother would like it.

As soon as April sunlight began to dry up the puddles of melted snow on the dirt roads, Frost extended his daily walks, into Franconia, searching for a small farm that would be suitable. He soon found what he was looking for.

Although mountains flanked all sides of the Franconia village, the panorama that appealed strongly to Frost was the one seen best from the southern outskirts, the entire Franconia range, dominated by the rocky peak of Lafayette. Using that peak for orientation in his wanderings, he had been attracted to a little farm only a mile or so from the center of town. The serious hitch was that of displacing the present owner, whom he found raking dead leaves away from the front of the house.

Entering the dooryard and striking up a conversation, the intruder explained he was just out tramping, but wasn't a tramp; he wanted to buy a farm, and this was the one he liked best. The owner, Willis E. Herbert, amused by the bluntness of the visitor's approach, said maybe they could help each other. Herbert, needing more pasturage for his livestock, had taken a fancy to a larger farm, half a mile farther up the road. So, if the blunt-spoken visitor wanted this little farm and was willing to pay $1,000 for it, Herbert would move in a hurry.

A few days later Frost brought his wife and children over for a tour of inspection. Although the house was extremely small and had neither bathroom nor furnace, the entire family liked it. The water supply came from an uphill spring and was fed into the house by gravity, leaving enough surplus to fill a brook that flowed down into the Ham Branch of the Gale River. The barn was not so large as the one the Frost children remembered from their Derry days, but Frost was looking only for space enough to winter a few hens and a cow or two. Up beyond the barn were a hayfield and a pasture. Above them were woodlots with good stands of white birch, maple, poplar, tamarack, and (most attractive of all) a grove of spruces pretty enough to be marketable for Christmas trees. One of those woodlots was a sugar orchard, with a sugarhouse.

As soon as Frost had gained the approval of his family, he began to talk finances with Herbert. Apologetically, he said he couldn't find $1,000 very fast, although he might be able to draw on the trust fund from which he received an annuity, and he knew that John Lynch in Bethlehem would serve as reference for his credit. Herbert closed the deal with a handshake, "nothing down."

Frost and his family would stay with the Lynches in Bethlehem until a carpenter could make a few alterations and additions. The carpenter, when found, went about his task with such deliberation that the Frosts continued renting rooms at the Lynch farm throughout the spring of 1915. Before the actual move could be made, all of these pastoral arrangements were interrupted by two invitations that frightened the poet almost as much as they pleased him.

The chapter of the Phi Beta Kappa Society at Tufts College, in a suburb of Boston, wrote to Frost requesting him to read at least one unpublished poem at its annual meeting on May 5, 1915. Back of this invitation was Nathan Haskell Dole, who simultaneously prompted Sylvester Baxter and the Boston Authors' Club to urge that Frost talk before its members after a luncheon on the fifth of May. These invitations added fuel to a disagreement that had smoldered between Robert and Elinor Frost since the publication of *A Boy's Will* in England.

There were times when it seemed to Frost that the sharp differences of opinion between his wife and himself had seriously injured their marriage. Even prior to their marriage she had misunderstood him to such an extent that she had mistakenly hoped to make him over into an ordinary and responsible citizen. When this hope failed, she decided to throw her life away with his, self-sacrificially, and to honor him as a good poet who had failed to win attention. As long as he remained a failure she seemed to luxuriate in the sadness and loneliness of their predicament. But as soon as he began to be noticed in England, with his first book, she seemed to become jealous of the success that threatened to destroy what she had accepted as her ideal. Now the double invitation from Tufts College and the Boston Authors' Club caused her to reproach him with charges that he was too eager to win the wrong kinds of attention—that he was willing to buy attention and flattery at the expense of the time and energy he should conserve for writing more poems.

In his own defense, Frost tried to explain that he never had been and never could be content to write poetry merely for his or her enjoyment. Since the time he first began writing, he had hoped his poems would someday win acclaim. He was willing to admit it would be easier for him to refuse all invitations from those who wanted to see him and hear him. Never before had he stood facing a large audience for the purpose of reading or talking about his poems. He knew it would be painful for him. Nevertheless, he was determined to suffer whatever torture such an experience would inflict. He would do it not only to advance his own standing as a poet, but also to earn money for the support of his family.

Accepting these two invitations would give him a chance to improve relations with influential editors and critics, such as his "ancient enemy" Ellery Sedgwick and his new friend William Stanley Braithwaite. In addition, he looked forward to meeting other literary figures who were still strangers to him. One such was the poet and critic Louis Untermeyer, who, not long after Frost reached New Hampshire from England, had written a friendly letter to convey his admiration for *North of Boston* and to say he would soon be giving the book strong praise in *The Chicago Evening Post*.

There were obvious advantages in cultivating the friendships of such men as Untermeyer and Braithwaite, and soon after his arrival in Bethlehem he had kept his promise to send Braithwaite a copy of *A Boy's Will* and a long letter containing biographical information for the article Braithwaite was going to write. On the same day, he answered Untermeyer's letter, with a cordiality calculated to flatter.

Untermeyer's response clearly indicated that, with proper cultivation, he could be counted on to give continuing and vigorous support. Frost, in acknowledging the *Chicago Evening Post* review, and adding that there were "a dozen things in your article that I should like to thank you for in detail," expressed the wish that Untermeyer might, indeed, be in Boston near the time when Frost would be performing there. He hoped they might meet at Sylvester Baxter's house and, then, "steal away somewhere by ourselves" to talk about their mutual literary interest.

The Boston visit began unpleasantly. As soon as Frost reached the Authors' Club he learned he was sharing honors with another poet, Josephine Preston Peabody, whose lyrics and plays were far too conventional and old-fashioned to please Frost. He had not previously met her, but since the nineties he had been reading her sweet lyrics in magazines, and he had come to think of her as an outmoded sentimentalist who wrote too many poems about the moon. He resented the prospect of having her read poems just before he spoke on the topic of his choice, his theory of sound-posturing—or the sound of sense.

He might have taken consolation in his knowledge that the poetry of Josephine Preston Peabody would serve to illustrate, implicitly, his complaint against the persistent use of an outworn musical vocabulary. Instead, he worried over the fact that she was bound to cast him in the role of an outsider; everyone admired her and bowed down before her as Boston's best. As soon as he met her, all his suspicions seemed to be confirmed. She seemed to Frost coy and insincere. He sulked through the luncheon, became increasingly nervous as Dole introduced the first speaker, listened scornfully as the lady read several of her latest poems—and, then, he began to shake.

When he was introduced, Frost was in such a dour, frightened mood that his voice trembled and his words came awkwardly. As he listened to himself fumbling along, he was inclined to think that perhaps his wife was correct; he should not be here. He felt he did not even say his own poems well. And when he finished he was miserable. In spite of assurances given by Dole and Baxter, in spite of praise expressed by strangers who shook his hand, he was disgusted with himself for having botched the assignment.

There was one way to make amends, and Frost took it. Having promised to have a session with Braithwaite, to help him shape materials for a second *Transcript* article, Frost arranged to explain his theory of poetry to Braithwaite, at great length, during two interviews; and the article appeared while Frost was still in Boston. It conveyed all of the essential points the poet feared he had spoiled in his talk before the Authors' Club.

Braithwaite began: "The success which has immediately come to the poetry of Robert Frost is unique. It has no exact parallel in the

experience of the art in this country during the present generation."
After the preliminaries, the article settled into direct quotations from
Frost:

"'First,' he said, 'let me find a name for this principle which will
convey to the mind what I mean by this effect which I try to put into my
poetry. And secondly, do not let your readers be deceived that this is
anything new. Before I give you the details in proof of its importance, in
fact of its essential place in the writing of the highest poetry, let me quote
these lines from Emerson's "Monadnoc," where, in almost a particular
manner, he sets forth unmistakably what I mean:

> *Now in sordid weeds they sleep,*
> *In dulness now their secret keep;*
> *Yet, will you learn our ancient speech,*
> *These the masters who can teach.*
> *Four-score or a hundred words*
> *All their vocal muse affords;*
> *But they turn them in a fashion*
> *Past clerks' or statesmen's art or passion.*
> *I can spare the college bell,*
> *And the learned lecture well;*
> *Spare the clergy and libraries,*
> *Institutes and dictionaries,*
> *For that hearty English root*
> *Thrives here, unvalued, underfoot.*
> *Rude poets of the tavern hearth,*
> *Squandering your unquoted mirth,*
> *Which keeps the ground and never soars,*
> *While Dick retorts and Reuben roars;*
> *Scoff of yeoman strong and stark,*
> *Goes like bullet to its mark;*
> *While the solid curse and jeer*
> *Never balk the waiting ear.*

"'Understand these lines perfectly and you will understand what I
mean when I call this principle "sound-posturing," or more literally,
getting the sound of sense. What we do get in life and miss so often in
literature is the sentence sounds that underlie the words. Words in
themselves do not convey meaning, and to . . . [prove] this, which may
seem entirely unreasonable to any one who does not understand the
psychology of sound, let us take the example of two people who are
talking on the other side of a closed door, whose voices can be heard but
whose words cannot be distinguished. Even though the words do not

carry, the sound of them does, and the listener can catch the meaning of the conversation. This is because every meaning has a particular sound-posture, or to put it in another way, the sense of every meaning has a particular sound which each individual is instinctively familiar with, and without at all being conscious of the exact words that are being used is able to understand the thought, idea or emotion that is being conveyed. What I am most interested in emphasizing in the application of this belief to art, is the sentence of sound, because to me a sentence is not interesting merely in conveying a meaning of words; it must do something more; it must convey a meaning by sound.'

" 'But,' I queried, 'do you not come into conflict with metrical sounds to which the laws of poetry conform in creating rhythm?'

" 'No,' the poet replied, 'because you must understand this sound of which I speak has principally to do with tone. It is what Mr. Bridges, the poet-laureate, characterized as speech-rhythm. Metre has to do with beat, and sound-posture has a definite relation as an alternate tone between the beats. The two are one in creation, but separate in analysis. If we go back far enough we will discover that the sound of sense existed before words, that something in the voice or vocal gesture made primitive man convey a meaning to his fellow before the race developed a more elaborate and concrete symbol of communication in language. I have even read that our American Indians possessed besides a picture-language, a means of communication, though it was not said how far it was developed, by the sound of sense. And what is this but calling up with the imagination, and recognizing, the images of sound? When Wordsworth said, "Write with your eye on the object," or in another sense, it was important to visualize, he really meant something more. That something carries out what I mean by writing with your ear to the voice.

" 'This is what Wordsworth did himself in all his best poetry, proving that there can be no creative imagination unless there is a summoning up of experience, fresh from life, which has not hitherto been evoked. The power, however, to do this does not last very long in the life of a poet. After ten years Wordsworth had very nearly exhausted his, giving us only flashes of it now and then. As language only really exists in the mouths of men, here again Wordsworth was right in trying to reproduce in his poetry not only the words—and in their limited range, too, actually used in common speech—but their sound. . . .' "

Frost had reason to be satisfied with Braithwaite's assistance in conveying to the public these extremely important principles concerning the sound of sense. In addition, the *Transcript* article enabled the proponent of these principles to reach a larger audience than the Authors' Club.

The visit to Tufts College in Medford was far more pleasant than he had expected. He was a guest for the night at the home of Charles Ernest Fay. A professor of modern languages at Tufts, Fay was more widely hailed as the "dean of American mountaineering." He had climbed the mountain trails on those peaks visible from the porch of Frost's new home, and he talked enthusiastically about the Franconia region. But he was equally enthusiastic in his conversation about the New Poetry, and he proudly said he had first heard the name of Robert Frost during a recent visit to England.

At dinner the main subject for conversation was the news that the English poet Rupert Brooke had just died in the war. Asked to tell of his friendship with Brooke, who had helped to edit the Georgian publication *New Numbers* from Abercrombie's thatched cottage in Gloucestershire, Frost easily participated in the grief over the young soldier's death—and as easily managed to keep silent about his jealousy of Brooke.

Throughout dinner he found it easier to talk than to eat. The prospect of reading before the chapter of Phi Beta Kappa brought on an attack of nervous indigestion. But the reading went well, and notice was later given of "the pleasing impression made by the poet, of the simplicity of his manner, the sincerity of his voice and the beauty of his three poems." He read "Birches," written in Buckinghamshire during a phase of homesickness; "The Road Not Taken," inspired by Edward Thomas and only recently completed; and "The Sound of Trees," written at Abercrombie's cottage in Ryton.

Among those whom Frost met at the reception that followed was George H. Browne, who made an attractive offer. If the poet would give a reading of some poems, without remuneration, at the Browne and Nichols School in Cambridge the following Monday, Browne would arrange for Frost to receive $50 for each of four other readings at schools in the Boston area. Although he had not intended to linger in Boston this time, Frost could not resist the opportunity to advertise his poetry, while picking up $200.

As he returned to Boston from Tufts the next morning, he had in mind another financial scheme. He wanted to see whether he could sell to Sedgwick the three unpublished poems in his pocket. Sedgwick's previous show of friendliness had not caused Frost to forgive the fact that the *Atlantic* had never yet accepted any of his poems.

Again Sedgwick surprised Frost, by greeting him in the *Atlantic* office with the announcement that the poet had arrived just in time to share some news about himself. The news could wait, Sedgwick said, until he found out if Frost had brought some poems for the *Atlantic*. Pretending to be hurt, Frost reproachfully asked if he looked like the sort of beggar who went around to editors pleading with them to take a poem. Of course not, Sedgwick said. He just wanted Frost to remember that whenever he had some poems available, the *Atlantic* would be glad to publish them—and would pay well for them. Did he mean he'd take a Frost poem sight unseen? To Sedgwick it must have seemed safe to reply as he did: "Yes, sight unseen."

Frost reached toward his coat pocket as he went on to explain that he was just returning from Tufts, where he had read three poems at the annual Phi Beta Kappa meeting, and that as a consequence he did have with him the manuscripts of these three poems. He took them out of his pocket, held them high, as though he were an auctioneer, and carried on his teasing. "Are you sure—that you want to buy—these poems?" Sedgwick had no choice but to say that of course he was sure. Slowly, Frost lowered the manuscripts into Sedgwick's hand and said, with finality, "They—are—yours."

It was Sedgwick's turn for teasing, and he had his own gift for it. The news, he said, was that the *Atlantic* had just received a letter from one of England's most distinguished critics, Edward Garnett. With the letter, Garnett had sent an article entitled "A New American Poet," and it was devoted entirely to Robert Frost. After Sedgwick settled his visitor in a chair, he read aloud a portion of Garnett's letter:

"Of Mr Frost I know nothing personally, but a few particulars given me by Mr Edward Thomas who sent me 'North of Boston.' Possibly you know more than I do—which is simply that he hails from a New England farm, has paid a long visit to England, & has returned only a few weeks ago to the States. Mr Frost as a poet, however, *is a very considerable figure indeed,* not to be classed in any way with Mr Undermeyer & his associates, who I see are vociferously advertizing the claims of 'The New Poetry,' or with the class of poetic dilettanti who contribute to Miss Harriet Monro's magazine 'Poetry'.

"From what Mr Thomas told me I fancy these fellow poets, or poetlings, are not particularly anxious to herald Mr Frost's achievment; the former, if I may judge from my examination of 'their' work in 'Poetry,' are *negli[gi]ble,* whereas Mr Frost is really *representative,* carrying on those literary traditions of New England, which are associated with talents as diverse as Hawthorne, Thoreau & Sarah Orne Jewett. If anything I have erred in *understating* Mr Frost's claims to the attention of American readers; but I prefer that my verdict should be cool & unabiassed. Although I rely entirely on my own judgment in this matter, I understand from Mr Thomas that the few notices 'North of Boston' received on this side, though short, owing to the War, practically confirm my belief that since Whitman's death, no American poet has appeared, of so *unique a quality,* as Mr Frost. . . ."

Frost was elated, until Sedgwick explained, with a straight face, that arrangements had already been made for a reviewer to include *North of Boston* in a general survey of poetry. It might not be possible, therefore, to use Garnett's article. But, Frost protested, how could the *Atlantic* refuse to print an article by Garnett? Ah, but the article hadn't been requested. Still teasing, Sedgwick went on to explain that the situation was awkward and nothing could be decided, for the present. Frost left the *Atlantic* office in a rage.

Two evenings later, while a guest in Sylvester Baxter's home in Medford, he was in no mood for recognizing or enjoying the next move in Sedgwick's game of counterteasing. Sedgwick telephoned Frost, with mock seriousness, that although he had read and liked the poems, he would have to consult his poetry editor before he could say for certain whether the *Atlantic* would publish any of them. If Frost had been on the giving end of such tantalization, he would have enjoyed it. Now he bellowed over the phone: "Oh, no, you don't! You accepted those poems for publication, sight unseen, and I'm going to hold you to it." Sedgwick, pretending reproach, ironically urged Frost not to get too excited. "I'm not excited," Frost said, again bellowing, "I'm—inexorable!" With this pronouncement he ended the conversation, by slamming the receiver into place.

One of the guests at Baxter's that night was Louis Untermeyer, who had accepted Frost's invitation to meet him there. Frost liked the breezy manner in which this New Yorker handled gossip about literary matters. Only twenty-nine years old, he seemed to Frost a witty jester. He had a hawklike nose, a fondness for outrageous puns, and surprising ease in joking casually about his Jewish heritage.

Frost, using his knack for getting strangers to talk about their past, quickly obtained the most picturesque details of Untermeyer's story. As a boy, he had become impatient with formal education and escaped from it before he finished high school. He had written his first poem when he was thirteen, entered his father's jewelry business when sixteen, married a poet named Jean Starr when he was twenty-two, and published a book of lyrics when twenty-six. Early in his career as an author he had begun writing reviews for various newspapers, and he was now an editor of a leftist periodical, *The Masses*.

Sylvester Baxter, when given a chance to add some literary news, informed his guests that all the recent stirrings among the New England poets had caused him to join Braithwaite, Edward J. O'Brien, and others in planning to organize a poetry club of New England. The first meeting was to be held a few nights hence, on May 11, 1915, and it would be an advantage for Frost if he could attend. Frost, having committed himself to remain in the Boston area for the readings arranged by George H. Browne, accepted the invitation.

The pleasant literary gossip in Baxter's home was darkened by arrival of the news that a German submarine had torpedoed the British luxury liner *Lusitania,* without warning, earlier that day off the Irish coast. According to the first estimates, the ship had gone down so fast that over a thousand passengers (including at least a hundred American citizens) had lost their lives. Up until this time there had been considerable American sympathy for Germany, but it was clear there would soon be strong demands for an immediate declaration of war by the United States. Frost was certain he would be in favor of such. He later conveyed his views to Untermeyer quite strongly: ". . . Nothing is true except as a man or men adhere to it—to live for it, to spend themselves on it, to die for it. Not to argue for it! There's no greater mistake than to look on fighting as a form of argument. To fight is to leave words and act as if you believed—to *act* as if you believed. . . ."

During the next few days the shock of the *Lusitania* sinking was almost eclipsed for Frost by the excitement when the New England Poetry Club met on May eleventh. Warfare broke into the open as soon as the business session began, and Frost was amused by all these frictions between celebrated literary personalities—partly because it provided such a wealth of material for gossip. ("I like the actuality of gossip, the intimacy of it," he had told Braithwaite.)

Present at this meeting of New England poets was Edwin Arlington Robinson, whom Frost had already met under awkward circumstances. Braithwaite, in his first *Transcript* article on Frost, had begun clumsily, with a survey of those New England poets who had attracted special attention during the nineteenth century. He continued: "One came . . . much later, who is today our foremost poet in whom the very fundamental substance of New England life burns with extraordinary intensity. This poet is Edwin Arlington Robinson. . . . There comes now another poet to help Robinson uphold the poetic supremacy of New England: . . . Robert Frost." Braithwaite's manner of putting Frost in second place was, at least, indelicate. And soon thereafter Braithwaite made another mistake.

Frost said he also considered Robinson one of the best of the living American poets and would like to meet him. Braithwaite volunteered to introduce them, and while Frost was visiting Baxter during this second visit to Boston, Baxter went with Frost and Braithwaite to Robinson's apartment in Cambridge. Unfortunately, the introduction was handled with a crudeness that must have been as embarrassing to Robinson as to Frost. When the two stood face to face, Braithwaite began by saying, "Frost, when anybody thinks of poetry in America, he always thinks of Robinson as our greatest poet." (In his reminiscences, Braithwaite said of this awkward moment, "So I introduced them, and I don't think Frost ever forgave me the fact that I, before Baxter, made the statement that Robinson was the greatest of our poets." Frost never did.)

Robinson tried to make amends. After the organization meeting of the New England Poetry Club, he waited for a chance to speak again with Frost. With his typically owlish humor, he said he detected a slight hoarseness in Frost's throat and that bitters would be a good lubricant; there was a bar nearby where they could have a drink. Frost accepted the invitation, although he was not accustomed to frequenting bars.

When the two men parted that evening, each promised to send the other a book. Robinson had just published his second prose play, *The Porcupine,* and he quickly mailed a copy to Frost in Bethlehem. Frost, in his belated letter of acknowledgment, used the play as a springboard for discussing his own theories about the sound of sense:

"Don't think I have been all this time trying to decide what your play is if it isnt a comedy. I have read it twice over but in no perplexity. It is good writing, or better than that, good speaking caught alive—every sentence of it. The speaking tones are all there on the printed page, nothing is left for the actor but to recognize and give them. And the action is in the speech where it should be, and not along beside it in antics for the body to perform. I wonder if you agree with me that the best sentences are those that convey their own tone—that haven't to be described in italics. . . . This in no spirit of fault-finding. I merely propose a question that interests me a good deal of late.

"I have had to tell a number of people in my day what I thought of their writing. You are one of the few I have wanted to tell—one of the very few. Now I have my chance to tell you. I have had some sort of real satisfaction in everything of yours I have read. I hope I make that sweeping enough.

"I owe Braithwaite a great deal for our meeting that day."

Even when he tried to conceal his jealousy of Robinson, Frost was unable to do any better than make awkward motions. Friendship between these two major New England poets of the twentieth century never developed. After these preliminaries they rarely saw each other, and their correspondence with each other was limited to only a few brief letters.

CONCERNING FRIENDS
AND ENEMIES

(1915–1916)

ROBERT FROST did not go straight home after his second round of campaigning in Boston. He stopped overnight in Derry, New Hampshire, to visit John and Margaret Bartlett. Until the start of the war, John had done well enough as a newspaper reporter in Vancouver. Forced out by wartime curtailments, he and his wife made a discouraged retreat, with their year-old son, to the Derry farm owned by Margaret's parents. Frost, full of his latest triumphs, sympathetically gave the young people reassurance that he would stand by them and help in any way he could. His response to their problems was deepened by the analogies he saw between John's predicament and those Frost himself had suffered through during the days when he had first come to Derry, ill with asthma—or perhaps tuberculosis—and convinced that his grandfather had wanted him to "go on out and die."

His own immediate problem was to learn from Willis Herbert where they stood concerning the Franconia property Frost hoped to buy. While Frost had been in Boston, Herbert had called on John Lynch, to say he'd decided this newcomer was famous enough to pay a little more than a farmer would ordinarily pay. (Frost explained this awkwardness to Untermeyer: ". . . the farm I was to have had for a thousand dollars has gone up a hundred or two owing to the owner's having seen my picture in the paper. . . .") Nevertheless, the family eventually moved to the Herbert farm, early in June 1915. (The price finally paid was only $1,000.)

For a time the poet devoted all his energies to farming. But into the idyllic atmosphere of the farm came too many reminders, by mail, that such an enjoyable retreat could be only *part* of the poet's life henceforth. Early in June, Ellery Sedgwick made his peace, by writing to say he was going to publish in the August issue of the *Atlantic* not only Edward Garnett's article in praise of Frost, but also the group of new poems:

"Birches," "The Road Not Taken," and "The Sound of Trees." He said he
had been planning to do this from the start and that Frost should have
seen through his teasing. Greatly relieved, the farmer-poet passed the
news along to Untermeyer: "The three poems you have interested
yourself in are with Ellery to stay. Ellery has said it: he is going to be good
to me. He is even going to print the article by my new-found friend
Garnett. He says it overpraises me, but never mind, it may not hurt me:
he has never known a man's head turned when his hair was turned
already."

Wanting to thank Garnett, Frost had difficulty in doing so without
showing too much bitterness against American editors and critics who
had either ignored or misinterpreted him. The letter to Garnett, when
finally written, still retained some traces of impatience:

". . . Most of the reviewers have made hard work of me over here. That
is partly because they use up their space groping for the reason of my
success in England. (I was rather successful, though not with the editor
of The English Review—as you observe.) What you are good enough to
call my method they haven't noticed. I am not supposed to have a
method. I am a naive person. They get some fun out of calling me a
realist, and a realist I may be if by that they mean one who before all else
wants the story to sound as if it were told the way it is because it
happened that way. Of course the story must release an idea, but that is a
matter of touch and emphasis, the almost incredible freedom of the soul
enslaved to the hard facts of experience. I hate the story that takes its rise
idea-end foremost, as it were in a formula such as It's little we know what
the poor think and feel—if they think and feel at all. I could name you an
English poet the editor of The English Review admires, all of whose
stories are made on just that formula. The more or less fishy incidents
and characters are gathered to the idea in some sort of logical arrangement, made up and patched up and clothed on. . . ."

The polemical undertone in his letter to Garnett was inspired partly by
the way Garnett's article upbraided American readers and editors for
their failure to be first in recognizing this "New American Poet" who was
"destined to take a permanent place in American literature." No American reviewer had dared make a statement so sweeping as that. Garnett
admitted, with ironic condescension toward American readers, that
"originality of tone and vision is always the stumbling-block to the
common taste when the latter is invited to readjust its accepted standards." After praising "The Death of the Hired Man" for its "exquisite
precision of psychological insight," the English critic again bore down on
the common taste: "Yes, this is poetry, but of what order? the people may
question, to whom for some reason poetry connotes the fervor of lyrical

passion, the glow of romantic color, or the play of picturesque fancy. But it is precisely its quiet passion and spiritual tenderness that betray this to be poetry of a rare order. . . ."

Pleased by the prospect of this article, Frost worried over Garnett's tone and over its effect on American critics and reviewers.

Frost himself had helped to precipitate a concern for this question when he provided information for use in Braithwaite's first article. It contained this: "It must be remembered that Mr. Frost had no influence to attract this critical attention except what the work itself commanded. He has accomplished what no other American poet of this generation has accomplished, and that is, unheralded, unintroduced, untrumpeted, he has won the acceptance of an English publisher on his own terms, and the unqualified approbation of a voluntary English criticism." Other American critics had gone out of their way to stress the same point —until Frost had begun to worry that such praise might backfire. The backfire came. It was directed by Jessie B. Rittenhouse, recording secretary of the Poetry Society of America:

". . . When an American poet comes to us with an English reputation and prints upon his volume the English dictum that 'his achievement is much finer, much more near the ground, and much more national than anything that Whitman gave to the world,' one is likely to be prejudiced, not to say antagonized, at the outset. Just why a made-in-England reputation is so coveted by the poets of this country is difficult to fathom, particularly as English poets look so anxiously to America for acceptance of their own work. . . ."

Miss Rittenhouse also called the British praise of his works "fulsome and ill-considered," and Frost made his first complaint against her to Sidney Cox:

"The only nastiness in Jessie B's article is the first part where she speaks of the English reviews as fulsome. There she speaks dishonestly out of complete ignorance—out of some sort of malice or envy I should infer. . . .

"She has no right to imply of course that I desired or sought a British-made reputation. You know that it simply came to me after I had nearly given up any reputation at all. . . ."

It would be necessary, Frost decided, to find some way of publishing his own answer to these charges—to quiet the claim, first made by Pound (who was actually quoting Frost), to the effect that Frost had gone to England only after he had been snubbed by American editors and publishers. Appealing to Alfred Harcourt, Frost used the same methods already used in manipulating Braithwaite and Untermeyer as voices for his views. If Harcourt could exert his influence to get something published in denial of the current thrusts at American publishers, Frost would be grateful. Harcourt knew the ropes, and within a few days after the request was received, he planted an editorial in *The New York Times*:

"That Mr. ROBERT FROST's volume of poems, 'North of Boston,' made its first appearance under the imprint of an English instead of an American publisher has disturbed some of our reviewers and revived the old complaint that we are unappreciative of true excellence when it knocks at the door of our native literature. Mr. FROST's poems are pre-eminently worth while, they are thoroughly original in theme and treatment, they are genuinely interpretive of certain phases of American life—why, then, were they published first in England? The query has suggested dire possibilities by way of answer. But now Mr. FROST himself comes to the rescue with an explanation the simplicity of which should allay at once any international jealousies or suspicions. Writing to his present American publishers he tells them that he happened to be in England when the idea came to him of collecting his poetry manuscripts into a volume. He did this, and, with the manuscript in his pocket, went up to London and left it with a publisher, who promptly accepted it. He declares, moreover, that he 'never offered a book to an American publisher, and didn't cross the water seeking a British publisher.' The thing 'just happened.' And, so, there is not 'another case of American inappreciation' to record."

That this editorial did not contain the whole truth, and that Frost was willing to differentiate between what he would say in private and in public, he very quickly demonstrated in his letter of thanks to Harcourt for assistance: "If I ran away from anything when I went to England it was the American editor. Very privately in the inmost recesses of me I suppose my Hegeira was partly a protest against magazine poets and poetry. We wont insist on that now; but please remember it when I am dead and gone."

In spite of his nervousness, worries, and fears over the public responses, Frost enjoyed the private game of jockeying for position and of demonstrating his power to manipulate those he could use. He further enjoyed noticing that, as the controversy continued, the sale of his books increased. Long before the summer of 1915 was over, Harcourt proudly informed him that *North of Boston* was on the best-seller list and that a fourth printing had been ordered. This was enough to start the poet on a new campaign.

In a flattering letter to Braithwaite, he built up to his point by urging that the poet-critic should come and visit him in Franconia, where they could fill a week of days walking and talking. He concluded: "If you dont come I shall be sure it is because you are too nice to have anything to do with the author of a Best-seller (non-fiction) which is what I am told I have become. Isn't it—well hard to know how to take?"

There were reasons for strengthening his ties with Braithwaite. Having published no new poems since his return from England, except the three in the *Atlantic,* he wanted Braithwaite to pick up at least one of these for his *Anthology of Magazine Verse for 1915.*

Inviting Braithwaite to visit the Frosts in New Hampshire was successful as strategy. Braithwaite sent his regrets, saying he was so busy compiling his *Anthology* that he could not get away just now. But he did hope Frost would be willing to let him use in the *Anthology* "Birches," "The Road Not Taken," and (because it had appeared in *The New Republic*) "The Death of the Hired Man." Frost replied expansively, ". . . I shall be honored if you will use the poems in your book, honored enough if you will use two, honored beyond dreams if you will use three. . . ."

A more important honor came from the "dean of American letters," William Dean Howells, in his column in *Harper's Magazine* for September. After condemning *vers libre* as having newness only in the sense of being "what we may call the shredded prose," and after treating harshly not only Amy Lowell's *Sword Blades and Poppy Seed,* but also Edgar Lee Masters' extremely popular *Spoon River Anthology,* Howells gave almost unreserved praise to *A Boy's Will* and *North of Boston:* "Here is no *vers libre,* no shredded prose, but very sweet rhyme and pleasant rhythm, though it does not always keep step (wilfully breaks step at times, we should say), but always remains faithful to the lineage of poetry that danced before it walked." Continuing at some length, Howells singled out for praise one aspect no other critic had mentioned:

". . . His manly power is manliest in penetrating to the heart of womanhood in that womanliest phase of it, the New England phase. Dirge, or idyl, or tragedy, or comedy, or burlesque, it is always the skill of the artist born and artist trained which is at play, or call it work, for our delight. Amidst the often striving and straining of the new poetry, here is the old poetry as young as ever; and new only in extending the bounds of sympathy through the recorded to the unrecorded knowledge of humanity. One might have thought there was not much left to say of New England humanity, but here it is as freshly and keenly sensed as if it had not been felt before, and imparted in study and story with a touch as sure and a courage as loyal as if the poet dealt with it merely for the joy of it.

"But of course he does not do that. He deals with it because he must master it, must impart it just as he must possess it. . . ."

Howells gave Frost more than public praise. He wrote a personal letter, in advance of his article, and asked Frost to call on him whenever the poet was next in New York. He did, and the visit with Howells was far more intimate than Frost had expected. Howells had a secret to confide. The triumph of *North of Boston* amounted to a fulfillment of a hope Howells had entertained forlornly in 1909, when he had published what he now considered to be a similar volume of blank-verse poems, *The Mother and the Father: Dramatic Passages.* Apparently, Howells said, the reading public had not been ready for the poetic realism he had offered at that time. Glad that Frost had succeeded where he himself had failed, the poet-novelist inscribed a copy of *The Mother and the Father* as a gift, which Frost proudly accepted.

Neither in his conversation nor in his article did Howells raise one question that bothered so many conservative reviewers: whether the dramatic narratives in *North of Boston* might have been handled just as well as short stories or sketches, in prose. Frost was still chafing under Amy Lowell's having compared his poetic tales with the prose stories of Alice Brown, and under the additional claim that while Alice Brown had "a rare sense of humor," Frost seemed to have none.

Commenting sarcastically on this latter point, in one of his letters to Edward Thomas, Frost wrote: "Amy Lowell says I have no sense of humor, but sometimes I manage to be funny without that gift of the few. Not often, you know." Often enough, he thought, to have woven comic touches into more than half the poems in *North of Boston*. And as for his earlier book, he had supposed his best readers would notice how the entire structural arrangement of poems in *A Boy's Will* conveyed his own retrospective detachment and humorous objectivity concerning poems that reflected his immature moods. His "program notes" had been calculated to heighten an awareness of the humor there. As for his humorous employment of irony and sarcasm, even Ezra Pound had laughed sympathetically over the five lines of "In Neglect."

Tones, tones, tones. He was certain he had succeeded in building enough humorous tones of voice into his poems to spare him too much concern over Amy's apparent tone-deafness. But he was seriously annoyed when others repeated her insinuation that he was a writer of short stories in verse. And an editorial in the New York *Evening Post* carried the insult further by insisting that "It was hardly necessary to run Robert Frost's lines solid in order to show that they are essentially prose. . . . Disguised as poetry, the . . . short story is finding a market."

It seemed to Frost that Edward Garnett had answered these insults best when he had come to Frost's defense by declaring him to be "a master of his exacting medium, blank verse." Going even further, Garnett had restated the question raised by readers who were deaf, and had answered well:

"But why put it in poetry and not in prose? the reader may hazard.

Well, it comes with greater intensity in rhythm and is more heightened and concentrated in effect thereby. If the reader will examine 'A Servant to Servants,' he will recognize that this narrative of a woman's haunting fear that she has inherited the streak of madness in her family, would lose in distinction and clarity were it told in prose. Yet so extraordinarily close to normal everyday speech is it that I anticipate some academic person may test its metre with a metronome, and declare that the verse is often awkward in its scansion. No doubt. But so also is the blank verse of many a master hard to scan, if the academic footrule be not applied with a nice comprehension of where to give and when to take. . . ."

Frost was always conscious of the need for conveying his criticisms subtly—even, for concealing them entirely—whenever his opponent was being useful to him. His newly made friend Untermeyer, for example, had already established himself as a defender of Frost's against those who belittled his poetic abilities, and Frost was as flattering to Untermeyer as to Braithwaite. For a time. His compliments obliquely reflected a desire to hold Untermeyer's hands so that the polemical critic couldn't strike Frost; and there were many times when Frost poured out his resentments against enemies real or imagined, knowing that some of his prejudices, thus expressed, would help to color Untermeyer's critical writings.

Oversensitive, and suffering too often under the delusion that he was being persecuted by those who might set the "whole nation" against him, Frost needed the playful and witty support given him by many of his understanding friends, including Untermeyer. But Edgar Lee Masters was one competitor who was praised too highly and too often by Untermeyer. Even worse, Frost noticed, Untermeyer and Braithwaite coupled Frost with Masters as the two best finds of the year 1915. Resenting the praise Untermeyer gave Masters, Frost tried to correct him: "It grieved me a little that you shouldnt have felt that what I wanted to say about Masters but couldnt say because it would sound strange coming from me—couldnt say in so many words at least—was that he was too romantic for my taste[,] and by romantic I'm afraid I mean among other things false-realistic. . . ." Masters' next book, *Songs and Satires,* disappointed all the critics, including Untermeyer. Delighted by this development, Frost privately gloated over his belief that Masters was dead as a competitor. A blurb, written by Masters for Sandburg's *Chicago Poems,* gave a chance for extra gloating to Untermeyer:

". . . Meanwhile and till I can go to join him here's a sigh and a tear for poor old Masters. That stuff on the outside of Sandburg's book is enough to prove my original suspicion, not that Masters is just dead but that he was never very much alive. A fellow that's that way can't ever have been anyother way. But we wont labor that. We wont labor or belabor any thing and so we shall save ourselves from all things dire. Nothing but what I am 'forced to think' forced to feel forced to say[,] so help me[,] my contempt for everything and everybody but a few real friends.

"You are of the realest of these. Who else has struck for me so often in swift succession. I had seen what you wrote in Masses. The devil of it is I am getting so I rather expect it of you. Don't fail me!"

Moods of scorn and condemnation were indulged by Frost whenever his lack of confidence in his own abilities to sustain his own powers was intensified by other fears that also drained his energies. Throughout the fall of 1915 he was frightened by a serious illness that overtook Mrs. Frost, and seemed related to her being pregnant. From the time her first child was born, she had been warned repeatedly by various physicians that she had a heart ailment that made childbearing dangerous. Now that she was carrying her seventh child, she was told by her new doctor in Franconia that her heart was not in good condition and she must be very careful. Frost, writing to Lascelles Abercrombie, confided: "You will be sorry to hear that Elinor is altogether out of health and we are in for our share of trouble. . . . It is the old story—what she has been through so many times. . . . The doctor frightens me about her heart. But this is something you mustnt mention in your letters."

Late in November, Mrs. Frost suffered a miscarriage, and Frost quickly conveyed the news to Abercrombie in a brief note: "Just a word to you and Catherine to let you know that we are out of those woods —though perhaps not yet far enough to feel safe in crowing. We are still six in the family, no more and, thank God, noless. . . ."

After telling Untermeyer that the crisis had passed, he added: ". . . We are lucky in all being still alive. I am nurse cook and chambermaid to the crowd and that discouraged it would do my enemies (see roster of the Poetry Society of America) good to see me. . . .

"You needn't tell anyone I am so down or I shall have everybody on top of me. You know what a wolf pack we are."

While this bitter mood lasted, he gave way to new outbursts aimed at those he viewed as enemies. A copy of Braithwaite's *Anthology of Magazine Verse for 1915,* received from Untermeyer, annoyed Frost so much he had to find a special way to vent hostility. While he had been on friendly terms with Braithwaite, and indebted to him for the two long *Transcript* articles they had collaboratively written, Frost had completely ignored the fact that Braithwaite, who appeared to be a white man, was in part a Negro. Largely because of Braithwaite's preference for Robinson, however, Frost turned against Braithwaite, and began to make remarks that revealed some of his deep-seated prejudices. Near Christmas 1915 he sent Untermeyer a one-sentence foreshadowing: "Sometime at a worse season I will tell you what I think of niggers and having said so much to pollute this letter I will break off here and begin over on a fresh sheet which I will mail under a separate cover." The continuation was a tirade against Braithwaite and others whom he now considered to be his enemies:

"And again: to be niggerly is not necessarily to be niggardly. It is niggerly for instance to single out Fannie Stearns Davis for dispraise, but it cant be called niggardly to name nobody else in the world but to praise him. In the case of Fannie you can't help suspecting something in the woodpile, a nigger scorned or slighted or not properly played up to.

"Mind you I haven't read Fannie and I havent read Braithwaite's g.d. book—I got one of the children to read it for me and tell me about it. All that saved the fat obstacle from the worst fate that overtakes paper was your name and mine on the flyleaf."

After he digressed to tell a story, he continued:

"Maybe you dont like me to talk this way. I can see that I am going to make enemies if I keep on. Still that wont be anything new or strange. I had nothing but enemies three years ago this Christmas.

"Why go into details? Granted that there are a few good poems in the book—I read yours and liked it because it *says* something, first felt and then unfolded in thought as the poem wrote itself. That's what makes a poem. A poem is never a put up job so to speak. It begins as a lump in the throat[,] a sense of wrong, a homesickness[,] a lovesickness. It is never a thought to begin with. It is at its best when it is a tantalizing vagueness. It finds its thought and succeeds, or doesnt find it and comes to nothing. It finds its thought or makes its thought. I suppose it finds it lying around with others not so much to its purpose in a more or less full mind. That's why it oftener comes to nothing in youth before experience has filled the mind with thoughts. It may be a big big emotion then and yet find nothing it can embody in. It finds the thought and the thought finds the words. Let's say again: A poem positively must not begin thought first. . . .

"You mustn't mind me. Some days you would think I knew it all[,] to see me on paper. In reality I am only a poor man on ration. Its a hard winter and I'm hard up and sometimes I harden my heart against nearly everything. . . ."

Untermeyer didn't mind. It frequently happened that when Frost was roiled by his uncontrolled hatreds he could depart from them and (either because of them or in spite of them) could give expression to some of his best insights concerning the constructive relation of art to life.

VENTURING OFF
FROM FRANCONIA

(1916-1917)

IN THE middle of the winter of 1916 a problem that continued to worry Robert Frost, during these early days of success, was how to prepare a face for the faces that he met. The problem called for some acting, some pretending, and some masking of what seemed to him to be his essential weaknesses.

During the years on the Derry farm, when he was trying to discover who he was and what he might become, he had explored such a gamut of hopes and fears, that he had confronted others with a variety of faces. At times his best protection had been to treat the whole world with scorn. At other times, when he needed help, he had not hesitated to wear a mask of ingratiating obsequiousness, although he hated that posture. On the farm, if neighbors appeared in the yard so that he could see them before they saw him, there had been times when he hadn't even bothered to prepare a face; he had often stayed behind a closed door or he had hit for the woods.

When he began teaching at Pinkerton Academy, he had hoped that nobody could guess the pain and anguish required by the act of walking into the classroom to face those boys and girls who knew him only as a local "hen-man," now teaching because he had failed at farming.

In England, all the old cringing and furtiveness had overwhelmed him anew. He had been almost overcome by his inner fears and outer tremblings when he had carried the manuscript of *A Boy's Will* into Mrs. Nutt's London office. Of course, the success of that visit had given him courage enough to seek out literary friendships. His growing confidence had been strengthened by the success of *North of Boston,* and even before he returned to America from England, he had been provided with a public image by the British reviewers: a Yankee farmer who had made admirable poetry out of his farming experiences. All he needed to do after that, to play the self-assigned part, was to become "Yankier and Yankier."

After he landed in New York, he had performed so well, in his confrontations with strangers, that this had given him new assurance; Sylvester Baxter had even said in print, in Boston, that Frost was "a most agreeable personality."

If he had resisted public talks and readings, he might have protected the easygoing, agreeable image. But he would never forget how those first invitations—from Tufts College and the Boston Authors' Club—had made him turn over inside. Frost had been almost ill at the very thought of standing before a large audience, to read his poems or explain his theories. Having determined to suffer whatever the cost to his nerves, so that he might improve his own poetic stature, through making such public appearances, he had done his best to assert courage, boldness, daring. Yet, at the Authors' Club, before he uttered a single word he could feel his lips trembling, and his voice had actually quavered; he had seen that some of his listeners were suffering with him.

Nevertheless, during this trial period he was the one who found most fault with the ways in which he performed. He put himself through a variety of paces, in a tour that had forced him to behave like a grasshopper, jumping in contrary directions: from Franconia to the Boston area for several appearances; then, up to Hanover, New Hampshire; then, all the way down to New York City; then, back to Boston; and to Exeter, New Hampshire. The geographical changes had not bothered him so much as the necessary changes in manner.

At the start of these gyrations, an afternoon performance before a group of elderly Bostonians, in the Hotel Vendome, went well enough to satisfy him. His next appearance, before the girls of Abbot Academy in Andover, Massachusetts, was much more difficult. Then, there was a sort of homecoming ritual in Lawrence, where many of the faces in his audience were so familiar to him that he was able to relax more than usual. At Dartmouth he had the advantage of being introduced as one who had suffered through part of a semester there, back in 1892; this helped establish a rapport with the students. The townspeople in Exeter made him feel relatively comfortable. But a few nights later, when he attended a huge banquet in Boston to read one poem at the end of the annual meeting of the Dartmouth alumni association, he felt miserably out of place; and the cigar smoke became so thick, before he stood to read his poem, he felt suffocated.

The worst misery in this extended schedule of performances occurred in New York City, where he made the mistake of trying to give the hostile Poetry Society of America a serious defense of his poetic theory. As the third of four speakers, he was followed by Untermeyer, who read some uproariously successful parodies of peculiarities in the works of Robinson, Masters, Frost, Amy Lowell, and Vachel Lindsay. Frost tried to conceal his annoyance. But there was no pleasure in sitting there, after the failure of his own performance, and listening to the mossbacks laughing over a parody of the poetry he had just been trying to defend. Home he went to Franconia, sick in spirit, heart, head, stomach; and his illness was serious enough to keep him in bed for a week.

He had not yet learned to cope with his new task of performing adequately under different public circumstances. He was working on precisely this problem when he wrote in a letter to Bartlett:

"The Exeter evening was better than the Dartmouth Dinner. I never can tell when I am going to like my job. Lawrence was rather a success: most of the schools and colleges have been. The Dartmouth Dinner was for the politicians. I felt rather lost with my brief poem in all the smoke and noise. I would do better another time; for I would bargain for an early place on the program and should know from experience how to make more of my voice and manner. I wasnt particularly good at the New York Dinner either. There I struck too serious a note. Dinners are all new to me."

He ran into more that was new when the next round of readings took him to Mount Holyoke College. In that performance he followed his usual custom of reading some of his poems before he talked on his theories of poetry. Both parts of the program were well received, but his hostess, Jeannette Marks, a professor of English, caught him off guard when she asked him to serve as a judge in a poetry contest she was conducting for undergraduates in the New England area. Dreading the amount of work he might be letting himself in for, he saw no way of backing out. He stayed overnight at Mount Holyoke, and the next morning Miss Marks again took advantage of his generosity by persuading him to talk informally, about some of his favorite nineteenth-century poets, before one of her classes. Although the assignment was not difficult, it increased the drain on his nervous energies.

An entirely different exercise awaited him when he went from Mount Holyoke to Boston for his next engagement. His newly made friend and admirer George H. Browne had made him promise, months ahead of time, that he would talk before the New England Association of Teachers of English, in the Boston Public Library, on March 18, 1916. His announced subject was "Having a Literary Moment," and he had decided he would attack the customary way of teaching literary composition in secondary schools, the approach of the rhetoricians who harped on figures of speech, grammar, syntax—and, even, spelling.

Speaking from his own experience as a teacher at Pinkerton Academy, he told of how he had encouraged his pupils to write from their own experience and of how he had picked out words or phrases or sentences or paragraphs he could praise by saying, simply, "There you did it." Such encouragement, he said, provided the best stimulus to greater effort. Of course, the teacher who had never had literary moments of his own would have difficulty in detecting one in the uneven writing of a pupil. Paraphrasing what Emerson had said in "Monadnoc" about rude poets of the tavern hearth, Frost described what he meant by figures of speech. Students could be shown how to use their ears in gathering materials for their literary compositions. They could be shown various ways in which contexts would serve to fasten tones of voice to a page so readers could hear them.

At the conclusion of his talk to the teachers he was questioned in ways that made him know he had offended and puzzled some of his listeners. He was glad for the chance to rumple the prejudices of the rhetoricians; but, again, he did regret the amount of energy he had spent on what seemed to him a nearly hopeless cause. As soon as he got back to Franconia he began his next letter to Untermeyer: "I wish I could remember where-all I've been in the past week or so and who-all I've baptized into my heresies. Here I am home again in disgrace with those who see through me[,] and ready with pen and the same kind of note paper to resume inkling."

In disgrace he was, with his wife, who saw through him to the extent of knowing he was too exhausted to do anything more with pen and paper than waste his time writing letters.

In less than two weeks after this return, he was packing his bag in readiness for another strenuous peddling of heresies, this time in Philadelphia. The invitation that took him there had been made especially attractive by the circumstances that built up to it. One of the earliest letters of praise for *North of Boston,* received shortly after the return from England, had come from Cornelius Weygandt, a professor of English literature at the University of Pennsylvania. Weygandt and his family spent their summer vacations in the White Mountain village of Wonalancet. From Wonalancet, in August of 1915, Weygandt had brought his family by car to spend an afternoon visiting with the Frosts in Franconia, and the friendliness quickly established between the two families had been exceptionally warm.

After this visit Weygandt offered Frost the chance to earn money by extending his bardings farther south than previously. The invitation took him to Philadelphia on April 3, 1916. He stayed with the Weygandt family in Germantown, gave a reading of his poems to a group of friends in Weygandt's home (as a sort of warm-up) and, then, performed before an audience of 500 students at the University of Pennsylvania the next day. A luncheon was held in his honor at the Philadelphia Art Club, where he was interviewed by a reporter.

During this interview he was given another chance to practice discretion while conveying his literary and educational prejudices. He surprised the reporter by saying that New England puritanism could provide some hints useful to literary theory, if only one could get back to the root-meanings: purification from unscriptural and corrupt forms of ceremonies, renewal of original meanings in words, disciplined simplification of human responses. For the benefit of the reporter, he offered an example of what needed to be purified in the gushing, undisciplined verse of many modern lady-poets; and he added:

"Never larrup an emotion. Set yourself against the moon. Resist the moon. If the moon's going to do anything to you, it's up to the moon. . . .

"Love, the moon, and murder have poetry in them by common consent. But it's in other places. It's in the axe-handle of a French Canadian woodchopper. . . .

". . . The curse of our poetry is that we lay it on things. Pocketsful of poetic adjectives like pocketsful of peanuts carried into a park for the gray squirrels! You can take it as gospel, that's not what we want.

"But people say to me: 'The facts themselves aren't enough. You've got to do something to them, haven't you? They can't be poetical unless a poet handles them.'

"To that I have a very simple answer. It's this: Anything you do to the facts falsifies them, but anything the facts do to you—yes, even against your will; yes, resist them with all your strength—transforms them into poetry."

Frost had reason to feel content with the quality of his performances in Philadelphia, and he foresaw no difficulty in handling his next important commitment. A group of undergraduates at Amherst College had invited him to give a reading of his poems, and they had offered a satisfactory honorarium. Frost had accepted.

When he reached Amherst, on his way home from Philadelphia, he found that his host and guide was the attractive and witty Stark Young, a thirty-five-year-old Mississippian. During the previous ten years, Young had published two novels, several short stories, and some poems. He had recently been brought to Amherst from the University of Texas by the provocative and controversial new president of Amherst, Alexander Meiklejohn. Although Young proved to be a genuine admirer of Frost's poetry and a gracious host, he embarrassed Frost by asking favors. In the quiet of Young's prettily decorated apartment, he asked for permission to read aloud some of his own poems. Frost listened politely, was not impressed, and had some difficulty in finding enough kind words. Then, Young further embarrassed him by asking for help in securing a publisher for a book that would contain these poems. Still trying to be polite, Frost suggested that Young send his manuscript to Alfred Harcourt at the office of Henry Holt and Company; Frost would do what he could. Not long after he returned to Franconia from Amherst he received a letter from Harcourt: "Stark Young of Amherst writes that he has had two fine days with you and that you went over his verses and liked them, and wanted him to bring them down to me. . . ." Frost answered by telegram in two words: "THUMBS DOWN."

The accumulation of all these distracting experiences annoyed Frost, because he had half-promised Harcourt another volume of poetry, which might be published in the fall of 1916—even though it seemed impossible that he could have the manuscript ready by then. The Phi Beta Kappa Society at Harvard had invited him to be the poet for its annual public meeting in June of 1916, and he had already set aside for that occasion two almost-completed poems, "The Ax-Helve" and "The Bonfire." Both needed further revision, and he seemed unable to find the right mood for making revisions.

His wife, understanding the ways in which his intermittent moods of grouchiness and sulking were heightened by the strain of his barding ventures, continued to say his first loyalty should be to his writing. Each time he returned from another tour, her silences were sufficient reminders of her belief that the gains from these trips did not offset the losses. She understood all his needs for public attention and recognition. She also knew how important it was to him to flaunt his heresies before assemblies of old-fashioned poets and academicians. But she kept urging him to put the poetry first.

After he came back from Amherst he was apparently overcome by a new wave of depression and discouragement. Repeatedly, he told himself and others that the best work of any poet is completed before he reaches thirty. If he had outlived his poetic powers he might as well be dead. This dark mood passed, and although it was followed by other moods just as dark, he was soon lifted by a sequence of events that honored and cheered him. One of these events was an invitation from Untermeyer to serve as a contributing editor on the staff of a projected monthly periodical to be called *The Seven Arts*. Another was his triumphant visit to Harvard, as Phi Beta Kappa poet, at commencement in June 1916.

Even before the Harvard visit occurred, preparations for it included pleasant surprises. A retired professor of philosophy there, George Herbert Palmer, wrote to say that when the poet appeared in Cambridge he should bring Mrs. Frost with him and they both would be welcomed as guests in the Palmer home over the commencement weekend. Palmer's invitation was complicated, however, by the question of whether the Frost children were old enough to keep house for themselves while the Frosts were away.

Franconia neighbors solved the problem. Not too far beyond the Frost farm, and on the same side of Iron Mine Hill, was a farm (more nearly an estate) occupied in summer by a wealthy retired minister, J. Warner Fobes of Peace Dale, Rhode Island. Mr. and Mrs. Fobes had been among the first to call on the Frosts after the move to Franconia, and the friendship begun between the two families was exceptionally cordial. Mrs. Fobes, learning of the Palmer invitation, insisted the four Frost children could easily be cared for in the spacious Fobes summer home.

The attentions given the Frosts by the Palmers in Cambridge were flattering, and the poetry readings went well. At the public meeting of the Phi Beta Kappa Society, Frost said his war poem entitled "The Bonfire," and at the Phi Beta Kappa dinner that evening he said his education poem "The Ax-Helve."

The poet's confidence was further strengthened by another invitation accepted that summer. Ernest Silver asked him to give five lectures in one week at the Plymouth Normal School—and to bring the entire Frost family with him, to stay as Silver's guests in the home where they had lived while Frost was teaching there. The week at Plymouth went happily, and the six Frosts were next escorted to nearby Wonalancet as guests of the Weygandts for a few days. By the time this flurry of events ended, Frost was in the proper mood for settling down in Franconia to complete the manuscript of *Mountain Interval*. (*Mountain Interval* was published on December 1, 1916—later than planned.)

The mood was broken when a visitor came unexpectedly to Franconia. He was Stark Young, and he brought from President Meiklejohn at Amherst the request that the poet serve as a member of the Amherst faculty for at least one semester, with the rank of full professor, for a salary of $2,000, starting in January of 1917. The sudden move was caused by the election of Prof. George Bosworth Churchill to the Massachusetts state legislature.

Frost was at once attracted and repelled by the prospect. He had almost convinced himself he had risen above the need to teach, now that he could supplement his income from royalties by going about the country as a bard. And if he should crawl back into teaching, under the excuse that he needed more money to support his family, could he tolerate the academic? In spite of his occasional doubts concerning the wellsprings of his creative abilities, he wanted to keep trying to write more poems. If he assumed the voice and manner of a professor, might it cause him to lose the voice and manner of the poet, completely?

His recent visit to Amherst had made him realize that it was an exceptional college, newly dedicated to certain goals Frost admired. And it was easy for Frost to assume that Meiklejol..n was a boldly independent rebel whose procedures in handling a small college like Amherst could make room, comfortably, for Frost's own brand of individuality. Now that the poet had gained some literary recognition, he was able to look back over his first forty years of life and interpret them as containing proofs that he had successfully declared his independence from all the conventional responses to educational, economic, social, and political programs. The years of isolation on the Derry farm had heightened his awareness of his being separate. He had even run away from America long enough to complete his first two volumes of poetry. Instead of aligning himself with any literary schools or movements when he returned to America, he had again deliberately isolated himself on a small farm in the White Mountains; and the friends who meant the most to him were those who showed their own individuality.

Even in assuming that his own brand of rebelliousness would mix well enough with Meiklejohn's, Frost hesitated for fear the president's leanings toward logic and philosophy might indicate a lack of appreciation for literary art. But in a college as small as Amherst there should be a chance to show the students the way in which literature should be approached, provided the academicians would not be too much of a hindrance.

The Amherst offer was made attractive by other factors Frost was just then considering. Although mountain air helped him and other hay-fever victims during the pollen season, he and his family had discovered that so much below-zero weather during the winter was harsh on sensitive lungs. He had been confined to his bed repeatedly, with feverish colds that plagued him too often; and his son, Carol, had developed a sore throat and cough that was so persistent the boy had been taken to Boston for medical examinations by a specialist.

Carol wanted to become a full-time farmer as soon as he finished high school, and his interests helped to persuade his father that there was no sense in trying to raise crops at a mountain level where freezing temperatures occurred even in summer months. If the Amherst offer were accepted, Frost and his family would be in a good position to search for a more practical farm, in the region of the Connecticut River valley.

After more soul-searching, he decided that he would make no choice until he had gone to Amherst once more, to lay all his doubts and fears before President Meiklejohn. The president's considerateness and warmth of personality made the opportunities very attractive, and he accepted the offer. Soon after he returned to Franconia, following the second visit, he heard from the president: "This morning at the chapel service I read 'The Road not Taken' and then told the boys about your coming. They applauded vigorously and were evidently much delighted at the prospect. I can assure you of an eager and hearty welcome by the community. . . ."

Shortly before Robert Frost started for Amherst College in January of 1917, he began a successful effort to find an American publisher for the poems of his Welsh friend Edward Thomas. Unable to proceed earlier in this effort because Thomas felt he had not yet achieved maturity as a poet, Frost had tried to overcome the reluctance by repeating his claim that the genuine poetry in so many of the prose essays published during the past ten years by Thomas stood as convincing evidence that Thomas had curiously denied himself the right to be the one thing he couldn't help but be. Once, when Thomas expressed fear he was a fool to hope he could ever establish himself in this field that was new to him, Frost replied impatiently: "You are a poet or you are nothing. . . . I told you and I keep telling you. But as long as your courage holds out you may as well go right ahead making a fool of yourself. All brave men are fools."

This help and friendship meant so much that Thomas repeatedly hoped he might move, with his family, to New Hampshire and live next door to Frost. At the same time, he was frank in admitting that, much as he dreaded the thought of physical combat, he felt he should fulfill his responsibilities as a British subject, by enlisting in one of the armed services.

Frost was familiar with all the excruciations through which this dour Welshman went each time he was required to make a choice. Repeatedly, while the two botanized together—Thomas leading the way through his favorite countryside, in the hope of showing his American friend an extraordinary station of rare plants—these ventures had ended with self-reproachful sighs and regrets. Even the most successful of these walks failed to satisfy Thomas's fastidiousness. He blamed himself for having made the wrong choice of location, and would sigh wistfully over the lovely specimens he might have shown if only he had taken Frost to a different place.

Frost, disciplined by his mother's puritanical and stoic insistence on quoting the biblical adage that the worthy plowman never looks back, was amused by these laments. Teasing gently, he accused Thomas of being such a romantic that he enjoyed crying over what might have been. After one of their best flower-gathering walks, he had said to Thomas, "No matter which road you take, you'll always sigh, and wish you'd taken another." It seemed to Frost such an amusing attitude should provide the makings of a poem that could represent, with dramatic and ironic subtlety, the very human and familiar posture of his romantic friend. Near the end of his stay in Gloucestershire he had written at least one stanza:

> *I shall be telling this with a sigh*
> *Somewhere ages and ages hence:*
> *Two roads diverged in a wood, and I—*

I took the one less traveled by,
And that has made all the difference.

Not until he reached New Hampshire, and began to find in the many letters from Thomas further reflections of the same wistful brooding over alternatives, did Frost complete this poem, which he first called "Two Roads." As soon as it was done to his satisfaction he sent a fair copy of it to Thomas, as a letter, with nothing else in the envelope. The hope was that Thomas would take the poem as a gentle joke and would protest, "Stop teasing me." Instead, Thomas praised the poem in ways that indicated he viewed the speaker of this dramatic lyric as Frost, not as Thomas. Although he liked the poem and, even, said he found it "staggering," he stopped there. Frost, in his next letter, asked why Thomas called the poem "staggering." The answer, when it came, clearly revealed that Thomas had not yet suspected that his own viewpoint—or any viewpoint like his—had been parodied and quietly mocked. It was embarrassing to Frost to explain this joke that had failed, but he did explain. Thomas replied: "You have got me again over the Path not taken & no mistake. . . . I doubt if you can get anybody to see the fun of the thing without showing them & advising them which kind of laugh they are to turn on. . . ."

If failure of insight rested with Thomas, part of his blindness was caused by his being in no mood for laughter of any kind at this particular time. In July 1915 he said quite simply, "I am going to enlist on Wednesday if the doctor will pass me. . . ." Thus ended the days, weeks, months of his agonizing over this particular choice.

As soon as Thomas announced he was in uniform, Frost responded sympathetically:

"I am within a hair of being precisely as sorry and as glad as you are.

"You are doing it for the self-same reason I shall hope to do it for if my time ever comes and I am brave enough, namely, because there seems nothing else for a man to do.

"You have let me follow your thought in almost every twist and turn toward this conclusion[.] I know pretty well how far down you have gone and how far off sideways. And I think the better of you for it all. Only the very bravest could come to the sacrifice in this way. . . .

"I have never seen anything more exquisite than the pain you have made of it. You are a terror and I admire you. For what has a man locomotion if it isnt to take him into things he is between barely and not quite standing.

"I should have liked you anyway—no friend ever has to strive for my approval—but you may be sure I am not going to like you less for this.

"All belief is one. And this proves you are a believer.

"I cant think what you would ask my forgiveness for unless it were saying my poetry is better than it is. You are forgiven as I hope to be forgiven for the same fault. I have had to over rate myself in the fight to get up. Some day I hope I can afford to lean back and deprecate as excessive the somewhat general praise I may have won for what I may have done.

"Your last poem Aspens seems the loveliest of all. You must have a volume of poetry ready for when you come marching home. . . ."

As Thomas moved from one training camp to another, he still found time to keep writing poetry, and he relished this creative experience as an exciting, fearful, breathtaking adventure. By the time he was transferred to the Royal Artillery Barracks, where he was trained as a gunner-cadet, some of his poems had already appeared in print under the pseudonym Edward Eastaway. In December of 1916 he volunteered to go out to France with the next draft, and before he went he had seen eight of his poems in print. He also arranged for the publication in London of a sixty-four-page book to be entitled *Poems,* by Edward Eastaway, and asked that it be dedicated to Robert Frost. (He was at home on leave, with his wife and children, for Christmas of 1916, just prior to his departure for France; and his letters, then, were in part the inspiration for Frost's imaginative war poem entitled "Not to Keep.")

At Frost's suggestion, Alfred Harcourt arranged with Thomas's London publisher to bring out an American edition of the book. The good news was sent to Helen Thomas by Frost in a letter that began:

"I am writing this to you because I think it may be the quickest way to reach Edward with questions I must have an answer to as soon as possible.

"I have found a publisher for his poems in America. But there are several things to be cleared up before we can go ahead."

One of the questions was whether, for the American edition, Thomas might be willing to use his own name and to give up the pseudonym.

She answered, in March:

"What a bit of luck to get your letter at all. I thought all the mails had gone down in the Laconia, but evidently not. Im *so* excited & happy about your splendid news, & Ive already written to the dear man & told him. . . . Im not at all sure that Edward Eastaway will consent to be Edward Thomas. . . . Its all very good news & you sound as pleased & you knew we would be. . . .

"Ill leave this letter open for details to be added about the book.

"Edward will be 39 tomorrow March 3rd, & we are hoping our parcels of apples & cake & sweets & such like luxuries will get to him on the day. . . ."

Two weeks later, Helen Thomas continued the letter:

". . . Eastaway will not be Thomas & thats that he says. . . . Edwards letters are still full of interest & life & satisfaction in his work. He's back at his battery now in the thick of it as he wanted to be, firing 400 rounds a day from his gun, listening to the men talking, & getting on well with his fellow officers. He's had little terms of depression & home sickness. He says 'I cannot think of ever being home again, & dare not think of never being there again' & in a letter to Mervyn he says 'I want to have six months of it, & then I want to be at home. I wish I *knew* I was coming back. . . .'"

There was a postscript, added by Helen Thomas:

"This letter was returned by the Censor ages after I posted it. I have had to take out the photographs.

"But today I have just received the news of Edward's death. He was killed on Easter Monday by a shell. . . ."

Jack Haines and Lascelles Abercrombie had already sent other details. The big British attack had opened to the east of Arras on the morning of April 9, 1917. Thomas had been among those who watched from his artillery post the first waves of British troops crossing no-man's-land. A few minutes later, he was killed by the concussion from an exploding shell.

Until Frost received word of the death of Edward Thomas, he had managed to keep himself from being too deeply involved with even his own secret hopes and fears. No other war loss could have affected him more profoundly. The bond between these two men had been forged not so much by their common tastes in literature as by far-deeper similarities in temperament. Now, just after the soldier had found himself as a poet and had begun what amounted to a new and more valid way of life, all the mutual hopes of the two had been obliterated by that shell. The immediate task was to say something to the bereaved widow:

"People have been praised for self-possession in danger. I have heard Edward doubt if he was as brave as the bravest. But who was ever so completely himself right up to the verge of destruction, so sure of his thought, so sure of his word? He was the bravest and best and dearest man you and I have ever known. I knew from the moment when I first met him at his unhappiest that he would some day clear his mind and save his life. I have had four wonderful years with him. I know he has done this all for you: he is all yours. But you must let me cry my cry for him as if he were *almost* all mine too.

"Of the three ways out of here, by death where there is no choice, by death where there is a noble choice, and by death where there is a choice not so noble, he found the greatest way. There is no regret—nothing that I will call regret. Only I can't help wishing he could have saved his life without so wholly losing it and come back from France not too much hurt to enjoy our pride in him. I want to see him to tell him something. I want to tell him, what I think he liked to hear from me, that he was a poet. I want to tell him that I love those he loved and hate those he hated. (But the hating will wait: there will be a time for hate.) . . .

"It was beautiful as he did it. And I don't suppose there is anything for us to do to show our admiration but to love him forever."

There was one thing left to do for Edward Thomas, and Frost threw himself genuinely into the task of making other people realize that the dead man deserved the recognition he had not yet been given as a poet. Two days after writing to Helen Thomas, he wrote to Garnett, who had learned from Thomas about *North of Boston*:

"Edward Thomas was the only brother I ever had. I fail to see how we can have been so much to each other, he an Englishman and I an American and our first meeting put off till we were both in middle life. I hadn't a plan for the future that didn't include him.

"You must like his poetry as well as I do and do everything you can for it. His last word to me, his 'pen ultimate word,' as he called it, was that what he cared most for was the name of poet. . . . His concern to the last was what it had always been, to touch earthly things and come as near them in words as words would come.

"Do what you can for him and never mind me for the present. . . ."

With the same intensity of anguish, Frost sought assistance from his friends in America. As soon as the American edition of Thomas's *Poems* was published, he helped his newly made friend George Whicher at Amherst write an essay for publication in *The Yale Review*. He collaborated with Louis Untermeyer in another carefully written and comprehensive essay on Edward Thomas. Wanting to write his own tribute, he could not trust himself, immediately, to keep his grief under the severe artistic controls required by his temperament. The poem he finally wrote was simply entitled "To E. T."

22

ON THE
AMHERST COLLEGE FACULTY

(1917–1920)

ROBERT FROST and his family enjoyed the process of getting acquainted with the village of Amherst, which had grown up around a broad and parklike common shaded by elm trees. In the center of town, the Dana Street house rented by the Frosts stood within easy walking distance of the campus. Friendly neighbors helped the poet and his family settle into the village routine, which included public-school schedules for the four Frost children.

Of the courses the poet had agreed to teach, the most attractive to him was the special seminar devoted to the appreciation and writing of poetry. A group of students who had elected the seminar explained to their new professor that there was no classroom on campus that could provide the atmosphere suitable for such a course. They asked him to consider holding class one night each week in a large room shared by four of them on the second floor of the Beta Theta Pi fraternity house. The offer was accepted, although the atmosphere was rather precious for the tastes of Robert Frost.

Each of the seminar sessions held in this room was unpredictably different, and the students quickly discovered that their new teacher was, indeed, set against the customary academic approach to literature. He seemed to begin each evening casually, with whatever thought might cross his mind. He was blunt in his attacks on what he viewed as the inexcusable procedure of trying to separate form from content, in the study of how to write poetry or how to appreciate it. As a corrective he preached the Emersonian doctrine of the instant dependence of form on soul—the Emersonian insistence that a poem grows out of heartfelt thoughts, finds its expression in sentence tones, and in this way creates its own architecture.

The students, invited to read their own poems aloud, were relieved to find that Frost was gentle with any offering that was not pretentious. He had his own quiet ways of teasing and mocking anyone who tried to lean, for purposes of creating sublime poetic effects, on the musicality of words.

There was a regular time during each of these seminars when the class, as class, was dismissed; those who could not linger for informal conversation were given the chance to leave. The students who stayed were usually entertained with a brilliant flow of monologue, in which Frost revealed to them his prejudices concerning many subjects. (One evening he surprised them with his denunciation of Greenwich Village life in New York City. It was talk that, as one of them later said, "would have delighted the ears of any fundamentalist preacher in that wicked town.") At the end of each evening—usually well after midnight—one or two of the students escorted the poet-professor to his front door on Dana Street.

Other surprises awaited those taking the course in pre-Shakespearean drama. Frost, given permission to handle the subject in any way he chose, made it clear, when first he met the class, that he would be giving no lectures on historical backgrounds; he preferred to talk about the plays as plays.

One of the first assignments was *The Four P's* by John Heywood. Students to whom parts were assigned followed instructions to modernize their lines by removing didactic passages and rewriting archaic constructions. When ready to demonstrate, the students stood before the class and read their parts with so much feeling, for the dramatic tones of voice, that the old interlude became "surprisingly lively and entertaining." Within three months the class had made similar adaptations from *Gammer Gurton's Needle*, Kyd's *Spanish Tragedy*, Marlowe's *Doctor Faustus*, and Shakespeare's *Othello*. The results pleased the students so much that they gave public presentations of the five abridgements.

From the start, Frost conducted these experiments with the hope that he could heighten literary tastes and insights, but he was soon disappointed. In spite of the warm enthusiasm shown by some students in this good-sized class, he was hurt to find that the good work was done by only a few and that too many seemed indifferent.

One of his best students, a Colorado boy named Gardner Jackson, felt that part of the difficulty grew out of the casual way in which Frost handled requirements. Retrospectively, Jackson gave this account: ". . . he required virtually no papers. He hardly gave any tests or examinations. His class was the most loosely run and undisciplined class of any of the classes I attended in college. I used to talk with him about that, because the boys in the back row would actually be playing cards together while he was holding forth. It wouldn't disturb him at all. He said, 'If they want what I have to give, they can take. If they don't, that's all right.' It was a 'gut' course. I don't believe he flunked anybody in that course. . . ."

Frost was disturbed by the failure of his experiments, not only in this course, but also in his section of the freshman composition course. Part of the trouble, as he saw it, was that the elderly professor in charge of composition was content to demand that his instructors drill the students in differentiating between the literary forms of exposition, description, narration, while giving proper attention to grammar, spelling, and punctuation. Frost was indignant. Here, again, he was eager to convey his belief in the Emersonian concept that good writing, in either prose or poetry, grows out of having something to say. He urged the freshmen to write brief compositions based on their own observations and insights, and he expected that the students would relish this freedom to fashion their descriptions or narrations out of their own experiences. When the boys seemed at a loss to know how to follow these general instructions, he blamed their previous instructors.

Frost was also annoyed to discover that so many of these young men who had nothing to say seemed to have no capacity for thinking with any originality and were, therefore, willing to have their professors do their thinking for them.

Given repeated opportunities to share his teaching problems with President Meiklejohn, Frost received sympathetic encouragement to continue whatever provocative forms of experimentation he chose. Meiklejohn was quite frank in admitting that the most serious hurdle he himself faced, in trying to develop new methods of approach for the undergraduate program of study at Amherst, was the deadwood on the faculty—deadwood he had inherited from his predecessor and could not get rid of.

One of Meiklejohn's first ways of applying leverage against the lethargic intellectual atmosphere created by faculty and students had been to require that each freshman take a course in logic, a course taught by Meiklejohn himself. Another stimulus calculated to awaken concern for living issues of the day was a newly instituted course entitled "Social and Economic Institutions," taught by a brilliant young professor, Raymond G. Gettell. With Meiklejohn's encouragement, Gettell was soon taking his students on field trips to the nearby cities of Northampton and Holyoke to study living and working conditions of the laboring classes. Meiklejohn was also trying to provoke thought and debate among students and faculty by bringing to the campus as lecturers a few dedicated radicals. All these stratagems were designed to shock the boys into having something to think about, talk about, write about.

To Frost, such an unusual array of experiments seemed dangerous, because it ran counter to his own fondness for preaching the gospel of self-reliance and rugged individualism. He expressed criticism of President Meiklejohn and of Professor Gettell for what seemed to him their socialistic and, even, communistic leanings.

The students at Amherst were aware that Meiklejohn consciously and deliberately endowed the words "intellectual" and "anti-intellectual" with special meanings. To assist him in this, he not only carefully selected the newcomers to his faculty, but also steadily increased the parade of visiting lecturers. One of these was a young Columbia professor, John Erskine, who had previously taught at Amherst and who attracted special attention in 1915 when he published a volume entitled *The Moral Obligation to Be Intelligent and Other Essays*. Previously, his title essay had been delivered as a paper before the annual public meeting of the Amherst chapter of Phi Beta Kappa, and Meiklejohn had said that Erskine's ideas fitted nicely into those of the educational program at Amherst.

Frost, who later became well acquainted with Erskine, had no more sympathy for this notion of moral obligation to be intelligent than he had for Meiklejohn's notions of the need for social amelioration. Whenever his intolerance was stirred by such currents of thought, he tried to counteract them by preaching another aspect of his doctrine. In classroom and out, he told students there was no valid connection between real life and the artificiality provided through academic programs that pretended to fit young men for what lay ahead. And it seemed to him that the brightest and most independent students ought to find reasons for escaping from all the poisonous nonsense peddled as "the Amherst idea."

One sympathetic listener to this advice was the junior from Colorado, Gardner Jackson, who disliked seeing lazy students playing cards in the back row of the drama class. His almost-worshipful admiration of Frost was rewarded by special attentions, and Frost became better acquainted with him than with any other student during that spring term of 1917.

Like several other students, Jackson was surprised to discover that Frost took an extraordinary pleasure in gossiping about teachers close to him, particularly his colleagues in the English department. Stark Young remained a special target for Frost, and Jackson was cross-examined concerning Young's ways of dealing with the students. Part of the difficulty, here, was that Young was the wittiest and most skillful teacher in the department at that time, and Frost was jealous.

Unintentionally, Jackson gave Frost the weapons needed for acts that went beyond gossip. During Jackson's freshman year he and another boy had been amused, rather than annoyed, by the unsuccessful attempts of Young to educate them in forms of eroticism that did not appeal to them. As their instructor in freshman composition, he had invited them several times to his apartment. With lights dimmed and incense burning,

Jackson said, he read them homosexual passages while "trying to induce us into the joys of the abnormal business." It was difficult for Jackson to understand why Frost seemed so eager to collect more and more details about the seductive habits of Stark Young, and it never seemed to occur to him that Frost might use the information for the purpose of urging President Meiklejohn to dismiss Young.

There were some students at Amherst who were attracted to Frost because he kept protesting that atheism was one of the evils encouraged by Meiklejohn's liberalism. A few of them, after hearing him make remarks that might, indeed, have "delighted the ears of any fundamentalist preacher," invited him to talk before the members of the Amherst Christian Association. Accepting, he built his talk around a selection of poems largely available to him in *The Oxford Book of English Verse*, seeming to take as his topic the romantic belief that "the world is a place to get away from"—through love or art or nature or science or religion.

Before the first term of the poet's stay at Amherst was completed, the United States declared war against Germany and her allies; and those who upheld any form of pacifism aroused his outspoken and scornful disgust. "Glorious war, isn't it?" he wrote to one of his friends. To another he said: "Write a lot. Enjoy the war. I've made up my mind to do the second anyway. I dont see why the fact that I can't be in a fight should keep me from liking the fight."

Not even the war could help him ignore the accumulation of campus annoyances, which got on his nerves so much that he was sorry he had accepted the Amherst offer. "I'm sick as hell of this Stark Young imbroglio," he wrote to Untermeyer, "and I'm thinking of going out and getting shot where it will do some good." And in another letter to the pun-loving Untermeyer:

". . . I was melancholy when I wrote [last] and disposed to play with sad things. I'm still melancholy. He may be stark young but I'll say this[:] if he was much stark younger I should go stark crazy before I got back to my sidehill. He has spoiled everything here that the coming of the war hasn't spoiled. And he's so foxy about it. He walks up close to me on the street and passes candy from his pockets to mine like a collier passing coal to a warship at sea. It makes everybody think that he must say with sorrow everything he says against me when he loves me so much in spite of all. But it will make a melodrama."

He might have added "another melodrama," for he had published a little one, entitled "A Way Out," in *The Seven Arts* for February 1917. (It was later produced in Northampton by some of his Amherst students.) The writing of "A Way Out" could have drained off, temporarily, some of his bitterness.

The setting of the piece is a "bachelor's kitchen bedroom in a farmhouse with a table spread for supper." The owner and sole occupant, Asa Gorrill, shuffles across the stage to answer a knock and is confronted by a stranger who pushes into the room. The stranger hastily cross-examines Asa, as though he has reason for wanting to learn much, fast, about this hermit. The two men are the same height and have features so much alike they might pass for twins, but Asa has never before seen the stranger and can't imagine what he wants. Gradually, Asa learns the intruder has killed someone and is trying to escape from those in pursuit. Having been told he looks like Asa, the stranger has decided his best means of escape—his best "way out"—is to cast himself in the role of Asa Gorrill. Practicing, he puts on some clothes that belong to the hermit, and he imitates the way the hermit talks. By the time the posse begins hammering at the door, the intruder has killed Asa and hidden the body offstage. Shuffling to the door and opening it cautiously, he successfully deceives the posse by playing the role of Gorrill very well.

Many times, when Frost indulged his hatred, he couldn't resist imagining he had used murder as a means of liberating himself from a torturing enemy. Escape of some kind—real or imaginary—was his favorite solution for many of his problems. In 1917 one strong temptation was to run away from every care at Amherst by escaping to Franconia and refusing to go back.

To Franconia he did go, just as soon as the school year was over for him and for his children. He had not made up his mind whether he would return to Amherst in the fall, but he carried with him an attractive offer. The offer, based on a wartime reorganization of the Amherst course program, gave the poet a chance to teach only two (instead of three) courses, to choose these courses, to continue in the rank and salary-scale of a full professor—even, to be absent from the campus, whenever convenient, to give readings of his poems.

The decision to reject such an offer might have been possible could he support himself and his family from the proceeds of his writings. But royalties from his third book, *Mountain Interval,* were disappointingly small. Payments for poems sold to magazines might have amounted to more if he had found more time or inclination at Amherst to write, but during the semester just completed he had not offered a single poem to any magazine. How, then, to earn a living? The last thing he wanted to do was to try to make a go of it by earning a living as a farmer. Under the circumstances, Meiklejohn's generosity would provide a comfortable subsistence (more than he had ever made before); and in August of 1917, Frost wrote John Bartlett, "We are all going back to Amherst next month."

Where the Frosts would live during their first full academic year at

Amherst was a problem nicely solved by one of the most pleasant real-estate dealers Frost had ever met. His name was Warren R. Brown.

Brown knew what Frost wanted (the place had to be just far enough out of town to give the Frost family a chance to escape from the villagers, the students, the faculty), and he showed him an attractive property on the Pelham Road—just across the Amherst town line, in West Pelham. It was a two-story, shingled cottage, nestled in against a grove of tall pines. Large enough for a family of six, the cottage had a picturesque setting that immediately appealed to Frost. The region offered a fine variety of places for botanical explorations or just casual walking. He was well satisfied and looked no further.

After his return to Amherst in the autumn of 1917 the poet, made irritable by campus duties and regulations, was in no mood for devoting his newly acquired budget of spare time to writing poetry; and soon an extraordinary sequence of rages piled up like dark thunderclouds—and took so much out of him that he may not entirely have avoided mental illness.

One serious upset was caused by Amy Lowell. After she had given a course of lectures on modern poets, she published them in the fall of 1917 under the title *Tendencies in Modern American Poetry*. Frost was infuriated because the chapter devoted to him came second and Robinson came first. Nevertheless, Amy Lowell's essay on Frost stood out as the most extended and most favorable critical treatment given him by an American. He was aware of its value in this regard, and he wrote a restrained letter of thanks. Without restraint, a few days later he cut loose to Untermeyer, complaining that Amy's fumbling approach was a dreadful misrepresentation. Halfway through the letter, he once again took issue with her claim that he lacked a sense of humor, and he continued:

"I really like least her mistake about Elinor. That's an unpardonable attempt to do her as the conventional helpmeet of genius. Elinor has never been of any earthly use to me. She hasn't cared whether I went to school or worked or earned anything. She has resisted every inch of the way my efforts to get money. She is not too sure that she cares about my reputation. She wouldnt lift a hand or have me lift a hand to increase my reputation or even save it. And this isnt all from devotion to my art at its highest. She seems to have the same weakness I have for a life that goes rather poetically; only I should say she is worse than I. It isnt what might be expected to come from such a life—poetry[—]that she is after. And it isnt that she doesnt think I am a good poet either. She always knew I was a good poet, but that was between her and me[,] and there I think she would have liked it if it had remained at least until we were dead. I don't know that I can make you understand the kind of person [she is]. Catch her getting any satisfaction out of what her housekeeping may have done to feed a poet! Rats! She hates housekeeping. She has worked because the work has piled on top of her. But she hasn't pretended to like housework even for my sake. If she has liked anything it has been what I may call living it on the high. She's especially wary of honors that derogate from the poetic life she fancies us living. What a cheap common unindividualized picture Amy makes of her. . . ."

While Frost was growling over the faults of Amy Lowell, he was building up a rage over what he viewed as the stupid mistreatments of his eldest daughter, Lesley, during the first term of her freshman year at Wellesley College. Her choice of Wellesley had been stimulated by Charles Lowell Young, who taught a course in American literature there and whom her father had met during a climb up Mt. Lafayette in the summer of 1917. Young had assisted Lesley in making application for admission. He had also given her counsel in choosing courses. But because she had acquired her father's knack for expressing furious indignation against anyone who found fault with her independent ways, she soon began to complain that she was being mistreated by two of her Wellesley professors, Miss Fletcher in Latin and a man in French, both of whom gave her mid-term marks she considered disgracefully low and unfair.

Her father, responding with sympathy, wrote a diatribe to Miss Fletcher. Professor Young did what he could to soothe all of the contestants, but Frost was still angry at the so-called "linguists" when he sent his thanks to Young:

"You are a great friend and we are fortunate in our misfortunes to have one so great. You may not know all you have done to be called great. Among a lot of other things you have given us support, and what is better and harder to give, self-support.

"As for that precisian in syntax [Miss Fletcher] I can't quite get over her. She is nothing new mind you. If I showed surprise in running into her it is not because I had never seen her before, it is because I hadn't seen her for so long I had begun to fool myself into the notion that I had talked her off the face of the earth—laughed her off the face of the earth. I had fallen into a mellow reminiscent way about her in my public utterances that was almost good-natured and forgiving. Now I get my punishment (and not alone) for letting myself believe even for the least division of an hour that there is any such thing as progress. Mea culpa. The fault is mine and the punishment is half Lesley's. I gave a lecture somewhere once upon a time on 'The Waiting Spirit: How Long Will It Wait,' in which I showed how I thought we had revised our teaching in English and ought to revise it in other subjects to give the spirit its chance from the very first day in school and every step along the way, not counting on it to wait at all. I asserted that there wasnt an English teach[er] left who would be for putting off the day of the spirit in reading and writing till the hard mechanics of the subject could be learned. It has been found that the spirit won't be put off. Either it will be engaged at once and kept engaged or it will take sanctuary in the sun returning unto the God who gave it. So I said in folly and so I made Lesley believe we all believed. And then on top of all the pains your Latin department takes to make Latin painful, comes your French department to exclaim against a child for so far forgetting herself as to write a poem in French before she had studied French prosody. 'Let the spirit wait,' says your Whitechapel Frenchman: and the spirit can wait to go—it is all one to him. . . . I never wrote exercises in my life. I was the same sixpence then as now and so is Lesley's Latin teacher the same old scourge blight and destitution that held marks over me for seven years of Latin and then left me nowhere in the end. It's sure she's an argument against taking Latin as literature but isnt she just as much an argument against taking it as a discipline in the hope that the close thinking it calls for in accurate translation will serve in any other walk of life than Latin. Precise in syntax, you would say, precise in business, precise in justice. But not so. I say I have seen Miss Fletcher before. And never in all the years have I found her able to think closely of anything but Latin. I have always found her miserably minded. Was Miss Fletchers handling of the crime she thought she had caught Lesley at precise? It was slovenly. I hope I made her look ridiculous to herself. And it didnt take me five questions. Yet I hardly feel as if I had had satisfaction. She may have to hear further from me. She is a bad woman. . . .

"Lesley says you had a talk with the Whitechapel Frenchman. I wonder if you found him implacable in his magisterial self-importance. Has Lesley the least hope of success with him? Prosody! I was hoping the mere word might be kept from Lesley as long as possible. I've been telling Lesley how little embarrassed Wilfrid Gibson was when he had to confess before all the assembled professors at Chicago last winter that he didn't know one form of verse from another. I believe I don't know a single poet who knows any prosody, except always Robert Bridges. I once asked De la Mare if he had noticed anything queer about the verse in his own The Listeners and he answered that he hadnt noticed anything at all about the verse in it queer or unqueer.

"But blast all this. What a father I am! I promise never to talk to you about my children again—any of them. That is if you will forgive my having talked this time and the last time and the time before that and so on back to the day on top of Lafayette. . . ."

Lesley pleased her father by withdrawing from Wellesley at the end of her freshman year and by doing wartime work with other girls in an airplane factory. As soon as classes ended at Amherst and the summer vacation of 1918 began, Frost made a quick retreat to Franconia. "Two weeks' farming has made me think better of teaching than I did when I left it at Commencement . . . ," he wrote to Whicher.

President Meiklejohn had found several ways to make the restless poet "think better of teaching," even prior to commencement. The undergraduate newspaper for May 6, 1918, carried the announcement that an honorary degree had been given Professor Frost by Amherst; that he had been "reappointed professor of English Literature with the understanding that he is to teach in the first semester only, giving two courses." The seniors had given him a further honor by inviting him to be their speaker at the traditional senior-chapel exercises. Perhaps in no mood for addressing them, he begged off at the last moment on grounds of illness. The students, accustomed to the poet's knack for getting out of his academic obligations, were given to making jokes about it; and the satirical speaker in the class-day address, at commencement time, delighted his audience by paying special attention to such by Frost during the year.

By the time the Frost family returned to Amherst in the fall of 1918 there was one important diversion. President Meiklejohn had asked Frost to give a new course that was to be merely a series of discussions, designed to appeal to those Amherst students who were thinking primarily of when they might be called into one of the armed services. The course was to be called "War Issues," and the president was confident such a seminar, devoted to the exploration of conflicting attitudes toward the war, toward pacifism, toward the draft, toward freedom of speech, could be made stimulating by Frost's reactionary prejudices. Frost explained his attitude, in a letter to Untermeyer:

". . . This is a war college and I am teaching war issues: so it's a lucky thing I have always taken a sensible view of the universe and everything in it. Otherwise I might have to knuckle to the war department were it ever so little or else go to jail like good old Gene Debs. I am out to see a world full of small-fry democracies even if we have to pile them two deep or even three deep in some places. . . .

"Too much war! I swear if there's another war on top of this one I shall refuse to know anything about it. I have ordered all my papers and magazines discontinued after July 4 1919. No more politics for me in this world, once I am sure all throwns are throne down."

As it happened, the war was blamed for one epidemic Frost did not escape. During the fall of 1918 the spread of influenza became so serious that during one day—the first of October—209 people died in the city of Boston. Frost, confined to his bed with a severe case of the disease, was too ill to celebrate Armistice Day. He remained seriously ill during the

next two months, but by the fourth of January he had recovered
sufficiently to joke about his ordeal:

"Here it is as late as this (1919 A.D.), and I don't know whether or not
I'm strong enough to write a letter yet. The only way I can tell that I
haven't died and gone to heaven is by the fact that everything is just the
same as it was on earth (all my family round me and all that) only worse,
whereas, as I had been brought up in Swedenborgianism to believe,
everything should be the same only better. Two possibilities remain:
either I have died and gone to Hell or I havent died. Therefore I havent
died. And that's the only reason I haven't. I was sick enough to die and no
doubt I deserved to die. The only question in my mind is could the world
have got along without me. . . ."

A serious question kept troubling him throughout the spring of 1919
and, again, when he returned to Amherst College that fall. He kept
asking himself how and why he had made the mistake of nearly giving up
being a poet—and of becoming a mere teacher. As soon as he decided he
had, indeed, made a mistake and that he should fight his way out of
Amherst, he began to seek excuses for resigning. His capacity for rage
was always helpful to him under such circumstances, and he liked to say,
repeatedly, "I always hold that we get forward as much by hating as by
loving."

Late in January of 1920 he brought to the boiling point his indignation
against Stark Young and President Meiklejohn, particularly because their
talk about "freedom" seemed to him far too academic, far too liberal, to be
tolerated. It also seemed to Frost that Meiklejohn was so obsessed with
the pleasures of debate and argument that he encouraged Amherst
students to express, freely, treasonable attitudes. In addition, he became
convinced Meiklejohn's leanings were immoral, undemocratic, and
atheistic.

As soon as the poet's rage was hot enough to satisfy him, he demanded
a private session with Meiklejohn and delivered an ultimatum: Stark
Young must be fired, because he was a bad moral influence on the
students; if he stayed, Frost would quit. Meiklejohn tried to reason with
Frost by asking where the boys were likely to go, in later life, without
coming into contact with individuals who had moral imperfections. The
president was willing to let the boys build their own defenses against
such imperfections, in this Amherst atmosphere where men like Frost
would counteract whatever might be immoral in the influence of men
like Young. Frost took the opening thus offered. "I did not come here to
counteract," he said. Then, he resigned.

No public announcement was made of Frost's resignation, but the poet
himself spread the word privately. Having been asked to serve as an
after-dinner speaker before a group of Amherst alumni, and having made

a provisional acceptance, he wrote that there were circumstances that made it impossible for him to accept:

"I am forced after all to give up the idea of speaking at the Amherst dinner, and I owe you something more than a telegram in explanation. I have decided to leave teaching and go back to farming and writing. Strangely enough, I was helped to this decision by your invitation. It was in turning over in my mind my subject chosen for the dinner that I came to the conclusion that I was too much out of sympathy with what the present administration seems bent on doing with this old New England college. I suppose I might say that I am too much outraged in the historical sense for loyalty. I can't complain that I haven't enjoyed the 'academic freedom' to be entirely myself under Mr. Meiklejohn. While he detests my dangerously rationalistic and anti-intellectualistic philosophy, he thinks he is willing to have it represented here. But probably it will be better represented by some one who can take it a little less seriously than I. . . ."

After making his decision, Frost gathered his family and retreated with them to Franconia in February of 1920. Words of solicitude sent to him by Wilbur Cross at Yale gave him another chance to clear his own mind, concerning what he had learned at Amherst and why he had decided to break away:

"I should have answered your letters sooner, but I have been busy retiring from education. I discovered what the Amherst Idea was that is so much talked of, and got amicably out. The Amherst Idea as I had it in so many words from its high custodian is this: 'Freedom for taste and intellect.' Freedom from what? 'Freedom from every prejudice in favor of state home church morality, etc.' I am too much a creature of prejudice to stay . . . [and] listen to such stuff. Not only in favor of morality am I prejudiced, but in favor of an immorality I could name as against other immoralities. I'd no more set out in pursuit of the truth than I would in pursuit of a living unless mounted on my prejudices. There was all the excuse I needed to get back to my farming. . . ."

23

TROUBLES WITHIN
THE FAMILY

(1920)

SOON AFTER Robert Frost withdrew from Amherst College and took
refuge in Franconia, he received word that his sister, Jeanie, was in jail.
He had heard nothing from her, and very little about her, for more than a
year; and when last they had met they had exchanged harsh words and
had quarreled bitterly. Wilbur Rowell, who regularly sent each of them
annuity payments from their grandfather's estate, kept in far-closer
touch with Jeanie than her brother did.

In Portland, Maine, using a public telephone in a drugstore, she had
tried to place a call to Rowell in Lawrence. Failing to reach him, she
became hysterical, and the druggist summoned the police. Jeanie,
obsessed for years by the notion that she was in constant danger of being
captured by underworld characters who wanted her for their white-slave
trade, fought the policemen and protested that she was being kidnapped
by criminals who were only pretending to be officers of the law. She was
subdued by force, taken to the police station, and locked in a cell. A
physician gave her sedatives, pronounced her demented, and said she
should be placed in an asylum for the insane.

Whatever her condition may have been, she did have enough presence
of mind to ask that word of her plight be sent to her friend Louie
Merriam, with whom she had been living—and wandering from one
teaching position to another. Miss Merriam came quickly, explained that
she understood Jeanie's case, and offered to assume complete responsibility for her care if the police would let her go. The police, unwilling to
accede until they had instructions from the nearest of kin, asked about
relatives. Both women had their reasons for avoiding any mention of
Jeanie's brother. Instead, they named Rowell as Jeanie's lawyer and
guardian. Frost learned of Jeanie's predicament only when he received
Rowell's letter of March 29, 1920. Answering, he wrote:

". . . I am too shaken at the moment to know what to propose. It may not be an incurable case. My hope is that what has been pronounced insanity may turn out no more than the strange mixture of hysteria and eccentricity she has shown us so much of. If so, she might be perfectly manageable at large in the company of somebody like Louis Merriam. But I should want them to come to rest somewhere and should feel obliged to contribute a little to make it possible. . . .

"We are just back from Amherst and in here where letters seem forever in reaching us. Will you wire at my expense if you wish to see me to instruct me as to how I shall approach the Portland police without assuming more responsibility than I am equal to? I may say that there isn't the haste that there would be if my personal attendance could do anything to soothe or comfort Jean. It's a sad business."

Frost gained additional instructions from Rowell before starting alone by train to Portland. The long and tedious journey gave him time enough to weigh his responsibilities to his sister. From childhood he and Jeanie had been so much alike, in so many ways, that they had found special methods of taunting and tormenting each other. While their mother was alive she had managed to serve as a buffer between them. After their mother died, Jeanie and Rob became increasingly hostile toward each other; and he would never forget the dreadful scenes she had created, in the presence of his baffled children, at the Derry farm while occasionally visiting there.

Frost had written her from England, at least once, to tell of his triumph in getting two books published. He had also sent her some of the most favorable reviews. When he returned to the United States and tried to create a new basis of rapport between them, she seemed particularly grateful to him for his urging that she should stop teaching, long enough to acquire a college degree.

While Jeanie was trying to complete the University of Michigan examinations that would enable her to be graduated at the end of two and a half years, her brother and Wilbur Rowell frequently shared their acquired evidences that she gave the impression of "extreme eccentricity" at Ann Arbor. She was consistent only in making appeals for gifts, loans, or advances on her annuity; and both men continued to help her financially. Her brother became increasingly disturbed, however, by her radical opinions concerning social and political questions. (She bitterly opposed the entry of the United States into the war and participated in protest marches.) Nevertheless, she did complete her course of study and was graduated in August of 1918, adequately prepared to teach German, Latin, and French at the high-school level.

The high-school position she obtained was at New Marlboro, adjacent to Mill River, Massachusetts, where she took up residence—so near to her brother that he was displeased. In Mill River her indiscreet ways of expressing her pacifist views and her sympathies for Germany precipitated a series of persecutions calculated to drive her out of town. The worst moment occurred on the morning of Armistice Day, 1918, when one of the teachers demanded that Miss Frost celebrate with them, by saluting the flag. She refused and was nearly mobbed by students and teachers alike. Fearing violence, she called a taxi and gave directions to the home of her brother in Amherst.

Frost, sick in bed with influenza, had been in no mood to learn that his sister had arrived unexpectedly—with a request that he pay the taxi fare. Jeanie, storming into his bedroom, infuriated him with her account of how she had barely escaped being murdered by the brutes in Mill River. She had no money, and her brother gave her a few dollars. But when she asked if he would help her find another teaching job, he refused. Taunting her with sarcasms, he said he had friends who wrote for the socialistic-communistic sheet called *The Masses,* in New York City, and maybe he could get her a job with those who thought as she did. Enraged by his mockery, she fled again. That evening she telephoned her sister-in-law to say there was no need to worry about Rob's influenza; people as bad as he never died of illness. That was the last word from Jeanie until Frost learned she had been locked up in Portland as demented.

If Frost, during his ride through the mountains to Portland, did use his leisure to review these past relations with his sister, he may have been in no mood to sympathize with her for what subsequently happened. He expected to find her still held in custody by the police. Instead, he learned that Miss Merriam had rescued her, by finding a doctor in West Pownal, Maine, who had taken Jeanie into his own home for observation and treatment. The police told Frost about the decision of the other doctor, who had insisted Miss Frost should be placed in a mental institution. On the strength of this information, Frost began to suspect the motives of Miss Merriam, who might want control of Jean's annuity.

Having decided his sister should be taken to the state hospital in Augusta, he obtained the necessary papers for commitment and was accompanied to West Pownal by a woman authorized to serve as a sheriff. He was not well received. Miss Merriam clung to Jeanie and insisted that Frost's decision was further proof he was cold and cruel. After an unpleasant fracas, in which Miss Merriam used her fingernails enough to draw blood on Frost's face, he and the sheriff managed to force the hysterical Jeanie into a taxi. They took her to the state hospital, and the understanding there reached with the doctors was that Frost would be notified if or when his sister was able to leave. Not long after he returned to Franconia from Maine, he confided to Untermeyer:

"I must have told you I have a sister Jeanie two or three years younger than myself. . . .

"She has always been antiphysical and a sensibilitist. I must say she was pretty well broken by the coarseness and brutality of the world before the war was thought of. This was partly because she thought she ought to be on principle. She has had very little use for me. I am coarse for having had children and coarse for having wanted to succeed a little. She made a birth in the family the occasion for writing us once of the indelicacy of having children. Indelicacy was the word. Long ago I disqualified myself for helping her through a rough world by my obvious liking for the world's roughness.

"But it took the war to put her beside herself, poor girl. Before that came to show her what coarseness and brutality really were, she had been satisfied to take it out in hysterics, though hysterics as time went on of a more and more violent kind. I really think she thought in her heart that nothing would do justice to the war but going insane over it. She was willing to go almost too far to show her feeling about it, the more so that she couldnt find anyone who would go far enough. One half the world seemed unendurably bad and the other half unendurably indifferent. She included me in the unendurably indifferent. A mistake. I belong to the unendurably bad.

"And I suppose I am a brute in that my nature refuses to carry sympathy to the point of going crazy just because someone else goes crazy or of dying just because someone else dies. As I get older I find it easier to lie awake nights over other people's troubles. But thats as far as I go to date. In good time I will join them in death to show our common humanity."

The first trip Frost made to Augusta to call on Jeanie, after she had been committed, was in May of 1920, and he found her sane enough to express her bitterness against him for his decision to have her put away. Answering his questions as briefly as possible, she sat rigidly on a straight-back chair, facing him, her eyes closed. After his next visit, about two months later, he wrote to Rowell:

". . . I have been over twice to see Jean, and should have been oftener if the journey weren't so long and expensive. When I was with her she was nearly rational—not quite. But she is in a semi-violent ward and the doctors tell me she is noisy and destructive at times. Her general health is bad. I should think she might not live long. . . ."

Jeanie lived for nine years in the state hospital in Augusta, Maine, and died there from natural causes at the age of fifty-three, on September 7, 1929. Her brother, a few years after her death, talked to his friend John Bartlett concerning her, and Bartlett made the following notes:

"The talk had turned to the subject of adjustment and mal-adjustments...R.F. . . . observed how he could look back, probably JTB could look back and see times when it seemed a miracle they had 'come through'...Will had something to do with it...He could contemplate his sister's life . . . and see half a dozen times when by making the right decision she could have saved herself...to an extent, it was a matter of choice...one could run away from things in cowardice, or one could run away from them and retreat into the ego, in the direction of paranoia. . . .

"INSANITY. We all have our souls—and minds—to save, and it seems a miracle that we do it; not once, but several times he could look back and see his hanging by a thread. His sister wasn't able to save hers. She built the protecting illusion around herself and went the road of dementia praecox."

During the summer of 1920, Robert Frost felt himself surrounded by too many troubles in Franconia, and he began to look for avenues of escape. He and his sister had acquired from their mother a romantic habit of idealizing distant scenes, particularly when immediate irritations became annoying. His running away, on this occasion, was motivated in part by a young man from New York City, Raymond Holden, whom Frost had first met in Franconia during the summer of 1915.

Invited to read his poems and talk before a group of summer visitors at a nearby hotel, Frost had felt that most of his listeners treated him as a mere curiosity. By contrast, young Holden's attention had been so rapt and sympathetic that Frost instinctively made him the focal point of that audience. At the conclusion of the reading, Holden was introduced as one who wrote poetry and aspired to become a poet. Liking Holden, Frost cultivated a friendship with him. The Frost farm was only a mile or so from where Holden was staying, and he was encouraged to become a regular visitor at the farm. During the remainder of that summer he became well acquainted with all of the Frosts.

Holden was absent from Franconia during the summers of 1916, 1917, and 1918. However, he and Frost corresponded, and Holden confessed in his letters that, as soon as he could return, he hoped to take up residence in Franconia. By the time he did return, in the summer of 1919, he had married and had acquired a substantial inheritance from his grandfather. After gaining his wife's consent, he announced that they would live in Franconia, year round, so he might be near Frost while continuing his effort to establish himself as a poet.

Frost offered to sell him the uphill half of Frost's own fifty-acre farm. Delighted with the possibilities thus made available to him, and considering himself richer than he was, the young man did not even realize that Frost was driving a hard bargain. Having paid $1,000 to Willis Herbert when he bought the farm, Frost offered to sell Holden twenty-five acres for $2,500—on the condition that if Frost should be forced by circumstances to sell the other half of the farm, containing house and barn, Holden would buy it from him for an additional $2,500. The terms were immediately accepted.

Although Frost might have hesitated over gouging a worshiper, his attitude toward the wealthy was controlled, in part, by his pleasure in bolstering his own ego through outsmarting any one of them. In this case, his liking for Holden and for the young man's poetry was apparently counterbalanced by his eagerness to get back at him for being rich, at a time when Frost needed money.

Holden began building his house before the summer of 1919 ended. Immediately, the friendship between the two men seemed much closer than it had been, and Holden was glad for the excuse to spend more time with the Frost family.

The better acquainted he became with the Frost children, the more deeply Holden recognized the tensions in the relationships of all four with their father. The spirited and attractive Lesley, twenty years old, seemed to become increasingly capable of standing up to him, in asserting her own wishes and prejudices. Dour and frequently sullen Carol, seventeen, was inclined to use silence and withdrawal as his best defenses against his father's persistently harsh faultfinding. The attractive Irma, sixteen, had odd mannerisms that seemed to reflect the prudishness of both her parents concerning sexual matters. Fourteen-year-old Marjorie, fragile and shy, seemed to be her father's favorite. Each of these young people showed artistic gifts, and all spent considerable time in writing—although their father did not seem enthusiastic over their attempts to write poetry. He implied, half humorously and half seriously, that one poet in the family was enough.

In spite of Holden's reticence, Frost soon correctly guessed that Holden's wife, accustomed to the city, had grown unhappy over the prospect of living in the woods, year round, and had begun to look for ways to escape. What worried Frost was that Raymond's marital estrangement seemed to be reflected in his becoming too intimate with Lesley. These fears and suspicions were heightened, during the summer of 1919, when Lesley announced she and Carol were going to climb Mt. Washington, with Raymond and a male guest then visiting the Holdens.

The four of them carried blankets, together with enough food for the two-day trip, and slept under the stars, near the top of the mountain. Not long after their return to Franconia, Holden wrote a poem inspired by this experience. It was entitled "Night Above the Tree Line," and when he sold it to *Poetry* magazine he dedicated it to Lesley. Pleased, Lesley told her father about it, and Frost sternly demanded that Holden must wire Harriet Monroe instructions to cancel the dedication. The demand was carried out, but Holden was hurt.

Although the underlying awkwardness gradually increased between Frost and Holden, there were many days when their friendship seemed to remain at a high level of mutual cordiality. During one of their longest hikes—over Mt. Moosilauke and down into the township of Warren —Holden told Frost a story he had recently found in a history of Warren, a story about a woman who had become a pauper there and had been accused of being a witch, with evil powers over her husband and other men. Frost, fascinated by the possibilities of poetic extensions in the story, asked if he might borrow the local history. The book was lent as requested, and Frost used the story as the basis for his dramatic monologue "The Pauper Witch of Grafton."

During all of their pleasantly shared experiences, Frost said nothing to Raymond Holden about the development of a plan to look farther south in New England for another farm. He actually began looking at property in Connecticut and southern Massachusetts early in May of 1920. After two exploratory trips his interests shifted to the region around Arlington, Vermont, where Alfred Harcourt spent his summers. The first nudge in that direction had been given by Dorothy Canfield Fisher, the attractive and successful poet-novelist, whom Frost had met in Boston in December of 1915. Soon after that meeting she had written him from her home in Arlington:

"That was by far the best part of my Boston trip—meeting you and hearing you voice my secret and up-to-the-present-time humble views about poetry!

"I'm writing to tell you how much good it did me. . . ."

In the summer of 1919, Frost had received from Mrs. Halley Phillips Gilchrist, secretary of the Poetry Society of Southern Vermont, a gracious letter inviting him and Mrs. Frost to visit friends and admirers in Arlington, to stay as guests with the Gilchrists there, and to give a reading of his poems at a meeting of the society, in the Gilchrist home. He had answered that if the society would be willing to wait until the hay-fever season had passed, he and Mrs. Frost would gladly accept the invitation; they would plan to stop at Arlington en route to Amherst. He added, "We shall look forward to the ride across states and to seeing you all at Arlington—even a little to reading to you, though I'm not the minstrel I sometimes wish I were and don't pretend to give or experience the pleasure Vachel Lindsay does in public performance. . . ."

The plan had been carried out, and the genuinely affectionate reception given the Frosts during their visit in Mrs. Gilchrist's home was pleasurably different from the response provided by the curious and quickly bored summer people to whom Frost had first read in Franconia. He was flatteringly told that his Arlington reading was an historic event, and in this cordial atmosphere, the Frosts confided they were planning to move down out of the White Mountains to a region where their son might be more successful as farmer and apple-raiser. This beautiful Green Mountain valley, flanked by relatively low and tree-covered or, even, pasture-crowned mountains, made the Frosts wonder if any suitable farms might be available in or near Arlington. The very next day they were escorted through the region to consider possibilities. Although they reached no decision before they drove on to Amherst, they returned to Arlington at the start of the Christmas vacation. And they returned again during the early summer of 1920.

Dorothy Canfield Fisher was the one who finally showed the Frosts the farm they chose to buy, the Peleg Cole place, at the brow of a hill not far below the village of South Shaftsbury (halfway between the towns of Arlington and Bennington), with impressive views of the Green Mountains to the eastward and of the Taconic Mountains to the west. The farmhouse itself was an oddity, built in 1779: a half-stone cottage, the thick and rough-hewn blocks of stone reaching up to the eaves of the steeply pitched gable roof, front and back; the same stone structure rising to the same height on the sides, with wooden clapboards and trim, painted dark red, ascending above to the gable peaks; a large wooden gable and window thrusting out through the roof directly over the front door; all windows and doorways deeply recessed.

The immediate setting heightened the charm of the cottage, shaded by ancient maple, horse chestnut, and elm. Behind the house was a small apple orchard, almost too old to be worth much. To the south of the orchard stood an unpainted, weather-beaten barn; and across the road in front of the house stood another barn that belonged with this ninety-acre farm. Downhill, to the west of the farmhouse, there was a good-sized pasture, with a brook running through it.

Several factors made the Frosts hesitate. The old farmhouse had no furnace, no running water, no bathroom—and the roof leaked. If they bought it, they could not make the necessary repairs and improvements before time for Marjorie to start her sophomore year in the high school at nearby North Bennington. Mrs. Fisher, serving as cheerful assistant to the Frosts during their deliberations, overcame their doubts by offering them free rooms in what had been, before her marriage, her family home. Called The Manse, or Brick House, it was conveniently located on the main street in Arlington, not far from South Shaftsbury. Her offer was accepted.

The bargaining for the Peleg Cole place was completed, and Frost had an easy way of getting money for the new farm. All he needed to do was to inform Raymond Holden that the Frosts were leaving Franconia and that, under the terms of their agreement, it was now necessary to ask

Holden to buy the other half of the Frost farm, for $2,500. Holden later said:

"I did not in 1919, and I do not now, know how much planning to take himself away from Franconia he had done before we reached our agreement. I do know that if I had believed that he would be gone from Franconia almost before the home I built on the land I bought from him was completed, I should have thought twice about making such a deal. . . . This turn of affairs affected me deeply. I reluctantly felt that he had used me as a convenience. I even, for a time, believed that his friendship for me was insincere and motivated by what he thought he could get out of me. This feeling did not persist. . . ."

Early in the fall of 1920, Holden's Franconia home was so nearly completed that he was able to move into it, with his estranged wife and, by then, their two children. At about the same time, Frost was stripping his Franconia house and shipping his furniture to South Shaftsbury, Vermont. Lesley was, according to Frost, sent away for her own safety; she spent the summer of 1920 working as a bookseller in New York City. Carol and Irma departed for South Shaftsbury first, in the Frosts' newly acquired secondhand Overland car, loaded with belongings.

A few days later, near the end of September, Raymond Holden used his own car to carry the Frosts and their daughter Marjorie from their emptied Franconia home to the Littleton railroad station. It was an awkward leave-taking, for reasons Holden stated, regretfully, years later: "It turned out . . . that I had not only contributed to his desire to leave the place he really loved but had given him the means of doing it."

Even after all the Frosts, except Lesley, were gathered in Arlington, repairs and renovations at the Peleg Cole house took longer than had been expected. There was a well with a hand pump in the front yard, but a better supply of water was found: a hillside spring, some distance across the road from the house. A storage tank had to be built below the spring, and pipes to the house had to be sunk deep enough to keep from freezing in winter.

Not until near the middle of November 1920 was Frost able to write: ". . . We're at South Shaftsbury at last. Part of the roof is off for repairs, the furnace is not yet under us and winter is closing in. But we're here. . . ."

SETTLING ONTO A
VERMONT FARM

(1920–1921)

ROBERT FROST was scarcely in his new home at South Shaftsbury before he began to have reservations about the farm he and his family had chosen to buy. He made the announcement of his decision to one of his friends, who had been urging him to look for a farm in the Berkshires, and added: "To you alone I will confess I am still looking for a home. I may settle down and like this place. My present agony may be homesickness for the home I've left behind me rather than for the home that never was on land or sea. . . ."

Another cause for hesitation at this time was the poet's financial status. Having walked out of Amherst, he was now forced to calculate how he could earn the equivalent of that Amherst salary—$4,000 a year. Returns from public readings would help. He was receiving either $50 or $100 for each reading, but at that rate of pay he would be required to give forty to eighty performances in order to gross $4,000 a year from them. Royalties from his three books had never brought him more than a few hundred dollars each year, even when *North of Boston* had been a best seller. The individual poems he sold to magazines (when asked) brought prices ranging from fifteen to thirty dollars apiece, but after the publication of *Mountain Interval* his reputation had declined so sharply that few editors seemed eager to ask. Only three new poems of his had appeared in magazines during 1917, only one in 1918, none in 1919, and none in 1920 up to the time of his decision to buy the Peleg Cole place in South Shaftsbury.

Easily victimized by his fears, he worried so much about his future, even before he moved from Franconia, that he seemed to make himself ill—the symptoms: irritability, peevishness, grouchiness, nervous depression, and lack of appetite.

One fact afforded cautious encouragement. During the past years, while fewer and fewer poems of his were appearing in print, he had written enough to increase his confidence in his having improved his capacities. He needed this confidence, for there continued to be moments when he was nearly paralyzed by the fear that the period of his best writing had ended. He was now accumulating so many new poems, he thought he might be ready to start planning for another book.

What he liked best was his recently developed knack for making some of his lyrics almost as tight as the classical epigrams he so greatly admired. One of them he called "Fire and Ice." Here was a new style, tone, manner, form for him; and he had never before managed to achieve such powerful compression. (The nearest he could remember was his five-line sarcasm entitled "In Neglect," where the tone and posture differed sharply from "Fire and Ice.") Another new poem, "Dust of Snow," satisfactory to him in its terse manipulation of opposites, was a quietly symbolic study in blacks and whites, all in a single sentence.

While these and other poems had just begun to accumulate, and while he had still been teaching at Amherst, in December of 1919 two other cheering events had occurred. The first was the appearance of a perceptive article in *The Nation*. The author, a complete stranger to him, was George Roy Elliott, a Canadian teaching at Bowdoin College. Frost, describing the article as "one of the most understanding things ever written about me," believed it to be responsible for the second event.

Also in December, to visit him in Amherst came another stranger, Joseph Anthony, requesting that *Harper's Magazine* be allowed to publish in one issue several new Frost poems. Given considerable time to decide how he would meet the request, he sent to *Harper's* from Franconia, soon after the retreat from Amherst, two long poems and two short ones: "Place for a Third," "Good-by and Keep Cold," "Fragmentary Blue," and "For Once, Then, Something." In response, *Harper's* had done more than pay well for the poems received. The editor-in-chief requested another cluster of poems at Frost's convenience. Delighted, he had sent four more: "Fire and Ice," "Wild Grapes," "The Valley's Singing Day," and "The Need of Being Versed in Country Things."

When Wilbur Cross sought one poem for *The Yale Review*, Frost replied: ". . . Do you think you could stand an unrelated group such as Harpers is about to publish? My plan would be to return to print hurling fistfulls right and left. You may not be willing to fall in with anything so theatrical. I wonder if I know you well enough to ask you to let me wait till some number when the poverty of your material would thrust me automatically into the place of prominence in your make-up. . . ." A few months later, the *Review* printed in one issue "Dust of Snow," "The Onset," "Misgiving," and "A Star in a Stoneboat."

Frost had taken these bunched events as omens. He told himself they marked a turning point in his career, and he began to say so, to his friends. At the same time, he was about to begin all over again as lecturer and bard, with an eye to the necessity for crowding several public appearances into each month. Before the workmen had completed repairing and improving the Stone Cottage in South Shaftsbury, he was off to give a reading at Bryn Mawr College. And on his way back he stopped in New York City, long enough to discuss his financial problems with his publishing firm.

Henry Holt and Company had been suffering through a crisis during the past few years. A senior member of the firm, Edward N. Bristol, had been elevated to the position of chief director. The younger men, Alfred Harcourt and Donald Brace, had resigned in May of 1919 to establish their own publishing house, hoping to take with them some of Holt's most valuable authors, including Robert Frost.

A legal point was ingeniously invoked to keep Frost from going. Bristol informed him that Holt had worked hard to obtain copyright for *A Boy's Will* and *North of Boston*; Holt also had *Mountain Interval* under copyright. If Frost chose to go with Harcourt, and planned someday to have a volume of collected poems, it would be impossible to include under a Harcourt imprint the contents of the three books on which Holt held the copyright. Sullenly, Frost chose to stay with Holt.

To make amends, Bristol had sent to Franconia for a visit with Frost the new head of Holt's trade department, an attractive young Harvard graduate, Lincoln MacVeagh; and during his visit he had greatly impressed Frost by displaying a genuine delight in and knowledge of Greek and Latin literature—and an equally genuine admiration for the classical and nonclassical elements in the poetry of Robert Frost.

To MacVeagh's office Frost went on November 9, 1920, as he was returning home from Bryn Mawr, and to MacVeagh he described the financial worries that had been bothering him since his resignation from Amherst. Hoping simply for an agreement on higher royalties from Holt, the poet was not prepared for MacVeagh's sympathetic proposal that Frost should be helped immediately with a sinecure, as consulting editor on the Holt staff, at a regular salary of $100 a month. Frost was relieved and encouraged by this development.

But before heavy snow began to fall on the Green Mountains in the winter of 1920, the Stone Cottage in South Shaftsbury became for Frost more like a hostelry, intermittently visited, than a permanent home. He rested briefly there between trips to far-scattered colleges that invited him to read his poems before large audiences and to talk with small groups of undergraduates concerning his poetic theories. Then, early in December of 1920 he stopped in New York City just long enough to learn, quite by accident, that at least one Midwestern university had gone so far as to establish a poet-in-residence on its campus. His informant was the poet and dramatist Percy MacKaye.

Miami University in Oxford, Ohio, had honored MacKaye in the fall of 1920 by appointing him poet-in-residence. A studio had been built for him on campus, and he had been promised freedom from too much academic intrusion. The plan had been developed through the initiative of President Hughes of Miami, and shortly after MacKaye was settled on the campus, Hughes had proposed to the annual meeting of the National Association of State Universities that other institutions of learning should follow this example.

MacKaye's story was a revelation to Frost, who said he would certainly like to find an institution that would ask him to do nothing except serve as poet-in-residence. If he were seriously interested, MacKaye said, President Hughes should be informed, because he knew the colleges and universities that had responded favorably to his proposals. MacKaye promised to talk with Hughes, and soon thereafter the University of Michigan made preliminary overtures to Frost.

Before he felt confidence that anything would eventuate from the Michigan preliminaries, Frost began making other exploratory gestures. In Vermont the most recent educational innovation that had attracted him was a summer school newly started by Middlebury College. Middlebury had inherited some real estate that offered an ideal setting for an unusual school of English, not far from Bread Loaf Mountain in Ripton, and Frost was so taken by the possibilities for conducting an extraordinary program in such a mountain retreat that he apparently asserted his own initiative in trying to make a rapprochement. To Prof. Wilfred E. Davison, head of the Bread Loaf School of English, Frost wrote on December 19, 1920:

"I have been a good deal interested in your new Summer School from afar off. I have been wondering if what is behind it may not be what has been troubling me lately, namely, the suspicion that we aren't getting enough American literature out of our colleges to pay for the hard teaching that goes into them. After getting a little American literature out of myself the one thing I have cared about in life is getting a lot out of our school system. I did what in me lay to incite to literature at Amherst. This school year I shall spend two weeks at each of two colleges talking in seminars on the same principles I talked on there. School days are the creative days and college and even high-school undergraduates must be about making something before the evil days come when they will have to admit to themselves their minds are more critical than creative. I might fit into your summer plan with a course on the Responsibilities of Teachers of Composition—to their country to help make what is sure to be the greatest nation in wealth the greatest in art also. I should particularly like to encounter the teachers who refuse to expect of human nature more than a correct business letter. I should have to cram what I did into two or at most three weeks. . . ."

Professor Davison answered promptly, accepting the plan and apparently offering to pay $150 for the proposed course on "Responsibilities of Teachers of Composition." Frost replied: "We are agreed on everything but the money. I suppose you offer what you can. But I really couldn't give of my time and strength at that rate—particularly of my strength, which I find I have more and more to consider. It would be stretching a point to offer to come for a week and give five lectures for $150 and my expenses. I am sorry if that seems too much, for I wanted the chance to show my belief in what you have undertaken in literature and teaching." Shrewdly, Davison answered by saying he would like to visit Frost, at such time as might be convenient, to discuss the Bread Loaf idea and ways of bringing Robert Frost to Bread Loaf. The visit occurred late in January 1921.

There were conflicting motives behind Frost's aggressive concern for what might be going on at the Bread Loaf School of English. They included his desperate fear that his purchase of the new farm, while he was trying to get along without the benefit of a regular salary, might place on him financial burdens heavier than he could meet. Shortly before Davison's visit to the Stone Cottage, Frost had been forced to borrow money, even though it hurt his pride to do so. New complications were caused when the University of Michigan made a formal proposal, as a result of MacKaye's hints. Although Frost was reluctant to leave New England, even temporarily, the $5,000 offered him for a one-year stay at Michigan was very attractive. A few days prior to Davison's visit, Frost wrote Harriet Moody, widow of the poet William Vaughn Moody, in Chicago, "We want to see you . . . before we do or don't decide to take this step into Michigan." The visit from Davison made the poet consider the possibility of aligning himself on a full-time basis with Middlebury College, but he feared that if he did, he might go into another writing slump as bad as the one caused by his going to Amherst in 1917.

Feeling nervously upset by all these considerations, and while recovering slowly from illness (the local physician said his aches seemed caused by a combination of grippe and neuralgia, but Frost imagined the ailment must be caused by something worse), he received a special invitation to praise American literature in a way that appealed to him. The novelist Hamlin Garland wrote saying he hoped Frost would take part in a memorial service to be held in the New York Public Library on March 1, 1921, to honor the late William Dean Howells. Frost answered: "Sick man as I am (I am just up from a week in bed) I am tempted to accept your invitation for the chance it would give me, the only one I may ever have, to discharge in downright prose the great debt I owe Howells.

"Howells himself sent me The Mother and the Father after he saw my North of Boston. It is beautiful blank verse, just what I should have known from his prose he would write. My obligation to him however is not for the particular things he did in verse form, but for the perennial poetry of all his writing in all forms. I learned from him a long time ago that the loveliest theme of poetry was the voices of people. No one ever had a more observing ear or clearer imagination for the tones of those voices. No one ever brought them more freshly to book. He recorded them equally with actions, indeed as if they were actions (and I think they are).

"I wonder if you think as I do it is a time for consolidating our resources a little against outside influences on our literature and particularly against those among us who would like nothing better than to help us lose our identity. I dont mean the consolidation so much in society as in thought. It should be more of a question with us than it is what as Americans we have to go on with and go on from. There can be nothing invidious to new comers, emigrant Russians Italians and the like, in singling out for notice or even praise any trait or quality as specially American. . . . Our best way to define to ourselves what we are is in terms of men. We are eight or ten men already and one of them is Howells. . . ."

Frost's concern for giving support to a truly American literature always found best expression when he saw the chance to oppose "those among us who would like nothing better than to help us lose our identity." That concern had been heightened while he was living in England from 1912 to 1915, and he repeatedly, after he returned to the United States, made outspoken protests against the various ways in which some of his countrymen seemed to pay too much attention to British poets.

Frost recovered from his illness soon enough to give three performances in New York and Philadelphia before the end of February. Early in March he was able to return to New York and to Philadelphia for two more performances. He spent a week as poet-in-residence at Queen's University in Kingston, Ontario, before the end of March. Then, after having been away from home so much during the fall and winter, he was glad to forget literature long enough to spend most of the spring improving his acquaintance with his farm.

Observing and participating in rural pleasures, during the spring and summer of 1921, gave Robert Frost the relaxation he so much needed. But his playing at farming was spoiled when the pollen began to float. As early as July seventeenth he wrote to Raymond Holden in Franconia: ". . . I am beginning to sniff the air suspiciously[,] on the point of taking flight from these weedy regions. It can't be long before you hear me come crashing through the woods in your direction. Don't shoot till you're sure who it is anyway. . . ."

Back of the humor was a guilty awareness that Holden might feel he had new reasons for shooting. Frost had arranged to borrow, during the approaching hay-fever season, the same farmhouse Holden had, less than a year earlier, bought from Frost at a fancy price and under disappointing circumstances.

In anticipation of the drive to Franconia, Frost had already completed plans to give one reading en route. Having initially offered his services to the Bread Loaf School of English for two or three weeks, he ultimately settled for just one evening's performance; but he had decided to give the school something more than had been bargained for. When he appeared, he read generously from his poems, then launched into a serious talk in which he foreshadowed what later became the basic idea for the Bread Loaf Writers' Conference.

He began his talk by saying that what Bread Loaf wanted for a teacher was an author with writing of his own on hand, one who would be willing to live for a while on terms of equality—almost—with a few younger writers. He said he was not suggesting that such an author-teacher need go so far as to carry his own manuscripts to the students, but rather, that they would be free to bring theirs to him. In such a course, the teacher would no more think of assigning work to the students than they would think of asking him to write something for them. A teacher should address himself mainly to the subject matter of the younger writer, but conversations would take the place of lectures. Instead of correcting grammar, he would try, insofar as an exchange of ideas was possible, to match experiences of life and of art with his students. Individual conferences could best be conducted during long walks into the country or talks before a fireplace. And the manuscripts offered to the author-teacher would not be "exercises," because the young writer's whole nature should be in every piece he set his hand to; his whole nature should include his belief in the real value that the piece would have when finished.

Four years passed before Robert Frost's ideas concerning the possibility of conducting a writers' conference along these lines became an actuality at Bread Loaf, quite apart from the Bread Loaf School of English. For the present, Davison's program was moving in another direction.

A FELLOW IN CREATIVE ARTS

(1921–1922)

MARJORIE FROST had already started her junior year at North Bennington High School, sharing a rented room in the village with her closest friend, Lillian LaBatt, when the rest of the Frost family set off for Ann Arbor early in October of 1921. They knew nothing about what it would be like to live on the edge of a large, state-supported Midwestern campus, but when they reached Ann Arbor they were all delighted. This hilly town on the Huron River seemed to be built in a forest of trees, and the surrounding countryside was a fruit-growing area. The entire setting reminded them so much of New England, they felt very much at home.

As soon as they had settled in, they were curious to know how the poet-in-residence would be asked to carry himself for the purpose of living up to whatever was expected of him. President Marion LeRoy Burton had said that the poet would be paid $5,000 for the year, but had not said how much time he should make available to the students, faculty, and community. Frost was prepared to grope his way, but feared he might spend the entire year in this large institution without having any effect.

He did have one old friend to whom he turned for counsel at Michigan: Morris P. Tilley, the English-department professor who had spent many summers, with his family, in Franconia while the Frosts were living there. Through him the poet gradually became acquainted with the senior members of that department, but introductions had not progressed far before Frost heard of resentments on the part of certain drones who disapproved of paying a mere poet $5,000 to sit around and do nothing all year while they slaved in classrooms.

Reporters who called at his elegant rented house on Washtenaw Avenue gave him chances to make it plain that he did not want to play the role of poet-in-retirement. Only, not all of the publicity was flattering. One interviewer expressed surprise over some theological implications of certain things the poet had said:

"The attention of Mr. Frost was drawn to the fact that some of the squirrels in Ann Arbor were dying; that a mysterious disease was carrying them to 'timely' graves; 'timely,' because they were getting too numerous. So speaking of the lessening number of squirrels he remarked:

" 'That is nature's way. Animals breeding rapidly after a time become a menace for one reason or another. Then comes a scourge and they die off. It is true of humans. When the world becomes so over-populated that its organizations can no longer protect its peoples there will come a pestilence, a famine, a scourge of disease—possibly a war—and men die by the thousands or are killed by the hundred[s] of thousands; and then once more organization is able to care for the people of a great world.' "

The reporter, amazed, completed the article sarcastically:

"How simple. The great world war was nothing to be regretted, but simply God's way of thinning us out! Poor, ignorant man may think he blundered, but Mr. Frost doesn't think so. The black plague, tuberculosis, gripp[e,] smallpox, scarlet fever—these must be looked upon as God's blessings in disguise to prevent over[-]population.

"God first creates too many stomachs and backs to get along comfortably, and then He sends His servants in the shape of wars and pestilence to thin us out!

"One might well argue that man has no right to try to interfere with God by endeavoring to cure diseases, or to prevent wars. Doesn't God know best?

"The University of Michigan is welcome to Mr. Frost and his theory of God's ways. . . ."

It was true that the Christian doctrine of acceptance, taught so early to Frost by his mother, continuously enabled him to rationalize oddities in his view of God's ways, but such a view did not hinder Frost from playing his own godlike role in designing and, then, helping accomplish a near-miracle at Ann Arbor. It all began with the suggestion that it might be possible to arrange a series of readings by several celebrated proponents of the New Poetry—including Amy Lowell, Vachel Lindsay, and Carl Sandburg. (Frost, with characteristic furtiveness, chose to stay behind the scenes in making the arrangements for the series and to do any necessary wire-pulling through private correspondence.)

Padraic Colum, fresh from Ireland, was the lead-off poet. Colum drew a good crowd, and before he read some of his own poems he talked on "The Development of Irish Literature," with special emphasis on the rise of the Abbey Theatre and the presentation of plays written in the peasant vernacular.

Next in the series came Carl Sandburg, whom Frost had met in Chicago in 1917—and had immediately disliked. The New England poet correctly assumed the Chicagoan would appear in Ann Arbor affecting his Whitmanesque mannerisms and garb, in order to show his deep sympathy with the working classes: the blue shirt, with the collar open at the throat, and the prematurely gray hair tumbling over his forehead. His announced topic was "Is There a New Poetry?" By way of answer he praised free verse as the surest indication of what was new. Then, accompanying himself on his guitar, he sang several American folk songs. Sandburg had scarcely left town when Frost reacted bitterly in a letter to MacVeagh:

"We've been having a dose of Carl Sandburg. He's another person I find it hard to do justice to. He was possibly four hours in town and he spent one of those washing his white hair and toughening his expression for his public performance. His mandolin pleased some people, his poetry a very few and his infantile talk none. His affectations have almost buried him out of sight. He is probably the most artificial and studied ruffian the world has had. Lesley says his two long poems in The New Republic and The Dial are as ridiculous as his carriage and articulation. He has developed rapidly since I saw him two years ago. I heard someone say he was the kind of writer who had everything to gain and nothing to lose by being translated into another language."

Following Sandburg came Louis Untermeyer, who chose for his subject "Certain American Poets." If the talk had been written by Frost as a deliberate parody of self-advertising, it could scarcely have been improved. It was summarized in *The Michigan Daily*: "Untermeyer placed Robert Frost as the greatest of American contemporary poets. . . ."

One of Untermeyer's remarks was saved, by an undergraduate reporter, for use in announcing the arrival of the next poet in the series, Amy Lowell: ". . . no individual has been more fought for, fought against, and generally fought about than Amy Lowell. She has been hailed and hooted in the triple capacity of person, propagandist, and poet. Nothing is so characteristic of Miss Lowell as her power to arouse. . . . " Frost had especially wanted her to appear in the series, partly because she could be counted on to give a show that might ascend to genuine histrionics or descend to vaudeville. Onstage, she was always a spectacle—stout, pompous, officious.

When she appeared, on the night of May 10, 1922, she was in fine spirits. Everyone was amused by her, and as she began her talk she announced, with customary arrogance, that she would talk about herself, her theory of poetry, and her practice of it. The crowd took all her remarks in good-humored fashion. When she began to read her poems, however, and to explain her meanings as she went, she gave the effect of talking down to her listeners, as though they were grammar-school children; and many of them were indignant.

Although it would have been difficult for any poet to follow Amy Lowell, the next one scheduled was the best showman in this higher-vaudeville business: Vachel Lindsay. Naïve and childlike in his ability to lose himself in the spirit of such poems as his "General William Booth Enters into Heaven" or "The Congo," he acted out and chanted them. Awkward in his long-armed, long-legged struttings about the stage, he never seemed to guess that anyone might find an element of clowning in his performance.

President Burton, addressing an alumni dinner in Louisville, Kentucky, said (before the poet series was over) he was uncertain whether the most popular man on the Michigan campus was Coach Yost or Robert Frost. When asked to comment, Frost said he was willing to demonstrate which man had the stronger drawing power. He would wait until the next football game and would schedule for that same Saturday afternoon a Robert Frost reading in the Hill Auditorium. On that afternoon the stadium, he declared, would be filled and nobody would be in the Hill Auditorium—"not even myself, because I'll be at the football game."

President Burton's remark was taken more seriously by an undergraduate who wrote an editorial on it for *The Michigan Daily*:

". . . Of course, the President made this remark more or less in a spirit of fun, but nevertheless it did drive home with particular effectiveness the realization of the University's progress during the present year towards the general appreciation of things cultural.

"The interest in literature and in any pursuit which deals with the arts has become widespread, and perhaps the best example of this is the enthusiastic attendance at the Poets' Lecture series, [requiring] . . . Hill auditorium in order to accommodate the crowds.

"President Burton attributes the cultural spurt largely if not entirely to the stimulating influence of Robert Frost in our midst, and few can deny that the fellowship made possible through the generosity of Chase S. Osborn has produced excellent results. . . ."

Frost was able to measure the success of his performance at Michigan in another way. As the end of the spring term approached he confided to one of his friends, "Terrible pressure being put on me to bring me back to Ann Arbor." Although he kept speaking of himself as being merely a part of "President Burton's window-dressing," he enjoyed the attentions showered on him during the year. He also liked sitting on the platform during the commencement exercises and, with Secretary of State Charles Evans Hughes and others, receiving an honorary degree. Although he grumbled pleasantly over the fact that he was asked to settle for a mere M.A., he found no fault with the citation: "Robert Frost, M.A., poet and teacher; trained at Dartmouth and Harvard; yet more truly a fashioner of his own education through sympathetic and penetrating studies of man and nature. As a Fellow in Creative Arts, Mr. Frost has been a welcome sojourner in our academic community—wise, gracious, and stimulating."

Few people outside the immediate family of Robert Frost could imagine the expenditure of nervous energy that had gone into such an extraordinary performance. He had found little time for the one thing the fellowship had been calculated to advance, work on his own poetry; indeed, not enough time to participate in the lonely and frustrating activities of his own children. Lesley, having dabbled once again in academic life and having joined a sorority, quickly became hostile toward the professors in her classes and toward the girls in Alpha Phi. Lesley's father could have explained her predicament by confessing that his habit of caustic disparagement, reflexively employed as a form of self-defense and aimed at human beings more often than at institutions, had proved to be so contagious that all his children had acquired that habit from him.

Lesley was not the only member of the family who wanted to escape from Ann Arbor at exactly the time when the poet was reveling in attentions there. Irma had been miserable from the start and had spent much of her time sulking. Marjorie, lonesome in Vermont and discouraged by her high-school assignments, had written letters that had so upset her mother that Mrs. Frost had twice gone back to North Bennington to visit with her. Carol, inclined to be suspicious of strangers, had grown restless as soon as Yost's very successful football season ended. One spring night, after his father had harshly criticized Carol, the boy simply walked out of 1523 Washtenaw Avenue and did not come back. His parents and sisters could only guess where he had gone, but as the hours of his absence turned to days, there was general agreement that he was probably hitchhiking eastward, toward the Stone Cottage in South Shaftsbury.

His parents phoned Marjorie in North Bennington and suggested that she might be on the lookout for her brother. A few days later they received word from her that Carol was keeping house alone in the Stone Cottage—and seemed to be having a fine time building a hen house. Carol's independent return to South Shaftsbury was enough to precipitate a further exodus from Ann Arbor. Irma and Lesley, pleading for permission to go home and keep house for their brother, were allowed to leave.

When Frost returned to South Shaftsbury in June of 1922 he felt thoroughly exhausted. The whirl of activities during the spring term had shaken him physically and made him regretful he had ever let himself in for such an ordeal.

Unfortunately, he now complained, his various performances had been so highly successful that the students, the faculty, and the townspeople hoped the one-year appointment was but a beginning. President Burton, in their final conversation before Frost's departure, had said that if money could be found for carrying on the experiment, Frost would certainly be invited back for at least one more year of residence at the university. In his state of weariness, the poet had not been elated by the prospect. He told the president, bluntly, that if he came back he would expect the arrangement would contain provisions for protecting him from being overwhelmed by intrusions that in the year just ending had kept him from doing his own work.

Frost had fled to his farm, glad to escape from the academic by helping Carol with work in spraying the new orchards, hoeing in the small vegetable garden, splitting wood, caring for the newly hatched chickens, cleaning the fancy-stepping Morgan, and occasionally milking their one cow. His daughter Lesley, at home for the summer, found another way to divert him.

She had heard that the Green Mountain Club had nearly completed making a 261-mile "Footpath in the Wilderness" across the longitude of Vermont, from Massachusetts to Canada. This Long Trail, as it was usually called, appealed to Lesley as a challenge for anyone who enjoyed packing blankets and food, sleeping on mountaintops, cooking meals over campfires, and enjoying kaleidoscopic changes in scenic views. More than that, the Frost family—at least the mountain climbers in it—could set a new record by being the very first to walk all the way along what was completed of the new trail, and she estimated that the expedition would take not more than two weeks.

Lesley's father was ready for such an outing. If any record-breaking was to be done, he wanted to be in on the excitement. More than that, he was eager to escape from the nervousness he had brought home with him. Carol promised to go if the others would wait until the middle of August, when he could best leave his farm work. Marjorie, also enthusiastic about the venture, gained permission to invite her friend Lillian LaBatt to join the hiking party. And their father suggested adding one more member to the group, a young man named Edward Ames Richards, who had just been graduated from Amherst. Irma, who did not like to climb, was glad to stay at home with her mother.

After elaborate preparations, the six started for the Long Trail on the fifteenth of August, each with a knapsack and blankets. According to the plan, the hikers would cover 225 miles of the 261-mile trail—from the other side of Bald Mountain (the foot of which rose not far to the east of their own dooryard) to Smuggler's Notch in Johnson, Vermont, where the trail then ended.

Unfortunately for Frost, his mountain-climbing shoes kept bothering him painfully. His feet swollen, he took his jackknife and cut slits in each boot; but even this desperate remedy did not entirely relieve the pain. Then, he replaced the slashed hiking boots with a pair of sneakers. But the boots had done their damage; and new complications developed when one of his knees began to bother him.

Before he decided he might as well admit failure, Frost had covered, he estimated, sixty-five miles on the Long Trail and fifty more miles on the valley road from Warren to Wolcott: a total of 115 miles. That was farther than he had ever walked before in one expedition—and good enough for the old man he suddenly felt he was.

Entitled to boast, he wrote to Untermeyer, with poetic license and playful hyperbole. The heading was "Wolcott Vermont nr Canada," and the message: "I walked as per prophesy till I had no feet left to write regular verse with (hence this free verse) and that proved to be just one hundred and twenty-five miles largely on the trail. Here I am stranded here without Elinor's permission to go on or come home. I slept out on the ground alone last night and the night before and soaked both my feet in a running brook all day. That was my final mistake. My feet melted and disappeared down stream. Good bye."

Then, a postscript: "I should admit that the kids all did two hundred and twenty miles. I let them leave me behind for a poor old father who could once out walk out run and out talk them but can now no more."

Frost knew that this longest walking venture of his life had been a major event for him, partly because it had enabled him to get so far away from all that was eating at him. He had gone into the Green Mountains with a congenial group of his own choosing, and although he had been forced to separate himself even from that company, he had enjoyed traveling incognito, at the time when he had been punishing himself for being older than he wished. His double-edged retreat into the wilderness, with plenty of time for meditation and contemplation, had somehow purged all the rancor and bitterness he had brought back from Ann Arbor.

The prospect for returning to Michigan had seemed dim, and Frost, hearing nothing further during August and September, had begun to protect himself against the apparent eventuality by accepting various invitations to give readings or talks, from Vermont to Texas. Unexpectedly, on October 6, 1922, he received a telegram from Burton: "VERY HAPPY TO SAY THAT WE HAVE SECURED $5,000 FOR FELLOWSHIP IN CREATIVE ART ASSUMING THAT YOU CAN BE WITH US AS ARRANGED LAST SPRING. WE ARE HOPING THAT BOTH MRS. FROST AND YOU CAN BE WITH US FOR OUR FIRST RECEPTION WEDNESDAY AFTERNOON, OCTOBER ELEVENTH. IN ANY CASE PLEASE WIRE ASSURANCES THAT THE WHOLE ARRANGEMENT IS AGREEABLE TO YOU. . . ."

Frost hesitated. While still trying to decide, he received another telegram from President Burton: "OUR WHOLE ENTERPRISE CONTINGENT ON YOUR ACCEPTANCE. YOU WILL BE DEEPLY INTERESTED TO KNOW CONFIDENTIALLY THAT UNNAMED DONOR IS PREPARED SERIOUSLY TO CONSIDER PERMANENT ENDOWMENT OF ONE HUNDRED THOUSAND DOLLARS IN LIGHT OF THIS SECOND YEAR'S EXPERIENCE. YOU MUST COME FOR SAKE OF CAUSE. STUDENTS[,] FACULTY, REGENTS AND CITIZENS UNITE IN INVITATION. . . ."

That settled it, and Frost replied by telegram: "ARRANGEMENTS MOST AGREEABLE AS YOU MUST KNOW[.] THANKS FOR OURSELVES AND WHATEVER WE MAY BE SUPPOSED TO REPRESENT[.] HAPPY TO BE WITH YOU AT RECEPTION ON WEDNESDAY[.]"

During the reception at the university on the eleventh of October, Frost had no difficulty in explaining to President Burton that prior commitments would force the poet to be absent from Ann Arbor during the next few weeks. He stayed only two days, meeting old friends and making plans for continuing the work he had begun so successfully during the previous year. Then, he went back to South Shaftsbury, en route to his first engagement, a reading in Rutland, Vermont, under circumstances he regretted.

The Vermont State League of Women's Clubs had caused the circumstances. It had voted on June 7, 1922, to name Robert Frost as its choice for the title of Poet Laureate of Vermont. Reactions occurred quickly, even as far away as New York City. An editorial in the *Times* had noticed the event, with mild sarcasms:

"If one of our States is to have a poet laureate, a natural expectation is that he would be a native, or, at the very least, a long-time resident of that State. It is more than a little curious, and an incitement to considerable thought, therefore, that the Vermont State League of Women's Clubs, in annual convention this week, selected ROBERT FROST to be Vermont's official representative of the Muses.

"To be sure, the choice is a credit to the critical judgment of these women, for the man they chose to be their laureate is a real poet. . . . But Mr. FROST was born in California, and his college days were passed partly at Dartmouth and partly at Harvard. He was a farmer for a while, or Who's Who says so, though one wonders, and then, after teaching in several New Hampshire schools, he finally landed at last as Professor of English Literature in Amherst. His home is set down as Franconia, N.H., but he does have a Summer place in South Shaftsbury, Vt., and that seems to be his only connection with the Green Mountain State. . . ."

The editorial writer in the *Times* went on to make further mistakes, including the claim that Robert Frost, as a writer of free verse, should not appeal to such traditionalists as Vermonters. The first corrections were

sent down to New York by Mrs. Halley Phillips Gilchrist, who had
arranged for the Frosts to make their 1919 visit to Vermont.

Writing from Arlington, she began by saying that the *Times* editorial
had interested her because of its errors. Robert Frost had been able to
vote as a citizen of Vermont for two years, she said, and he was certainly
no mere "Summer resident." She continued, "Here he maintains a farm,
for he is a good farmer in spite of your doubts." As for the mistake in
calling him a writer of free verse, she answered that one by quoting
"unofficially from Mr. Frost" as follows: "I know of no critic in America,
England, France or Vermont who supposes me to have written any free
verse."

The next defender of the ladies of Vermont was Sarah Cleghorn, who
wrote from Manchester that the *Times* "paragrapher" seemed ignorant
concerning Frost's place of legal residence, his activities as a farmer, and
his way of writing poetry. On the last point, she bore down with
considerable scorn: "Blank verse, as Mr. Frost uses it, is so natural in its
cadences and language that it is nothing strange if careless readers call it
'free.' But that is really a very free use of the word 'free.' Look at the lines,
and they will be found regular, according to the best traditions of English
poetry." As for the decision made by the women of Vermont, Miss
Cleghorn concluded, ". . . I take a sentimental pleasure in the credit they
have done themselves in formal recognition of the greatness of our best (I
think) American poet."

Although Robert Frost had been in Michigan when these little
skirmishes occurred, he acknowledged the honor by accepting an
invitation from the Rutland Women's Club to give a reading on the
evening of the eighteenth of October. Even that occasion stirred up a
local controversy. There were some who jealously protected the reputation of an Edgar Guest–like rhymer named Daniel L. Cady, author of a
book of doggerel, *Rhymes of Vermont Rural Life;* others scornfully
rejected any literature that could be viewed as merely local. Not long
after his reading in Rutland, Frost touched pleasantly on these matters in
a letter to Untermeyer:

". . . in Detroit I was bidden to a feast with Eddy Guest; even so in
Vermont I am bidden to a feast with Daniel Cady. Haply you never heard
of Daniel Cady. Stop your ears with wax or you will hear. . . . I heard in
Rutland Vt that the wife of the President of the Rutland Railroad
regarded Dorothy Canfield as local talent and as such refused to be
interested in her. 'Why she hasnt a reputable publisher, has she?' was
her question. Tell Harcourt that. The years we waste!"

Next after Rutland, in his autumnal round of readings, came several
Boston commitments made delicate by jealousies there. Always above
jealousy, however, was the unassuming Katharine Lee Bates, poet and

professor, who had previously brought Frost to Wellesley College as often as she could. This time, in making arrangements for another reading at Wellesley, on the twenty-fourth of October, she enlisted the help of another poet, Gamaliel Bradford, who had made most of his literary success with his prose "psychographs." Bradford had played host to Robert Frost in the fall of 1919 during Frost's first visit to Wellesley, and as a result of that meeting the two men had established an affectionate friendship. With the best of intentions, Frost had tried to help Bradford find outlets for his poems, his plays, and his novels. Following the first of these attempts, Bradford had written him: ". . . What strange perversity is it that induces a man to set his heart on doing those things which he has not succeeded in. . . . Yet the witchery, the infatuation of fiction and especially of poetry torment me in my dreams. . . ."

Immediately under way was his research on such figures as P. T. Barnum, Aaron Burr, John Randolph, Thomas Paine, and others, for psychographic treatment in a projected volume to be called *Damaged Souls*. Frost had already been shown an early draft of the chapter on Aaron Burr and had written from South Shaftsbury on January 18, 1922: "I've just been reading your Aaron Burr. He's a beauty. On with the job. Don't spare to be a little wicked yourself over these wicked people. Not that I would have you make the judicious grieve, but you can afford to make the judicious guess. Tease us."

When the Frosts spent the evening of the twenty-second of October with the Bradfords in Wellesley there was a woman and poet, known personally to all of them, whom the two men discussed with little sympathy. Amy Lowell, having published her *Critical Fable* anonymously, earlier that fall, was continuing to pretend she was not the author of it. On the title page she had described A *Critical Fable* as "A *Sequel* to the 'FABLE for CRITICS,'" in which James Russell Lowell had wittily balanced praise and faultfinding, throughout his treatment of popular poets of his day, including Emerson, Longfellow, Holmes, Whittier, Poe, and himself.

It seemed to Bradford and Frost that Amy greatly lacked her cousin's critical insights and poetic gifts. She had fumbled and stumbled through her supposedly balanced appraisals of Frost, Robinson, Sandburg, Masters, Lindsay, and herself; then, had placed in a lesser category such authors as Sara Teasdale, the Untermeyers, Pound, Eliot, Wallace Stevens, and Edna St. Vincent Millay. She had offended Frost because she found so many nice things to say about herself and so many uncomplimentary things to say about him. Perhaps her most barbed criticism was her treatment of him as an Emersonian poet-prophet who claimed a direct communication line from the Source of all inspiration.

Frost didn't have to explain to Bradford why such mockery infuriated him. Bradford, agreeing with Frost that Amy was probably the author, had his own reasons for being annoyed. His name had not even been mentioned in *A Critical Fable,* and yet, he had received from Houghton Mifflin a prepublication copy, with a note from Amy's editor, Ferris Greenslet, saying several critics to whom advance copies had been sent had guessed Bradford was the author. Whatever his weaknesses as a poet, Bradford was so fastidious in his conventional handling of meter and rhyme that he was horrified to have anyone try to dump this foundling on his doorstep. He had answered Greenslet curtly, "I could never possibly have been satisfied to write such shambling slouchy verse."

Frost was given his own chance to unmask Amy Lowell during his visit to Boston in the fall of 1922. The Frosts went from Wellesley to Brookline, to spend one night with Amy, and Frost thought he could use banter and irony as traps that would make her admit she was the author of *A Critical Fable*. He failed.

Robert Frost was forced to lick a few of his prejudices before he could be persuaded to go so far South as New Orleans. The stimulus had been provided by an extraordinary Browning devotee, A. Joseph Armstrong, teaching a course in contemporary literature at Baylor University in Waco, Texas. Armstrong had carried to Texas a hope that he could attract a parade of visiting poets and lecturers. His method was to promise he would arrange several well-paid performances for each prospective visitor, so that the long trip would be financially profitable. In 1920 he had succeeded in bringing to Waco a cluster of poets, and the next year he scheduled many readings for Carl Sandburg in Texas and the Southwest.

Frost had ignored Armstrong's many letters of invitation, until one of them prompted him to answer, from Ann Arbor on December 28, 1921: "You scare me. I could never think of being away from home anything like 'the greatest part of the year.' Poor Vachel has thus far failed to get married, and so one place is unhomelike as another to him. I can boast of no such artistic detachment." Given this opening, Armstrong used the assistance of Sandburg, who wrote to Frost; and Sandburg's encouragement came at the time when Frost was doubtful whether Michigan would be offering him a position for the academic year 1922–1923.

The double prospect of bunching several performances and of increasing the sales of his books had made him overcome his prejudices. He let Armstrong arrange a schedule that was to begin with a reading at H. Sophie Newcomb College in New Orleans on Friday, the tenth of November; continue with readings in Austin, Dallas, Fort Worth, San

Antonio, and Waco, in Texas; and end with a reading in Columbia, Missouri, on the twenty-third of November—ten readings in fourteen days.

Frost's talk and reading at the regular assembly at Newcomb College impressed his listeners in ways that amounted to a triumph for him. No longer did he permit audiences to see signs of his nervousness. And now a reporter called particular attention to Frost's sense of humor: "Not only did he give selections from his own works, but he also explained the origin and characteristics of modern poetry, including references to other modern poets, thus giving the audience an intimate glimpse of every contemporary in the art. And besides these things, and something which many will remember longer probably than the context of his lecture, his charming sense of humor."

As he moved on from New Orleans to Fort Worth, a journey of more than 500 miles, the change in the audience was as surprising to Frost as the change in the landscape. For the first time, he encountered a front-row heckler, who upset him dreadfully from the very beginning. The costume worn by the heckler suggested he was an ancient Confederate soldier, and yet, he seemed to dislike Frost for reasons other than that the poet was a Damnyankee.

"Do you call that stuff poetry?" he asked, in a plainly audible voice, before Frost had finished his first selection. Trying to ignore the questioner, Frost went on reading—through the sound of grunts and growls that came intermittently from his critic. When the same question was asked again, even more audibly, Frost felt he had to answer it. "*I* call it poetry," he said, and tried to explain. When "the very old and well-known local character" continued his interjections, ushers appeared and escorted him out. But the damage had been done, and Frost was upset more than his audience realized.

The next stop, Dallas, where he was cordially received, renewed his confidence and prepared him for his more important appearance at Baylor. Dr. Armstrong had a flair for making elaborate preparations. As Sandburg had predicted, the bookstores in Waco had ordered extra copies of Frost's books, and the local newspapers heralded the event well in advance of Frost's arrival.

In his class on contemporary poetry Dr. Armstrong made further preparations. He not only helped his students to become familiar with the poetry of Robert Frost, but also coached a few of them to be ready with particular questions they might ask when the discussion period began at the end of the poet's reading.

The hundreds of students, faculty members, and townspeople who gathered for the reading were too many for the chosen hall, and the excitement became almost riotous when announcement was made that the crowd would move to the university chapel. By the time Frost was introduced the atmosphere approached the gaiety of a carnival. He set the tone for his talk and his reading when he reminded them that one of their previous speakers, Miss Amy Lowell, had publicly accused him of having no sense of humor.

Mixing with his readings gay reminiscences and caustic asides on other modern poets, the Yankee won his Southern audience completely. He kept returning to Amy Lowell's interpretations, and after he had read his blank-verse narrative concerning the irate farmer who dumped a load of hay on his boss, Frost reminded his listeners that Miss Lowell had called this one a "grim tragedy." The next day, the local newspapers devoted unusual space to praising his performance.

After such a triumph, Frost found the remainder of his ten readings anticlimactic, at least for him. But before he reached Ann Arbor, where Mrs. Frost was waiting, he knew he would, for all this gallivanting, pay the price of another illness. To Lincoln MacVeagh, who had expected him to return to Ann Arbor by way of New York City, he wrote:

"I saw before I had gone many miles on the Katy that I wasn't going to last to get to New York. . . .

"What I suppose I felt coming on was the dengué (pronounced dang you) fever from a mosquito bite I got on my first day at New Orleans (pronounced differently from the way I was accustomed to pronounce it): Or it may simply have been the influenza. I was fighting a bad sore throat when I got to Columbia—fighting it without medicine you understand. And now here I am at Ann Arbor in bed with a temperature. . . ."

His letter of thanks to Dr. Armstrong, for having arranged the trip so carefully and for having served as host with such gracious hospitality, was genuinely warm: "You surely gave me The Great Adventure down there towards Mexico, and I have only myself to blame if it was too fast and furious for my faculties to take in. . . . You are the master manager, and I was ready to say so with my latest breath, which was what I was about down to when I wound up in Missouri. . . ."

FROM MICHIGAN BACK
TO AMHERST

(1922–1923)

ROBERT FROST was so ill with influenza when he returned to the University of Michigan after his round of readings in Louisiana, Texas, and Missouri that he was confined to bed for more than a week. Alternately enraged and depressed by his illness, he viewed it as a well-deserved punishment for his having once again frittered away so much time and energy on what he now viewed as trivialities.

The requirements waiting for him would be deterrents to his immediate goal of writing enough, while at Michigan, to complete the manuscript for a new volume of poetry. As soon as he did recover he was pulled from one diversion to another—to teas and receptions and plays. And the undergraduates once again began to ask for help in making plans for another series of readings or talks by poets and novelists.

Prof. Roy Cowden, supervising the undergraduate literary magazine and carrying on, with the staff, traditional evenings at his home, urged Frost to be present at each of them. He liked these evenings best, because he was always the star performer, and he enjoyed amusing his listeners with reminiscences that inevitably included gossip concerning the private lives of his friends and enemies.

Frost, during his absence for the Christmas vacation, went back to Vermont eager to make a retreat from any and every pull that might disturb him. But he had agreed to give a reading at Clark University in Worcester, Massachusetts, on January 5, 1923, and then to go to New York City.

He foresaw less pleasure than business during his trip to New York. Carl Van Doren had attracted him by requesting a new poem and a chance to interview him for a *Century* magazine article. And MacVeagh, at Holt, had been trying for months to discuss with him plans for a volume of selected poems that, early in the fall of 1922, Holt had announced would appear in the spring of 1923. Some teasing reactions to this announcement upset Frost, and while still sick in bed in November he had written MacVeagh a somewhat grouchy note of protest: "Please, please if you love me can this selected poems thing. Everybody is misunderstanding. . . . I want the field clear for my new books. It is going to break my heart to have this old dead horse talked about and reviewed as if it were my present bid for notice. I'll write more when I feel less upset. I'm sure its a mistake. . . ."

There were other pieces of unfinished business to handle in New York City. Ridgely Torrence, poetry editor for *The New Republic*, had asked for regular contributions of new poems; and it was, therefore, important to Frost to keep in close touch with Torrence. Untermeyer, on whom Frost counted most for favorable notices and reviews of anything he published, was planning to go abroad. He had urged Frost to visit him in New York during this vacation, lest they should fail to see each other until after Untermeyer's return.

All of these visits were arranged and made, but Carl Van Doren apparently took Frost to one literary celebration that disgusted him. The affair was a raucous cocktail party, given by Lawton Mackall in the new office of Mackall's magazine, *Snappy Stories*; and Frost had reason to feel out of place. As part of the entertainment, Christopher Morley read his own snappy parodies of a few modern poems, including "The Waste Land." Eliot's newly published poem had already created such a splash that Frost was made nervous and jealous by this newcomer's rapidly increasing fame. The literary controversy evoked by "The Waste Land" had been equaled only by that attending the appearance in Paris of Joyce's *Ulysses*, also published in 1922, and Frost quickly sided with those who found ways of trying to dismiss, as pretentious fakers, both Eliot and Joyce.

Immediately after Mackall's party Frost fell into argument, concerning Eliot and Joyce, with a young reporter named Burton Rascoe, who wrote a weekly column for the book department of the New York *Tribune*. By the time Frost and Rascoe parted they had worked each other into animosities that were mutually infuriating. Rascoe, instead of dropping the matter, pursued it, further, in his literary column; and after Frost returned to South Shaftsbury, Untermeyer sent the article to him. Frost was enraged by finding therein some direct quotations from his conversation with Rascoe—about "obscurity in poetry," Eliot, Joyce, and *Ulysses*. Frost immediately wrote a letter of reprimand.

On occasions like this, his chronic vindictiveness caused the poet to hammer away at his opponent as though he were throwing words for punches, and this time he struck so furiously that when he showed the letter to his wife she urged him not to send it. Still angry, and unwilling to waste his long tirade, he sent it to Untermeyer, with the following explanation: "Elinor thinks perhaps I ought not to send a letter like this. You judge for us. If you dont think I'll live to be sorry just put it into another envelope and send it along to Burton. . . ."

Untermeyer's response was one of dissuasion, and Frost accepted it. The unsent letter, preserved by Untermeyer, did more than serve as a safety valve for rage. It contains glimpses of certain characteristics in Robert Frost never suspected by those who saw him only during his affable moods:

"You little Rascol: Save yourself trouble by presenting my side of the argument for me, would you? (My attention has just been called to what you have been doing in the *Tribune*.) Interview me without letting me know I was being interviewed, would you?

"I saw you resented not having anything to say for yourself the other day, but it never entered my head that you would run right off and take it out on me in print.

"I don't believe you did the right thing in using my merest casual talk to make an article of. I shall have to institute inquiries among my newspaper friends to find out. If you did the right thing, well and good; I shall have no more to say. But if you didn't, I shall have a lot to say.

"I'm sure you made a platitudinous mess of my talk—and not just wilfully to be smart. I saw the blood was ringing in your ears and you weren't likely to hear me straight if you heard me at all. I don't blame you for that. You were excited at meeting me for the first time.

"You seem to think I talked about obscurity, when, to be exact, I didn't once use the word. I never use it. My mistake with the likes of you was not using it to exclude it. It always helps a schoolboy, I find from old experience, if, in telling him what it is I want him to apprehend, I tell him also what it isn't.

"The thing I wanted you to apprehend was obscuration as Sir Thomas Browne hath it. Let me try again with you, proceeding this time by example, as is probably safest. . . .

"I thought you made very poor play with what I said about the obvious. The greatly obvious is that which I see the minute it is pointed out and only wonder I didn't see before it was pointed out. But there is a minor kind of obviousness I find very engaging. You illustrate it when, after what passed between us, you hasten to say you like me but don't like my books. You will illustrate it again if, after reading this, you come out and say you like neither me nor my books, or you like my books but not me. Disregard that last: I mustn't be too subtle for you. But aren't you a trifle too obvious here for your own purpose? I am told on every hand that you want to be clever. Obviousness of this kind is almost the antithesis of cleverness. You should have defended your hero's work on one Sunday, and saved your attack on mine for another. You take all the sting out of your criticism by being so obvious in the sense of easy to see through. It won't do me the good you sincerely hoped it would. . . .

"When my reports are in on your conduct, I may be down to see you again.

"I shall be tempted to print this letter some time, I am afraid. I hate to waste it on one reader. Should you decide to print it take no liberties with it. Be sure you print it whole."

In spite of his resentment against Rascoe, Frost derived one major consolation from the New York visit. His discussions with MacVeagh, concerning future publications, clarified plans on both sides. The poet was eager to give primary emphasis to a projected volume of new poems, and MacVeagh assured him that if he had a book ready for publication during the autumn of 1923 it could be sold alongside *Selected Poems* in such a way that each title would help the other. Frost immediately promised that the new book would be completed in time for such publication, and he returned to South Shaftsbury convinced that he could make a start in organizing the manuscript before he returned to Ann Arbor late in January.

Unfortunately, illness spoiled those plans, and by the time he got back to Michigan, feeling guilty for having been absent too long, he was again caught up in his own conscientious attempts to make amends.

Robert Frost did not want to be adopted by Michigan—did not want to continue there for the rest of his life. The arrangement that had brought him back had promised nothing more than a single year, and he was glad when the year was ended. President Burton and many others were grateful to him for all he had done, and the farewells were extremely cordial. But he returned to South Shaftsbury early in June 1923 wishing for nothing more than a chance to proceed with work on his new volume of poetry, as soon as he could get done with one final public commitment.

The University of Vermont had invited him to appear at commencement, to receive an honorary degree, and he had been so pleased (the first bona fide offer of a degree, as he thought—because there were strings attached to those awarded him by Amherst and Michigan) that he sent his grateful acceptance. Someone had apparently confided the news to the elderly Henry Holt, whose summer estate was not far from Burlington, and Holt had immediately written to request the privilege of playing host when the poet came north to receive the degree.

Returning from that occasion, Frost reported to MacVeagh, "I had a good evening with your Mr Henry Holt at his place between the mountains and the lake when I was in Burlington. . . ." Holt showed enthusiasm for the news that Frost would have another book of poems in the fall, and this visit seemed to be the last engagement, social or academic, that stood between him and his intended work on the book—if nothing unexpected came along.

The unexpected had already happened, without his knowing it. President Meiklejohn had been dismissed by the trustees of Amherst, with startling local results. Several faculty members hired by Meiklejohn submitted their resignations, in protest; and because his enmity toward Meiklejohn had been openly expressed, and because his resignation from Amherst had been made in protest against Meiklejohn's policies, Frost was one of the first to receive a telegram from the trustees asking if he would accept a position as a member of the heavily depleted department of English. Again, he was forced to reconsider all his arrangements for restricting his energies primarily to the writing of poetry. To MacVeagh he confided his quandary: "Its going to be embarrassing to stay out of the row or to go into it."

While he was trying to decide, he received a visitor. The newly designated successor in the presidency of the college, George Daniel Olds, elevated from his position as a professor of mathematics, drove up to South Shaftsbury to persuade Frost. Before Olds returned to Amherst he succeeded in winning Frost's acceptance, and a few days after his visit the president made public the names of those newly appointed to the college faculty, including Robert Frost.

In all this excitement Frost did not quickly get back to the manuscript on which he had done much while at Ann Arbor. Determined to complete it for a publication date that would occur soon after he began his duties at Amherst, he tried again to ignore all the other holds on him. He had already decided the book would be entitled *New Hampshire.*

The entire plan for Robert Frost's fourth book, *New Hampshire,* grew out of an event that had occurred during the spring of his first year at Ann Arbor. Invited to give a talk before the local Rotary Club and aware that he would be addressing businessmen, he decided to be playful and satirically amusing with a discourse on two attitudes toward selling. One of these was the notion that a true lady or gentleman should never get hands dirty by working for money or by selling anything; the other, the communistic complaints against bourgeois profits achieved through competitive capitalism.

The talk went well enough—although Frost belatedly realized he had pitched his remarks over the heads of the businessmen. His game had been to strike an ironic posture of claiming that New Hampshire is the purest noncommercial state in the Union; while it has a splendid variety of precious and admirable things for show, it does not have enough of anything to sell. He had supposed his listeners would recognize the ways in which he only pretended to make that claim, for the purpose of mocking the two opposed categories of snobs: those among the pseudo-aristocratic capitalists and those among the pseudo-aristocratic communists.

The most important gain he derived from giving the talk was in manipulating a cluster of images and anecdotes that he viewed, in retrospect, as materials for a long poem quite different from any he had previously written. In some of Horace's satirical discourses there was classical precedent for such a poem. The *Sermones* always scattered friendly banter through a rhapsody of anecdotes, exempla, dialogue, self-appraisal, self-disparagements, epigrams, and proverbs.

When he had returned to Vermont in the late spring of 1922 he was in no mood for writing, although he kept thinking about details he might use when he got around to it. At last, one July night after everyone else in the Stone Cottage had gone to bed, he sat down at the dining-room table, knowing vaguely what the shape of the poem would be. As a starting point, he pretended to agree with a lady from the South who implied that commercialism of any kind was disgraceful. Such a start was designed to be a parody of both forms of snobbishness that annoyed him. And from this beginning he went on to give three examples of individuals, from states other than New Hampshire, who had sullied themselves through different forms of salesmanship. He added, "It never could have happened in New Hampshire."

Continuing, he admitted he had once found a person "really soiled with trade" in New Hampshire; but this person "had just come back ashamed / From selling things in California." Then, Frost stated: "Just specimens is all New Hampshire has, / One each of everything as in a showcase, / Which naturally she doesn't care to sell."

To illustrate he gave examples, within discursive contexts, ironically pretending to praise some details that were obviously not praiseworthy. Foreshadowing the last line of the poem, he boasted that New Hampshire was "one of the two best states in the Union." Vermont, of course, was the other.

As he continued, he half-seriously and half-playfully defended New Hampshire against criticisms made by the Massachusetts poets Emerson and Amy Lowell. And he teasingly pretended to explain his own position, using words that could be misleading if taken merely at face value.

At this time in his life he was often complaining about Russia, and in the writing of the poem he made a few satirical thrusts at Russia. The next target was what he viewed as the cheap Greenwich Village talk to which he had been exposed repeatedly. Then, he digressed long enough to bring under satirical criticism some opposed notions concerning nature and human nature. And he struck a posture of pretending to agree with what he considered to be false religious notions.

To Frost, nothing built with hands was sacred—not even poems—unless the creative act was performed with a devout awareness of continuities between the parts, in the divinely ordained scheme of things. He might confide, privately, that the preacher in him would eventually triumph over the poet; but so long as he struck these equivocal postures of pretending to agree with views he was intent on satirizing, he hoped nobody would accuse him of preaching. He concluded the helter-skelter satire by returning to the demand of a "New York alec" that Frost characterize himself by deciding whether he would rather be childishly immature or prudishly puritanical: "I choose to be a plain New Hampshire farmer / With an income in cash of, say, a thousand / (From, say, a publisher in New York City). / It's restful to arrive at a decision, / And restful just to think about New Hampshire. / At present I am living in Vermont."

Fatigued and yet elated, after finishing the rough draft of the poem "New Hampshire" in one stretch of work, Frost was not immediately aware he had written straight through the night. When he put his pen down and stretched, looking out through the window, he was surprised to see there was light in the east and that the syringa bush at the end of the front lawn was already coming out of darkness. With a sense of unusual excitement, he stood up, walked stiffly to the front door, opened it, descended the stone steps to the dew-heavy grass, and stood marveling less at the dawn than at his night's work. Never before, in all his years of sitting up late to write, had he worked straight through until morning. Even now, with the poem tentatively finished, he was not ready to stop. There was something else he wanted to write—or felt impelled to write—although he had nothing immediately in mind as a starter.

Back into the house he went, moving through the living room to the dining room almost as though he were sleepwalking. He picked up his pen, found a clean page, and began a lyric that had nothing to do with the dawn of a July day. He seemed to hear the words, as though they were spoken to him; and he wrote them down as best he could, in his fatigue, even though they came so indistinctly at times that he was uncertain what he heard. In a short time, and without too much trouble, he completed a rough draft of these four quatrains:

> *Whose woods these are I think I know.*
> *His house is in the village, though;*
> *He will not see me stopping here*
> *To watch his woods fill up with snow.*
>
> *My little horse must think it queer*
> *To stop without a farmhouse near*

Between the woods and frozen lake
The darkest evening of the year.

He gives his harness bells a shake
To ask if there is some mistake.
The only other sound's the sweep
Of easy wind and downy flake.

The woods are lovely, dark, and deep,
But I have promises to keep,
And miles to go before I sleep,
And miles to go before I sleep.

Pivoting on the word "promises" and, therefore, suggesting innumerable extensions, this new poem, "Stopping by Woods on a Snowy Evening," immediately seemed to him one of the best he had ever written. The tensions between his promises to himself as artist and to his wife and family (and others who made demands he often resented) continued to make him feel guilty. Equally serious to him was the feeling that although he had promised himself, years ago, he would do everything in his power to succeed as a poet, he often doubted whether he had the creative energy to keep adding elements of newness to his poetic performance.

This night's accomplishment gave him new courage to face the miles he hoped to go before he slept. New in this experience was the odd juxtaposition of the tight lyric form, with its unusual rhyme scheme, and the sprawling, discursive, conversational form of "New Hampshire." The incentive provided by the excitement of this night's work made him begin to think he could build around this doubly centered nucleus enough pieces to make a book more to his liking than *A Boy's Will* or *North of Boston* or *Mountain Interval.*

Unfortunately, he had another set of promises to keep during that summer of 1922; and his plans for the new book advanced no further until the Christmas vacation, when he began to select and arrange poems. By the time he returned to Ann Arbor from South Shaftsbury, he had progressed far enough to confide to Untermeyer: "It might be a good idea to call the explanatory poems Notes. I'm pretty sure to call the book New Hampshire. The Notes will be The Witch of Coos, The Census-taker, Paul's Wife, Wild Grapes, The Grindstone, The Ax-helve, The Star-splitter, Maple, The Witch of Grafton (praps), The Gold Hesperidee (praps) and anything else I can think of or may write before summer. . . ."

In "a larking mood," he did have fun, with reference to his academic relationships, by adding to "New Hampshire" passages that served as undeveloped hints that needed explaining. These passages justified his use of mock-scholarly footnotes, containing merely the titles of the so-called "explanatory poems." His next decision was to give the book a three-part structure: Part one would be devoted exclusively to the title poem; part two, the explanatory poems, grouped as "Notes"; and part three, lyrics that could be referred to as "Grace Notes" (in the sense that they were added for pure ornamentation).

When he began to assemble the poems to be used as "Notes," he gave first place to "A Star in a Stoneboat." Obliquely, this poem did provide extensions of the self-revealing and self-concealing equivocations in "New Hampshire," concerning polarities in his religious beliefs and unbeliefs—and pleased him because it was a newly approached subject handled with a freshness of supporting imagery and because it reaffirmed his posture of standing apart from the ordinary run of those who "may know what they seek in school or church."

In spite of all his teasings, aimed at the doubts (or, even, the beliefs) of those whose opinions differed from his, Frost was essentially concerned with using his poetry for the purpose of affirming his own religious belief (and the element of dialogue, in his poems, sometimes reflected the conflicts in his own consciousness). He liked saying, repeatedly, that he was a dualist in his thinking and a monist in his wishing. He was at least emotionally sympathetic with anyone, like Plato, who made the leap beyond the dualism of the known to the all-controlling One of the unknown.

Among the "Grace Notes" he chose to add to the manuscript of "New Hampshire" was a mood poem reflecting his emotionally sympathetic belief in oneness. He called it "I Will Sing You One-O," and he thought the intensity of that hymn to Oneness should offset any doubts raised, in the minds of religious readers, by his own teasing expressions of doubt in so many of his other poems.

Just the variety of tones and meters in all these new poems, assembled for this prospective volume, pleased and encouraged him. He was content to let his readers notice the consistency with which he intermingled with the humorous or comical or satirical elements the serious hints of his physical and metaphysical affirmations.

The next task, after he had roughly completed the assembling, was to get the entire manuscript typed in time to meet the summer deadline set by MacVeagh. In Ann Arbor, throughout the spring of 1923, he worked on the manuscript with the aid of Lawrence Conrad, the young man who had been his favorite student the year before.

Conrad, serving as typist, was amused to have Frost sit at his elbow and make last-minute revisions. Occasionally, the poet would invoke the services of his wife, in helping him reach decisions concerning lines or stanzas that troubled him. While Conrad waited, Frost would carry a page to the bottom of the stairs and call to Elinor, invisible above, to ask if she would listen while he read something aloud, so she could give him her decision as to which of two passages was the better. (Occasionally, the question would be, "Elinor, how did we decide to spell this word . . . ?")

Elinor Frost took pride in the part she played as adviser to her husband—the part she had played ever since she herself stopped writing poetry. Her strong admiration for his work found expression while Frost and Conrad were still preparing the typescript of the new book. When MacVeagh wrote to Frost just prior to the publication of *Selected Poems* and added to his business letter a special tribute to the poems themselves, Mrs. Frost assumed the responsibility for answering:

"I have wanted to write to you ever since your last letter came, to thank you for what you said at the end of it about Robert's poetry. Robert was greatly pleased, and I myself felt it deeply that you should realize how much there is in the poetry that those who have written about it either don't see at all, or touch on very lightly. There is in it all the truth, vigor and humanity that they emphasize, but there is also a clear beauty, and even 'glamour' in line after line, and poem after poem, which his own particular way of expressing seems to have blinded them to so far. . . ."

When the book was published, on November 15, 1923, some of the reviewers considered *New Hampshire* the best of Frost's work; and John Farrar was ecstatic in parts of his review:

". . . It is difficult for me to write sanely of Robert Frost; for, in my opinion, he is one of the few great poets America has ever produced.

". . . This volume . . . should be hailed with any amount of hand-shaking and cheers.

"Perhaps this is the perfection of Frost's singing. Perhaps this is the fruit of his ripest powers. It is a book of which America may well be proud. . . ."

The highest tribute paid *New Hampshire* occurred when the newly established Pulitzer Prize for poetry was awarded to it, as the best book of poems published in America in 1923.

IN AND OUT OF
AMHERST AGAIN

(1923–1925)

A FEW MONTHS before *New Hampshire* was published, Robert Frost
carried out one of the promises he had made to President Olds of
Amherst College: to be a scout for the department of philosophy. Frost
had in mind a particular type of teacher, one whose knowledge concerning the history of philosophy could be adapted to the limitations of
undergraduate responses. Influenced by William James in this regard,
the poet was willing to admit that for him there had to be a blend between
the realms of philosophy and theology. A professor who was an atheist
would never serve to offer the philosophy course Frost wanted for
Amherst.

After a futile search, Frost could not resist confiding the outcome to
Lincoln MacVeagh:

". . . I have to report having found the philosopher I was on the hunt
for in myself. On my way home from our talks together I said Why not?
And the next day being called on the telephone from Amherst to say what
courses I would announce for this year in English, I proposed to give one
in philosophy on Judgements in History, Literature, and Religion—how
they are made and how they stand, and I was taken on by the department
like odds of a thousand to one. Well the debacle has begun. He[re] begins
what probably won't end till you see me in the pulpit."

Not required to teach more than two courses (of his own choosing) and
having made up his mind to proceed with bold innovations, he announced that his English-department offering would expose a selected
group of seniors to an unusual assortment of forms from American,
English, and European literature. While making up his reading list in
advance of the fall term, he concentrated on the writings of rebels.

He would start the boys off pleasantly, by giving them as their first
assignment Melville's more-or-less-autobiographical (and highly romantic) narrative concerning a rebel who jumped ship in the South Seas and

lived for a time among cannibals, *Typee*. Thoreau was another rebel who should be taken under consideration, and *Walden* was placed early on the schedule of assignments. Thoreau could be used to pave the way for Emerson, and the students would be asked to read all of *Representative Men*—essays on such bold adventurers-in-ideas as Plato, Swedenborg, Montaigne, Shakespeare, and Goethe.

From English authors Frost selected George Henry Borrow, who imbibed infidel ideas before he became a Bible salesman, and Edward Gibbon, whose education was so irregular and independent that it made a special appeal to Frost. The only translation placed on the projected list of readings was of the violently wrathful and vengeful genius Benvenuto Cellini. The only author chosen to represent poetry was one of Frost's secretly cherished favorites (and by no means a rebel), Christina Rossetti, who found her own ways of blending mysticism with passionate sensuousness.

The Frosts, in their move back to Amherst, rented a house at 10 Dana Street, not far from the campus. They enjoyed the cordiality of the welcome given them by old friends, and Frost discovered that the enrollments in his two courses proved he was among the most popular of the newly appointed professors.

He began this course on "Judgments" by expressing two of his own. A philosopher, he said, gets up one metaphor and spends all his life studying and amplifying it; a poet tosses off metaphors at the rate of one a day. The danger that should be feared most is imprisonment within one hard-and-fast metaphor.

Part of his purpose, in both courses, was to decontaminate students who might have become infected by the disease he chose to call "Meiklejaundice." The boldness he prided himself on, as teacher, was partly that of provocation, achieved by knocking established ideas into cocked hats. By contrast, what he disliked most strongly was the conventional orthodox procedure of spoon-feeding facts and accepted ideas, through the lecture method.

In his English course, "Readings," he gave special emphasis to that title. He hoped that his own reading-aloud in class, from an assigned text, and his original comments on inseparable relationships between what was said and how it was said, in a passage under consideration, might encourage freshness of insight on the part of his students.

One cluster of insights, partly assembled through his articulations in the classroom, he passed to Untermeyer in the form of a letter:

"Since last I saw you I have come to the conclusion that style in prose or verse is that which indicates how the writer takes himself and what he is saying. Let the sound of Stevenson go through your mind empty and you will realize that he never took himself other than as an amusement.

Do the same with Swinburne and you will see that he took himself as a wonder. Many sensitive natures have plainly shown by their style that they took themselves lightly in self-defense. They are the ironists. Some fair to good writers have no style and so leave us ignorant of how they take themselves. But that is the one important thing to know: because on it depend our likes and dislikes. . . . I am not satisfied to let it go at the aphorism that the style is the man. The man's ideas would be some element then of his style. So would his deeds. But I would narrow the definition. His deeds are his deeds; his ideas are his ideas. His style is the way he carries himself toward his ideas and deeds. Mind you if he is down-spirited it will be all he can do to have the ideas without the carriage. The style is out of his superfluity. It is the mind skating circles round itself as it moves forward. Emerson had one of the noblest least egotistical of styles. By comparison with it Thoreau's was conceited, Whitmans bumptious. Carlyle's way of taking himself simply infuriates me. Longfellow took himself with the gentlest twinkle. I don't suppose you know his miracle play ['The Flight into Egypt'] in The Golden Legend, Birds of Killingworth, Simon Danz or Othere."

So far, Frost had avoided any direct comment on his own style, but as he continued he closed the focus, until he included himself in one important regard:

"I own any form of humor shows fear and inferiority. Irony is simply a kind of guardedness. So is a twinkle. It keeps the reader from criticism. Whittier when he shows any style at all is probably a greater person than Longfellow as he is lifted priestlike above consideration of the scornful. Belief is better than anything else and it is best when rapt[,] above paying its respects to anybody's doubts whatsoever. At bottom the world isnt a joke. We only joke about it to avoid an issue with someone; to let someone know that we know he's there with his questions: to disarm him by seeming to have heard and done justice to his side of the standing argument. Humor is the most engaging cowardice. With it myself I have been able to hold some of my enemy in play far out of gunshot. . . ."

In the fall of 1923 the Frosts went up to South Shaftsbury from Amherst for an important wedding, that of Carol Frost to Lillian LaBatt. Shortly after the wedding, Frost sent MacVeagh an account:

"Carol's marriage was only a little of a surprise. He and Lillian had been engaged for some time. They were such children that I didnt want to commit them to each other by taking much notice of the affair or saying much about it. I doubt if I thought it would survive Lillian's first year at college. But it turned out in a way to show that I was no judge of the intensity of children. Lillian's first year at college it was that didn't survive. She quit, homesick, and Carol went right to her mother and got her. It was all done in a week. I may be frosty, but I rather like to look on at such things. And I like children to be terribly in love. They are a nice pair. Lillian is an uncommonly pretty little girl. She is pretty, quiet and unpractical. She has been a great friend of the girls in the family for some years. All she . . . [has] done is transfer herself from the girls to the boy. We'll see how completely she deserts the girls."

In spite of the demands made on him at Amherst, Frost still found time to meditate wistfully on all that Wilfred Davison was trying to accomplish with his summer program at the Bread Loaf School of English. When Davison wrote asking about a man to hire for the Bread Loaf staff, Frost did more than answer the question:

". . . You've done something with Breadloaf to make it different from the ordinary American school in more than location, but, as I look at it, not nearly enough. You're missing a lot of your opportunities up there to make a school that shall be at once harder and easier than anything else we have. I'd be interested to tell you more about it if you should come down for a visit overnight; and I'd be interested in coming up for longer than my stay of last summer . . . , if you would excite me with something rather more advanced in educational experiment. . . ."

Davison accepted the invitation, visited the Frosts in Amherst on December 22, 1923, and commemorated the event in a journal entry:

". . . Mr. Frost kept up a steady stream of comment and anecdote. How he does like to talk! There were things I wanted to say, but there was little opportunity. I asked a few questions, answered a few, and listened. And such talk! It makes an average person despair. Mainly it was Mr. Frost's ideas about the teaching of English. . . .

"In general, I found Mr. Frost somewhat less unspoiled than when I first saw him four years ago. He is feeling his oats a bit, I fear. He said he was vindictive, and the comments he made showed it. But his fighting blood is up, and for the most part, he is apparently in the right.

"He scored many things about teaching, especially the new notion that the students should teach themselves, which he called 'Nonsense'. He said he told his boys that if he should leave his left leg lying on the desk for them to use, they wouldn't know what to do with it. He thought it absurd to assume that students knew better than their teachers what they needed.

"But at the same time he has all his old zeal for reform. He said that English teaching is in a bad way generally and especially scored graduate work, which he called futile. He thinks we are too much bound to books. . . .

"For proper growth, there must be idleness. Mr. Frost said that idleness had been the making of him. He thought that in all our school work there was too much 'busy work.'

"Specifically regarding Bread Loaf, Mr. Frost's idea was that we should have there a Pastoral Academy, where freedom should abound. He would have no formal restraint, but he would feel free to send students home at any time when they failed to take advantage of their opportunities. He would have very few formal lectures and recitations. For these he would substitute conferences and discussions. Instead of final examinations of the usual sort, he would substitute various tests, for he said students even in graduate work must be checked up. He would assign ten students to every teacher and ask each teacher to form his estimate of them through informal association in walks, talks, and from those general observations by which we form estimates of people in ordinary life. In fact, he said he would always 'freshen' method by bringing into the schoolroom as much of the atmosphere of life outside as is possible. For tests to take the place of examinations, Mr. Frost would substitute oral examinations, pieces of creative work, lectures by students before the class, with an occasional written examination. . . .

"Sometimes I think Mr. Frost is a great man, and sometimes I think he is only a neer-do-well who has happened to find fame. When his gray eyes are upon you, you cannot get away from them. His mind is fertile in thought; his conversation was brilliant, but racy. He chose words with more precision than I ever noticed before. But I believe his range of ideas is comparatively narrow; that is what I mean when I say he is not great. I doubt whether the spiritual makes any very deep appeal. Certainly he is not conventionally religious. He damned quite a few things, including 'those bloody papers.' But the way that mind unfolds idea after idea on the topic he is thinking about, is marvelous. He sees ideas from many angles, and he illustrates everything to himself as he thinks, in specific instances and anecdotes. His talk was full of digressions, as one thing suggested another to him. I came away with a somewhat confused impression of it all; I was mentally weary, in fact, from the strain. . . ."

Davison was only one of the many who marveled at the ways in which Robert Frost unfolded his ideas, saw them from different angles, and illustrated them vividly with specific instances. These extraordinary exercises of mind, which the poet demonstrated in his best appearances, increased the public demand for him—to such an extent that President Olds was occasionally forced to let him be absent briefly from the Amherst duties.

In late February and early March of 1924 he gave talks and readings in Baltimore, in Boston, and in Philadelphia. Next, he went out into western Pennsylvania to Allegheny College; then, to the University of Michigan, during the Amherst spring vacation.

He had been asked, somewhat mysteriously, to spend a week on the campus as guest of the university; and as the week progressed he was honored and feted in some extraordinary ways. Finally, after all these attentions had been enjoyed, President Burton made the confidential revelation that he was empowered by the regents of the university to offer Frost a lifelong appointment at Michigan, as a poet-in-residence, with the title Fellow in Letters. If Frost accepted, he would have absolutely no faculty duties on committees, no teaching duties other than those he might voluntarily arrange in the form of occasional conferences or seminars on writing.

He was tempted to accept at once. But he had promises to keep, at Amherst. The question he faced, inwardly, was how bold he could be in making this choice between the permanent appointment so recently accepted (with four hours of classes a week) and this even-better offer (with no hours of teaching required—and a salary of $5,000).

After considerable exercise of mind, he informed Burton he would accept the offer and would begin in the fall of 1925, provided no announcement be made until after he had begun the next year of teaching at Amherst.

During the remainder of the term he tried to justify his secretly made contract, by finding local targets for disparagement; and throughout the summer he continued to brood over the boldness of his decision to break with Amherst. President Olds, aware Frost was not happy with the way things had gone during the past year, tried to smooth his feathers by giving him additional freedom. That generosity heightened Frost's discomfort, caused by conscience; and what he dreaded most was the unspoken reproach that might await him when he told Olds, and others, he was leaving Amherst for Michigan.

On edge, and almost sick with a case of nerves, he made two hay-fever retreats, with Mrs. Frost, that summer, and used his hay fever as excuse for asking permission to return to Amherst after the beginning of the term. What ailed him, inwardly, was far more distressing than hay fever, and when he finally did return to Amherst, a full week after classes had begun, he felt cross and ugly.

Early developments that fall gave Frost new reason and means for justifying his decision to accept the Michigan offer. He was ready to say quite pointedly, to anyone who might accuse him of having broken his word to President Olds, that his primary obligation must be to his own writing and to his career as poet. His idea of avoiding regular classes and requiring students to come to him, separately, had seemed good in theory. In practice, it made him the victim of any boy who felt free to knock on the door at 10 Dana Street, at any hour of the day or night, and stay as late as he chose. Mrs. Frost became impatient with these worshipful intrusions, even before her husband did; and she was even more concerned over how he was to find time for his writing.

He had been offered, finally, a way to get a living through casual and occasional participation in the educational processes of a great university. Under the circumstances, he felt fully justified in breaking his connection with Amherst. This, at any rate, would be his defense when assailed.

The announcement, made in November of 1924, placed stress on the new freedom made available to the poet:

"Robert Frost, professor of English at Amherst College since 1923, has resigned, his resignation to become effective at the end of the present academic year. . . . His fellowship at the University of Michigan has been created especially for him, and will exist for life. The fellowship entails no obligations of teaching and it provides for all living expenses. He will have entire freedom to work and write.

"In accepting the fellowship Professor Frost feels that he will be able, not only to write, but also to carry on, as he has done in this college, his theory of 'detached education.' This theory of education is one in which the students are encouraged to do more and more work for themselves, and to expect from the teacher more of guidance than of tutoring.

" 'It takes me one step further along in the kind of teaching I have done here at Amherst,' Professor Frost is quoted as saying. . . . 'It might be described as no more than a slight interference with students in their self-teaching. I have never been able to care much about following boys up with detailed daily questions. I have wanted to sit where I could ask everything of them at once, where by a challenge I could ask them to go the whole length in some one of the arts, for example. . . .'

"Commenting upon his departure from Amherst, the poet declared that 'it will cost me something in broken ties to leave Amherst, but I haven't seen how I could refuse the advantages offered me at Michigan. Chief of these will be the freedom to get my writing done. The fellowship will give me practically all my time to do with it as I please.' "

Frost was relieved to discover that, as soon as word was out, the students and his colleagues on the faculty at Amherst were more inclined to congratulate than criticize, and things went well during the fall term of 1924.

Amy Lowell was at the center of one worry. Frost, having told the Amherst students he would give them a chance to hear and see this picturesque monster in action, tried to make arrangements for her to read there, and a plan was worked out successfully. Miss Lowell arrived in late February of 1925, talked to a capacity audience, amused the students with her haughty mannerisms—and, even, pleased some of them with her poems. After the performance, she made another occasion of the reception given her at the Frost home.

Mrs. Frost told Mrs. Fobes about the "little party" and went on to tell about an event that promised to be far more spectacular: ". . . Some literary people in Boston are getting up a big dinner for her in Boston, just before she sails the 1st week in April, in honor of the Keats book, and Robert has got to make a ten minute speech in praise of her on that occasion. Robert and I and the Untermeyers are going to stay with her two or three days at that time, and I am sure we'll have a lot of fun. Robert and Louis will be joking about everything and everybody. . . ."

But the joking had already begun, and some of it involved plans for another dinner. Frederic G. Melcher, editor of *Publishers Weekly,* had proposed to celebrate Robert Frost's so-called fiftieth birthday (actually, his fifty-first) with a dinner in New York City on March 26, 1925—not much more than a week prior to Miss Lowell's dinner in Boston. Although Amy had permitted Melcher to use her name as a member of the committee sponsoring the Frost birthday party, she insisted from the start of these preparations that because of her chronic ailments and the complicated plans not only for her own dinner, but also for her impending departure for England, she could not get down to New York on the twenty-sixth. Bantering, Frost had said that of course if she couldn't attend his party, he wouldn't attend hers. Mrs. Frost, as though to make amends for such a threat—or, at least, to place the terms in a better light—wrote to Miss Lowell soon after her reading in Amherst:

". . . Robert says to tell you that he'll be on hand for your party if there is anything left of him by that time. He has twelve or thirteen reading engagements between now and then (which means a lot of travelling, as you know) besides keeping up his college work, and I just don't know just how he is going to manage it. Then there is his own party on the 26th, which will, of course, be a nervous strain, though a pleasure at the same time. I wonder if anyone will come to *his* party. Please change your mind and come yourself. . . ."

It was to Untermeyer that Frost had written, "I always hold that we get forward as much by hating as by loving," and now that he was placed in a position where there would be some competition over whether more guests of distinction would gather for Amy Lowell's dinner than for his, envy and jealousy turned banter into a renewal of his disgust for what he viewed as her charlatanism. While she continued to treat as a joke his claim that he wouldn't attend her party if she didn't attend his, he became increasingly serious. Next, he persuaded Untermeyer to join him in the plot to stay away.

The Frost birthday dinner, held at the Hotel Brevoort, was a modest success. The master of ceremonies was Carl Van Doren, and one of the tributes he read aloud was from the absent Miss Lowell. She gave an account of the start of her acquaintance with Frost and described it as "a friendship, which, on my part, has been an ever-increasing admiration of his work, and a profound attachment to the man."

More playfully, the after-dinner speakers combined praise with teasing. They included Dorothy Canfield Fisher, Wilbur Cross, Walter Prichard Eaton, and Louis Untermeyer. (Frost, in his reply, added to the spirit of playfulness by offering his listeners a little one-act drama inspired by John Lynch of Bethlehem: "The Cow's in the Corn.") The ladies among the guests included the novelist Willa Cather, the poet Jean Starr Untermeyer, the poet and novelist Elinor Wylie, the journalist Elizabeth Shepley Sergeant; and the atmosphere of the entire evening was thoroughly pleasing to Frost. But the absence of Amy Lowell gave strength to his decision that he would absent himself from her dinner. While still in New York, immediately after his birthday celebration, he persuaded his wife to make excuses to her for him: "I am writing to say what we ought to have said decidedly in the first place—that it's simply out of the question for Robert to speak at your dinner. He just isn't able to. He is tired now, and has three lectures ahead of him this week, with much travelling. He is sorry, and we hope very much that it won't greatly disarrange your plans. . . ."

Even without Robert Frost, the dinner in honor of Amy Lowell was a spectacular triumph. The two-volume *John Keats,* on which she had worked with so much devotion, had already gone through four large printings. The sponsors of this celebration were distinguished Bostonians, including authors, scholars, and artists.

Miss Lowell, although she pronounced the party a "huge success," was scarcely able to maintain her poise to the end of the evening. She suffered great pain, in spite of sedatives given her by her physician, and the strain of the occasion was too much. She became so ill she was forced to cancel her accommodations aboard the *Berengaria,* scheduled to sail for England on April 15, 1925. A few weeks later, on the twelfth of May, she suffered a stroke and died.

Frost, conscience-stricken, made the only amends possible. He immediately sent a telegram of condolence to Ada Russell. Mrs. Frost wrote at length to her.

Soon after Amy Lowell's death, President Olds called on Frost to make a commemorative statement before the students in chapel. He could not refuse. In his remarks he discriminated precisely between what he admired about her "liveliness of mind and spirit" and what he did not like about her poetry. A day later, a reporter from the *Christian Science Monitor* appeared at 10 Dana Street to ask for a tribute that might be published. Made uneasy by the request, Frost explained he would prefer to write out such a tribute, rather than dictate it on the spur of the moment. If the reporter would wait a few minutes, he would try to gather his thoughts. Retreating alone to his study, he found paper and pen, still wondering what he could write that would not mock him when he saw it in print. He remembered a pair of thoughts he had recently formulated in conversation, and decided to put them down, even though he had not previously associated them with Amy Lowell—or with each other. As he wrote he patched in a few additional statements that might be taken as praise, provided the reader did not look too closely. What he gave the reporter was adequate:

"It is absurd to think that the only way to tell if a poem is lasting is to wait and see if it lasts. The right reader of a good poem can tell the moment it strikes him that he has taken an immortal wound—that he will never get over it. That is to say, permanence in poetry as in love is perceived instantly. It hasn't to await the test of time. The proof of a poem is not that we have never forgotten it, but that we knew at sight that we never could forget it. There was a barb to it and a tocsin that we owned to at once. How often I have heard it in the voice and seen it in the eyes of this generation that Amy Lowell had lodged poetry with them to stay.

"The most exciting movement in nature is not progress, advance, but expansion and contraction, the opening and shutting of the eye, the hand, the heart, the mind. We throw our arms wide with a gesture of religion to the universe; we close them around a person. We explore and adventure for a while and then we draw in to consolidate our gains. The breathless swing is between subject matter and form. Amy Lowell was distinguished in a period of dilation when poetry, in the effort to include a larger material, stretched itself almost to the breaking of the verse. Little ones with no more apparatus than a tea-cup looked on with alarm. She helped make it stirring times for a decade to those immediately concerned with art and to many not so immediately.

"The water in our eyes from her poetry is not warm with any suspicion of tears; it is water flung cold, bright and many-colored from flowers gathered in her formal garden in the morning. Her Imagism lay chiefly in images to the eye. She flung flowers and everything there. Her poetry was forever a clear resonant calling off of things seen."

Frost did not immediately hear how Untermeyer had reacted to the news of Amy Lowell's death, and he suspected Untermeyer might hold him responsible for the awkwardness that had developed in their warm friendship. He let more than a month pass before writing him:

". . . I suspect that what lies at the bottom of your schmertz is your own dereliction in not having gone to her Keats Eats just before Amy died. She got it on us rather by dying just at a moment when we could be made to feel that we had perhaps judged her too hardly. Ever since childhood I have wanted my death to come in as effectively and affectingly. It helps alway[s] anyway it comes in a career of art. Whatever bolt you have shot you have still, as long as you are alive, that one in reserve. But of course it always does the most good on a world that has been treating you too unkindly.

"I didnt rise to verse but I did write a little compunctious prose to her ashes. And I did go before the assembled college, to say in effect that really no one minded her outrageousness because it never thrust home: in life she didnt know where the feelings were to hurt them[,] any more than in poetry she knew where they were to touch them. I refused to weaken abjectly."

Far more important to Frost was another death that had occurred while he and Amy Lowell were still bantering over who would or would not appear at whose dinner. On February 19, 1925, newspapers throughout the country bore the announcement that Marion LeRoy Burton of the University of Michigan had died the day before. For Frost the death of Burton raised questions of whether his unnamed successor would have enough sympathy for a Fellow in Letters, appointed for life.

Frost was asked to be the main speaker at a memorial service held in Ann Arbor on May twenty-eighth. Accepting the honor, he chose that occasion to review for his listeners what he described as some of President Burton's ideas on education:

". . . Administration was never enough to satisfy the idealism of his nature. He brushed it aside in his mind for something beyond, which as I came to see, was no less than the advancement of learning through magnanimous teaching. Buildings, discipline, entrance requirements, professional schools were but the spread and ramification of the tree. His heart was really in some slight branch away at the top by which alone the tree was gaining height. The height of teaching was what concerned him[—]how far up it could be carried. We talked of nothing else the last few times I saw him. . . .

"Remember now that I am telling you almost his very words. No one was ready to give a name yet to the change that was coming over education. He preferred to describe it himself in terms of teachers. He built the future on teachers who would know how to get more out of a student by throwing an atmosphere of expectation around him than by putting the screws on him. They would ask without asking. How? By implication, by challenge, by example, by presence.

"What would they ask? First of all that the student make his own trouble and not wait for teachers to make it for him. Second, they would ask the student to . . . [grasp] the idea that telling over a story he read last night, in nearly the order in which he read it, is no more good recitation than is polite conversation. And they would prejudice him against intruding with the sciences into art. They would prejudice him against having to tell teachers what the teachers already knew. They would prejudice him against putting a poem or book to any use except that it was intended to be put to by the man who wrote it. They will remind him that, in both the arts and sciences, a man shows the quality he is to be known by, strikes what is called his note, young, or, almost certainly, not at all. He has no time to waste dawdling with nothing but good marks for an excuse. Between 15 and 25 are the springing years. And, last of all, they will turn their claim on him into his claim on them, and ask him, by implication, to use it. . . .

"President Burton's plan was just unfolding. It was all his own. Others will go on with it. But that will not be the same to his friends who sympathized with him in his ambition. Our loss may be great, but his loss was great too, interrupted in what he could not help feeling was a great enterprise."

Robert Frost hoped none of his listeners at the memorial service would realize that he had placed many of his own opinions, concerning education, in the mouth of the dead president. The poet had stretched the truth considerably when he assured these listeners, "Remember now that I am telling you almost his very words." In a sense, his primary theme throughout his address had been the justification of the unorthodox stance he had taken at Amherst and would take when he returned to Ann Arbor that fall. If anyone saw through his machinations, Frost could at least say he himself deeply believed in these notions and that he had already talked them over with Burton, who seemed to like them.

In spite of his unorthodox methods as a teacher, Frost had already made several important contributions to the educational programs at Michigan and Amherst. Even before he attended the Amherst commencement of 1925 a great many of the students, the faculty, and the townspeople found occasions for expressing gratitude to him, personally. And an editorial concerning his plan to go to Michigan praised him warmly; it made only one complaint: "The wish has been expressed from more than one source that such an opportunity had been created for Prof Frost here at Amherst, so that we might have benefited by his progress in the kind of teaching he has been doing in Amherst college."

28

FURTHER SHIFTS— NEW VOLUMES

(1925–1930)

WHEN ROBERT FROST and his wife made the train journey from Vermont to Michigan in the fall of 1925, he knew she was reluctant to go. "Neither Carol or Lillian seem well enough to please me," she had written to Mrs. Fobes a few weeks earlier, "and I am rather worried and tired." Her husband thought she worried unnecessarily about their children, and all these fears and worries concerning the children were, indeed, debilitating. But some of her nervousness and fatigue, now, stemmed from the aftereffects of a serious illness during the previous June—an illness her husband had misrepresented, for reasons of delicacy.

Awaiting Mrs. Frost in Ann Arbor was the problem of furnishing the house that friends of the Frosts' had chosen and rented for them at 1223 Pontiac Road, across the Huron River from the campus. Taking the life appointment seriously, the Frosts had sent their furniture by freight from Amherst, and as they had been slow in making arrangements for its shipment, delivery would be late. Dean and Mrs. Joseph A. Bursley, two of their closest friends, insisted that the Frosts plan to be their guests until the house on Pontiac Road was ready for occupancy. Mrs. Frost could count on obtaining some rest while waiting for the furniture to arrive.

Almost as soon as the Frosts reached Ann Arbor, other friends were quick to extend hospitalities, so they were promptly caught up in too many social engagements. During the past three years his stature as poet had grown in the eyes of these admiring people, and new luster was provided by his having been given so unique a position at Michigan and by his having served as the major speaker in the memorial service for the late president.

One of the first social invitations came from Burton's successor, Clarence Cook Little, a New Englander who had specialized in biology and genetics while doing graduate work at Harvard and who had become a professor in the Harvard Medical School before serving as president of the University of Maine. When the Frosts went for dinner they discovered that Mrs. Little was strongly sympathetic toward Frost's new appointment. Herself a poet, she was eager to organize an informal group of nonstudents who might enjoy sharing their literary enthusiasms. Frost, trying to show more interest than he felt for such a plan, made and later kept a promise to meet with this group as soon as Mrs. Little could assemble it.

Much of the conversation with President Little was tactfully directed to the subject of biology and to questions concerning the president's work in that field. Frost spoke with sincerity about his early delight in reading and rereading Charles Darwin's book on the famous voyage of the *Beagle*. His host, impressed, later took from a shelf in his own library, and presented to Frost as a gift, the first edition of Darwin's *Journal of Researches*. The rapport established seemed mutually gratifying, but Frost knew he could never develop with this cold-mannered scientist the same cordial friendship he had formed with President Burton.

One of the boys who called on the Frosts soon after they moved into their new home at 1223 Pontiac Road was a young poet, Wade Van Dore, whom they had first met in New Hampshire several years earlier. Van Dore was not a registered student. A rebel, he had never gone further than the ninth grade in his formal education. Writing poetry was his primary concern; and he had consciously taken Thoreau's *Walden* as his gospel, because it preached freedom and protested that the mass of men lead lives of quiet desperation, enslaved by dispensabilities.

In 1922, Van Dore discovered the poetry of Robert Frost and wrote the author to say he admired it. Touched by unusual elements in the letter, Frost had replied:

"First about Thoreau: I like him as well as you do. In one book (Walden) he surpasses everything we have had in America. You have found this out for yourself without my having told you; I have found it out for myself without your having told me. Isn't it beautiful that there can be such concert without collusion? That's the kind of 'getting together' I can endure.

"I'm going to send part of your letter to a farmer in Franconia N. H. where I lived and owned a small property until last year. The farmer is a friend of mine and will listen sympathetically to what I shall say about you. I dont know just what your plan would be. Would it be to camp out for a while on his land and then find a few boards and nails to build a shack of for the winter? . . ."

Pleasant contacts with the young people on or near the campus at Ann Arbor were interrupted by reports of illness from the children back home. And another interruption marred the newly established serenity of the

Frosts in their hideaway on Pontiac Road. Not long after they moved in, the poet made a considerable journey to give a series of readings, the first being in New Hampshire. From New Hampshire, he started southward; first, to Philadelphia; then, to Baltimore; then, Chapel Hill, North Carolina. Within ten days he was back in Ann Arbor. The trip had been so arduous, however, he was once again suffering from an ailment that threatened to be influenza. He spent the next few days in bed, regretting his attempts to crowd too many diversions into a period that was supposed to be a withdrawal from all that might interfere with poetry-writing.

Even on Pontiac Road he could not withdraw from newspaper reporters who sought him out and prodded him with questions that often were annoying. Fortunately, one pleased him by leading into a discussion of a favorite topic. The reporter asked whether the scalpel of modern science might have probed so deeply into the mysteries of earth, air, and water that there was no longer room enough for poetic genius to find free play in the imaginative explorations of the unknown.

To Frost, the word "science" could be simultaneously fascinating and repulsive. He was always deeply absorbed by details concerning any new scientific discovery. At the same time, he could be offended by any cocksure scientific manner that chose to use human revelations for purposes of mocking poetic and religious concerns for true mysteries. On this occasion, he answered the reporter in ways that hinted at how and where Frost took his position on the old-new battle line between science and religion.

". . . Life has lost none of its mystery and its romance. The more we know of it, the less we know. Fear has always been a great stimulus to man's imagination. But fear is not the only stimulus. If science has expelled much of our fear, still there is left a thousand things from which to shape our dreams.

"Keats mourned that the rainbow, which as a boy had been for him a magic thing, had lost its glory because the physicists had found it resulted merely from the refraction of the sunlight by the raindrops. Yet knowledge of its causation could not spoil the rainbow for me. I am so sure that it is not given to man to be omniscient. There will always be something left to know, something left to excite the imagination of the poet and those attuned to the great world in which they live.

"Only in a certain type of small scientific mind can there be found cocksureness, a conviction that a solution to the riddle of the universe is just around the corner. There was, for example, Jacques Loeb, the French biologist, who felt he had within his grasp the secret of vitality. Give him but ten years. . . .

"He had the ten and ten more, and in ten more he was dead. Perhaps he knows more of the mystery of life now than ever he did before his passing. . . ."

One cause of his immediate brooding over the tugs and pushes between science and religion was his uneasiness over the presence of the science-oriented President Little, in the place of the religion-oriented President Burton. He had spent only a few weeks of his permanent appointment in this new atmosphere before he began to doubt he could last until spring. In a sense, he did not even last through the fall term. Family illness again interfered.

Mrs. Frost had gone East, to Pittsfield, Massachusetts, because of news Marjorie was in a hospital there with pneumonia. Although she had passed the crisis before Mrs. Frost arrived, she was also suffering from a pericardial infection, from chronic appendicitis, and from a nervous breakdown. Her condition became so critical that Frost himself went to her bedside before the middle of December.

Other members of the Frost family gathered in Pittsfield, and braced for a somewhat-forlorn celebration of Christmas: Irma came up from her art studies in New York City; and Carol and Lillian drove from South Shaftsbury, with their one-year-old son, Prescott. Lesley drafted her father to help during the final Christmas rush at the bookstore she and Marjorie had opened in Pittsfield in the spring of 1924. And New Year's Eve found Frost writing, despondently, in a letter to John Bartlett:

"I am not sure of hanging on long at Ann Arbor though the position is supposed to be for life. It's too far from the children for the stretch of our heart strings. . . . We dont like to be scattered all over the map as long as we dont have to be. Elinor stands being separated from the children worse than I do. What I want is a farm in New England once more."

During the same evening, yet in an entirely different mood, he wrote to Sidney Cox. He began by scolding the young professor for trying to build a teaching method on a foundation of contentiousness, and gradually brought the letter around to that subject on which he himself was always contentious: modern science, in its opposition to religion. Letting himself unwind through writing such a letter was one of Frost's favorite ways of keeping his mind off whatever worried him most.

Marjorie's slow recovery from nervous exhaustion and pericarditis caused a postponement of the scheduled operation for chronic appendicitis. Her father, perplexed to know which of his responsibilities should be given priority, lingered in Pittsfield until the middle of January—then, departed to give three readings, before returning to Ann Arbor.

The most important of the three engagements was at Bryn Mawr. In his talk there, before reading, he began by teasing his audience in a typically provocative way. He said the current excitement over the New Poetry had caused him to look carefully at a few poems called to his attention by Sir Arthur Quiller-Couch. At this moment he deceptively held aloft a small, fat volume to which he had added a flamboyant dust jacket, cut to fit the book: his old copy of *The Oxford Book of English Verse*, edited by Quiller-Couch. He wanted to share his discovery of these poems.

The first one he read (without naming author or title or book) brought gasps of delight from the girls. Would they like to hear another, by the same author? Oh, they would! Again he read. Again there were murmured sounds of approval. Just one more, from the same author? Yes, please. When he had finished the third poem, which everyone admired, he asked if anyone could name the author. No, but it was plain they were breathless to hear; and he told them: Henry Wadsworth Longfellow. Groans.

When the noise had subsided, Frost teasingly asked the girls to decide for themselves when they had been correct in their evaluations—when they had liked the poems, without knowing who wrote them, or when they reacted to an unpopular name?

From this teasing start he went on to discuss his announced topic, "Metaphors." Praising Longfellow's fresh uses of metaphors in the poems he had read, and also honoring Longfellow's quiet refusal to snap metaphors like whips, he borrowed from his Amherst course in "Judgments" some examples of poor metaphors used by philosophers. Then, he offered some examples of metaphors employed by critics and interpreters, in their attempts to describe the motives of poets. Some critics liked to say that some poets, trying to "escape" from life, wrote their poems as forms of retreat, after they had been wounded by life. Other critics claimed that the realistic poet deserved most praise, because he used poetry as a means of "grappling" with what bothered him in his private or public experiences.

Escape? Grappling? He moved on, by offering a definition of poetry, with the aid of a metaphor borrowed from his recent reading in science. Poetry is "tropism," he said, in the sense that the biologists use the word. He reminded them that tropism may be defined as an orientation of an organism, usually by means of growth rather than movement, in response to external stimulus. Tropism, then, may be growth toward light: an *aspiration* toward light. Poetry, considered in this way, might be defined as aspiration.

Having established this ambiguous definition, he invoked a homely image—the housefly—to suggest two different ways of looking at the word "escape." If you wish to rid a room of houseflies, he said, all you must do is darken it and let a small crack of light appear at an open window. The flies will go to and through that crack of light, not because they want to "escape" from the room, but rather, because the attraction of the light is too much for them; they *aspire* toward it.

His listeners, fascinated, were slightly bewildered, and he was ready to make his point. Aspiration, he said, is belief, faith, confidence. There are, of course, many different kinds of belief, and poetry may deal metaphorically with any one or all of these beliefs. A poem may be an unfolding of an emotion that is at first purely implicit. It may begin merely as a vague lump in the throat, and out of that tension the images of a poem may be used for purposes of passing from the implicit to the explicit. The poem itself might be the quiver of the transition from belief to realization.

Having, thus, guided his Bryn Mawr listeners up a little flight of stairs that amounted to his own subtle version of Plato's ladder in the *Symposium*, he began to read some illustrative poems of his own— starting from images he himself had endowed with metaphorical hints of aspiration, in "Birches." By the time he finished, the girls were captivated, although some of them were not exactly sure they understood the points he had tried to make.

At this stage in his career as a performing bard, Frost increasingly enjoyed teasing and tantalizing his audiences by making bold statements that meant much to him and, also, by aiming his remarks just high enough over the heads of his listeners to make them stretch for his meanings.

His schedule of readings led Frost from Bryn Mawr to Union College in Schenectady, New York, and, then, back to Amherst. He had promised President Olds he would not desert Amherst; he would return for two-week stays, occasionally, and place himself at the disposal of professors who wanted him to talk in their classrooms—or, even, at the mercy of students who just wanted to talk. During this two-week stay, he gave one public reading in Johnson Chapel.

He also renewed his acquaintance with G. R. Elliott, whom Frost had pried away from Bowdoin by helping him obtain a position in the department of English at Amherst. To Elliott, Frost confided that the permanent fellowship at Michigan was not working out so well as had been expected; he seemed too much of a Yankee to enjoy the prospect of living permanently in the Midwest; he might resign from the university at the end of the year and offer his service at various colleges for a week or two, using his Vermont farm as base.

By the time he returned to Ann Arbor, late in January of 1925, the second semester was about to begin. According to the agreement he had made, Frost was to have only one formal obligation at Michigan each year. He was to offer a second-semester course intended chiefly for those students who would be writing even if they were not in the course.

At first he met the class, limited to twelve students, in one of the seminar rooms in the library—and was tolerant of the uninvited. After three sessions he said there was no need to meet as a group anymore; each of them should write something new and, when ready to show it, should telephone to make an appointment for a conference at his home. Those who accepted the arrangement were the serious ones. The others were merely eliminated by this Gideon's test.

One advantage thus gained by Frost was that he could protect the hours he liked best for writing. As long as Mrs. Frost remained in Pittsfield with Marjorie, he found that any hour of day or night (except the morning) was good for his own writing.

A Boston reporter had asked him whether the "flat country" around Ann Arbor, presumed to be so different from New England, might have a bad effect on his writing poetry. His polite answer: "I never write about a place in New England, if I am there. I always write about it when I am away. In Michigan I shall be composing poetry about New Hampshire and Vermont with longing and homesickness better than I would if I were there, just as [I did when I was] in England."

One night he sat alone before the fireplace in the house on Pontiac Road, feeding branch after branch of black walnut to the flames and enjoying the fragrance. The signs of spring in Ann Arbor reminded him of what must be happening back in Vermont and New Hampshire —reminded him in particular of images that asked to be caught in a poem. Truly homesick, he reached for pen and paper and wrote "Spring Pools."

Much of his loneliness and homesickness disappeared when Mrs. Frost returned, bringing with her not only the slowly recovering Marjorie, but also the strong-willed Irma, grown tired of studying art in New York. The presence of the girls in the household required a certain amount of social activity for entertainment. One family of visitors brought with them an attractive young man, John Paine Cone, who had grown up on a wheat farm in Kansas. To the surprise of everyone, John Cone and Irma Frost so quickly fell in love that they were engaged to be married before Irma went back to Vermont and John returned to Kansas.

As the end of the term approached, another visitor brought another surprise. President Olds of Amherst had been informed by Elliott that there might be a possibility of persuading Frost to give up his position at Michigan and go back to Amherst on a part-time basis. Olds appeared in Ann Arbor, found Frost amenable to such a proposal, and completed the arrangements. Frost was so relieved, the tone of his letter of thanks to Elliott ascended to the almost-lyrical.

On the farm in South Shaftsbury, before Robert Frost returned there in June of 1926, Carol Frost and his wife, Lillian, had set out a hundred dwarf Astrachan trees and sixty cultivated highbush blueberry plants. The young people had thrown their efforts into such a variety of experiments, and with such eagerness, it was difficult to keep track of their plans. His father, boasting of Carol's earnestness, wrote, "He's such a worker as I was never suspected of being though I may have been." Of course, the poet never had been such a worker, but he took extraordinary pleasure in watching the farm prosper.

One drawback to this pleasure was that the family was getting too big for the Stone Cottage. Frost's grandson, Prescott, was just reaching the age when he could walk and talk well enough to charm and exhaust those who tried to protect him from his own garrulous boldness. Marjorie continued to require the worried attentions of her parents. Irma was buzzing with plans for her wedding. Then, Lillian became unexpectedly ill and was hospitalized in Bennington, where she underwent major surgery early in July.

The pressures thus placed on Frost, as head of the family, were enough to make him talk about getting away; and Mrs. Frost, writing to Mrs. Fobes, explained the plans for an unusually early departure for Franconia: "Robert and I have decided to go up to the mountains next Monday. . . . Robert has become very nervous, and it is necessary for us to be by ourselves, without the children, for a little while, so that he may recover his equanimity. . . ."

The escape to Franconia afforded so much relief, Frost soon found himself in the mood for writing new poems and revising old ones. The longest of his unfinished poems, started in the spring of 1920, had been inspired in part by Edward Ames Richards, the Amherst student who had subsequently gone partway with the Frosts on the Long Trail hike in 1922. Richards had published in *The Amherst Monthly* for March 1920 a meditative lyric in which two lovers talked briefly about a brook's name. In discussing the poem with Richards, at the time of its publication, Frost had said that if he were to build either a lyric or a dramatic dialogue around the name of a brook, he would make something quite different.

The only help needed or gained from Richards was a particular memory-jog. Back in his Derry days Frost had often admired a stream that flowed westward, as though it were deliberately ignoring its eventual destination to the east, the Atlantic Ocean. On all the Derry maps, old and new, that stream was officially designated West-Running Brook. Never before had Frost considered building metaphors around the contrary direction of that stream, but Richards had shown him possibilities, and a good start had been made.

Returning now to this unfinished poem, he brought to it a new stimulus afforded by the scientists with whom he had quarreled at the University of Michigan. He had boasted of his own Socratic contrariety in merely asking those men questions about the Darwinian theory, but he had confided to Untermeyer something else concerning his artistic pleasure in reacting against more than evolutionary formulas:

". . . [I am very] fond of seeing our theories knocked into cocked hats. What I like about [Henri] Bergson and [J. Henri] Fabre is that they have bothered our evolutionism so much with the cases of instinct they have brought up. You get more credit for thinking if you restate formulae or cite cases that fall in easily under formulae, but all the fun is outside[:] saying things that suggest formulae that won't formulate—that almost but don't quite formulate. I should like to be so subtle at this game as to seem to the casual person altogether obvious. The casual person would assume that I meant nothing or else I came near enough meaning something he was familiar with to mean it for all practical purposes. Well well well."

What Frost liked, in addition, about Bergson and Fabre was that each had acquainted himself with the results of modern science and, then, found his own ways to attack some of the most cherished scientific hypotheses.

One image in Frost's gradually developing poem, "West-Running Brook," owed far more to Bergson than to Richards. In *Creative Evolution,* Bergson had extended the Lucretian view of life as a river: the stream of everything that runs away to spend itself in death and nothingness, except as it is resisted by the spirit of human beings. Bergson had added another analogy, built around a wave-image: "Life as a whole, from the initial impulsion that thrust it into the world, will appear as a wave which rises, and which is opposed by the descending movement of matter." And he had written: "Our own consciousness is . . . continually drawn the opposite way, obliged, though it goes forward, to look behind. This retrospective vision . . . must detach itself from the *already-made* and attach itself to the *being-made* . . . , turning back on itself and twisting on itself. . . ."

To Frost, one of the most important elements in Bergson's highly poetic philosophy was the denial of essentially deterministic elements in the Darwinian theories. In his gently contrary manner, Bergson insisted that the human spirit has the freely willed power to resist materialism through creative acts that pay tribute to God. Frost, in bringing his poem to completion, made it a study in Bergsonian contraries.

"West-Running Brook" begins as a dramatic narrative in which a New England farmer and his wife notice similarities between themselves and the brook: " 'It must be the brook / Can trust itself to go by contraries / The way I can with you—and you with me. . . .' "

Then, they notice another contrariety: "The black stream, catching on a sunken rock, / Flung backward on itself in one white wave, / And the white water rode the black forever. . . .″

Immediately, the man and wife express pleasantly contrary views concerning whether the wave should be endowed with masculine or feminine symbolism; but the wife encourages the husband to say how he interprets it, and he does. Although, as he goes on, the husband seems to be expressing a purely materialistic view of biological devolution and of eventual annihilation, the continuing motion of the poem is contrary to such a view.

Within this Bergsonian poem the act of resistance is primarily motivated by sorrow or remorse over that which is happening, as all substance seems to be lapsing unsubstantial in the universal cataract of death. At the same time, the act of resistance is represented as being sacred, in the sense that it is an assertion of belonging and dedication and consecration to the Source of the *élan vital*. The husband seems to be manipulating, metaphorically, such Heraclitean-Lucretian-Pauline contraries as that the death of the earth gives life to fire, the death of fire gives life to air, the death of air gives life to water, and the death of water gives life to earth—thus, figuratively suggesting the endless cycle of birth, death, rebirth, and continuity, in nature and in human nature.

The motion of the metaphors is one of circling back to the beginning of beginnings, in the cautiously ambiguous statement, " 'And there is something sending up the sun.' " Such a statement might or might not be made to fit the Darwinian formula of evolution, but the husband's concluding lines endow the statement (and the entire poem) with religious overtones that are contrary to a purely scientific interpretation of evolutionary theories: " 'It is this backward motion toward the source, / Against the stream, that most we see ourselves in, / The tribute of the current to the source. / It is from this in nature we are from. / It is most us.' "

Robert Frost knew that in "West-Running Brook" the metaphors he had borrowed and adapted to his own uses had provided him with the most incisive and expansive poetic expression he had yet given his deepest religious belief concerning death and the possibilities of eternal salvation after death. Nevertheless, he knew he had conveyed these beliefs with enough artistic indirection to let him escape any self-conscious embarrassment.

At Franconia the serenity of the Fobes cottage encouraged Frost to work further on the cluster of manuscripts he was shaping toward a book. But too soon he was forced to put aside his manuscripts and begin his next series of performances. He was scheduled to begin his promised ten-week stint at Amherst early in January 1927 (he had rented the Tyler

[311]

house at 34 Amity Street). And, then, he made an uneventful spring tour to Michigan, Maine, and New Hampshire.

Marjorie's perplexing condition failed to improve, and in May of 1927, as the three of them returned to the Stone Cottage in South Shaftsbury, the parents tried to cheer her by discussing the possibility of a voyage to England and France that summer. But she remained so weak the plans had to be abandoned.

One innovation, made in the hope of providing more serenity for all three, was a retreat from the Stone Cottage to nearby summer quarters —a place that came to be known as the Shingled Cottage—on a back road in North Bennington, within the area that became the campus of Bennington College. Another reason for this move was awareness that Carol and Lillian, given title to the farm at South Shaftsbury as a wedding present, had been forced to share it with so many other members of the Frost family that cumulative frictions had become unpleasant.

Carol's father wrote, during the summer and fall of 1927, enough new poems to make him think about the shape he might give his next book. The structural problem was not unlike the one he had faced when he tried to assemble a scattering of lyrics for *A Boy's Will*. There, he had established a progression through moods of escape, retreat, doubt, denial, negation—to moods of pursuit, love, hope, and affirmation. This time he chose to divide his latest assemblage of poems into six carefully arranged parts, each illuminating different ways of looking at "contraries." Centrally, as part three, he placed by itself the unifying study-in-contraries, "West-Running Brook," title-poem for the projected volume.

Part one, containing eleven lyrics, was made to foreshadow the cumulative emphasis on contraries, by carrying on its section-title page this juxtaposition: "I / SPRING POOLS / *From snow that melted only yesterday.*" And at the close of part one he placed a sonnet built around contrary responses to darkness, a sonnet that gave metaphorical expression to the poet's firmly stoical-puritan belief in the Christian doctrine of submission, "Acceptance."

He made part two continue this theme of responses to light and dark, by using as the section title for it a pair of words that might at first glance seem directly contrary to God's "Let there be light." Then, as balance, he borrowed from the preceding poem a motto that set up another contrariety on its section-title page, thus: "II / FIAT NOX / *Let the night be too dark for me to see / Into the future. Let what will be[,] be.*"

He placed first in part two the darkly imaged poem entitled "Once by the Pacific," and followed it with nine other poems in which the moods were predominantly dark. Again, however, he chose as concluding poem a meditative lyric calculated to convey further hints of metaphysical submission and acceptance, "Acquainted with the Night." Here was one of his recurrent themes: ideally, he had been forced to confront some of the worst forms of darkness, and he liked to think he had coped with them in ways that enabled him to avoid the extremes of self-deceptive pessimism or optimism. Immediately following this poem he placed "West-Running Brook."

In part four, entitled "Sand Dunes," he permitted six lyrics to extend the affirmations implicit throughout the title-poem; and into part five, bearing the section title "Over Back," he placed four brief rural poems that were the least useful to his design. Part six was made up of seven much stronger poems, each manipulating contraries, by further balancing attitudes of negation against attitudes of affirmation. The section title and motto, here, were calculated to set the pace for this concluding parade of tantalizations: "VI / MY NATIVE SIMILE / 'The sevenfold sophie of Minerve.'" Although he borrowed this motto, somewhat perversely, from an obscure sixteenth-century poet, he enabled his readers to find the source of the section's title merely by turning the page and reading the playfully serious first poem in part six, "The Door in the Dark."

Thus placed, as the first poem in the final structural unit of *West-Running Brook,* "The Door in the Dark" provided more than the source for the title of part six. It hinted that the poet had begun to approach the sevenfold wisdom of Minerva only after he had suffered through a jarring and a disillusioning experience; that this experience, no matter how painful, had given freshness and originality to all the subsequent poetic comparisons he made, all the implied or stated analogies between seemingly dissimilar things.

In concluding his arrangement of this manuscript, he chose to place in last position a poem satirically aimed at one of his favorite targets, man's arrogant quest for scientific knowledge. This final poem, entitled "The Bear," had been inspired in part by events in the Franconia region. But if Franconia bears provided one element of inspiration for the poetical satire he chose to use as a set piece for the conclusion of his new volume, Alexander Pope's "Essay on Man" provided other elements—including the appropriateness of using mock-heroic couplets.

The total manuscript of *West-Running Brook,* finally including thirty-nine poems, was as different from *New Hampshire* as that volume had been from *Mountain Interval* or *North of Boston* or *A Boy's Will.* The range and variety of forms was heightened by the freshness of metaphors in the rhymed lyrics, by the metaphysical reach of the blank-verse title poem, and by the mingled play and seriousness of the couplets in "The

Bear." Quite boldly, Frost had also combined new and old, by sprinkling throughout the manuscript a few poems written so early he could have included them in *A Boy's Will.*

Although his new manuscript contained far more hints of his religious faith than any of his other books had done, he could not resist this artistic game of hinting at the importance to him of his puritan heritage—which he sometimes mocked and sometimes defended—and he had grown increasingly aware that one artistic gain made available to him from his religious belief was that it enriched and extended the ulterior meanings of his best metaphors, that it permitted him to talk about at least two worlds simultaneously. ("I almost think any poem is most valuable for its ulterior meaning," he once said; and he, then, puckishly added a mocking salute to Adler: "I have developed what you might call an 'ulteriority complex.' ")

Long before he completed the manuscript of *West-Running Brook,* he began to doubt whether he would give it to Henry Holt and Company for publication. His friend Lincoln MacVeagh, who had played such a valuable part in making *New Hampshire* an attractive book and a financial success, had resigned from the Holt firm late in 1923. As a consequence, there had been a cooling-off in Frost's relations with his publisher. At the same time, he had acquired an increasingly sophisticated attitude toward author-publisher relations. He had even decided that he should have driven a harder bargain over royalties prior to the publication of *New Hampshire.*

Remembering the difficulties he had met when he had tried to leave Holt and go with Alfred Harcourt, he cautiously weighed possibilities during the winter of 1927–1928. He discussed the entire problem with his best-informed friends, and (perhaps through no accident) word of these discussions reached his publisher, with the result that some hurried moves were made. Richard H. Thornton, successor to MacVeagh as Holt representative, was sent to call on Frost in South Shaftsbury late in May 1928.

In the negotiations, Frost knew that he had the advantage of being a Pulitzer Prize–winner with a new manuscript. His royalties on *New Hampshire* had been fifteen percent of the retail price; he asked and was promised fifteen-percent royalties on the first 5,000 copies of *West-Running Brook,* and twenty percent on all copies thereafter. There would be a limited, as well as a trade, edition; and an advance of $2,000 would be paid on request. Thornton also promised that a new and enlarged edition of *Selected Poems* would be published alongside *West-Running Brook,* in the fall of 1928, and all five of Frost's books would be brought together in a *Collected Poems,* either in the fall of 1929 or the spring of 1930.

Thornton carried back to Holt's office, and gained approval for, a proposal that Frost should be guaranteed a monthly payment of $250 throughout the next five years, with the understanding that he would also receive whatever royalties his books might earn above that annual amount of $3,000. Having gained far more contractual advantages than he had expected, he was thoroughly satisfied to stay with Henry Holt and Company.

But while Robert Frost was carefully working on the revisions of his manuscript for *West-Running Brook,* he kept looking out of the corner of one eye at progress being made on another manuscript, a biography of himself. He had been told that a study of him was to appear in a series to be published by the firm of George H. Doran in New York City. The editor in charge of the series was John Chipman Farrar, who had been an undergraduate at Yale when Frost first met him.

Farrar, combining the talents of a businessman with those of a poet, had chosen to earn his living as a publisher. He had made a good start with Doran and had been asked to serve as director of Middlebury's new addition to the Bread Loaf School of English, the Bread Loaf Writers' Conference. Frost, who had participated in the arrangements for this development, also attended the first session, in the summer of 1926.

At Bread Loaf, Farrar told Frost of the plan for the series of monographs and asked him to help by naming an author who might acceptably write the Frost study in the series. Farrar may have made the mistake of anticipating the choice, for they both knew that Wilfred Davison, director of the School of English at Bread Loaf, was gathering materials for a biographical study of Frost. Nevertheless, the decision was to rest entirely with Frost, who was so completely caught off guard that he asked for time to consider possibilities.

As it happened, another man named Davison called on Frost at Bread Loaf during the Writers' Conference in the summer of 1926, a poet who had come to the United States from England in 1925. Edward Davison and his wife had visited the Frosts at South Shaftsbury early in June 1926, and Frost had been much impressed by this young Englishman —who, in turn, showed a flattering admiration for Frost. As a consequence, Davison was urged to stop briefly at Bread Loaf, and there Frost somewhat impulsively asked him if he would like to write the book Farrar wanted. No decision was immediately reached, but shortly after the close of the conference, Edward Davison provisionally agreed to write a trial chapter, which he would submit to Frost.

In the trial chapter, Davison made an introductory survey of the New Poetry movement in America and brought in a few references sufficiently uncomplimentary to reveal that Davison had a strong dislike for the poetry and the personality of Louis Untermeyer. Frost was dismayed. He explained that there was no reason Davison should like Untermeyer for Frost's sake, but there was an obvious reason he should not express his dislike in a book on Frost. Davison took the criticism well, promised to rewrite the chapter, and assumed Frost had forgiven him for the blunder. But Frost had not forgiven, and had secretly decided someone else must be found to write the monograph. While Davison was continuing his revision, Frost went ahead to make other arrangements.

Frost's attention had been called to a *Saturday Review* essay carrying the declaration: ". . . we realized quite suddenly that the purest classical poet of America was Robert Frost." The essay continued by pointing out that while several of Frost's critics had mistakenly viewed him as a romantic poet of nature, nobody had paid sufficient attention to his being deeply rooted in Hellenism. The author of the article, Gorham B. Munson, could have made an equally strong case to support the claim that Frost was even more deeply rooted in puritanical Hebraism. Temporarily, however, Frost preferred to think of himself—and to have others think of him—as a classicist; and if Munson could be persuaded to write the biography under Frost's guidance, Munson could also be helped to shape the classical image even more pointedly than he had already done. Years earlier, under Frost's guidance, Untermeyer had strenuously attacked those who were inclined to view Frost as a romantic, rather than as a realist. Frost was now eager to help Gorham Munson, or anyone else, heighten the stature of the Frost image as that of a "good Greek."

In the autumn of 1926, Frost spent a few days in New York City. While there, he went around to Munson's quarters and, not finding him at home, left a note asking that he telephone the signer the next day. During the phone conversation Frost told this man he had never met that Munson was his choice for the writing of the monograph, and when Munson showed interest he was invited to dinner that evening. At this meeting Frost promised to have John Farrar offer Munson a contract.

As Frost became better acquainted with Munson some reservations were felt concerning this hasty choice, and it soon became obvious that Munson would need some careful tutoring before he could satisfactorily complete the biography. At the same time, Frost was troubled by the awkwardness of his relations with Edward Davison, who had to be let down as gently as possible. He insisted that Davison should continue his work on his own version of the biography—for which he could easily find a publisher when he next returned to London.

Farrar sent Frost a tactful plaint that hinted at the predicament caused by Frost's artful dodgings:

". . . I find the Edward Davison situation is becoming a bit of a mare's nest. . . . You must know I was far from planning anything that would 'hurt' Ted. That isn't the way I work. . . . It is, therefore, quite disquieting to me to have Ted Davison accusing me of a deep-laid-and-dyed plot against him. . . .

"So far as Dean Davison is concerned, he is now all up in the air for fear somebody or other will think he had antagonistic motives. For the matter of that, he had been planning for years on this work, and his disappointment is great. . . .

"This is the first time I have been involved in a literary imbroglio and I don't like it any more than I imagine you do. . . ."

Munson moved ahead so rapidly on the little biography that he completed the manuscript before the first of June 1927. Writing to Frost, he announced he had delivered one copy to Farrar, and was mailing another to Frost in the hope that any mistakes could be caught and corrected before Farrar sent the manuscript to the printer.

Not satisfied with the manuscript, Frost took the blame for certain mistakes. They amounted to faithful reportings, on Munson's part, of misrepresentations Frost had somehow conveyed, in trying to give an impression of what life had been like on the Derry farm during the years from 1900 to 1909. These years were particularly important to Frost, because he thought they provided the turning point in the whole story. Munson's account endowed the Derry venture with a sadness of deprivation, Frost thought, and such handling would give the wrong impression. He did now try to give a few more details that might convey the freshness and originality and luck of the cherished and (at least, in retrospect) perfect hiatus on the Derry farm.

Frost was apparently slow in getting his suggestions to Munson. Although the corrective information was gratefully received, the manuscript given Farrar had already been sent to the printer. Under the circumstances, Frost could only hope the reviewers would be kind.

The little book was published on November 1, 1927, under the title *Robert Frost: A Study in Sensibility and Good Sense,* and the reviewers made too much out of the last chapter. In his suggestions for revision Frost had apparently failed to notice and comment on the fact that the last chapter, entitled "Against the World in General," amounted to an expanded version of the *Saturday Review* essay and that Munson, in his revised attempt to strengthen the claim that Frost was a classicist, rather than a romantic, had invoked the support of the New Humanist leader Irving Babbitt. Munson was so sympathetic toward Babbitt's position in the current humanist controversy, he unintentionally encouraged critics to view Frost as a disciple of Babbitt's.

Scornfully opposed to being called the disciple of anyone, Frost had even-deeper reasons for wanting to separate himself completely from the New Humanists and Babbitt's version of humanism. To Frost, Babbitt's views were offensive because they contradicted his own cherished belief in the essentials of Christian teaching, especially the belief in God's mercy after death. Babbitt further offended by dismissing William James and Henri Bergson in arrogant and querulous ways, insisting that they were pure romantics who inherited too much nonsense from Rousseau. Such an approach heightened Frost's distaste for those meanings Babbitt assigned to the opposed terms "romanticism" and "classicism."

What Frost admired most about James and Bergson was that no matter how theologically heretical they might be, they did view life as God-centered. What he disliked most about Babbitt was the insistence that human life should be man-centered. Hence, the misery in finding that some reviewers of Munson's book hailed Frost as a humanist, while other reviewers damned him—for the same reason.

It was too late to make any protest to Munson, the man chosen to help improve the image of Frost as a classicist. But just when it seemed that the less said the better, Munson made another unintentional mistake. He had given journalistic assistance to Babbitt from the start of the controversy between the New Humanists and the theists, and he now tried to give additional support by publishing a *Bookman* essay entitled "Robert Frost and the Humanistic Temper."

Further linking the names of Frost and Babbitt, he wrote: "Not by theory but by practice as a poet is Mr. Frost truly a contemporary humanist," adding, "To illustrate: Mr. Babbitt says. . . ." Then, to clinch his point, Munson analyzed "West-Running Brook" as evidence that "the poet's sense of contraries is not far from the humanist's declaration that in man there is a duality of consciousness, a struggle between his impulse to unify himself and his impulse to drift with the stream of life."

That was too much for Frost to take without protest. He wrote Munson a letter that combined reprimand with oblique self-explanation, beginning, "We know each other so well that it seems as if we ought to go on and know each other better." In reply, Munson tried to defend himself, but the harm done to their friendship was irrevocable, and thereafter Frost merely went through the motions of courtesy.

29

A TRIP ABROAD AND
AID TO WRITERS

(1928–1930)

WHENEVER THE Frosts talked about going abroad for Marjorie's health, France was given special consideration, because Marjorie wanted to live there and learn to speak French. Advice was sought from Dorothy Canfield Fisher, who knew France almost as well as she knew Vermont. For several months during the First World War she had lived in Bellevue, near Sèvres, southwest of Paris, and she had remained on intimate terms with a family in Sèvres. If Marjorie would enjoy living with this family, Mrs. Fisher would make all the arrangements with Madame Marguerite Fischbacher.

The offer was accepted, and Mrs. Fisher kept her word. The only remaining drawback was fear that Marjorie might not be strong enough to stay with the Fischbachers while her parents left her there and went over to England to visit friends.

Frost, in uncertainty about how to make plans for such a precarious trip, had notified only one of his friends in England, the barrister-poet-botanist-bookcollector John W. Haines. Responding with his persistent friendliness, Haines assured the Frosts that he and his wife would enjoy having the Americans stay with them as guests as often and as long as possible during the proposed return to England. On July 29, 1928, Frost replied:

"We have the tickets and that is nearer you and England than we have been for thirteen years. The only thing that can keep me from walking a path with you this year will be the failure of Margery to come up to the mark on sailing day. . . . We plan to put her in charge of a nurse companion in France to see if the interest in picking up French and the society of some one young enough to laugh a lot wont help her case. So we are sailing, if we sail[,] directly for France. The ship leaves Quebec Canada with or without us on August 4th. Don't set your heart too much

[319]

on seeing us. . . . I will bring Elinor to your house inside of a few weeks now, though, if it in me lies. You dont care how old we look. . . ."

They did sail as planned, and the voyage was spoiled for them because all three suffered intermittently from seasickness. When they reached Paris they lingered for a few days before going on to Sèvres, and Frost dutifully tried to enjoy the wicked city he was predisposed to dislike. For Marjorie's sake, he spent an afternoon with her in the Louvre and an evening at the Opéra. When they moved out to Sèvres, Mrs. Frost was so fearful Marjorie would have difficulty in making adjustments to the Fischbacher family that she insisted on taking up residence for a short time in a Bellevue pension. For several days, Marjorie's parents took her on brief sight-seeing trips. They visited the famous ceramics museum that specialized in Sèvres ware. They even went to Versailles and peeked into the palace, the gardens, the park.

Frost was embarrassed by his inability to read or speak French and feared that any Frenchman speaking to another in his presence must be making fun of his ignorance. At Versailles his greatest enjoyment came when he found a portrait of George Washington in the palace gallery of noted generals. "Everything is American to him who looks with American eyes," he shamefacedly confessed.

Having expected to stay only a few days in France before crossing the channel, Frost was ready to leave France and start for England. What kept him was Mrs. Frost's distress over Marjorie's recurrent depressions and physical weaknesses. But early in September the parents felt safe in committing her to the care of Madame Fischbacher. They started for Gloucestershire, got as far as London, and stayed at the Imperial Hotel for several days while Mrs. Frost tried to overcome her own fatigue and depression.

As soon as Mrs. Frost felt strong enough to continue the journey, they went on to Gloucester, were welcomed by the Haines family, and spent the next ten days there, in hiding. The affection of the Haineses had a salutary effect on Mrs. Frost. While she was regaining her strength, Haines and Frost walked those roads and footpaths of the Dymock region they had often explored with Edward Thomas, Lascelles Abercrombie, and Wilfrid Gibson.

Haines still kept in touch with the Abercrombies and the Gibsons, but he could give no cheerful news about them. Lascelles and Wilfrid continued to write and publish verse, without attracting any attention from the newcomers. The Abercrombies were living at Leeds, and he was giving lectures at the university there. The Gibsons lived in the town of Letchworth, over in Hertfordshire. Frost, still bearing a grudge against Gibson for his failure to help Edward Thomas establish himself as a poet, could not make up his mind whether he would bother to get in touch with Gibson. Haines thought he should.

While the Frosts were staying with the Haines family, encouraging letters came from Marjorie, strengthening their hopes that they had been correct in leaving her with strangers in France. Mrs. Frost, slightly buoyed by the prospect of remaining longer in England, returned with her husband to London, knowing that he was far more eager than she for the renewal of other friendships.

The best London clearinghouse for information concerning fellow poets was Harold Monro's Poetry Bookshop (which had been moved in 1926 from 35 Devonshire Street to 38 Great Russell Street, near the British Museum). Frost telephoned the dour Monro and was surprised at the warmth of Monro's response. He insisted that Frost give a reading of his poems, in a room at the back of the bookshop; and when Frost hesitated, Monro sweetened the invitation. If Frost would promise to read, Monro would give him a stag dinner with his fellow American T. S. Eliot. Both offers were accepted, and the date of the reading was set for the eighteenth of October.

Other telephone calls prepared the way for several additional visits. The Frosts went up to Buckinghamshire to spend a night with the de la Mares at Taplow. They entertained Mr. and Mrs. John Gould Fletcher. They spent two nights in the home of the Georgian poet John Freeman.

An unexpected awkwardness developed when the Frosts called on the widow of Edward Thomas. She had recently shocked many of her friends by publishing some intimate, autobiographical reminiscences in a volume entitled *As It Was*. The book attracted international attention—had, even, been suppressed in Boston—and it had greatly eased her financial difficulties. But the Frosts, during their visit with her, severely expressed regret that she had gone into so much detail about her marital difficulties. They feared she might have injured, rather than strengthened, Edward's literary reputation.

In his next letter to Haines, Frost wrote: "We saw Helen Thomas and that ended one passage in our lives. . . . I decided before I had listened to her long that Edward had worse enemies to his memory than poor old simple Wilfrid [Gibson]. It needed only that decision to make it easy to visit Wilfrid at Letchworth. . . ."

Frost felt guilty for the hostile ways he had ignored Gibson; but the visit was carried through with ease, because both of the Gibsons crowded the conversation with their favorite recollections of events in Gloucestershire, and Frost was glad the small talk enabled him to conceal his dislike for this man who specialized in sentimentalities. Within a few days after the visit, Gibson sent him thirty-three lines of blank verse commemorating their reunion—a poem in which, as Frost told Haines, "he stoutly excuses us all for looking so horribly old."

There was one other comparable occasion when Frost was embarrassed and amused by being given a poem written in his honor. His call on the one-legged supertramp, W. H. Davies, was made entertaining by the old man's garrulousness, and yet, the beginning of the visit was so quaint that Frost could not resist reporting it to a friend who could appreciate: "Davies was the same old Davies. The minute Elinor and I got there he rose and presented us with an autographed poem as a 'souvenir of our visit.' He hasnt aged a hair. Still harping on why he isnt read in America. Wants to come over lecturing."

The saddest of these brief calls occurred one night when Frost went alone to a shabby Lincoln's Inn apartment to surprise John Cournos. Back in 1914 this Russian Jew from Philadelphia had been struggling to establish himself as a literary figure in London, and he was still struggling. Delighted to receive such an unexpected visitor, Cournos was in need of comfort. His wife was to undergo surgery the next day, and there was the possibility, at least the fear, she might not survive the operation. As usual, Cournos was also worrying about where he would find money enough to pay the expenses. The next morning Frost enclosed a check for fifty dollars with a note to Cournos and took to the hospital a bouquet of yellow roses for Mrs. Cournos.

Long before the Frosts started for England and France, Frost had informed his Irish friends Padraic Colum and George William Russell ("AE") that he wanted to visit them. He wrote Colum from London in an attempt to set up a mutually convenient time, and arrangements were soon worked out. Frost went to Ireland for five days, leaving his wife alone in London. During one evening Frost was taken to a gathering of literary notables, including William Butler Yeats. Once again, however, there was disappointment for Frost in the way he was barely noticed by his favorite Irish author.

Back in London, Frost soon realized that Harold Monro had done him a considerable favor. Even before the reading at the Poetry Bookshop, mailed announcements had spread the news to officers of the International P.E.N. Society (of which Frost had a few years earlier been made an honorary member) and of the English Speaking Union. Each group began making plans to honor him.

Those who gathered to hear him read at the bookshop were mostly strangers, and he was disappointed to be told by Monro that T. S. Eliot had sent his regrets. The night after the reading, however, Monro kept his word and took Frost to dinner with Eliot, whom he had not previously met. The two Americans entered into conversation easily, comparing notes on how their host had and had not assisted them, more than a decade earlier. During the summer of 1914, while Frost was living in Gloucestershire, Monro had been given his first opportunity to help Eliot, and had failed him. Conrad Aiken, then a stranger, appeared at the Poetry Bookshop, offered Monro a manuscript entitled "The Love Song of J. Alfred Prufrock," and explained that the author of it was his Harvard classmate, just then in Germany. After considering the manuscript for *Poetry and Drama,* Monro returned it to Aiken, dismissing it as being, according to Aiken's later telling of the story, "absolutely insane, or words to that effect."

There was something strained about the entire evening, and what annoyed Frost most was the way in which this native of St. Louis affected an English accent. Long before the evening was over, Frost decided to go on disliking Eliot as a tricky poet—and as a mealymouthed snob.

Late in October of 1928, just as Frost was beginning to be noticed by individuals and groups who had belatedly learned of his presence in England, disturbing news came from Madame Fischbacher. Marjorie was not well. Mrs. Frost, knowing of her husband's many commitments in England, insisted on going alone to France. Frost promised to meet her there in a week or ten days, and they planned to sail home from Le Havre before the middle of November.

In making his commitments he had accepted an invitation from Abercrombie to give a reading of his poems at the University of Leeds. He had also promised to go as far north as Edinburgh, to visit the Spenser scholar James Cruickshanks Smith and his family, whom the Frosts had met at Kingsbarns in Scotland during the summer of 1913. And Mrs. Smith's sister, Mrs. Jessy Mair, had arranged to have Frost give a talk and reading before the literary society of the London School of Economics. (Recently widowed, Mrs. Mair was later to marry the British economist William Henry Beveridge, director of the school.)

After his appearance at the London School of Economics he went to Edinburgh, spent a night with the Smiths, and then, stopped briefly at Leeds with the Abercrombies. Back in London, he found word that Mrs. Frost had decided to bring Marjorie over to England. The three of them would, therefore, sail for home from Southampton, and Frost seized one more chance to renew another old friendship, that with the poet F. S. Flint.

Flint had attended the reading at Monro's bookshop and, subsequently, made arrangements for Frost to meet him on an appointed evening. After dinner at the Garrick Restaurant, he took Frost to the apartment of Edward Garnett. No other critic in England had written of Frost's poetry more appreciatively or had been a closer friend of Edward Thomas's, and there was every reason for assuming Frost would enjoy this first meeting with Garnett. Unfortunately, Frost was in a grouchy mood, and he soon arranged to make sparks fly. He wondered if Garnett had ignored him, after one article, because he thought *Mountain Interval* a failure, made up of poems not good enough for *A Boy's Will* or *North of Boston*. When Garnett frankly answered that *North of Boston* was his favorite among Frost's four books, Frost took offense.

Flint tried to change the subject by introducing names of other poets, and immediately Frost fell into disagreement with Garnett over what qualities were best in the New Poetry. Although Frost's belligerence spoiled the evening, Garnett made a gracious and tactful gesture when his visitors were leaving. No matter what their differences of opinion might be, he said, he felt sure they could agree that Frost had written one nearly perfect pastoral poem, which discerning people would not soon forget, "The Mountain." That was enough to mollify Frost, and the parting was friendly.

By the time Mrs. Frost and Marjorie reached London, the two most important events remaining on Frost's calendar were the dinners arranged for him by the P.E.N. Society and by the English Speaking Union. As frequently happened, however, when Frost set too fast a pace for himself and was forced to risk having his sensitivities scraped raw by too many contacts with friends and strangers alike, he became ill, just before the scheduled dinners, and both had to be canceled.

One of the prime movers of these occasions was the Irish-American poet Norreys Jephson O'Conor, and when it became apparent Frost was recovering from his illness (he had only one more call to make, on Poet Laureate Robert Bridges), the O'Conors asked permission to arrange a small farewell party at their home on Sunday evening, November eleventh, the day after his appointment for tea with the poet laureate. Given permission, Mrs. O'Conor soon telephoned the Frosts, to relay another invitation.

Miss Edith Sitwell was not certain she would be able to meet the Frosts on the Sunday evening, and she did so want to make their acquaintance, she wondered if they would come to her home Saturday afternoon, the tenth. She had already invited Mr. and Mrs. T. S. Eliot and Mr. and Mrs. W. B. Yeats. Regretfully, the Frosts declined.

Frost went alone to Oxford to call on Bridges, with whom he had, in England in 1913, enjoyed discussing the sharp differences between their theories of poetry. The two men had briefly seen each other, again, at the University of Michigan in 1925. On the strength of these previous meetings, Frost had written Bridges shortly after reaching London and said he wished to call just long enough to pay his respects.

When Frost arrived it was immediately apparent that this distinguished eighty-four-year-old gentleman, who had published his first book of poems before Frost was born, was in no mood to discuss poetic theories. The poet laureate did have much to say, somewhat pompously, about his work on the long poem he was going to call "The Testament of Beauty" and about his brief stay at the University of Michigan. The conversation was too cold and formal to satisfy Frost. Taking his leave as soon as he dared, he was sorry he had not accepted the invitation to be with the Eliots and the Yeatses at Edith Sitwell's.

After the farewell evening at the O'Conors', there was time enough to show Marjorie a few more of the scenes in London she remembered from childhood. Then, they sailed for home aboard the SS *Olympic* on November 14, 1928.

In retrospect, Frost could not be sure the trip to France and England had been at all successful for Marjorie. He was certain Mrs. Frost had lost more than she had gained from all these adventures—that one serious cause of her suffering had been his insistence on making so many final social engagements, when she would have preferred taking Marjorie home weeks earlier. "I've made Elinor unhappier keeping her on than I think I ever made her before," he guiltily wrote to Haines. He was more philosophical in writing Davison, "Some things have disappointed us as much as we were afraid everything might (we were prepared for the worst). . . ." This was a favorite posture of his: always expecting the worst, and counting as pure gain anything better than that.

When Frost disembarked from the SS *Olympic* in New York, previously scheduled engagements awaited him, and he could not accompany his wife and daughter to South Shaftsbury. As soon as he had started them toward home, he went to Baltimore to give a talk before a convention of teachers. Then, he journeyed even farther South, to give a reading of his poems at the North Carolina College for Women, in Greensboro.

On his return trip he stopped in New York City long enough to autograph several copies of his newly published *West-Running Brook*, and while there he was interviewed by a reporter who asked if he would be willing to predict which of the younger poets might achieve prominence. He named five: Robinson Jeffers, Raymond Holden, Archibald MacLeish, Joseph Moncure March, and Stephen Vincent Benét.

Had he helped any of his own students to get a firm start as a poet? No, he supposed not. In fact, he was doubtful about the value of trying to ease the ordeal youngsters had to pass through if they were to establish themselves. Nothing he had said or done, nothing he had failed to say or do, was likely to have a lasting effect on the making or unmaking of a poet.

But hadn't he received help from his own teachers when he was just getting started with poetry? No, he thought not: "I never owed anything to a teacher and I don't want anyone to owe anything to me."

He considered young Joseph Moncure March a good example of how any poet might get started. While he had been an undergraduate at Amherst, March had wasted some time in trying to write like Frost, and then, he had gradually discovered his own idiom. His fresh narrative poems, which had been published in books entitled *The Wild Party* and *The Set-up*, had already made reviewers pay attention to him, and Frost was certain March would continue to improve.

A few weeks later, when Frost returned to Amherst, he kept talking about his hopes for the future of March. Some undergraduates asked him to conduct one of the regular faculty-student poetry discussions, and he said he would give them a reading from "an Amherst poet," although he refused to name the poet in advance. Those who mistakenly guessed he would read from his own poems were surprised to hear him offer the entire text of March's narrative poem "The Set-up," the story of a Negro prize fighter whose ambitions and abilities are crookedly misused by his manager. Frost concluded by saying he believed March would eventually become an important literary figure.

Frost had actually done much to help March with his poetry; and there were many other students at Amherst, Bowdoin, Dartmouth, Michigan, and Wesleyan whom Frost had assisted far more than he was willing to admit. Some of them continued to call on him at his home, long after their graduation, and they always found him willing to stay with them in conversations about poetry late into any night. Many kept sending him manuscripts—only a few of which he read, and acknowledged in letters that combined firmness with gentleness.

Once, he wrote an introduction to a volume of poems by some Dartmouth undergraduates, and his remarks were gentle:

"No one given to looking under-ground in spring can have failed to notice how a bean starts its growth from the seed. Now the manner of a poet's germination is less like that of a bean in the ground than of a waterspout at sea. He has to begin as a cloud of all the other poets he ever read. That can't be helped. And first the cloud reaches down toward the water from above and then the water reaches up toward the cloud from below and finally cloud and water join together to roll as one pillar between heaven and earth. The base of water he picks up from below is of course all the life he ever lived outside of books.

"These, then, are the three figures of the waterspout and the first is about as far as the poet doomed to die young in everyone of us usually gets. He brings something down from Dowson, Yeats, Morris, Masefield, or the Imagists (often a long way down), but lifts little or nothing up. If he were absolutely certain to do as doomed and die young, he would hardly be worth getting excited over in college or elsewhere. But you can't be too careful about whom you will ignore in this world. Cases have been known of his refusing at the last minute to abdicate the breast in favor of the practical and living on to write lyric like Landor till ninety.

"Right in this book he will be found surviving into the second figure of the waterspout, and, by several poems and many scattered lines, even into the third figure. . . .

"We are here getting a long way with poetry, considering all there is against it in school and college. The poet, as everyone knows, must strike his individual note sometime between the ages of fifteen and twenty-five. He may hold it a long time, or a short time, but it is then he must strike it or never. School and college have been conducted with the almost express purpose of keeping him busy with something else till the danger of his ever creating anything is past. Their motto has been, the muses find some mischief still for idle hands to do. No one is asking to see poetry regularized in courses and directed by coaches like sociology and football. It must remain a theft to retain its savor. But it does seem as if it could be a little more connived at than it is. I for one should be in favor of the colleges setting the expectation of poetry forward a few years (the way the clocks are set forward in May), so as to get the young poets started earlier in the morning before the freshness dries off. Just setting the expectation of poetry forward might be all that was needed to give us our proportioned number of poets to Congressmen."

Among the contributors to this volume of Dartmouth verse was a student named Kimball Flaccus, who eventually abandoned poetry for scholarship; but while he continued to write verse, he sent Frost occasional samplings, in and out of print. One of these offerings inspired Frost to give more than casual encouragements:

"The book has come and I have read your poems first. They are good. They have loveliness—they surely have that. They are carried high. What you long for is in them. You wish the world better than it is, more poetical. You are that kind of poet. I would rate as the other kind. I wouldnt give a cent to see the world, the United States or even New York made better. I want them left just as they are for me to make—poetical on paper. I dont ask anything done to them that I dont do to them myself. I'm a mere selfish artist most of the time. I have no quarrel with the material. The grief will be simply if I can't transmute it into poems. I dont want the world made safer for poetry or easier. To hell with it. That is its own lookout. Let it stew in its own materialism. No, not to Hell with it. Let it hold its position while I do it in art. My whole anxiety is for myself as a performer. Am I any good? That's what I'd like to know and all I need to know. I wonder which kind of poet is more numerous, your kind or my kind. There should have been a question in the census-taking to determine. Not that it should bother us. We can be friends across the difference. You'll have me watching you. We must meet again and have a talk about poetry and nothing but poetry. The great length of this letter is the measure of my thanks for the book."

To Frost, there was always the delicate question of where to draw the line between too much encouraging and too much discouraging a beginner. He tried to make each student find his own way to develop his own manner of excellence. He was sure such had to begin with the simple process of discovering new analogies, new metaphors: putting two and two together, out of space and time, in ways nobody had previously thought of. He liked to call it a process of connecting the unconnected, and it depended on the ability of the individual to disconnect himself from others, so he could have the freedom of his own meditations, away from anybody's company.

Frost tried to treat his poetically inclined students in such ways that they would gradually feel his purpose was to leave them alone, even to force them into isolation: "Give him that terribly abandoned feeling, left to the horrors of his own thoughts and conscience." These were the circumstances that, he knew from his own experience, forced the poet in on his own meditations concerning possibilities.

Sometimes a student who asked for advice was a complete stranger. One of these was Burrhus Frederic Skinner, a senior at Hamilton College who sent manuscripts of short stories, with his request that Frost say whether he found enough promise in them to warrant Skinner's continuing. Even a stranger was honored with a reply if his writing showed something unusual, and young Skinner received one:

"My long delay with these stories has given you time to think of some things about them for yourself, alternating between doubt and confidence. It has probably done you good: so I wont apologize for it.

"You know I save myself from perfunctory routine criticism of ordinary college writing on purpose to see if I can't really help now and then someone like you in earnest with the art. Two or three times a year I make a serious attempt to get to the bottom of his work with someone like you. But it's all the good it does. I always come a long way short of getting down into it as far as the writer gets himself. Of course! You ask me if there is enough in the stories to warrant your going on. I wish I knew the answer to that half as well as you probably know it in your heart. Right at this moment you are very likely setting your determination to go on, regardless of anything I say, and provided only you can find within a reasonable time someone to buy and read you. I'd never quarrel with that spirit. I've a sneaking sympathy with it.

"My attempt to get to the bottom of a fellow writer's stuff this time put this into my head: All that makes a writer is the ability to write strongly and directly from some unaccountable and almost invincible personal prejudice like Stevensons in favor of all being as happy as kings no matter if consumptive, or Hardy's against God for the blunder of sex, or Sinclair Lewis' against small American towns or Shakspeare's mixed, at once against and in favor of life itself. I take it that everybody has the prejudice and spends some time feeling for it to speak and write from. But most people end as they begin by acting out the prejudices of other people.

"Those are real niceties of observation you've got here and youve done 'em to a shade. 'The Laugh' has the largest value. That's the one you show most as caring in. You see I want you to care. I dont want you to be academic about it—a writer of exercises. Of course not too expressly, overtly care. You'll have to search yourself here. You know best whether you are haunted with any impatience about what other people see or dont see. That will be you if you are a you. I'm inclined to say you are. But you have the final say. I wish you'd tell me how you come out on thinking it over—if it isnt too much trouble—sometime.

"I ought to say you have the touch of art. The work is clean run. You're worth twice anyone else I have seen in prose this year."

Frost, ending the letter, had scarcely signed his name to it when he thought of another way to explain his feeling about all "that makes a writer." He added a postscript: "Belief belief. You've got to augment my belief in life or people mightily or cross it uglily. I'm awfully sure of this tonight."

Of all the students Frost met, one who augmented his belief mightily by showing a determined capacity for disconnecting himself from society, for the purpose of cultivating poetic growth, was the young man who had hung around the edge of the campus at the University of Michigan—and, yet, resisted the academic: Wade Van Dore. Van Dore sometimes sent Frost new poems, with accounts of his latest peregrinations, and Frost could rarely resist answering, in ways such as this:

"Two of these last four you sent are thrust home, High Heaven and The Seeker. The Silence and The Moment before and after Moonrise are less merciless. You are finding out. You are going to do it—if you dont let up on yourself—if you dont get to[o] conceited to watch yourself and everybody else who ever attempted it. Dont miss any tricks or arts, traits or ingredients. Look and then look some more. Its your funeral. Little I can do to help except say 'em as I see 'em. . . ."

When Van Dore showed too much eagerness to get his poems into print, and wrote to tell of those who might give him a hand in finding a publisher, Frost tried to slow him down:

". . . It is pleasant to have those folks out there so kind to you. But remember nothing counts but the sheer goodness of your own thought and art. Weight is what you must achieve to make a place for yourself in the ruck of rhymsters. The visitors at the Bread Loaf School of English made a great fuss discovering a certain young Charles Malam last summer and already he is out with a book, the only really good poem in which I enclose you. From that culture spot he might have spread out pretty far. Whats now to prevent his spreading out from his other and worse poems. . . ."

As soon as Van Dore really had the makings for a first volume, Frost helped him select the best poems and found a publisher for him. When the book appeared, under the title *Far Lake*, it bore this dedication: "To the sunlight on the pines near Far Lake; to the sound of the aspen leaves at Shebandowan Lake; and to Robert Frost."

Among the poems Frost advised Van Dore to hold back was one entitled "The Echo," which the older poet criticized as being merely sentimental. And part of what seemed unsatisfactory and sentimental to Frost about "The Echo" and other poems by Van Dore was a recurrent unwillingness to accept the loneliness of that wilderness life Van Dore claimed to like best. Occasionally, Frost was inspired to answer, in a poem of his own, a particular attitude he found annoying in the work of another poet. Van Dore apparently provided one such inspiration, in that Frost grew impatient with Van Dore's wistful attitude of asking nature for something nature could not give. One sought the solitude of wilderness, Frost believed, to make the most of it, in terms of natural wonders (whatever they might be), without cultivating a "troubled heart" over such companionship as it would obviously fail to provide. His ironic reply to Van Dore was first entitled "Making the Most of It." Later, the title was shortened to "The Most of It."

Such a poem, stimulated by the intensity of Frost's reaction against an attitude taken by someone else, in or out of verse, did not often occur to Frost. Usually, he found release in outspoken, and sometimes vituperative, complaints. Yet, with undergraduates and former students who were still trying to establish themselves, he seemed to remember so strongly his own long years of apprenticeship, and of neglect from others, that he was inclined to give them support along with criticism.

Just how much literary education Frost might manage to impart, in genuinely sincere and sympathetic efforts to be of help, he continuously refused to estimate. His only certainty was that if an undergraduate had been led, through the study of literature, to reconsider his attitude toward the important uses of analogy and metaphor, in any form of human response to experience, such a student could use this knowledge to advantage in any profession he might later choose. He had tried to find different ways of talking about this topic, and of extending it, on many occasions subsequent to his talk on "Metaphor" at Bryn Mawr College. When the alumni council at Amherst invited him to address them on any subject he liked, he entitled his talk "Education by Poetry."

He began by saying he could name several colleges where the study of poetry was barred; he supposed that such a ruling took the onus off poetry completely, by keeping it from being misused. In some schools and colleges, where poetry was assigned, it was used primarily for the study of syntax, language, or technique. To Frost, however, it seemed it could better be read for purposes of discovering how beautifully enthusiasm could be brought under artistic control—enthusiasm "taken through the prism of the intellect and spread on the screen in a color, all the way from hyperbole at one end—or overstatement, at one end—to understatement at the other end. It is a long strip of dark lines and many colors. Such enthusiasm is one object of all teaching in poetry. . . .

"I would be willing to throw away everything else but that: enthusiasm tamed by metaphor. . . . I do not think anybody ever knows the discreet use of metaphor, his own and other people's, the discreet handling of metaphor, unless he has been properly educated in poetry."

Continuing, he tried to suggest the range and scope of metaphor, inside and outside formal poetic utterance:

"Poetry begins in trivial metaphors, pretty metaphors, 'grace' metaphors, and goes on to the profoundest thinking that we have. Poetry provides the one permissible way of saying one thing and meaning another. People say, 'Why don't you say what you mean?' We never do that, do we, being all of us too much poets. We like to talk in parables and in hints and in indirections—whether from diffidence or some other instinct.

"I have wanted in late years to go further and further in making metaphor the whole of thinking. I find some one now and then to agree with me that all thinking, except mathematical thinking, is metaphorical. . . ."

He would not make exception for scientific thinking; and to demonstrate his point he reviewed certain scientific uses of metaphor, starting with the Greeks and coming down to the Einsteinian theory of relativity and, even, down to Niels Bohr on the structure of the atom. Having mocked some of the scientific uses of metaphor, he went on to praise the uses of it in religion and philosophy:

"Greatest of all attempts to say one thing in terms of another is the philosophical attempt to say matter in terms of spirit, or spirit in terms of matter, to make the final unity. That is the greatest attempt that ever failed. We stop just short there. But it is the height of poetry, the height of all thinking, the height of all poetic thinking, that attempt to say matter in terms of spirit and spirit in terms of matter. It is wrong to call anybody a materialist simply because he tries to say spirit in terms of matter, as if that were a sin. Materialism is not the attempt to say all in terms of matter. The only materialist—be he poet, teacher, scientist, politician, or statesman—is the man who gets lost in his material without a gathering metaphor to throw it into shape and order. He is the lost soul."

He had warned his friends that as he grew older he seemed more and more likely to become a preacher, and at this moment he did not hesitate to say some things, more openly than he had said them before, concerning the all-encompassing importance to him of poetry:

"The person who gets close enough to poetry, he is going to know more about the word *belief* than anybody else knows, even in religion nowadays. There are two or three places where we know belief outside of religion. One of them is at the age of fifteen to twenty, in our self-belief. A young man knows more about himself than he is able to prove to anyone. He has no knowledge that anybody else will accept as knowledge. In his foreknowledge he has something that is going to believe itself into fulfilment, into acceptance.

"There is another belief like that, the belief in someone else, a relationship of two that is going to be believed into fulfilment. That is what we are talking about in our novels, the belief of love. And the disillusionment that the novels are full of is simply the disillusionment from disappointment in that belief. That belief can fail, of course.

"Then there is a literary belief. Every time a poem is written, every time a short story is written, it is written not by cunning, but by belief. The beauty, the something, the little charm of the thing to be, is more felt than known. . . .

"Now I think—I happen to think—that those three beliefs that I speak of, the self-belief, the love-belief, and the art-belief, are all closely related to the God-belief, that the belief in God is a relationship you enter into with Him to bring about the future. . . ."

The members of the alumni council, watching Frost and listening to his thoughts concerning the importance to him of education by poetry, were more convinced than ever that Amherst College should continue to afford the luxury of having this man on campus—not as a regular teacher, but simply as a poet-in-residence, as a man whose attitudes toward the close relationship between art and life must have a fertilizing effect on the hearts and minds of the undergraduates. One of them began his praise by writing: "You did a most difficult thing last Saturday. You captured completely the people of your own Amherst family."

30

A NEW FARM,
NEW BOOK, NEW GRIEFS

(1929–1934)

FOR FROST, there was a special fascination in any country real estate with a "For Sale" sign on it. He always seemed to be looking for a farm he could buy at a reasonable price, particularly if the house was attractively old and the view panoramic.

Since the fall of 1923, when Carol married and had brought Lillian to live at the Stone Cottage, Frost had really been without a farm of his own. He had given the bride and groom that farm as a wedding present, but without immediately realizing that something was wrong about continuing to live in a house one had given away. There was no need to feel crowded out, even after the birth of Prescott, but there had been a growing sense that the young people ought to have that home for themselves, without the presence of their elders. In addition, so long as the Stone Cottage remained the gathering place for the grown-up children—Marjorie, Lesley, Irma—the frequent noise and hubbub put a strain on Frost's nerves and made him want to find a farm to which he could steal away.

In South Shaftsbury one of his favorite walking companions, who understood real estate, was the bearded mail clerk and beekeeper, Charles Monroe. He knew the owner of every outlying farm in the district, and he made it easy for Frost to find a farm—a farm tucked away in a high hollow, or gully, between two ridges of land (as though the original builder had thought of ways to protect himself from northeast and southwest winter gales). Frost liked the small, eighteenth-century house and the view up the Batten Kill valley and, westward, far into New York state. And if one wished to climb hillside fields, beyond the clutter of barns and sheds and corncribs surrounding that old farmhouse, one could gain other views to the south and west. There was also a pretty stand of paper birches right on the edge of one high field. Before

[333]

Frost and Monroe had completed a leisurely walk around the boundaries, Frost was ready to buy.

The newly considered farm was only a mile and a half from Carol's farm if one went by road; only three-quarters of a mile distant if one walked crosslots, through fields and pastures. It was not nearly so far away as the Shingled Cottage in North Bennington, which the Frosts had rented in the summer of 1927, and which they rented again in the summer of 1928, staying there until they went abroad with Marjorie. As soon as Frost found that the owner of the farm in the hillside gully was willing to sell and that he could give the tenants of the farm a six-month notice at any time, all that was needed was $5,000 in ready cash. Frost could count on much more than that as royalty earnings from *West-Running Brook*; and, moving rapidly, he was soon able to boast:

"I bought a farm for myself for Christmas. One hundred and fifty three acres in all, fifty in woods. The house a poor little cottage of five rooms, two ordinary fireplaces and one large kitchen fireplace all in one central chimney as it was in the beginning. The central chimney is the best part of it—that and the woods. . . . We have no trout brook, but there is a live spring that I am told should be made into a trout pond. There is a small grove of white paper birches doubling daylight. The woods are a little too far from the house. I must bring them nearer by the power of music like Amphion or Orpheus. . . ."

As soon as the property was his, Frost made a game out of going there as often as he could, puttering around while making plans to tear down useless outbuildings and to renovate as soon as the house was vacated. By around the first of October in 1929, when the Frosts moved into what Frost began calling the Gully House, there was still much work to be done. But they were delighted with the lofty isolation of it.

They left, to take up their tasks in Amherst, early in January, and after they returned to South Shaftsbury in June of 1930, Frost wrote:

". . . I dont know whether I've told you the big barn is clean gone (except for the stone foundations), we have a good rush of water from the faucets—Carol built the spring all over and laid on iron pipes last winter, the north porch is floored with brick 24 ft by 9 ft and new tin-roofed, the road had an easy winter and came through in very decent condition, the house is all papered and painted inside. . . . Elinor and I are alone here with nothing but a black New Foundland pup—in breathless quiet after our stormy life. Having failed to educate my own children and other people's children I propose to end up as a teacher training a pup. . . ."

Long before the appearance of his *Collected Poems,* in the fall of 1930, Robert Frost began to suffer dreadfully over his belief that the reception given this volume would bring his career to some kind of turning point. If the critics were favorable in their reappraisals of such poems as he chose to save from the forty years of effort, to be represented in *Collected Poems,* his immediate position would be strengthened. If not, he might be swept into the discard, along with so many other so-called New Poets who were either fading or already forgotten. "I tremble and am never too happy at being exposed to the public with another book," he confided to his publisher.

Given the choice, however, of passively awaiting the verdict or of trying to influence those who might help to make it, he once again exerted himself. Privately, he was willing to admit that, during the fifteen years since his return from England, he had cultivated many friendships with an eye to favors.

Frost's nervousness, just prior to the appearance of his *Collected Poems,* was heightened by his desire to protect himself from several of the "isms" then being touted in ways that annoyed him: humanism, humanitarianism, romanticism, socialism, communism, anarchism. When the New School for Social Research, in New York City, invited him to give a series of lectures on poetry during the first three months of 1931, he accepted. To Frost, the New School was a hotbed of radicalism-socialism-communism, and he was determined that before he finished giving these lectures the radical humanitarians among his listeners there would know more about him than just his theory of poetry.

As for the humanists, they still kept moving in on him uncomfortably, as a result of Munson's biography. In protest, Frost kept insisting that Babbitt's way of preaching the gospel of the New Humanism made it no less sentimental than the gospel of humanitarianism. Frost had his own way of hurling the word "romantic" at anyone who crowded him too hard, and just at this time he was jealous enough of Edwin Arlington Robinson's recent success, to take pleasure in condemning him as a romantic.

What infuriated Frost most about Robinson, now, was the way in which the commercial success of Robinson's *Tristram* had been assured, prior to publication, by a group of literary salesmen. Carl Van Doren, as editor of the Literary Guild, had hired a theatre for the Sunday evening nearest publication day; and friends of Robinson's had persuaded the celebrated actress Mrs. August Belmont (Eleanor Robson) to come out of retirement and read, to a large audience of guests, passages from *Tristram.* The next day, newspapers across the country told the story of how America had at last found and honored a great poet. The publicity thus gained was excellent, the timing perfect. The Literary Guild distributed 12,000 copies of *Tristram,* and within a year Macmillan sold over 75,000 copies. Then, Macmillan brought out a volume of Robinson's *Collected Poems,* which won a Pulitzer Prize.

To Untermeyer, Frost could not resist striking a few verbal blows at

Robinson, while worrying about the prospects for his own *Collected Poems*:

". . . Where have I been the last six months in abeyance? But where was I the eighteen years just preceding—the years I mean from 1912 to 1930? In no very real dream. The book of all I ever wrote, when it comes out this fall, ought to do something toward accounting to me for those false years. But I have seen it in proof and it looked like no child of mine. I stared at it unloving. And I wonder what next. I dont want to raise sheep[;] I dont want to keep cows[;] I dont want to be called a farmer. Robinson spoiled farming for me when by doubting my farm he implied a greater claim on my part to being a farmer than I had ever made. The whole damn thing became disgusting in his romantic mouth. How utterly romantic the ennervated old soak is. The way he thinks of poets in the Browningese of 'Ben Johnson'[;] the way he thinks of cucolding lovers and cucold husbands in 'Tristram'! Literary conventions! I feel as if I had been somewhere on hot air like a fire-balloon. Not with him altogether. I haven't more than half read him since The Town Down the River. I simply couldnt lend a whole ear to all that Arthurian twaddle twiddled over after the Victorians. A poet is a person who thinks there is something special about a poet and about his loving one unattainable woman. You'll usually find he takes the physical out on whores. I am defining a romantic poet—and there is no other kind. An unromantic poet is a self contradiction like the democratic aristocrat that reads the Atlantic Monthly. Ink, mink, pepper, stink, I, am, out! I am not a poet. What am I then? . . ."

It was easier for Untermeyer to understand these signs of running scared than for Frost to explain to himself what anxieties drove him to such venomous pronouncements. He felt he had dropped behind Robinson in the race for public attention, and he was as angry at himself as at Robinson.

When, finally, the first prepublication copy of *Collected Poems* arrived in South Shaftsbury, Frost was delighted by the format. Pronouncing it perfect, he returned to his worries over what the reviewers might say. One of his worst fears was that some of the attacks made against *West-Running Brook* would be repeated, even elaborated. He was inclined to suspect that one of his own colleagues on the Amherst faculty had been the author of one of those attacks, an anonymous review that had challenged Frost's insights and outlooks:

". . . This construction of an adequate philosophy raises Frost above other contemporary poets, and it has given him, one suspects, a feeling that the outcry, raised by many poets, against this particular era or this particular country, is senseless. He has a poem entitled 'Acquainted With the Night,' which begins with a description of the experience of loneliness and recognition of suffering, and ends by telling of the clock which 'proclaimed the time was neither wrong nor right.' Frost evidently believes it is the artist himself that matters and not the time in which he happens to live. He may be right, but we must still remember that he has created the ordered world in which he lives only by the exclusion of many, many chaotic elements in the real world. Perhaps it is this fact that explains why Frost is, even at his best, a very perfect minor poet, not the major poet for whom American is looking."

The thing he feared came unto him. One of the first reviews of *Collected Poems* appeared in *The New Republic,* and it seemed to be a close paraphrase of that anonymous reviewer who claimed Frost had created his make-believe world only by excluding from his attention so many "chaotic elements in the real world." The *New Republic* reviewer was Granville Hicks, one of Frost's communistic enemies, who also pounced on Frost's claim that the time was "neither wrong nor right." Then, Hicks began to probe:

"This is vigorous doctrine in an age that has been fertile in self-analysis and self-commiseration. Frost's credo, however, runs counter to the consensus of opinion of the critics of all ages as well as to the temper of his own era. Matthew Arnold summarized the verdict of most students of letters when he said, 'For the creation of a master work of literature two powers must concur, the power of the man and the power of the moment, and the man is not enough without the moment.' . . .

"So strong is the case for this view of literature that we may omit the task of defending it in detail, and, instead, ask ourselves how it is possible for Frost to hold the contrary opinion. . . ."

Continuing, Hicks surveyed Frost's *Collected Poems,* to discover three important subjects were missing. He found "nothing of industrialism," nothing of "the disrupting effect that scientific hypotheses have had on modern thought," and nothing of "Freudianism." After admitting that Frost used less-pertinent ways to exercise his poetic imagination, Hicks returned to his complaints, in making a conclusion:

"There is one thing, of course, Frost cannot do: he cannot contribute directly to the unification, in imaginative terms, of our culture. He cannot give us the sense of belonging in the industrial, scientific, Freudian world in which we find ourselves. The very limitations that are otherwise so advantageous make it impossible. That is why no one would think of maintaining that he is one of the great poets of the ages. To that extent the time, even though he refuses to lay the responsibility at its door, is not right. . . ."

Still pretending he never read reviews of his books, and yet, rarely missing the important ones, Frost did not miss this one. He immediately began to formulate his answer. Just when or where he would deliver that answer, he could not foresee, but he apparently watched for an occasion. Some of his students at Amherst gave it to him, some time later, by sending him birthday greetings. His acknowledgment was published in the campus newspaper. Starting with thanks to those who had shown "sympathy with me for my age," he went on to offer an essay on "ages" in another sense:

"But speaking of ages, you will often hear it said that the age of the world we live in is particularly bad. I am impatient of such talk. We have no way of knowing that this age is one of the worst in the world's history. Arnold claimed the honor for the age before this. Wordsworth claimed it for the last but one. And so on back through literature. I say they claimed the honor for their ages. They claimed it rather for themselves. It is immodest of a man to think of himself as going down before the worst forces ever mobilized by God.

"All ages of the world are bad—a great deal worse anyway than Heaven. If they weren't the world might just as well be Heaven at once and have it over with. One can safely say after from six to thirty thousand years of experience that the evident design is a situation here in which it will always be about equally hard to save your soul. Whatever progress may be taken to mean, it can't mean making the world any easier a place in which to save your soul—or if you dislike hearing your soul mentioned in open meeting, say your decency, your integrity.

"Ages may vary a little. One may be a little worse than another. But it is not possible to get outside the age you are in to judge it exactly. Indeed it is as dangerous to try to get outside of anything as large as an age as it would be to engorge a donkey. Witness the many who in the attempt have suffered a dilation from which the tissues and the muscles of the mind have never been able to recover natural shape. They can't pick up anything delicate or small any more. They can't use a pen. They have to use a typewriter. And they gape in agony. They can write huge shapeless novels, huge gobs of raw sincerity bellowing with pain and that's all that they can write.

"Fortunately we don't need to know how bad the age is. There is something we can always be doing without reference to how good or how bad the age is. There is at least so much good in the world that it admits of form and the making of form. And not only admits of it, but calls for it. We people are thrust forward out of the suggestions of form in the rolling clouds of nature. In us nature reaches its height of form and through us exceeds itself. When in doubt there is always form for us to go on with. Anyone who has achieved the least form to be sure of it, is lost to the larger excruciations. I think it must stroke faith the right way. The artist[,] the poet[,] might be expected to be the most aware of such assurance. But it is really everybody's sanity to feel it and live by it.

William Prescott Frost, Jr., 1872
(Courtesy of Mrs. Jean Moodie Rau)

Isabelle Moodie Frost, 1876
(Courtesy of Mrs. Jean Moodie Rau)

Robert and Jeanie Frost, c. 1879
(Courtesy of Mrs. Jean Moodie Rau)

Part of Mrs. Frost's Salem School class, 1887. Front row, extreme left:
Jeanie Frost; front row, extreme right: Sabra Peabody; back row, wearing hat:
Robert Lee Frost
(Courtesy of Mrs. Nelly Hall Fry)

Robert Lee Frost, 1892
(Courtesy of the Jones Library, Amherst, Massachusetts)

Elinor Miriam White, 1892
(Courtesy of Mrs. Lesley Frost Ballantine)

The poet using his homemade writing-board in his parlor,
Franconia, New Hampshire, 1915
(Courtesy of the George H. Browne—Robert Frost Collection,
Herbert H. Lamson Library, Plymouth State College)

The Frost family in Bridgewater, New Hampshire, 1915. Front row, left to right: Marjorie, Carol; middle row: Lesley, Irma; back row: Elinor, Robert. (Courtesy of the George H. Browne—Robert Frost Collection, Herbert H. Lamson Library, Plymouth State College)

The farmer-poet at the Stone Cottage, 1921
(Courtesy of *Yankee* magazine, Dublin, New Hampshire)

Fellow in Letters at Michigan, 1925
(Courtesy of Wade Van Dore)

The poet at Bread Loaf, August 1938
(Photograph by Bernard DeVoto, courtesy of Mrs. Bernard DeVoto)

The Bread Loaf Writers' Conference staff, 1939. Top row, left to right: Fletcher Pratt, Gorham Munson, Herbert Agar, Richard L. Brown, Bernard DeVoto, Robeson Bailey, Herschel Brickell. Middle row: John Gassner, Louis Untermeyer, Robert Frost, Edith Mirrielees, Theodore Morrison. Foreground: Mrs. John Gassner, Mrs. Fletcher Pratt, Kathleen Morrison, Mrs. Herbert Agar, Mrs. Robeson Bailey.
(Courtesy of Middlebury College News Bureau)

Sitting for Walker Hancock, 1950
(Photograph by Hyde Cox)

Dartmouth's George Ticknor Fellow in the Humanities, with Gillie, 1944
(Courtesy of Dartmouth College Library)

At the inauguration of President John F. Kennedy, January 1961
(Photograph by George Silk, *Life* magazine, © Time Inc.)

With Soviet Premier Nikita Khrushchev, Gagra, 1962
(Courtesy of Stewart Udall)

A stop on "the last go-round," November 1962
(Photograph by Joe Clark)

Frost's last Thanksgiving at the Homer Noble farm, 1962
(Photograph by Anne Morrison Smyth)

Fortunately, too, no forms are more engrossing[,] gratifying, comforting, staying than those lesser ones we throw off, like vortex rings of smoke, all our individual enterprise and needing nobody's co-operation; a basket, a letter, a garden, a room, an idea, a picture, a poem. For these we haven't to get a team together before we can play.

"The background . . . [is] hugeness and confusion shading away from where we stand into black and utter chaos; and against the background any small man-made figure of order and concentration. What pleasanter than that this should be so? Unless we are novelists or economists we don't worry about this confusion; we look out on [it] with an instrument or tackle it to reduce it. It is partly because we are afraid it might prove too much for us and our blend of democratic-republican-socialist-communist-anarchist party. But it is more because we like it, we were born to it, born used to it and have practical reasons for wanting it there. To me any little form I assert upon it is velvet, as the saying is, and to be considered for how much more it is than nothing. If I were a Platonist I should have to consider it, I suppose, for how much less it is than everything."

To Frost, idealists like Granville Hicks were Platonists, in that they measured the immediate realities of life against human perfection, which would never exist on earth, and then, complained that there was something horrendously wrong about the present.

In explaining his own attitude to his friend the leftist Genevieve Taggard, Frost had been so persuasive that her review of *Collected Poems* could scarcely have been more sympathetic to his position had he written it himself. He had apparently complained to her that Munson should not have tried to crowd him into a pigeonhole with humanists like Irving Babbitt, and she began by explaining Munson's mistake:

"The humanists have been trying to pigeonhole Robert Frost. Long, long shall our humanists sit with their rubber bands in their hands ready and waiting to snap them around the quotations they want from his works. The rest of Frost they would undoubtedly discard. Texts from this book laid neatly on four sides of him may serve the two-dimensional critic and the literal-minded reader; but not even his own texts nicely dove-tailed, can box the intelligence expressed here so sure of its goings-out and its comings-in. Frost is too cussedly non-conformist to trust even his own words as texts five minutes after he has uttered them. His mind is too seasoned, too humorous, to relish the owlish solemnity of dicta and dictations. He trusts his poems as poems, as metaphors spread to catch meaning, as words that have become deeds. He has given them speech that suggests not one meaning but many. Any effort, therefore, to strip Frost down to singleness of meaning in the interests of propaganda must be opposed. The wisest and most mature poet of our time should not be hacked at and shaved down to suit a pigeonhole. If, in their text-gathering, the humanists had paid more attention to Frost's behavior with his poems, if they had understood the meaning of tone and intention—if, in other words, they had known how to read poetry and not merely how to collect texts, they would have abandoned the attempt."

As she continued, Miss Taggard revealed that she had also listened carefully to Frost's boast concerning his own rebel attitudes and his abhorrence of systems:

". . . Toil has dignity in this poetry; it is universal human experience portrayed concretely, in locality, in Yankee accent.

"Then lest toil become a doctrine, Frost abandons it. Like Thoreau, he rebelled in his life, and he here and there rebels in his verse, from the morality of work-for-its-own-sake. He loafs. We see him insisting on leisure for meditation—rejecting toil for something better, and more active—creation. . . . Frost accompanied the swing of his scythe with the . . . [ease] of his thought for many years. When the time came he knocked off work and called it a day. . . .

"Frost is a mature artist in a society of clever mechanical youngsters."

As other reviewers lined up unevenly on the opposed sides represented by Miss Taggard's praise and Mr. Hicks's faultfinding, it quickly became apparent that the admirers were making the publication of *Collected Poems* the major triumph Frost had nervously hoped it might be. Even his British friend Hugh Walpole helped the cause, by publishing a single sentence of evaluation, in which he said that *Collected Poems* "is for me more sure of immortality than any other book of the last five years, whether in England or America." It was awarded the Pulitzer Prize, as being the best volume of verse published during 1930 by an American author. An even-more-important honor, not unrelated to the appearance of *Collected Poems,* was Frost's election to membership in the American Academy of Arts and Letters. Among the five members who nominated him to this membership, he later learned, one was E. A. Robinson.

Late in the autumn, when Frost was beginning to relax under the praise given his *Collected Poems,* he received the frightening news that his daughter Marjorie was a patient in the Baltimore hospital where she had been training to become a nurse. At first the doctors thought she was again suffering from her previous ailment, pleurisy. A few days later they said they had found definite evidence she had tuberculosis and that she ought to be placed in a sanatorium as soon as possible.

Her parents, after some groping and indecision, remembered that John Bartlett had moved from New Hampshire to Boulder, Colorado, partly because of his asthma, but primarily because of the fear that his wife had tuberculosis. Marjorie knew the Bartletts well, and if a place could be found near them, so they might visit her occasionally, she would like that. A telephone call was made, and Mrs. Bartlett assured them the Mesa Vista Sanitarium, only three blocks from the Bartlett home, would be the perfect place. Further consultation revealed that the Baltimore authorities supported Mrs. Bartlett's judgment. Arrangements were quickly made, and as soon as Marjorie was strong enough to make the long journey, she went alone by train to Denver.

Frost, trying to carry on as casually as though he were not frightened by Marjorie's plight, went through his performances remarkably well. As soon as he completed his obligations at Amherst he followed his usual pattern of going the rounds of readings—but with a new sense of his need to earn more, to pay Marjorie's expenses in Colorado. He gave readings at Wesleyan, Yale, Harvard, Bowdoin, Bates, and Clark University; he carried out his promise to give six lectures at the New School for Social Research.

The strain of all this barding-about wore him down, and he became ill. Then, fell another unexpected blow. Elinor Frost, informing Mrs. Fobes, reflected her own grief:

". . . since coming home [to South Shaftsbury], there have been a great many things to do—and besides that, I have been much disheartened and sad. Not about Marjorie, for just lately, the improvement has been very marked. . . . For quite a while, the gain in her condition was slower than with ordinary tuberculous patients whose symptoms are worse than hers were, so they concluded that a partial nervous break down was complicating the case. She has felt from the first that it was just the right place for her to get strong in, and lately she is very happy and cheerful, I can see by her letters. . . .

"The reason I have been almost crushed with discouragement lately is that Lillian, Carol's wife, also has tuberculosis. . . . You know Marjorie and Lillian were intimate friends in High School. Isn't it extraodinary that they should both have the same thing at the same time, after being separated most of the time for several years?

"Well—Carol and Lillian have decided to sell their farm, and move to a sunnier climate. . . .

"After getting information about a good many places, and considering the matter a long time, they have decided to go to San Bernadino, Cal. . . . You can imagine what a blow it is to me to have them go so far away. I have always wanted to watch Carol a little on account of his lack of vigorous health, and he is very dear to me—while Prescott has become very precious to us. . . ."

Frost, for his part, tried to cheer the family with talk of compensations: His children were giving him an excuse to go West, even to the state of his birth. But before they could start West, the elder Frosts were called on to show solicitude for one of their married daughters, Lesley—expecting her second child in June, at almost the same time she hoped to complete proceedings for her divorce. Writing to Untermeyer on June 12, 1931, Frost hinted at his state of mind:

". . . I am in no mood to estimate myself or anything I ever did. Lesley is at the hospital in Southampton (L.I.) in ineffectual pain and has been for three days now. We dont understand whats the matter. The doctor says nothings the matter[.] We'll be convinced of that after everything comes out all right. All our children are an anxiety at once it happens. Marj gains very slowly. . . . Carol must sell his farm just when it is coming into productiveness. . . . Irma is on the strain of having a husband at college[.] . . . And here is Lesley in trouble too. Elinor just interrupted me to say on the telephone that it is bad but the worst of it is it doesnt get worse. . . ."

Lesley gave birth to her second daughter, Lesley Lee, and as soon as the elder Frosts were convinced the ordeal had ended successfully, they started for Colorado. A few days later Frost took his wife and Marjorie by car, some thirty miles southwest of Denver, to the mountain town of Evergreen, for a ten-day stay. Trying to carry his family responsibilities as graciously as he could, he wrote from there one letter that gave Untermeyer a chance to see beneath the surface of the verbal gaiety:

"I am up here 8000 feet high gasping for oxygen, my walk slow and vague as in a world of unreality. Anything I say feels as if someone else said it. I'm told its not my heart but the size of my lungs thats to blame. . . .

"We came here to give Marj a vacation from the sanitorium. We[']re having a fine time all to ourselves in spite of the uneases of altitude. (Marj and I are the sufferers as it turns out[,] though Elinor was the only one we feared for beforehand.) . . . I'm botanizing all over in an almost entirely different flora. Up one ravine today there were masses of larkspur and monkshood. Its a very flowery country. . . . Three weeks ago I was settled for a month but as if forever in the sand dunes of extreme Montauk. Such lengths our children drag us to. Im glad none of the family are foreign missionaries or we should be snatched back and forth very likely from continent to continent instead of as now from state to state. I dont care if God doesnt care. . . .

"I, we all, go back to Boulder next Wednesday for my talks to the summer school. I may live to be sorry I got into those. Sometimes I do well and then again I get too tired from the strain leading up to a performance. I mustnt complain . . . I dont manage myself very well. I don't care if God doesn't care.

". . . Sometimes I almost cry I am afraid I am such a bad poet. But tonight I don't care if God doesnt care. . . ."

The anxiety shared by Frost and his wife found more open expression in her letters to Mrs. Fobes:

". . . Marjorie doesn't seem as well as I had hoped to find her. She must rest in the sanatorium several months longer, I think, before she goes about much or undertakes any mental or physical work. But she seems happy, and I know she will recover—if she cannot be considered already recovered.

"With Lillian it is different. I am afraid she may not live, and the great concern I feel for her, and for Carol and Prescott, stretches my endurance almost to the breaking point. Why are we so unfortunate? I have worked so hard for my family all these years, and now everything seems tumbling around me. I do not lament this way to everyone, of course. I am too proud, and with Robert I have to keep cheerful, because I mustn't drag him down, but sometimes it seems to me that I *cannot* go on any longer. . . ."

Before his parents reached San Bernardino, Carol and his family were already established at the California Hotel and had begun to search for a house to rent. Frost joined in the hunting, and they with some difficulty found a house in Monrovia that gave a superb view of the San Gabriel mountain range. The elder Frosts stayed for only a week, establishing contacts with recommended medical specialists and gaining assurances that the best care would be given Lillian. Then, they started homeward, by way of San Francisco.

There was an odd excitement for Frost in anticipating this return to his birthplace. On the train, as they approached, he drew for his wife an outline map of the city, putting in such names of streets and landmarks as he could remember, with special attention to those on and around Nob Hill. As soon as his wife lay down to rest in their hotel room, he went out to prowl streets so changed only the names were familiar to Frost.

Mrs. Frost was not well enough to go with him, but before they were to take the ferry to the train shed in Oakland, he could not resist going all the way across the peninsula. His goal was to walk again on the beach below the old Cliff House—nearly four miles southwest of the spot that would soon anchor one end of the already-projected Golden Gate Bridge.

Back once more in South Shaftsbury, during the autumn of 1931 the writing of poetry was interrupted by several trips to give previously scheduled readings in various parts of New England and as far south as Philadelphia. More complicated interruptions were caused by decisions involving a major real-estate transaction. The Frosts had decided they were tired of renting quarters in Amherst and would purchase a house.

A relatively small, two-and-one-half-story building, typically Victorian in architecture, it was more elegant and expensive than any home they had previously owned. (It was said to have been designed by the celebrated Stanford White.) The address was 15 Sunset Avenue, and the view to the west included the lower Berkshires, with Mt. Warner in the near distance. Frost completed the purchase late in November, then hired a decorator who was asked to advise in making the furnishings appropriately Victorian. When finished, the living room was elegantly done, with lace curtains and damask drapes, an Axminster rug, a horsehair sofa and a chair to match.

The Frosts moved in on February 1, 1932, just before he was to take up his duties at the college. By that time, however, he had worn himself out with all the tasks of moving, and became seriously ill. His ailment was influenza, complicated by inflammatory rheumatism and nervous exhaustion.

While still in a dark mood and depressed by his ailments, Frost hopefully shared with his wife the announcement from Marjorie that she had fallen in love with a student at the University of Colorado, Willard Fraser, and that they were engaged to be married.

There were three important obligations to be attended to before any definite time could be set for a return to Colorado and California. Frost was at Columbia University on May 24, 1932, as Phi Beta Kappa poet, reading for the first time his new poem "Build Soil." He was also present at the university commencement on June first, to receive his ninth honorary degree. Later in the month he went to Williams College to receive his tenth, and as soon as these events were behind them, the Frosts departed for Colorado.

Marjorie and Willard were waiting for them at the station in Denver when they arrived, and Marjorie's parents became increasingly impressed by their daughter's choice of this quiet and straightforward young man. When Willard left Boulder for his summer work, digging with the distinguished Colorado archaeologist Earl Morris, Marjorie and her parents started for California.

In Monrovia, Carol had carried out instructions that he find a house his parents could rent inexpensively for several months. They particularly liked the place he chose, because it again afforded them a fine view of the foothills of the San Gabriel Mountains, rising steeply to the north, and because it was within walking distance of Carol's temporary home.

The elder Frosts tried to stay in hiding throughout the summer, and they succeeded until an ardent Frost collector gave away their secret. Not too reluctantly, Frost let himself be persuaded to give three readings in the Los Angeles area late in September: at Occidental College, the University of Southern California, and California Institute of Technology. Then, early in October, they started home.

Constantly worrying about the heavy expenses he had agreed to meet, in the attempt to restore his children to health, Frost had accepted several invitations to give lectures and readings on the way back across the continent, and by the time he and Mrs. Frost reached South Shaftsbury he had completed arrangements for another miscellaneous group of readings and talks, all mixed in with unavoidable social engagements.

The most memorable of these engagements was a banquet in honor of T. S. Eliot, at the St. Botolph Club in Boston on November 15, 1932. Eliot, having come from England to spend the fall semester at Harvard, had quickly become an object of adulation. As the dinner started, Frost's initial reaction was one of disgust at what he viewed as the obsequiousness with which the younger men fed questions to Eliot, hung on his words, and bowed to all his pontifications.

If Scotland had not been slighted by Eliot in one of his comments, Frost might have managed to remain silent. With a British tone of superiority, Eliot announced that no good poetry had ever been written north of the Scottish border, except perhaps for one poem, William Dunbar's "Lament for the Makers." Trying to conceal his indignation, Frost challenged that pronouncement by asking if an exception to it might be made for Burns. No, Eliot thought not. Then, said Frost, might it be said that Burns was, at least, a good songwriter? "One might grant that modest claim," Eliot acknowledged, in a tone that seemed deliberately condescending. Frost wanted to leave the table and not come back.

Nothing about the affair pleased him until, over coffee and brandy, someone produced a copy of "The Hippopotamus" and asked the guest of honor to read it aloud. (To Frost, the request seemed accidentally funny, for Eliot had already retracted the satirical attitude he had held when he had written that poem.) Eliot graciously answered that he would read his poem if Mr. Frost would read one of his. Mischievously, Frost agreed to do more; he'd *write* a poem while Eliot was hippopotamizing. The other guests were amused, and Frost made a show of collecting a few place cards, on which he immediately started to scribble. When Eliot's sepulchral droning ended and attention turned to Frost, he stopped writing. He'd have to improvise the end of his poem, he said, because he hadn't quite figured out the last quatrain. Then, he announced his title: "My Olympic Record Stride." None of his listeners knew he had actually completed the poem months earlier, that he had already said all nine quatrains of it, from memory, earlier in the fall, or that he had chosen it, now, for purposes of criticizing what he considered to be the pomposity of this visitor—this native of St. Louis, this son of a Boston girl, who had run away from the United States and who had apparently worked hard to develop an English accent.

Frost, after reading from his penciled place cards, and finding the last quatrain on the ceiling of the private dining room, was not prepared for the polite solemnity with which his listeners praised his accomplishment. He had hoped his game would be taken as a practical joke and that someone would challenge his claim that he was improvising, but their seriousness deprived him of any chance to confess.

This performance at the St. Botolph Club cost him more nervous energy than he could afford. He had scarcely returned to Amherst before he became ill with a condition the doctor called grippe. But as Christmas approached, he recovered sufficiently to be up and around the house.

During the next few months, Frost carried on his public commitments at Amherst and elsewhere under the burden of tension. An elaborate schedule of readings in Texas, arranged to help his children pay their bills, found him near exhaustion. After he returned, he tried to meet other engagements—and kept trying, until he was again ill. His wife described their predicament as it existed late in May of 1933:

"We are still in Amherst. . . . We have lingered here because of Robert's health. Two days after he was in New York, he came down with a bad cold. It was a queer cold, with temperature, and has been followed by a prolonged period of temperature and prostration. He has very little appetite, and is intensely nervous. The doctor is watching him, with tuberculosis in mind, and advises absolute quiet for an indefinite period, that is, an avoidance of whatever might be a physical or nervous strain. He stays in bed until dinner time, and then dresses and then wanders around the house, and if it is sunny, sits a little while outdoors. I expect that after we get up to the farm, he will improve, as the air is really better up there, and probably his digestion and appetite will improve. I hope I am mistaken, but my opinion is that he is in for real trouble this time. His cough has settled into something that seems to me to have a permanent quality in it. He has been overdoing too much these last two years. . . .

"Marjorie is to be married in Billings on Saturday. The young man she has been engaged to for a year, has got a job on a weekly newspaper in Helena. He . . . cannot come east for a wedding. As Robert hates ceremonies, it is just as well not to have to have it in our house. It will be a very quiet affair in his father's house in Billings, and then they will drive to Helena. Marjorie is a lot stronger, and looks fine, but I am rather anxious about the effect of housekeeping on her. . . ."

Intermittently, throughout the next twelve months, Frost was incapacitated by a series of ailments that depressed him and frightened his wife. During the summer of 1933 they were visited briefly by Carol and Prescott, who drove East from California and brought good news about Lillian's progress toward recovery. There was still talk that Frost himself might have contracted the disease. That fall, he suffered extremely from hay fever, ran a temperature for several days, and was forced to stay in bed for some time immediately after reaching the sanctuary of the Fobes guest cottage in Franconia. Doctors had repeatedly urged him to protect himself against winter cold, by spending the worst months in Florida, and there were times during the winter of 1933–1934 when he was tempted to go. But always there was the problem of whether he could afford such an expensive trip, and he was still needing all the money he could earn from such public readings as he could manage to give.

Marjorie and Willard had urged the Frosts to visit them in Montana during the approaching summer of 1934, but these expectations were suddenly changed by frightening events. Mrs. Frost, knowing Marjorie was expecting a child in mid-March, decided to go alone to Montana to be with her daughter during her confinement. On March 16, 1934, the child was born and was named Marjorie Robin Fraser. Mrs. Frost thought her daughter was recovering normally, and she hurried back to Amherst, because of word that Frost was ill again. She was home only two weeks when Willard telephoned to say Marjorie was seriously ill with puerperal fever.

The elder Frosts left for Montana by train as soon as they could, knowing the dread ailment was frequently fatal. When they reached Marjorie's bedside, it was difficult for them to tell whether she recognized them. The fever made her delirious. Day after day they lived in a confusion of hopes and fears that grew increasingly dreadful.

Frantically trying to learn whether there was any new way to combat the fever, Frost was told that the Mayo Clinic in Rochester, Minnesota, had developed a serum that was still in the experimental stage. Telephone calls were made, and the doctors at the clinic urged that the patient be brought to Rochester by private plane. These arrangements were quickly completed, but Marjorie died there on May second. Her body was taken back to Billings for burial, and it was not until Frost returned to Amherst that he could bear to express his anguish. On May fifteenth he wrote Untermeyer:

"I told you by letter or telegram what was hanging over us. So you know what to expect. Well the blow has fallen. The noblest of us all is dead and has taken our hearts out of the world with her. It was a terrible seven weeks' fight—too indelibly terrible on the imagination. No death in war could more than match it for suffering and heroic endurance. Why all this talk in favor of peace? Peace has her victories over poor mortals no less merciless than war. Marge always said she would rather die in a gutter than in a hospital. But it was in a hospital she was caught to die after more than a hundred serum injections and blood transfusions. We were torn afresh every day between the temptations of letting he[r] go untortured or cruelly trying to save her. The only consolation we have is the memory of her greatness through all. Never out of delirium for the last four weeks her responses were of course incorrect. She got little or nothing of what we said to her. The only way I could reach her was by putting my hand backward and forward between us as in counting out and saying with overemphasis *You—and—Me*. The last time I did that, the day before she died, she smiled faintly and answered [']All the same,['] frowned slightly and made it [']Always the same.['] Her temperature was then 110 the highest ever known at the Mayo Clinic where as I told you we took her but too late. The classical theory was not born out in her case that a fine and innocent nature released by madness from the inhibitions of society will give way to all the indecencies. Every thing she said[,] however quaint and awry[,] was of an almost straining loftiness. It was as if her ruling passion must have been to be wise and good or it could not have been so strong in death. But curse all doctors who for a moment let down and neglect in child birth the scientific precautions they have been taught in school. We thought to move heaven and earth—heaven with prayers and earth with money. We moved nothing. And here we are Cadmus and Harmonia not yet placed safely in changed forms."

It was even longer before Marjorie's mother could bring herself to tell even her closest friends about the unacceptable loss. On June 12, 1934, she wrote to Mrs. Fobes, merely giving the facts. Mrs. Fobes, in reply, tried to console her, but she refused to be comforted:

". . . It is true that her two years in training at Baltimore were a great satisfaction to her—and her marriage a great happiness, but somehow the thought of all that does not help me. She wanted to live . . . , and yet she was so brave and noble. The pathos of it was too terrible. I long to die myself and be relieved of the pain that I feel for her sake. Poor precious darling, to have to leave everything in such a cruel and unnecessary way.

"I cannot bear it, and yet I *must* bear it for the sake of the others here. . . ."

31

HARVARD ENGAGEMENTS
AND BOOK SIX

(1934–1936)

WHEN ROBERT and Elinor Frost returned to Vermont after the funeral service for Marjorie in Montana, they were accompanied by their inconsolably bereaved son-in-law, Willard Fraser, and his baby daughter, Robin. Although the Frosts felt they did not have enough strength to take charge of the child indefinitely, they knew Willard needed such immediate help as they could give him, and they insisted he leave Robin with them when he returned to Montana. Lillian, who had regained her health remarkably after her siege of tuberculosis, offered her assistance. She assumed primary responsibility for taking care of the baby, at the Stone Cottage, during the summer of 1934, and the grandparents returned Robin to Willard early in the fall.

This return was easily arranged, because Frost had agreed to participate in ceremonies connected with the inauguration of Gordon K. Chalmers as president of Rockford College, in Illinois, where Lesley had obtained a teaching position after her divorce from Dwight Francis. Willard and his mother were waiting for the Frosts at Rockford and took Robin from there to Montana. By the time the Frosts returned to Amherst, near the middle of October 1934, it was plain that Mrs. Frost had overtaxed herself. Early in November she was prostrated by a severe heart attack, angina pectoris, and several days passed before she was out of danger. Although warned by her doctor that she must carefully reserve what little strength she had, she seemed not to care whether she recovered.

The doctor urged that, because Mrs. Frost's condition was so precarious and because Frost himself had suffered from severe pulmonary ailments throughout the previous winter, they escape the coldest months of the approaching winter, by going to Florida. Lillian's doctor had given her similar advice. Therefore, cooperative plans were developed, and just for the novelty and adventure of it, Key West was chosen as their joint destination. Early in December the elder Frosts went to Miami and down across the Keys by train. Carol and his family drove from Vermont by slow stages, arriving in Key West shortly after Christmas.

Frost, trying to keep his mind off griefs and fears, did whatever he could to keep his wife from brooding over Marjorie's death and over her own condition. She remained so physically and nervously tired, even the least exertion was hard for her; nothing seemed attractive to her in the picturesque shabbiness of the palm-shaded streets or in the quaintly varied architecture of the houses. A convenient diversion to which Frost devoted himself while in Key West was the writing of an introduction he had promised for the humanitarian socialist-reformer-poet Sarah Cleghorn, his Vermont neighbor. In this assignment he permitted the introduction to tell more about himself than about Miss Cleghorn or her autobiography, *Threescore*.

Frost may not have realized that as his literary reputation increased he was growing bolder in asserting his prejudices concerning social, political, and religious matters. So far, however, he had not published any prose statement that indicated so clearly as this one the close relation between his underlying puritan bias and his social-political conservatism. In his comment he went into his concern for abstract opposites; and increasingly, during these days, Frost kept finding more-detached and more-philosophic ways of manipulating opposites, in his poetry and in his conversations.

Invited up to speak at the University of Miami, he talked about the outside extremes of a poem. In the creative act, he said, a certain impulse or state of mind precedes the writing of the poem. Next comes what Stevenson had called a visitation of style, a power to find words that will somehow convey the impulse. The subject matter is provided by a combination of "Things that happen to us and things that occur to us." And, gradually, out of this happy process the poem gets made, leaving something more implied than stated: "It is what is beyond that makes poetry—what is unsaid. . . . Its unsaid part is its best part."

Not long after the Frosts returned to Amherst from Key West, in April of 1935, he chose to make further extensions of his thoughts concerning opposites. Stanley King, who had become president of the college in 1932, felt that the students were not being given sufficient opportunity to become acquainted with their poet-in-residence, and he arranged to have Frost make three public appearances that spring.

The first of these was devoted largely to a reading of his own poems. The second was more nearly a lecture on two different kinds of originality—good and bad—in modern poetry. And in the third he addressed the seniors at the opening of commencement week; his topic, "Our Darkest Concern." This time he worked out his talk in terms of political or social opposites: the extreme left and the extreme right. His target was the New Deal, with its goal of achieving social improvement by protecting and directing the lives of its citizens toward what Frost viewed as a Utopian ideal of society. His darkest concern was that "Utopia will get us yet," and he offered as the opposite of Utopia his concept of freedom:

"True freedom is the privilege of meeting the emergencies of life by apt recalls from the past; enough of these good recalls, scattered and freely had, form future mental figures which lead to reason. Personal freedom has always been considered by the world as too remotely unsocial; this personal freedom has now vanished in favor of a new freedom of relationships, of social rights and cont[r]acts.

"Men have always dreamed of Utopia in the past; I suppose Utopia will get us yet. Life wastes away into death, insanity, poverty and crime; Utopia aims to alleviate or stop these sorrows. There are too many things to be done before Utopia can be attained, yet writers from Plato to Spenser and even later have crusaded in this seemingly hopeless cause. Our lives are an attempt to find out where we are standing between extremes of viewpoint; in politics and in education we are now shifting between the extreme left and the extreme right. Twenty years from now I shall expect to find education still leaning a bit to the left—but still human."

As soon as Frost could escape from Amherst to his farm in South Shaftsbury, he tackled another literary assignment, by manipulating another variety of opposites. Edwin Arlington Robinson had died on April 6, 1935, just after he had completed reading proof on a new narrative poem that was to be published under the title *King Jasper*. A few weeks later Robinson's publisher asked Frost to write an introduction for it, and he accepted the invitation. In working on the first draft, he used some of the ideas he had played with in his recent talks at Amherst and elsewhere. He began:

"It may come to the notice of posterity (and then again it may not) that this, our age, ran wild in the quest of new ways to be new. The one old way to be new no longer served. Science put it into our heads that there must be new ways to be new. Those tried were largely by subtraction —elimination. Poetry, for example, was tried without punctuation. It was tried without capital letters. It was tried without metric frame on which to measure the rhythm. It was tried without any images but those to the eye; and a loud general intoning had to be kept up to cover the total loss of specific images to the ear, those dramatic tones of voice which had hitherto constituted the better half of poetry. It was tried without content under the trade name of poesie pure. It was tried without phrase, epigram, coherence, logic and consistency. It was tried without ability. I took the confession of one who had had deliberately to unlearn what he knew. He made a back-pedalling movement of his hands to illustrate the process. It was tried premature like the delicacy of unborn calf in Asia. It was tried without feeling or sentiment like murder for small pay in the underworld. These many things was it tried without, and what had we left? Still something. The limits of poetry had been sorely strained, but the hope was that the idea had been somewhat brought out."

So far, Frost had conveyed his own prejudices against modern poetry, without mentioning Robinson. As he began the next paragraph, he briefly digressed to include Robinson—and, then, quickly turned to his own meditations concerning religious matters:

"Robinson stayed content with the old-fashioned way to be new. I remember bringing the subject up with him. How does a man come on his difference, and how does he feel about it when he first finds it out? At first it may well frighten him, as his difference with the Church frightened Martin Luther. There is such a thing as being too willing to be different. And what shall we say to people who are not only willing but anxious? What assurance have they that their difference is not insane, eccentric, abortive, unintelligible? Two fears should follow us through life. There is the fear that we shan't prove worthy in the eyes of someone who knows us at least as well as we know ourselves. That is the fear of God. And there is the fear of Man—the fear that men won't understand us and we shall be cut off from them."

Frost now moved to attack poets who were making poetry "a vehicle of grievances against the un-Utopian state." A distinction should be made, Frost said, between grievances and griefs. He preferred having griev-ances restricted to prose, "leaving poetry free to go its way in tears." After saluting Robinson as one who understood this differentiation and as one who was "a prince of heartachers amid countless achers of another part," Frost again returned to expounding his own prejudices:

"Grievances are a form of impatience. Griefs are a form of patience. We may be required by law to throw away patience as we have been required to surrender gold; since by throwing away patience and joining the impatient in one last rush on the citadel of evil, the hope is we may end the need of patience. There will be nothing left to be patient about. The day of perfection waits on unanimous social action. Two or three more good national elections should do the business. It has been similarly urged on us to give up courage, make cowardice a virtue, and see if that won't end war, and the need of courage. Desert religion for science, clean out the holes and corners of the residual unknown, and there will be no more need of religion. (Religion is merely consolation for what we don't know.) But suppose there was some mistake, and the evil stood siege, the war didn't end, and something remained unknowable. Our having disarmed would make our case worse than it had ever been before. Nothing in the latest advices from Wall Street, the League of Nations, or the Vatican incline me to give up my holdings in patient grief."

Giving so much sarcastic airing to some of his own grievances—when he was pleading that the poet should restrict himself to griefs—he concluded by placing in Robinson's mouth some more of Frost's often-repeated opinions:

"There were Robinson and I, it was years ago, and the place (near Boston Common) was the Place, as we liked afterward to call it, of Bitters, because it was with bitters, though without bitterness, we could sit there and look out on the welter of dissatisfaction and experiment in the world around us. It was too long ago to remember who said what, but the sense of the meeting was, we didn't care how arrant a reformer or experimentalist a man was if he gave us real poems. For ourselves, we should hate to be read for any theory upon which we might be supposed to write. We doubted any poem could persist for any theory upon which it might have been written. Take the theory that poetry in our language could be treated as quantitative, for example. Poems had been written in spite of it. And poems are all that matter. The utmost of ambition is to lodge a few poems where they will be hard to get rid of, to lodge a few irreducible bits where Robinson lodged more than his share."

Frost was not sure Robinson's publisher would find such an essay appropriate, but he was certain he had never before given so compressed a statement of his own position. Macmillan did, indeed, feel that the essay was perhaps too much Frost, and politely asked him to bring Robinson in a bit more. He obliged by adding some quotations from "Miniver Cheevy," "Old King Cole," "Mr. Flood's Party," and "Dear Friends." But his most revealing addition was an expression of his own belief in the need for stylistically counterbalancing seriousness with its opposite, humor:

"The style is the man. Rather say the style is the way the man takes himself; and to be at all charming or even bearable, the way is almost rigidly prescribed. If it is with outer seriousness, it must be with inner humor. If it is with outer humor, it must be with inner seriousness. Neither one alone without the other under it will do. Robinson was thinking as much in his sonnet on Tom Hood. One ordeal of Mark Twain was the constant fear that his occluded seriousness would be overlooked. . . ."

To Frost, the experience of writing a tribute to his friend-and-enemy Robinson had been an ordeal, and he suffered much over the various stages of revising it. Before the summer of 1935 was over, however, he was caught up in several other ordeals that were even more painful.

Edward Davison had asked him to serve once more on the staff of the

Rocky Mountain Writers' Conference, which Davison would be supervising as program director, that summer. Frost agreed to go, partly because his wife urged him to do so. She hoped they could extend their travels, by going from Boulder to Billings, to visit Marjorie's grave and see Robin again. He doubted she was strong enough for the emotional strain such a visit would entail. "Elinor is not fit for anything," he wrote. "She is trying to save up energy for a melancholy journey to the terrible scenes in Colorado and Montana. I am doing my best to dissuade her from such a pilgrimage."

Frost was unable to dissuade his wife. Late in July they made the long journey by train to Colorado. Willard Fraser and his mother brought Robin down to Boulder for the reunion that meant so much to Mrs. Frost, and while she took charge of caring for her granddaughter during the week the Frasers remained, her husband turned to his duties at the Writers' Conference. Then, when his public appearances there were completed, he left his wife with the Bartletts and made a brief trip southward to Santa Fe, where he had been invited by fellow poet Witter Bynner to give a reading under the auspices of a local group.

Frost and Bynner had known each other since 1921, although the differences between them were sharp enough to make genuine friendship unlikely. The visit began pleasantly, because Frost was given a chance to indulge his archaeological enthusiasms. On the morning after his arrival he went by automobile far enough into the desert, with some of Bynner's friends, to see the prehistoric cliff dwellings of the Pueblo Indians. Unfortunately, this expedition did cause him to be late for a special luncheon at Bynner's home, where the painter John Sloan was one of the waiting guests.

Frost had scarcely made his apologies, when Bynner showed the assembled guests a recently published volume of poems by his Harvard classmate Horatio Colony, holding the work aloft as though it were a newly found Pentateuch. Frost recognized the book. He had received an advance copy and had read far enough to find in it what seemed to him a repulsively Whitmanesque glorification of homosexuality. As soon as Bynner began to praise it, Frost maliciously pretended to side with him, saying of course they might not agree on which poem in the volume was the best—so, Frost would read one of his favorites aloud, if Bynner would give him the chance. Bynner, momentarily deceived, put the book in Frost's hands; and he selected what seemed to him a subtly insinuative paean to homosexuality. As he finished, he turned to Bynner and said, "Of course, Witter, you wouldn't understand that, because you're too young and innocent."

The jeer was taken as intended, and Bynner lost his temper. Seizing a full mug of beer, he shouted, "Colony is a better poet than either one of us," and poured the beer over Frost's head. Instead of going into a rage, Frost remained serene. Knowing he had scored, he could afford to shrug off the beer. While some of the ladies in the party solicitously mopped him, he merely smiled at Bynner and said, "You must be drunk."

There was no other incident. The public reading was attended by a large audience and was well received. But after he returned to Boulder and told Bartlett of his adventures with Bynner, he concluded, "I shouldn't have gone down there."

Not long after the Frosts returned to Vermont from Colorado, in August of 1935, he began to think and talk about plans for a new book of poems. During the seven years since publication of *West-Running Brook,* he had not even bothered to keep track of how many pieces he had scattered through various magazines. Yet, he felt he must have enough to make a volume. How he would shape it or what he would call it, he could decide after spreading out his manuscripts and moving them around until some sort of pattern emerged. It was certain that his gradual play with the political scene, since the beginning of the New Deal, would add novelty. It might even force him to collect the more satirical ones into a section by themselves, apart from the lyrics.

The most polemical was the "political pastoral" he had read as the Phi Beta Kappa poem at Columbia in 1932, "Build Soil." He knew anyone who looked at that dialogue would understand his social prejudices well enough. Emerson had helped to inspire "Build Soil," but it owed even more to Frost's own experience as isolated poet and farmer in Derry. Less than a year before he had written "Build Soil," a reporter asked Frost's opinion about the increasing drift of country people toward the city—and got a better answer than he could have expected:

"Poetry is more often of the country than of the city. Poetry is very, very rural—rustic. It stands as a reminder of rural life—as a resource, as a recourse. It might be taken as a symbol of a man, taking its rise from individuality and seclusion—written first for the person that writes and then going out into its social appeal and use. Just so the race lives best to itself—first to itself, storing strength in the more individual life of the country, of the farm—then going to market and socializing in the industrial city. . . .

"We are now at a moment when we are getting too far out into the social-industrial and are at the point of drawing back—drawing in to renew ourselves. . . .

"I think a person has to be withdrawn into himself to gather inspiration so that he is somebody when he comes out again among folks—when he 'comes to market' with himself. He learns that he's got to be almost wastefully alone. . . ."

Another inspiration for "Build Soil" had been provided by some of

Frost's city friends who had made a posture of withdrawing into the country—for the wrong reasons. One of them was Untermeyer, who purchased a large farm in a valley of the Adirondacks and had tried to set himself up as a gentleman farmer. Frost, visiting him there, had found him so completely out of character that he tried to send him some advice, in the form of metaphors drawn from the act of farming:

"The land be your strength and refuge. But at the same time I say this so consonant with your own sentiments of the moment, let me utter a word of warning against the land as an affectation. What determines the population of the world is not at all the amount of tillable land it affords: but it is something in the nature of the people themselves that limits the size of the globulate mass they are socially capable of. There is always[—] there will always be[—]a lot[,] many lots of land[,] left out of the system. I dedicate these lots to the stray souls who from incohesiveness feel rarely the need of the forum for their thoughts[;] of the market for their wares and produce. They raise a crop of rye, we'll say. To them it is green manure. They plow it under. They raise a crop of endives in their cellar. They . . . [eat] it themselves. That is they turn it under. They have an idea. Instead of rushing into print with it, they turn it under to enrich the soil. Out of that idea they have another idea. Still they turn that under. What they finally venture doubtfully to publication with is an idea of an idea of an idea. The land not taken up gives these stay-outers[,] these loosely connected people[,] their chance to live to themselves a larger proportion of the time than with the throng. There is no law divine or human against them when you come to think of it. The social tyranny admits of squatters tramps gypsies because it cant make itself tight if it wants to. It isnt rebellion I am talking. It isnt even literary and intellectual detachment. It is simply easy ties and slow commerce. Refuse to be rushed to market or forum. Dont come as a product till you have turned yourself under many times. We dont have to be afraid we wont be social enough. Hell, havent I written all that in my first book? But the point is the unconsidered land makes the life I like possible. Praise be to the unconsidered land. That's all. . . ."

His pleasure in writing "Build Soil" had stimulated many further poetic excursions into social and political satire. The risk in such adventurousness was obvious. Just how these attitudinizings would be accepted by reviewers of his new book would depend largely on which critics were chosen by which editors. He kept reminding himself that the making or breaking of a book could depend on those choices, and he was unwilling to leave such matters entirely to chance.

For practical purposes, he also used some other strategies than those of cultivating the goodwill of editors and reviewers. His trip northward to Miami from Key West, to take part in the Winter Institute of Literature at the University of Miami, had enabled him to establish new contacts that deserved further cultivating. As a result, when his Amherst doctor advised him that he and his wife should again escape the New England winter in 1935, he accepted an invitation to participate in the next institute.

He planned to offer at the institute a three-day series to writers, under the title "Learning to Have Something to Say"; and another lecture would be on "The Uses of Ambiguity." But before he had begun these talks—in fact, before he had even reached Miami, shortly before Christmas—he received three invitations that overshadowed anything likely to happen in Florida. Each came to him from Harvard. He was asked to deliver an ode at the Harvard tercentenary celebration, in the autumn of 1936, to be the Phi Beta Kappa poet at ceremonies also scheduled to occur that autumn, and to deliver the Charles Eliot Norton lectures in the spring of 1936. He accepted the first two immediately; he hesitated over the third, for reasons he explained in his answer:

"As you may imagine, I should be most happy to be your Charles Eliot Norton Professor next spring; and that not alone for the honor of the appointment. I should value also the compulsion the lectures would put me under to assemble my thinking right and left of the last few years and see what it comes to. I have reached a point where it would do me good.

"But let me tell you my situation. Your letter overtakes me on my way to Florida, where, after my last bad influenza I promised the doctor I would spend a couple of winters sunning on the tennis courts. I might as well be in Florida as in bed. (No reflection on Florida intended. Even Florida is no doubt somebody's home. And nothing but good of any of these States ever out of me.) I have already served one of my half terms down there. I am superstitiously afraid I ought to serve the other. If I served it clear out, I could hardly be back before the middle of March. I might risk the first of March. But even that is too late for your purposes. Or is it? I don't suppose I should ask that a Harvard thing so important should be reshaped somewhat to fit a mere person. Nevertheless I am tempted to ask. I am going to be greatly disappointed to see this opportunity pass from me. . . ."

The agreement was made that he would not be required to take up his duties as Norton Professor until the first of March, and Frost awkwardly secured from President Stanley King permission to absent himself once again from his Amherst duties. The awkwardness grew out of his contractual promise that during the three months each year he spent as poet-in-residence at Amherst College he would accept no invitations requiring him to be away from the campus for any considerable length of time. During each of the years since King had been president, Frost had violated the terms of that promise in ways that had caused some members of the faculty to protest that their poet-not-often-in-residence was a luxury the college should not afford. This time it was easy to persuade King that honor would accrue to Amherst if a member of her faculty were given leave to serve at Harvard.

At Miami, a colleague on the staff of the 1936 Winter Institute was a part-time Harvard tutor whom Frost had newly met, a maverick from Utah named Bernard DeVoto. After his graduation from Harvard, DeVoto had returned to Utah and begun his literary career as a novelist, then moved to Cambridge, partly in the hope of acquiring a position at Harvard.

Frost, having read and admired one of DeVoto's articles, entitled "New England: There She Stands," went alone and unannounced to call on him at his hotel room in Miami one evening, ostensibly to discuss the Westerner's views of New England. DeVoto was flattered. At the end of this visit Frost said they would soon be seeing each other in Cambridge. Disclosure of the Norton professorship appointment was news to DeVoto, and immediately he offered to serve as handyman and guardian for the Frosts as soon as they reached Cambridge. His assistance was accepted. Frost was relieved to know he would now have another friend in the Boston region, where he felt he had several dangerous enemies.

He had already been warned that the favorite modern poet among students and faculty at Harvard was the previous Norton Professor, Thomas Stearns Eliot. And there were other reasons Frost suspected he might find more enemies there than friends. He had been outspokenly critical of the way some Harvard reformers had helped to organize a strike of floor-scrubbing charwomen a year earlier. The subsequent fracas had seemed to Frost a typical example of that sentimental humanitarianism recently brought into fashion by the New Deal, and the incident had been enough to inspire his bitterly sarcastic poem "Provide, Provide."

At Harvard, Prof. John Livingston Lowes and the committee in charge of the Norton lectures to be given by Frost, completely miscalculated the public appeal the poet would make in his lecture series on "The Renewal of Words." The first lecture was entitled "The Old Way to Be New," and well before starting time on the evening of March 4, 1936, over 1,000 people managed to crowd into New Lecture Hall. Some of them stood in the side aisles, others sat in the center aisle, and the boldest standees draped themselves along the edge of the platform.

When Frost was introduced he began to speak in a nervously restrained voice. For several minutes he seemed to grope for words and ideas, as though he were not sure of himself. He used no notes, but he knew precisely what he was going to say. The lecture was a reworking of the introduction he had written for Robinson's *King Jasper,* except that he would illustrate his points by using his own poems. As soon as he had made a few caustic remarks about some ways in which the present age sought new ways to be new, the laughter of the audience seemed to reassure him, and he soon established his winning platform manner.

Like Mark Twain, Frost had learned to enthrall by deliberately interrupting himself with well-timed silences, and whenever he paused, the expectant hush of the entire audience was extraordinary. By the time he completed his performance—a truly professional piece of acting—he was called back repeatedly to read one more poem. Afterward, students pursued him, requesting his autograph in copy after copy of his books.

Bernard DeVoto kept all the promises he had made in Miami. He did serve as guardian, and he had arranged for the Frosts to rent a furnished home at 56 Fayerweather Street, not far from the Cambridge common. DeVoto had also persuaded his close friends Mr. and Mrs. Theodore Morrison to hold a small reception for Frost after each lecture, in their home at 8 Mason Street. The Frosts had previously met the Morrisons. A tutor in English at Harvard, Morrison had been serving as director of the Bread Loaf Writers' Conference since 1932. His wife, formerly Kathleen Johnston, had been a leader in the small group of Bryn Mawr undergraduates who had brought Frost there for three give-and-take discussions, in 1920, and had also been editor-in-chief of the Bryn Mawr *News* during her senior year.

Mrs. Frost, because of illness, was unable to attend either the first lecture or the first reception. The sudden change from semitropical weather in Florida to the winter chill of Cambridge had been too much for her, and she was confined to bed for several days immediately after their arrival in Cambridge. Her husband, usually far more vulnerable than she, and frequently victimized by respiratory ailments, remained extraordinarily well. He seemed too excited to have time for illness.

The second lecture, entitled "Vocal Imagination—the Merger of Form and Content," was a concise summing-up of what he had said during the past twenty years about his belief that the living part of a poem is the intonation entangled somehow in the syntax, idiom, and meaning of the sentences.

The third lecture was entitled "Does Wisdom Signify?" and Frost talked on both sides of this question, starting with the claim that in poetry the vividness with which the mood or viewpoint was conveyed was more important to the success of the poem than the question of whether the poet's insights were wise. (Such was his ideal posture, in moments of detachment. Privately, however, he was inclined to insist that whenever he came across a poem that reflected merely trivial insights on whatever subject might be under consideration, he grew impatient.) Unfortunately, on this occasion his talk became such a rambling and helter-skelter collection of thoughts, one Boston newspaperman had difficulty seeing how they had anything to do with the announced topic.

The fourth of the lectures was on "Poetry as Prowess (Feat of Words)"; and, again, Frost made it summarize much he had previously said—this time about how the words in a poem must become deeds, as flat and final as a showdown in a poker game. The fifth and sixth lectures, "Before the Beginning of a Poem" and "After the End of a Poem," were largely repetitions of the talks he had given at the institute at Miami in 1931.

All six lectures were attended by overflow audiences that were unusually sympathetic, and Frost received so many flattering attentions from President James Bryant Conant and various members of the faculty that he began to believe Harvard was going to offer him a permanent appointment.

As soon as Mrs. Frost recovered from her illness, the Conants invited the Frosts to dinner, and this gesture seemed auspicious. Unfortunately, Frost and Conant did not find ways to make science and poetry congenial. In addition, they quickly established sharp differences in their political views. Conant, admiring Roosevelt, praised him for recently bringing representatives of the teamsters to the White House to receive assurances that he would support their union. Frost, disgusted by this latest sign of New Deal largesse, sarcastically suggested that a good title for that speech of assurances might be "Every Man's Home His Own Poorhouse," because all of those teamsters would eventually be living on government charity. Not amused, Conant answered gruffly, "You have a bitter tongue."

Frost's newly made friend Bernard DeVoto had, when speaking of Conant, an even-more-bitter tongue, for reasons that soon became apparent. Having served as tutor and lecturer at Harvard for six years, DeVoto kept hoping for a permanent appointment. In the autumn of 1935 he had been offered the editorship of *The Saturday Review* and tried to use that offer as leverage. Six months later, when the same offer was made again, on even-better terms, DeVoto went directly to President Conant and said he felt compelled to accept the offer unless he could get the Harvard appointment he preferred. Conant studied the matter for a few days, then wrote that the previous Harvard decision must stand; if DeVoto really did have another offer, he should accept it. Enraged by the insinuation that he had not told the truth, DeVoto turned to Frost, who was genuinely sympathetic. Frost insisted that if DeVoto wanted to keep the respect of others and of himself, he should immediately resign his lectureship. Reluctantly, he did resign.

Frost achieved several favors from non-Harvard friends while at Harvard. Three were on the editorial board of the Book-of-the-Month Club, and in early spring of 1936 it was announced that his forthcoming book of new poems, *A Further Range,* would be the club choice for June. The news came to Frost through Richard Thornton at Holt, together with assurance that 50,000 copies would be distributed by the club. A few days later Frost's wife confided to Thornton's wife: "It is certainly *grand* about the Book-of-the[-]Month Club. I rather thought they would take it, because Henry Canby and Dorothy Canfield are always such staunch friends of Robert's work, and Christopher Morley has shown much friendliness the last year."

There was another prize worth fishing for: the Pulitzer. This award, for the best book of poems published by an American author in 1936, would not be made until May of 1937, but Frost already knew of one factor that would work in his favor. His friend Untermeyer had been appointed to the committee.

In the previous year Untermeyer's volume of *Selected Poems and Parodies,* in the running for a Pulitzer Prize, had lost out; and Frost tried to offer philosophical consolation:

"Just a word about the outcome. I know you were prepared not to mind it. So that if you do mind it you dont mind it so much. I hate this being automatically entered for prizes by the mere act of publication. I have suffered nervous collapse in my time from the strain of conscious competition and learned from it how to pretend at least that I am below or above it for the rest of my life. And I'm a good stout pretender when I set out to be. Nobody can catch me setting my heart on any rewards in this world. I'd as soon be caught breaking and entering. My days among the dead are passed. The only comparison I suffer gladly would be with them by them. Conflicting claims and the clamor that goes with these among our contemporaries are next to nothing to me. *Next* to nothing. I know too well the personal politics. So do you. We have our farms and our poems to cultivate. . . ."

Untermeyer knew how to read between the lines of this "good stout pretender" who might suffer another nervous collapse if *A Further Range* should be mistreated too harshly by the critics. Part of what bothered Frost was his recent tendency to let his poems reflect too many of his murderous thoughts. The newness was all on the surface, but now he permitted his killer instincts to find expression in only-slightly-veiled poems. The problem was how to justify this in the eyes of those who liked to think of him as the personification of old-fashioned New England virtues.

If he had seemed lately to go beyond New England in the subject matter of his verse, some of the reason was that the lives of his children had drawn him away from the White Mountains to the Green, away from the Green Mountains to the Rockies, beyond the Rockies, and even beyond the Sierras, to his birthplace in California. Why not use as metaphor the fact that his experiences had caused him to look across all the ranges of mountains in the United States—and, thus, to endow his poetry with a further range of themes, even social and political?

For the present, however, Frost's great fear was that his chance to receive a permanent appointment at Harvard might have been spoiled. He gave Untermeyer some hints of this fear:

"I dont feel I made too big a hit with the dignitaries and authorities. There was a moment in March when I thought perhaps they were giving me back my father's Harvard. But probably I was fooling myself. I'm imperfectly academic and no amount of association with the academic will make me perfect. It's too bad for I like the academic in my way, and up to a certain point the academic likes me. Its patronage proves as much. I may be wrong in my suspicion that I havent pleased Harvard as much as I have the encompassing barbarians. My whole impression may have come from the Pound-Elliot-Richards gang in Elliot House here. I had a really dreadful letter of abuse from Pound in which he complains of my cheap witticisms at his expense. . . . I suspect the same dirty sycophant of having reported me to him as reported me to Wallace Stevens. I think its Mattison. Never mind. Peace hath her victories no less renowned than war."

He had other reasons for worrying about the enmity between himself and Prof. F. O. Matthiessen, whose communist sympathies were plainly reflected in his published writings. It was clear that the most dangerous criticism of *A Further Range* would come from such closely organized liberals as Matthiessen and his crowd. Frost felt a sense of the danger the leftists might cause his literary position.

The strength of these critics was becoming so unified that one could predict the savagery of the attacks they would make on such a poem as "Build Soil," and considered within a hostile framework, *A Further Range* would not get far, Frost knew.

As it happened, the first attack on it was made by Newton Arvin in the *Partisan Review*. He began by saying, with obvious disparagement, that the poems of Robert Frost gave a precise rendering of one aspect of New England:

". . . It is the New England of nasalized negations, monosyllabic uncertainties, and non-committal rejoinders; the New England of abandoned farms and disappointed expectations, of walls that need mending and minds that need invigoration, of skepticism and resignation and retreat. . . .

"It exists, and Robert Frost is its laureate. He has . . . found the perfect metaphor and the perfect cadence for that Yankee renunciation which, whatever else it is, is certainly what the Buddhists would call his own *dharma*. . . . And—since no one expects that . . . Robert Frost will change his tune—everyone will be prepared to find the sentiment recurring, as it does more and more quaveringly, in this sixth volume of his. . . ."

Apparently, part of Arvin's purpose was to deflate the current literary reputation of Robert Frost. His article, entitled "A Minor Strain," contained the clarifying statement that Frost's poetry, instead of giving "the true essence of the New England spirit," was "expressive much more of the minor than of the major strain in Yankee life and culture; or of a strain that perhaps seemed almost the major one in a late, transitory, and already superseded period."

The next attack was by Horace Gregory, in *The New Republic,* and another harsh criticism of *A Further Range* appeared in *The Nation,* by Richard Blackmur. But the harshest of all the assaults occurred in *New Masses,* where Rolfe Humphries titled his review "A Further Shrinking."

In the midst of these attacks Frost gave a reading at the Bread Loaf Writers' Conference, stayed there over a weekend, and suffered abnormally from the good intentions of those who commiserated with him over the unpleasant reviews *A Further Range* had been receiving. Such a display of sympathy was enough to make him suspect that he was surrounded by jealous enemies. He and Mrs. Frost had made their annual retreat to the Fobes cottage in Franconia early in August, and the trip to Bread Loaf was made from Franconia. By the time he returned to the White Mountains he was far more disturbed and upset than he had been before. Now he was even more worried that he might not be able to settle in and write the two poems he had promised to read at Harvard in September. Unfortunately, his resolve was not so firm as his distaste for writing occasional verse, and he became nervously upset when he failed to find inspiration for either of the pieces.

Mrs. Frost was not surprised when he became ill, and Frost was actually relieved by the doctor's insistence that he send telegrams to the Harvard authorities. Mrs. Frost explained to Thornton at Holt:

". . . he came down with a severe attack of shingles on his face. Shingles is a nervous disease, you know, and the doctor here said he was suffering a nervous exhaustion, and that if he didn't stop trying to work, he would get into a condition that might take a year to recover from. He *couldn't* work, anyway, the pain in his head was so acute. So he had to give up doing the Harvard poems. . . ."

He also had to give up his promise to be at Amherst College when the fall term started, and he knew President King had already grown impatient with him for dodging responsibilities at Amherst, year after year. Although the Frosts did return to the college late in September, he was quickly overtaken by another illness and was again bedridden.

Shortly before Christmas of 1936 he felt well enough to read his poems before students and faculty at the New School in New York. Assuming that some of his leftist critics were in his audience, he reviewed some of the epithets hurled at him, and singled out the one used by Rolfe Humphries: "counter-revolutionary." If such cheap name-calling was in order, he said, he could easily cap that one. His opponent was merely a "bargain-counter revolutionary." Most of his listeners seemed to enjoy this retort, but as Frost was leaving he was stopped by an excited, long-haired, scraggly bearded creature who said he happened to be a friend of the man Frost had called a bargain-counter revolutionary; maybe Frost didn't know what a firecracker was, but if he didn't he'd soon find out.

Frost laughed off the threat—without forgetting it. Shortly after he returned to Amherst, he received through the mail a crudely wrapped package, bearing no return address. The package felt as though it contained a cigar box, and Frost knew homemade bombs were often concealed in cigar boxes. None of his friends would be sending him cigars; they all knew he didn't smoke them. His wife tried to reassure him by saying it was so light it couldn't possibly contain a bomb. He didn't know what to do, but perhaps there would be no danger in removing the string and wrapping.

As soon as he had cautiously unwrapped the package, his suspicions were confirmed. It was a cigar box, the tax stamp seemed to be deliberately broken, and the cover was held down by what seemed to be an oddly shaped tack. He said to his wife that, as a one-man demolition squad, no matter how great the risk, he'd carry the bomb into the backyard, tie a stone to it, and hurl it against a tree. He did—and scattered cigars all over the yard.

32

"I . . . GO FORTH
COMPANIONLESS"

(1936–1938)

IN THE autumn of 1936, when the Frosts were advised by their Amherst doctor that they should once again make plans to escape southward before the arrival of winter, they decided against going back to Florida. The two winters already spent there had been spoiled by too many intrusions, and even Key West had not provided the isolation they desired. Their enjoyment of California during their previous visits encouraged them to consider the possibility of finding a place to hide somewhere below Los Angeles—perhaps near Long Beach. But, there again, they knew they would be within reach of possible intruders. The southern part of Texas was discussed, because they had enjoyed the countryside around Austin and San Antonio in 1933; and, after much talk about it, they finally decided to gamble on a winter in San Antonio.

Hating to be separated from their children and grandchildren at Christmastime, the elder Frosts proposed a family reunion in San Antonio on Christmas Day and offered to pay expenses. Although Lillian had recovered well from her long siege with tuberculosis, her doctor continued to advise that she escape New England winters as much as she could. It was, therefore, easy to persuade Carol, Lillian, and the twelve-year-old Prescott. Irma was not interested. Living in Hanover, New Hampshire, where her husband was establishing himself in a successful architectural firm, she was threatening to obtain a divorce; and she got along no better with her father than with her husband.

Lesley, divorced, had already decided to spend the winter near Mexico City, in company with her two daughters. She arranged to reach San Antonio, en route to Mexico by car, on or before Christmas. Willard Fraser was invited to bring Robin from Montana to Texas and to leave her under Lillian's care during the winter.

Lillian was able to write in a letter to a friend, "On Christmas day we all—Father, Mother, Lesley, Elinor, Lee, Willard, Robin, Carol, Prescott, and I—had dinner together at our hotel, the Saint Anthony, here in San Antonio."

A few days later, after Willard had started back alone to Montana and Lesley had continued, with her children, toward Mexico, Carol and his parents began house-hunting. A furnished apartment on the edge of the city was rented for Carol and his family. Less than two miles away, at 113 Norwood Court, the elder Frosts found and rented an apartment to their liking. The real-estate agent who helped them was almost successful in persuading Frost he should buy property on the edge of a little canyon wilderness not too far outside San Antonio, but Mrs. Frost dissuaded him.

In no mood to write poems, after the fiasco caused by his failure to produce those he had promised for Harvard, Frost entertained himself by writing letters, the most serious to the new editor-in-chief of *The Saturday Review,* Bernard DeVoto. He had not forgotten DeVoto's offer, made during the fall, to publish an essay that would rebuke those critics who had attacked *A Further Range* and its author so harshly. Frost had demurred, but by the time he was settled in San Antonio for the winter of 1936–1937, he changed his mind and wrote: "I am going to have you strike that blow for me now if you still want to and if you can assure your wife and conscience you thought of it first and not I. The Benny-faction must be beyond suspicion of procurement on my part or I will have none of it. All depends on the sequence of events; which I leave to your memory. I am not above asking favors, but principle if not delicacy forbids that it should be too soon in a friendship. . . ."

Whiling away the winter in San Antonio, and waiting for DeVoto to "strike that blow" for him, Frost had leisure to follow an entirely different controversy. Edmund Wilson had published in *The New Republic* some complaints against DeVoto; DeVoto answered in *The Saturday Review* and went on to attack Wilson. Frost, troubled at the prospect of getting mixed up in this combat, wrote DeVoto:

"On third thought and after reading what you did to Edmund Wilson I have decided to have you leave me out of it a while yet, so that my enjoyment of your editorship may be unmixed with self-interest. You go ahead and let me applaud under no obligations. Don't think I dont realize what I am foregoing.

"I believe you came into the world to save me from trying to write social moral and esthetic criticism by making me feel a failure at it before I got started. You can see the temptation I have been trembling on the verge of in my old age. I have caught myself in time. I draw back. You write the criticism who can really write it. . . ."

DeVoto protested against this restraint. Because of illness, he had not yet been able to write what he had in mind, on Frost and his critics, but he briefly outlined the article for Frost and asked permission to continue. Frost answered: "All right, let's hear how good a poet I am. Perhaps it was to tell me and the world your flu spared you. The article as you block it out is too much for me to deny myself. . . ."

Frost had already used his influence with Middlebury College to secure the promise of an honorary degree for DeVoto that June. He had also arranged to have DeVoto rent the Shingled Cottage on the Bennington College campus as a temporary summer home, and he wrote to him early in May of 1937: ". . . Fine to have you in Vermont. I'll be there just ahead of you. . . . I have one lecture to give. Its at Oberlin for commencement. Heaven is My Destination. My self assigned subject: What Became of New England? Then for some much needed self-indulgence. For a person who set out to have his own way in the world I am ending up a horrible example of duteous unselfishness. Dont tell anybody in that article—which by the way I really ought not to see till it's in print if I dont want to feel guilty of having written it myself. . . ."

In his address at Oberlin College, "What Became of New England?" he was eager to claim that New England had given the Oberlin area of Ohio a certain puritan moral fiber that it still retained, and to make a defense of the broader puritan heritage. Part of his claim would be that, even as the whole function of poetry is to refresh and renew the meanings in words, so the function of puritan culture remained to purify some fundamental meanings.

In his commencement address he explained how the puritan tradition, spreading outward from New England, had given itself to this cause of stubbornly clinging to meanings that needed purification:

"New England, now,—what's become of it? It's not necessarily to be found in a literature to be restricted to New England. The little nation that was, and was to be, gave itself, as Virginia gave herself, westward, into the great nation that she saw coming, and so gave help to America. . . .

"And the thing New England gave most to America was the thing I am talking about: a stubborn clinging to meaning,—to purify words until they meant again what they should mean. Puritanism had that meaning entirely: a purifying of words and a renewal of words and a renewal of meaning. That's what brought the Puritans to America, and that's what kept them believing: they saw that there was a meaning that was becoming elusive."

Frost reached back across forty years for an illustration, back to his undergraduate days at Harvard, when he had sat in a lecture hall and heard Santayana mock puritan-Christian doctrine:

"You can get out a theory that meanings go out of things. You can call it disillusionment. You can get disillusionment of a phrase, such as 'fearing

God,' and 'equality.' And then you can form a religion, like George Santayana. He lets you see that there is nothing but illusion, and it can just as well be one kind as another: there is the illusion that you are conscious of, and there is illusion that you become conscious of later. But you should go right on anyway, because there's no proof: all is illusion. You grow to be a sad person.

"Some people pity a person who loses his hero. Who suffers the worse, the person who loses his hero, or the lost hero? You must seek reality forever in things you care for.

"Witchcraft was an illusion, wasn't it? And so is all this Industrialism. And so is the New Deal. You can make it all illusion with a little help of Santayana. He says right out in his philosophy that there are two kinds of illusion, two kinds of madness: one is normal madness, the other is abnormal madness!"

Then, as though he had surprised and embarrassed himself by devoting too much time to Santayana, Frost plunged abruptly to an unexpected conclusion. Choosing one final word, in order to show how poetry could and did refresh meaning, he used as illustration a pair of stanzas from one of his favorite poems, "A Song to David" by Christopher Smart—without naming either the poem or its author:

"Let's take one more: 'prayer.' I'll tell you one of the poems which comes out of the eighteenth century, and ought by rights to be dead by this time. . . ."

Although this commencement address at Oberlin College did amount to one of Frost's most outspoken public utterances concerning his religious belief, just ahead of him waited something for which he could find little consolation, either in religious belief or in poetry.

After an unusually busy summer he returned to Amherst, with his wife, and learned that she needed immediate surgery for cancer. He took her to a hospital in nearby Springfield and was advised that her heart was so weak she might not be able to survive an operation. The desperate decision was made, and the next day Frost wrote to Untermeyer:

"I tried two or three times yesterday to tell you that Elinor had just been operated on for a growth in her breast. I doubt if she fully realizes her peril. So be careful how you speak in your letters. . . . You can see what a difference this must make in any future we have. She has been the unspoken half of everything I ever wrote, and both halves of many a thing from My November Guest down to the last stanzas of Two Tramps in Mud Time—as you may have divined. I don't say it is quite all up with us. We shall make the most of such hope as there is in such cases. She has come through the operation well, though there was delay over her for a day or so at the Hospital for fear her heart wouldn't stand the ether. Her unrealization is what makes it hard for me to keep from speaking to somebody for sympathy. I have had almost too much of her suffering in this world."

Since the early days of their marriage, Frost and his wife had differed in their attitudes toward suffering. She had often chided him for acting like a spoiled child when he was ill, and he admitted that she was much braver than he. But in writing, "I have had almost too much of her suffering in this world," he had betrayed himself to such an extent that he regretted the confession almost as soon as he had mailed the letter. The next day he wrote asking Untermeyer to destroy it.

After Mrs. Frost recovered sufficiently to return home to Amherst, she insisted her husband must keep his promises to give readings in various parts of New England that fall. Then, having been disappointed with their winter in Texas, and still hoping to find a congenial atmosphere in which to hide, the Frosts chose to spend the coldest months of the approaching season in Gainesville, Florida. Plans were made for Carol and his family to drive down from Vermont and for Lesley and her children to join them when she could. Early in December, while staying temporarily at the Thomas Hotel, they began the process of hunting for a house to rent. The one chosen, at 734 Bay Street North, had two furnished apartments, and Lesley insisted that she and her children should take the upstairs apartment, so that her mother would not have to exert her weak heart by climbing the stairs. Mrs. Frost insisted that the downstairs apartment would never do for her husband; he would be constantly annoyed by the sound of the children's busy feet overhead. The arrangement was carried out as she wished, and a house nearby was found for Carol and his family.

Soon after Christmas, Frost received from DeVoto the long-awaited article, "The Critics and Robert Frost," already set in type and scheduled to be published in the issue of *The Saturday Review* for January 1, 1938. As soon as Mrs. Frost had read it aloud to her husband, he wrote DeVoto:

"I sat and let Elinor pour it over me. I took the whole thing. I thought it couldnt do me any harm to listen unabashed to my full praises for once in a way. I said to Sidney Cox years ago that I was non-elatable. While I wasn't actually fishing I suppose I hoped he might see I wanted to be contradicted. All I got out of him was [']That's a serious thing for a poet to confess.['] He was plainly by his tone crediting me with courage in self betrayal. After hearing all you said in my favor today, I tried it at the wistfullest I could command on Elinor. 'What a lie,' she answered. 'You can't talk in public or private without getting elated. You never write but from elation.' . . ."

DeVoto's article was ostensibly a review of *Recognition of Robert Frost,* a collection of notices, reviews, and tributes to Frost, chronologically arranged under subject headings. Using as his point of takeoff Amy

Lowell's review of *North of Boston,* and calling it the worst early piece of criticism, DeVoto added:

". . . When Miss Lowell reworked her piece in 'Tendencies in Modern American Poetry' she brought it down from the higher to the middle strata of the inane, but in the review you get the pure stuff and it is one of the most idiotic pieces written about poetry in this generation. It is screamingly silly. Nothing approached it until the publication of 'A Further Range' impelled a group of muddled minds to tell us about Mr. Frost without bothering to read him. At that time Newton Arvin and Horace Gregory crowded Miss Lowell hard, only to lose in the end to Mr. Blackmur. His piece in the *Nation* may not be quite the most idiotic review our generation has produced, but in twenty years of reading criticism—oh, the hell with scholarly reservations, Mr. Blackmur's *is* the most idiotic of our time. It is one of the most idiotic reviews since the invention of movable type. The monkeys would have to tap typewriters throughout eternity to surpass it, and Mr. Blackmur may regard his immortality as achieved. . . ."

Some friends were delighted with DeVoto's ways, in the article, of thumping all of Frost's enemies. Ridgley Torrence wrote that he didn't see how Arvin, Blackmur, and Gregory "would ever get up from the slaughterhouse floor." But others were not so pleased with the almost-apoplectic manner in which DeVoto had thrown his punches. Theodore Morrison felt another kind of defense should be written. Frost answered Morrison: "I wish you could see that by lingering over them too long we make those fellows more important than I for my part like to think they are. I have read not one of their criticisms, but I can't pretend not to know what they think of me. . . . As you may imagine I hate all this. It is a vexation of the spirit that cant help me write any more prose or verse. I should think Benny had dealt with it sufficiently for the time being. . . ."

Another friend and poet, R. P. T. Coffin, planning to lecture on Frost, wrote to him in Gainesville and asked for any self-definition Frost had written. Coffin had made notes on a talk given by Frost in New York on April 1, 1937, and hoped that Frost might be able to send him a transcript of it. In his reply Frost explained that he could not even remember the subject of those remarks, and he added:

"The nearest I ever came to getting myself down in prose was in the preface to Robinson's *King Jasper.* That is so much me that you might suspect the application to him of being forced. It was really no such thing. We two were close akin up to a certain point of thinking. He would have trusted me to go a good way in speaking for him particularly on the art of poetry. We only parted company over the badness of the world. He was cast in the mold of sadness. I am neither optimist nor pessimist. I never voted either ticket. If there is a universal unfitness and unconformity as of a buttoning so started that every button on the vest is in the wrong button hole and the one empty button hole at the top and the one naked button at the bottom so far apart they have no hope of getting together, I don't care to decide whether God did this for the fun of it or for the devil of it. (The two expressions come to practically the same thing anyway.) Then again I am not the Platonist Robinson was. By Platonist I mean one who believes what we have here is an imperfect copy of what is in heaven. The woman you have is an imperfect copy of some woman in heaven or in someone else's bed. Many of the world's greatest—maybe all of them—have been ranged on that romantic side. I am philosophically opposed to having one Iseult for my vocation and another for my avocation; as you may have inferred from a poem called Two Tramps in Mud Time. You see where that lands me on the subject of Dante's Beatrice. Mea Culpa. Let me not sound the least bit smug. I define a difference with proper humility. A truly gallant platonist will remain a bachelor as Robinson did from unwillingness to reduce any woman to the condition of being used without being idealized. . . .''

Coffin wanted more, and he got it by reminding Frost that he had talked on "Crudities":

"Your letter brings back my animus of that April 1st. I was gunning for the kind of Americans who fancied themselves as the only Americans incapable of crudity. I started off with some crudity I knew they could join me in laughing at and I ended up with some they might not be so incapable of themselves. But I protested all the way along my love of crudity. I thank the Lord for crudity which is rawness, which is raw material, which is the part of life not yet worked up into form, or at least not worked all the way up. Meet with the fallacy of the foolish: having had a glimpse of finished art, they forever after pine for a life that shall be nothing but finished art. Why not a world safe for art as well as democracy. A real artist delights in roughness for what he can do to it. He's the brute who can knock the corners off the marble block and drag the unbedded beauty out of bed. The statesman (politician) is no different except that he works in a protean mass of material that hardly holds the shape he gives it long enough for him to point it out and get credit for it. His material is the rolling mob. The poet's material is words that for all we may say and feel against them are more manageable than men. Get a few words alone in a study and with plenty of time on your hands you can make them say anything you please. . . .''

Coffin had done well to approach Frost when he had plenty of time on his hands, to express himself on his attitudes toward crudities and on his non-Platonic attitude toward woman. Shortly after he had explained himself in this manner, he was agonizingly forced to reconsider.

The Frosts were so pleased by their stay in Gainesville, they decided to buy a small house they could occupy annually during their winter retreats. Carol used his car to drive them through the countryside, and Frost was particularly happy to indulge once again in his game of prospecting for property. At last they found a house all of them liked, and on Friday afternoon, March 18, 1938, they went to make one final inspection.

As they returned and were climbing the stairs to the second-floor apartment, Mrs. Frost suddenly complained of her chronic ailment. She had suffered so many minor heart attacks, no immediate fear was felt, but a doctor was called. He listened to her heart and pronounced her condition alarming. He told Frost she was too ill to be moved. Within a few hours a more severe attack occurred, and she became unconscious. The doctor, happening to be present, quickly revived her. He told her husband, however, that her condition was precarious and she would almost certainly have another attack, which might be fatal.

Frost's anguish was inseparable from his guilt. Distraught, he told himself he was to blame, for dragging her about the countryside, house-hunting, when he should have been more considerate of the weakness she had shown since her cancer operation. And he should never have permitted her to insist they take the second-floor apartment, should never have let her climb those stairs, day after day. If she was going to die, there was so much he must say to her. He had to ask forgiveness for all the wrongs he had done her since the days of their courtship. She had nearly died when their first child was born, and her physician had told Frost her heart was so weak she might not be able to stand the strain of giving birth to another child. When that first child had died, at the age of four, something in her spirit had seemed to die. Now, remembering that his own passionate demands had brought six children, he felt that, in a sense, he had killed her.

But she was not dead, and it would be like her to disprove the doctor's prophecy. When she lived through the night, there seemed to be hope she would recover. Frost, intermittently pacing the corridor outside her bedroom, could occasionally hear her answering the doctor's questions. Certainly she would ask to see him as soon as she was permitted. He wanted her to say, at least with her eyes, that she forgave him—that all the pain and suffering he had caused her had been more than offset by the joys and triumphs of their years together. But she did not ask to see him, and as the hours of the second day passed he began to wonder if she had perhaps found her ultimate way of punishing him for what was unforgivable.

She did suffer additional heart attacks, one after another—seven in all. And after each she grew weaker. When, finally, he was admitted to her room, she was either asleep or unconscious, and all he could do was hope she would recover long enough to look at him. On Sunday afternoon, she simply stopped breathing.

At first, the most painful element in her death was that she had gone without giving him the chance to ask and receive her forgiveness. Throughout their life together she had continued to refine her extraordinary capacity to reprimand or tease him with eloquent silences. Always, before, he had found ways to achieve ultimate clarifications of those silences, no matter how long or how mysterious they had been. What remained, now, was an irrevocable silence on which his imagination worked, to perplex and torture him with uncertainties of whether she had deliberately refused to say anything to him or had been unable to speak. His ever-present sense of guilt provided the answer that hurt most, and the longer he brooded over her final silence, the more certain he became that he deserved it as punishment.

While the final rites were being arranged, Frost was so ill he could not immediately participate. He had been suffering from a sore throat and cold even before Mrs. Frost was stricken, and the pain in his throat had become worse during the two days she lingered. The doctor, quickly realizing he had another potentially serious condition confronting him, insisted that if Frost did not go to bed, and stay there for some time, there was danger of pneumonia.

From his bed he talked with his children about the necessity for postponing any funeral. But he knew what Elinor wanted him to do. For years she had said she would rather be cremated than buried; she wished her ashes taken to the farm in Derry, New Hampshire, and scattered along the bank of Hyla Brook, in that little grove of pines where she had spent so many idyllic hours with her young children. Because the doctor would not permit Frost to attend the formalities of the cremation, Lesley and a friend accompanied the body to Jacksonville, Florida; and during the identification ritual there, she was granted permission to place in the casket an envelope given her for that purpose by her father.

Lesley, almost overcome by grief after the cremation, unintentionally revealed a habit of vindictiveness she had acquired from her father. When he asked if he might make his home with her during the remainder of his life, she bluntly said no; and she burst into an almost-hysterical accusation that further amazed him. She said she had seen him cause so much injury to his own children, she would not permit him to move into her home, where he might also injure the lives of her two daughters. Her rage increased as she went on to insist, through her tears, that she could not forgive him for his having ruined her mother's life. It was his fault that her mother was dead, for his selfishness had forced her mother to climb, repeatedly, those stairs to the upper quarters. Lesley, then, hurt him most by concluding that he was the kind of artist who never should have married—or, at least, never should have had a family.

Frost was so deeply wounded by these accusations, he could not answer. Lesley's outburst increased the pain caused by what he had said to himself—and what Elinor had not said. What he needed now was someone who might contradict him, by saying his self-condemnation was far too harsh. There were no comforters in his own family, however.

Irma, far away in New Hampshire, would have given him no help if she were present. She had disagreed and argued with him bitterly during the past few years. Carol was less hostile than his sisters, only because he was less articulate. There had never been any sustained affection between him and his father, and on many occasions each had antagonized the other in ways that had built up lasting enmities. He had been his mother's special care, and he had leaned on her so completely that he suffered his own collapse when she died. As soon as he could leave, after his mother's cremation, he made haste to start North, with Lillian and Prescott, to whatever consolation the farm in South Shaftsbury might give him.

During the several days Frost was confined to his bed in Gainesville, he kept going back over the spoken and unspoken reproaches. Although he had long ago rejected the trite saying that an artist should never have a family, Lesley's bitter use of it forced him into reconsiderations. Repeatedly he had said, in moments of impatience, that his devotion to his art had been spoiled by his devotion to his family; but he had been genuinely attentive to his wife and children.

Most of his poems had been written for Elinor, first; and all his books had been dedicated to her. As for the children, he wondered how many fathers had spent as much time with their children as he had with his. Back on the Derry farm, where three of them had been born and all of them had learned to walk and talk, he had certainly given more of himself to them than to his farming or his writing. And when he and his wife decided their own experiences as teachers qualified them to keep their children out of public schools, he had enjoyed his parts of the teaching. Throughout all, he had also tried to help them understand the differences between right and wrong.

He wondered whether Lesley had any justifiable reason for saying she would not permit him to injure her children as he had injured his own. He hoped not. And yet, he knew some of the specific charges she might make. All four of his children had been taught by him to write poetry, but in later years Elinor had scolded him for refusing to help get their poems published, even in magazines. His defense had been that if they were to succeed as poets they must make their own way among editors and publishers. There was one way in which he had unintentionally failed them. He had tried to develop in them courage to overcome the fears that had beset him in his childhood, but it did seem that he had accidentally taught them more fear than courage.

Each of them had grown up somehow victimized by a peculiar set of fears. The succession of nervous breakdowns that had overtaken Marjorie after her graduation from high school might be explained, he thought, by fears not unlike those that had ruined the life of his sister, Jeanie. Marjorie's pure idealism had made the evils in the world seem so intolerable that she had cringed in her attempts to make adjustments. Carol's oddities, apparent since boyhood, had expressed themselves in his cumulative suspicion that everyone (including his father) was trying to take advantage of him, or persecute him. Many of Irma's difficulties, not easily understandable until after her marriage, seemed traceable to a prudish notion that the sexual act was bestial. Her father was unwilling to take the blame on himself for that distortion. Lesley's bundle of fears were not unlike Carol's, and yet, she had plunged into a variety of experiences with more courage and boldness than any of the other children. If he had injured them by communicating his fears to them, such an act had been just the opposite of what he had intended.

He was willing to grant that Lesley or anybody else could make a case for the claim that the artist should never have a family. It was obvious to him that there must always be a conflict between a man's devotion to his art and his devotion to wife and children.

Before Frost had recovered from his illness, visitors began arriving in Gainesville to express condolences. Among the first was the poet and novelist Hervey Allen. A good listener, he helped most by giving Frost a chance to pour out his self-condemnations, against which Allen made the needed protestations. After his visit, Allen received from Frost a brief note of thanks, made up largely of two quotations from Tennyson. The first was from Sir Bedivere's speech to King Arthur after surviving the last battle: "And I the last go forth companionless / And the days darken round me." The other ("But it is written also," he noted, "by the same hand"—in "In Memoriam"): "Let darkness keep her raven gloss."

Another visitor who came unexpectedly, with sympathetic offers of assistance and consolation, was President Stanley King of Amherst College. Frost had written King to say his illness following Mrs. Frost's death had made him realize the need, once again, to beg off from his Amherst obligations; that under the circumstances, he wished to tender his resignation. He also asked for permission to have a service in Johnson Chapel some time in April. President King responded by going directly from Amherst to Gainesville and offering whatever assistance he could give in making arrangements for the memorial service.

Practical assistance was provided by Louis Untermeyer, who went to

Gainesville as soon as he could, and stayed long enough to help address envelopes containing the printed announcement of the service at Amherst.

Bernard DeVoto's expressions of sympathy evoked this reply:

"I expect to have to go depths below depths in thinking before I catch myself and can say what I want to be while I last. I shall be all right in public, but I can't tell yet how I am going to behave when I am alone. She could always be present to govern my loneliness without making me feel less alone. It is now running into more than a week longer than I was ever away from her since June 1895. You can see how I might have doubts of myself. I am going to work very hard in May and be on the go with people so as not to try myself solitary too soon.

"I suppose love must always deceive. I'm afraid I deceived her a little in pretending for the sake of argument that I didnt think the world as bad a place as she did. My excuse was that I wanted to keep her a little happy for my own selfish pleasure. It is as if for the sake of argument she had sacrificed her life to give me this terrible answer and really bring me down in sorrow. She needn't have. I knew I never had a leg to stand on, and I should think I had said so in print. . . ."

And just before Frost started North, from Gainesville, he wrote to the George Roy Elliotts at Amherst:

"I am coming back to Amherst on Tuesday or Wednesday for some more of the finalities I haven't yet learned to accept with the flesh. Otto and Ethel [Manthey-Zorn] have asked me to their house since I dont seem to want to see the inside of my own. . . . I shall probably wander round . . . for a while till I can decide who I am now, and what I have to go on with. Some of the old ambitious resolutions may come back to me in some form. The danger will be that they may too openly concern her. Pretty nearly every one of my poems will be found to be about her if rightly read. But I must try to remember they were as much about her as she liked and permitted them to be. Without ever saying a word she set limits I must continue to observe. One remark like this and then no more forever."

33

THE URN AND ITS ASHES

(1938)

THE ENTIRE Frost family gathered for the service in Amherst on April twenty-second. Sitting directly behind them in Johnson Chapel were the nineteen men invited to attend as honorary bearers. Frost was more attentive to these men, most of whom had come long distances, at his request, to honor Elinor, than he was to the service itself. He knew that she, as a nonbeliever, would have scoffed at having any memorial for her in a house of God.

After the service, before the children left that afternoon, Frost called them into brief and private conclave. He had been unable to complete the plans for carrying out the final pagan ritual Elinor had requested. All of them had heard their mother say, more than once, that she wanted her ashes scattered along Hyla Brook; but that would have to be postponed, he said, until he could make preliminary arrangements. He would go alone to Derry and request permission of the present owner, whoever he was, so that when they gathered there, at a later time, their appearance would not seem an act of trespassing. For the present, Frost must remain in Amherst long enough to make formal his resignation from the college and to sell the Sunset Avenue house.

His decision to resign from Amherst College had been taking shape for several years and was not precipitated hastily by his wife's death. Unpleasant frictions had been developing with various faculty members who resented his being paid a salary for doing next to nothing. Several had complained to President King that Frost had not even tried to live up to his terms of contract. Others complained that he used the treasury of Amherst as a source for unearned gifts to friends whom he brought to Amherst for trivial lectures.

Frost had expressed his own counter-resentment to DeVoto, from Gainesville, just two weeks before Mrs. Frost died:

". . . Wait till I tell you all that has been happening at Amherst to make me sick of the smallness of academic ways. I dont blame the professors too much for their hostility to the writers out in the world. They have their own positions to magnify and defend. I have to remember the college is the whole of their life whereas it is only a very small part of mine. But my English department werent very good to me about the incursion of Louis [Untermeyer]. George Whicher attended all four lectures; none of the others, even for my sake, would show the least interest. I was all right, but deliver them from my friends. It is not enough consolation that Louis had a triumph with the house-full that came. I say Love me love what's mine. And I am in a position to enforce that rule. What puts me in that position and keeps me there is my recklessness of consequences. . . ."

Mrs. Frost's death, making him even more reckless of consequences, had given him excuse enough to resign. In the days immediately following the funeral service, he talked informally with President King about his wish not only to resign, but also to sell his Amherst home. The president expressed his genuine regret and urged him to reconsider. But he said that if Frost was certain he wanted to sell the house, the college would buy it from him. Arrangements were made, and Frost began the sad task of packing.

". . . Closing myself out of Amherst has taken more time than I expected," he wrote to Dorothy Canfield Fisher. "The college is buying my house; so I have had to empty it." There were other obligations, including talks and readings, made just to keep busy. On June third Amherst College completed the transaction of purchasing the Sunset Avenue house, and the next day Frost wrote King a letter of resignation.

After he had completed the details of what he referred to as "closing myself out of Amherst," Frost had not forgotten his promise to make arrangements for spreading Elinor's ashes alongside Hyla Brook in Derry. He went alone, both wanting and dreading the "ache of memory" there. He had kept the images of that farm so vivid in his consciousness, during all the years since he had last seen it, he was not prepared for the shock of finding everything changed.

As the side door opened to his knock, he introduced himself to the woman of the house, and could see she neither knew nor cared who he was. When he explained why he had come, she listened with an expression of puzzlement and indifference. She supposed what he asked would be all right, but she'd have to consult her husband and he was not at home. To his request that he be permitted to walk through the alders to the brook and up through the mowing-field to the orchard, she said that would be all right. Then, she closed the door. Already, this woman's indifference had spoiled the ritual. It seemed to him Elinor, if she could have overheard that chilly conversation, would have changed her mind about wanting her ashes scattered where such a stranger might tread.

As he went down the steps near the front of the barn, he instinctively set his course toward the little corduroy bridge he had built across the brook—and, suddenly, knew the bridge could no longer be there; it must have rotted out years ago. The alders had been permitted to grow, without trimming, and when he tried to find the footpath he and she and their children had worn, he wasn't sure where it had been. But getting through the rank alders, he found where the bridge had been, even found part of the little dam of stones they had built just above the bridge. He looked into the branch-cluttered opening among the pines, and saw the piece of plank he had wedged and nailed between the forked trunks of two pines as a special seat for her.

Picking his way beyond the grove, along the bank of Hyla Brook, he noticed wild orchises still growing there. He turned at the stone-wall boundary mark and climbed the hill, into the mowing-field, so he could look through and over the orchard, at the backsides of barn and house. The apple trees were past their prime; nobody had bothered to trim them for years. And he noticed the forlorn appearance of weather-beaten clapboards on the back of the barn.

As he climbed back up the stone steps and into the yard, he knew he still owned everything he wanted of this farm. What was left was merely a profanation—a desecration—of what was his. He could never scatter the ashes in this desecration.

When he got back to South Shaftsbury and told Carol and Lillian the story of his visit to the Derry farm, he was relieved to find that they quickly accepted his decision. There still remained the problem of what to do with the ashes, and the urn. There was a good-sized empty cupboard in the Stone Cottage bedroom that had been made available to him when he found he could not sleep in the ghost-filled Gully farmhouse. Because he didn't know where else to keep the urn, he put it in the cupboard. Then, he tried to think of other things. Occasionally, he offered help with daily chores around the farm, always feeling he was in the way; and for many days he wasted daylight walking up through the fields and woods of the Gully farm, wasted sleepless nights writing letters to those who might understand his loneliness enough to share some part of it. One of these letters went to J. J. Lankes, whose woodcuts had been used to illustrate *New Hampshire* and *West-Running Brook*:

"I was over at the Gulley Gulch today trying to get used to it enough to use and keep it. . . . The place is bad with good memories, but so's the whole world. I suppose you saw no one ever got far into my affairs and friendship that didn't succeed with Elinor. Her favor was the final test. I did a few things she was opposed to, but that was only because she wasn't seriously opposed to them. . . . I am going over in my mind the special places where we were at one. There are a good many of them fortunately to console me for the suffering I must have caused her sometimes. I'm afraid I dragged her through pretty much of a life for one as frail as she was. Too many children, too many habitations too many vicissitudes. And a faith required that would have exhausted most women. God damn me when he gets around to it. I refused to be bowed down as much as she was by other deaths. But she has given me a death now that I cant refuse to be bowed down by. Here I am brought up short when in every way you can name I was still going full tilt. I'm not behaving very well. I shall have to look for examples of good behavior in my predicament. And then I dont know about my ability to follow them. I have been relatively prospered in an outrageously self-indulgent life. I have been given absolutely my own way. You might not notice it from the outside, but such are the facts. . . . Probably I'll have thought this all out and worked it off before I see you in the fall. So we can talk of ordinary things then. . . ."

He kept trying to talk of ordinary things with Carol, Lillian, Prescott; also kept trying to find a satisfactory way of rearranging his life. Much as he had talked about stealing away and staying away from other people, he was convinced by his loneliness that he could never live alone unless friends or relatives were near. Cut off from Amherst, he now had greater freedom to devote more of himself to writing, but since Elinor's death he felt paralyzed. He was not sure he could ever again write a good poem; he was almost sure he didn't care. He could earn his living with talks and readings. But where would he live? Carol and Lillian talked about building an ell for him on the Stone Cottage; and yet, Carol might not want him underfoot that much.

Day after day he set out alone, aimlessly walking. He botanized enough to discover that in the grove of red pines he and Carol had set out as seedlings, seventeen years earlier, some wild orchises were beginning to grow. Down on one side of this grove he found one showy orchis and picked it. Without saying anything to Carol or Lillian about his find, he took it to his bedroom in the Stone Cottage, placed it in water, in a thin vase, and stood it next to the urn on the closet shelf—as though he were trying to make amends for his failure to carry out her wish. He supposed he would stop this guilty brooding after awhile and get back into something like his old form, at least in public. Just now, there were moments when he felt so completely crushed by loneliness, he wished the urn in the cupboard held his ashes, with hers.

THE
LATER
YEARS

34

RESCUED FROM A
DANGEROUS SELF

(1938–1939)

ONE MORNING late in July 1938, Robert Frost watched from a front-room window as a car made its way up the dirt road toward his Gully farmhouse in South Shaftsbury, Vermont. When it was close enough for him to see the Massachusetts license plate, he waited only a moment before taking his customary evasive action. Hurrying outside, through the kitchen door, he hit for the woods and was safely out of sight before the uninvited visitor drove into the yard.

As so often happened, however, his curiosity forced him to circle back to a vantage point where, through a screen of leaves, he could study the intruder. Someone he could not immediately make out—a woman, perhaps forty years old, rather slight of build, with bright auburn hair—was apparently writing a note she planned to leave. When she finished it, wedged it between the kitchen door and the jamb, and turned to walk back to her car, he recognized Kathleen Morrison, wife of Theodore Morrison of Harvard and Bread Loaf. Before he had time to come out of hiding and greet Kay, she started her car and drove off.

Her note explained the purpose of her visit. Her husband, as director of the Bread Loaf Writers' Conference, was now preparing for the August session, and he wanted Frost to know he was welcome as ever to a job at Bread Loaf, welcome to remain on campus for the two weeks of the conference and to give as few or as many lectures as he wished. Also, Kay's note continued, she and her children—Bobby, aged eight, and Anne, almost two—were staying with friends whom the Frosts had met, the Nathaniel Sages, in West Dover, Vermont; and they wanted Frost to spend a few days with them.

Frost had known Mrs. Morrison longer, if not better, than he had her husband. As Kathleen Johnston, a student at Bryn Mawr College in the Class of 1921, she had been a member of the "Reeling and Writhing Club," which in 1920 brought him to Bryn Mawr for a private, three-session course in the arts of reading and writing poetry. During the next several years, they had met little or not at all. Then, in 1936, Frost had come to Harvard, and Kay had joined her husband, a Harvard English instructor, in inviting Frost back to their Cambridge home for small receptions after each of his Norton lectures. Frost's growing affection for the Morrisons had led him to invite Ted to participate in the service for Elinor, and the Morrisons' reciprocated friendship had led Kay, now, to call on the grieving poet at his home in the Gully.

If there was some concern for his well-being reflected in Kay's visit and the Sages' invitation, it was not without reason. As the Morrisons and other close friends knew, Elinor's death continued to haunt him; and when Mrs. Morrison returned, several days later, Frost told her he was not yet ready to leave South Shaftsbury. He did, however, agree to participate in the Writers' Conference.

Convinced Frost's solitude was doing him no good, Mrs. Morrison returned to convey the Sages' invitation again. This time, impulsively, the poet chose to accept. Hastily packing a suitcase, he climbed in Mrs. Morrison's car and rode with her to the Sages' summer home. On the way, he confessed to Kay that he had brought with him a sheaf of unanswered correspondence to which he would sooner or later have to attend. If he could wait until the end of the Writers' Conference, said Mrs. Morrison, she would be happy to type his answers for him.

In West Dover, at the Sages' suggestion, Kay joined Frost for long hikes, taking part in his favorite pastime, botanizing—and listening sympathetically as he unburdened himself of his accumulated troubles. Frost enjoyed these walks, but in the emotional havoc that was the aftermath of Elinor's death, their time together produced a result neither of them had anticipated. Lonely and desperate for companionship, Frost soon began to imagine not only that the gratitude and affection he felt for Kay was love, but that she might be prevailed upon, despite her married status, fully to reciprocate that feeling.

When he returned for a second visit to West Dover, he astonished Kay by professing his love and by following that with a proposal—amounting almost to a demand—that she leave her husband and become his wife. In his excited state of mind, he was hardly daunted when Kay told him that, happily married as she was, marriage to him was out of the question; that, much as she might care for him as a friend, she would never consent to be his wife.

On the Bread Loaf campus the staff Ted Morrison had assembled included two of Frost's closest friends, Bernard DeVoto and Louis Untermeyer, who were delighted to see Frost apparently emerging from his long period of bitter mourning. His first talk and reading was a spectacular performance, and Charles H. Foster, a young poet from the

University of Iowa, later recorded: "Last night, Frost gave the best lecture I have ever heard him give. His mind was seething and rolling with metaphors and humor and he was exhausted when he was finished. . . ."

It was clear from this talk, and from others he gave in the week that followed, that Frost had made a successful escape from one set of problems connected with his wife's death. But to many of the participants at Bread Loaf it was equally plain he was by no means a man enjoying emotional peace. "Frost told me," wrote Foster in his journal after his first private conversation with the poet, "that he was a God-damned son-of-a bitch, a selfish person who had dragged people rough-shod over life. People didn't understand [him] who wanted to make him good. His rebellion looked so good, he said, but he was always a person who had his way, a God-damned son of a bitch, Charlie, and don't let anyone tell you different. . . ."

A week later, on the night of August twenty-seventh, Frost conducted himself in a manner seemingly calculated to convince his colleagues that what he had said of himself was true. The occasion was a lecture and poetry reading by Archibald MacLeish, who had just arrived at Bread Loaf for a brief visit, and Frost found himself sharing the limelight with a poet whose reputation rivaled his own. Wallace Stegner, one of the members of the staff, has described what happened:

". . . Early in the proceedings . . . [Frost] found some mimeographed notices on a nearby chair and sat rolling and folding them in his hands. Now and again he raised the roll of paper, or an eyebrow, calling the attention of his seat mates to some phrase or image. He seemed to listen with an impartial, if skeptical, judiciousness. About halfway through the reading he leaned over and said in a carrying whisper, 'Archie's poems all have the same *tune*.' As the reading went on, to the obvious pleasure of the audience, he grew restive. The fumbling and rustling of the papers in his hands became disturbing. Finally MacLeish announced, 'You, Andrew Marvell,' a tour de force that makes a complete thirty-six-line poem out of a single sentence. It was a favorite. Murmurs of approval, intent receptive faces. The poet began. Then an exclamation, a flurry in the rear of the hall. The reading paused, heads turned. Robert Frost, playing around like an idle, inattentive boy in a classroom, had somehow contrived to strike a match and set fire to his handful of papers and was busy beating them out and waving away the smoke."

The fire was quickly extinguished, but Frost's jealousy continued to burn. After MacLeish had finished his reading, the group adjourned for drinks and conversation, and at the urging of several, MacLeish began to read his new radio play, *Air Raid*. Again, Frost began baiting the speaker, with murmured comments. MacLeish refused to take offense, and the audience sat in embarrassed silence, afraid to look predator or prey in the face. Finally, DeVoto, less inclined to patient acquiescence than his fellows, said something in reproof of his misbehaving friend (something like, "For God's sake, Robert, let him read!"). Frost said nothing in reply, but a short time later he himself took offense at a remark clearly intended for someone else, and abruptly left the room.

Next morning Herschel Brickell of the Bread Loaf staff received the summons of the troubled poet. He wanted to be driven at once to Concord Corners, Vermont, where he had a house in which his daughter Irma and her family were staying. But if Frost was seeking in Concord Corners refuge from emotional conflict, he found none. Irma refused Brickell permission to spend the night and insisted on putting her father in a room the only access to which was through the bedroom where she and her husband slept. Hurt and angered, Frost called Brickell in the morning and said he now wanted to go back.

He returned to a Bread Loaf alive with rumor and speculation as to the reasons for his erratic behavior. Charles Foster agreed with Brickell's suggestion that Frost was now "raping his personality"; and they concurred that all the unaccustomed whiskey-drinking, all the self-abasement, all the ugliness were unlike the man they had long known and loved. Foster could not help thinking that the explanation, whatever it might be, somehow went beyond the death of Elinor Frost, five months before. But he had no idea what else might account for so much turmoil.

Bernard DeVoto and Louis Untermeyer, both of whom were privy to Frost's thoughts, had a better understanding of the situation. They knew that much of Frost's behavior that week was related to what he felt for Kathleen Morrison. Untermeyer's natural sympathy enabled him to maintain his loyalty to his friend, even though he did not approve the course he was taking. But DeVoto was deeply disturbed by the recklessness with which Frost seemed determined to interfere with the Morrison family. As he bade farewell to Frost at the end of the conference, he scolded him for the second time in a week by saying, "You're a good poet, Robert, but you're a bad man."

DeVoto was gone before Frost could find an appropriate way of responding to his reprimand, and soon the Bread Loaf campus was deserted, except for Frost and the Morrisons. At the Morrisons' invitation, Frost moved into the house where Ted and Kay would continue to stay until the start of the Harvard semester, in late September. Now, Kay would do the secretarial work she had promised.

Even before Kay set up her typewriter, however, Frost began to realize that whatever help she gave him before he left Bread Loaf could only provide temporary relief for a problem that, as long as he remained active as a poet and lecturer, was bound to be a continuing nuisance. Living alone was one thing; he could get used to that, in time. But he would

need help with lecture-scheduling, proofreading, book-balancing, with
the flood of routine correspondence.

The solution to his dilemma dawned on him suddenly, and was so
clearly the answer to all his needs that he wondered at not having
thought of it sooner. Who could be his secretary, his manager, better
than the woman who was even now answering his mail? Kay Morrison's
willingness to help him, as a favor, might easily be turned into a
permanent and formal relationship in which he would pay her a salary
for so many hours a week, all the year round, for—why not?—all the
remaining years of his life. He decided he would bring up the idea before
he left Bread Loaf.

When he did bring it up, he was delighted to find that both Kay and her
husband thought his proposal worthy of trial. Kay said she would give up
her job as a part-time reader for the Atlantic Monthly Press and Little,
Brown and Company, and would get in touch with Boston friends to see
about finding Frost an apartment within commuting distance of her own
home in Cambridge. Then, as Frost suggested, she would begin coming
to him every weekday morning around half past nine, performing
whatever secretarial or managerial chores needed to be done, and
returning to her home and family around four in the afternoon.

It was not the salary Frost offered that induced Mrs. Morrison to take
the job. Kay had seen enough of Frost before, during, and after the
Writers' Conference to know he was desperately in need of looking after
and that unless someone came forth to take him in hand he might never
write poetry again. There was a risk, Kay knew, in continuing their
association on a daily basis, but it was a risk she was prepared to run.
Frost meant too much to her, as a friend and as a poet, for her to decline
to help him at this critical juncture of his life.

Enjoying the Morrisons' company, Frost spent the last weeks of the
summer vacation exploring the Vermont countryside in their old Plymouth. Then, he decided it was time to go on to Concord Corners; and
among his first acts on settling in there was to write a letter to his new
secretary, containing much he had been unable to express adequately
face to face:

"Dear Kay: I try you with pencil to see if a change of tool won't give me
the release that a change of paper sometimes does. I am like an ocean
that in its restlessness may have brought up every imaginable shape to
the surface, but won't be satisfied till it brings up the sea serpent. You two
rescued me from a very dangerous self when you had the idea of keeping
me for the whole session at Bread Loaf. I am still infinitely restless, but I
came away from you as good as saved. I had had a long lovers' quarrel
with the world. I loved the world, but you might never have guessed it
from the things I thought and said. Now the quarrel is made up. Not that

it ought to matter to anyone but me, but I can't help hoping it matters a little to my friends. The turning point for the better was on that Sunday when I seemed to behave so much worse. Stanley King's charge against me was ingratitude. It will be a sensitive subject with me the rest of my life. I must be careful to avoid even the appearance of ingratitude. I am grateful to you two for your ministrations. Never doubt me. Let us pray the sea-serpent I feel so big with and about may prove to be a poetic drama. . . .

"Tears in my heart when I left you people. I wish you were in the house I am looking at over there above the lake where it in turn looks at the White Mts across the lake. Its a place I have had in mind for you. . . . Since you wont have it as a loan I am going to sell it to Benny. . . ."

But the DeVotos had no great desire to live in a place as remote as Concord Corners. Even if they had, the Writers' Conference had spoiled forever Benny's notion of Frost as a kind of father who could do no wrong. Nothing Frost did or said could make DeVoto take back, implicitly or explicitly, what he had said at the end of the conference. He still thought him "a bad man."

Frost's liking for Concord Corners collapsed. "You ask where I am," he wrote to his Harvard friend David McCord. "I am where the wind never ceases blowing. . . ." And he added, "I am not going to stay up here in a bath of memories very long—I am damned if I am[,] not for any hay fever. . . ." A few days later he left Vermont for Louis Untermeyer's farm, Stony Water, in Elizabethtown, New York, which he had visited briefly before the Writers' Conference.

In writing to invite himself back to Stony Water, Frost had also announced the success of Mrs. Morrison's efforts to find him a place to live in Boston: "at 88 Mount Vernon Street overlooking Louisburg Square." He remained more than a week in Elizabethtown, then left with Untermeyer for the train station in Springfield, Massachusetts, stopping in Amherst to arrange for the transfer of his possessions to his new home. Soon after his train left for Boston, however, a severe hurricane swept across the state, and resulted in an adventure Frost later described in a letter to his son, Carol:

". . . I set out from Springfield to go to Boston at a little afternoon. Already the water was too high for the direct route. So my train was sent to New Haven to aim for Boston by the Long Island shore tracks. It never got further than New Haven and it was twelve hours getting there. I waited in it for half the next day and then went up to Pierson College at Yale for the next night. I had a pleasant time with friends. But I was restless to get where I could be located by Lesley should she be in trouble, so hired a taxi for thirty dollars and came from New Haven by the Post Road one hundred and fifty miles to the St Botolph Club 4

Newberry St Boston Mass which will remain my address for some time to come. I saw a lot of ruin the whole way, but we had no trouble in getting through and were in no danger. The wildest time was in the train during the hurricane. The train stood still and let it blow the trees down all around. The train shook and the passengers joked. Luckily the train was a sleeper from St Louis with not many left in the sleeping cars. That gave everybody in the chair cars a chance to hire beds for the night. . . ."

Frost's apartment was not to be ready for occupancy until mid-October, and since there was work to be done in preparation for his forthcoming lecture tour, now just three weeks away, Kay Morrison called on him at the St. Botolph Club as soon as she had returned from Vermont. When she tried to enter the club, however, she was stopped and informed that women were not permitted on the premises; she could not even speak to her employer in the downstairs parlor. Infuriated, Frost abruptly moved out of his room and took another in the nearby Ritz-Carlton hotel. But after a few days, exhausted by his recent exertions and apprehensive about his first lecture tour since Elinor's death, he came down with a cold that soon worsened until it was serious enough to send him to Massachusetts General Hospital. He remained there for several days, before deciding he had endured hospital routine long enough. Then, he walked out, undismissed.

It was the second week of October when he moved in at 88 Mt. Vernon Street. It was a small flat, smaller it seemed to him than any place he had lived in since his childhood in San Francisco. But Kay assured him that with the proper furnishings, and with his books lining the walls, it would be comfortable enough, at least until a larger apartment, or perhaps a small house in Cambridge, could be found. With less than a week before his first appearance, at Columbia University on October sixteenth, Frost decided not to finish unpacking until he returned from his tour.

By mid-November he was back, and he soon began to usurp Mrs. Morrison's time and attention in ways she had not anticipated when she agreed to become his secretary. "Be moderately sorry for a poor old man of iron will," he wrote to Untermeyer in late November. "Nothing I do or say is as yet due to anything but a strong determination to have my own way. . . ." And he spoke directly of Kay, who had so quickly become the real center of his new life:

"This year I have worked hard in the open, and I think it has done me good. My secretary has soothed my spirit like music in her attendance on me and my affairs. She has written my letters and sent me off on my travels. It is an unusual friendship. I have come to value my poetry almost less than the friendships it has brought me. I say it who wouldnt have believed I would ever live to say it. . . . I was thrust out into the desolateness of wondering about my past whether it had not been too cruel to those I had dragged with me and almost to cry out to heaven for a word of reassurance that was not given me in time. Then came this girl stepping innocently into my days to give me something to think of besides dark regrets. My half humorous noisy contrition of the last few months has begun to die down. You have heard a lot of it and you are hearing it still a little here. I doubt if it has been quite dignified. I am told I am spoken of as her 'charge.' It is enough to be. Lets have some peace. You can figure it out for yourself how my status with a girl like her might be the perfect thing for me at my age in my position. I wish in some indirect way she could come to know how I feel toward her."

It was not long before Frost found a way of informing Kay Morrison how he felt toward her; and, appropriately, it was by means of poetry: a sonnet of just one sentence, the central image of which was a carefully constructed metaphysical conceit. His eventual title for the poem was "The Silken Tent," but when he first presented it to Kay, Frost called it "In Praise of Your Poise." As he realized when he wrote it—and Kay when she read it—it was not only the first poem he had written in many months, but one of the best he had written in his life.

On the last day of November, Frost delivered a lecture at Harvard University, and it met with a response for which the Harvard authorities had not adequately prepared. The planners had scheduled it to take place in Room D of Emerson Hall, capacity 300. More than 1,000 came. The mob scene was particularly pleasing to Frost, for he knew it would prove to skeptics that he was still in demand at Harvard. That, in turn, would aid David McCord and the "Friends of Robert Frost" in their effort to raise $4,000 for a two-year appointment for him at Harvard.

Even Frost was surprised by the ease with which he now approached public appearances, after years of being terrified. A few hours before the Harvard lecture, he had written Lesley: ". . . My fear of these things beforehand has largely left me. I have done my ten or fifteen this fall in Ohio Pennsylvania New York and Massachusetts with almost perfect calm. Something strange has come over my life. I shall never be the scared fool again that I used to be. Nothing can more than kill me."

Lesley knew her father too well to take his remark as indicating he had also overcome his lifelong fear of death. But his letter suggested that he took comfort in believing the dread event was still many years off: "I happened to remark at the DeVoto table that I might turn to prose in ten years from now and their eight year old piped up 'You, you'll be dead in ten years.' I really enjoyed the rudeness. The devil of it is that except for the flu threat I seem more alive than I ever was. You should see me in trials of strength and suppleness with men much younger. I even excel in some events. . . ."

In reminding his daughter that his mental and physical powers had not diminished with age, Frost was obliquely defending the way he had ordered his life in the months since Elinor's death. Lesley, he knew, was not sure he had been wise in declining the offer of Carol and Lillian to build an ell on the Stone Cottage for his use. She was even-less sure that Kay Morrison was the perfect solution to his difficulties. Knowing Lesley's disapproval of Kay would create family tensions with which he could ill afford to cope, Frost tried hard to assure his daughter her fears were groundless.

When he visited Lesley in Washington, D.C., a week later, Frost again found it necessary to justify himself and defend Kay, in the face of Lesley's persistent questioning. The course of the discussion can be inferred from the letter Frost sent her after his return to Boston:

". . . You kids count with me and having you to think of and see something of means a great deal. But there are things I have to look for outside where there are no family memories for complication. You must come to be grateful to Kathleen for her ministrations[.] The closest criticism will discover no flaw in her kindness to me I am sure. We must all be a lot together when we can. She will press nothing of course—as she has pressed nothing. If I find myself almost a member of the Morrison family (in my entire detachment) the pressure has been all mine from the moment when both Kathleen and Ted together merely suggested that I come and live near them in Cambridge. They had forgotten the idea when I picked it up to decide me against going to live in New York. . . ."

Besides his defense of his relationship with Kay, Frost's letter contained good news concerning his recent negotiations with Henry Holt and Company, from whom, for a variety of reasons, he had lately been seriously disaffected.

In February 1938 economic difficulties in the Holt trade department were compounded by a power struggle between Holt's president, Richard H. Thornton, and its treasurer, Edward N. Bristol, who was seeking Thornton's removal. To put pressure on his adversary, Bristol urged a reduction in the monthly payments of $250 to Frost, which for several years had been given as a guaranteed advance against his royalties. Frost learned of the threat to Thornton's position, and since the level of his royalty earnings was such that there was no danger of his experiencing any real reduction in income, he went along with the reduction as a gesture of loyalty to the man who had championed his cause at Holt for the past ten years. But Thornton was unable to save himself, and by the fall of 1938, Frost was thoroughly disgusted with the firm.

"Whats eating me at the last moment," he confessed to Untermeyer in October, "is how to compose a tactful letter . . . to get a friendly release from Henry Holt and Co." The response of the Holt management was prompt and decisive. As intent as ever to keep Frost with the firm, T. J. Wilson, the acting president, hastened to inform him that Blue Ribbon Books wished to publish a cheap reprint edition of the forthcoming Holt book *Collected Poems of Robert Frost 1939*, from which Frost stood to reap a guaranteed advance of $2,000.

At the same time, Edward Bristol wrote to assure him that, contrary to the fears he had lately expressed, Holt had absolutely no intention of closing down the trade department of the company. "On the contrary," said Bristol, "we are seeking a man of enterprise to develop it from a source of annual loss of over $30,000 (the other branches prospering) to at least its pre-depression place. Otherwise we should not have been so firm in our response to your suggestion of withdrawing your books." He added: "I don't know what passed between you and Mr. Thornton when your monthly stipend was reduced from $250. Your royalty earnings by and large seemed to justify the larger sum, and we are of course ready to continue it until you would call for a change. It would, of course, make the future more certain if you cared to include your prose as well as poetry, so long as you are satisfied that we are doing our part well. Mr. Wilson is trying to see you personally shortly, and can arrange details in person. . . ."

Frost received from Wilson a concrete proposal: "If you will give us all your future books, whether in verse or in prose, for publication by us, we will pay you a royalty of twenty per cent of the published price on all copies sold. We will also pay you henceforth a royalty of twenty per cent of the published price on all copies sold of those books by you which we published prior to the present date, December 12, 1938. Furthermore, we will pay you, during the remainder of your lifetime, the sum of $300 monthly, until you consider such a payment an unfair burden to us. These monthly payments to you shall not be considered returnable to us under any circumstances. . . ."

Never before, as Frost well knew, had an author been offered so munificent a contract. The fifteen-percent royalty he had been receiving was unusually good. Twenty percent was unheard of.

It was the new head of Holt's trade department, William M. Sloane III, who detected a serious flaw in the agreements for Frost's new *Collected Poems*. Sloane was disturbed to find that Holt had agreed to permit Blue Ribbon Books to publish an edition textually identical to Holt's own, at a list price only about a third of that of the Holt edition. Considering this a situation likely to damage sales of Holt's volume, Sloane asked Frost, in their first meeting, if he would be willing to write a special preface to be added to the *Collected Poems* Holt was bringing out, to distinguish it from the cheaper edition.

Because he saw the validity of Sloane's argument, but more because he liked this young man who wrote books himself and loved classical literature, Frost put aside his long-standing aversion to writing to order. Within three weeks he had completed a 1,500-word preface, a highly compressed, richly metaphorical essay on the art of poetry, "The Figure a Poem Makes."

He began with a discussion that reflected his continuing interest in the relationship of the sound of a poem to the sense the sound conveys. The object in writing poetry, he asserted, "is to make all poems sound as different as possible from each other," but the "greatest help towards variety" lies less in what the poet does with his words than in what he does with his "meaning," his "subject matter." In our language, Frost said, the poet has but two meters to choose from, "strict iambic and loose iambic," but the "possibilities for tune from the dramatic tones of meaning struck across the rigidity of a limited meter are endless." Beyond the sound of a poem, there is its quality of "wildness" to consider, but the wildness must be pure, the poet must be "wild with nothing to be wild about." "Just as the first mystery was how a poem could have a tune in such a straightness as meter, so the second mystery is how a poem can have wildness and at the same time a subject that shall be fulfilled." He, then, described the "figure a poem makes":

"It begins in delight and ends in wisdom. The figure is the same as for love. No one can really hold that the ecstasy should be static and stand still in one place. It begins in delight, it inclines to the impulse, it assumes direction with the first line laid down, it runs a course of lucky events, and ends in a clarification of life—not necessarily a great clarification, such as sects and cults are founded on, but in a momentary stay against confusion. . . ."

Frost was pleased with the piece, and particularly so by the success with which he had adapted ideas about wildness and love—important private concerns of the moment—to the needs of an essay on poetry. As he was putting the finishing touches on it, in January of 1939, he was further pleased by the arrival of a letter from the National Institute of Arts and Letters, informing him he had just been awarded the institute's gold medal, for "distinguished work in poetry." The writer extended an invitation to the annual dinner in New York on January eighteenth, at which time the institute would formally present the award.

Frost had planned to leave for Florida well before the dinner in question, and he had undertaken lecture obligations in the South. But the medal, awarded only twice before for poetry, was worth a special trip back to New York; and he cheerfully made plans to go there after a speaking engagement in Richmond, Virginia. On the evening of the eighteenth, after accepting the medal, he addressed the membership of the organization and chose to speak on a subject that was both a personal favorite and appropriate to the occasion:

" 'Have you ever thought about rewards,' I was asked lately in a tone of fear for me that I might not have thought at my age. I don't know what I was supposed to think, unless it was that the greatest reward of all was self-esteem. Saints, like John Bunyan, are all right in jail if they are sure of their truth and sincerity. But, so, also, are many criminals. The great trouble is to be sure. A stuffed shirt is the opposite of a criminal. He cares not what he thinks of himself so long as the world continues to think well of him. The sensible and healthy live somewhere between self-approval and the approval of society. They make their adjustment without too much talk of compromise.

"Still an artist, however well he may fare, within and without, must often feel he has to rely too heavily on self-appraisal for comfort. For twenty years the world neglected him; then for twenty years it entreated him kindly. He has to take the responsibility of deciding when the world was wrong. He can't help wishing there was some third more disinterested party, such as God, or Time, to give absolute judgment. . . .

"The scientist seems to have the advantage of him in a court of larger appeal. A planet is perturbed in its orbit. The scientist stakes his reputation on the perturber's being found at a certain point in the sky at a certain time of night. All telescopes are turned that way, and sure enough, there the perturber is as bright as a button. The scientist knows he is good without being told. He has a mind and he has instruments, the extensions of mind that fit closely into the nature of the Universe. It is the same when an engineer has plotted two shafts to meet under the middle of a mountain and make a tunnel. The shafts approach each other; the workmen in one can hear the pickaxes of the workmen in the other. A sudden gleam of pickaxe breaks through. A human face shows in the face of the rock. The engineer is justified of his figures. He knows he has a mind. It has fitted into the nature of the Universe."

The artist, he said, concluding his remarks, must look elsewhere for proof of his excellence:

"I should be sorry to concede the artist has no such recourse to tests of certainty at all. His hope must be that his work will prove to have fitted into the nature of people. Beyond my belief in myself, beyond another's critical opinion of me, lies this. I should like to have it that your medal is a token of my having fitted, not into the nature of the Universe, but in some small way, at least, into the nature of Americans—into their affections, is perhaps what I mean. I trust you will be willing to indulge me here and let me have it so for the occasion. But whatever the medal may or may not symbolize, I take it as a very great honor."

Immediately following the institute dinner, Frost boarded a train for Key West, Florida, where he was joined after several days by the Morrisons. They stayed at the hotel where Frost had stayed during previous trips to the island, slept late, took long walks around the picturesque town, and played tennis with Mrs. Ernest Hemingway, whose husband was then in Havana. Returning to the mainland, they spent a second week visiting their mutual friend of Bread Loaf summers, Hervey Allen.

A highly successful novel, *Anthony Adverse,* had enabled Allen to build a good-sized estate in Coconut Grove, and the property had on it a number of prefabricated houses in which Allen's guests stayed. The addition of Frost and the Morrisons to the two couples already there put a considerable strain on the hospitality the Allens could provide. That, however, was nothing compared to the strain Frost himself felt. By the time the Morrisons left him and returned to Cambridge, he was tense and exhausted. "There is nothing much new about me," he wrote Lesley on February third, "except that I came through the two weeks with the Morrisons pretty well considering all there was on all sides to dissemble. I am alone now in a rather desolated house. The plan of my well-wishers is to ship me off for a few days' change to Cuba in the company of Mr and Mrs Paul Engel who are my neighbors in another of the Allen houses."

Compounding the tensions that grew out of his relationship with Kay were Frost's concerns for Carol and his family, who had also come down to Florida. Carol was planning to buy a house and settle permanently somewhere in southern Florida, hoping thereby to break out of the pattern of failure and dependency on his father. Frost knew well that Carol's problems were more psychological than economic, but he was powerless to do much more than observe the way in which Carol seemed to flirt constantly with self-destruction.

Worried over Carol, Frost could not help thinking once again of the way in which he had seemingly damaged his children. Exposed from their earliest years to the high-strung personality of their father, all had developed personalities that were also high-strung. Beyond that, they all had been obliged to live with the heavy burden of a father whose fame and success they could scarcely hope to duplicate. Marjorie, Irma, Carol, and Lesley had all tried or were trying to express themselves through art, but even Lesley, the strongest of his children, seemed unable to break free of his unintended domination. "It is as if I was always present when you wrote," he told her, alluding to the children's stories she had recently seen through publication. "You have me to get over."

He finally managed to assuage his sense of guilt by reminding himself—and Lesley—that if his children were unhappy, he was too. "Me—," he complained, "I am miserable living round with people all the time. I have always had hours and days to myself alone. I feel on draught from dawn to dark. It can't last. I have no idea how it is going to be stopped though. Not as yet. My entanglement has had critical moments when it looked near openly declared trouble. The future of Europe is easier for me to see into than my own future. . . ."

Hervey Allen had quickly realized that his friend's spirits were disturbingly low, and he displayed just the right combination of wit, wisdom, and commiseration to give Frost some comfort amidst the problems that beset him. According to Frost's later account, Allen was:

". . . the same old historical philosopher as of old only more so. He has many figures, parallels, and ancient and modern instances. To show his sympathy with me he says he hates to see one of the most powerful engines of the country wracking itself to pieces from running wild after the loss of its fly wheel: also I remind him of a big steam boat with all its lights ablaze and the band on it playing as it passes Goat Island toward the roar of Niagara Falls. I, who never sang played read or wrote a note of music have learned for consolation to play on a 'recorder' by ear entirely the whole of The Linden Tree and Wanita. What is to become of me? Will I end up on the concert platform? That is for my friends and well-wishers to puzzle out. I am past feeling that it is any concern of mine."

Continuing the account, which was contained in a letter to Louis Untermeyer, sent on February 17, 1939, Frost reported he had just received word of the publication of his new book, *Collected Poems*: ". . . I got a telegram partly in Latin from the Holts yesterday saying it was their pride to let me know that my latest book was that day on the market. The Latin gave me a stir that I never expected to have again in this world from publication. . . ."

Modesty prevented Frost from repeating the text of the telegram, but it had indeed been a moving tribute from William Sloane. "You have erected a monument more lasting than bronze," went Sloane's adaptation of Horace. Next day, Frost thanked his publisher, and added significantly, "I am happy to be in your hands."

35

PROPERTIES IN
VERMONT AND FLORIDA

(1939–1940)

As SOON as he was back in Boston, Robert Frost began preparing for a series of five lectures in Lawrence, Massachusetts, given the general title "A Prospective Anthology of British and American Verse." He was still so downcast by personal frustrations, however, that when he gathered his thoughts toward the first lecture, on March second, "The Success of a Single Poem," he found himself reflecting with some bitterness that for all the success of his own poems, his private life had little of what might be called success.

How successful Carol and his family were, Frost had summed up in his last letter to Lesley: "They are not lucky so far in life. They catch no fish." Irma and John Cone caught no fish either. Despite John's growing success as an architect, Irma seemed to find married life excruciatingly difficult, and in recent months she had been subject to an increasing number of emotional and physical disorders. Lesley, divorced and with two young daughters, was trying to succeed as a teacher at a private school in Washington, D.C., but she was not immune from the Frost traits of extreme nervousness and irritability. And the discovery, among his papers, of a letter Elinor had sent to Lesley back in 1917 gave Frost a further opportunity to reflect on why the members of his family seemed to "catch no fish."

". . . Somehow mixed with my own recent mail," Frost wrote to Lesley after reading it, "I found this letter of Elinor's. I suppose you must have given it to me when I was away from my desks and files and I must have put it into one of my traveling bags with the confusion of letters and manuscript I always carry around. It belongs to your early days at Wellesley. My, my, what sorrow runs through all she wrote to you children. No wonder some thing of it overcasts my poetry if read aright. No matter how humorous I am[,] I am sad. I am a jester about sorrow. She colored my thinking from the first just as at the last she troubled my politics. It was no loss but a gain of course. She was not as original as I in thought but she dominated my art with the power of her character and nature. I wish I hadnt this woeful suspicion that toward the end she came to resent some thing in the life I had given her. . . . It seems to me now that she was cumulatively laying up against me the unsuccess of the children I had given her. She was a person of the soundest realistic judgement. But here I think she was radically wrong for once. She failed to see she wasn't giving you the time she patiently gave me. You are coming out all right in your way. Irma will come out all right too. . . . A way will be found to put Carol on his feet. You'll see. . . ."

The first Lawrence lecture was a pleasurable relief from family worries (and the audience did not have to be reminded it was in their town, fifty years before, that Frost had discovered his interest in reading and writing poetry). He began by assuring his listeners his talks would be informal, with no explicit criticism of the poets in question, but with a wide-ranging selection of the verse of such men as Collins, Emerson, Longfellow, Poe, Bryant, and Sill.

The format was a departure for him, he continued, because he was usually expected to read only his own verse. He would follow his usual practice of saying nothing against any poem or poet, but would let his selections indicate his preferences—for, as the title of the fourth lecture suggested, he considered "The Anthology as the Highest Form of Criticism." After lecturing on many poets, English and American, past and contemporary, he would return to his own verse, in a lecture entitled "If the Anthologist Includes His own Writing; with liberal quotation from his latest book."

Frost's humorous, mildly ironic platform manner delighted the Lawrence audience, and the series was a great local event. His Lawrence engagements, however, were spread out over a period of two months, and he interspersed with these, other lectures in Massachusetts, New York, New Jersey, and Pennsylvania. In early April he embarked on the major phase of his lecture season, traveling to the University of Iowa for a long visit he had postponed from the previous winter, before going on to other colleges in Wyoming and Colorado.

Arrangements for the Iowa lecture had been made by Norman Foerster, the director of the university's School of Letters, and the lecture was to begin at seven-thirty, in a room Foerster's colleagues had repeatedly warned was too small to accommodate the number of people likely to seek admission. By seven o'clock, the 300-seat Senate Chamber was nearly filled. By seven-fifteen, it was jammed. By seven-thirty, the stairs leading to the hall were so crowded Frost himself could not get in. Finally, with considerable difficulty, he made his way to the podium, only to be delayed further while an amplifier system was set up for the hundred or more students who had been unable to gain entry.

Forty-five minutes later he began his lecture, betraying no sign that the preliminary confusion had upset him. When it was over, he attended a party given in his honor at Foerster's home, and still he made no reference to the events of the evening. When, however, all the other guests had at last departed, Frost turned on Foerster and tore into him in a fury. "What the hell do you think I am," he demanded, "a rural schoolteacher that nobody wants to hear? Last week I talked to two thousand in Philadelphia, and they turned five hundred away!"

A more serious, though less dramatic, upset was occasioned by Paul Engle, who, though absent from Iowa City during the week of Frost's visit, had previously contributed a pair of poems, and a brief eulogy honoring his friend, to the April number of *American Prefaces,* the university's literary journal. The eulogy was beyond reproach, and the title-page poem, "Homage to Robert Frost," was good enough to win Frost's admiration for Engle's poetic gifts. But the second, longer poem, "For an Apple Grower," contained—to his shock and dismay—a lengthy, poeticized version of much he had said to Engle during their visits together in Gainesville not long before Elinor Frost's death and in South Shaftsbury not long after. Engle had obviously intended to honor both the Frosts when he wrote the poem, but it was hard for Frost to see it that way. What he did see was Engle's apparent intention to represent him as a doddering old man, tied to his past and with no discernible future. He made up his mind that Engle had turned against him—and once his mind was made up, he rarely (if ever) allowed it to be changed.

From Iowa City, Frost went directly to Laramie and the University of Wyoming. After attending a dinner in his honor on the night of April eighteenth and lecturing the following day, he went by train to the Central State Teachers College in Edmond, Oklahoma. By the time he arrived in Denver, Colorado, on the morning of April twenty-third, he was ill and worn out. Fortunately, his friend John Bartlett had heard in advance that Frost was to be in the vicinity, and he had written volunteering his services and his Boulder home while Frost was in the area.

During their drive together to Boulder, Frost and the Bartletts talked of all that had happened since they had last seen each other, in 1935. Almost at once the talk turned to Elinor's last years and death, and John and his wife, Margaret, unaware of the Engle incident at Iowa, were disturbed and saddened to see how painfully fresh these still were in Frost's mind. By afternoon his emotions were sufficiently under control for him to attend the honors convocation at the University of Colorado and receive an honorary degree, but his illness forced him to cut short his acceptance speech before he had really finished. Afterward, he retired to rest, and he was well enough by evening to perform again, longer and far better, at a dinner.

By prearrangement, Frost stayed that night at President George Norlin's home, but he moved in next day with the Bartletts and permitted John Bartlett to drive him back and forth to his other area engagements in Denver, Fort Collins, and Colorado Springs. Of these, the most important was his talk on April twenty-eighth in Colorado Springs, at the opening session of a conference on the fine arts, arranged by his English poet-friend, the director of the Rocky Mountain Writers' Conference, Edward Davison. After a warm introduction by Davison, Frost spoke on "The Trial by Market." His remarks were a further development of the ideas he had expressed at the January meeting of the National Institute of Arts and Letters.

On the last day of April, after visiting his old friend, the Denver poet Thomas Hornsby Ferril, Frost headed home, making several stops for more lectures along the way. When he arrived, safe but exhausted, at 88 Mt. Vernon Street, he found a letter waiting for him that was a demonstration of the affections of his friends at Harvard University. The writer was Harvard President James B. Conant:

"A group of men and women, calling themselves the 'Friends of Robert Frost,' have donated to the University a sum of money to provide for the creation for two years of the 'Ralph Waldo Emerson Fellowship in Poetry.' It is their hope and mine that you will be willing to accept appointment to this Fellowship for two years, beginning September 1, 1939. I have ventured to have this appointment made by the Corporation and sent to the Board of Overseers for confirmation next Monday. If you accept this appointment, you would be quite free to do whatever work you desired in the University during these two years. It was the hope of those who founded this Fellowship that after consultation with the Chairman of the English Department you might make arrangements for meeting groups of young men interested in poetry and possibly give a series of lectures if you so desire. From my own point of view, you are quite free to come and go as you wish and I only hope that you will enjoy this method of coming in contact with some of the students in the College who are interested in poetry. I am sure that you will have much to give them. . . ."

Frost's reaction to the Harvard invitation, which was the culmination of more than a year of work on the part of David McCord, Robert Hillyer, and others, was curiously unenthusiastic. Perhaps because he was exhausted from the rigors of his Western trip, perhaps because he and President Conant had not got along well during the Norton professorship in 1936, or perhaps because the break from Amherst had soured him on all college employment, Frost procrastinated for more than six weeks before sending his formal acceptance. When he finally did get around to drafting a letter to Conant, he did not try to conceal his misgivings about the appointment he was accepting.

While Frost was worrying over the details of his new job, he was also taking steps to find a happier place to spend his summers. The Morrisons, as they had informed Frost in the fall of 1938, had arranged to rent a farm between Bread Loaf and the nearby village of Ripton. The Homer Noble Farm, as it was known locally, was owned by the widowed Mrs. Noble. She also had for rent a cottage across the road from where she now lived in Ripton, an easy walk from the farm and the Bread Loaf campus; and Mrs. Noble provided dinner for summer guests. After some consideration, Frost decided to rent the cottage, and he made arrangements with Mrs. Noble to be included at her table when she served dinner.

On many occasions, however, he dined with the Morrisons at the farm, and the more he saw of it, the more he liked what he saw. He was impressed by the gently rolling land and, situated in the upper pasture, a hundred yards or more above the main farmhouse, its attractive little guest cabin. The entire farm was something more than 150 acres, surrounded on three sides by part of the vast Green Mountain National Forest. Frost had reason to believe Mrs. Noble was willing to sell her farm, and he decided early that if she were, he might well be willing to buy.

In Frost's plans for the Homer Noble Farm the Morrisons, of course, were central. He knew they were as fond of the farm as he was, and he doubted that either Kay or Ted would object to living in a house of which he was landlord. For compensation he would ask only the same rent the Morrisons were paying Mrs. Noble, and to be fed and looked after, mostly by Kay, while he made his own home in the three-room cabin. With considerable misgivings, but sensible of how much it would simplify their summer housing problem, the Morrisons agreed to join him, beginning next summer, in the arrangement he had in mind. When he spoke to Mrs. Noble about selling the place, he found she was willing to accept the figure he proposed.

The 1939 session of the Bread Loaf Writers' Conference began on August fifteenth, and Frost carried out his plan of the previous November by "teaming up" with Louis Untermeyer in classes on poetry criticism, four or five a week, for the two weeks of the conference.

Despite his unusually extensive participation in the teaching activities at Bread Loaf, Frost continued to doubt that the conference did much to improve the productions of would-be artists. He expressed his ambivalent views on the value of Bread Loaf in a preface, "The Doctrine of

Excursions," he had reluctantly agreed to write for the forthcoming *Bread Loaf Anthology,* a collection of previously unpublished poetry and prose.

"You who are as much concerned as I for the future of Bread Loaf," it began, "will agree with me that once in so often it should be redefined if it is to be kept from degenerating into a mere summer resort for routine education in English, or worse still for the encouragement of vain ambition in literature. We go there not for correction or improvement. No writer has ever been corrected into importance. Nor do we go to find a publisher or get help in finding a publisher. Bringing manuscript to Bread Loaf is in itself publication. . . ."

At the end of the conference Frost returned to Boston, rested for one month, and then, set out on a whirlwind lecture tour in which, by his own count, he "did fourteen lectures and travelled two thousand miles in fifteen days." When he returned he was exhausted, but he at once began preparing for his debut as Harvard's Emerson Fellow. His plans for his course in "Poetry" were revealed in an interview he gave before the first class meeting, in mid-November:

". . . Mr. Frost has not thrown in the sponge on his ideas that education should be a take-it-or-leave-it business instead of a day-after-day quizzing of boys with questions to which he already knew the answers.

"His belief is in an 'education by presence'—the stimulation of students to enterprise by the mere presence in their midst of men who have done things and have wide intellectual horizons.

"He will give marks, of a sort, but they will be secondary. Mr. Frost will do most of the talking, but if mere talking will not stir up some enterprise among his hearers, he will 'just keep silent, or even lie down on the desk until it is realized that what I want is self-starters, not followers of a set routine. . . .' "

Further developing the automotive metaphor, he said his objective was to help colleges become "factories for turning out human self-starters." The interview included Frost's thoughts on a variety of subjects, among them the world political situation in the wake of the recent German invasion of Poland:

"The world is swaying to the left and to the right. It is a drunken world, going home we know not where, but the important thing to realize is that it is not swaying too far to the left or too far to the right. . . .

"My life has been all holidays, whether it has been work or play. The secret? I say it is this: Never allow yourself to become a 'case' if you can help it; and never froth at the mouth about things.

"That's the trouble with too many people. They froth at the mouth because they're reading the same newspaper too much. They get all scared about what they think Germany's going to do. They get all worried about 'reds' in the country. They get frothed up about what's going to become of democracy. And all the time they forget that there are limitations to all things; that there always is a balance to everything. . . ."

Frost's notion that there was "a balance to everything" was strongly reminiscent of the Emersonian doctrine of compensation, and while thinking about his new job he may well have been rereading Emerson's essay on the subject. The interview concluded, however, with ideas that were pure Frost. Although the Harvard catalogue listed his course as "Poetry," he remarked: "I can talk politics under that heading. I'll tell the boys the world speaks to them and they have to answer back. I'll tell them always to have something to say or they will be on their way to become 'cases.' Say something to Hitler, to Chamberlain or to the drama, but say something—something with a kick in it."

The "Poetry" seminar, consisting of forty undergraduate and graduate students, met Thursday nights in the Upper Common Room of Adams House. Late in the semester, as Frost taught the closing weeks of his course, he was suffering from an increasingly painful and debilitating illness. The trouble had started in October. At first, he had dismissed it. Left untreated, however, it had continued to worsen, and by early December the pain was so intense that Frost did see a doctor, before taking to bed.

From the Morrison home on Walker Street, Cambridge (where Kay had put him up and engaged two nurses to help her give him full-time care), he dictated to Louis Untermeyer, on December thirteenth, an account of his condition: ". . . My disease I guess is accidia (Fr. acedie) contracted I fear from having tried to get too much meaning out of the word in a lecture . . . at the Grolier Club recently. It is closely related to acidosis, for which I am being treated by a doctor. He has a right to complain that I have held something back from him and not laid all my cards on the table. But accidia it really is. . . ."

Frost assumed Untermeyer would know what he meant by "accidia" (or "acedia," as properly spelled), a disease not of the body, but of the spirit—the symptoms of which, as first diagnosed in students, monks, and other medieval contemplatives (and as formulated by one modern scholar), were "a loss of faith, undue retreat into one's self, a sense of futility, and a paralyzing estrangement from God and man." In his Grolier Club talk, on November sixteenth, Frost had discussed "accidia" in a more secular sense, as the affliction he and other artists suffered in periods of "sullen lethargy" between spells of creative effort. "Loafing has a good deal to do with being an artist," he asserted. "No good writing [can be done] as a continuous stream. All writers who have struggled with ideas have suffered from these terrible lulls. It is called temperament."

The cure for acedia, traditionally, was hard and unremitting prayer. For Frost it was "honest work." With his own "accidia" complicated by acidosis, however, he was beginning to worry about what would happen in the event his illness kept him away from the income-producing lectures he had planned for the months ahead. Though the purchase of the Homer Noble Farm was well within his means, it did represent an expense. His intention to buy property in Florida would involve further outlays. Considering, also, his financial commitments to Carol, Irma, and the rest of his family, he began to realize that if he did not recover quickly, his funds would soon be dangerously low.

In the context of these worries over money and illness, the recent proposition of a man named Earle J. Bernheimer had begun to seem more attractive than it had at first. An avid collector, Bernheimer had since 1936 been sending Frost items from his collection, to be signed and returned. When the collector visited him at Bread Loaf in August 1939, however, their association had taken a new direction. Bernheimer was eager to discuss an item he did not possess, but coveted. It was the slender little volume called *Twilight*, which Frost had had privately printed in 1894 in an edition of two copies, only one of which survived.

Was there any possibility, Bernheimer inquired, that Frost might be willing to part with the precious volume? Frost said no; the book had been a gift to Elinor and, in a way, still belonged to her. If he parted with it at all, it must be to some college or university library where it would be safely and permanently preserved. With that, the conversation turned to other subjects.

A few days after Bernheimer's departure Frost received an interesting letter from the collector. ". . . Driving my car the long road home," Bernheimer wrote, "I thought many times of your conversation—especially of the volume of your poems titled 'Twilight'. I planned plans and thought of many things so that I might eventually own it. I hope you will not be perturbed when I bring up the subject again. . . ."

Away from the pressures and frictions of the Writers' Conference, Frost had found himself giving Bernheimer's offer more thought than he had first intended. Whatever the book had meant to Elinor, whatever it now meant to collectors like Bernheimer, *Twilight* for him had always been surrounded by intensely unpleasant associations. Why not, then, sell the book?

Thus, Frost answered Bernheimer's letter with a short one of his own: "I might not be able to refuse serious money for the unique Twilight, but it would have to be really serious money that would mean something to my family. You say what you think could be done. There may be merit in your suggestion that you could buy or lease the book with an agreement to leave it in the end to some person or institution by me designated."

Bernheimer arrived in Boston on January 6, 1940, and went directly to 88 Mt. Vernon Street. Frost, still ill with acidosis, at first talked only about the history of the volume. Finally, Bernheimer suggested they discuss figures. Frost knitted his brow and said he had four families to take care of (Marjorie's, Irma's, Carol's, and Lesley's); what would Bernheimer say to a thousand for each of them? Having come prepared to spend a good deal more for the volume—as Frost was prepared to take considerably less—the collector immediately agreed to the figure. He telephoned his business partner in Kansas City and instructed him to send Frost at once a check for $4,000. Then, receiving Frost's assurance that the volume, suitably inscribed, would soon be mailed to him, Bernheimer happily departed.

If Frost had any sense of triumph for having sold *Twilight,* he did not have long to enjoy it. The next night, while alone in his apartment, he suffered a violent gastroenteritic attack. Had he been left alone for long in this condition, the consequences might well have been grave. But by a fortunate coincidence, his friend the poet-psychiatrist Merrill Moore happened to call, and Frost's voice on the telephone was so strange that Moore rushed over at once. He found Frost almost unconscious and immediately ordered an ambulance, which took him to the emergency room of Massachusetts General Hospital.

By morning Frost had recovered considerably. The attack may have been brought on by intestinal flu, by food poisoning, or (most likely) as a reaction to sulfa drugs that had been prescribed for his cystitis. Whatever the cause, it had aggravated an already-present hemorrhoid condition, and surgery would have to be performed. After another day at the hospital, for observation, and one day more at the Morrisons' home, Frost re-entered Massachusetts General and underwent a hemorrhoidectomy.

The operation was successful, and within a few days Frost was well enough to begin joking about his condition and treatment. On January twelfth he supplemented the terse hospital reports on his condition with a "bulletin" of his own. "Mr. Frost," it went, "is resting on his laurels after a legal operation for asteroids at the hands of Dr. Henry Faxon."

Slowly regaining his strength after the operation, on February first he left Boston with Mrs. Morrison and her son, Bobby, to complete his recuperation in Key West. Kay, able to remain with him for only the first two weeks of his stay, had arranged to have Frost looked after for another month by his newly appointed "official biographer," Lawrance Thompson, who met him in Coconut Grove the day after Kay's departure from

Miami. On the morning of February seventeenth Frost rode back, with Thompson, in a hired limousine, for another few weeks in Key West, where they arrived after dark.

They enjoyed a leisurely dinner; then, Thompson left to unpack and Frost went to sit by the hotel's open fireplace. After a few minutes, a man in his early twenties came up and stood by the fire. "You're Robert Frost, aren't you?" he inquired. "Yes," Frost smiled, happy to be recognized in such an out-of-the-way place. "Who are you?" The young man said his name was Hyde Cox and added that he had attended Frost's Norton lectures at Harvard in 1936. Prompted by Frost's questions, he then explained what had brought him to Key West.

He had, he said, inherited from his grandfather enough money to make him financially independent. But after graduation from Harvard, he had decided to travel around the country, living on what he could earn by hawking newspapers on street corners and by other menial jobs. He craved this kind of experience as an antidote to his sheltered and bookish childhood, a need Frost understood perfectly. Cox had been on the road now for several months and planned to visit all forty-eight states before going home to New England.

Frost listened, fascinated. Curious to know more about this young man and wishing to help him in any way he could by sharing his own experiences, he took him for a long walk around the island and invited him for breakfast the next morning. As they talked that night and during several days and nights following, Frost took pleasure in discovering all he could about his new friend; and before Cox left Key West, Frost made him promise to call on him in Boston.

By the end of his first week in Key West after Kay's departure, Frost engaged in a practical joke that was designed to punish Kay for her apparent failure to write to him, as she had promised she would do. On February twenty-second Frost decided he had waited for Kay's first letter long enough and that retaliatory action was in order. He knew Kay had given Thompson instructions not to permit him to buy property while he was in Key West. He also knew, or at least suspected, she had told Thompson to telegraph her should Frost suffer a physical relapse or a serious emotional depression. Summoning Thompson, Frost instructed him to send Kay at once a telegram of only two words: "GETTING SERIOUS"—which she could take as referring to an impending purchase of real estate, or in any other way she liked.

Thompson did as he was told, and Frost awaited the results. If his intention was to cause Kay agonies of worry over what had happened to him, he could not have been disappointed. Not knowing if the apparent crisis in Florida was mental or physical, she telephoned doctors of the mind and body, in Boston and Miami, seeking advice and making contingency arrangements for treatment. She telegraphed Hervey Allen, to say the situation in Key West was out of hand, and telegraphed Thompson for further information. Finally, after a day of uncertainty, she received a telegram of explanation. Nothing was wrong with Frost. It had all been an unfortunate misunderstanding.

On February twenty-fourth, the day the flurry subsided, Hervey Allen appeared unexpectedly, with his friend Henry Seidel Canby. Happy to see Allen again, Frost was equally happy when Allen invited him back to Coconut Grove for another visit. On the twenty-sixth Frost, Thompson, Canby, and Allen drove together in Allen's car to the Florida mainland.

His telegram notwithstanding, Frost had failed to find a house to his liking in Key West, and he soon began scouting the neighborhood around Hervey Allen's estate. One lot he and Allen examined, belonging to a man named Paige, adjoined Allen's, but Paige was asking a steeper price than Frost was willing to pay. He continued his search elsewhere, without success. Finally, in mid-March, he announced it was time for him to go. Mrs. Morrison, he said, had made arrangements for him to lecture his way up the Atlantic coast, and he was expected to speak shortly at a women's club in Palm Beach.

To satisfy herself there was nothing wrong with Frost, Kay had also arranged for him to see a Palm Beach doctor named Waterman, before he subjected himself to the rigors of another series of lectures. Kay's fears were groundless, but Frost was too eager to return to his home and secretary to permit good health to delay him. After his return to Boston, he described to Louis Untermeyer the result of his examination:

". . . I was willing the doctors down in Florida (Dr Waterman to be precise) and the doctors up here (Dr Moore to be precise) should have me as sick as they pleased if it would get the prescription out of them that I wanted, namely, that I should 'go back north where I was born bred look to die.' I told Dr Watermans wife in his presence and hearing that he had better look out for me: I wasnt above using him merely to get out of work or get round a woman. She answered I would have to be a pretty smart man to get anything out of her husband that he didnt see me getting and intend me to get. I ventured to say I was a pretty smart man when I had been up awhile and was well awake. Well the result of our fencing was that my aches and pains were authenticated and I got my order to go North for my health instead of further South. Looking each other wickedly in the eyes we both laughed. . . ."

He wrote at the same time to Hervey Allen, with remarks relating to his real-estate plans in Coconut Grove:

". . . Soothing converse and time have brought me along till I begin to believe I may yet live to resemble my old self. But never mind if I dont. You and I won't care will we, please? All I need is a very few friends to set their hearts right on me just as I am without one plea. I refuse to be taken as promising. I have been all through that and I have had enough of it. It makes me sick in the nerves to be counted on for anything. Cheers for my moral improvement would start me down hill on the road to ruin. This time with you I began to be sure you understood. And I was encouraged to advance a step toward buying the Page acres. I dont see how we could hurt each other by being conterminous. Your neighborhood would give me pleasure. . . ."

The deal with Paige did not materialize, but in late April, with the help of a local real-estate agent, Allen found a five-acre tract of undeveloped pineland on Davis Road in South Miami, within a mile of his estate. It was available for purchase at $400 an acre, and Allen recommended it to Frost as the property he should buy. A month later, having rejected several other possibilities that arose, Frost informed Allen of his decision to buy, sight unseen, the property on Davis Road.

By mid-June, Frost and the Morrisons were installed at the Homer Noble Farm in Ripton, Vermont; and within a short time a pattern of living had been established there. Frost slept late and, rising, fixed himself a breakfast of raw egg, orange juice, and coffee or milk. Then, he worked for a few hours, awaiting the arrival of Mrs. Morrison, carrying a basket lunch. They talked or conducted whatever business needed to be done; and in midafternoon she returned to the farmhouse, leaving Frost to amuse himself with his garden, with a walk, with his chickens, or with training his new and remarkably intelligent companion, a Border collie he had given the name Gillie. Descending in late afternoon for dinner with the Morrison family, Frost, then, returned to his cabin with any guest who might be visiting, talking and walking until well past midnight.

Before the end of the summer, Frost increased his property holdings in Ripton by purchasing the thirty-seven-acre Euber farm, a mile through government land from his own, which commanded from its farmhouse a fine view of the Adirondack Mountains, to the west. The house was badly in need of repair, and Frost arranged for extensive renovations to be made so that the "U-Bar" could be used next summer by one of his friends. He was equally concerned with his Florida property, on which he hoped to have erected some kind of living quarters by the time he went South for his winter vacation.

THE END OF A SON'S LIFE

(1940–1941)

ROBERT FROST'S son, Carol, had from childhood been plagued by persistent fears and anxieties, which his parents, and later his wife, eventually came to recognize as symptoms of mental illness. His paranoia led him to suspect potential friends of seeking to take advantage of him, and he suspected strangers of plotting to spy on him—or worse. He refused to believe, at times, that even the closest members of his family loved him, and he found little to love in himself. Craving perfection, much as his father had done, he found that his achievements always fell far short of his expectations. When they did, frequently he was plunged into deep depression. What was most disturbing, he would often speak of taking his own life—not just to escape the demons that tormented him, but whenever he felt his life had attained "fulfillment."

Much in his son's troubled mind seemed to have no specific origin, but Frost believed he could trace the source of Carol's obsession with suicide. In June of 1911 the Frost family was living in Derry Village, New Hampshire, in a house owned by an affable young lawyer named Lester Russell. One day Russell was arrested for misusing funds that had been entrusted to him, and before he was taken to jail he drank enough arsenic to cause his death next day. Frost tried to comfort and reassure his children by telling them Russell's life had been a happy one, that it had reached a kind of fulfillment, and that God had called him home to heaven. But the children, in their play with neighborhood friends, soon heard the word "suicide," and gradually they picked up the details of how Lester Russell had killed himself. For nine-year-old Carol there seemed to be a curious problem in trying to correlate his father's word "fulfillment" and the other word, "suicide." Thereafter, at various turning points and crises in his life, he often spoke of committing suicide, when it seemed to him that he, too, had reached fulfillment.

The most recent episode of such talk, prior to 1940, had followed the death of Carol's mother, in 1938. When Elinor died Carol's grief was so intense he began to speak vehemently of suicide, until his wife, Lillian, feared that the son would not long survive the mother.

The two and a half years that had passed since Elinor's death had not been happy ones for Carol. He had tried to succeed at various business ventures, all centered on the farm in South Shaftsbury, but at none of them had he even reached the break-even point. Sinking deeper than ever into his delusions of persecution and into financial dependence on his father, he became increasingly morose and withdrawn, as he despaired of ever achieving the success he coveted for the sake of his wife and son. Frost had already begun to wonder if Carol would not eventually be better off, and safer, in a mental institution.

In the summer of 1940, Lillian Frost developed a condition that made a complete hysterectomy advisable in the near future. Carol's apprehensions for her safety were entirely reasonable. But as he continued to brood over the approaching operation, Carol became more and more obsessed by its obvious corollary: Lillian would never again be able to bear a child. Once again he began to speak of suicide.

Carol's talk so frightened Lillian that a few days before she entered the hospital in Pittsfield, Massachusetts, on October 1, 1940, she wrote to her father-in-law asking for help. Could Frost, she inquired, possibly spend a few days with Carol and Prescott when she underwent surgery? Frost immediately made arrangements to join his son and grandson as soon as he could leave Boston.

When he reached South Shaftsbury he was shocked by how completely Carol had slipped into the depths of a suicidal depression. For the next two or three days he listened to a litany of failures, fears, and frustrations. He reasoned, cajoled, and argued with his son, trying to make him give up the idea that he was a hopeless failure, that his life had reached fulfillment now that Lillian would never again have a child, that everyone would benefit if he were no longer alive. Carol's reasoning was so mired in confusion, however, Frost could not be sure his son even understood what he was saying and hearing. Finally, when he had exhausted all the arguments he could think of, Frost persuaded Carol to repeat to him the promise he had made to Lillian just a few days before: that under no circumstances, whatever he might wish to do, would he ever do more than talk about taking his own life.

Having visited Lillian on several successive days following her operation, and having spent an entire Saturday night in close conversation with his son, Frost was convinced the worst of their two very different crises had passed and that it was safe for him to leave. Carol's last sullen remark, "You always win an argument, don't you?" was disquieting, but seemed at least to indicate his grudging willingness to go on with life.

Two days later, however, Carol appeared in an agitated state in Lillian's hospital room and stayed just long enough to blurt out a few ill-connected remarks. One of them was that he was going to break two promises he had made.

Carol returned that night to his home and son in South Shaftsbury, and in the upstairs bedroom they shared in Lillian's absence, he began to talk to Prescott about suicide. Hours passed and more hours, until finally, when it was almost dawn, Prescott could stay awake no longer. As the boy slept, Carol went downstairs and loaded the rifle he had given Lillian as a wedding present seventeen years before. Some time later Prescott was startled from sleep by the sound of a shot. He ran downstairs, to find his father lying dead on the kitchen floor, the rifle by his side.

"I'm cursed. God, if I don't believe I'm cursed."—So the bereaved father had complained in Frost's early poem "Home Burial." When Prescott telephoned his grandfather on the morning of October ninth, Frost had reason enough to say the words anew. He had lost his favorite daughter, Marjorie, in 1934; his wife in 1938; and, now, his last surviving son. But too many people were depending on him—and too many plans needed to be made—for Frost to permit himself, as yet, the luxury of mourning in bitter solitude. By early afternoon of the same day, he was in South Shaftsbury making arrangements for a funeral and cremation, comforting Prescott, and planning the best way to break the tragic news to Lillian.

As for Prescott, Frost was pleased to learn that throughout his ordeal he had conducted himself with remarkable character for one so young. He had immediately telephoned the police, his grandfather, the family doctor; then, waited at home until the police came. Following the funeral, Frost wrote a letter to his grandson, praising him for having shown so much of the quality Frost had always valued most in life:

"Disaster brought out the heroic in you. You now know you have the courage and nerve for anything you may want or need to be, engineer, inventor or soldier. You would have had plenty of excuse if you had gone to pieces and run out of that house crying for help. From what Lesley reported to me of her talk with Lillian in Pittsfield Friday I judge you were in actual danger there alone with your unhappy father—unhappy to the point of madness. You kept your head and worked your faculties as coolly as a clock on a shelf. You've been tried more than most people are in a whole lifetime. Having said so much, I shan't bring up the subject again (for a long time anyway) either of your bravery or the terrible occasion for it. Let's think forward—I don't mean in big terms all at once, but just taking the days as they come along with a more natural and comfortable interest than I fear you have been permitted for some years past. . . . The spell you and Lillian have been under is broken. You and she can think with some sanity now. So can I with you. . . ."

At the same time, Frost wrote a letter to Lillian, which began with an assurance that she and her son could continue to count on him for support now that Carol was dead: "You're going to make it easy for me from now on by telling me always right straight out what you think best for yourself and Prescott and then if it is within my means and ability I will do it. I shan't have to guess so miserably any more. That is the great gain for me from our tragedy. I'll make suggestions if you want me to and I won't if you dont want me to. I suspect you will be making plans as you lie there in bed. But don't think you have to hurry. The immediate future is taken care of. . . ."

There was no use going over and over the circumstances surrounding Carol's death, but as Frost brooded alone in his Boston apartment, searching for the reasons his son had been driven to unreason, he found it impossible to avoid doing just that. Within three weeks he wrote to Louis Untermeyer expressing, more openly than he could to a member of his own family, his conscience-stricken sense of failure as a father:

"I took the wrong way with him. I tried many ways and every single one of them was wrong. Some thing in me is still asking for the chance to try one more. There's where the greatest pain is located. I am cut off too abruptly in my plans and efforts for his peace of mind. You'll say it ought not to have come about that I should have to think for him. He really did most of his thinking for himself. He thought too much. I doubt if he rested from thinking day or night in the last few years. Mine was just an added touch to his mind to see if I couldn't make him ease up on himself and take life and farming off-hand. I got humbled. Three weeks ago I was down at Merrills telling Lee [Simonson] how to live. Two weeks ago I was up at South Shaftsbury telling Carol how to live. Yesterday I was telling seven hundred Harvard freshmen how to live with books in college. Apparently nothing can stop us once we get going. I talk less and less however as if I knew what I was talking about. My manner will be intended to indicate henceforth that I acknowledge myself disqualified from giving counsel. Kay says I am not to give myself up. Well then I'll be brave about this failure as I have meant to be about my other failures before. But you'll know and Kay will know in what sense I say things now. . . .

"I failed to trick Carol or argue him into believing he was [in] the least successful. Thats what it came down to. He failed in farming and he failed in poetry (you may not have known). He was splendid with animals and little children. If only the emphasis could have been put on those. He should have lived with horses. . . ."

Heartbroken as he was, Frost was determined not to let Carol's death disrupt, as had the death of his wife, his normal activities. Only a week after the tragedy in South Shaftsbury he informed his publisher, William

Sloane, that he would have two books to offer him for publication in the coming year: one, a volume of prose that would be a selection of his previously published prefaces, talks, and essays; the other, a new volume of poetry. Frost worked so hard at putting together the new verse volume, after Carol's death, that by the time he was ready to leave for a visit to the University of Iowa in late October, he was able to tell Mrs. Morrison just where in his study she would find the completed manuscript should anything happen to prevent his return.

He came back refreshed and ready to take up his duties at Harvard for the second and last year of his Emerson fellowship. By Christmas 1940 he had gone so far toward regaining his equilibrium that he was able to send out to his friends and associates a Christmas poem asserting that, taken all in all, the forces of light still held a slight edge over the forces of darkness in the world. Against the dark backdrop of the Nazi advance across Europe, the title, "Our Hold on the Planet," had many levels of possible meaning.

On January 15, 1941, after dismissing his Harvard students at the end of his second course in "Poetry," Frost headed for Florida to direct the installation of the two prefabricated houses he had ordered from a firm in New England some months before. When he arrived at Hervey Allen's estate, however, he discovered that the houses had not yet been delivered, having been delayed in transit for reasons related to the heavy flow of war materials up and down the coast. He had, thus, to content himself with clearing unwanted palmettos from his property and planting the first young orange trees in what he hoped would someday be a grove. So, between gardening, relaxing, and visiting with Allen, just a short walk away, Frost spent his winter vacation at the Florida "farm" he had already decided to call Pencil Pines.

The delay in the erection of his prefabricated houses might have been more disappointing had Frost not decided, even before leaving for the South, to look for a new home in the North. The lease on his Mt. Vernon Street apartment was just about up when he concluded that, instead of renewing it, he would ask Mrs. Morrison to find him a house, with more room and with stairs front and back on which he could exercise by climbing and descending. By the time he came back to Boston, Kay had succeeded in finding him a place that perfectly suited his needs. It was an old, Victorian-style double house of three stories, in a quiet, residential neighborhood of Cambridge. After a two-week lecture trip to Texas, early in March, Frost moved to his new residence at 35 Brewster Street.

On the twenty-sixth of March, the day he celebrated his "sixty-sixth" birthday, Frost went to Washington, D.C., to visit with his daughter Lesley, to inspect an exhibition of his works that she had helped prepare in the Library of Congress, and to talk the following day in the Coolidge

Auditorium of the Library of Congress. The title he gave his talk was "The Role of a Poet in a Democracy."

His position, he began, was analogous to what "a good churchman" had once said regarding Jesus Christ: "Thou art the Way. / Hadst Thou been nothing but the goal, / I cannot say / If Thou hadst ever met my soul." Democracy as a way, he said, had always interested him more than democracy as an end in itself. He was not one to say, as some parents did of their children, that the more he loved it, the more he saw its faults. "Hell! You know. It's a lie to begin with—it's an affectation. And the more I love my country the *less* I've seen its faults, and I'm not ashamed to say it. It is the way; had it been nothing but the goal, democracy and I would probably never have met. I'm not far-seeing enough for goals."

The focus of his remarks was the truncated pyramid, with an eye at the apex, that appears on the great seal of the United States. It was a figure, he said, and "all figures—all figurative things in verse or prose—can be taken, probably, more than one way." The way he preferred to take it was as meaning "democracy would always mean refraining from power, beyond a certain point; that we would never in this country have anybody at the apex but God." That was why he so admired George Washington: because he had had the chance to seize power, but had refused to go beyond a certain point.

The Library of Congress talk did much to bring Frost into public notice as a commentator on the American political scene, a role to which he had increasingly aspired in recent years. He received further help and encouragement in that direction a few months later when President Conant invited him to stay on at Harvard for an extra year as Fellow in American Civilization—or, as the president described it, "a roving consultant in History and Literature." The annual stipend of $3,000 was half again as much as he had received in his Emerson fellowship, and the duties were no more rigorous. All he would have to do was make himself more or less regularly available in each of Harvard's seven houses, for "group discussions on American Civilization in the larger sense of the word." Frost cheerfully accepted Conant's invitation.

His first opportunity to speak on American civilization came little more than a month later. On the twentieth of June he delivered to the Phi Beta Kappa Society at Harvard a new poem on which he had been working, irregularly, since 1935. It was called "The Lesson for Today," and in it Frost took a stand—in his half-joking, half-serious way—against those poets and prophets of doom who were suggesting that the world was, beyond question, passing through the darkest age in human history. Such people, Frost said, were off the mark. First, it was impossible for them to judge how bad the times really were, without the perspective of hundreds of years of ensuing history. Second, in their condemnation of human suffering and adversity, they failed to realize that "The ground-work of all faith is human woe."

Frost was inclined to scoff at those who shed "literary tears" over the fact that they, the nation, the human race—even, the earth itself—were "doomed to broken-off careers." The epitaph that Frost would choose to be remembered by would be no more bitter than the single line: "I had a lover's quarrel with the world."

After his Harvard appearance Frost returned to Ripton, where Lillian and Prescott were spending part of the summer. With Frost's assistance and encouragement, both Lillian and her son had emerged as successfully from the dark period of Carol's death as Frost himself had done. But there was still one more duty to be performed before they could feel that the whole sad business was behind them. Carol's ashes, as well as Elinor's, were still in the possession of the Bennington undertaker where they had been since Carol's cremation. Interment had yet to take place.

Some months before, Frost had purchased a large plot in the cemetery of Old Bennington's First Congregational Church, for use as the Frost burial ground. He had also arranged for several stones to be made that would bear the names of all the Frosts, including those already buried elsewhere, and his own.

In September he learned that the stones had been delivered to the cemetery and that two recesses had been prepared, to receive the urns of Carol and his mother. He completed arrangements with the minister of the church and set a time for the interment. As they entered the churchyard at the appointed hour, they caught a glimpse of the minister talking to a parishioner. They walked on to the gravesite to await his arrival. Ten minutes passed, then twenty, then thirty. Thinking the minister was for some reason deliberately ignoring them, Frost became increasingly furious—until, at last, he decided they had waited long enough. "We don't need any help to do what we came here for," he said to Lillian and Prescott. He instructed his grandson to place Carol's urn in the space that had been prepared for it. He did the same with the long-unburied urn of his wife. As they watched, two workmen who were standing by came forward and set the stones in place. Then, the three Frosts turned and walked away.

37

WAR, A BOOK,
A POST AT DARTMOUTH

(1941–1943)

THE EUROPEAN war that had begun in the fall of 1939 was two years old
when Robert Frost began his third consecutive year at Harvard, as its
Fellow in American Civilization. Thus far, the United States had managed to stay out of the fighting, and many at home were content that
America should continue to isolate itself from the conflagration abroad,
whatever the consequences. Frost was not one of these. He was willing to
see his country go to war. He needed, however, a better reason for doing
so than merely the salvation of Great Britain.

"Our seaboard sentimentalists think of nothing but saving England,"
he wrote to Willard Fraser in November 1941. "Some of them would go
so far as to sacrifice America to save England. They are the Anglophiles
with an English accent. One of the seven colleges of Harvard is presided
over by such a patriot. Only one. But there are more who act and talk
from a fear that to save America we must save England. I brush all this
aside. We are able to fight and we are not afraid to fight. My only doubt is
whether we need to join in Englands fight. I should like it better if we had
it all to ourselves so the issue would be something I could understand and
if we won we would get the loot the glory and the self-realization. That
last is the great thing. I dont want to see a lot of bloody trouble unless we
are going to bring America out a nation more distinct from all other
nations than she is already. . . . I am not much worked up over politics.
There are some people round I cant bear to listen to—thats all that ails
me. I heard two commencement addresses the argument of which was
that this was a war to make the world safe for Shakespeare. The
Athenians might have made the rhetorical claim that the object of their
war with Sparta was to make the world safe for Thucidides and
Sophocles. They lost to Sparta, but the great dramatists were still the
great dramatists over and above the conflicts of politics and nations.
Theres where the only peaceful brotherhood of man will ever be, above

opinions and parliaments in the real[m] of music poetry science and philosophy. Religion ought to be included in my list and might be if it would only behave religiously and cease to try to pray God in on one side or the other. Men should be able to kill each other in settling differences of opinion, but at the same time recite and sing to each other the same poems and songs of international greatness. . . ."

Lest his son-in-law conclude from his remarks that he was hoping for the defeat of England, Frost added a postscript to help clarify his position:

"I dont know whether I made it clear in all the foregoing that my international politics were in no way hostile to England. I admire England beyond any great power since Rome. Benny DeVoto goes round saying he wishes the war was over so we could go back to hating England. He means twisting the Lions tail. I have never been a Lions-tail-twister. I am for the moment impatient with the mighty nation that it should be crying baby to us to come and save it again. I wish it would try to keep my admiration by winning its own war: or else get clear off the field and out of our way so we could win the war not for England but for ourselves."

On December 5, 1941, Frost went to Williamsburg, Virginia, to serve as the Phi Beta Kappa poet at the annual meeting of the society's mother chapter at the College of William and Mary. He read three short poems he had written over a period of many years. The earliest, "To a Moth Seen in Winter," dated from the turn of the century, and the latest, "Time Out," had been written within the past three or four years. The third poem, written around 1935, had like the other two never before been given to the public. Unlike the others, however, its theme was clearly historical, in a way that no poem of his had been since his first poetic composition, "La Noche Triste," back in 1890. He called it "The Gift Outright," and in it he celebrated the process by which America had ceased to be merely a group of English colonies and had begun to take shape as a nation in its own right.

Two days after Frost's Williamsburg visit, the Japanese attacked Pearl Harbor and thrust the United States overnight into active participation in the Second World War. In his excited reaction to the declaration of war, Frost bitterly blamed President Roosevelt for getting the United States into a fight for which the country was not adequately prepared. Even more bitterly, he accused England of starting something she could not finish—and, then, appealing to America for help. He despised the way in which Prime Minister Churchill had come to America to tell how it could be of help, and he saw the whole thing as connected with America's insistence on commercial expansion into parts of the Pacific where it did not belong. But whatever or whoever the cause or culprit, Frost felt sure the outbreak of war was likely to result in the serious curtailment of his lecture schedule, upon which he greatly depended to help provide an income for his financial outlays to his family and for his farm.

Fortunately, relief was available in the form of an unusual arrangement he had recently entered into with Earle J. Bernheimer, the collector who had purchased the unique copy of *Twilight* just a year ago. Back in June, Frost had sent Bernheimer a proposal: "I am rather in need of about two thousand dollars right now and would like to sell you two of my most valuable manuscripts at one thousand dollars apiece. One would be the original manuscript of my only full length play to date ['The Guardeen'] with all its emendations crude upon it. The other would be the Robinson preface [to *King Jasper*]. I thought perhaps your interest in collecting me would go to this length. . . ."

There was little that Bernheimer would not have done to please Frost or to improve his own collection, but $2,000 for those particular items seemed a steep price. He had, moreover, become enmeshed in a legal quarrel that for the moment made such an outlay next to impossible. He replied, therefore, by offering Frost a loan of $1,000, to be canceled in the near future by the "purchase" of literary manuscripts such as those Frost had already offered. Then, Bernheimer requested a personal interview with Frost.

They met in Ripton on July twenty-eighth. Frost's manner was so cordial Bernheimer made bold to suggest an arrangement with the poet that would be mutually profitable. Bernheimer would take the two manuscripts and would give Frost the $1,000 of his counteroffer. But he was willing to go further. In return for whatever literary documents or anything else Frost felt he could spare, with whatever personal signature or inscription he might choose to add, Bernheimer would quietly and regularly send him a monthly check for $150, until such time as one or the other of them saw fit to terminate the arrangement.

Frost had scarcely believed the collector would be willing to relieve him, so handsomely, of materials he would otherwise have merely stored or destroyed. He accepted Bernheimer's proposal and sent him off to await the first bundle.

Much as Bernheimer's checks were a comfort to Frost, they did not remove his deep fear that, because of the war, his old age would be marked by the same kind of want he had known earlier in his life. The new book he was working on, he believed, contained some of his best poetry; but what would that matter, from the standpoint of financial worries, if the war made money even tighter than it already was? Frost's fears continued to build, until Kay Morrison decided to reveal them to William Sloane at Holt, in the hope he might be able to reassure the poet. Sloane responded early in January 1942:

". . . Kay tells me that you are worried about the situation as regards the way it may effect the reception of this book. . . . I believe that the next months are going to see an intensification of the better kind of patriotism in this country, a renewal of the average American's love for the things which are distinctly his own. Your poetry is one of those things, and I do not believe that in the case of this book of all others the situation is going to prove unfavorable. Of course heavier taxes will mean less luxury money, and books are to a certain extent luxuries; but I think this will be more than offset by the other tendency which I have mentioned. We are planning our sales campaign so as to secure an *advance* sale of 7500 copies of THE WITNESS TREE if we can, and I can see no reason why we cannot. . . ."

Under the circumstances, Frost could hardly have wished for a stronger vote of confidence from his publisher. The size of the anticipated advance sale was scarcely smaller than it would have been if there had been no war at all. But whether such confidence was justified remained to be seen.

In the early weeks of America's involvement in the war, a personal crisis of unclear nature, but apparent major seriousness, threw him into a depression deep enough for him to toy—though, surely, no more than toy—with the idea of committing suicide. The mood soon passed, and in a few days he returned to business as usual—at least outwardly.

After attending a P.E.N. Society banquet in his honor on the night of January 20, 1942, he headed for Florida to inspect his newly erected prefabricated houses and to await the arrival of Mrs. Morrison. Frost living in a small rented cottage on Ohio Street in Coconut Grove, and Kay in a boardinghouse nearby, the poet and his secretary were presently hard at work furnishing, planting trees, and otherwise improving his future winter headquarters.

"We've brought the two small houses on a little way further," he reported to Lesley in February; "we've had three and five weeks in them and now leave them to our neighborly neighbors the Hjorts to keep an eye on till we come back next year. . . . The three-room house is already almost too pretty to abandon. The two room house exactly twenty five feet across a grassy and flowery court from it is comfortable and convenient. The three-room is to have an open fireplace soon. The two room has a small woodstove against the blue northers. . . ."

Mrs. Morrison left Florida for Cambridge on the twenty-fifth of February, and Frost remained behind to fulfill a few lecture commitments in the South. A summer cold, however, soon forced him to return to South Miami for a few days, before starting North once again.

Shortly after he came home to 35 Brewster Street, Mrs. Morrison showed him an article by Carl Sandburg in the March issue of *The Atlantic Monthly*. The aging poet whom Frost had long since decided was one of his major rivals had taken issue with Frost's recently quoted statement that he would as soon write free verse as play tennis with the net down. Without mentioning Frost by name, Sandburg had written what amounted to a self-defense, as well as a defense of free verse against its detractors. Frost's reaction was as full of sarcasm as the Sandburg remarks that had prompted it. In a letter to Lawrance Thompson he wrote: ". . . Kathleen says I am challenged to single combat by Carl Sandburg in an article in the Atlantic for March. His works prove you can play tennis more imaginatively with the net down, or so he maintains. He suspects me of having meant him in my witticism: and merely incidentally to his patriotic campaign to help Archie [Mac-Leish] save the country he rushes to the defense of himself as an American poet. Sauve qui peut (sp.) It is something if he saves one poet in the general wreck. . . ."

Though Frost always found some excuse to mock poets who, like Sandburg, presented what seemed to him a threat to his literary reputation, he was often willing to do what he could to help a young and promising writer. One such was the subject of a letter Frost sent to William Sloane on the occasion of his own so-called sixty-seventh birthday, on March twenty-sixth:

"I'm sending you separately some poems I have had on my mind on my conscience and on the shelf for too long a time. I didn't write them. But I like them rather well though not nearly as well as I like the fellow who did write them. He is the interesting Iowa farmer I may have spoken to you about. Many of us are his admiring friends including the Iowan Vice president of the United States [Henry Wallace]. His name is James Hurst [Hearst] and it is already known for one volume of verse (Prairie Press publishers) that went throug[h] an edition. The story that goes with him helps sell the verse. He is partly paralized from a diving accident and only holds up his end with his brother farming a big Iowa farm by virtue of what he can do with the big machinery once he is lifted into his seat by someone else. His brother has devoted himself to giving him a share in the farm life and has stayed unmarried, I suspect, at a sacrifice. They are a noted pair. Their farm is one of the best in Iowa. I tell you all this for obvious reasons. And I might add that I have wondered if Henry Wallace mightnt be induced to go on the jacket of his book with the idea of bringing Hurst out of his regional existance into a national. Now you've got all the elements, you can be left to judge for yourself. Only please deliver judgement quickly—Hurst mustnt be kept waiting cruelly long. Mind you I am not pressing. Some of the poems I like well. Maybe the book would gain by the elimination of the poems that echo Spoon River."

Within a month Frost's interest in the careers of young poets was pushed into the background by the appearance of his own book, *A Witness Tree,* his first collection of new verse since 1936. Dedicated "TO K. M. / FOR HER PART IN IT," *A Witness Tree* contained forty-two poems grouped in five sections, with two introductory poems that gave readers to understand just what Frost meant to imply by the book's title. The first introductory poem, called "Beech," Frost fancifully attributed to "The Moodie Forester" (Moodie having been, of course, his mother's maiden name), and in it he provided essential clues for understanding the symbolic levels of the witness-tree metaphor that governed the organization of the entire book.

Having evoked the simplest secular dimension of the witness tree, as the scarred-trunk-and-iron-stake marker identifying the corner of a piece of country property (in this case the Homer Noble Farm), and the symbolic dimension of the tree, as marker between the poet's finite, troubled inner world and the only-less-chaotic world around him, Frost added a second tree poem he borrowed from *The New England Primer* —to which he added his own title, "Sycamore." Here, the witness tree became not a marker, but a vantage point—from which to see beyond the finite world to the infinite, God.

With these two poems, Frost established for his readers the notion that the others that followed were themselves, taken separately and as a whole, a kind of witness tree—demarcating the secular and spiritual boundaries of the poet's life and times. It was an ambitious design; yet, he felt it was fully justified by the poems he had chosen to include.

The first of the book's five sections, after the two introductory poems, was called "One or Two," and it included fourteen poems (beginning with "The Silken Tent"), each of which contributed a different perspective to the question implied by the section's title. The second grouping, "Two or More," began with "The Gift Outright" and contained five poems, including "Triple Bronze," "Our Hold on the Planet," and "The Lesson for Today." Next was "Time Out," with eight poems, including "To a Moth Seen in Winter," "A Considerable Speck," "November," and "It Is Almost the Year Two Thousand."

In "Quantula," the next section, Frost grouped nine short poems, ranging from the gnomic couplet "The Secret Sits" to two eight-line ventures into political commentary, "An Equalizer" and "A Semi-Revolution." As much as any poem in the collection, "A Semi-Revolution" was linked thematically to the second of the introductory poems, "Sycamore." Throughout his life, Frost consistently scoffed at the notions of social planners who believed imperfection could be legislated out of existence. For him, there was only one "salve," and it was the same "Secret" who sat in the middle and knew: God. But only one who, like

Frost, had climbed the tree "our Lord to see" would know that. All others must endlessly "dance round in a ring and suppose," spinning out one theory after another to repair what it was God's pleasure to set asunder.

The last section, entitled "Over Back," began with a poem linked even more closely to "Beech" than "A Semi-Revolution" was linked to "Syca-more." Entitled "Trespass," it concerned one who had chosen to ignore the message of the speaker's witness tree. Five poems more and the book was complete.

By mid-June sales stood at 10,000 copies. Informing Frost of the great success of *A Witness Tree,* William Sloane added that he had decided to let Louis Untermeyer go ahead with a project he had proposed some time ago, a selection of Frost's poems especially designed for young and new readers. And at Holt, Sloane's plans included the soon-to-be-published *Fire and Ice: The Art and Thought of Robert Frost,* written by Lawrance Thompson, the first full-length study devoted not to Frost the man, but to his poetry.

So much excitement gave Frost a feeling of elation as great as the misgiving he had once felt for the success of *A Witness Tree.* He did not conceal his enthusiasm when he wrote to Sloane on the sixteenth of June: "Really ten thousand in less than two months beats everything. . . . You were right about publishing this Spring and we are glad you stuck to it—war or no war. . . ."

The success of *A Witness Tree* freed Frost from enough of his anxiety, over how the war would affect his career, to permit him to regard the war effort with far less cynicism than before. By the late summer of 1942, he was willing to admit to Thompson, who had recently been commissioned an officer in the Navy, that the British were "all right as allies," though he could not resist qualifying that statement with the wry observation, "You have to take comfort from any animal heat you can snuggle up to in a cold storm." He was even willing to express limited praise for the third major partner in the anti-Axis alliance, the Russians.

Many of Frost's fellow artists, Louis Untermeyer, Archibald MacLeish, and Carl Sandburg among them, had decided to turn their own views on the war to useful purpose by joining in the propaganda efforts of the Office of War Information. Untermeyer, in particular, wanted—and, even, expected—Frost to do likewise. But Frost, aware of what an artist lost by yoking himself to any official line of reasoning, flatly rejected all invitations to hurl his words and thoughts as weapons against Japan or Nazi Germany. In a letter to Lesley a few days before Christmas 1942, he wrote:

". . . Once you start reasoning you never know where you will end up.

"That's why I refrain from reasoning too much about the Germans. . . . Why are we at war? The best construction I can put on it is that we and the British have a property and a position the Germans would give anything to get away from us: and that we arent fools enough to let them. The position and the airs of easy assurance that go with it are even more enviable than the property. They would fain try how it feels to sit on top of the world—recline on top of the world. It gives beautiful the manners of the non-upstart and non-climber. Well if I dont look out I'll be writing a primer myself. Whence the Natziism? That grows naturally and swiftly out of the desperation of what the poor fools are attempting against a world roused from peace and comfort to meet them in arms. Louis now speaks with the official We. He says We expect the war to last about another year. I am only too willing to have them proved right. I wonder how much of a soldier Prescott will have been made into by then. I'm glad he got in in time to choose his service. . . ."

Prescott Frost, just turned eighteen, had chosen to enlist on December 7, 1942, in the Army. But in mid-January 1943, a few weeks after arriving in Colorado for basic training, Prescott was overtaken by a serious illness, the details of which arrived in Cambridge only after the worst of the crisis had passed. By late January, Frost had heard enough of Prescott's improving health from Lillian, from Lesley, and from Prescott himself to be fully satisfied his grandson, though still weak from the effects of his illness, was out of all danger. He saw no reason, therefore, to delay further his departure for Florida, where he planned to spend the month of February at his five-acre "farm," gardening, relaxing, and writing. A few days after his arrival, he interrupted his activities long enough to write a letter to the grandson with whom he had communicated mainly through Lillian since the boy left home for basic training:

". . . I have n't heard from your mother for a week or so. When I do I hope it will be with good news about your health. The last was that you were up around and all right. I suppose the sulphur medicine may take longer to recover from than the pneumonia.

"I am down here again for the old climate. *My* exact address is Route 2 Coconut Grove Florida[.] I shall stay for about four weeks and Kathleen will keep me company most of the time. . . . The sun is warm here this year. I am getting more summer heat this winter in Florida than I got all summer in Vermont.

"Speaking of Vermont, I wonder if you have noticed the Govt report that Texas and Vermont lead all the states of the Union in percentage of enlistments. Your state is a proud little state to belong to. I wonder if the explanation isnt that Texas and Vermont were once nations by them-selves, won their own independence, and had each a flag of its own—a national flag not just a state flag. A history like that is bound to linger in the minds of its people and show itself in their character. That winter we all lived in Texas I heard plenty of proud talk about the state. When I told a Texan I thought Vermonters hated the idea of Govt relief, he said Texans were the same. Absolutely no one at first would volunteer to go on relief and a posse had to be organized to run some one down to be the first victim of Govt paternalism. Massachusetts is pretty well up on the roster and so is my birth state California. It surprises me to see states like Virginia and South Carolina once so warlike (in '61) now away down. New Hampshire was next below Vermont. . . ."

Prescott presently answered, announcing that he was about to begin a furlough home to South Shaftsbury. He hoped he would somehow be able to see his grandfather. He realized, however, that that would be next to impossible. Disappointed, Frost confirmed the bad news, in a letter addressed jointly to Lillian and her son:

"I am sorry sorry the furlough comes so soon and lasts such a short time. I wanted to see the soldier in uniform, the first in our family for a hundred years. I mean in the direct Frost line. But I have a lecture to give at the University of North Carolina (Chapel Hill) on March 1st which determines the date of my journey north. I am lucky to be getting lectures still at here and there a college and feel I mustn't pass any of them up. I shall miss the chance to hear about soldiering at first hand. You must write to me Prescott. My chief interest in the war comes from your being in it. I dont listen to the radio commentators and I hardly look at the papers. . . . I think of you every day."

Among the other things Frost thought about every day was whether and how he could find some kind of long-term teaching appointment to replace the now-defunct Emerson fellowship at Harvard. The fellowship in American civilization that had succeeded it was now entirely honorary, and was limited to only a few lectures during the academic year. So great was Frost's fear of running out of money, he was prepared to do much—even to swallow his considerable pride—to secure a job that would meet his requirements.

Several months went by during which it seemed to Frost that only an end to the war would bring about his return to college teaching on a regular basis. He had all but given up hope for an early appointment when, in March 1943, he had a visit at 35 Brewster Street from Ray Nash, a member of the faculty at Dartmouth College, whom he had befriended when Nash was teaching at the New School in New York. "In Cambridge the other night," Nash afterward wrote to Dartmouth President Ernest Martin Hopkins, "I had a long visit with Robert Frost. It transpired that he is finishing up his work there. . . . I said I wished Harvard's loss might be Dartmouth's gain. Then he surprised me by saying thoughtfully that it would be kind of nice to end up where he started out fifty years ago. . . ."

Hopkins readily agreed to take the matter up at the next meeting of the board of trustees. The exigencies of the war had obliged them to impose a freeze on new faculty appointments, except where "excessive demand" could be proved. But, according to Hopkins, the idea of appointing Frost to some position on the Dartmouth faculty was not a new one. It had been discussed in administrative circles on the several occasions when word of Frost's possible availability had reached them.

Frost's appointment to a position at Dartmouth was still under discussion when, in late March, he left New England for a three-week session as writer-in-residence at Indiana University in Bloomington. If he did not know it before his arrival, he learned soon afterward that another visitor to the campus was Bernard DeVoto, the end of whose series of lectures coincided with the beginning of Frost's Bloomington stay. Having never acknowledged the estrangement DeVoto so acutely felt, Frost was in a better position than his once-devoted friend to take the initiative during the three days in which they shared the campus. Seeking DeVoto out, Frost unburdened himself on three successive nights of talk so highly personal that DeVoto could not help wondering if he were being encouraged to undertake a biography. However, DeVoto felt as if Frost were trying to "ingest" him, and he could not wait to make his escape from Bloomington.

Soon after he returned to Cambridge, DeVoto received news from Bloomington that was even more upsetting. Frost, after saying good-bye to him, had entertained a dinner party with talk behind his back, and DeVoto minced no words in the letter he shortly directed to Frost:

"Various remarks you made about me in Bloomington have been faithfully reported to me. I find myself not liking one of them, one which you have been making for a number of years in various parts of the country. It is reported to me from Bloomington by one of the eight faculty men at the dinner where you made it in words which he says are exactly or substantially yours, as follows:

" 'DeVoto, you know, has been under the care of a psychiatrist, who has told him that I am not good for him, that if he is ever to succeed, he must not cultivate my company: I am too strong for him and have a bad effect upon him . . .' . . . .

"The statement is altogether false. No part of it is true. I think you know that. What satisfaction you get from circulating a false and damaging statement about me I don't know or care, but I have made no earlier protest out of respect to years of friendship with you. I have decided, however, that I no longer care to submit to it. I do not want to hear of your making that statement again in public or in private. Please see to it that I do not have to act any farther in the matter than thus calling it to your attention."

DeVoto clearly intended to leave no doubt in Frost's mind that he now considered their friendship finally and irreconcilably at an end. Frost, however, saw nothing in DeVoto's remarks that he could not defuse by providing his own version of the Bloomington evening in question. With the same mixture of surface humor and subsurface malice that had characterized his offending remark, Frost drafted a letter. "Benny Benny!" it began:

"The first thing Kay did when she got here was to give me what you in your unconventional Western way would call Hell for talking about you too much in company. (She did not say in public.) And now comes your letter to give me more Hell for the same thing. I feel injured and misunderstood. . . . I never speak of you but to praise. I have been mentioning you for membership in the Academy. I have predicted that you would have to be called back to Harvard. But I am nobody's propagandist. You know my danger. I am prone to think more things are funny than you would. . . . You say the story isnt true and I take your word for it but I had it on the best authority and your attitude toward me for the last two years has tended to make it seem plausible. . . . But true or not true I wouldnt for the world go on repeating the story if it bothered you or anybody else. . . . You want to be friends I could tell by your manner in Bloomington. I want to be friends as you can tell by my manner in this letter. Now lets forget differences and get to our writing again."

DeVoto failed to respond. Their relationship had suffered a blow from which it was unlikely, even with further conciliatory gestures, to recover.

In early May, following Frost's return to Cambridge from Bloomington, came the culmination of efforts by another friend who was willing by nature to forgive and forget differences. Louis Untermeyer in 1943, besides serving in the O.W.I., was also on the committee of Columbia University responsible for recommending to the board of trustees a winner of the Pulitzer Prize in poetry. As perturbed as he was by Frost's refusal to take any active part in the war effort, Untermeyer could not, and did not, deny that *A Witness Tree* deserved the coveted award more than any other poetry book published in 1942. His fellow committee members, Bliss Perry and Wilbur Cross, agreed *A Witness Tree* was the best volume under consideration. They believed, however, that the three Pulitzer Prizes Frost had already won were all any artist should receive in a lifetime—be his subsequent work ever so good. They voted, therefore, to recommend the volume that all three men agreed was the second best.

In a minority report, Untermeyer urged the trustees not to deny Frost his fourth Pulitzer Prize simply because he had won three before. Convinced by Untermeyer's argument, the board overrode the majority vote of the advisory committee and awarded *A Witness Tree* the prize.

By the end of the month Frost had another, though less dramatic, victory to celebrate: the culmination of his efforts to secure permanent employment in a college. For some time President Hopkins of Dartmouth had been perfecting his plans for Frost's appointment, and the last remaining obstacle was the position of Harvard University, conveyed through Grenville Clark, that that institution still had claims on Frost's services, and it would not relinquish them unless Dartmouth permitted Frost to deliver several lectures at Harvard during the coming academic year. The matter was resolved when Hopkins telephoned Clark, his good friend, and teasingly assured him Dartmouth would be glad to do anything it could, at any time, "for the cultural uplift of Harvard."

Ray Nash on June twenty-fourth stipulated what were to be the eventual terms of Frost's appointment. His duties would be: "Entirely extra-curriculum. Regular hours to meet students in his study three days each week (Friday, Saturday and Sunday) during autumn and early winter (October, November, December, January—until his usual trip South); again, in the spring, several visits for work with students or perhaps a public appearance; attendance at important gatherings like commencement. His responsibilities to Dartmouth would not interfere with occasional lectures elsewhere." The salary was to be $2,500 per annum, with an expense allowance of $500. The term of appointment would be one year, with the understanding that it might be renewable, from year to year, for an indefinite period.

In his letter of July ninth to President Hopkins (who had presented him with an honorary Litt.D. from Dartmouth ten years before), Frost expressed pleasure at and hopes for his latest role at Dartmouth:

". . . I am accepting your call back to Dartmouth with pride and satisfaction. Let's make it mean all we can. Call back, I call it. I once went to school at Dartmouth. As you know I am one of your alumni, though without benefit of graduation. I had my degree at your hands. I have been at Hanover to read many times in the last twenty five years and the boys have given me some of my best occasions.

"The idea is that, in addition to what I do at Dartmouth for Dartmouth, I shall belong to Dartmouth in what I do for my publishers and my public. . . ."

38

THE MASQUES
OF REASON AND MERCY

(1943–1946)

ROBERT FROST'S incumbency as Dartmouth's George Ticknor Fellow in the Humanities began on October 1, 1943, and was marked that evening by a reception. Frost's primary association was with Baker Library, and a room had been set up for his use as his private office and classroom. The program, according to the design of the Ticknor fellowship and following Frost's own academic preferences, was nondepartmental, with a leaning only to the humanities, in the broadest sense. How nondepartmental it proved found reflection in an account of the first regular meeting, written by Charles G. Bolté:

". . . That night his conversation ranged over war, politics, farming, poetry, education, social change, personalities, biography, autobiography, industrial developments in Vermont, the possibility of selling unsprayed apples, the advantages of living on a non-farming farm, the definition of democracy as the best form of government because power was divided against itself and no one could gather too much of it, the riddle of Jeffersonian policy, and the proper way to build a log fire. It went on for nine hours, goaded occasionally by his listeners, but mainly unwinding effortlessly and without the use of stimulants. . . ."

Bolté continued by summarizing what were probably Frost's opening remarks at the first meeting of his Ticknor seminar:

"Mr. Frost is interested in clear thinking, and thinks that one way to get it is to learn politeness—the kind of politeness which lets another man have his say without an angry rebuttal in the middle. He also wants his pupils to know when they're talking in quotation marks and when they're thinking for themselves—freshness again. They can write for him, but that's not the only thing; good conversation will be accepted, and good reading. Probably even good listening. The substance of his informal assignment is that he will be on hand in Hanover, to talk to anybody who cares to come in, alumni and faculty as well as undergraduates and trainees. . . ."

Of Nash's acts of devotion, none did more to win him a place in Frost's affection than the Baker Library exhibition he assembled, in collaboration with Harold Goddard Rugg, entitled "Fifty Years of Robert Frost." It included the most extensive collection of his books and manuscripts ever gathered together up to that time, and one item commanded particular interest, as a work representing the fiftieth year of Frost's artistic career. A play in blank verse, of one act and of some 400 lines, it was one of a pair Frost planned to write on the linked subjects of justice and mercy, and the reason men applied toward the understanding of both.

"Last night I finished writing The Forty-third Chapter of Job, A Masque of Reason," Frost had told a friend in April of 1943, in announcing completion of the first of the two plays. "You may have to listen to it sometime when I have done its companion piece The Whole Bible, A Masque of Mercy. Neither may ever see the light. I *will* dabble in drama."

From April to October, Frost had continued to tinker with the first masque, had made some progress on the second, and in the interest of succinctness had shortened the title of each. His attitude toward the eventual publication of *A Masque of Reason* and *A Masque of Mercy*, meanwhile, underwent considerable change from the position that "Neither may ever see the light." In October he impulsively went with Kay Morrison to speak to a leading director about possible Broadway production of the two masques. It was only after he returned that he realized how far ahead of his plays his ambitions for them had progressed.

The pair of masques, which had originally been conceived as poems in dramatic form, were like no such poems Frost had written or read before. He called them masques, but they bore little resemblance to the opulent court spectacles of sixteenth- and seventeenth-century England. Though nominally belonging to the same genre as Milton's *Comus,* they were closer in underlying purpose to *Paradise Lost*—if not quite to "justify the ways of God to men," at least (by retelling and extending familiar biblical stories in an engagingly witty fashion) to show men how to take the mysterious ways of God.

A Masque of Reason grew out of Frost's lifelong fascination with the Book of Job, whose basic narrative line, that of a man forced to suffer a prolonged period of undeserved adversity, carried for Frost great emotional appeal. Having suffered half a lifetime of frustration and neglect before achieving recognition as a poet, having lost (to cholera infantum) his first child, Elliott, and later a daughter, wife, and son (within a space of six years), Frost had little difficulty in identifying elements of his own experience with those of the archetypal sufferer of the Old Testament. Job's ultimate restoration to health and wealth also strongly appealed to his imagination and invited analogies with his own life. It was because of the opportunity it presented to explore the "reason" behind human suffering, however, that Frost had chosen, audaciously, to fashion a "Forty-third Chapter of Job."

Four characters—Job, his wife, God, and the devil—constitute the dramatis personae of the play, which is set in a "fair oasis in the purest desert" many centuries after the end of Job's earthly torments. The first extended speech is God's. "I've had you on my mind a thousand years . . . ," God says, addressing Job.

Job and his waspish wife, Thyatira, proceed to engage in a witty conversation with God, by means of which Frost, like the author of the Book of Job, is able to explore the complex of issues conjoined under the heading "The Problem of Evil." At times Job's position and God's are one. Generally, however, Frost represents Job as God's persistent questioner, continuing to search out the "reason" for his suffering, much as his biblical original did before finally repenting "in sackcloth and ashes."

Almost at once, answers to the mystery of Job's undeserved suffering do begin to appear. In one of them God says, "I was just showing off to the Devil, Job, / As is set forth in Chapters One and Two." Here Frost means God's remark to be taken as much more than a wisecrack. By it (and by the symbolic grouping of God, Job, and the devil onstage at the end of the play) he is suggesting what he felt to be a profound truth concerning the nature of evil: God requires the devil—or evil—to be present in the world. And for the same reason He needs man; both help Him realize His goals. Human reason, as Frost saw it, could not grasp what those goals were, but man must accept evil and suffering as an integral part of God's plan, one that no amount of "progress" would ever eradicate. It was a repudiation of the New Deal and the liberal reformers who were expecting science and government to invent and institute Utopia. Nowhere but in heaven, for Frost, and no way but by the grace of God, could one hope to realize the peace and contentment everywhere denied to living men and women.

In mid-December 1943, a month after he began another phase of the Ticknor fellowship by delivering a lecture in Hanover open to the general public, Frost came down with an illness he might have interpreted, had he been so inclined, as yet another in the Job-like series of torments that had marked his life. Indeed, when he contracted a case of pneumonia serious enough to require a month-long confinement in the Dartmouth infirmary, he could not help wondering, during the worst of it, if God had misunderstood his devout intentions in *A Masque of Reason* and decided to punish him for sacrilege he had never intended. After the fever passed, he convinced himself God had indeed understood and, so, had spared his life. But he decided that when he resumed work on the second play, *A Masque of Mercy,* he would leave no room for doubt in the mind of man or God that he continued to be what he had always been: a man who, though he had no use for calcified church ritual or narrowly pious orthodoxy, would not object to being regarded as one of the most profoundly religious men of his age.

By the end of January 1944 he had recovered sufficiently to go to Florida and to begin, only somewhat later than usual, his annual winter vacation at Pencil Pines. Lillian Frost and her son, who had been living in the two small bungalows since Prescott's medical discharge from the Army in July, moved into a cottage on the property of Frost's neighbor, Professor Hjort. From there they paid daily visits to see how Frost's recuperation was progressing and to help him with gardening chores around his modest orchard. Kay helped, too, and worked with him on the manuscripts and letters he had carried with him to South Miami. Because of family responsibilities in Cambridge and her promise to visit Lesley on her way home, she left without him, after three weeks, and left a gap behind that Lillian and Prescott could not completely fill.

When he wrote a long-owed letter to Earle Bernheimer in March, he favored the collector with his latest thinking on the war, carefully counting Bernheimer among those who, like himself, had rejected the liberal sentimentality that anticipated universal peace and brotherhood as one result of the approaching Allied victory:

". . . The war moves slow if it moves at all. I keep changing my expectations about it. At first I thought it would be long; then I thought it would be short; now it begins to look long again. Im not worried about it. Neither am I troubled about the future in general. Things are coming out our way. I feel more and more sure. Our kind of people are beginning to speak up for our kind of world. . . . I was coming to think there was no use in my contending in my unaggressive way against the Predominant Nonsense: I was so much alone in my instinctive prejudices. I was resolved not to lose my temper and get going. But I decided to give the immediate future up as lost to the bad thinkers eructed from the Social Settlements and leap forward to set my heart on vindication from the more distant future when I shant be here to triumph. I sold out too easily. There's more of us than just me and you. . . ."

The object of the letter was partly to breathe new life into a friendship that in recent months had suffered an apparent decline; and if his relationship with Bernheimer had deteriorated of late, Frost knew he had no one but himself to blame. For the past several months he had continued to accept, without compunction, Bernheimer's monthly checks for $150. By mid-1943, however, he had begun to take those "gifts" for granted and had come to concern himself less and less with the quality of those few items he sent in return. Mrs. Morrison, more often than not, was the one who acknowledged receipt of Bernheimer's checks, and Frost's personal letters to Bernheimer—collector's items of a sort themselves—became increasingly rare.

In August 1944, Frost found another of his friendships in trouble and requiring extraordinary measures to preserve. For some time he had been aware of Louis Untermeyer's displeasure at his refusal to take any formal role in the efforts to defeat Nazi Germany. At their infrequent meetings during the first years of the war, Frost had tried to explain to Untermeyer that he was no-less loyal in his sympathies, no-less opposed to Hitler, no-less sympathetic to the lot of the Jews of Europe, for all his determination to remain "above the battle."

Faced with the enormity of the Nazi crimes against his fellow Jews, however, Untermeyer was outraged by what he could not help interpreting as Frost's indifference. His hostility one weekend at Bread Loaf was so glaring that, in an effort to save their friendship, Frost wrote him a letter that, for added impact, he chose to write as an epistle in blank verse. He began by addressing himself to what was, for Untermeyer, the heart of the issue:

> I'd rather there had been no war at all
> Than have you cross with me because of it.
> I know whats wrong: the war is more or less
> About the Jews and as such you believe
> I ought to want to take some part in it.
> You ought to know—I shouldnt have to tell you—
> The army wouldnt have me at the front.
> And hero at the rear I will not be—
>
> . . .
>
> I could no more have taken pen to Hitler
> Than taken gun (but for a different reason).
> There may have been subconscious guile at work
> To save my soul from the embarrassment
> Of a position where with praise of us (US)
> I had to mingle propaganda praise
> Of a grotesque assortment of allies.
> False friendships I accept for what they're worth
> And what I may get out of them in peace and war,
> But always with a minimum of talk
> And not for long. I'm bad at politics.
> I was born blind to faults in those I love,

But I refuse to blind myself on purpose
To the faults of my mere confederates. . . .

Frost continued by deflating the paternalistic pretensions of the United States, England, and Russia, thereby implicitly demonstrating how unsuited he was to be a writer of wartime propaganda. He spoke of how he took "sides" with all peoples—including the Jewish—who wanted "a platform country" to "speak their language from." He spoke of "us (US) / The mighty upstart, full of upstart people / Or Shoe-string Starters as I like to call them" and of "the democracy in me" that demanded only that "I get surprised at where men come from." Then, as he brought his discursive epistle to a close, he appealed to Untermeyer not to give up, for mere political differences, the friendship they had shared, unbroken, since 1915.

Untermeyer could not help being moved by Frost's poetic peace offering. When he gave Frost's letter-poem the careful reading it demanded, he soon found himself writing to Frost that he was not only delighted with it, but amazed. "Once more," he said, "you accomplish that miraculous thing of saying profound things as though you were not saying anything at all, as though . . . [you] were musing for the sake of musing—and being amusing. I don't know when you have packed so much thinking in so lightly running a speech."

The praise was appreciated; the friendship, at least provisionally, restored. Untermeyer's words reminded Frost, however, he had miles to go on another undertaking that, he hoped, would draw a response not unlike Untermeyer's to his letter-poem. He was thinking not only of the *Masque of Reason,* the publication of which had by now been set to take place on the date of his "seventieth" birthday, but of the *Masque of Mercy,* which he had yet to complete.

The round of parties and social calls occasioned by his birthday left Frost so exhausted he came down with a cold, and spent much of the next few weeks in bed. But by April 12, 1945, he had recovered sufficiently to fulfill an engagement his friends at Amherst would have hated to see him miss: his first visit to and first reading at Amherst College since his resignation in the summer of 1938. George Roy Elliott, George Whicher, Reuben Brower, and others who had a hand in the invitation went out of their way to guarantee the success of Frost's visit. Knowing that the biggest risk they ran was a meeting between Frost and the man he blamed for his departure, President Stanley King, they declined King's offer to return from an out-of-town trip to be on hand. And they chose not to cancel the evening lecture when, hours before it was scheduled to begin, word came of the death of President Franklin Roosevelt that afternoon. They decided, as well, to keep from Frost news of the death, apparently assuming it could do nothing to improve his nerves or the quality of his public performance.

Leaving Amherst after the brief but successful visit, Frost spent three weeks in Hanover to conclude his second year as Ticknor Fellow. Then, he retired to the Homer Noble Farm for a summer of work on his unfinished *Masque of Mercy*. By August eighth he could report to Bernheimer that he had "at last had the idea I needed for the final touch" to the play—which he promised to add to Bernheimer's collection, after reading it at the impending session of the Bread Loaf Writers' Conference. He did read it at the conference, but he soon decided the "final touch" was not so final as he had thought and that something more was lacking in the second masque to bring it to a close on just the note he wanted. Except for a speech or two, in any case, the play was done.

Like the earlier masque, *A Masque of Mercy* was loosely based on an Old Testament story, this time the Book of Jonah. The action was set in a small bookstore in Frost's modern equivalent of Nineveh—New York City—where, just at closing time, a conversation between the store's owner, his wife, and a lingering customer, Paul, is interrupted by the frenzied entrance of a fugitive who announces fearfully, "God's after me!" He, shortly, introduces himself as the archetypal fugitive of the Bible, Jonas Dove—or Jonah.

The other characters quickly learn his motivation for flight, which, says Jonah, is that "I've lost my faith in God to carry out / The threats He makes against the city evil. / I can't trust God to be unmerciful."

The Keeper of the bookstore (his full name is My Brother's Keeper) can scarcely understand the nature of Jonah's Old Testament indignation. Keeper's wife, Jesse Bel by name, is a neurotic "solitary social drinker" who generally stays out of the discussion. Paul, however ("the fellow who theologized / Christ almost out of Christianity"), has much to say about Jonah's demand—not fundamentally unlike Job's—for divine justice. Speaking to Jonah early in the play, he overtly establishes the central theme of the masque: "You are the universal fugitive— / Escapist, as we say—though you are not / Running away from Him you think you are, / But from His mercy-justice contradiction. / . . . I'm going to make you see / How relatively little justice matters."

When Paul picks up Jonah's complaint that he cannot "trust God to be unmerciful," by asking him, "What would you have God if not merciful?" Jonah's response is clear: "Just, I would have Him just before all else. . . ." But Paul, in a speech reminiscent of God's remarks to Job early in *A Masque of Reason,* shows the prophet that he has not properly understood the import of his role in religious history.

If at any earlier time in his life Frost might have rested in Jonah's notion of the primacy of justice, now, at seventy, his sympathies leaned, rather, toward the position advanced by (Saint) Paul. By the end of the masque, Frost permits Paul to convince Jonah that the Sermon on the Mount was ". . . just a frame-up to insure the failure / Of all of us. . . ." Says Paul, "Mercy is only to the undeserving. / But such we all are made in the sight of God." Then, in a climactic moment of the play, Jonah is led to admit, "I think I may have got God wrong entirely. / . . . / Mercy on me for having thought I knew." As his Old Testament "sense of justice" begins to fade and die, so does he, with a plea for "mercy" on his lips.

Although the masque was all but finished by the end of the summer of 1945, the something Frost felt to be lacking in the final scene—in which Paul and Keeper, standing over the fallen Jonah, discuss the need for courage in carrying out human responsibilities—kept him from sending the masque off to Holt or to Bernheimer. He was still working on the scene when, in early August, a pair of events halfway around the globe gave him new food for thought on the paired subjects of justice and mercy. On August sixth an American airplane dropped an atomic bomb on the city of Hiroshima, Japan. Three days later a similar weapon was turned against Nagasaki. The atomic age had begun.

While Frost had mixed feelings about the use of such awful weapons of destruction against civilian populations, he rejoiced at the peace that soon followed. In mid-October, he visited in Hanover with the retiring President Hopkins and his newly named successor, John Sloan Dickey, discussing what form his third Ticknor year was going to take. He, then, hastened to Ohio for an honorary degree at Kenyon College. Upon his return to Cambridge he set down, at Hopkins's request, his recollection of their recent meeting: ". . . The possibilities came up in pairs—Should I come for week-ends part of the year or make a solid thing of it for a few weeks twice a year? We decided for the latter. Should we open the class to a large number or restrict it to a few? We decided for the latter. Should I mark like teachers of regular courses or should I merely tell the boys what I thought of them as in a progressive school. We decided for the latter. And then I'm to think of myself as belonging to the Library. . . ."

A few days later he interrupted his activities in Cambridge long enough to write a letter to Lesley. He had not, it was clear, been neglecting his own education on the subject of atomic power:

"With things like the atomic bomb I pride myself on putting them in their relative place a priori without ever having been in a physics laboratory. I said right off uranium was only a new kind of fuel. Wood will rot down to ashes in a few years. It can be touched off and reduced to ashes in a few minutes. It can be touched off and let down with a bump—exploded. Uranium will rot down to radium in a few million years if left to itself, and from radium to lead in a few thousand more. Lead is the ashes, the dead end. It can no more be touched off than the ashes of wood. Most of the matter we live with on and among has long since spent its radioactiveness. We don't have to be afraid of anybody's setting it going: any radiomaniac. Uranium is a strange rare survival from a world once generally active with alpha beta gamma delta and other rays. We live comfortably with practically nothing but the end products. Now Einstein speaks up and tells the hysterical: no new principle is involved. It is just a bigger explosive we have got. We have found a way to let uranium down all those million years with a bang. Of course very magnificent on the part of man. The mind keeps penetrating deeper into matter. I knew at once that the important question was how much uranium there was left in the world, and how many elements there were still left that hadn't levelled off. Einstein says not many. Maybe two or three of those in very small quantities like uranium. So the imagination can rest from getting up doomsdays. The new explosive can be bad for us. But it can't get rid of the human race for there would always be left, after the bomb, the people who fired it—enough for seed and probably with the same old incentive to sow it. There's a lot of fun in such considerations. . . ."

There was a lot of fun, as well, in trying to express in poetry his belief that the world was making far too much of a fuss over this new weapon that "let uranium down all those million years with a bang." By Christmastime 1945, Frost had written and sent to his friends a poem, "On Making Certain Anything Has Happened," in which he advised them (as he elsewhere put it) to "be sure they have something to get hysterical about before they do it." In this poem Frost adopted a posture of effortless equanimity. Other poems he was writing at about the same time suggested that the slightly bemused detachment he now felt, had been achieved only after some not-insignificant difficulty.

"One Step Backward Taken," published early in 1946, presented the powerful, nightmarish vision of a world being swept off its foundations, and of a destruction only survived by a last-minute strategic retreat. A related poem of the same period, the genesis of which can be traced to the same sense of terrifying dislocation, was "Directive." Where the speaker in "One Step Backward Taken" had saved himself *from* going, by spatial retreat, salvation here is to be achieved *by* going, on a ritualized journey the direction of which is backward in time—but also inward, to levels of perception unaffected by external circumstances.

Even as he was articulating ways of coping with the confusion and hysteria of the "universal crisis," Frost found himself faced once again with a family crisis that demanded a practical, rather than a poetic, solution. In the fall of 1944, Irma and John Cone, having passed through a series of marital crises since their marriage in 1926, separated—Irma remaining with her two children at their home in Hanover, New

Hampshire, and Cone moving to New York City. After nearly two years of estrangement Cone, in May 1946, wrote to his father-in-law explaining the reasons he felt compelled to seek a divorce. Frost had seen enough to sympathize with Cone, and he promptly informed his son-in-law he would do nothing to impede a divorce action. When Irma learned of her husband's plans, however, she insisted on leaving Hanover and going to Ripton, where her father could look after her and her younger son, five-year-old Harold. Though he did not relish the prospect of "protecting" Irma from the phantoms that beset her, Frost stoically agreed to her coming.

Irma's tendency to hysterical displays of temper, and other unmistakable signs of her worsening mental condition, made Frost sure he did not want his daughter living under the same roof with him. He put her in Mrs. Homer Noble's boardinghouse for the summer, while he considered how he should take care of her thereafter. But even this temporary arrangement did not succeed. Suffering increasingly from paranoid delusions and expressing her fears and obsessions in a number of unpleasant ways, Irma became more and more difficult to manage.

Over the next several months Irma was a constant source of anxiety to her father. With Mrs. Morrison's help, he found one place after another for her to stay, always with like results. Irma would find her present situation unbearable, or the proprietors of her current home would find her so. Frost finally decided he would have to find Irma a home she could not be asked to leave; he would have to buy her a house of her own. By October, when he had to leave New England for a series of engagements in the Midwest, his search had narrowed down to a few towns in the vicinity of Boston. A satisfactory house, however, had not as yet been found.

The major stop in Frost's Midwestern trip was Gambier, Ohio, where Kenyon College had arranged a week-long conference on "The Heritage of the English-Speaking Peoples and Their Responsibility." Arriving in Gambier, he soon wished he had stayed away. Harold J. Laski, the British socialist, was, he learned, to be the speaker he would follow to the rostrum. Laski had lately been expressing publicly his conviction that Russian foreign policy was primarily motivated by a desire not for global hegemony, but for national security—a conviction for which Frost had little sympathy. A last-minute change in the order of speakers saved the day.

Frost's topic was one he had spoken on often in recent months, in lectures entitled, as this one was, "The Separateness of the Parts." Running directly counter to the views expressed by most of the conference participants, Frost began by delineating what he considered a fundamental human dichotomy. On one side there was "the Western idea that we must master nature, and get such a grip on it that we can make ourselves all happy and make the universe a brotherhood of unconflicting love." In opposition to this, he said, was the Eastern belief that "nature is too much for us, and that we may as well throw ourselves on God and Christ or some saviour." His own inclination, he freely admitted, was "toward Asia."

Continuing, he explained what he meant by "the separateness of the parts" and its opposite—another way of discussing his basic dichotomy: "I won't go any further than to say that the separateness of the parts is as important as the connection of the parts. That is my gospel. There are those who were called to take care of the connection of the parts and there are those who were called to take care of the separateness of the parts, and I don't believe I am called upon to do either. I was just watching those things with a little anxiety for the separateness because everybody is talking unity so hard—just a little anxiety, that's all, and a little bit of fear of mob thinking."

Despite his disclaimer, few participants in the conference doubted that Frost leaned markedly toward the separateness of the parts, and that he looked not to the infant United Nations Organization or other political inventions, but heavenward, for answers to the political and economic disunity that was of so much concern to the liberal members of the conference.

After Gambier, Frost went on to Cincinnati, where his plans included a visit with one of his Ripton neighbors and friends, Rabbi Victor E. Reichert. During summers in Vermont, Frost and Reichert, leader of Cincinnati's Rockdale Avenue Temple, had passed many evenings discussing the relative merits of the Old and New Testaments and other theological matters. In inviting Frost to spend an evening with him and his wife, Reichert knew they would be likely to engage in yet another lively discussion on some problem of biblical interpretation or comparative religion. Reichert also knew that Frost's interest in the Jewish religion went further than that of most other Christian believers.

After several hours of talk, Reichert announced that he was giving a sermon next day, the first day of the Feast of Tabernacles. With studied casualness, Frost announced, in turn, that he himself had once preached for a friend at a Congregational church back home. "You never preached for me," the rabbi ventured. "You never asked me," answered Frost. "I'm asking you now."

Next morning Robert Frost delivered a sermon at the Rockdale Avenue Temple. He began by saying he sometimes found himself thinking courage was the greatest of all virtues. But he had read an ancient Roman poet, Ennius, who said that it was only the second greatest of virtues. Many bad men have been brave; wisdom is better than bravery.

"Now religion," Frost continued, "always seems to me to come round to something beyond wisdom. It's a straining of the spirit forward to a wisdom beyond wisdom. Many men have the kind of wisdom that will do well enough in the day's work, you know, living along, fighting battles, going to wars, beating each other, striving with each other, in war or in peace—sufficient wisdom. They take their own side, naturally, and do well enough. But if they have religious natures . . . they constantly tremble a little with the fear of God. And the fear of God always has meant the fear that one's wisdom, . . . one's own human wisdom is not quite acceptable in His sight. Always I hear that word 'acceptable' —'acceptable' about offerings. . . . Always the fear that it may not quite be acceptable. That, I take it, is the fear of God, and is with every religious nature, always. . . ."

Frost had heard the word "acceptable" used in a specifically religious context only minutes before, during the reading by Rabbi Reichert of a passage from *The Union Prayerbook*: "Look with favor, O Lord, upon us, and may our service be acceptable unto Thee. Praised be Thou, O God, whom alone we serve in reverence." When Frost heard this, he knew he had a focus for his talk to those who were gathered there that morning. Only later did he realize that he also had more: a way of bringing his *Masque of Mercy* to just the kind of conclusion he wanted, but which he had heretofore been unable to find.

Soon after he returned to Cambridge, he drafted speeches for his characters Paul and Keeper that were a kind of benediction to his ventures into religious drama. *A Masque of Mercy* was now finished. Within a month Frost had not only sent it to Holt, for publication in a separate volume early in the new year, he had also gathered together many of his wartime lyrics and decided to bring out a collection of these, as well. Two books in one year; not bad for a poet just turned seventy. He could only hope that his offerings would be found acceptable to the critics and reading public and—not least of all—in the sight of heaven.

39

TROUBLES, STRAINS, RAPPROCHEMENT

(1946–1949)

IN 1946, Robert Frost spent the last hours of the old year and the first of the new composing a long letter to his old friend Untermeyer. On one page, beneath the printed letterhead of "The George Ticknor Fellowship in the Humanities," Frost underscored "Humanities" and penned: "and in opposition to the sciences by contract. I am not supposed to use electric light to read or write by. I use Roman Candles in preference to tallow candles." The letter began:

"As I sit here alone watching the old year out with nobody to get ahead of me in exclaiming Happy New Year on the last stroke of twelve (or should it be on the first? Has any custom been established?), but after all come to consider me by and large, none so forlorn in my emotional life (There would be no mockery in my being wished a Happy New Year or at any rate a Happy-go-lucky New Year—nor in your being, either[,] I take it)—let's see where was I?—as I sit here on this aniversary of nothing but one of Time's new beginnings it comes over me with a young freshness to write one more letter to the friend I have written more letters to than to any one else. . . ."

For several pages he rambled on, with a succession of jokes and witticisms. When fatigue began to overtake him, however, he remembered that he had not yet said a word about the "family troubles" this letter had helped him, temporarily, to forget. They concerned Irma, who, divorced now from John Cone, showed every sign of heading for a mental breakdown:

". . . My daughter Irma has lived in ten houses in the last six months from sheer unhappiness. Kay and I have found most of them for her. We are buying her a small one right now in Acton Mass where her ancestors on the other side landed from the Mayflower. The wear and tear on Kay and me has been considerable. Merrill [Merrill Moore, the poet who was also a practicing psychiatrist] is for having Irma brought to rest in an institution or at least under a guardian. I find it hard to end anyone's freedom to range to waste and to ruin. Take that away from anyone and what is there left? Let them run I say till they run afoul. . . ."

Having got Irma settled in the house he had found for her in Acton—a town just near and far enough to and from Cambridge—Frost prepared to leave for a much-needed, month-long vacation at his winter retreat in Florida. At the end of February he returned for two weeks to his home on Brewster Street, and on March sixteenth he left by train for the West Coast. His main reason for going to California was a charter-day ceremony on March twenty-second at the Berkeley campus of the University of California. He attended, listened with interest to an address by Douglas Southall Freeman, the biographer of his namesake, Robert E. Lee, and received an honorary degree (his seventeenth). Afterward, he had a look at San Francisco; and he visited Blanche Rankin Eastman, his mother's closest friend, whose telephone call the night before revealed to him that, at nearly one hundred, she was still alive. In the evening he attended, as guest of honor, the annual California alumni banquet.

A gala prebirthday party was celebrated on the following evening (for his so-called seventy-second birthday) at the Hotel Mark Hopkins in San Francisco. Robinson Jeffers and Gertrude Atherton were among the sponsors, and the guest list of one hundred included Alfred Harcourt, Frost's first Holt editor, and Governor Earl Warren.

The balance of Frost's time in California was spent, in roughly equal parts, with Earle Bernheimer and Bernheimer's principal Frost-collecting adversary, Louis Mertins, the Redlands poet-teacher-collector, whose ranch home overlooked the San Bernardino Valley. On his actual birthday, Bernheimer gave him a second party, in Beverly Hills, of almost-embarrassing opulence, to which he had invited an assortment of minor literary figures, businessmen, editors, and actors—few of whom Frost knew. Two days later he returned to Redlands for a final lecture he had, as he now regretted, agreed to deliver at the university there. Fatigue, boredom, and homesickness had long since got the better of him. He wanted nothing more than to be back under the protection of his secretary in Cambridge.

As he stopped at Ann Arbor for a talk-and-reading during the long ride East, he managed to put the California visit in the best possible light: "I have just been out in California, the 'state where I was born in, early on one frosty morning,' as the song goes. They were very nice to me out there—so nice they only embarrassed me once. The Governor of the state asked me why I had left. I said I was very young—and I was carried out screaming."

After a week of rest at his home in Cambridge, Frost went traveling again: to Hanover for the first spring session of his popular Ticknor seminar; then, to Amherst for what was only his second visit to the college since his resignation from the faculty in 1938. Stanley King, whom Frost had never forgiven for the way he had—as Frost saw it—plotted to get him off the faculty, was now gone himself, having resigned and been replaced by one of Frost's former (and favorite) Amherst students, Charles Woolsey Cole.

The Amherst visit began with an appearance before an overflow audience in Johnson Chapel, where Frost described for his listeners "the way to approach a scientist"—one of his favorite subjects in recent months of lecturing around the country: "You say to him, science is domestic science and that is all it is. It all comes down to keeping house, cooking, eating, keeping warm and, of course, domesticating ourselves on the planet, so to speak. You can always get a rise by saying that. They tell you that, don't you know, science is a good deal pure science and of no earthly use."

Frost did not have to be told by a scientist, he continued, that pure science—or "curiosity"—had resulted in the penetration of space and the splitting of the atom. But he was afraid that, with all the modern talk about pure and applied science, the notion of "pure" and "applied" would be carried too far, until there would be distinctions made between pure and applied religion, athletics, motherhood—or, even, pure and applied poetry: "Some people have talked about reducing poetry to more immediate use. Maybe it is not useful if it is only in a book." Of his own poems, he said, "Mending Wall" had been spoiled by being "applied"; and a committee had once been sent to him to find out "what those promises were" in "Stopping by Woods on a Snowy Evening."

In early May, less than a week after his return to Cambridge, Frost answered a knock at his door and opened it to find, to his amazement, T. S. Eliot standing before him. "I was in town," Eliot explained simply, "and I couldn't leave without coming to pay my respects." Frost showed him in, and the visitor soon explained, further, how he had come from England to visit his ailing brother and had decided to make his passage-money by giving a few lectures and readings.

Sitting at his ease in the living room at 35 Brewster Street, Eliot was pleasantly modest and natural. They chatted about the old days in London before the Great War and about their most recent poetic efforts. After an hour or so Eliot said he must go, adding that he had greatly enjoyed the visit. Flattered by Eliot's interest in seeing him and by the esteem Eliot accorded his verse, Frost had to admit, to his visitor and to himself, that he had enjoyed the unexpected visit too.

A source of anxiety for Frost that spring and on into the summer was associated with the publication on May twenty-eighth of *Steeple Bush*, his first collection of new lyrics since *A Witness Tree* in 1942. Good as he felt the poems in the new book to be, he knew that the critics, and readers in general, would be on the lookout for signs that he was now past his poetic prime—too old to turn out verse that invited comparison with his best work.

He had tried in *Steeple Bush* to branch out in new directions, taking more direct cognizance, than in previous collections, of the issues affecting the contemporary world. The final grouping of six poems, for example, was called "Editorials" and contained several poems that referred in some way to that new subject for treatment in poetry, the atomic bomb. When read sequentially, however, the poems of *Steeple Bush* contributed to a thematic whole dominated not by secular, but by spiritual concerns.

Frost's anxieties continued to mount until, by mid-June, he was nearly sick with worry. Knowing how Frost went into a tailspin at the least hint of an unfavorable notice, Kay protected him by screening reviews, reading to him the best ones and reporting (sometimes with selective discrimination) on most of the rest. Inevitably, there were times, however, when even Kay's best efforts were insufficient to protect her employer from emotional knocks at the hands of reviewers.

The review of *Steeple Bush* in *Time* magazine was not kind. Kay decided it would not do to let him see it. It was, she told Frost, a typical "smart-alecky" *Time* review; he had best leave it alone. He agreed. Later that afternoon, however, out he went and bought a copy of *Time*.

"Robert Lee Frost," he read, "is the dean of living U.S. poets by virtue of both age and achievement. At 72, the four-time Pulitzer Prizewinner has lost little of his craftsmanship and none of his crackling vigor. But what was once only granitic Yankee individualism in his work has hardened into bitter and often uninspired Tory social commentary. The 43 poems of *Steeple Bush* do nothing to enlarge his greatness and no one of them could begin to displace the best of his *Collected Poems*. . . ."

In Ripton, a few days later, Frost began to complain of pains in his wrists and chest. One afternoon Mrs. Morrison came up to his cabin and found him on the floor, in front of the fireplace. His head was resting on his arms, and these were draped across the seat of his Morris chair. When she went over to speak to him, he winced, and said, "Don't touch me." Where does it hurt? she demanded. "In my heart."

Familiar enough with Frost's psychosomatic ailments not to be unduly alarmed, Kay suggested he remain in bed the rest of the day. Next day he was still complaining of pains in his chest and arms, and when Kay went to the cabin the day after that, she found him still in bed. Although he agreed to get dressed, he soon returned to his bedroom to lie down.

William Branch Porter, a frequenter of the Bread Loaf Writers' Conference and a medical specialist, arrived next day. He told Kay that

Frost was suffering from what was commonly known as "soldier's heart," a problem more of mental and emotional strain than of physical malady. Returning for another visit a few days later, he invited Frost to tell him something of his recent physical and emotional history. After listening for some three hours, he offered an opinion.

He could, he told Frost, give a medical explanation for the pains he had been suffering. But before he went into that, he wanted to say something else. He said he gathered from everyone, everywhere he went, that Frost was considered the poet laureate of the United States. As such, he was in a position earned by his accomplishments, and it gave him certain rights he should accept. But one right he should accept, he did not; and this refusal amounted to a basic flaw in his character. He had never developed his ego to the extent that he could be free from concern for what other people thought of him.

Having been told by Mrs. Morrison and by Frost himself of his reaction to the *Time* review, Dr. Porter continued: Who was the author of this dread review? A nobody. Yet, Frost—the poet laureate of the United States—had permitted himself to be upset by him. After assuring Frost that his physical condition was excellent for a man of his age, that he was physiologically younger than Porter himself, the doctor took his leave. Frost was soon out of bed, feeling much better in body and in mind.

A few days later, having just learned that Jacky Cone had recently spent two days with his mother in Acton, Frost wrote his grandson. Replying almost at once, Jacky assured his grandfather their views were the same, and it was agreed that the state hospital in Concord, New Hampshire, was the best place for her to be committed, should such become necessary.

The matter rested until the thirtieth of July, when Mrs. Morrison received a call from Jacky, saying his mother had asked him to come up from New Jersey, where he was staying with his father, to take her away from the Acton house. Young Harold, she had explained, was about to go and visit some of his father's relatives; and she was afraid to stay alone in the house, because there were plots afoot to kidnap her. Only a few days before, Frost had asked Kay to take especially good care of him for the next two weeks, for if she did not, *he* would go crazy. On the strength of this, Kay decided not to tell him about her conversation with Jacky.

Her protective efforts, however, soon proved to be in vain. The day after Jacky's call, Irma was found wandering on Brattle Street in Cambridge, looking for the house of her cousins, Vera and Hilda Harvey, nearby. When she arrived at her destination, the Harvey sisters telephoned 35 Brewster Street, where Lillian, the only present occupant, had Irma brought by taxi. Lillian quickly realized Irma's condition was much worse; and, almost fearful of violence ensuing, she called Frost's lawyer-neighbor, Erastus Hewitt, who in turn called Frost.

On August sixth Frost and Kay took a train down from Vermont and went directly to Hewitt's home in Cambridge, where they were soon joined by Merrill Moore. In the discussion that followed, Moore said he had considered the various alternatives and that the only acceptable option was to take Irma to the state hospital in Concord, where he had already made the preliminary arrangements for her admission. Now, said Moore, they must all go to Frost's house and take Irma up to Concord.

While Frost waited outside in Moore's car, Moore went to the house and knocked on the door. Lillian Frost let him in and told him Irma was upstairs in bed. Please tell her to get up, he said. A few minutes later, Irma appeared in the living room, a wrapper over her night clothes. She listened as Moore explained why he had come. He had decided, he said, that she needed the protection and rest a good hospital would afford, and he had come with her father to take her to one. Irma refused to go, but he insisted. If she did not dress, he gently but firmly told her, he would carry her upstairs and dress her himself. Two hours later, having dressed and packed her bag, Irma emerged from the house.

With Irma in front, between Moore and his wife, and Kay, Frost, and Hewitt in back, they set off on the drive to Concord. Irma, as they drove through the fog and cold, rocked forward and back in the seat, sighing to herself, as if trying to figure out a means of escape. At last they arrived at the hospital, shortly before dawn. Frost, Kay, and Hewitt waited as Moore and his wife took Irma inside.

After some time a doctor came out to speak to Frost. Frost asked if he might speak to his daughter before he left. Of course, said the doctor. Going inside, Frost thought to explain to his daughter the necessity of bringing her to Concord. Only this way, he wanted to say, could she ever hope to regain her health, rid herself of all the fears she was plagued by. Only this way could she hope to get her son Harold back. When he tried to talk to her, however, she would have nothing to do with him. After listening intransigently to his pleas for understanding, all she would say was, "Get out of here."

"Cast your eye back over my family luck," Frost wrote to Louis Untermeyer a few days later, "and perhaps you will wonder if I haven't had pretty near enough. That is for the angels to say. The valkyries and the eumenides."

After all Frost had been through in the troubles over Irma's commitment, neither Kay nor Ted Morrison had the heart—or courage—to tell him that another potential source of upset awaited him at the 1947 session of the Bread Loaf Writers' Conference: the presence of Benny

DeVoto, who had not participated in the conference for the past five years. Frost wondered, when he learned elsewhere what the Morrisons had failed to tell him, for what purpose DeVoto had come back to join the Bread Loaf staff. His questions were soon answered.

Entering the Little Theater on the evening of August thirteenth, to deliver his first public lecture, he had just reached the front of the hall when DeVoto fairly jumped out of his seat and rushed toward him. "Robert," he said in a stage whisper, over the din of applause at Frost's entrance, "you've been a damn fool and I've been a damn fool. Let's forget it and be friends." Permitting DeVoto to lead him to the seat he had saved beside his own, Frost turned to see where Kay was seated and said, in another stage whisper, "Now, wasn't that nice of him." The evening, and the week that followed, proceeded as free of unusual stress and difficulty as Frost could have wished. Though the friendship was by no means fully restored, the Frost-DeVoto feud, at least, was over.

Less happy were his relations that fall with Earle Bernheimer. Frost knew Bernheimer had been embroiled in a divorce and child-custody suit as costly as it was complicated. In California in March, Bernheimer had hinted that he had begun considering the liquidation of his assets, including his extensive literary collection. It was bad enough to hear Bernheimer speculating that *Twilight,* for which he had paid Frost $4,000 in 1940, might now fetch more than twice that amount, by virtue of Frost's increased fame. What was worse, by far, was hearing him say that the auction block might be the destiny of the collection Frost had spent a decade helping him build.

Frost was in Florida on his winter vacation when, in early February 1948, a letter reached him that represented the best news he had had from any quarter in several months. It was from the president of Amherst College: "It is a profound satisfaction to me to advise you that the Trustees of Amherst College at their meeting on January 24 voted to confer upon you the degree of Doctor of Letters, *honoris causa,* at our next commencement, on Sunday, June 20, 1948. You know how happy this action of the Trustees will make all your Amherst friends and what a great satisfaction it will be to me to confer the degree upon you. I hope your plans will permit you to be with us at the commencement. . . ."

What plans could Frost have had to render impossible his going to Amherst under such circumstances? If his April visit to the college had proved he still had many friends there, this invitation from President Cole seemed almost to prove that, given time and the right kind of hinting on his part, his return to the Amherst family—his final victory over Stanley King—might soon be made complete.

In June, having fulfilled his Ticknor obligations at Dartmouth, and fresh from an honorary-degree ceremony at Duke University, Frost journeyed to Amherst and called on President Cole. As the commencement ceremony was still a few days off, they began their visit by going to another kind of ceremony in Marlboro, Vermont, at the fledgling college recently founded there by Frost's onetime Amherst student and sometime friend Walter Hendricks. Hendricks's installation as president of Marlboro College provided the basis for Frost's extemporaneous talk, after his return to Amherst, on a subject currently very much on his mind. Later printed as "Speaking of Loyalty," his remarks may well have been calculated to plant ideas in the minds of Cole, the trustees, and their fellow Amherst graduates.

"Charlie Cole and I, and George Whicher," Frost began, "are just back from having inaugurated the first president of a brand new college. The extenuating circumstance is that it is a seedling from Amherst. . . .

". . . And I'd like to say a little bit in connection with this. . . . There someone is starting a new thing to be loyal to. . . .

"You often wonder about that. There are talkers abroad who confuse the word loyalty, make confusion with the word loyalty. They use Emerson and they use Josiah Royce to prove that you can be as loyal as Benedict Arnold or Aaron Burr, we'll say, and still be a loyal person. Loyal to something else, that's all they mean. . . .

". . . Lately I've been thinking more and more about it. All there is is belonging and belongings; belonging and having belongings. You belong and I belong. The sincerity of their belonging is all I have to measure people by. . . .

"You have to ask yourself in the end, how far will you go when it comes to changing your allegiance."

Despite the extensive hints he dropped in his talk, Frost waited in vain for a hint from Cole—or anyone else—that his reappointment to the faculty at Amherst was under active consideration. Week after week went by with no word out of Amherst. Finally, in mid-September, came a break in the silence. It was a letter to Kay Morrison, who had done her part on Frost's behalf by dropping some hints of her own into the receptive ears of George Whicher: ". . . I have made some discreet soundings and as far as I can discover there is a unanimous and excited hope that a way may be found to attach Robert again to Amherst. But securing authorization, working out financial adjustments, and the like take more time than anyone would suppose. . . ."

In early November, some weeks after Frost began his sixth consecutive year at Dartmouth, President Cole wrote to inform him that the trustees of Amherst had, at last, made the decision for which he had been waiting. He outlined a proposal: Frost would "come to Amherst and stay in residence there for at least one month each semester"; his title would be Simpson Lecturer in Literature; his annual stipend would be $3,000; "no faculty duties requiring attendance at meetings, service on committees, or the like"; at least one lecture and reading to the entire college each year; other duties consisting of "visiting classes and seminars as a guest teacher, informal conferences with faculty and students, and such other engagements as might seem desirable to the faculty and students and acceptable to you." Finally, "It would be our intention to continue this arrangement as long as you were willing and able to maintain it but the appointment might well be on an annual basis."

Good as the proposal was, there were some drawbacks. The salary was roughly the same as that of the Ticknor fellowship at Dartmouth, and no mention was made of an annual pension, payable upon his retirement. But when Frost and Mrs. Morrison paid a call at the president's office, they were happy to learn that Cole was willing to be "flexible." He soon wrote back to propose a straight five-year contract at $3,500 per annum, renewable annually thereafter. He also said that "if at any time after July 1, 1954 it should be decided . . . that you should not continue your duties on a year-to-year basis . . . , the College would thereafter pay you an annual retirement allowance of $2500 a year."

Frost quickly decided to accept, but postponed notifying President Cole until he had told President Dickey that he would be resigning the Ticknor fellowship. His letter to Dickey skirted the fact that it was he himself, as much as anyone, who had instigated the change of loyalties:

"You have something to listen to that I hope will give you a little pain if only because it gives me a good deal of pain. I am being asked back to the college of my first and longest employment and on terms so extravagantly generous that I couldnt expect anyone else to match them. My recent five years back at the college of my first attendance has meant much to me under both you and Mr Hopkins and my admiration for you both in your different ways will always come out in my talk wherever I go. . . . But I must beg you to let me leave you now with your blessing. Please understand that what takes me away is not just more money, though that has to be considered even by the improvident. It is largely the appeal of being provided for at one stroke for the rest of my time in and out of education. . . . There is sentiment in the situation and even something of rapprochement. . . . I will tell you the rest when we meet in April. I speak now merely to prepare you to receive me with forgiveness."

SUCCESS, HONORS, AND
EIGHTY YEARS

(1949–1954)

WHILE STILL in South Miami on his annual vacation, Robert Frost was presented with an opportunity to review other of his loyalties. His publishers, Henry Holt and Company, had been in a period of upheaval, begun in 1946 by the wholesale resignation of the trade department to follow its departing manager, William Sloane. It had not been easy for Frost to decline his friend's invitation to cast his lot, as a number of Holt authors had done, with the new organization called William Sloane Associates. However, his decision to continue with Holt was aided by an officer who declined to shift his allegiance to Sloane's firm, Alfred C. Edwards.

Edwards had come to Holt from a career in banking. As treasurer of Holt, and subsequently as executive vice-president and president, on numerous occasions he showed the good sense and business acumen Frost wanted to see in those responsible for the production and market-ing of his literary enterprises. More than that, Edwards showed qualities and had a background that soon resulted in his becoming Frost's friend. Above all, Edwards was a doer; he knew how to get things done, and done right. Although he was not a particularly bookish man, he could command the respect of men who were. And he had always had a great admiration for the poetry of Robert Frost.

Despite his developing friendship with Al Edwards, Frost was less than totally pleased with Sloane's successors in the Holt trade department, beginning with his immediate successor, Denver Lindley. In 1948, Lindley's place was taken by Glenn Gosling; and the new publishing contract worked out shortly after Gosling's accession was, by and large, a good one from Frost's point of view. It took away from him, however, the voice he had always exercised in deciding when, and which, books of his should be brought out, and this loss Frost was reluctant to accept.

Early in April 1949, having fulfilled a number of obligations elsewhere,

Frost went to Dartmouth to deliver, for the last time as Ticknor Fellow, a lecture in the Great Issues course President Dickey had established in 1947 as a requirement for graduating seniors. Next day he concluded his participation by attending a question-and-answer session and expanding upon his remarks of the night before. On the following evening, April thirteenth, he was in Amherst where, after his talk-and-reading, President Cole announced that Frost would rejoin the faculty in the fall.

At Holt, meanwhile, Frost's new collected edition had gone through the necessary steps of production and was ready for publication on May thirtieth. The title Holt had chosen for the book was *Complete Poems of Robert Frost 1949*. Like the 1939 collected edition, this one began with "The Figure a Poem Makes." Then followed, in chronological order, the texts of each of the eight volumes of verse Frost had published from *A Boy's Will* (1913) to *Steeple Bush* (1947). Preceding the masques of *Reason* and *Mercy,* with which the volume ended, was a section called "An Afterword," containing three poems, each of recent origin and each having appeared in some fashion prior to 1949.

The book was well reviewed, and advance sales soon indicated *Complete Poems* was going to do very well indeed. In the fall of 1949 he wrote to Lesley:

". . . I have a vague sense of having had this year the height of my success. It is entirely beyond anything I ever dreamed of or set my heart on. Its our elders that despise our unpromising youth. So they get dead and safely out of the way before they are proved wrong in their misjudgement of us. There are a few people I regret not triumphing over. But it is with a mild regret that seldom comes over me in its unworthiness. Now would be the time for them to have to reappear and face my facts. Any earlier it wouldnt have been so hard on them. Any later we dont know what the situation might have become. 'For we are poised on a huge wave of fate. And whether it will roll us out to sea' etc etc as it is written in Sorab and Rustum—if I remember rightly. I haven't my Arnold here to verify it. . . ."

As he approached his "seventy-fifth" birthday, Frost had a gathering body of evidence that the "wave of fate" would not roll him out to sea, but would deposit him, triumphant, on dry land. In November, at a Waldorf-Astoria luncheon, the Limited Editions Club awarded him its gold medal, for *Complete Poems*—the book that, published within the past five years, was judged "most likely to attain the stature of a classic." Early in 1950 he was informed that a committee of the American Academy of Arts and Letters had nominated him as a candidate for that year's Nobel Prize for literature.

When the Nobel Prizes were announced, Frost's name was not among the winners. On March twenty-fourth, however, two days before his birthday, the United States Senate bestowed an honor upon him that was a satisfactory alternative to the Swedish award—a resolution passed by unanimous consent:

"Whereas Robert Frost in his books of poetry has given the American people a long series of stories and lyrics which are enjoyed, repeated, and thought about by people of all ages and callings; and

"Whereas these poems have helped to guide American thought with humor and wisdom, setting forth to our minds a reliable representation of ourselves and of all men; and

"Whereas his work through the past half century has enhanced for many their understanding of the United States and their love of country; and

"Whereas Robert Frost has been accorded a secure place in the history of American letters; and

"Whereas on March 26 he will celebrate his seventy-fifth birthday: Therefore be it

"*Resolved,* That the Senate of the United States extend him felicitations of the Nation which he has served so well."

But the year marked so magnificently for Frost by the birthday resolution of the Senate also brought to a bittersweet resolution the long legal battles of his principal collector, Earle J. Bernheimer. While Bernheimer was by no means reduced to poverty, his assets had greatly diminished, and he was forced to a series of painful decisions. One of these, he told Frost in a letter in March, was that he was disposing of his art and literary collections—foremost among them his books and manuscripts of Robert Frost. Unable now to give this assemblage to an academic library, as he had always hoped and intended, he would sell it, he told Frost, to any library willing to pay his price of $18,000.

Hoping it was not too late to dissuade Bernheimer from the "absolute decision" he had made, Frost sent on March nineteenth an importunate letter:

". . . Throw collecting out of your life if you must and throw away your collections. But hold on a minute. You've been my friend and I've been yours. We've exchanged favors in the largest way. How many friends have you ever had who could speak to you as I am speaking now? I make no secret of it that I have had a romantic pleasure in your being my one and only Maecenas. If anybody else had bestowed on me with your generosity I might now be rich enough to take up with your offer of your Frost collection for sale. Surely our friendship has gone too far for you to want to chuck it along with the collection. Dont treat me like the women who have bedevilled you. Let's keep our kindness to each other in mind as the central fact in all this. You can see how you would hurt my sensibilities a little in seeming to assume that I would be willing to act for profit as a middleman between you and any purchaser of the books I have inscribed for you. You are in a petulant mood and not saying what you really mean. Of course I'll try to find you a purchaser in a creditable quarter if that is your insistance[.] But what I would very much rather do is what I have wanted to do all along—persuade you to end as you began ma[g]nificently. . . . How do I mean magnificently? I mean becoming a man of your means and intelligence. I mean by giving the whole big rubbish heap to some one library to be preserved in your name and mine as the Bernheimer Frost Collection. . . ."

Bernheimer's reply was friendly enough, but by no means was it the kind of turnabout for which Frost had hoped. He tried one last time to advise him against selling:

". . . There should be nothing more to say. Nevertheless I am going to indulge in one last word of protest. I still think it would be a real triumph of sentiment if you made yourself the final benefactor by conferring the collection in your name on one of the colleges I spoke of. That would be fine for us both. I wish I could get at you personally for a good old persuasive talk. Please go slow in taking your decision. Mind you the sale of the collection will give me no offence. I merely speak to save you from what you might come yourself to look on as a mistake. . . ."

Quite possibly Frost initially intended to behave in a manner consistent with his statement that "the sale of the collection will give me no offence." Once the auction became a certainty, however, and word began to circulate that Bernheimer possessed a considerable number of Frost books and manuscripts, all inscribed to him, Frost's self-defensive instincts outweighed his more generous impulses. In conversations with friends and book-collecting acquaintances, during the months preceding the December auction, he repeatedly hinted that Earle Bernheimer's decision to auction his collection constituted the most inexplicable kind of betrayal. He hinted—or said flatly—that much of what Bernheimer had to sell had been gifts from him, including the unique book, *Twilight*. He professed to have no idea why Bernheimer should abruptly decide to dispose of what he had accumulated.

The public auction of Bernheimer's "remarkable collection of the writings of Robert Frost" brought, at the Parke-Bernet Galleries in New York, a total approaching $15,000—in a market made bearish by the widespread belief that Bernheimer was selling for profit the gifts of a victimized poet. As a final irony, the unique *Twilight*, for which Bernheimer had paid Frost's price of $4,000 in 1940, was purchased for $3,500—a figure that, according to a brief account in *The New York Times*, was "thought to be the highest ever paid for a work by a contemporary American author."

In the months between his birthday in March and the auction in

December, the only major poem Frost wrote was "How Hard It Is to Keep from Being King When It's in You and in the Situation." The verse tale hinges on a son's sale of his father into slavery—in a public auction. First read on May twenty-fifth as the Blashfield Address of the American Academy of Arts and Letters, the poem was a humorous parable concerning a king and prince who have had enough of royal life and flee their palace "in the guise of men."

Two weeks before reading "How Hard It Is . . ." to the American Academy, Frost had broken the ice with a new communications medium, by appearing briefly on John Cameron Swayze's popular television program, "Watch the World." The Blashfield Address was to have been the matter of his second television appearance, later in the month. But after putting up with spotlights so blinding they almost prevented him from reading his poem, he was informed that, through a technical malfunction, the part of his reading that was to have been broadcast had been lost. Frost was so annoyed that he confined his activities for the next two years to more familiar avenues of public expression.

Thus, for the balance of 1950 and most of 1951, he did little that added more than footnotes to an already-impressive career. In the June following his American Academy appearance, he accepted honorary degrees from Colgate and Marlboro; and in August he participated, as usual, in the Bread Loaf School of English and the Writers' Conference. In October he attended another conference, in his honor, at Kenyon College—after which he returned to New England to spend a month in residence at Amherst in fulfillment of his duties as Simpson Lecturer in Literature. In the first months of 1951 he could be found at his winter retreat in South Miami; and in the spring the pattern of readings from Florida to New Hampshire began once again.

This regular cycle of activities was temporarily interrupted by an illness that, untreated, might well have posed a serious problem. In the summer of 1951 a wen Frost had long had on the right side of his face, near his right eye, began to grow and ulcerate. A local doctor he went to for advice suspected an allergic reaction to some food he had taken and told Frost to think no more about it. A week later, however, during the closing exercises of the Bread Loaf School of English, Frost was introduced to a Boston doctor named Ragle, whose son was a member of the graduating class. After an exchange of pleasantries, Dr. Ragle took Kay Morrison aside to say the lesion on Frost's face was cancer and must have immediate attention. A few days later Frost entered the Mary Hitchcock Memorial Hospital in Hanover, New Hampshire, and underwent facial surgery.

The operation was successful, and Frost remained in the hospital several days to give his wound a chance to mend. Scarred though he was by this most recent life-threatening disease, his general health was unusually good for a man approaching eighty. True, his gait had slowed a bit, his hearing and eyesight had begun to fail, and he did not have the excess of physical energy he had once had. But his mind remained undimmed, and his gift for monologue and memorization more than adequately made up for what he had lost in his ability to hear a low-toned conversation or read unfamiliar verse on the public platform. Rarely, now, did he "read" poems to an audience. Rather, he "said" them, and did so with equal facility—though occasionally with some initial fumbling —whether they were his own or those of Shakespeare or Milton, Emerson or Longfellow.

Survivor that he was, it was inevitable that he should outlive some of his closest friends. John Bartlett had died in 1947, followed by his wife, Margaret. Hervey Allen had died in 1949; early in 1952, Sidney Cox. Equally inevitably, a new generation of friends rose up, composed of young men and women who had come to know Frost as a teacher at Amherst, Dartmouth, Harvard, or on other campuses at which he spent some time each year. His students revered him, cherished his friendship and advice, and looked upon him as a benign, loving grandfather, full of wisdom and wit. It was an image Frost found particularly congenial.

One young man fortunate enough to have gained Frost's respect and affection was Hyde Cox, the wandering Harvard graduate Frost had first met and befriended in Key West early in 1940. In many subsequent visits by Cox to Ripton or Cambridge and by Frost to Crow Island, Cox's home on the coast in Manchester, Massachusetts, each provided the other with a kind of companionship neither could derive in quite the same way from anyone else. With Hyde Cox, as with many other friends over the years, Frost wanted to discover as much as he could about every aspect of his friend's existence, and to provide help and encouragement in any way he could.

Cox in personality probably reminded Frost of no one so much as his most cherished friend, Edward Thomas. Like Thomas, who at Frost's instance had turned to writing poetry before his death in the First World War, Hyde was extremely sensitive, easily depressed, and sometimes at a loss as to what direction his life should take. Intellectually gifted, he was obviously capable of doing almost anything he chose. Frost followed with interest his friend's circuitous route toward personal fulfillment, seeing in Hyde's developing career something of his own protracted struggle for self-realization. Often, when Hyde's spirits were low, Frost would manage to come forth with just the right word to set things right.

Cox was particularly happy when, in late 1949, another of his friends, the noted sculptor Walker Hancock, expressed an interest in doing a head of the poet. Cox soon conspired to bring Frost to Gloucester, Massachusetts, where the artist had his studio. The head was modeled in March 1950, and the experience was as rewarding for Frost as it was for Cox and Hancock. During many hours Frost watched Hancock demonstrate his prowess, as the head took shape. The poet talked all through the sittings—and displayed prowess of his own by composing, aloud, lines for the poem he would read in May to the American Academy, "How Hard It Is to Keep from Being King. . . ." When the head was at last completed, Frost agreed that his likeness had never been more successfully captured in any artistic medium.

Besides the poem he had read to the American Academy in 1950, his productions in the years immediately following *Complete Poems* rarely came to more than one a year, that one being the poem he sent in booklet form to friends at Christmastime. In 1950 it was "Our Doom to Bloom," the title of which referred to the inevitable proliferation of the welfare state; in 1951 it was "A Cabin in the Clearing," a dialogue between Smoke and Mist concerning the "inner haze" of a country cabin's occupants; in 1952, "Does No One But Me at All Ever Feel This Way in the Least," a complaint to the sea on its failure to isolate the New World from the Old; in 1953, "One More Brevity," concerning a dog much like Gillie (whose death in 1949 had robbed Frost of his most constant companion). Besides "How Hard It Is to Keep from Being King . . . ," the only poem he published between 1950 and 1953 that was not a Christmas offering was "For Columbus Day," first read at Amherst in December 1950 (and ultimately titled "America Is Hard to See"), which reflected his impressive knowledge of events in pre-colonial American history.

Despite a recurrence of face cancer, which necessitated a second operation in late December, the year 1953 was, by and large, a good one for Robert Frost. In March he was awarded the annual fellowship of the Academy of American Poets, which carried a stipend of $5,000. In June he accepted an honorary degree from the University of North Carolina. In December, a week before the cancer surgery, he concluded an active year of lecturing, by returning to California, where an audience of 2,500 at the university in Berkeley gave him an enthusiastic reception.

It was 1954, however, that was truly a milestone year. Only months before he reached what would have been celebrated as his "seventy-ninth" birthday, March 26, 1954, the researches of his biographer revealed that Frost would, in fact, be eighty years old on that day. Plans were quickly formulated by his friends in Washington, Amherst, New York, and elsewhere to mark the suddenly extra-significant date with appropriate kinds of public and private celebration.

The events connected with Frost's birthday began on March twelfth in Washington, where he had been invited to a White House reception by

President Dwight Eisenhower's assistant, Sherman Adams. Frost had first met Adams a year or two earlier. As Governor of New Hampshire, on a visit to Boston, Adams had been taken to the St. Botolph Club to hear Frost give a reading of his poems; and at the end of the evening he had been called on for remarks. Much to the poet's surprise, the Governor had quoted from memory several appropriate lines of Frost's poem "New Hampshire," and their friendship had thus begun. Adams's invitation to Frost to come to the White House implied that the President would be there to welcome him. Such proved not to be the case. But Frost's afternoon at 1600 Pennsylvania Avenue, where he read his poems to, and was toasted on his upcoming birthday by, the assembled staff, was an exciting experience that did much to further the friendship of the politics-loving Vermont poet and the poetry-loving ex-Governor of New Hampshire.

In New York on March twenty-fifth Frost's day began with a nine-o'clock press conference at his suite in the Waldorf-Astoria, where for nearly three hours he answered questions in a room crowded with television cameras, glaring lights, and some two dozen reporters. That evening he attended a Holt-sponsored dinner in his honor, to which had been invited some eighty guests—and each was given an autographed copy of *Aforesaid* (which, published that day, was Holt's own birthday gift to Frost: a new selection of his verse, in a limited edition of 650 copies).

On Friday, March twenty-sixth, Frost went to Amherst, Massachusetts, where a second major birthday party was held, in the dining room of the Lord Jeffery Inn. That night there was a touch of sadness in the gathering, for one of those who was to have spoken, George Whicher, had died of a heart attack three weeks before. (His remarks in praise of Frost, the last thing he did before his death, were read at the dinner by an Amherst colleague.) But sadness was not the reigning emotion of the party, at which the guest list of eighty included more of those Frost considered his close friends than had the Holt affair the night before.

One by one, the after-dinner speakers rose at the behest of toastmaster Archibald MacLeish and offered reminiscences and praise of the poet they had come to honor. While Frost, exhausted and ill from the day before, sat pale and impassive behind a bouquet of eighty red roses, President Cole spoke of how Frost had spent twenty-three of his last thirty-eight years at Amherst. After Cole it was Louis Untermeyer's turn to speak. He recalled how he had been one of the first in America to review the poetry of Robert Frost, whose work, in 1914, had just appeared in a British magazine. ("I was amazed," said Untermeyer, "that any Englishman could write with so pronounced a New England accent.") An encomium by Mark Van Doren followed, read in his absence by MacLeish. Then, it was Thornton Wilder's turn; then, MacLeish's; then, Whicher's stand-in, Curtis Canfield. When Canfield had finished, Hyde Cox presented to the poet his birthday gift, an Andrew Wyeth watercolor.

After Cox, Raymond Holden rose to say a few words, and to read a letter from the Governor of New Hampshire. Finally, it was time for Frost himself to speak. He began by commenting on the manifold tribute he had just been accorded. "I don't read about myself very much," he said, "but I hear about it, people tell me, word comes to me: then I spend all night wondering if it's true. I've heard a lot tonight to think over, and it makes me look back, think about my poems, and think about why I wrote them."

To the frequent comment that "poets die young" he answered that poets die in many ways; not just into the grave, but into businessmen, into critics, or into philosophers—"one of the noblest ways to die." This reminded him, he said, that "what begins more ethereal than substantial often tends to end more substantial than ethereal. . . . You might say that that's the curve from the lyric to the epic. . . . But when I think of myself (I'm made self-conscious about it all) I wonder if the curve hasn't been a little different from that; it's always been very substantial, I think, from the very earliest. . . . Ethereal growing more substantial till I may be too much of a thinker. I hear the praise of my wisdom—and I once threatened to think about that a little; what begins in delight ends in wisdom. . . ."

After talking about his late interest in "collecting absolutes" (universal truths just surprising enough to give delight, as well as inspire wisdom), he told of his press conference the day before; then, of an encounter he had had with a local grocer; and, then, to conclude, of what it was like to be called "great" so many times in one evening: "You know, people say you're this and you're that and you wonder if you're anything—and words are strange, aren't they? Hard to get out. Perfection is a great thing. All I've wanted is to write a few little poems it'd be hard to get rid of. That's all I ask. I heard somebody say, you know, that if you don't know you're great you can't be great. This word 'great' grates on my nerves!"

ADDED GLORY
AT HOME AND ABROAD

(1954–1957)

WHEN SHE came to Ripton in July 1954, Lesley Frost had a special purpose in mind. A former employee in Spain of the United States Information Agency and a frequent lecturer in South America, she had been asked by her friends in the Department of State to seek her father's participation in a forthcoming goodwill mission. In August an international writers' congress was to be held in São Paulo, Brazil, as one of the principal events in the city's quadricentennial celebration. The United States had been invited to send a poet and a prose writer to the congress, and the State Department's choice in the former category was Robert Frost. If he agreed to go, Lesley would serve him there as companion and interpreter.

Frost was at first reluctant, not only because it would require him to fly for the first time since 1939, but also because it would require a violation of one of his oldest maxims: "I only go—when I'm the show." Conversations with State Department officials convinced him, however, that this was no ordinary mission. In recent months, he was told, anti-Americanism had been on the rise in Brazil. The temporary denial, on political grounds, of a United States visa to Brazilian writer José Lins do Rêgo had exacerbated an already-precarious situation. By agreeing to attend the congress, Frost would be doing much to improve the image of his country throughout South America. For this everyone, from the American embassy in São Paulo to the White House itself, would be greatly in his debt. After some consideration, he decided to please both Lesley and the State Department by going.

The two Frosts left New York on August fourth. Then began ten days of poetry readings, sightseeing, parties, and press conferences, through all of which Frost moved with the easy assurance of a seasoned man of the world. In both São Paulo and Rio his lecture performances were received with great enthusiasm, with an adulation, in fact, usually reserved for the most-popular native poets.

His talk about poetry often wandered, as it did at home, into political subjects. At a Rio press conference, on August tenth, he offered his wry views on a favorite topic of his fellow congress-goers: the desirability of a "one-world" approach to solving political differences. "Decency, honor, and not too much deceit," he said, "are about the best one can aspire to in international relations." And "nationalism and internationalism are the same as personalism and interpersonalism. There cannot be anything interesting between persons unless they are persons. There cannot be anything interesting between nations unless they are both distinctly nations."

At the congress itself he came down hard on the frequently heard complaint that the United States, with its overwhelming economic power, dominated South America. "They spent most of their time worrying about us (the United States)—" he later reported, "not hating us so much as worrying. They worry about our materialism, think we lead them astray with our movies, automobiles, our chewing gum and Coca-Cola.

"I reassured them. If they don't trust us, they shouldn't buy our things. They shouldn't be so willing to be seduced."

Having completed his Brazilian itinerary, Frost agreed to Lesley's request to return by way of Lima, Peru. After a few days there, as guest of the American ambassador, he was happy, however, to return to Vermont. He delayed his homecoming only long enough to confer in Washington with Secretary of State John Foster Dulles, to whom he offered suggestions for the improved management of "inter-cultural affairs."

With scarcely a pause to catch his breath, Frost was soon back at work, talking and reading on native and familiar ground. The work consisted, as well, of accepting honors and awards—of which there were many in this, his eighty-first year. In October he received the distinguished-service award of the New Hampshire Education Association and a similar honor from the Theodore Roosevelt Association. In November he was made honorary associate of Harvard's Adams House and given an honorary LL.D. by the University of Cincinnati. The new year, 1955, began with an honor that was particularly gratifying. John Dickey, his good friend, wrote to say that the trustees of Dartmouth, in a move unprecedented in the history of the college, had voted to grant him a second honorary doctorate. To the doctorate of letters given him in 1933 would now be added a doctorate of laws.

The poet's occasional assertions to the contrary notwithstanding, honors and awards—the gathering of what he himself called "glory"— were very much what Robert Frost's later years were about. Having been deprived, almost totally, of any kind of recognition for the first forty years of his life, he carried with him into old age a need for approbation that was almost insatiable. Each new honor did more than gratify; it was a vindication—a proof of his personal and poetic worth. The doubters, now, were all believers, but the old inner doubts remained. Only the steady influx of objectified praise could quiet the fear he had that everything he had achieved would somehow slip away.

Frost's hunger for glory and his willingness to pursue it were nowhere better illustrated than in a series of events that, from their simple beginning in April 1956, culminated in one of the more glorious episodes of his life. His eighty-second birthday was some two weeks behind him when a letter arrived from President Eisenhower's assistant, Sherman Adams. It read:

"There is a matter in which the President is personally interested and about which we would like very much to talk with you in the near future.

"Mr. Conger Reynolds, of the U. S. Information Agency, will try to reach you for an appointment. . . ."

In his meeting with Frost, at the Homer Noble Farm, Reynolds had little to say about any matter in which President Eisenhower was, except in the broadest sense, "personally interested." Instead, he described various areas around the world where American prestige was threatened and various ways in which his own agency, the U.S.I.A., was working to defend the nation's image abroad. Among the more effective ways of doing so, Reynolds explained, was to have well-known and respected public figures write essays about American life, for international distribution. Perhaps Frost might wish to undertake such an essay.

It was the second request in as many weeks that Frost felt bound to decline. In early June, Sherman Adams had written him to invite his membership in a group called CASE, a committee of artists and scientists favoring President Eisenhower's re-election. In December, however (a month after Eisenhower had managed, without Frost's help, to win re-election), a letter arrived from the man who had been instrumental in his 1954 mission to South America, Harold Howland. "Our Embassy at London has informed us," he wrote, "that it is planning an exhibit concerning your life and work. . . . The Embassy has further stated that a personal visit by you would enhance immeasurably the effect of this exhibit on the English public.

"The Department of State, recalling your splendid cooperation in visiting Latin America . . . , wholeheartedly endorses the Embassy's suggestion. . . ."

The letter concluded with an invitation to visit Great Britain, at government expense, sometime between February and June of the coming year.

Howland's letter came as a surprise. Conger Reynolds, in his June visit to Ripton, had given not the slightest indication that anything like this trip to England was being contemplated by the State Department. Nor had Sherman Adams. Was this invitation unrelated, then, to the events and conversations of recent months? Frost could only guess.

What he did know was that he was interested in the proposed trip and wanted to hear more about it. But he did not sit back and wait for Howland's next letter. Instead, he wrote Amherst trustee Eustace Seligman, New York law partner of Secretary of State Dulles, and began on his own to elicit the "demand" that was his prerequisite for making the English trip. Further, on January 4, 1957, he wrote to Sherman Adams: ". . . without making too much fuss about it you might look into this request I have from the State Department to visit England for myself and for my country this spring. What I need to know is how much I am wanted and at what level. It would be no small undertaking for me to go abroad. I should want to be sure it would be worth the trouble all around. I suppose advice is what I am after. . . ."

As a result of Frost's prodding of Seligman and Adams, Secretary Dulles wrote him on February twelfth, urging that he "accept this new call upon your services as a distinguished representative of the American cultural scene." But Frost was not yet satisfied. What he still wanted —probably had wanted from the very first mention of this trip—was something only the English could provide. To round out the public career that had begun in England before the First World War, he wanted from the most honorable of British universities, Oxford and Cambridge, honorary degrees.

To achieve this end, Frost now turned his attention to England itself. Acting under his instructions, Kay Morrison spoke with John L. Sweeney, curator of the Poetry Room of the Harvard library, and suggested that he write to friends in England and Ireland to inform them Frost might be coming in the spring. This he did; and, as Frost had hoped, word soon began filtering back that both Oxford and Cambridge, as well as the National University of Ireland, were considering giving him degrees.

The time was now right to answer Dulles's letter. On February twenty-sixth, Frost wrote:

"Your letter helps me to a decision. I feel better with your assurance that the State Department and our Embassy will take care of me to see that I am kept reasonably busy. I wouldn't want to be shot off as an unguided missile. I have personal friends in England and Scotland, though not so many as once upon a time when I lived with them a while before the great wars. My books are over there too with Jonathan Cape and I must have some readers. But I wouldn't want it to look as if I had come over to laze around aimiably on vacation. I wish you could tell Mr. Howland that it is not overwork that I fear. I want my time planned for. . . ."

On March ninth Sir Douglas Veale, registrar of Oxford University, wrote to inform him that the Hebdomadal Council had "resolved to propose to the Convocation of the University that the Degree of Doctor of Letters, *honoris causa,* be conferred upon you." Brian Downs, vice-chancellor of Cambridge University, sent a similar message. Only two Americans before Frost had been accorded this rare double honor: Henry Wadsworth Longfellow, in 1868, and James Russell Lowell, in 1873. The goodwill mission would now be, as well, a major personal triumph.

A few weeks later, Frost shared his good news with Lawrance Thompson, whom he would shortly invite to serve as his companion on the English trip. The plans, as finally worked out, called for Frost to leave for England on Sunday, May nineteenth, and for Thompson to follow next day. In London, Frost was met at Heathrow airport by the head of the United States Information Service program, and by newspaper reporters and cameramen. He was rushed to a room at the airport terminal for a short television interview, shown that night on the B.B.C. news. Then, he was taken to the Connaught Hotel.

Tuesday was Frost's first public appearance, a reading at the University of London, scheduled for the afternoon. Before the performance, he was given a small reception attended, among others, by T. S. Eliot. "It would be a great disappointment if my more or less official return to England didn't mean furthering our acquaintance," Frost had on May second written his onetime "enemy," "and I should be less a respector of persons than I am if I didn't hope to give you before I get through with this here world the highest sign of my regard. You and I shot off at different tangents from almost the same pin wheel. We had America in common and we had Ezra in common though you had much more of him than I. If I was ever cross with you it was for leaving America behind too far and Ezra not far enough. But such things look less and less important as we age on. . . ." At the reception, Frost asked Eliot if the letter had given him any offense. Said Eliot, "I didn't mind the scolding."

The reading was attended by an overflow crowd of some 700 people. Frost began by recalling the Poetry Bookshop of Harold Monro, and he mentioned F. S. Flint—who, like Eliot, was present in the audience—as the first person in literary circles whom he had met during his visit to England in the period 1912–1915. Flint, he said, had introduced him to Ezra Pound. His reminiscences continued with an account of the publication of his first book, by the London publisher David Nutt, in 1913; his reasons for coming to England the year before; the poems and friendships he had written and formed during his four-year stay. He was in fine form, and the audience loved him. As he finished, the applause was sustained, and many came up to ask for autographs. His first performance was an auspicious beginning for the many more to come.

Wednesday, May twenty-second, Thompson took him to the American embassy for a visit with Ambassador John Hay Whitney. Their meeting, from Frost's point of view, was a failure. The ambassador seemed uninterested in initiating conversation, so Frost spent most of their visit educating him about his namesake, John Hay, author of *The Pike County Ballads*; but it was apparent to Frost the ambassador did not care much for poetry, or for him. The rest of the day was busy—too busy—and by the end of the day he was exhausted. Back at the hotel, he complained to Thompson of chest pains, and said he might have to give up the whole trip.

May twenty-third the schedule was built around Frost's talk-and-reading at Cambridge University. Fully recovered, Frost addressed an audience of some 400 that afternoon. The twenty-fourth was a day of travel, from Cambridge to Durham, and Frost in the afternoon addressed a capacity audience at the university.

The plan for the weekend was for Frost to do little but rest, in preparation for the activities of the days ahead. On returning to London he complained that his stomach was upset. He was well enough, however, to attend a dinner Monday in his honor, given by the staff of *The London Magazine*. On Tuesday, after dining at the Garrick Club with Rupert Hart-Davis, Frost returned to the Connaught and happened to see Adlai Stevenson, the unsuccessful Presidential candidate in the last election, crossing the lobby. He and Stevenson chatted about why they were in England. Then, still bothered by his indisposition, he attended a dinner at London University, and went to bed early.

Wednesday he had luncheon at the House of Lords with William Henry Beveridge (Baron Beveridge of Tuggal, architect of the British "welfare state"), a champagne party arranged by his English publisher, Jonathan Cape, and a dinner party given in his honor by Penguin Books.

Thursday, May thirtieth, Frost made his second excursion from London, for a two-day visit to Manchester, where his lecture was held in the largest available auditorium of Manchester University. Even here, the house was filled, with people sitting in the aisles and standing in the rear; and in another lecture hall nearby an overflow audience listened over a public-address system. Friday he attended a luncheon in his honor and spoke once again.

Back in London, after a short rest he set out for Sussex to visit one of his first English champions, Sir John Squire, once editor of the famous literary magazine *The London Mercury*. When the visit was over, Frost was subdued and saddened. His friend had fallen on hard times. Squire was now the mere shadow of what he had been.

June second, in the morning, Frost was to go with Eleanor Farjeon, once a close friend of Edward Thomas's, on a visit to the late poet's widow, Helen. When Thompson went to tell Frost that Miss Farjeon was waiting, Frost hoarsely announced he had caught a sore throat yesterday, on the way back from Sussex, and thus could not go. Nevertheless, he dressed hurriedly and went downstairs to greet Miss Farjeon and make his apologies.

On June third, when Thompson called on Frost at eleven in the morning, he found the poet still in his nightgown, complaining that he was sick. His face was pale, his words slurred and unconnected. He allowed Thompson to take his pulse, which was so weak that a doctor's visit seemed to Thompson imperative. Before calling the embassy, he asked Frost if he had taken any medicine for his throat. Yes, said Frost, he had taken quite a lot of morphine pills all day; and, then, when he couldn't sleep, two sleeping pills during the night.

The doctor confirmed what Thompson feared. The effect of the morphine and sleeping pills was synergetic—each reinforcing the strength of the other. Pneumonia, under such circumstances, was a real danger. The doctor suggested Frost spend the next twenty-four hours in bed. But the situation was not that simple. This was the day he was supposed to go to Oxford. In less than twenty-four hours he was to be accepting his first honorary degree.

It was decided that if he slept in the car, he could probably make it to Oxford later in the day. And sleep he did, all the way. They drove directly to the warden's lodge of Wadham College, where Sir Maurice Bowra awaited them. Sleeping some two more hours after his arrival, Frost was well enough recovered by evening to take dinner with Sir Maurice and to attend a reception in his honor later that evening.

On Tuesday, Frost walked in his red-and-gray academic robe to the Oxford convocation ceremony. The citation was read in Latin, and Frost seemed to follow it. He perked up when the statement occurred that "he would rather make a claim on our regard simply as a farmer and as a poet." The citation continued: "In truth he has for so long now devoted himself to the arts of the poet and the husbandman that his work has passed into his character, nay, into his features which reflect the genius of the poet, the sturdiness of the farmer, and the peace of old age. . . ."

That afternoon, at five, Frost was ushered into a large hall for what would be one of his best talks of the English trip. As he finished, after an hour and a half, Nevill Coghill thanked him from the floor, saying it had been a very memorable, amusing, and very moving experience. To sustained applause, Frost then was escorted up the central aisle.

Wednesday, June fifth, the schedule was relatively light. At noon Frost addressed the American Association, with W. H. Auden relaying questions. Later he dined with Lord and Lady Beveridge. Finally, he drove to Cheltenham where, after a visit with his old friend Jack Haines, he retired to prepare for next day's tour of "old haunts" in the Dymock region of Gloucestershire.

Thursday, after his return to London, he attended a dinner at the Savile Club, arranged in his honor by Stephen Spender and Irving Kristol of *Encounter* magazine. The guests included C. Day Lewis, Dwight Macdonald, Graham Greene, Isaiah Berlin, Arthur Waley, Laurie Lee, and E. M. Forster.

After four days of rest, on Tuesday, June eleventh, Frost went at noon to the B.B.C. office building and recorded a half-hour question-and-answer session. At five he gave a reading to the Poetry Society, attended by an overflow audience. And at seven-thirty he left for the major event of the day, a formal dinner in his honor, sponsored by Books Across the Sea, a committee within the English Speaking Union.

T. S. Eliot had agreed to serve as toastmaster, and after dinner, with Frost by his side, Eliot began to speak:

"Mr. Frost, . . . I would like, before proposing a toast, merely to drop one or two grains of incense before you.

". . . I never heard your name until I came to this country; and I heard it first from Ezra Pound, of all people. He told me about you with great enthusiasm. I gathered that you were a protégé of his of whom he expected a good deal! At the same time, I gathered that your work, or what had appeared at that time, was not in Ezra Pound's opinion required reading for *me*. He may have been right, at that time, because I was still in a formative period, and goodness knows what would have happened if you had influenced me at that stage. But, you know, as one gets older, one cares less about movements and tendencies and groups. We all have our own idiom and metric and subject matter, but I have long since come to feel that there are only two kinds of poetry—good and bad. And the bad poetry can be very much of one's own type, and the good poetry can be of a very different type.

"Mr. Frost is one of the good poets; and I might say, perhaps, *the* most eminent—the most *distinguished,* I must call it—Anglo-American poet now living. I have a special weakness, perhaps—no, I shouldn't call it a weakness—a special understanding of a great deal of his work, because I also have the New England background. But I think that there are two kinds of local feeling in poetry. There is one kind which makes that poetry only accessible to people who've had the same background, to whom it means a great deal. And there is another kind which can go with universality: the relation of Dante to Florence, of Shakespeare to Warwickshire, of Goethe to the Rhineland, the relation of Robert Frost to New England. He has that universality. And I think that the beginning of his career, and the fact that his first publication and reputation was made in this country, and that he is now hailed in this country universally as the most distinguished American poet, points to that fact.

"Ladies and gentlemen, I give you Robert Frost."

Frost was moved by Eliot's remarks, almost to tears. When he rose to acknowledge the tribute, the first thing he said was, "There's nobody living in either country that I'd rather hear that from."

Wednesday, June twelfth, Frost went to Cambridge. Thursday, after a morning stroll, donning his red gown, he was one of eight granted Cambridge honorary degrees. In the afternoon Frost returned to his hotel and was visited there briefly by Mr. and Mrs. I. A. Richards. He paid a visit himself to E. M. Forster, and late in the day Frost and his party left Cambridge and returned to London. They stopped on the way in Beaconsfield to examine The Bungalow, the house the Frost family had occupied in the period 1912–1914.

Farewells were the main business of Frost's last full day in England. At twelve-thirty on Friday, June fourteenth, a bon voyage luncheon party was given him by Sir Allen Lane of Penguin Books, at a French restaurant. Next, Frost went to a tea at the United States Information Service, attended, as well, by the staff of the American embassy, their wives and children. The day ended with a short interview for B.B.C. television.

Saturday, the fifteenth, Frost and Thompson flew to Dublin. They were met there by Michael Tierney, president of University College, Dublin, and Frost later dined with his host, the American ambassador to Ireland, William H. Taft III (whose father had once been Frost's choice for President of the United States).

On Tuesday evening Frost gave a talk-and-reading at University College. Wednesday he was awarded an honorary degree by the National University of Ireland, and presiding was the aged and renowned Prime Minister, Eamon de Valera.

Three degrees and many memories richer, Frost, at eighty-three, had successfully completed his mission.

IN THE SETTING
OF THE CAPITAL

(1957–1961)

IN THE first public appearance of his English trip, his afternoon talk at the University of London, Robert Frost had spoken of the "selfish generosity" shown him by Ezra Pound when they first met in England in 1913. Then Pound had taken it upon himself to "boom" Frost in the United States, by submitting a review of his first book, *A Boy's Will,* to Harriet Monroe's *Poetry* magazine. If Frost had thereby incurred a debt to the brilliant-but-erratic poet, it was one he eventually chose to forget. Pound's high-handed manner in London, his penchant for verbal indelicacy, and particularly his activities in the Second World War killed whatever sense of obligation Frost may at first have felt. Frost was satisfied that Pound was not only mad, but a traitor, deserving indefinite confinement in the government mental institution, St. Elizabeths Hospital in Washington, where he had been placed in 1946.

Not until 1954 did Frost's attitude toward Pound begin to soften. It was in that year that there appeared in *The New York Times Book Review* a review by Horace Gregory of *Literary Essays of Ezra Pound,* edited by T. S. Eliot. In it Gregory praised Eliot for reintroducing to the reading public "Pound the man of letters, who in 1913 and 1914 praised an unknown poet, Robert Frost, and another unknown writer, D. H. Lawrence. . . ." And the *Book Review* featured, alongside Gregory's commentary, a quote from a 1914 review by Pound of *North of Boston.*

"Mr. Frost," Pound had written, "is an honest writer, writing from himself, from his own knowledge and emotion; not simply picking up the manner which magazines are accepting at the moment, and applying it to topics in vogue. He is quite consciously and definitely putting New England rural life into verse. He is not using themes that anybody could have cribbed out of Ovid.

"There are only two passions in art; there are only love and hate—with endless modifications. Frost has been honestly fond of the New England people, I dare say with spells of irritation. He has given their life honestly and seriously. He has never turned aside to make fun of it. He has taken their tragedy as tragedy, their stubbornness as stubbornness. I know more of farm life than I did before I had read his poems. That means I know more of 'Life.' "

Frost was forced to admit, in seeing anew this statement of four decades past, that Pound had not only been one of his earliest critics, but one of his best. And while rereading the essay fragment scarcely left Frost with a feeling of love for Pound, it did make him feel something other than scorn. Perhaps, Frost admitted for the first time, Pound deserved a fate somewhat less extreme than to languish forever in St. Elizabeths Hospital, facing indictment—if he "recovered"—for the crime of treason.

Despite his new attitude, for nearly three years Frost did nothing to help his onetime champion. Then, early in 1957, he was asked by Archibald MacLeish, one of several writers who had long been campaigning for Pound's release, to join that effort in an important way. MacLeish had written a letter to Attorney General Brownell, which T. S. Eliot and Ernest Hemingway had agreed to sign. MacLeish did not intend, he explained, to sign it himself, for he was known in Republican Washington as a staunch New Deal Democrat. That, said MacLeish, was where Frost came in. He was on good terms with Sherman Adams and others within the Eisenhower administration. His views, if not explicitly Republican, certainly leaned toward that party's conservatism. He was, most important, the best-loved poet in the United States. His signature on the letter to Brownell, therefore, would very possibly prove decisive in winning Ezra Pound's release.

From the rising storm of opposition to Pound's continued confinement, Frost guessed it would not be long before Pound won his freedom, with or without his help. He saw no reason it should not be he who was remembered as having been instrumental in winning it. Demonstrating his own kind of "selfish generosity," Frost agreed to sign the letter MacLeish had drafted and to have his name appear first. Dated January 14, 1957, it read:

"We are writing to you about Ezra Pound who has been confined in St. Elizabeths Hospital in Washington for eleven years under indictment for treason.

"Our interest in this matter is founded in part on our concern for Mr. Pound who is one of the most distinguished American writers of his generation, and in part on our concern for the country of our birth. As writers ourselves we cannot but be aware of the effect on writers and lovers of literature throughout the world of Pound's continued incarceration at a time when certain Nazis tried and convicted of the most heinous crimes, have been released and in many cases rehabilitated.

"It is our understanding, based on inquiries directed to the medical personnel at St. Elizabeths Hospital, that Pound is now unfit for trial and, in the opinion of the doctors treating him, will continue to be unfit for trial. This opinion, we believe, has already been communicated to the Department of Justice. Under these circumstances the perpetuation of the charges against him seems to us unfortunate and, indeed, indefensible. It provides occasion for criticism of American justice not only at home but abroad and it seems to us, in and of itself, unworthy of the traditions of the Republic. Concerned, as we must be, with the judgments of posterity on this unhappy affair, we cannot but regret the failure of the Department thus far to take steps to nol pros the indictment and remit the case to the medical authorities for disposition on medical grounds. . . ."

The letter had just the effect MacLeish hoped it would. In late February, Brownell wrote Frost he had "asked that a review of the matter be made. . . ." He would communicate further with him when it had been completed. The promised response came on April eleventh. In a letter from William P. Rogers (soon to replace Brownell as Attorney General), Frost was invited to come to Washington, at his convenience and with his cosigners Eliot and Hemingway, to discuss Pound's case. Preoccupied by the English goodwill trip that was now just a month off, Frost made no immediate reply.

After his return to the States, Frost must have sensed MacLeish's anxiety, for on June twenty-fifth he wrote him:

"My purpose holds to help you get Ezra let loose though I won't say my misgivings in the whole matter haven't been increased by my talks with Eliot lately, who knows more about Ezra than anybody else and what we can hope to do for his salvation. I should hate to see Ezra die ignominiously in that wretched place where he is for a crime which if proven couldn't have kept him all these years in prison. So you go ahead and make an appointment with the Department of Justice. I suppose we must be prepared to answer for Ezra's relative sanity and ability to get himself taken care of out in the world. Neither you nor I would want to take him into our family or even into our neighborhood. I shall be acting largely on your judgment. I can't bear that anyone's fate should hang too much on mine. . . ."

MacLeish replied at once, with plans for a trip to Washington. From his home in Conway, Massachusetts, he wrote on June twenty-eighth: ". . . I have asked Miss Geffen at the [American] Academy [of Arts and Letters] to write the Deputy Attorney General asking whether July 19 (late in the

PM) . . . [or] the 20th would do. Of course I would go along if you want me. I have also written Ernest asking him to send you a full statement of his views and I shall ask Tom to do the same so that you will go fully armed. . . ."

On July nineteenth Frost and MacLeish met with Rogers at the Department of Justice and discussed the case. MacLeish soon reported to Pound that the main obstacle to his early release seemed to be his association with a segregationist poet named John Kasper, who had recently made headlines by helping to provoke a race riot in Clinton, Tennessee:

". . . What the conversations boiled down to was about what we expected: though maybe a little more hopeful than we feared.

"For the immediate future and so long as the Kasper mess is boiling and stewing the Department will not move. I have never understood— and neither, incidentally, has your daughter Mary—how you got mixed up with that character.

"Beyond that, though there are no commitments, the Department does not close the door provided somebody can come forward with a sensible plan for your future. . . ."

Dr. Winfred Overholser's cooperation was essential. As head of St. Elizabeths Hospital, he would be required to testify as to whether Pound would ever be fit to stand trial. Only with his negative answer, and his expert opinion that Pound would pose no danger to himself or others if set free, did the campaign on Pound's behalf have any chance of success. Frost made his second assault on Washington, this time without Mac-Leish, in the third week of October. Overholser was out of town on vacation, so no progress could be made on that important front. Rogers, however, while remaining annoyingly noncommittal, seemed willing to consider Frost's suggestion that if Pound could not be released outright, because of the "Kasper mess," he could at least be transferred to a private institution, until the civil-rights crisis had quieted down.

A month after his talk with Rogers, and having heard nothing from him in the interim, Frost renewed his efforts by sending Rogers a note blending his most charming manner and latest developments in the case: ". . . I assume people are less busy the higher up they get and the bigger the questions get or I would apologize for taking your time for the rest of this Pound business. . . . Archie MacLeish tells me this morning that he has Dr. Overholser's consent for Pound's transfer the minute he himself is released from holding Pound as a prisoner. I may have to call you on the telephone next. I grow impatient. The amnesty would be a good Christmas present."

Christmas, however, brought no change in the status of Pound's case, and Frost was forced to conclude that his efforts had reached an impasse.

Then, on January 16, 1958, a development unrelated to Pound suggested to Frost a new way of attacking the problem. At a dinner in his honor at the New York headquarters of the Poetry Society of America, at which he was awarded the society's gold medal for distinguished service, Frost was the subject of a telegram of greeting signed by President Eisenhower himself.

Frost was familiar enough with such laudatory messages to guess that Eisenhower was probably not its author—and very possibly was not even aware of its existence. More likely, he had Sherman Adams to thank. In writing to Adams on February twelfth, however, he glossed over the issue of authorship and used the telegram as a lever to gain access to the White House, obviously as much for his own ends as for any benefit to Pound: "That was a splendid telegram. . . . Of course I saw your hand in it. You have a great great influence up there. Few in your position have ever thought of the arts at all. Some day it seems as if you might want to have me meet the President to thank him in person at a meal or something, so that it needn't go down in history that the great statesman and soldier never dined socially with any but the big shots, and these preferably statesmen, warriors, business men and Hollywoodsmen. . . ."

Frost's letter brought incredibly rapid results. Four days later he received a telegram from the President inviting him to an "informal stag dinner" and "general chat" at the White House on February twenty-seventh. On the sixteenth Frost wired his acceptance of the President's invitation, saying he was "only too sensible of the honor." His telegram of the same day to Adams suggested that, amid the flush of excitement at the prospect of meeting the President, he had not forgotten his commitment to Pound: "BE IT UPON YOUR HEAD BUT I AM ACCEPTING THE PRESIDENT'S INVITATION BLACK TIE AND ALL. TRUST I DON'T HAVE TO PROVE MYSELF WORTHY OF THE HONOR. WHAT'S ON MY MIND WOULD BE MORE APT TO BE BROUGHT OUT IN TALKS WITH YOU SEPARATELY. . . ."

Adams came through, once again, by inviting Frost to lunch on the same day he would dine with the President. Accepting by telephone, Frost asked Adams to invite the Attorney General, as well. Clearly, the matter "more apt to be brought out . . . separately" was Ezra Pound. A word from Adams, Frost knew, and Rogers might well abandon his intransigent position.

Just as Frost had hoped, the meeting with Rogers and Adams was the beginning of the end of the logjam. When the three men met over lunch in the staff dining room of the White House, Frost learned that Rogers was at last beginning to lean toward Pound's early release.

On April first came two crucial developments. The Library of Congress, which had been charged in August to compile a report on the Pound case, released the completed document, "The Medical, Legal,

Literary and Political Status of Ezra Pound." The same day, Attorney General Rogers held a press conference and sent up a trial balloon. He said Pound might escape trial and be allowed to go to Italy, adding that his fate depended upon new diagnoses by his doctors, concerning his future competence to stand trial. "Is there any point in keeping him in there," Rogers asked rhetorically, "if he never can be tried?"

The public responded very satisfactorily to the test, and now all that was needed was a prominent figure to cut through the red tape. On April fourteenth, with MacLeish's prodding, Frost went again to Washington and called on the Attorney General. "I've dropped in to see what your mood is in regard to Ezra Pound," Frost said. "Our mood is your mood, Mr. Frost," Rogers replied. "Well, then," said Frost, "let's get him out right away."

At Rogers's suggestion, Frost now arranged an immediate appointment with William Shafroth, governmental expediter in legal matters. Shafroth recommended Thurman Arnold as lawyer for the defense.

On April eighteenth Arnold went to court to ask for the release of Pound; and, after legal and medical testimony had been presented, he read into the record a "Statement of Robert Frost":

"I am here to register my admiration for a government that can rouse in conscience to a case like this. Relief seems in sight for many of us besides the Ezra Pound in question and his faithful wife. He has countless admirers the world over who will rejoice in the news that he has hopes of freedom. I append a page or so of what they have been saying lately about him and his predicament. I myself speak as much in the general interest as in his. And I feel authorized to speak very specially for my friends, Archibald MacLeish, Ernest Hemingway and T. S. Eliot. None of us can bear the disgrace of our letting Ezra Pound come to his end where he is. It would leave too woeful a story in American literature. He went very wrongheaded in his egotism, but he insists it was from patriotism—love of America. He has never admitted that he went over to the enemy any more than the writers at home who have despaired of the Republic. I hate such nonsense and can only listen to it as an evidence of mental disorder. But mental disorder is what we are considering. I rest the case on Dr. Overholser's pronouncement that Ezra Pound is not too dangerous to go free in his wife's care, and too insane ever to be tried—a very nice discrimination.

"Mr. Thurman Arnold admirably put this problem of a sick . . . [man] being held too long in prison to see if he won't get well enough to be tried for a prison offense. There is probably legal precedent to help toward a solution of the problem. But I should think it would have to be reached more by magnanimity than by logic and it is chiefly on magnanimity I am counting. I can see how the Department of Justice would hesitate in the matter from fear of looking more just to a great poet than it would be to a mere nobody. The bigger the Department the longer it might have to take thinking things through."

Despite the ironic thrust at the thirteen years it had taken the government to think things through, the motion for dismissal went unopposed by the Department of Justice, and the next morning *The New York Times* carried a front-page story on the dismissal of the indictment against Pound. It concluded: "The person most responsible for today's announcement was not in court. He is Robert Frost, the poet, who had waged a persistent public and private campaign during the last two years for Mr. Pound's release. . . ."

Anyone who was aware of the behind-the-scenes efforts of Archibald MacLeish might well have said it was he, not Frost, who was "most responsible for today's announcement." When Frost spoke that evening at the Poetry Center in New York, however, he chose to take issue with another aspect of the newspaper's report. After finishing his reading he returned to the stage, apparently for an encore. Instead, he told his audience that though the papers said it had taken him two years to win Pound's release, it had taken him, in fact, only a week. Then, he waved good night and walked briskly offstage.

He had further reason to boast a few days later, when Librarian of Congress L. Quincy Mumford offered him a position in the library that would make possible his continued involvement in the life of Washington, as Consultant in Poetry—a nine-month appointment that would be available as of the fall of 1958 and paid the incumbent handsomely in money, as well as honor. Frost, asked to keep his discussions with Mumford in confidence, could not resist dropping a few broad hints when he wrote President Eisenhower thanking him, belatedly, for the White House dinner:

"To be stood up for and toasted alone in such august company by the ruler of the greatest nation in the world was almost more to me than being stood up for in acclaim by whole audiences of his people and mine. At any rate it left me with less to say for myself on the thrill of the moment and was so like the outcome of a life story[,] it leaves me with nothing to go on with but possibly some more of the same kind of very quiet poetry that seems to have started all this unquietness. I hope you will accept a book of it from me to take to your farm some day. I am a great advocate of some library in the farm house to mix with the life of the farm. Not that I would underestimate its value in the Capitol to mix with the life of the Capital. Books and paintings and music tend to temper the harshness of politics. . . ."

A few days later Mumford sent him a contract, specifying the terms and requirements of the post, with the request that he meet the press on

May twenty-first, the day the announcement of his appointment was to be made. He was only too happy to comply. In a high-spirited monologue-*cum*-press-conference at the library, he answered serious questions with engaging flippancy, gave hints of the kind of consultant he planned to be, and took every opportunity he could to steer discussion in the direction of his late triumph in the case of Ezra Pound.

In October, during his first week in Washington as Consultant in Poetry to the Library of Congress, Frost made it plain he intended to make his presence felt while he held his first official government position. Duties of lecturing at the library, helping to build up the poetry collection, and answering the queries of students, professors, and would-be poets were not nearly inclusive enough. He wanted the consultantship to be treated as an office in which his views would be listened to by the men who were running the country, and in which he could achieve significant results for his "cause": poetry, the arts—and (not inconsequentially) his own reputation.

When he returned to Washington in December for his second week of consulting, he called a press conference and explained: "I don't want to run for office, but I want to be a politician"; and he wished "some good Senator would resign about six months before the end of his term and let me finish it out."

He went on to complain—almost joking, but serious underneath —that the government had failed, so far, to employ him in a manner commensurate with his willingness to be put to use. Since assuming office, he said, he had been consulted only a handful of times—three by the White House, once by the Supreme Court, and not at all by Congress. Such neglect, he added, was not what he had anticipated in taking the job: "I wondered if I hadn't come down here on a misunderstanding. I thought I was to be poetry consultant . . . in everything—poetry, politics, religion, science. I'll tackle anything."

He said were he to be asked about education, on which he regarded himself as "the greatest living expert," he had a response already in mind:

"I have long thought that our high schools should be improved. Nobody should come into our high schools without examinations—not aptitude tests, but on reading, 'riting, and 'rithmetic. And that goes for black or white.

"A lot of people are being scared by the Russian Sputnik into wanting to harden up our education or speed it up. I am interested in toning it up, at the high-school level.

"If they want to Spartanize the country, let them. I would rather perish as Athens than prevail as Sparta. The tone is Athens. The tone is freedom to the point of destruction. Democracy means all the risks taken—

conflict of opinion, conflict of personality, eccentricity. We are Athens, daring to be all sorts of people. . . ."

Not until March of 1959, nearly four months later, did the calendar help him achieve what his own requests for attention did not. In that month he celebrated the eighty-fifth anniversary of his birth, and Senator Winston L. Prouty of Vermont rose on the Senate floor and proposed a birthday resolution honoring "America's great poet-philosopher, Robert Frost." In his introductory remarks was an excerpt from a recent article by J. Donald Adams of *The New York Times*: ". . . I can think of no better tribute to Frost on this coming birthday than for every American who admires his work to write a letter to the Nobel Prize Committee, asking why our foremost poet has not yet been recognized in Stockholm. It is a recognition long past due, and time flies on ever swifter wings."

Senator Prouty continued: ". . . the awarding of the Nobel Prizes is outside the prerogatives of the U.S. Senate. But the unanimous adoption of this resolution will inform Mr. Frost and the world of the esteem in which this great American poet is held by the Members of this body. . . ."

The resolution was quickly approved. The real celebration, however, took place in New York City, where Henry Holt and Company had arranged to give a gala dinner on the evening of the twenty-sixth at the Waldorf-Astoria hotel.

The day began with a press conference, where the questioning turned quickly to a subject on which Frost had much to say. With the rise of science, one reporter observed, poetry seemed to be playing a lesser role. "Poetry has always played a lesser role . . . ," Frost answered.

"I may say I've never got on by setting poetry in opposition to science or Big Business or academic scholarship, although some poets seem to live on that contrast. . . . Science cannot be scientific about poetry, but poetry can be poetical about science. It's bigger, more inclusive. . . . Get that right, you know," he said, and repeated his familiar remark.

Did these large birthday celebrations bore him? "They don't bore me, but sometimes they make me feel too old. The question of deserts might bother me at night. But I like to be made of, you know. I like to be made of."

Had he any wish for the world and his country that he would like to state on this eighty-fifth birthday? "For the world, no. I'm not large enough for that. For my country? My chief wish is for it to win at every turn in anything it does.

". . . People say that there's always room at the top. There isn't. There's only room for one at the top of the steeple."

Could not Mr. Frost afford to say that because he was at the top, and sitting pretty? "I was down under for many, many years," he said, "with no prospect of winning." Having "won," he gave his formula for success:

"Sneak up on things. And never be caught looking as if you wanted them."

Another question concerned the present state of New England. Was it in decay? "People ask me that on my travels," he replied. "Often they ask me in the South. And I ask, 'Where did you go to school?' And they say Harvard—or Yale. And then I say the successor to Mr. Dulles will be from Boston: Mr. Herter. And the next President of the United States will be from Boston. And then I ask, 'Does that sound as if New England is decaying?'"

But whom did Mr. Frost mean? "Can't you figure that one out for yourself?" The newsmen could, indeed, figure it out, but they wanted to hear Frost say the name himself. With a shrug, he obliged them: "He's a Puritan named Kennedy. The only Puritans left these days are the Roman Catholics. There. I guess I wear my politics on my sleeve."

The press conference over, Frost had the rest of the day free until the Holt dinner. The guest list included some one hundred "distinguished friends and admirers from all walks of life"; but the main after-dinner speaker was neither a close personal friend nor an admirer of long standing. He was the well-known critic Lionel Trilling.

Trilling began by addressing the audience at large, and speaking of how future archaeologists would regard Frost as something of a mythic figure, associable with Jack Frost, the vernal equinox, and the "rite" of commencement. He went on to say that any person called upon to speak at the "momentous" occasion of the poet's "Sophoclean" eighty-fifth birthday must approach the assignment with some diffidence: "Yet I must be more weighed down by diffidence than many others who might speak here. I must almost entertain a doubt of the appropriateness of my speaking here at all. For I cannot help knowing that the manifest America of Robert Frost's poems is not the America that has its place in my own mind. . . ."

Trilling described himself as a recent convert to Frost's poetry: "It is a fact which I had best confess as simply as possible that for a long time I was alienated from Mr. Frost's great canon of work by what I saw in it, that either itself seemed to denigrate the work of the critical intellect or that gave to its admirers the ground for making the denigration. It was but recently that my resistance, at the behest of better understanding, yielded to admiration. . . ."

He, then, began to speak of "my Frost," who was "anything but" a poet who "reassures us by his affirmation of old virtues, simplicities, pieties, and ways of feeling." Rather, Trilling asserted, he was "a terrifying poet"—"a tragic poet." And, finally, Trilling addressed Frost directly: "I hope that you will not think it graceless of me that on your birthday I have undertaken to say that a great many of your admirers have not understood clearly what you have been doing in your life in poetry. . . . And I hope that you will not think it graceless of me that on your birthday I have made you out to be a poet who terrifies. When I began to speak I called your birthday Sophoclean and that word has, I think, controlled everything I have said about you. Like you, Sophocles lived to a great age, writing well; and like you, Sophocles was the poet his people loved most. Surely they loved him in some part because he praised their common country. But I think that they loved him chiefly because he made plain to them the terrible things of human life: they felt, perhaps, that only a poet who could make plain the terrible things could possibly give them comfort."

When Trilling sat down, Frost rose to deliver some remarks of his own, and it soon became apparent he was having difficulty deciding whether to be flattered or insulted by what Trilling had said. He seemed upset.

The events of the evening had a strange aftermath. J. Donald Adams, one of the guests at the birthday dinner, denounced Trilling's speech, in his column in *The New York Times Book Review,* and denied that Frost was at all the "terrifying" poet Trilling had made him out to be. When a number of letters appeared soon after in the *Book Review,* all expressing curiously bitter support of Adams's rebuke, Trilling decided to have his talk printed in its entirety in the *Partisan Review,* together with a statement of his views on the meaning of the "cultural episode" to which it had given rise.

Having long since recovered his lost composure, Frost was delighted at the attention focused upon him by the Trilling-Adams debate. When he received from Trilling an advance copy of the *Partisan Review* piece, with a note apologizing for any distress the birthday talk had caused, he replied, in a letter dated June eighteenth: "Not distressed at all. Just a little taken aback or thrown back on myself by being so closely examined so close by. It took me more than a few minutes to change from thoughts of myself to thoughts of the difficulty you had had with me. You made my birthday party a surprise party. I should like nothing better than to do a thing like that myself,—to depart from the Rotarian norm in a Rotarian situation. . . ."

Of far-greater and more continuing interest to the national press and the general public was Frost's birthday prediction that the junior Senator from Massachusetts, who had not yet, even, formally declared his candidacy, would be the next President of the United States. Senator Kennedy was somewhat embarrassed to see Frost's remark widely taken as an outright endorsement. "I just want to send you a note," he wrote Frost on the eleventh of April, "to let you know how gratifying it was to be remembered by you on the occasion of your 85th birthday. I only regret that the intrusion of my name, probably in ways which you did not entirely intend, took away some of the attention from the man who really deserved it—Robert Frost. . . ."

Impressed by the young Senator's letter, as well as by the publicity the prediction concerning him had generated, Frost began repeating, in many, if not most, of his subsequent public lectures his forecast of Kennedy's election. He knew that if the Senator did go on to become President, Kennedy just might be grateful enough to offer him a job on the White House staff, perhaps by creating a tailor-made Cabinet position of the kind Sherman Adams had half-seriously mentioned before his fall from power.

In the middle of May, Frost returned to Washington for his fourth and last week at the Library of Congress job. Soon after he arrived he received a telephone call from Congressman Stewart L. Udall of Arizona, who said he had recently seen it reported that Frost had yet to be consulted by a member of Congress and who offered his home—including dinner—for a "Congressional consultation" later that week. Frost readily accepted and happily regaled Udall, his family, and four or five other members of Congress with three hours of observations on poetry and politics.

June was to bring an invitation from Quincy Mumford for Frost to prolong his formal relationship with the Library of Congress, by serving for three years, beginning in 1960, in a position that had been established just for him: Honorary Consultant in the Humanities. Frost was happy to accept. He wrote Mumford on the tenth of July: ". . . I am honored by the summons of your appointing me consultant in the humanities which I more or less arbitrarily take to mean practically everything human that has been brought to book and can be treated in poetry,—philosophy, politics, religion, history and science. Everything, everything. . . ."

Frost spent the remainder of the year doing the things he had been doing for so many years—lecturing around the country, visiting friends and being visited, teaching at Amherst, vacationing in Ripton, working on his poems—all at much the same tempo, now that he was in his mid-eighties, that he had maintained in his seventies, his sixties, and before.

Early in May 1960 he returned to Washington for the first series of lectures in his new role at the Library of Congress, and during the visit he testified, before a Senate subcommittee, for the bill to establish a National Academy of Culture. He disliked the overworked word "culture" intensely, but he liked the idea of an academy to honor the arts and was happy to be "consulted" on the matter. Frost told the Senators he wanted poetry declared equal to big business, to science, to scholarship:

". . . When I look down the list of scholarship in the university I sometimes land, in the end, looking for what's most akin to the arts. I land in the sports department. The performance—all art is performance.

It is not scholarship. The scholar people have tolerated us lately, been very nice to us. They admit that there might be such things as a living writer. Many of them used to boast they had read nothing later than the eighteenth century. . . . And the awareness is the great thing. . . . The foundations are getting aware of us, but I want my country officially to be aware of us so that we feel our equality. I do want you to declare our equality. We will take care of the rest. . . ."

He received a Congressional compliment in June when the Senate passed a bill that had first been introduced in late April by Leverett Saltonstall of Massachusetts, authorizing the creation and presentation to Frost of a $2,500 gold medal "in recognition of his poetry, which has enriched the culture of the United States and the philosophy of the world." The bill was then sent over to the House of Representatives where, after consideration in committee, it was passed and sent on to the White House.

President Eisenhower signed the "Robert Frost Medal" bill into law on September thirteenth. A short time later Frederic Fox at the White House called the director of the mint and asked when he thought the medal would be ready for presentation. Not for some time, said the director—if ever. He went on to explain that the mint had not yet received the $2,500 to strike it. While Congress had authorized the money, it had forgotten to appropriate it, and until someone came up with the amount, nothing could be done but to go ahead with plans for its design. Fox telephoned Mrs. Morrison in Cambridge and explained the situation.

While this was going on, Frost himself was in California on a lecture tour. He spoke on November ninth in Los Angeles, and there delivered his first public reaction to the news that John Kennedy had won the Presidential election the day before. It was, said Frost, "a triumph of Protestantism—over itself." He was delighted by the outcome, which had been close enough for him to feel, with some justification, that his predictions of Kennedy's victory had helped shape their fulfillment. Luckily, the victory margin was not small enough to depend upon Frost's own vote. He had neglected to arrange for an absentee ballot before leaving for the West Coast.

Frost made several stops on the way home, including Tucson, where he attended the opening of a new poetry center at the University of Arizona. While he was there Frost went to call on Congressman Udall, with whom he had become increasingly cordial during each of his visits to Washington. They speculated about the kind of President that Senator Kennedy, a friend of Udall's, would prove to be, and agreed he would very likely pay more attention to the arts, among them poetry, than any President had done in many years.

Kennedy demonstrated his willingness to give heed to the arts even sooner than Frost anticipated. On the first of December the President-elect summoned Udall to his Georgetown home and invited him to serve in his Cabinet as Secretary of the Interior. Udall accepted at once, and they continued to talk for some time. Then, as he rose to leave, Udall offered a suggestion: "You might consider having our mutual friend Robert Frost take part in the inauguration ceremonies." Kennedy registered surprise and asked, "Doing what?" "Why, reading a poem at the beginning, or in the middle, or at the end." "Oh, no," said Kennedy. "You know that Robert Frost always steals any show he is part of. . . ."

That the new President might be upstaged by the old poet was only a self-deprecatory joke. Senator Kennedy quickly followed it by saying he was interested in the idea; Udall should find out if Frost would be interested, and report back.

When Udall telephoned Frost with the good news of his own appointment to the Cabinet, he informed the poet of Kennedy's interest in having him participate in the inauguration. Frost was astonished by the idea—and delighted, both by Udall's good fortune and his own. Kennedy's invitation to Frost went out by wire a few days later, and Frost answered in kind the following day: "IF YOU CAN BEAR AT YOUR AGE THE HONOR OF BEING MADE PRESIDENT OF THE UNITED STATES, I OUGHT TO BE ABLE AT MY AGE TO BEAR THE HONOR OF TAKING SOME PART IN YOUR INAUGURATION. I MAY NOT BE EQUAL TO IT BUT I CAN ACCEPT IT FOR MY CAUSE——THE ARTS, POETRY, NOW FOR THE FIRST TIME TAKEN INTO THE AFFAIRS OF STATESMEN. . . ."

Kennedy soon telephoned to discuss what Frost was going to do when he appeared on the inaugural platform a month hence. Did he care to write a new poem for the occasion? No, said Frost, he could never be counted on for something like that. Then, would he read "The Gift Outright"—and alter the last line, if only for a day, from "such as she would become" to the more positive-sounding "such as she *will* become?" Yes, Frost supposed he could do that; and the matter was settled.

As the big day drew nearer, Frost forgot or overcame his reluctance to celebrate the new administration with a new composition. When he reached Washington on the eighteenth of January, he had a few dozen lines done, but it was still far from completion. By working feverishly into the first hours of the twentieth, he managed to write forty-two lines of a poem that, while not really finished, was at least presentable. When Udall picked him up at his hotel to take him to the ceremonies, he announced, "I've decided I want to say a few things besides reading my poem. Will that be all right?" Udall, somewhat taken aback by the surprising news, asked how long it would take. Frost was not sure; he would have to time it and see. Then, as Udall stood and listened through the door of Frost's room, Frost read aloud the poem he called simply "Dedication" (later retitled "For John F. Kennedy His Inauguration").

Frost emerged, to tell Udall he would need only so many minutes, and was told there was, therefore, no problem in having him read the new poem as a preface to his saying of "The Gift Outright." But as Udall drove him through the snow-covered streets to the Capitol, Frost admitted that one thing still worried him. The poem had been typed on one of the hotel's typewriters the night before, and he found it a bit difficult to make out, even in good light. In the bright sunlight of the outdoor ceremony, he might have considerable difficulty reading what he had written. Udall said he knew where there was an oversized-letter typewriter of the sort President Eisenhower used for his speeches and that he would have the poem typed at once on the special machine.

The ceremony began at noon. When, finally, it was time for what was listed in the program as "Poem by Mr. Robert Frost," Frost, who had been shivering in his place on the platform for nearly an hour, rose and slowly made his way toward the lectern, with several sheets of paper clutched in his hand against the stiff breeze. Taking his time, he anchored the pages with his outstretched hands; then, in a voice obviously nervous, said, "First, the 'Dedication.'"

The sun was glaring, and the reflected light from fresh-fallen snow and fresh white paint compounded the difficulty. These and his unfamiliarity with the poem he was about to read caused him to miss the first word: "Summing—— Summoning artists to participate / In the august occasions of the state / Seems something for us all to celebrate. / And—— And today is for my cause a day of days. / And his be poetry's old-fashioned praise / Who was the one—— Who was the first to think of such a thing. / This tribute—— for to—— to be his that here I bring / Is about——."

At this point, after a long pause, he interrupted himself to say, directly into his typescript (but plainly enough so that the microphone picked it up), "No, I'm not having a good light here at all." A few more broken phrases from the poem, and he paused again: "I can't see in the sun." Vice-President Johnson rose from his seat to try to shield Frost's papers from the glare with his top hat, but it did not seem to help. Half grabbing the hat away, Frost said, "Here, let me have it," a remark that broke the painful silence in the audience and brought a burst of laughter and applause.

Finally, he saw there was no point in trying to read the new poem. "I'll just have to get through as I can," he said, to himself; and, then, into the microphone, "I think I'll say, this was to be a preface to the poem I can say to you without seeing it. The poem goes like this. . . ." Another burst of applause. And, in a voice that was firm and unfaltering, he began "The Gift Outright": "The land was ours before we were the land's. / She was our land more than a hundred years / Before we were her people. She was ours. . . ."

He gave his altered version of the last line, and without pausing he continued to speak: ". . . and this poem—— what I was leading up to was a dedication of the poem to the President-elect, Mr. John Finley." Out of kindness, or perhaps because the last two words were delivered in much-lower tones than what preceded, the audience hardly remarked the final error of his uneven performance at the inaugural rostrum. Instead, it gave him a warm round of applause, and the ceremonies continued immediately with the administering of the oath of office to the President-elect. Frost's official part in the day's activities was over.

He remained in Washington long enough to see an article in *The Washington Post* that began, "Robert Frost in his natural way stole the hearts of the Inaugural crowd yesterday with a poem he recited and another which he couldn't read because the sun's glare hid the words. . . ." In a way, Senator Kennedy's joking prediction to Stewart Udall had come to pass.

Before leaving, he went with Mrs. Morrison to call on the new President and First Lady at the White House, to receive Kennedy's thanks for taking part in the installation and to thank him for permitting him to do so. Frost presented the Kennedys with a manuscript copy of the "Dedication" poem, on which he had written, "Amended copy. And now let us mend our ways." He also gave the President a bit of advice: "Be more Irish than Harvard. Poetry and power is the formula for another Augustan Age. Don't be afraid of power."

President Kennedy sent him a short thank-you letter a few days later, typed. But in signing it, he showed he had not forgotten the advice. The President wrote across the bottom of the page, "It's poetry and power all the way!"

43

MORE TRAVELS, ILLNESS, ANOTHER BOOK

(1961–1962)

LESS THAN two months after President Kennedy's inauguration, and only a few weeks before his own eighty-seventh birthday, Robert Frost packed his bags and prepared to embark on a trip that would carry him farther from home than he had ever been: a two-week trip, under State Department auspices, to Israel, Greece, and England. Unlike his last venture across the Atlantic, in 1957, there were no honorary degrees or promises of extraordinary recognition to entice him into making the taxing—and, at his age, potentially dangerous—journey. Indeed, he found himself wondering, before his departure on March ninth, whether it had been a mistake to accept the invitation to serve as first lecturer in a new program on American culture and civilization at Hebrew University of Jerusalem. But it was one further opportunity to add to his store of that intangible commodity he called "glory."

Another reason, which in itself would have been insufficient to justify so ambitious an undertaking, was that it would permit him to view, firsthand, two cultures from which, as he had said in his poem "Kitty Hawk," Western civilization had taken its "running start." At a farewell luncheon in New York he said as much: "I am going to make a bee-line from where the human race has come for 2,000 years. And it has come in many ways—language, the alphabet from that end of the Mediterranean, the Bible, from which so much of our own literature is made. . . . Right there, that was the beginning of it all." And at a press conference following the luncheon, Frost's remarks suggested that his nationalism had something to do with his going, as well: "I look on Israel as an American colony. They all speak English there. They have so much of the American people's spirit. They have many, many things in common with us—more than anybody else."

He had a few surprises in store for him when he reached the "American colony," but the surprises of the journey began much sooner than that. Only when Frost and his traveling companion for the trip, Lawrance Thompson, boarded the El Al Israel Airlines jet that evening did they learn that their flight was the "Sheraton–Tel Aviv Special," carrying a group of reporters and executives to the opening of the first American-owned hotel in Tel Aviv. Surprised by the prospect of an impromptu press conference as he made his way across the Atlantic, Frost was equally surprised to learn—after a nerve-racking, four-hour delay in takeoff—that Holt and El Al had joined in preparing a souvenir folder for the first-class passengers, "Honoring the Distinguished American Poet Robert Frost."

When the plane was safely airborne, the predictable occurred. By ones and twos, the reporters and executives began congregating around Frost's seat, until he was surrounded by eager eyes and ears. One writer, Harry Golden, made himself something of a nuisance with his show of admiration. Frost knew that he was the author of a collection of essays called *Only in America,* but he also knew Golden was a friend of Carl Sandburg's—thus, as he saw it, not one to be much suffered.

When Golden presented him with a paperback copy of his book, inscribed "To Robert Frost, may you live to 120, like Moses," the poet was amused enough to reply, "And like Moses with all his powers unimpaired." Golden persisted with his talk, comparing Frost and Sandburg as artists and, finally, as Frost awoke disheveled from a nap, observing that the poets had the same kind of hair. Frost's patience wore thin. "What's he always talking about Sandburg for?" he snapped, at no one in particular. "And how dare he say I have the same kind of hair as Carl? My hair's my own and I don't copy anybody else's haircut."

Realizing the reporters were hanging on his every word, he decided to continue his verbal barrage—aiming, now, not at Golden, but Sandburg himself: "I've been cutting my own hair now for twenty years. Haven't been to a barber since then. Got sick and tired of those fellows. I didn't mind them talking to me. I guess every barber's supposed to do that. But I did mind them always telling me my hair was falling out. So I started cutting my own hair. As you grow older, you don't care about those things. Of course, Carl's a very careful fellow. I'm sure he goes to the barber."

The attack soon turned from Sandburg's hair to his poetry: "We're entirely different in our work. He has a good heart. He says in his poetry, 'The People, Yes.' I say 'The People, Yes—and No.' I'd say Sandburg has written some good Whitmanesque verse, but I don't think he knows what form is. Our great difference is our approach to poetry. . . . But I have no quarrel with him. He's out there in Hollywood now with his name on the door writing that five-million-dollar picture about Christ, and I suppose that's all right if you want to do that sort of thing. But I don't like people telling me we have the same kind of hair."

By the time the plane approached Paris for a refueling stop, the conversation had turned to politics—but, even there, Sandburg was susceptible to attack. The New Deal and the Fair Deal, Frost complained, had "aimed only to send all children to school, and all people over 65 to hospitals. They worried only about the helpless.

"I'm over 65, and I don't feel helpless. Damn the helpless. That's for Sandburg."

Thirteen hours out of New York, the plane landed in darkness at Lod airport, and Frost and Thompson were whisked through the immigration office, from which they went on to their rooms at the King David Hotel in Jerusalem, ten miles away.

Next morning the two visitors decided to spend part of their free time exploring the neighborhood around the hotel. North, across the wadi, they could see Mount Zion in the distance. For recent history, they needed to look no farther than the hotel walls, pockmarked with bullet holes from the 1948 war, following Israel's declaration of statehood. After lunch, they were taken on a motor tour along the boundary separating the Israeli from the Jordanian sector of Jerusalem.

On Sunday morning, thanks to the American consul in Jerusalem, Frost and his companion were accorded the rare privilege of passing through the Mandelbaum Gate and exploring Jordanian territory. For the next few hours Frost and Thompson were in a fabled land. They retraced the Stations of the Cross, with their genial Arab guide pointing out historic sites along the way. There on that wall was where Jesus was tempted by Satan; here was the Petra Hotel (named, Frost recalled, after the place he had written about, in 1891, in "Petra and Its Surroundings," an essay published in the Lawrence *High School Bulletin*); there ahead was the Mount of Calvary, where a church had been built upon the reputed site of the True Cross. The guide showed them where, in the church, the Cross was said to have stood. The hole was there to see, and Christian believers, said the Arab, thought it beneficial to reach down into it and to pray. Did Frost wish to do so? "Oh, no," said the poet, with a mixture of amusement and embarrassment. "I'm not good enough."

On the way back to the Israeli sector Frost observed to Thompson that he was perfectly willing for anyone else to believe all the "historical" accounts the guide had been providing, even if he did not believe them himself. At least, he said, they offered greater elevation and moral significance than the evolution myths created by Charles Darwin.

During the next few days Frost participated in a number of "talking sessions" at Hebrew University, his chief appearance there coming on the night of March thirteenth. He announced at the outset that he did not intend to talk *about* American civilization, because he *was* American civilization; with that, he said some of his poems and, then, offered to take questions from the audience.

Of his own poems, he said they all began with the same thing: "An idea—now ask me what that is." But without waiting for the question to be asked, he answered it by repeating one of his time-tested formulas: "An idea is a thought-felt thing." Then, forgetting how many times he had used the definition—or for heightened effect—he added he had never said that before.

"Yesterday I met a lot of professors and we discussed education," he continued. "Education, I said to them, elevates trouble to a higher plane. I had never said that before, either. It surprised *me*. Maybe one day it will start a poem."

After two hours of what was essentially a running monologue, the session ended, and the poet retired to his hotel to rest before his meeting with the English faculty later that evening.

Over the next few days Frost left Jerusalem for a visit to Tel Aviv, a look at the new Hadassah Medical Center, and a brief, cordial visit with the President of the country, Itzhak Ben Zvi. An all-day drive down the seacoast was planned, as were more talks and social calls. But halfway through his ten days in Israel, fatigue, intestinal illness, and—most important—homesickness began to get the better of him. Israel had proved to be far less an American colony than he had anticipated. It was hotter than South Miami ever got, had more rocks everywhere than Vermont had anywhere, and fewer of the natives spoke fluent English than Bostonians spoke proper Bostonian. What he wanted now was to go home at once.

He was expected to spend a few days in Athens and to lecture there, expected to spend his eighty-seventh birthday with E. M. Forster in Cambridge a week hence. But he did not know whether he had either the strength or the desire to continue. Accordingly, as soon as he reached Athens, Frost asked Thompson to telephone Alfred Edwards in New York and say he was seriously considering an immediate return, for reasons of illness. He might have done just that, had not the wife of the American ambassador solved his digestive problem with a diet of tea and custard. So dramatic was his recovery that within hours of his arrival in Athens he was well enough to hold a press conference for a score of Greek newsmen, and well enough to amuse and amaze them with his comments on international politics and his command of Greek history and literature. He was also well enough to participate in a reception in his honor held at the ambassador's residence.

On three successive days he gave public lectures in Athens, all of which went extremely well. At his talk on March twenty-second, before the Archaeological Society, the subject on which he chose to speak was Plato—and, more particularly, his own sympathy for Platonic philosophy. Plato, he said, was of course "more of a mythologist than he was a philosopher. He made his own myths, and he was sort of a link between the almost-unconscious metaphors of the earlier times to the conscious philosophy of his time and on. But he still makes myths. . . . I like to think that I'm not quite a Platonist, and then, all of a sudden I find myself saying something that I myself trace right back to Plato. For instance, I say: 'There's more religion outside the church than in; there's more love outside of marriage than in; there's more poetry outside of verse than in; and there's more wisdom outside of philosophy than in.' . . ."

Before he left Athens for London on March twenty-fourth, Frost joined vacationing friends from Amherst to climb the Acropolis, which meant much to him as a symbol of Athens' ancient greatness. If he had been bored and homesick at times in Israel, he could not be so in Greece. Greek history, Greek literature meant too much to him. Coming to Athens seemed to him, he said, a kind of homecoming.

In England, Frost began a limited schedule by attending a prebirthday party in his honor, on the afternoon of March twenty-fifth, at the residence of American Ambassador David K. E. Bruce. After a short nap, he attended, as well, what he supposed would be another party honoring him, at the home of Sir Charles Tennyson (leading member of the society "designed," according to Frost, "for the prevention of forgetting Tennyson"). When the party proved to be no more than an ordinary high tea, the homesickness that had repeatedly overtaken Frost earlier in the trip came back in full force. He quickly returned to his hotel, where he told Thompson to make reservations for a flight home. Then, tired and ill, he went to bed.

Next morning, his birthday, Frost was in no condition for any kind of celebrating. Indeed, the poet looked so unwell that Thompson suggested a doctor be called in. The diagnosis gave little comfort. "I can tighten up his bowels all right," said the Englishman to Thompson, "but it's his heart that worries me." It was slow and irregular, and the doctor advised that Frost be taken back to America at once.

Back in Massachusetts by the end of March, Frost recovered quickly from the various ill effects of his trip, and within a few days' time was well enough to look forward eagerly to an event in Washington for which he had Stewart Udall to thank. Called "An Evening with Robert Frost," it was a reception and reading scheduled for the first of May. Much to Frost's disappointment, a crisis involving Communist military advances in Southeast Asia prevented President Kennedy and Secretary of State Rusk from attending. But despite their absence and the crisis mood that overhung Washington, his talk was a triumphant success. The audience included ambassadors to and from the United States, generals, Supreme Court justices, and members of the Cabinet and the Congress. The Secretary of the Treasury, C. Douglas Dillon, began by introducing Secretary Udall, who introduced Frost. Then, for more than an hour the audience was completely his. He spoke on his favorite subject of science-versus-poetry and read a wide selection of some of his best-known poems. He was not permitted to leave the hall until he had returned to the stage for several encores, each preceded by a standing ovation—nor until he had spent a full hour, in the lobby, accepting the personal tribute of many of the guests.

When the time came to return to Vermont for the summer, he had high hopes of finishing the collection of new poems he had been promising Holt for the past several years. The importance of finishing the book before death overtook him or his powers failed was given a special urgency, in early July, when he learned of the death by suicide of Ernest Hemingway. Frost felt sure he knew just why Hemingway had done what he had done: he had become convinced that he had lost his ability to write. And he would not tolerate any criticism of Hemingway's action; he insisted that he had shown great courage in killing himself when the thing he had lived for was gone. He even spoke of doing the same.

In his darker moods, in the weeks following the Hemingway suicide, he made a gesture more than once of throwing his almost-completed book into the fireplace—not so much because he feared his powers had failed him as because he dreaded seeing his poems attacked by the critics. He did not want to be told that they were not up to his best work.

The Vermont legislature in late June passed a bill designating him Poet Laureate of Vermont, and the Governor invited him up to Stowe in July to receive a citation thanking him for his contributions to the life of his adopted state. By the time he arrived at Stowe, Frost had written a four-line poem to thank the state for the honor, "On Being Chosen Poet of Vermont." But his feelings of warmth toward his fellow Vermonters were considerably cooled by a sequence of events that began in October 1961.

Stewart Udall had caught the hint when Frost had written, in April, that he might want a park made someday out of his place in Vermont. In subsequent conversations the poet and the politician agreed that it would be a fine idea to have a Robert Frost Memorial Park created in Ripton, as a living monument to the state's laureate. During a visit by Udall to the farm, they further agreed that the best plan of attack was to arrange a trade of some of the government acreage bordering Homer Noble Farm for another piece of property Frost would purchase in or near Ripton. It seemed simple enough, and Frost did prepare to purchase some acreage known as Beaver Meadow, north of Ripton, in order to trade it for the government land in question. But when the government land was appraised in anticipation of the trade, the value assigned to it was so astronomically high that the entire scheme had to be abandoned. For Frost, who had long hoped to see a park set up that would preserve the memory of his association with Ripton and vicinity, the disappointment was acute.

A plan that did not fall through was one initiated by the citizens of Lawrence, Massachusetts. A year or two earlier, they had authorized the construction of the Robert Lee Frost Elementary School. The school opened in September of 1961, but the dedication was delayed until early January of the new year, so Frost could attend. In the course of the afternoon, he spoke about poetry and his experience as a student at Lawrence High School.

On January eighteenth, before leaving for his winter vacation in Florida, he attended the annual Poetry Society dinner in New York, where another form of homage was awaiting him: a recently completed portrait bust by lawyer-sculptor Leo Cherne. But Frost was so far from being pleased by the finished product that the affair, for him, was a dismal failure. Next evening he found himself at a party at the apartment of his daughter Lesley. But, again, he came away feeling angry and out of sorts. Lesley had told him of her decision to sell the third of Pencil Pines he had in 1953 given her and her husband, Joseph Ballantine, as a wedding present; it seemed to Frost that Lesley was deliberately setting out to hurt him—and hurt, indeed, he was.

His feeling of persecution was still strong enough, several days later, to convince him that even his most devoted admirers were turning against him. At Agnes Scott College in Decatur, Georgia, to which he had paid almost yearly visits since 1935, he was sure there was disrespect intended in some of the questions he was asked after his talk; and he vowed privately that he would never again return.

Even before he reached South Miami, on the night of January 26, 1962, exhaustion and sheer rage combined to make him virtually ill. Within a few days he had contracted a cold and sore throat and was feeling so poorly he telephoned Kay Morrison in Cambridge and tried to tell her just how sick he was. But his deafness prevented him from hearing what she was saying in response, and in disgust he cut her off by hanging up. Disturbed, Mrs. Morrison immediately phoned one of her Miami friends, Helen Muir, and asked her to see what the matter was. One look at the poet was enough to convince Mrs. Muir a doctor was needed. His diagnosis was probable influenza, but he was unable to persuade Frost to enter the hospital. In the end, the doctor prescribed appropriate medication and arranged for a nurse to come and take care of him at Pencil Pines.

By February third he was feeling much better in body, if not in spirit. When the doctor returned and found his temperature was normal, he suggested that Frost go outside to enjoy the sunny, mild weather with a short walk. While he was dressing, however, a brief shower left the grass soaking wet. Going out anyway, he got his feet wet and returned to the house with a chill. When the doctor came back, he assured Frost his temperature was still normal and that he was "coming along fine." The poet did not agree and said he felt terrible. When he got up to shave a few hours later, he began to cough violently and saw blood in his phlegm. Without a moment's hesitation, he walked unsteadily to the telephone, dialed Mrs. Morrison once again, and growled darkly: "If you want to see me again, alive, you'd better get down here fast. And tell Al Edwards the same." He, then, hung up.

The nurse, who had overheard all this, phoned the doctor and told him that her patient was behaving "like a crazy man. He's trying to kill himself." Returning at once, the doctor found that Frost's temperature was now alarmingly high and that his lungs were filled with congestion. The new diagnosis was inescapable: pneumonia.

An ambulance was called, and he was taken to the hospital. There being no time to await results of tests, the doctor made an educated guess that Frost's pneumonia was of the pneumococcus variety. That the guess was correct very likely saved Frost's life. Within a few days he was well enough to joke with the doctor about the penicillin treatments without which he would surely have died. "They say pneumonia is 'the old man's friend,'" Frost observed. "I guess that makes penicillin the enemy of the old man's friend."

Despite a relapse that temporarily threw his survival in doubt, Frost was sufficiently recovered by the sixteenth of February to leave the hospital and retire for a month of convalescence to Pencil Pines. While there, he occupied himself by going over, with Kay, page proofs of the long-awaited book he had recently submitted to Holt. His South Miami farm, nestled as it was in a clearing of scrub pine, was a particularly appropriate setting for applying the finishing touches to the new volume. The title Frost had given it (after years of intending to call it *The Great Misgiving*) was *In the Clearing*.

Frost, as more than one scientist of his acquaintance had had occasion to observe, had an unusual command of the facts and principles of modern science; and several poems in this, as in previous volumes, suggested he had little patience with those—in or out of the sciences —whose "fond faith" it was that learning, generally, and science, in particular, could so reduce the world to quantifiable, rational data, that God would be quite left out of the universal equation. That God's purposes were served, even in the most apparently accidental of natural and human events, was the theme of a poem in *In the Clearing* entitled "Accidentally on Purpose."

The notion that human instinct was man's "best guide upward further to the light" was extended in the poem "Kitty Hawk," which (despite its three-beat lines sounding half like *Beowulf* in translation and half like doggerel) Frost regarded, properly, as one of his most important poems. Beginning it in 1953 after a visit with his friends the Huntington Cairnses at Kitty Hawk, North Carolina, Frost reworked and expanded the poem until it had grown to almost 500 lines, and it included both a partial autobiography of his early life and the philosophy of his maturity.

It was clearly Frost's intention to include the discoveries of science and technological developments among the ways men had emulated God by "risking spirit in substantiation." But it is also clear that he considered poetry, in particular, a meritorious endeavor to apply mind, or spirit, toward the deeper penetration of the universe; and he considered the poems of *In the Clearing* to be examples of how he himself had followed God's example by risking his spirit—in verse.

Frost was well enough by the third week in March to go to Washington for the celebration of his eighty-eighth birthday, on March 26, 1962. The birthday activities began with a press conference. Later, the poet called on President Kennedy, to receive from him the gold medal he was once to have received from President Eisenhower. In return, he gave the President the first copy of *In the Clearing,* published later that day, which carried an affectionate inscription. And that evening Frost went to the Pan American Union for his birthday dinner.

Two hundred guests helped him celebrate in his grandest party to date, and the after-dinner speakers who rose to praise him included Chief Justice Earl Warren, Robert Penn Warren, Adlai Stevenson, Justice Felix Frankfurter, and Mark Van Doren. Stewart Udall, who, with Alfred Edwards, had arranged the affair, then rose to introduce the guest of honor. At five past midnight it was the poet's turn to speak, and for twenty-five minutes he did just that. He recited some of the poems in his new book, interspersed with his accustomed comments, and closed by praising the woman who had been his devoted secretary for more than twenty years, Kay Morrison. After a recitation of the sonnet he had written for her, "Never Again Would Birds' Song Be the Same," he sat down. Another great evening was over.

44

THE ADVENTURE TO RUSSIA

(1962)

IN SPITE of his cherished belief that the battlefield was one of the best places to test the relative strength of opposing ideas, Robert Frost eventually became convinced that, in a nuclear age, it made no sense for the superpowers to go to war over some transitory trouble spot or a difference of political ideology. His rejection of atomic combat implied, however, no acceptance of the petty squabbling of the Cold War. Rivalry between the great powers was, he believed, inevitable; but the best, the highest kind of rivalry was on the level of intellectual, creative, and athletic competition. I had, moreover, to contain a good measure of something Frost had come to value much in recent years: magnanimity.

President Kennedy, Frost was sure, believed as he did. But what of the Russian leader, Nikita Khrushchev? Frost believed Khrushchev, too, could be persuaded to give up "blackguarding," for "magnanimous rivalry," if asked to do so in the right way; and an autocratic ruler like the Soviet Premier could, if he chose, do more to effect change in the conduct of world politics than even the President of the United States.

In May 1962, Frost received a call from Stewart Udall, who began by saying he was going to Russia in the fall to inspect Soviet hydroelectric facilities. Also, Udall continued, he was shortly to entertain the new Russian ambassador, Anatoly Dobrynin, in his Georgetown home. Would Frost care to come? Yes, said Frost, very much.

Udall's party led to unexpected developments. After a spirited discussion between Frost and the ambassador, in which Frost presented his case for "the right kind of rivalry," Udall observed that it would be greatly beneficial to international understanding if Frost could share his views with the Russian people. Perhaps, he said, an exchange could be worked out, in which some Russian poet might visit the United States in return for a visit by Frost to the Soviet Union. Ambassador Dobrynin said he liked the idea very much. Half-elated and half-terrified, Frost said he would have to give the matter careful thought.

He eventually decided he was willing to go to Russia if there was a chance—even a small one—that in so doing he might be presented an opportunity to meet Khrushchev and share with him his vision for a better world. He was past being interested in visiting new lands, seeing new people—even, winning new converts to his verse. But to take a part in the shaping of history, a part that might far transcend even his participation in the Presidential inauguration, that indeed was *something*!

He would go, he said, if the President wanted him to; and in July, after the Department of State had successfully completed preliminary arrangements, Kennedy sent Frost the word he wanted: his personal invitation, along with an expression of his high esteem. Frost's letter, accepting, only hinted at his hope to see Khrushchev. He made no secret, however, of his boyish delight at the prospect of going.

The choice of a traveling companion had by now been made: Frederick B. Adams, Jr., a friend who was director of the Morgan Library in New York City. But as Adams spoke no more Russian than did Frost, it had also been decided someone must be brought along to serve as interpreter: Franklin D. Reeve, a young professor at Wesleyan University who had an excellent command of the Russian language. The entourage complete, Frost left it to Adams and Reeve to work out an itinerary with the State Department. He himself had only one fixed goal for the Russian expedition—and that goal appeared nowhere in his itinerary: to talk to "the great man" and to present to him his vision of a magnanimous rivalry that just might alter the course of history.

In Washington, on August twenty-seventh, Adams and Reeve joined Frost for dinner at the home of the Udalls. Even now, Frost's nervousness was beginning to get the better of him. Next morning Adams found him in his hotel room complaining of pains in his chest—the kind of pains he often got when something or someone was causing him anxiety. But he quickly recovered from his "heart trouble," and lunch with the Dobrynins, at the Soviet embassy, took place without incident.

The flight to Russia, with Frost, Adams, and Reeve accompanied by Udall and his party, was uneventful; and late in the afternoon of August twenty-ninth, the Americans disembarked at Sheremetyevo airport, outside Moscow. There, Frost was greeted by a pair of American diplomats, a delegation representing his official host on the trip, the Soviet Writers Union, and a group of Russian and foreign reporters who had come to welcome his arrival.

"I am here to talk with you about science, art, athletics, great music and, of course, poetry," he told the Russians. "We can talk about these things because there is no rivalry.

"We admire each other, don't we? Great nations admire each other and don't take pleasure in belittling each other." But, he added, "If the Russians beat my country in everything, then I will become a Russian."

His writer-hosts broke into nervous laughter, but they seemed not to comprehend him when he continued: "You've got to have power to protect the language, to protect the poetry in it. You've got to be strong to protect poetry. Poetry's the most national of the arts, not so much painting or music. A great nation makes great poetry, and great poetry makes a great nation. It works both ways."

He told his questioners: "Sometime I'll go a little deeper into our approach to each other. I've got some rather bald things to say."

After a brief interview Udall and his engineers left, and "the three" were taken to the Sovietskaya hotel, accompanied by Jack Matlock of the American embassy and Aleksandr Tvardovsky, who was to be the other half of the Russian-American cultural exchange. Frost knew that much about the Russian, but he was unaware of just how important a man Tvardovsky was. As editor of *Novy Mir* he was a powerful figure in determining which Russian artists enjoyed the approval of the Soviet government—and which did not.

Next morning Matlock reappeared to say that the embassy was working to arrange an interview with the Soviet Premier, but that it was too early to tell if their efforts would be successful. A lengthy program of things for Frost to do and see during his ten days in Russia was soon shortened considerably. "There isn't much time," Reeve had explained, "and we must arrange things so Frost sees some people and reads his poems. He doesn't like just sight-seeing and staring at monuments." That, nevertheless, was what he did for much of the morning. After several interviews with Russian newspaper reporters, he was taken in a sedan provided by the Writers Union and shown around the city.

Next day, after more interviews with the press, the trio was driven to dinner with Kornei Chukovsky at his dacha in Peredelkino, the writers' colony outside Moscow. At eighty, Chukovsky was Frost's counterpart among Russian writers, the grand old man.

Back in Moscow, Frost paid a visit to an "English" school, where the children were exposed to a curriculum that emphasized instruction in the English language. But, obviously, Frost was disappointed. He had been in Russia for almost four days, and it seemed to him that he was no closer to doing what he had come for—to see Khrushchev—than he was when he arrived.

Frost, Adams, and Reeve visited the Aelita, a "youth café," as the guests of Yevgeny Yevtushenko. Afterward the party adjourned for dinner at Yevtushenko's apartment, where several other poets and friends of the Russian's were waiting. Each, including Frost, recited a few of his poems; and the evening ended at midnight on a much more favorable note than the day had begun. But Frost could not help wondering at what sacrifice Yevtushenko managed to satisfy what were, to him, the irreconcilable demands of his art and his revolutionary politics.

Sunday, following dinner, the Americans boarded a sleeper for Leningrad, where Frost would give the first public poetry reading of the trip. But the reading filled Frost with nothing like eager anticipation. He saw no point in talking to an audience that did not understand what he was saying. Khrushchev was on his mind, still. If he did not see the Premier before he went home, then (as he had said more than once during his first days in Russia)—"What the hell am I doing here?"

Returning to Moscow, Frost gave another public lecture. Like the first, it was received politely, but with restraint. The Russian audiences did not seem to trust themselves to laugh at the mild witticisms he aimed toward their society and their leadership. At the informal reception that followed his reading, a reporter, David Miller, came up to Adams and asked if he, Frost, or Reeve had heard from Stewart Udall. Adams said he assumed that the Interior Secretary was on his way back from his tour of Siberian hydroelectric stations. "No," Miller informed him, "he's in Moscow, and he'll be leaving by plane early tomorrow morning for Gagra to visit Premier Khrushchev." He paused, and added, apologetically, "I thought you'd like to know."

Adams told Reeve and Matlock—but not Frost—what he had learned. By now it was too late in the evening to call Udall and ask him to communicate his plans to the poet, with perhaps a promise to do what he could toward arranging a meeting between Frost and the Premier. Matlock offered to get up at dawn and try to intercept Udall at the airport. But by the time he got there Udall had left, and Matlock returned disconsolately. Frost would have to be told.

Adams broke the news as gently as he could. As expected, Frost saw Udall's unheralded departure for a visit with Khrushchev as a desertion, if not an outright betrayal. Adams tried to pacify him with assurances that, even if he did not see Khrushchev, his Russian visit had been a triumph. Frost, however, would have none of it, and icily refused to talk about it any further.

That afternoon while Frost was resting alone in his room, his telephone rang repeatedly, but he chose to ignore it. Adams and Reeve returned to the hotel in the early evening and learned at the front desk that someone had been trying to reach Frost all afternoon with no success. Fearing something had happened to him, they rushed to his room. When he let them in they asked if he had not heard the telephone. "Yes," he answered, "it rang quite a lot, but I didn't bother to answer it. I knew there'd just be a voice on the other end speaking Russian, and I couldn't do anything about it."

They called the American embassy and asked if there were any messages for Frost. There were none. They called the Writers Union, but no one was there. Somewhat baffled, they awaited the arrival of Matlock for dinner. When he appeared, however, he could provide no information about the mysterious telephone calls. Finally, as they sat over cocktails in Matlock's apartment, the diplomat received a call from which he returned with a broad smile. He had just been informed, he said, that Premier Khrushchev would see Frost tomorrow in the Crimea.

The good news came as such a shock to the old poet that soon he became, as Adams later described it, "actively sick." His nervous illness was, indeed, so violent it was decided to defer until morning the final decision as to whether or not he would go at all. Several hours of sleep, they hoped, would help him recover. Unfortunately, when Adams and Reeve called on him before six next morning, he told them he had hardly slept and that he felt even worse than he had the night before. He knew, and his companions knew, he was in no condition to go anywhere. But Frost remarked as they debated a course of action, "It would be hard to face my friends at home if I had a chance to do what I came to do, and then didn't do it." With a little further discussion, it was decided Frost would go, taking with him the Russian-speaking Reeve.

By eleven o'clock, after a three-hour flight on a regularly scheduled jet, Frost, Reeve, the poet Alexei Surkov, and an interpreter named Myshkov landed at the airport outside Sochi in the Crimea. They were driven across the border into Georgia and taken to the guest house of the Georgian S.S.R. Ministry of Health. Premier Khrushchev's dacha, to which they were to continue after a little time to eat and rest, was a twenty-minute drive away.

Frost, who had napped during much of the flight to Sochi, lay down in his room and told Reeve that he was feeling worse than ever. Reeve told Surkov of the situation over lunch in the dining room, and they wondered uneasily what their next move should be. Returning to Frost's room, Reeve asked if the poet wanted a doctor to be summoned. After some hesitation, he said yes. Twenty minutes later, a white-frocked woman appeared. She took Frost's temperature (it was 101.5°), listened to his chest and back, and made her diagnosis: Frost was neither very sick nor quite well; he seemed to be suffering from nervous indigestion, probably brought on by too much traveling; if his illness became any worse he should be returned at once to Moscow. Frost, from his bed, made his own pronouncement: he could go no further.

Once again, Reeve informed Surkov of how things stood; and, then, returned to Frost's room. A few minutes later Surkov appeared and said he had just spoken by telephone with Khrushchev. The Premier was sending his personal physician to look at Frost, and would soon come himself. The meeting was still on.

Frost was pleased—and, in a way, relieved—but the imminence of his long-sought confrontation with the Russian leader made him edgier with every passing minute. Through his mind ran all the things he wanted to say, had been planning to say. He tried to doze, but could not. Khrushchev's doctor now arrived, confirming his colleague's diagnosis of the poet's illness. Then, after a few minutes, the Premier himself appeared at the house. Reeve thanked him for coming, thanked him for sending his own doctor, explained Frost's illness, and said how anxious the poet was to meet him. After a word with the doctor about the state of Frost's health, the Premier, accompanied by his secretary, entered the room.

Forewarned by Reeve, Frost had sat up on the edge of his bed and put on his shoes and socks. Reeve, Surkov, and Myshkov stationed themselves around the room, as did Khrushchev's secretary and the host of the guest house. After an exchange of greetings with the poet, Khrushchev sat on a chair beside Frost's bed. Then began the conversation, an account of which was later published by Reeve:

"[Khrushchev] asked about Frost's health, chided him for not taking care of himself, expressed admiration at Frost's traveling so far, said how pleased he was to see him, reminded him to be sure to follow the doctors' orders if he was going to live to be a hundred. Frost, for his part, said that he was very glad to have come, that he was very pleased by the invitation, that you could never trust doctors anyway, and that he was certainly going to live to be a hundred because in the year he would be a hundred his country would be two hundred. It was something, he said, being half as old as your country.

"Khrushchev asked him how he had found his stay in Russia, how he had been received. Frost replied that he had had a fine time, that the Premier certainly had done a lot for poetry, judging by all the poems that were published and by all the poets around. They talked briefly about art and poetry and the artist's relation to his society. Frost conveyed the President's greetings to the Premier and expressed his gratitude to those who had arranged his trip.

"And with that the real conversation began. Khrushchev wondered if Frost had anything special in mind, and Frost started talking about what had long lain closest to his heart: a way for working out an East-West understanding. . . ."

He had said much of it already, in his letter to President Kennedy, to Ambassador Dobrynin at Udall's dinner party, to the Russian literary men during his week in Russia, to the press. There must be no petty squabbling in the relations between Russia and America, but rather, a noble rivalry on the level of sports, science, the arts, democracy. "God wants us to contend," he told Khrushchev, and the superpowers were destined for a hundred years of competition that would determine which political system, the American or the Soviet, would come out on top. The central element had to be magnanimity; neither side must seek to blackguard the other to gain political advantage.

To much of this Khrushchev readily agreed, but he also seemed particularly eager to demonstrate the logic of Soviet international politics. In Reeve's words:

"Premier Khrushchev said that the fundamental conflict between the two countries was peaceful economic competition. He said that the Soviet Union and all the Warsaw Pact nations were young countries, healthy, vital, full of energy. He said that they had made extraordinary strides forward. The United States and Western Europe, he said, were thousands of years old with a defunct economic system. This reminded him, he said, of an anecdote reported in Gorky's memoirs of Tolstoy, where Tolstoy told about being too old and too weak and too infirm to do it but still having the desire. Frost chuckled and said that might be true for the two of them but that the United States was too young to worry about that yet. . . ."

Frost now came as close as he would come in the conversation to making the hard request of Khrushchev that he had been keeping a secret from even his closest friends for months. He began by saying the Premier was a man of great power, and he was, therefore, in a position to do great good toward effecting a solution to the Berlin problem that had troubled East-West relations for the past fifteen years. All Khrushchev had to do, said Frost, was to propose a kind of horse-trade with the United States, something given up somewhere in the world by the Soviet Union in return for something given up in the matter of Berlin by the United States. He was sure the United States would accept the terms of any proposal he made. Khrushchev listened to the old man's words, and replied simply, "You have the soul of a poet." Then, the conversation moved on to other subjects.

The meeting lasted ninety minutes. Finally, the Premier asked if Frost were not tired, if he had not overstayed his time. Frost said he had not, and added he was glad to have had such a frank, high-minded discussion. Khrushchev asked that Frost give his greetings to President Kennedy and the American people, and suggested, also, that Frost talk to Kennedy about the issues they had just raised. "It is a great pleasure to have met such a famous poet," said the Premier. After some further exchange of pleasantries and a clasping of hands, Khrushchev, followed by his secretary and doctor, withdrew from the room.

"Well, we did it, didn't we?" Frost said to Reeve as he fell back, exhausted, on the bed. "He's a great man, he knows what power is and isn't afraid to take hold of it. He's a great man, all right."

When the group returned to Moscow the following morning, a number of reporters were waiting for the poet. Apparently fully recovered from the illness that had overtaken him two days earlier, Frost declined to take the hotel elevator to his second-floor apartment, but walked upstairs, shaved, and twenty minutes later invited the correspondents into his sitting room to hear the story of his meeting with the Soviet leader. "He's our enemy, but he's a great man," said Frost of Khrushchev. "He's a ruffian. He's ready for a fight. He's not a coward. He's not afraid of us and we're not afraid of him."

A Russian reporter suggested that perhaps he meant to say the Premier was "rough," but not that he was a "ruffian." Frost apparently did not hear her, for he kept right on talking. But it was clear he used "ruffian" as a term of admiration.

"I sat on the edge of the bed, and we had a good talk and went at it." He said he had been disappointed only by Khrushchev's apparent unwillingness to cut the Gordian Knot of world problems—particularly in the case of Berlin. "I told him he ought to be like Alexander the Great, who didn't believe in fussing with Gordian Knots and untying them. He believed in cutting . . . [them]. I just hoped a man as mighty as Khrushchev might do something even if we didn't."

"I was like a tramp poet who visits a great monarch. 'I've got just one little request,' the tramp asks the monarch. 'Will you grant it to me before I ask it?' Well," he conceded, "I didn't get that far."

He said he had gone to Khrushchev hoping to convince him to compete with America in "strife and magnanimity" and that the Premier was amenable: "He agrees with strife and with magnanimity. He's no saphead. No liberal sapheads for me."

Did he have any message from Premier Khrushchev for President Kennedy? he was asked. "Yes," he replied, "in a way." Adams and Reeve counseled him to save his "message" for the President's ears, but he kept on. The Premier had told him to say to the President "not to do this, and to do that, and that he mustn't do this and must do that, quite a few things." When pressed, he assured the reporters that the conversation had not been "on a low level of partisanship," but "all high level." He would say no more.

Later, over lunch, Adams asked Frost if he wanted to send a cable to Mrs. Morrison, informing her of his safe return from Gagra. He thought a moment and told his friend what to send: "BACK FROM CRIMEA, ALL CRIMES ACCOMPLISHED."

On Sunday, September ninth, the Americans flew home; and the story should have ended there, but it did not. When the jet carrying Frost,

Udall, and their companions touched down in New York, Frost had not slept for eighteen hours and was physically and mentally exhausted. Aware of Frost's condition, Alfred Edwards, who had come to meet him, did his best to reach the plane before Frost emerged to face the waiting press. Inexplicably, Secret Service agents prevented him from approaching the plane. A few minutes later, Frost stepped out on the arm of Stewart Udall and happily complied with the request of the reporters that he answer just a few short questions.

What had he discussed with Premier Khrushchev? What had the Premier said? "Khrushchev said he feared for us modern liberals," Frost answered. "He said we were too liberal to fight. I suppose he thought we'd stand there for the next hundred years saying, 'On the one hand—but on the other hand.' " Did he have any message from Khrushchev to deliver to President Kennedy, and if so, when did he plan to deliver it? "Yes," Frost replied, "I have a message from Khrushchev for the President. I don't 'plan' to see him. I wait for the President."

In the days and weeks ahead Frost waited for his summons to the White House or, at least, a note from the President thanking him for representing his country on the cultural mission to Russia. Nothing came. Instead, Frost began to receive mail from various quarters asking if it were true, as the newspapers all reported, that Khrushchev had said the United States was "too liberal to fight." One letter came from Charles H. Lyttle, pastor of the First Unitarian Society of Geneva, Illinois:

"Owing to the very high regard in which you are held in our church circle, several of our members have felt a bit distressed over certain aspects of the enclosed newspaper account of a purported interview with you on your arrival in New York from your visit to Russia.

"Your remarks concerning your attitude toward socialism did not puzzle or disturb us—some of us feel as you do on that subject—but your (alleged) report that 'Premier Khrushchev believes the United States will not fight to protect its rights . . . he thought that we are too liberal to fight,'—is the cause of our dismay.

"For the John Birchers in our community this is most welcome grist for their mill!

"For those of us who are striving to prevent war, the report is confusing and distressing—if the press item is accurate.

"We would be greatly obliged if you woul[d] . . . inform us of the accuracy or inaccuracy of the press notice. Some of us suspect that the press deliberately misrepresented you, on this point at least. . . ."

Unwilling to admit he might have distorted Khrushchev's words to unburden his own obsession with "liberals," Frost answered Lyttle on September twentieth:

"The Sun gets me right. Surely you can have no objection to my getting

Kruschev exactly right. He is power personified ruling over four hundred million people seemingly of one accord. My stay was too brief for penetrating into any dissidence, if such exists. The Russian nation expects to try us out in one way or another. The stage or arena is set (by you-know-Whom) for a rivalry between us for the next hundred years in athletics, art, science, business, and in democracy, our kind of democracy versus their kind of democracy (so to call it by courtesy). Mr. Kruschev agreed to all this magnificently. We are confronted with a Gordian Knot in the problem of whether it is as important for them to achieve great things as for us to achieve them. Liberals would rather fuss with that Gordian Knot than cut it. They're wasting time in an emergency. That's the way Mr. Kruschev sees it as a Nationalist. He and I didn't talk about peace or love or coexistence. We talked about surpassing excellence and the survival of the fittest. His amusing and slight contempt was for people who enjoy wanting something they haven't the force to get. . . ."

When he answered a letter, similar to Lyttle's, from the former Socialist candidate for President, Norman Thomas, Frost came close to, but fell short of, admitting he had put the word "liberal" in Khrushchev's mouth:

"Everyone seems to want to start joking with me about the word 'liberal' but as you say it's no joking matter. It was almost that with Kruschev. Shall I try to tell you the affable way he used it with me in Gagra. He was just being good-natured and literary when he expressed concern for American liberality. He was quoting either Gorky to Tolstoi or Tolstoi to Gorky, I forget which, when he said there was such a thing possibly as a nation's getting like the bald-headed row at a leg show so it enjoyed wanting to do what it could no longer do. I was interested to find the great old powerhouse so bookish. . . . I think I broke down his figure by answering we were too young a nation for that worry.

"There are all sorts of liberals and I have amused myself with defining them. Kruschev's was a good crack. My own latest is that they are people who have had the liberal education that I fled and have come back to assert my difference with in their own strongholds, the colleges. If Matthew Arnold is their gospel, I come pretty near being a liberal myself. I have teasingly described them as people who can't take their own side in a quarrel and would rather fuss with a Gordian Knot than cut it and as 'Dover Beach-combers' and as Matthew Arnold's wisest 'who take dejectedly their seat upon the intellectual throne'. They are never arbitrary enough 'to bid their will avouch it' like a real leader. But all that aside . . . , I yield to no one in my admiration for the kind of liberal you have been, you and Henry Wallace. One of the great moments of my life was when . . . I stood between you and Henry for a chance photographer

[501]

to take our picture. . . . I can't see how Kruschev's talk got turned into what you quote[:] that we weren't men enough to fight. I came nearer than he to threatening: with my native geniality I assured him that we were no more afraid of him than he was of us. We seemed in perfect agreement that we shouldn't come to blows till we were sure there was a big issue remaining between us, of his kind of democracy versus our kind of democracy, approximating each other as they are, his by easing downward towards socialism from the severity of its original ideals, ours by straining upward towards socialism through various phases of welfare state-ism. I said the stage or arena is set between us for a rivalry of perhaps a hundred years. Let's hope we can take it out in sports, science, art, business, and politics before ever we have to take it out in the bloody politics of war. It was all magnanimity—Aristotle's great word. I should have expected you to approve. Liberal in a good sense of the word. Browning tells of a post-office bulletin notice in Italy 'two liberal thieves were shot'. If only a word would stay put in basic English."

President Kennedy remained silent. Frost could not have known how resentful he had been when informed by Udall that the remark attributed to Khrushchev was, beyond question, the sentiment not of the Soviet Premier, but of Frost himself. The only word from the White House on the subject of the Russian trip came not from the President, but from August Heckscher, special consultant on the arts—a position that had been created partly as a result of Frost's prodding. "I am among the many millions of your countrymen," wrote Heckscher, "who have been proud and delighted by your remarks and observations on your trip through the Soviet Union. You did wonderfully. You helped set a framework for broad and magnanimous discussion.

"I am sure that on both sides of the Iron Curtain your visit will be long remembered."

Frost hoped that Heckscher's kind words were true. But he would have preferred, and he continued to hope, that he would soon hear similar ones from President Kennedy.

CONCLUDING THE STORY

(1962–1963)

ROBERT FROST had survived grave illness to make the trip to Russia, and had survived the trip itself; but as he entered the fall of 1962 he was an ill and tired man. Even before leaving for the Soviet Union, he had been told by Dr. Hartwell Harrison of the Peter Bent Brigham Hospital in Boston that he had a prostatic condition that was threatening sooner or later to require surgery. He hardly needed to be told the cystitis from which he had been suffering intermittently for more than twenty years had also grown worse in recent months; the constant discomfort it caused him, if not exactly a harbinger of death, at least served to remind him he had lived a very long life. He was determined, however, not to slow down, not to end his days in retirement. He had expressed to one friend, as they walked on a secluded path near the Homer Noble Farm, the ideal he conceived for himself. "I often think that the best way to die," he said to Hyde Cox, "would be to die like this someday, out on the trail." And it was, indeed, to the well-worn academic trail that Frost returned, as he entered the seventh month of his eighty-ninth year.

Dartmouth was the first stop of his fall itinerary. A few days later he called at Amherst, where his talk before the national committee of the Amherst capital program was preceded by President Plimpton's announcement that an anonymous gift of $3.5 million would be used to construct a new edifice: the Robert Frost Library. Lectures at other colleges followed until, after another talk at Amherst on October twentieth, he headed for Washington to speak at the first National Poetry Festival on the evening of the twenty-third.

Washington was in anything but a festive mood that week. The Cuban missile crisis, suddenly and unexpectedly, had brought the country and the world to the brink of nuclear war. Frost, in his Library of Congress talk, demonstrated a new willingness to admit that Premier Khrushchev had not, in fact, said quite what he had earlier reported. "I've joked about liberals a great deal," said the poet midway through his remarks, "and there's been something going around. I wonder how many of you've heard it: that I was told in Russia that Americans were too liberal to fight, or something like that. Nothing like that did I hear. What I heard was, rather, a pleasantry from the greatest ruler in the world, you know, the almighty, and in his genial way he just said, 'As Tolstoi said to Gorki'—or vice versa, I've forgotten which; it was a very literary conversation—'As Tolstoi said to Gorki, "There's such a thing as a nation getting so soft it couldn't—wouldn't fight."' See, that's all. He was just saying there was such a thing, and he might be suggesting that we better look out. See, that's all, it was a pleasantry. It wasn't a defiant thing, nothing was defiant. I'd like that straightened out, whatever happens. . . ."

Clearly, Frost was concerned that the present crisis might somehow be taken as having arisen from his inaccurate reporting of Premier Khrushchev's remarks to him in Gagra, that President Kennedy had taken such a strong stand against the installation of missiles in Cuba to demonstrate that the country was not, in fact, "too liberal to fight" in defense of its principles. But it did not escape Frost that Premier Khrushchev, very possibly, had deliberately misled him by agreeing to his formula of "magnanimous rivalry," free of the kind of "blackguarding" that the Cuban situation seemed to represent.

"Well, there were no lies, see," the poet continued; "it's very interesting. I couldn't go to him and say I was lied to, but I could say that there was a sort of loss of faith, that we understood each other, that I was led to understand what probably I was partly mistaken about. I wasn't very deeply, just a little. I could make that charge, that 'You've broken faith with me,' a little. I'd like to say that to him, like to see him here tonight. I admire him, admire the power and all that; but I feel a little hurt that way."

As much as he might have liked to have Premier Khrushchev in the audience that night, Frost would have liked even more to have President Kennedy before him as he admitted, at last, that Khrushchev had not said what he had attributed to him after returning from Russia. It grieved him deeply that he had angered the President by his remarks, and he seemed to want Kennedy to know he was sorry for what he had said and sorry for the confusion, if not the crisis, his "liberal" remark had occasioned.

Frost left Washington for Gambier, Ohio, and Kenyon College. In November—an unusually active month, even for Frost—he was in New York to receive the MacDowell Colony medal, to say his poems, and to hear a number of congratulatory telegrams that included one from President Kennedy, laudatory but quite impersonal. Less than a week later he was in Michigan, to receive an honorary doctor of laws degree from the University of Detroit, after reciting his poems to an audience of 8,500 people. From Detroit he went on to Chicago, for the celebration of the fiftieth anniversary of the founding of *Poetry* magazine; then, back to Greenwich, Connecticut, for a lecture and a family Thanksgiving dinner at the home of Willard Fraser's sister, Jean, attended by Lesley, her two daughters, and their husbands.

Frost went up to Hanover for another talk, on the evening of November twenty-seventh, in the handsome new Hopkins Center of Dartmouth College, named after the president who had brought Frost to Dartmouth in 1943.

"I think the first thing I ought to speak of," he began, "is all this luxuriance: all in easy chairs and a beautiful hall—and nothing to do but to listen to me. Pretty soft, I call it. Pretty soft.

"I was so made that I—though a Vermonter and all that—I never took any stock in the doctrine that 'a penny saved is a penny earned.' A penny saved is a *mean* thing, and a penny spent is a generous thing and a big thing—like this. (It took more than a penny to do this. There's nothing mean about it.) . . .

"And I was thinking . . . of the extravagance of the universe. What an *extravagant* universe it is. And the most extravagant thing in it, as far as we know, is man—the most wasteful, spending thing in it—in all his luxuriance.

"How stirring it is, the sun and everything. Take a telescope and look as far as you will. How much of a universe was wasted just to produce puny us. It's wonderful . . . , fine.

"And poetry is a sort of extravagance, in many ways. It's something that people wonder about. What's the need of it? And the answer is, no need—not particularly. That is, that's the first one.

"I've always enjoyed being around colleges, nominally as a professor, you know, and a puzzle to everybody as to what I was doing—whether anything or not. . . . And people say to me occasionally, 'Where *does* poetry come in?' Some of you may be thinking it tonight: what's it all for? 'Does it *count*?'

"When I catch a man reading my book, red-handed, he usually looks up cheerfully and says, 'My wife is a great fan of yours.' Puts it off on the women.

"I figured that out lately: that there's an indulgence of poetry, a manly indulgence of poetry, that's a good deal like the manly indulgence of women. We say that women rule the world. That's a nice way to talk. And we say that poetry rules the world.

"There's a poem that says: 'We are the music makers, / And we are the dreamers of dreams . . . / World-losers and world-forsakers,' . . . and all that. We are 'the makers' of the future. We: 'Built Nineveh with our sighing, / And Babel itself with our mirth; / And o'erthrew them with prophesying / To the old of the new world's worth; / For each age is a dream that is dying, / And one that is coming to birth.' That's a big claim, isn't it? An exaggerated claim.

"But I look on the universe as a kind of an exaggeration anyway, the whole business. That's the way you think of it: great, great, great expense—everybody trying to make it mean something more than it is. . . ."

Toward the end of his talk, he turned to some poems of his own composition, beginning with one from his most recent volume, *In the Clearing,* and called simply "Away!" Nowhere else had Frost with so much seeming equanimity looked forward to his own death. And if it were true that he had managed to overcome much of his fear of dying, he had done so partly by returning to some of the religious beliefs he had learned in childhood from his devout mother—principally the belief that life did not end with the grave, but went on in a life after death.

In former years, he was frequently inclined to protect his religious convictions with a superficial layer of skepticism and mockery that would protect his sensitive ego from the skepticism and mockery of others less religious than himself. But now, in "the last go-down," he seemed less inclined than ever before to play at being a skeptic. His Dartmouth talk, for example, contained what almost amounted to a sermon, the text of which was the key passage in his poem "Kitty Hawk": "But God's own descent / Into flesh was meant / As a demonstration / That the supreme merit / Lay in risking spirit / In substantiation."

"That's a whole of philosophy," he said. "To the very limit, you know." He, then, repeated a conversation he had had a few years before with his Ripton friend Rabbi Victor Reichert, who had started it off by observing that the best passages in the New Testament were merely quotations from the Old. Frost had asked him what, if that were so, was the best statement to be found in both Testaments. "Love your neighbor as yourself," said Reichert.

"But it isn't good enough," Frost countered.

"What's the matter with it?" asked the rabbi.

"And *hate* your neighbor as you hate yourself."

"Do you hate yourself?"

"I wouldn't be religious unless I did."

He extended his remark to Reichert in the gloss he provided of a biblical passage and a Matthew Arnold poem, as he continued his Dartmouth talk:

"In the Bible twice it says—and I quote that in a poem somewhere, I think; yes—twice it says, 'these things are said in parables . . .'—said in this way that I'm talking to you about: extravagance said in parable, '. . . so the wrong people won't understand them and so get saved.'

"It's thoroughly undemocratic, very superior—as when Matthew Arnold says, in a whole sonnet, only those who've given everything and strained every nerve 'mount, and that hardly, to eternal life.' 'Taint everybody, it's just those only—the few that have done everything, sacrificed, risked everything, 'bet their sweet life' on what they lived. . . . And only those who have done that to the limit, he says, 'mount, and that hardly . . .'—they barely make it, you know—'. . . that hardly, to eternal life.'"

Frost had bet his own life on poetry—sometimes at considerable expense both to those around him and to himself. By the logic that shaped his Dartmouth "sermon" he could hope to "mount, and that hardly, to eternal life." But everything depended on whether God found his poems "acceptable" (the word he had used in *A Masque of Mercy*), and only by dying could he know how God judged his work and, through it, himself. It was, therefore, entirely appropriate that in closing this talk at Dartmouth he quoted his somber poem "The Night Light." "Suppose I end on that dark note," he said. "Good night."

Two days later Frost went with Kay by train to New York City to participate in a closed-circuit television broadcast raising funds for the proposed National Cultural Center in Washington. As they were leaving the train, he suddenly felt faint and very nearly collapsed. He recovered at once and went through with his small part in the program. But Mrs. Morrison, suspecting that the momentary vertigo was related to Frost's cystitis problem, was glad she had, a month before, made an appointment for him to see Dr. Harrison at the Peter Bent Brigham Hospital on December third.

On Sunday, December second, Frost delivered an evening lecture at Boston's Ford Hall Forum, after which he returned home to await his examination by Dr. Harrison next day. But when Kay telephoned him at half past nine in the morning, Frost told her he felt so ill she would have to cancel his hospital appointment. Kay telephoned the office of Frost's personal physician, Dr. Roger Hickler, to ask if he could come at once to 35 Brewster Street. As Hickler was out of town, his colleague Dr. James Jackson arrived in his stead.

It was soon agreed between Kay and Jackson that the best course of action would be to have Frost admitted to the Brigham, not just for the planned examination by Dr. Harrison, but also in order that extensive tests could be made. When Frost was presented with the suggestion, however, he put up more of an argument than Kay had anticipated. His initial comment, after a conversation alone with Jackson, was disturbing in its finality: "If I ever go into that place, I'll never come out alive."

Mrs. Morrison and Dr. Jackson persisted in arguments favoring hospitalization, until Frost abruptly rose from his chair, glared at his secretary, and in his darkest voice said, as he swept upstairs to his bedroom, "This is when I walk out of your lives—all of you." The doctor was astonished, and Mrs. Morrison had to explain that such displays of temper were not unfamiliar. She suggested that Jackson go upstairs. He found Frost stretched out on his bed, immobile. After trying several times to elicit some response from the old man, the doctor came down and said, "He won't talk to me."

Jackson soon left, as did Mrs. Morrison. When she returned after an hour or two at her home, however, she found Frost in the kitchen, calm now, eating a late breakfast. He asked her to help him pack his bag and to drive him to the hospital. As Kay left him in his hospital room, he turned to her and said, "I will do this on the highest plane—don't fear."

Later that day, his examination and tests began. They revealed that the prostate was not abnormally enlarged for a man of his age, but that the bladder was obviously infected. The initial diagnosis, of which Mrs. Morrison was informed on December fifth, was that Frost's problem was, indeed, chronic cystitis. But the hospital telephoned again, next day, to say further tests had revealed a stoppage in the bladder. Colon bacilli had collected there, which if not removed would poison Frost's entire system. They recommended surgery to correct the problem. Frost was told he had a choice: either wear a catheter for the rest of his life or permit a complete prostate operation. Having endured a catheter for the past few days, he chose the operation.

The surgical procedure took place on December tenth, and it lasted much longer than the doctors had expected. The prostate proved to be cancerous, and the cancer had spread into the bladder. But the surgeon believed that all of the cancerous tissue had been removed, and Frost came through the operation without difficulty. For two weeks, as he mended, his spirits were high, he was comfortable, and the chances of a complete recovery seemed excellent. Then, on December twenty-third, he suffered a pulmonary embolism.

He lived through it, but only barely. His heart was damaged by the attack, and he did not have to be told by his doctors that another such was likely to be fatal. On New Year's Day 1963 came another setback, but not nearly so serious as the first. Two days later he was well enough to issue a statement that supplemented the terse releases of the hospital describing his "serious" condition: "With all these countless friends in the hospital and without I find myself better than a little less than bad." His wit, and his courage, had not failed him.

Two days later he was provided with another reason for feeling "better than a little less than bad," when he learned that he had just been awarded the Bollingen Prize for poetry. Next day another statement came forth from his hospital room:

"A sweet coincidence to have the great doctors of this great hospital —Dr. J. Hartwell Harrison, Dr. George W. Thorn, and Dr. Roger B. Hickler—hand me a virtual new lease on life; and on the same day and hour, the Bollingen Prize Committee of Yale University Library one new reason to live. . . .

"This year, or so, has been a year for me—taken to the President's side for his inauguration, and allowed to stand around listening when Premier Khrushchev declared Russia a Western nation to be trusted as such in heroic rivalry.

"The overwhelming wave of letters and telegrams have given me assurance of the friendship I never felt before."

On the night of January seventh Frost was stricken by another pulmonary embolism. With the help of an oxygen tent and anticoagulants, he again survived. Next day the doctors operated to tie off the veins in his legs, in an effort to prevent further blood clots from reaching the lungs.

Mrs. Morrison and her daughter had been Frost's only visitors up to now, but after the second embolism, with its inevitable result of weakening him still further, the doctors saw no reason to deprive him of what they knew—and he sensed—were likely to be his final meetings with his friends. Each day, as his strength permitted, he would receive one or two visitors at a time, as he sat up in bed or briefly in a chair next to it, telling them of his determination to recover, and saying things his reticence would not have permitted him to say were he not so obviously on the verge of death.

Lesley had been one of the first to see him immediately after the first embolism, and she had returned to New York a few days later, when it appeared that his condition had stabilized. But in the first week of January, she sent him a note in which she said: ". . . Someone just suggested you be dubbed Robert the Lion-Hearted. It suits." Nothing else she could have said would have pleased him more. In one of the few letters he dictated from his hospital bed, he returned Lesley's praise with some of his own:

"You're something of a Lesley de Lion yourself," he said. "I am not hard to touch but I'd rather be taken for brave than anything else. A little hard and stern in judgement, perhaps, but always touched by the heroic. You have passed muster. So has Prescott. You have both found a way to make shift. You can't know how much I have counted on you in family matters. It is no time yet to defer a little to others in my future affairs but I have deferred not a little in my thoughts to the strength I find in you and Prescott and Lee, and very very affectionately to K. Morrison and Anne Morrison Gentry, who are with me taking this dictation in the hospital, and to Al Edwards in all his powerful friendship. I trust my word can bind you all together as long as my name as a poet lasts. I am too emotional for my state. Life has been a long trial yet I mean to see more of it. We all liked your poems. It must add to your confidence that you have found a way with the young."

When he was not enduring the attentions of his doctors and nurses, receiving visitors, or resting, he was busily engaged in composing a poem that was a sequel to one he had finished shortly before entering the hospital. The first one, "The Prophets Really Prophesy as Mystics The Commentators Merely by Statistics," had been sent out as Frost's Christmas poem for 1962. The new poem, or as much of it as he had composed by the beginning of the third week in January, was perhaps more redundant of the Christmas poem than Frost was entirely aware. Mrs. Morrison's daughter recorded it during her attendance at the poet's bedside. But the visits of his friends left him little time or energy to carry the poem much further or to polish the draft he had begun.

On January twenty-second Louis Untermeyer spent more than an hour, talking about the trip to Russia, politics and poetry, and the early days of their friendship, when Untermeyer had been one of the first to champion his verse. They spoke of the recent evening at the National Poetry Festival, when Untermeyer had introduced him and he had begun his talk by observing he sometimes thought he was "sort of a figment" of Louis' imagination; of how, long ago, the editors of *The Atlantic Monthly* had returned some of his poems, with the terse note of regret that the *Atlantic* had no place for his "vigorous verse"; of the disappointment that, once again, someone else had won the latest Nobel Prize for literature.

Also on the twenty-second, Frost was visited by three Russians who were members of a Soviet writers delegation under the same U.S.-U.S.S.R. cultural-exchange agreement that had taken him to Russia: Viktor Rozov, Valentin Katayev, and Frida Lurye. They presented him with gifts from their homeland and toasted him with champagne. They also listened as, once again, he explained why he had gone to their country:

"I went over to Russia to confirm an idea I had, a feeling that Russia was drifting westward. We're rivals, in the end, in everything, war and all, to the end.

"One of my greatest experiences was to talk to Khrushchev, to have a heart-to-heart talk with him and to see if he was the man I thought he was. I was there to get some things corrected or confirmed. I got things confirmed but not corrected." Then, with a look at the State Department interpreter who had come with the Russians, he added, "Don't cheat on me!"

In a final speech, Katayev summed up for the delegation: "I am happy to hold the hand of a genius and a wonderful man. If all humanity had men like Frost there would be no wars. Life would be different." Frost liked that, but he could not let the statement go uncorrected. "Men are men," the Russians later quoted him as saying. "I'm not always so hopeful. War has its rules. We must not cut down the apple trees and we must not poison the wells."

The visit of the Russians touched Frost deeply. It made a proper ending to one of the great adventures of his life. But after they had gone he kept referring to the fact that not one word had come to him from President Kennedy since his return from Russia, not one word since his entering the hospital.

On Sunday, January twenty-seventh, Frost was surprised by a visit from Ezra Pound's daughter, Princess Mary de Rachewiltz. "I've come to thank you," began the princess. "I thought it was high time some member of the family did."

"This is a happy occasion for me," said Frost. "You're a dear and so is Ezra. He's a wonder. . . . A great poet and a great romantic. . . .

"Politics make too much difference to both of us. Love is all. Romantic love—as in stories and poems. I tremble with it. I'd like to see Ezra again. . . ."

Later in the day, Frost went back to working on his new poem about the prophet and the king, but aside from laying out the direction in which he hoped to take it, he made little progress. It was then, apparently, that he dictated to Mrs. Morrison's daughter a letter to Roy and Alma Elliott, answering a recent one of Elliott's that praised his Christmas poem as "one of your very best."

"Oh Roy and Alma," Frost said to his old friends:

". . . I'm mighty glad you like this poem for Christmas. Why will the quidnuncs always be hoping for a salvation man will never have from anyone but God? I was just saying today how Christ posed Himself the whole problem and died for it. How can we be just in a world that needs mercy and merciful in a world that needs justice. We study and study the four biographies of Him and are left still somewhat puzzled in our daily lives. Marking students in a kind of mockery and laughing it off. It seems as if I never wrote these plunges into the depths to anyone but you. I remember our first walk to Harpswell (?) together.

"This is being dictated to Anne Morrison Gentry who writes shorthand and her mother Kathleen Morrison who devises all my future. They are helping me through these hard days in a grand and very powerful hospital. . . . If only I get well, with their help, I'll go deeper into my life with you than I ever have before."

But it was by now too late for that. About the twenty-seventh he began to lose strength rapidly, and it became inescapably clear that there would be no recovery.

The physician-in-chief of the Peter Bent Brigham Hospital was George W. Thorn, and by the end of January he had become something of a personal friend to the ailing poet. He had been introduced to Frost some years before by their mutual friend Hyde Cox, who wanted to be sure Frost had a doctor he could turn to in the Boston area. The choice of Thorn could not have been a happier one. Soon after their introduction Frost had taken sick in Boston, and Dr. Thorn not only made an immediate visit to 35 Brewster Street, but had insisted on staying at the house overnight.

After Frost's admission to the Brigham, Dr. Thorn, knowing that Frost really trusted himself only at the Mary Hitchcock Memorial Hospital in Hanover, had come up to welcome and reassure him, and to say, "As long as you are here, Mr. Frost, you must regard Peter Bent Brigham as an annex of Mary Hitchcock." That was the kind of man Thorn was.

As the head of the teaching hospital of Harvard Medical School, it was Dr. Thorn's custom to lead his interns and residents, as part of their medical education, around to the rooms of his patients every morning. Frost doubtless looked forward to the brief visitations of Thorn and his young men, as they looked forward to seeing him. But the morning of January twenty-eighth was to be different. About dawn, Thorn awoke at home with an ill-defined feeling that something with Frost was not right. He drove to the hospital and went directly upstairs. Frost saw him standing in the doorway of his room, hours earlier than usual and without his usual retinue. He seemed instantly to understand what Thorn's presence signified. "Traveling light today, aren't you?" was all Frost said.

That day, he felt no better than he had the day before. He was unable to eat, and the doctors were at a loss as to what to do. About five in the afternoon he felt somewhat better, and a brief visit was permitted with Mr. and Mrs. Jack Sweeney. But before they left Frost told them, "I feel as though I were in my last hours."

He was. About midnight, new blood clots reached his lungs, and within a few minutes he lost consciousness. In Manchester, shortly before two, Hyde Cox awoke in his bedroom. He walked to the window and looked out, across the sea, to where Boston glowed in the distance. Then, he somehow realized that his great friend was dead. Anne Morrison Gentry's telephone call an hour later only confirmed it.

IN TRIBUTE

(1963)

THE TRIBUTES that had long since become an established element of Frost's life came forth in a deluge of praise after his death—the death at eighty-eight of "America's poet laureate," the "national bard," the "best-loved poet in the United States." Not just in his own country, but around the world, the news of Robert Frost's death elicited eulogies that would doubtless have gratified their subject—as well as amused him. This poet who, though singing, had remained unsung for the first forty years of his life, this Job-like man so often tested by family tragedy, by personal doubts and frustrations, had by the time of his death reached enviable heights of public esteem.

On the afternoon of January thirty-first, two days after the poet's death, a private memorial service was held in Appleton Chapel of Memorial Church in Harvard yard. While knots of students and curious onlookers idled outside, Frost's longtime acquaintance the Rev. Dr. Palfrey Perkins read selections of poetry and from the Bible and Prof. G. Wallace Woodworth of the Harvard music department performed organ pieces well chosen by Anne Morrison Gentry.

On the afternoon of February seventeenth a public memorial service was held in Johnson Chapel of Amherst College, attended by 700 guests ranging from the Chief Justice of the United States, Earl Warren, to many of the poets and professors, the politicians and publishers, the relatives and friends who had touched and been touched by Frost's life and art. Mark Van Doren read a selection of the poet's verse, and remarks were delivered by President Plimpton of Amherst and the Rt. Rev. Henry Wise Hobson, who spoke, with an understanding born of friendship, of Frost's character and the nature of his "strong and deep religious faith."

Four months later, on June sixteenth, the poet's ashes were buried in the Frost family lot of the Old Bennington cemetery. The simple ceremony, conducted by the pastor of the First Congregational Church of Old Bennington, was attended only by Mrs. Lesley Frost Ballantine and a family friend.

On October 26, 1963, many of those who had been present at the Amherst memorial service returned to the town for another ceremony, a convocation associated with ground-breaking exercises for the Robert Frost Library of Amherst College. Frost would have been particularly pleased by the choice of principal speaker. He was the man whose friendship he had, after his return from the Soviet Union, apparently lost forever, the young President whose own death was now less than a month away, John F. Kennedy. After praising the contributions of Amherst College to the life of the nation, and asserting the importance of colleges generally to that life, the President spoke of Frost in words that suggested no lingering animosity, but only genuine respect and a deep sympathy for those principles by which Frost himself had lived and written.

"This day," said the President, "devoted to the memory of Robert Frost, offers an opportunity for reflection which is prized by politicians as well as by others and even by poets. For Robert Frost was one of the granite figures of our time in America. He was supremely two things—an artist and an American.

"A nation reveals itself not only by the men it produces but also by the men it honors, the men it remembers.

"In America our heroes have customarily run to men of large accomplishments. But today this college and country honors a man whose contribution was not to our size but to our spirit; not to our political beliefs but to our insight; not to our self-esteem, but to our self-comprehension.

"In honoring Robert Frost we therefore can pay honor to the deepest sources of our national strength. That strength takes many forms and the most obvious forms are not always the most significant.

"The men who create power make an indispensable contribution to the nation's greatness. But the men who question power make a contribution just as indispensable, especially when that questioning is disinterested.

"For they determine whether we use power or power uses us. Our national strength matters; but the spirit which informs and controls our strength matters just as much. This was the special significance of Robert Frost.

"He brought an unsparing instinct for reality to bear on the platitudes and pieties of society. His sense of the human tragedy fortified him against self-deception and easy consolation.

"'I have been,' he wrote, 'one acquainted with the night.'

"And because he knew the midnight as well as the high noon, because he understood the ordeal as well as the triumph of the human spirit, he gave his age strength with which to overcome despair.

"At bottom he held a deep faith in the spirit of man. And it's hardly an accident that Robert Frost coupled poetry and power. For he saw poetry as the means of saving power from itself.

"When power leads man toward arrogance, poetry reminds him of his limitations. When power narrows the areas of man's concern, poetry reminds him of the richness and diversity of his existence. When power corrupts, poetry cleanses.

"For art establishes the basic human truths which must serve as the touchstones of our judgment. The artist, however faithful to his personal vision of reality, becomes the last champion of the individual mind and sensibility against an intrusive society and an officious state.

"The great artist is thus a solitary figure. He has, as Frost said, 'a lover's quarrel with the world.' In pursuing his perceptions of reality he must often sail against the currents of his time. This is not a popular role. . . .

"Yet in retrospect we see how the artist's fidelity has strengthened the fiber of our national life. If sometimes our great artists have been the most critical of our society it is because their sensitivity and their concern for justice, which must motivate any true artist, makes him aware that our nation falls short of its highest potential.

"I see little of more importance to the future of our country and our civilization than full recognition of the place of the artist. If art is to nourish the roots of our culture, society must set the artist free to follow his vision wherever it takes him. . . .

"I look forward to a great future for America—a future in which our country will match its military strength with our moral restraint, its wealth with our wisdom, its power with our purpose. . . .

"Robert Frost was often skeptical about projects for human improvement. Yet I do not think he would disdain this hope."

The President, now nearing the close of his address, quoted lines he identified as having been written by Frost "during the uncertain days of the Second War." The lines were from the poem entitled "Our Hold on the Planet," which ends: "Take nature altogether since time began, / Including human nature, in peace and war, / And it must be a little more in favor of man, / Say a fraction of one percent at the very least, / Or our number living wouldn't be steadily more, / Our hold on the planet wouldn't have so increased."

Then, in conclusion, President Kennedy declared, "Because of Mr. Frost's life and work . . . our hold on this planet has increased."

APPENDIX

⇥⇥⇤⇤

VERSE & PROSE COMPOSITIONS
BY ROBERT FROST

THE ENTRIES below constitute an index to all of Robert Frost's verse and prose works mentioned in the present volume and, also, a guide to the location of complete texts thereof, as contained in the sources given.

Accompanying each title are: first, an indication of the page or pages on which reference is made herein to an individual composition; and, secondly, a citation of the composition's presence if included in one or more of the following volumes: *The Poetry of Robert Frost* (1969), the standard edition of the poet's collected verse; *Robert Frost: Poetry and Prose* (1972), a selection of writings in both forms, ranging in date across the full span of the author's career; *Selected Prose of Robert Frost* (1966), a gathering of essays and statements initially published during the years 1924 through 1959; *Robert Frost and the Lawrence, Massachusetts, 'High School Bulletin'* (1966), containing facsimile reproductions of the writer's earliest literary efforts in print; and *Robert Frost: Farm-Poultryman* (1963), a compilation of prose that originally appeared in two poultry journals in the interval 1903–1905. The index-guide entries cite these five books by abbreviated titles.

Also potentially of particular usefulness as sources are *Interviews with Robert Frost* (1966) and five major collections of letters: *Selected Letters of Robert Frost* (1964), *The Letters of Robert Frost to Louis Untermeyer* (1963), *Robert Frost and John Bartlett: The Record of a Friendship* (1963), *Family Letters of Robert and Elinor Frost* (1972), and *Robert Frost and Sidney Cox: Forty Years of Friendship* (1981).

B

"Bear, The," 313–14
  The Poetry, 268
  Poetry and Prose, 109
"Beech," 421–22
  The Poetry, 331
  Poetry and Prose, 134
"Bereft," 73, 91
  The Poetry, 251
  Poetry and Prose, 99
"Birches," 170–71, 212–14, 218, 221,
  307
  The Poetry, 121
  Poetry and Prose, 54
"Birds Do Thus, The," 98
"Black Cottage, The," 169
  The Poetry, 55
"Bonfire, The," 231–32
  The Poetry, 129
"Build Soil," 344, 355–56
  The Poetry, 316
  Poetry and Prose, 125

C

"Cabin in the Clearing, A," 455
  The Poetry, 413
  Poetry and Prose, 164
"Census-Taker, The," 287
  The Poetry, 174
"Class Hymn," 62, 64
  High School Bulletin, 21
"Clear and Colder," 56
  Poetry and Prose, 199
"Code, The," 175, 279
  The Poetry, 69
  Poetry and Prose, 36
"Considerable Speck, A," 421
  The Poetry, 357
  Poetry and Prose, 150
"Cow in Apple Time, The," 190
  The Poetry, 124
  Poetry and Prose, 56
"Cow's in the Corn, The," 298

D

"Death of the Hired Man, The," 169,
  198–99, 202, 218, 221
  The Poetry, 34
  Poetry and Prose, 17
"Dedication"
  See: "For John F. Kennedy His
    Inauguration"
"Design," 155
  The Poetry, 302
  Poetry and Prose, 122
"Despair," 119
  Poetry and Prose, 226
"Directive," 436
  The Poetry, 377
  Poetry and Prose, 156
"Doctrine of Excursions, The," 401–02
  Poetry and Prose, 397
"Does No One But Me at All Ever Feel
  This Way in the Least?" 455
  The Poetry, 446
"Door in the Dark, The," 89, 313
  The Poetry, 265
  Poetry and Prose, 107
"Dream of Julius Cæsar, A," 52
  Poetry and Prose, 195
  High School Bulletin, 14
"Dream Pang, A," 132
  The Poetry, 16
  Poetry and Prose, 8
"Dust of Snow," 261
  The Poetry, 221
  Poetry and Prose, 89

E

[Editorials], 55–56, 59
  Poetry and Prose, 204
  High School Bulletin, 18, Facs.
"Education by Poetry," 330–32
  Poetry and Prose, 329
  Selected Prose, 33
"Encounter, An," 99
  The Poetry, 125

L

M

N

O

INDEX

INDEX

INDEX

G

Index prepared by Lisa McGaw.